出版说明

人类历史的发展过程也是思想文化不断积累和沉淀的过程。在几千年的人类历史发展长河中，先贤们或在人文社科领域，或在科学技术领域创作出了无数经典名著。这些著作所蕴藏的思想财富和学术价值，早已为世人所熟知，它们无不体现了作者所处的特定时代的思想和文化。通过这些经典名著，读者不仅可以欣赏到流畅的文笔、生动的描述和详细的刻画、深邃的思想，更可以领悟它们各自独特的历史与文化内涵。可以说，这些作品深深地影响了世世代代的读者，也引导着当今的学人以此来充实和丰富自己的头脑。有鉴于此，我们邀请了专门研究世界历史文化的专家学者，精心挑选代表世界历史文化不同领域的经典作品，采取英汉双语对照的形式出版，一方面为读者提供原汁原味的世界经典名著，让读者自由地阅读，在此过程中逐渐提升自己的英语水平；另一方面通过这种阅读，以达到对世界历史文化的整体了解，开阔自己的视野，打开通往世界的心灵之窗，同时又获得思想文化、个人修养、伦理道德等多方面的提升。

我们衷心期待这套书成为大家学习道路上不可或缺的好伙伴！如果您在阅读中发现有疑问或错误之处，请不吝指正，以便我们更加完善这套书。

宽　容

（英汉双语）

[美]房　龙◎著　余　杰◎译

TOLERANCE

北京工业大学出版社

图书在版编目（CIP）数据

宽容：英汉对照 /（美）房龙著；余杰译. —北京：北京工业大学出版社；2017.7
ISBN 978-7-5639-5257-1

Ⅰ. ①宽… Ⅱ. ①房… ②余… Ⅲ. ①英语 – 汉语 – 对照读物 ②思想史 – 世界 Ⅳ. ①H319.4：B

中国版本图书馆CIP数据核字（2017）第060399号

宽容（英汉双语）

著　　者：［美］房　龙
译　　者：余　杰
责任编辑：李周辉
封面设计：同人阁文化传媒 · 书装设计
出版发行：北京工业大学出版社
（北京市朝阳区平乐园100号　邮编：100124）
010-67391722（传真）bgdcbs@sina.com
出 版 人：郝　勇
经销单位：全国各地新华书店
承印单位：大厂回族自治县正兴印务有限公司
开　　本：787毫米 × 1092毫米　1/16
印　　张：22.25
字　　数：547千字
版　　次：2017年7月第1版
印　　次：2017年7月第1次印刷
标准书号：ISBN 978-7-5639-5257-1
定　　价：39.80元

目录 Contents

PROLOGUE

HAPPILY lived Mankind in the peaceful Valley of Ignorance.

To the north,to the south,to the west and to the east stretched the ridges of the Hills Everlasting.

A little stream of Knowledge trickled slowly through a deep worn gully.

It came out of the Mountains of the Past.

It lost itself in the Marshes of the Future.

It was not much,as rivers go. But it was enough for the humble needs of the villagers.

In the evening,when they had watered their cattle and had filled their casks,they were content to sit down to enjoy life.

The Old Men Who Knew were brought forth from the shady corners where they had spent their day,pondering over the mysterious pages of an old book.

They mumbled strange words to their grandchildren,who would have preferred to play with the pretty pebbles,brought down from distant lands.

Often these words were not very clear.

But they were writ a thousand years ago by a forgotten race. Hence they were holy.

For in the Valley of Ignorance,whatever was old was venerable. And those who dared to gainsay the wisdom of the fathers were shunned by all decent people.

And so they kept their peace.

Fear was ever with them. What if they should be refused the common share of the

序　　言

在平静无知的山谷中，人类过着幸福的生活。

在东南西北各个方向，延伸着绵亘不绝的山脉。

一条知识的小溪，沿着幽深破败的溪谷缓缓流淌。

它发源于昔日的高山，消失在未来的沼泽。

它不像河流那样声势浩大，但对于村民的低级需求来说绰绰有余。

在晚上，当他们饮完牲口、灌满木桶时，就会心满意足地坐下来享受生活。

守旧的老人被从阴凉的角落里搀扶出来。他们在那里待了整个白天，对一本古书的神秘内容冥思苦想。

他们向子孙咕哝着一些奇怪的词，但孩子们更想玩自远方带来的漂亮卵石。

这些词的含意经常很不清晰。

但它们是1000年前由一个被遗忘的部族写的，因此很神圣。

在无知的山谷，古老的东西总是受到尊敬。敢于否认祖先智慧的人，正人君子会避之而唯恐不及。

所以，他们都和睦相处。

恐惧总是如影随形。如果他们得不到园中果实的应有份额，又该怎么办？

products of the garden?

Vague stories there were,whispered at night among the narrow streets of the little town,vague stories of men and women who had dared to ask questions.

They had gone forth,and never again had they been seen.

A few had tried to scale the high walls of the rocky range that hid the sun.

Their whitened bones lay at the foot of the cliffs.

The years came and the years went by.

Happily lived Mankind in the peaceful Valley of Ignorance.

※ ※ ※ ※ ※ ※

Out of the darkness crept a man.

The nails of his hands were torn.

His feet were covered with rags,red with the blood of long marches.

He stumbled to the door of the nearest hut and knocked.

Then he fainted. By the light of a frightened candle,he was carried to a cot.

In the morning throughout the village it was known:"He has come back."

The neighbors stood around and shook their heads. They had always known that this was to be the end.

Defeat and surrender awaited those who dared to stroll away from the foot of the mountains.

And in one corner of the village the Old Men shook their heads and whispered burning words.

They did not mean to be cruel,but the Law was the Law. Bitterly this man had sinned against the wishes of Those Who Knew.

As soon as his wounds were healed he must be brought to trial.

晚上，在小镇狭窄的街道里，人们低声讲着情节模糊的故事——那些敢于质疑的男男女女。

这些人后来走了，再也没有回来。

还有些人曾试图攀登挡住太阳的岩石高墙。

但他们的白骨堆积在崖脚下。

岁月如梭。

在平静无知的山谷中，人类过着幸福的生活。

※ ※ ※ ※ ※ ※

漆黑的外面爬着一个人。

他手上的指甲已经被磨破。

他的脚上缠着因长途跋涉而被染成血红色的破布。

他步履蹒跚地来到最近一座棚屋的门前，敲了敲门。

然后，他昏死过去。在颤动的烛光下，他被抬上了一张吊床。

早上，整个村子都知道了这条消息：“他回来了。”

邻居们站在周围，全都摇头。他们明白，这是注定的结局。

失败和屈服总在等着那些胆敢离开山脚的人。

在村子的一个角落，守旧的老人们摇着头，低声说着恶毒的话。

他们并非天性残忍，但律法毕竟是律法。这个人犯了违背守旧老人意愿的罪过。

他的伤一好就必须接受审判。

They meant to be lenient.

They remembered the strange,burning eyes of his mother. They recalled the tragedy of his father,lost in the desert these thirty years ago.

The Law,however,was the Law;and the Law must be obeyed.

The Men Who Knew would see to that.

※ ※ ※ ※ ※ ※

They carried the wanderer to the Market Place,and the people stood around in respectful silence.

He was still weak from hunger and thirst and the Elders bade him sit down.

He refused.

They ordered him to be silent.

But he spoke.

Upon the Old Men he turned his back and his eyes sought those who but a short time before had been his comrades.

"Listen to me,"he implored."Listen to me and be rejoiced. I have come back from beyond the mountains. My feet have trod a fresh soil. My hands have felt the touch of other races. My eyes have seen wondrous sights.

"When I was a child,my world was the garden of my father.

"To the west and to the east,to the south and to the north lay the ranges from the Beginning of Time.

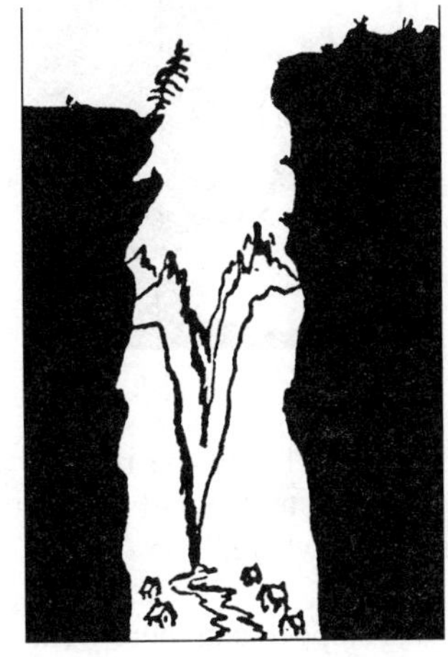

■ 无知的山谷

他们本想宽大为怀。

他们还记得他母亲那双奇异明亮的眼睛，也回忆起他父亲的悲剧——他30年前在沙漠失踪了。

然而，律法就是律法；律法必须遵守。

守旧的老人将执行律法。

※ ※ ※ ※ ※ ※

他们把这位漫游者抬到集市，人们恭敬而肃穆地站在周围。

漫游者因饥渴而仍显虚弱，老人们就让他坐下来。

他拒绝了。

他们命令他闭嘴。

但他偏要说话。

他转身背对守旧老人，双眼在人群中搜寻那些不久前还与他志同道合的人。

“听我说，”他恳求道，“听我说，大家都高兴起来吧！我刚从山那边回来。我踏上了一块新土地，感受到了其他民族的亲切抚摸，看到了奇妙的景象。

“我还是个孩子的时候，我的世界是父亲的花园。

“自从创世以来，东南西北四面疆界早就确定了。

“当我问疆界后面藏着什么时，人们就会嘘声连连，不断摇头。当我坚持要问时，我就被带到岩石这边，让我看那些敢于蔑视上帝的人的白骨。

“我大声哭喊道：‘撒谎！上帝喜欢勇敢的人！’守旧的老人就会走过来，给

■ 孤独的漫游者

"When I asked what they were hiding,there was a hush and a hasty shaking of heads. When I insisted,I was taken to the rocks and shown the bleached bones of those who had dared to defy the Gods.

"When I cried out and said,'It is a lie! The Gods love those who are brave!' the Men Who Knew came and read to me from their sacred books. The Law,they explained,had ordained all things of Heaven and Earth. The Valley was ours to have and to hold. The animals and the flowers,the fruit and the fishes were ours,to do our bidding. But the mountains were of the Gods. What lay beyond was to remain unknown until the End of Time.

"So they spoke,and they lied. They lied to me,even as they have lied to you.

"There are pastures in those hills. Meadows too,as rich as any. And men and women of our own flesh and blood. And cities resplendent with the glories of a thousand years of labor.

"I have found the road to a better home. I have seen the promise of a happier life. Follow me and I shall lead you thither. For the smile of the Gods is the same there as here and everywhere."

※ ※ ※ ※ ※ ※

He stopped and there went up a great cry of horror.

"Blasphemy!"cried the Old Men."Blasphemy and sacrilege! A fit punishment for

我读他们圣书中的内容。并解释说，上帝的旨意已经通过律法表现出来，他已安排好了天地万物。山谷由我们拥有和掌管，百兽、花朵、果实、鱼虾都属于我们，并听从我们的安排。但大山是属于上帝的，就算到了世界末日，山那边的事我们也应该永远一无所知。

"他们这都是在撒谎。他们欺骗了我，更欺骗了你们。

"那边的山上有牧场，当然，牧草肥沃得很；那里的男人和女人们和我们拥有的血肉不差分毫，所有的城市经过上千年的经营，发展得非常好，灿烂辉煌。

"我已经找到了康庄大道，已经看到了幸福生活的曙光。来吧，我带你们去。那里也有上帝的笑容，因为上帝无处不在。"

※ ※ ※ ※ ※ ※

他刚停下来，人群里就响起了一声恐怖的吼叫。

"亵渎！"守旧的老人喊，"这是亵渎圣灵。要让他付出代价！他已经丧失理智，竟敢嘲弄1000年前定下的律法。他罪该万死！"

人们举起沉重的石头，杀害了漫游者。

他的尸体被扔到山崖脚下，以此警告所有敢怀疑祖先智慧的人。

※ ※ ※ ※ ※ ※

没过多久，遇上了一场大旱。知识的小溪很快干涸了，牲畜因干渴而毙命，粮食在田里枯萎，无知的山谷一片饥荒。

但守旧的老人并没有灰心。他们预言说，最后一切都会好的，因为他们眼里最

his crime! He has lost his reason. He dares to scoff at the Law as it was written down a thousand years ago. He deserves to die!"

And they took up heavy stones.

And they killed him.

And his body they threw at the foot of the cliffs,that it might lie there as a warning to all who questioned the wisdom of the ancestors.

※ ※ ※ ※ ※ ※

Then it happened a short time later that there was a great drought. The little Brook of Knowledge ran dry. The cattle died of thirst. The harvest perished in the fields,and there was hunger in the Valley of Ignorance.

The Old Men Who Knew,however,were not disheartened. Everything would all come right in the end,they prophesied,for so it was written in their most Holy Chapters.

Besides,they themselves needed but little food. They were so very old.

※ ※ ※ ※ ※ ※

Winter came.

The village was deserted.

More than half of the populace died from sheer want.

The only hope for those who survived lay beyond the mountains.

But the Law said"No!"

And the Law must be obeyed.

※ ※ ※ ※ ※ ※

One night there was a rebellion.

Despair gave courage to those whom fear had forced into silence.

Feebly the Old Men protested.

神圣的篇章就是这样写的。

况且，他们自己几乎不需要食物。因为他们太老了。

※ ※ ※ ※ ※ ※

冬天来了。

村庄上一片荒凉。

半数以上的人因饥寒交迫而死去。

幸存的人，把仅有的希望寄托在山那边。

但是律法告诉他们："不行！"

律法必须遵守。

※ ※ ※ ※ ※ ※

一天夜里，爆发了叛乱。

那些因恐惧而逆来顺受的人因失望而有了勇气。

守旧的老人极力地抗争着。

他们被搁置不理。他们开始抱怨命运，诅咒忘恩负义的孩子们。但是当最后一辆马车即将驶出村子时，他们拦住车夫，逼他带他们一起走。

未知之旅开始了。

※ ※ ※ ※ ※ ※

距那个漫游者回家之时已经有很多年，要探索出他当年开辟的道路并不容易。

在找到第一个圆石堆路标之前，成千上万人因饥渴而倒下死去了。

■ 新的家园

They were pushed aside. They complained of their lot. They bewailed the ingratitude of their children,but when the last wagon pulled out of the village,they stopped the driver and forced him to take them along.

The flight into the unknown had begun.

※ ※ ※ ※ ※ ※

It was many years since the Wanderer had returned. It was no easy task to discover the road he had mapped out.

Thousands fell a victim to hunger and thirst before the first cairn was found.

From there on the trip was less difficult.

The careful pioneer had blazed a clear trail through the woods and amidst the endless wilderness of rock.

By easy stages it led to the green pastures of the new land.

Silently the people looked at each other.

"He was right after all"they said."He was right,and the Old Men ,was were wrong..."

"He spoke the truth,and the Old Men lied..."

"His bones lie rotting at the foot of the cliffs,but the Old Men sit in our carts and chant their ancient lays..."

"He saved us,and we slew him..."

"We are sorry that it happened,but of course,if we could have known at the time..."

从那以后，旅途上的磨难少多了。

那位细心的先驱已在丛林和无边无际的乱石荒野中烧出了一条宽敞的大道。

它一步一步带人们轻松迈向新土地的绿色牧场。

人们相互看着，先是一片沉默。

■ 可怕的冬天

“终究还是他对了，”人们说，“他是对的，守旧的老人错了。”

“他说的是真的，守旧的老人撒了谎……”

“他的尸骨还在崖下腐烂，守旧的老人却坐在我们的车里唱他们的老歌……”

“他救了我们，我们却毁了他……”

“对此，我们很难过，但是如果我们当时就知道的话，当然……”

然后，他们解下马和牛的套具，把牛羊赶进牧场，建起自己的房子，规划出自己的土地。此后，他们幸福地生活了很长一段时间。

※ ※ ※ ※ ※ ※

几年后，人们准备把那位勇敢先驱埋在一座曾为智慧老人建的雄伟的新大厦里面。

一支肃穆的队伍来到已荒芜的山谷。但当人们到

Then they unharnessed their horses and their oxen and they drove their cows and their goats into the pastures and they built themselves houses and laid out their fields and they lived happily for a long time afterwards.

※ ※ ※ ※ ※ ※

A few years later an attempt was made to bury the brave pioneer in the fine new edifice which had been erected as a home for the Wise Old Men.

A solemn procession went back to the now deserted valley,but when the spot was reached where his body ought to have been,it was no longer there.

A hungry jackal had dragged it to his lair.

A small stone was then placed at the foot of the trail (now a magnificent highway). It gave the name of the man who had first defied the dark terror of the unknown,that his people might be guided into a new freedom.

And it stated that it had been erected by a grateful posterity.

纪念的石碑

※ ※ ※ ※ ※ ※

As it was in the beginning—as it is now—and as some day(so we hope) it shall no longer be.

达先驱者的尸体本该所在的地方时，尸体荡然无存。

一条饥饿的豺狗早将尸体拖进了洞穴。

人们把一块小石头放在那位先驱足迹所踏之处（现在它是一条大道），石头上刻着这个率先向未知世界的黑暗恐怖挑战的人的名字，是他把他的人民引向了自由的新生活。

石头上还写着它是由感恩的后代建的。

※ ※ ※ ※ ※ ※

这样的事情发生在过去——就像现在一样——不过将来（我们希望）不应该再发生。

CHAPTER Ⅰ THE TYRANNY OF IGNORANCE

In the year 527 Flavius Anicius Justinianus became ruler of the eastern half of the Roman Empire.

This Serbian peasant (he came from Uskub,the much disputed railroad junction of the late war) had no use for"book learning."It was by his orders that the ancient Athenian school of philosophy was finally suppressed. And it was he who closed the doors of the only Egyptian temple that had continued to do business centuries after the valley of the Nile had been invaded by the monks of the new Christian faith.

This temple stood on a little island called Philae,not far from the first great waterfall of the Nile. Ever since men could remember,the spot had been dedicated to the worship of Isis and for some curious reason,the Goddess had survived where all her African and Greek and Roman rivals had miserably perished. Until finally,in the sixth century,the island was the only spot where the old and most holy art of picture writing was still understood and where a small number of priests continued to practice a trade which had been forgotten in every other part of the land of Cheops.

And now,by order of an illiterate farmhand,known as His Imperial Majesty,the temple and the adjoining school were declared state property,the statues and images were sent to the museum of Constantinople and the priests and the writing-masters were thrown into jail. And when the last of them had died from hunger and neglect,the age-old trade of making hieroglyphics had become a lost art.

第1章 无知的暴虐

公元527年，弗雷维厄斯·阿尼西厄斯·查士丁尼成为东罗马帝国的统治者。

这个塞尔维亚农夫（他来自尤斯库布，这是第一次世界大战中引起激烈争夺的铁路枢纽）对书本知识一窍不通。正是因为他的命令，古代雅典的哲学学派才被最后压制下去。也正是他，关闭了唯一一座埃及神庙。自从信仰新基督教的信徒侵入尼罗河谷之后，这座神庙就一直延续香火，已有几百年了。

这座神庙位于菲莱小岛，离尼罗河第一瀑布不远。自从人类有史记载以来，这个地方就是朝拜伊希斯[1]的圣地；不知为什么，在非洲、希腊和罗马诸神早已悲惨地销声匿迹之后，这个女神还受人尊奉。直到公元6世纪，这个岛一直是理解古老而神圣的象形文字的唯一场所。在这里，一小部分教士继续从事着在其他地方已被遗忘的工作。

现在，因为一个文盲农夫（他被称为“皇帝陛下”）的命令，神庙和毗邻的学校变成了国家财产，神像和塑像被送到君士坦丁堡的博物馆里，教士和象形文字专家被投入大牢。当他们中的最后一个人因饥饿孤独而死去时，历史悠久的象形文字

[1] 埃及神话中掌管生育和繁殖的女神。——译注

All this was a great pity.

If Justinian (a plague upon his head!) had been a little less thorough and had saved just a few of those old picture experts in a sort of literary Noah's Ark,he would have made the task of the historian a great deal easier. For while (owing to the genius of Champollion) we can once more spell out the strange Egyptian words,it remains exceedingly difficult for us to understand the inner meaning of their message to posterity.

And the same holds true for all other nations of the ancient world.

What did those strangely bearded Babylonians,who left us whole brickyards full of religious tracts,have in mind when they exclaimed piously,“ who shall ever be able to understand the counsel of the Gods in Heaven?”How did they feel towards those divine spirits which they invoked so continually,whose laws they endeavored to interpret,whose commands they engraved upon the granite shafts of their most holy city?Why were they at once the most tolerant of men,encouraging their priests to study the high heavens,and to explore the land and the sea,and at the same time the most cruel of executioners,inflicting hideous punishments upon those of their neighbors who had committed some breach of divine etiquette which today would pass unnoticed?

Until recently we did not know.

We sent expeditions to Nineveh,we dug holes in the sand of Sinai and deciphered miles of cuneiform tablets. And everywhere in Mesopotamia and Egypt we did our best to find the key that should unlock the front door of this mysterious store-house of wisdom.

东西方的会面

工艺就成了一种消失的艺术。

这一切太遗憾了！

假如查士丁尼（这该死的家伙！）不做得那么决绝，把一些老象形文字专家抢救到一个类似“挪亚方舟”的安全地方，就会使历史学家的工作容易得多。虽然我们能再次拼写出奇怪的埃及文字（这全归功于商博良的天才），但要理解他们传给后代的内在含义仍然非常困难。

在古代社会的其他民族中，同样的事情太多了。

那些留着奇怪胡子的巴比伦人，给我们留下了整座整座刻满宗教文字的砖场，当他们虔诚地疾呼“将来谁能理解天国上帝的忠告”时，他们脑子里是如何想的？他们不断祈求圣灵的庇护，力图解释这些圣灵的律法，把这些圣灵的旨意刻在城市最神圣的大理石柱上，他们又是如何看待这些圣灵的？为什么他们会突然极其宽容，鼓励教士研究高高在上的天国，探索陆地和海洋，突然又变成残酷的刽子手，当他们的邻居对如今已无人在意的宗教礼节稍有疏忽时，就施以骇人听闻的惩罚呢？

我们至今尚未弄清楚。

我们派了探险队去尼尼微，在西奈沙漠中发掘古迹，解释了几英里（1英里=1.829米）长的楔形文字书板。在美索不达米亚和埃及各地，我们都尽了最大努力去寻找打开藏有神秘智慧的宝库大门的钥匙。

And then,suddenly and almost by accident,we discovered that the back door had been wide open all the time and that we could enter the premises at will.

But that convenient little gate was not situated in the neighborhood of Akkad or Memphis.

It stood in the very heart of the jungle.

And it was almost hidden by the wooden pillars of a pagan temple.

※ ※ ※ ※ ※ ※

Our ancestors,in search of easy plunder,had come in contact with what they were pleased to call"wild men"or"savages."

The meeting had not been a pleasant one.

The poor heathen,misunderstanding the intentions of the white men,had welcomed them with a salvo of spears and arrows.

The visitors had retaliated with their blunderbusses.

After that there had been little chance for a quiet and unprejudiced exchange of ideas.

The savage was invariably depicted as a dirty,lazy,good-for-nothing loafer who worshiped crocodiles and dead trees and deserved all that was coming to him.

Then came the reaction of the eighteenth century. Jean Jacques Rousseau began to contemplate the world through a haze of sentimental tears. His contemporaries,much impressed by his ideas,pulled out their handkerchiefs and joined in the weeping.

The benighted heathen was one of their most favorite subjects. In their hands (although they had never seen one) he became the unfortunate victim of circumstances and the true representative of all those manifold virtues of which the human race had been deprived by three thousand years of a corrupt system of civilization.

Today,at least in this particular field of investigation,we know better.

然后，突然，几乎是偶然的机会，我们发现宝库的后门一直敞开着，我们随时都可以进去。

然而，这扇方便的小门并不在阿卡德或孟菲斯附近。

它位于丛林深处。

它几乎被异教徒所修神庙的木柱遮挡住了。

※ ※ ※ ※ ※ ※

我们的祖先在寻找易于抢掠的对象时，接触到了他们乐于称之为“野蛮人”的人。

这种相遇并不愉快。

可怜的野蛮人误解了白人的用心，以投掷长矛、张弓射箭的方式欢迎他们。

来访者则用他们的大口径短枪回敬。

从那以后，平静而不带偏见的思想交流的机会就很渺茫了。

野蛮人总是被描写成肮脏懒惰的废物，他们信仰鳄鱼和枯树，任何灾难都是他们所应得的报应。

然后是18世纪的变化。让·雅克·卢梭开始透过朦胧的伤感泪水观察这个世界。同时代的人被他的思想所打动，也掏出手帕，加入到流泪的行列中来。

愚昧的野蛮人成为他们喜欢的话题之一。在他们看来（尽管他们从未见过一个野蛮人），野蛮人是环境的不幸牺牲品，是人类各种美德的真正体现，而3000年的腐败文明制度已经使人类丧失了这些美德。

We study primitive man as we study the higher domesticated animals,from which as a rule he is not so very far removed.

In most instances we are fully repaid for our trouble. The savage,but for the grace of God,is our own self under much less favorable conditions. By examining him carefully we begin to understand the early society of the valley of the Nile and of the peninsula of Mesopotamia and by knowing him thoroughly we get a glimpse of many of those strange hidden instincts which lie buried deep down beneath the thin crust of manners and customs which our own species of mammal has acquired during the last five thousand years.

This encounter is not always flattering to our pride. On the other hand a realization of the conditions from which we have escaped,together with an appreciation of the many things that have actually been accomplished,can only tend to give us new courage for the work in hand and if anything it will make us a little more tolerant towards those among our distant:cousins who have failed to keep up the pace.

This is not a handbook of anthropology.

It is a volume dedicated to the subject of tolerance.

But tolerance is a very broad theme.

The temptation to wander will be great. And once we leave the beaten track,Heaven alone knows where we will land.

I therefore suggest that I be given half a page to state exactly and specifically what I mean by tolerance.

Language is one of the most deceptive inventions of the human race and all definitions are bound to be arbitrary. It therefore behooves an humble student to go to that authority which is accepted as final by the largest number of those who speak the language in which this book is written.

今天，至少在特定的考察领域里，我们知道得更多了。

我们研究原始人就像研究比较高级的家畜，他和它们的区别其实并不大。

在大多数情况下，我们总能劳有所获。野蛮人只是没有被上帝感化而已，他实际上是我们自己在恶劣环境中的自我体现。通过对野蛮人的仔细研究，我们开始了解尼罗河谷和美索不达米亚半岛的早期社会；通过对野蛮人的深入彻底认识，我们窥见了人类诸多奇怪的天性，这些天性深埋在一层薄薄的礼仪习俗的外壳之下，而这些礼仪习俗是我们人类历经5000年变迁而形成的。

这些发现并不能一直提升我们的自豪感。另一方面，了解了我们曾经摆脱的环境，欣赏了我们取得的许多业绩，会增加我们的勇气来对待手中的工作；除此之外，就是促使我们对落伍的异族兄弟保留更多的宽容。

这本书不是一本人类学手册。

这是一本奉献给“宽容”的书。

但宽容是个范围很广的命题。

偏离主题的诱惑很大。一旦离开大道，天晓得我们将在哪儿打住。

因此，还是让我用半页纸的篇幅来恰如其分地解释我所说的宽容的意义吧。

语言是人类最具欺骗性的发明之一，所有的定义都是武断的。因此，卑微的学生应该拜倒在一本权威典籍之下，因为其权威性已被大多数说这种语言的人接受了，这本书也是用这种语言写成的。

我所指的是《不列颠百科全书》。

I refer to the Encyclopedia Britannica.

There on page 1052 of volume XXVI stands written:"Tolerance (from Latin tolerare—to endure):—The allowance of freedom of action or judgment to other people,the patient and unprejudiced endurance of dissent from one's own or the generally received course or view."

There may be other definitions but for the purpose of this book I shall let myself be guided by the words of the Britannica.

And having committed myself (for better or worse) to a definite policy,I shall return to my savages and tell you what I have been able to discover about tolerance in the earliest forms of society of which we have any record.

※ ※ ※ ※ ※ ※

It is still generally believed that primitive society was very simple,that primitive language consisted of a few simple grunts and that primitive man possessed a degree of liberty which was lost only when the world became"complex."

The investigations of the last fifty years made by explorers and missionaries and doctors among the aborigines of central Africa and the Polar regions and Polynesia show the exact opposite. Primitive society was exceedingly complicated,primitive language had more forms and tenses and declensions than Russian or Arabic,and primitive man was a slave not only to the present,but also to the past and to the future. in short,an abject and miserable creature who lived in fear and died in terror.

This may seem far removed from the popular picture of brave redskins merrily roaming the prairies in search of buffaloes and scalps,but it is a little nearer to the truth.

And how could it have been otherwise?

I have read the stories of many miracles.

该书第26卷1052页写道：“宽容（来源于拉丁字tolerare——容忍）：容许别人有行动或判断的自由，对有异于自己或传统观点的见解的耐心公正的容忍。”

也许还有其他定义，但就本书的目的，我不妨用《不列颠百科全书》的话来作为引导。

既然我已经（或多或少地）被束缚在某个明确的宗旨上，那么我还是从野蛮人时代开始，来向你们揭示我从人类有记载的最早期社会形态中发现的宽容是什么样的。

※ ※ ※ ※ ※ ※

人们一般都认为原始社会非常简单，原始语言由一些简单的咕哝组成，原始人拥有一定的自由，只不过在世界变得“复杂”以后就消失了。

过去50年，探险家、传教士和医生在中非、北极地区和波利尼西亚的土著居民中进行的调查表明，事实正好相反。原始社会极其复杂，原始语言的形式、时态和变格比俄语和阿拉伯语都多，原始人不仅是现实的奴隶，也是过去和未来的奴隶。简言之，他们是凄惨可怜的生灵，在畏惧中生活，在恐怖中死去。

我上面所说的和人们的通常想象——勇敢的红皮肤的人类在大草原上悠闲地漫步，寻找野牛和战利品——似乎相差甚远，但更接近事实。

事情怎么会是另外一种样子呢？

我读过许多关于描写奇迹的书。

但它们缺少一个奇迹：人类生存下来的奇迹。

But one of them was lacking:the miracle of the survival of man.

How and in what manner and why the most defenseless of all mammals should have been able to maintain himself against microbes and mastodons and ice and heat and eventually become master of all creation,is something I shall not try to solve in the present chapter.

One thing,however,is certain. He never could have accomplished all this alone.

In order to succeed he was obliged to sink his individuality in the composite character of the tribe.

※ ※ ※ ※ ※ ※

Primitive society therefore was dominated by a single idea,an all-overpowering desire to survive.

This was very difficult.

And as a result all other considerations were sacrificed to the one supreme demand—to live.

The individual counted for nothing,the community at large counted for everything,and the tribe became a roaming fortress which lived by itself and for itself and of itself and found safety only in exclusiveness.

But the problem was even more complicated than at first appears. What I have just said held good only for the visible world,and the visible world in those early times was a negligible quantity compared to the realm of the invisible.

In order to understand this fully we must remember that primitive people are different from ourselves. They are not familiar with the law of cause and effect.

If I sit me down among the poison

■ 忌讳

这些毫无防范能力的哺乳动物到底是如何抵挡住细菌、柱牙象、冰雪和灼热的侵袭，并最后成为所有生灵的主宰的，我在这一章就不多谈了。

但有一件事情是肯定的：一个人绝不可能独自完成这些。

为了获得成功，原始人必须把自己的个性融入复杂的独具特色的部落中。

※ ※ ※ ※ ※ ※

统治原始社会的只有一个信条——至高无上的求生欲。

做到这一点太难了。

因此，所有其他欲望都服从于这一最高要求——活下去。

个人算不了什么，集体高于一切。部落成了一个活动的堡垒，它要自己求生存，一切为了部落，一切归部落所有，只有排斥一切外来物才能获得安全的保障。

但问题比刚才说的还要复杂。我刚才说的只适合于能看见的世界；在人类历史初期，可预见世界与不可预见世界相比微不足道。

为了充分理解这一点，我们必须记住，原始人与我们不同。他们不知道因果法则。

ivy,I curse my negligence,send for the doctor and tell my young son to get rid of the stuff as soon as he can. My ability to recognize cause and effect tells me that the poison ivy has caused the rash,that the doctor will be able to give me something that will make the itch stop and that the removal of the vine will prevent a repetition of this painful experience.

The true savage would act quite differently. He would not connect the rash with the poison ivy at all. He lives in a world in which past,present and future are inextricably interwoven. All his dead leaders survive as Gods and his dead neighbors survive as spirits and they all continue to be invisible members of the clan and they accompany each individual member wherever he goes. They eat with him and sleep with him and they stand watch over his door. It is his business to keep them at arm's length or gain their friendship. If ever he fail to do this he will be immediately punished and as he cannot possibly know how to please all those spirits all the time,he is in constant fear of that misfortune which comes as the revenge of the Gods.

He therefore reduces every event that is at all out of the ordinary not to a primary cause but to interference on the part of an invisible spirit and when he notices a rash on his arms he does not say,"Damn that poison ivy!"but he mumbles,"I have offended a God. The God has punished me,"and he runs to the medicine-man,not however to get a lotion to counteract the poison of the ivy but to get a"charm"that shall prove stronger than the charm which the irate God (and not the ivy) has thrown upon him.

As for the ivy,the primary cause of all his suffering,he lets it grow right there where it has always grown. And if perchance the white man comes with a can of kerosene and burns the shrub down,he will curse him for his trouble.

It follows that a society in which everything happens as the result of the direct personal interference on the part of an invisible being must depend for its continued existence upon a strict obedience of such laws as seem to appease the wrath of the Gods.

如果我坐在有毒的常春藤上，我会责怪自己的粗心大意，派人去请医生，让我小儿子尽快铲掉那些东西。认识因果的能力告诉我，有毒的常春藤会引起皮疹，医生会给我一些能止痒的药，铲掉常春藤可以避免再次发生痛苦的事情。

真正的野蛮人反应会截然不同。他根本不会把皮疹和有毒的常春藤联系起来。他生活在一个过去、现在和将来盘根错节、纠缠不清的世界。所有死去的首领都变成了神灵，死去的邻居变成了精灵，他们仍然是家族中看不见的成员，一步不离地陪着每个活着的人。他们和他同吃同睡，站着看守大门。活人应考虑的问题，就是与他们保持一定距离或得到他们的友情。如果他做不到这一点，就会立即遭到惩罚。由于活人不可能知道如何一直取悦所有的精灵，因此他总是害怕神灵将不幸作为报复降临到自己头上。

所以，他不会把每件异常的事情归结于最初的原因，而是归结于看不见的精灵的干涉。当他发现胳膊上有皮疹时，他不是说："该死的毒藤！"而是小声嘟囔道："我得罪了神灵，他来惩罚我了。"他会跑到医生那里，不是要消除常春藤毒的药，而是要一道比愤怒的神灵（而不是常春藤）扔给他的符更加灵验的符。

至于常春藤这一造成他所有痛苦的根源，他却不理不睬，任其像往常一样生长。如果白人偶尔带来一桶煤油把它烧了，他还会骂白人招惹是非。

因此，一个所有事情都被认为是由看不见的生灵操纵的社会要想持续生存，必须有赖于人们严格服从能平息神灵怒火的律法。

Such a law,according to the opinion of a savage,existed. His ancestors had devised it and had bestowed it upon him and it was his most sacred duty to keep that law intact and hand it over in its present and perfect form to his own children.

This,of course,seems absurd to us. We firmly believe in progress,in growth,in constant and uninterrupted improvement.

But"progress"is an expression that was coined only year before last,and it is typical of all low forms of society that the people see no possible reason why they should improve what (to them) is the best of all possible worlds because they never knew any other.

※ ※ ※ ※ ※ ※

Granted that all this be true,then how does one prevent a change in the laws and in the established forms of society?

The answer is simple.

By the immediate punishment of those who refuse to regard common police regulations as an expression of the divine will,or in plain language,by a rigid system of intolerance.

※ ※ ※ ※ ※ ※

If I hereby state that the savage was the most intolerant of human beings,I do not mean to insult him,for I hasten to add that given the circumstances under which he lived,it was his duty to be intolerant. Had he allowed any one to interfere with the thousand and one rules upon which his tribe depended for its continued safety and peace of mind,the life of the tribe would have been put in jeopardy and that would have been the greatest of all possible crimes.

But (and the question is worth asking) how could a group of people,relatively limited in number,protect a most complex system of verbal regulations when we in our own day with millions of soldiers and thousands of policemen find it difficult to enforce a few plain laws?

在野蛮人看来，这种律法的确存在。他的祖先创立了律法，把它传授给了他，他最神圣的职责就是保持律法不受侵犯，并将它完美无缺地传给他的孩子。

这在我们看来似乎有些荒谬。我们坚信进步、发展和持续不断地改进。

但“进步”是近年才形成的概念，而所有低级社会形态的特点是，由于人们从不知道别的世界，因此他们认为现状已经完美无瑕，没有理由再做改进了。

※ ※ ※ ※ ※ ※

假设上面说的是真的，那么怎样才能防止律法和依此建立的社会形态发生改变呢？

答案很简单。

即刻惩罚那些拒绝将公共条例看作上天旨意的人；说得浅显一些，就是靠刻板的专制制度。

※ ※ ※ ※ ※ ※

如果我据此说野蛮人是最不宽容的人，并没有侮辱他的意思，因为我马上要补充说明的是，在他生存的环境中，专制是理所当然的。如果一味地容忍，那么他的部落赖以保护人身安全及保持头脑冷静的律法就会遭到践踏，部落生活便会遭受威胁，这是最大的罪过。

但是（这个问题值得探讨），相对有限的几个人又是如何保护一整套口口相传的律法条例的呢？我们今天拥有几百万军队和成千上万名警察，可是连推行一些普

Again the answer is simple.

The savage was a great deal cleverer than we are. He accomplished by shrewd calculation what he could not do by force.

He invented the idea of"taboo."

Perhaps the word"invented"is not the right expression. Such things are rarely the product of a sudden inspiration. They are the result of long years of growth and experiment. Let that be as it may,the wild men of Africa and Polynesia devised the taboo,and thereby saved themselves a great deal of trouble.

The word taboo is of Australian origin. We all know more or less what it means. Our own world is full of taboos,things we simply must not do or say,like mentioning our latest operation at the dinner table,or leaving our spoon in our cup of coffee. But our taboos are never of a very serious nature. They are part of the handbook of etiquette and rarely interfere with our own personal happiness.

To primitive man,on the other hand,the taboo was of the utmost importance.

It meant that certain persons or inanimate objects had been"set apart"from the rest of the world,that they (to use the Hebrew equivalent) were"holy"and must not be discussed or touched on pain of instant death and everlasting torture. A fairly large order but woe unto him or her who dared to disobey the will of the spirit-ancestors.

※ ※ ※ ※ ※ ※

Whether the taboo was an invention of the priests or the priesthood was created to maintain the taboo is a problem which had not yet been solved. As tradition is much older than religion,it seems more than likely that taboos existed long before the world had heard of sorcerers and witch doctors. But as soon as the latter had made their appearance,they became the staunch supporters of the idea of taboo and used it with such great virtuosity

通法律都很难。

答案同样简单。

野蛮人比我们聪明得多。他们精确地估算出了无法用武力推行的方法。

他发明了“忌讳”（taboo）的概念。

也许“发明”这个词文不达意。这种事情很少是灵光突现的产物。它们是长期实践和积累的结果。不管怎样，非洲和波利尼西亚的野蛮人创造了“忌讳”的概念，因此省去了许多麻烦。

“忌讳”这个词起源于澳大利亚。我们都或多或少地知道它的含义。我们自己的世界也充满了忌讳，也就是不能做的事或不能说的话，例如吃饭时提到我们刚做完的一个手术，或把小勺放在咖啡杯里不拿出来。但我们的忌讳绝不会那么严重，它们只是礼节的一部分，而且很少会干扰我们的幸福感。

但对原始人而言，忌讳极其重要。

它意味着某些人或没有生命的物体是超然于这个世界的，它们（用希伯来语说）是“神圣”的，人们绝不能冒即刻死去的痛苦危险或付出永恒磨难的代价去谈论或涉及它们。对于胆敢违抗祖先意志的人，可以痛斥。

※ ※ ※ ※ ※ ※

究竟是教士发明了忌讳，还是为维护忌讳才产生了教士这个职业，这还是一个未解之谜。也许早在男巫师和女巫婆出现之前就存在忌讳了。后来，宗教刚刚出现，他们就成为忌讳的顽固支持者，并以非常巧妙的手法滥用这个概念，从而使忌

that the taboo became the"verboten"sign of prehistoric ages.

When first we hear the names of Babylon and Egypt,those countries were still in a state of development in which the taboo counted for a great deal. Not a taboo in the crude and primitive form as it was afterwards found in New Zealand,but solemnly transformed into negative rules of conduct,the sort of"thou-shalt-not"decrees with which we are all familiar through six of our Ten Commandments.

Needless to add that the idea of tolerance was entirely unknown in those lands at that early age.

What we sometimes mistake for tolerance was merely indifference caused by ignorance.

But we can find no trace of any willingness (however vague) on the part of either kings or priests to allow others to exercise that"freedom of action or judgment"or of that"patient and unprejudiced endurance of dissent from the generally received cause or view"which has become the ideal of our modern age.

※ ※ ※ ※ ※ ※

Therefore,except in a very negative way,this book is not interested in prehistoric history or what is commonly called"ancient history."

The struggle for tolerance did not begin until after the discovery of the individual.

And the credit for this,the greatest of all modern revelations,belongs to the Greeks.

讳被推而广之，成为史前时代的“禁物”象征。

在我们第一次了解巴比伦和埃及时，那些国家仍把忌讳置于重要位置。没有一条原始的忌讳粗糙像后来在新西兰发现的那样，而是被严肃庄重地改造成了约束人类行为的否定准则，以“你不能”之类的法律形式出现，就像我们都熟悉的基督教《摩西十诫》中的六条一样。

不用说，在那些国家的早期历史中，宽容的概念根本无人知晓。

我们有时看到的宽容，不过是由于无知而表现出来的漠不关心而已。

我们从未发现国王或教士有一丝诚意（哪怕微不足道），来允许别人履行“行动或判断的自由”，或“对不同于自己或传统观点的见解的耐心公正的容忍”，而这一点已成为现代社会的理想。

※ ※ ※ ※ ※ ※

因此，除非以一种非常消极的方式，否则本书不会让研究史前史或通常所说的“古代史”的人产生兴趣。

为宽容而战，是在个性被认可以后才开始的。

在现代最伟大的发现中，个性发现的荣誉应归于希腊人。

CHAPTER Ⅱ THE GREEKS

How it happened that a little rocky peninsula in a remote corner of the Mediterranean was able to provide our world in less than two centuries with the complete framework for all our present day experiments in politics,literature,drama,chemistry,physics and Heaven knows what else,is a question which has puzzled a great many people for a great many centuries and to which every philosopher,at one time or another during his career,has tried to give an answer.

Respectable historians,unlike their colleagues of the chemical and physical and astronomical and medical faculties,have always looked with ill-concealed contempt upon all efforts to discover what one might call"the laws of history."What holds good of polliwogs and microbes and shooting stars seems to have no business within the realm of human beings.

I may be very much mistaken,but it seems to me that there must be such laws. It is true that thus far we have not discovered many of them. But then again we have never looked very hard. We have been so busy accumulating facts that we have had no time to boil them and liquefy them and evaporate them and extract from them the few scraps of wisdom which might be of some real value to our particular variety of mammal.

It is with considerable trepidation that I approach this new field of research and taking a leaf out of the scientist's book,offer the following historical axiom.

According to the best knowledge of modern scientists,life (animate existence as differentiated from inanimate existence) began when for once all physical and chemical

第2章 希 腊 人

位于地中海一个偏僻角落的一个岩石小半岛，在不到两个世纪的时间里，为我们今天的世界奠定了较完整的文化基础，包括政治、文艺、化学、物理及其他未知的领域，这是怎样实现的呢？多少个世纪以来，人们对这个问题都困惑不解，哲学家也在努力寻找答案。

令人尊敬的历史学家不像化学、物理、天文及医学领域的专家，他们总是以一种恶意隐藏的蔑视态度去看待人们力图发现“古老法则”的一切努力。在研究蝌蚪、细菌和流星中大有用武之地的东西，在人类领域的研究中似乎难有作为。

也许是我大错特错，但我认为这些法则一定存在。事实上，我们至今并没有发现多少东西，我们的探索也不够努力。我们一直忙着积累事实，而没有把它们煮一煮，使它们液化、升华，再从中提炼出智慧——这些智慧对于我们人类这种特殊的哺乳动物也许还真的有些价值。

我诚惶诚恐地投身于这个新的研究领域，在此借用科学家作品中的一页内容，提出如下原理。

根据现代科学家最杰出的研究成果，当所有物理和化学成分都达到形成第一个

elements were present in the ideal proportion necessary for the creation of the first living cell.

Translate this into terms of history and you get this:

"A sudden and apparently spontaneous outbreak of a very high form of civilization is only possible when all the racial,climatic,economic and political conditions are present in an ideal proportion or in as nearly an ideal condition and proportion as they can be in this imperfect world."

Let me elaborate this statement by a few negative observations.

A race with the brain development of a cave-man would not prosper,even in Paradise.

Rembrandt would not have painted pictures,Bach would not have composed fugues,Praxiteles would not have made statues if they had been born in an igloo near Upernivik and had been obliged to spend most of their waking hours watching a seal-hole in an ice-field.

Darwin would not have made his contributions to biology if he had been obliged to gain his livelihood in a cotton mill in Lancashire. And Alexander Graham Bell would not have invented the telephone if he had been a conscripted serf and had lived in a remote village of the Romanow domains.

In Egypt,where the first high form of civilization was found,the climate was excellent,but the original inhabitants were not very robust or enterprising,and political and economic conditions were decidedly bad. The same held true of Babylonia and Assyria. The Semitic races which afterwards moved into the valley between the Tigris and the Euphrates were strong and vigorous people. There was nothing the matter with the climate. But the political and economic environment remained far from good.

In Palestine the climate was nothing to boast of. Agriculture was backward and there was little commerce outside of the caravan route which passed through the country from Africa to Asia and vice versa. Furthermore,in Palestine politics were entirely dominated

细胞的理想比例时，生命（区别于无生物的有生物）就开始了。

把这句话翻译成历史学概念如下：

"只有当所有种族、气候、经济和政治条件在不健全的世界达到或接近一种理想状态和比例时，高级文明形态才会突然且貌似自发地出现。"

让我举几个反面例子来详尽阐述这句话。

大脑发育尚处于穴居人水平的种族不会繁荣昌盛，即使在天堂也是如此。

如果出生在乌佩尼维克岛附近因纽特人的圆顶茅屋里，醒着的时候大部分时间都必须双眼紧盯着冰上的海豹捕猎洞，那么伦勃朗就不会画画，巴赫就不会作曲，伯拉克西特列斯也不会创作雕像。

如果达尔文必须在兰开夏郡一家棉纺厂谋生，他就不会在生物学上做出贡献。如果亚历山大・格雷厄姆・贝尔是一个没有自由的农奴，住在罗曼诺夫王朝的一个偏僻村子里，他就不会发明电话。

作为第一个现代文明的发祥地，埃及气候宜人，但那里的土著居民体魄却不强健，进取心也不强，政治经济环境也很糟糕。巴比伦和亚述王国同样如此。后来迁居到底格里斯河和幼发拉底河流域的闪米特族倒是身强体壮、精力充沛，气候也没有问题，但政治和经济环境很不理想。

在巴勒斯坦，气候一般，农业落后，除了横穿该国连接亚非两洲的大篷车商业通道之外，其他地区商业凋敝。更何况在巴勒斯坦，政治完全由耶路撒冷寺院的教

by the priests of the temple of Jerusalem and this of course did not encourage the development of any sort of individual enterprise.

In Phoenicia,the climate was of little consequence. The race was strong and trade conditions were good. The country,however,suffered from a badly balanced economic system. A small class of ship owners had been able to get hold of all the wealth and had established a rigid commercial monopoly. Hence the government in Tyre and Sidon had at an early date fallen into the hands of the very rich. The poor,deprived of all excuse for the practice of a reasonable amount of industry,grew callous and indifferent and Phoenicia eventually shared the fate of Carthage and went to ruin through the short-sighted selfishness of her rulers.

In short,in every one of the early centers of civilization,certain of the necessary elements for success were always lacking.

When the miracle of a perfect balance finally did occur,in Greece in the fifth century before our era,it lasted only a very short time,and strange to say,even then it did not take place in the mother country but in the colonies across the Aegean Sea.

In another book I have given a description of those famous island-bridges which connected the mainland of Asia with Europe and across which the traders from Egypt and Babylonia and Crete since time immemorial had traveled to Europe. The main point of embarkation,both for merchandise and ideas bound from Asia to Europe,was to be found on the western coast of Asia Minor in a strip of land known as Ionia.

A few hundred years before the Trojan war,this narrow bit of mountainous territory,ninety miles long and only a few miles wide,had been conquered by Greek tribes from the mainland who there had founded a number of colonial towns of which Ephesus,Phocaea,Erythrae and Miletus were the best known,and it was along those

■ 希腊

士操纵，这当然无助于任何个人事业的发展。

在腓尼基，气候还行，人也强壮，经商条件也不错，但这个国家的经济严重不平衡。由船主形成的小阶层掌握了全部财富，还建立了森严的商业垄断政策。这样，早期的推罗和西顿政府就落入了富人手里。被剥夺了辛勤劳动这一最基本权力的穷人变得冷淡而漠然，腓尼基最终和迦太基一样，由于统治者的短视和自私而毁灭。

简言之，在每个早期文明的中心，成功的必要因素总是有所欠缺。

公元前5世纪，完美平衡的奇迹终于出现在希腊，它只存在很短时间；而且奇怪的是，它并不是出现在希腊本土，而是出现在爱琴海对岸的殖民地。

在另一本书中，我描述了连接亚欧大陆的著名的岛屿桥梁，在人类还没有文字记载的时候，埃及、巴比伦和克里特的商人就经过这些岛桥来到欧洲。他们这一行动既通了商，又把亚洲的文化带到了欧洲，他们的足迹留在了小亚细亚西海岸一个名叫爱奥尼亚的狭长地带。

在特洛伊战争之前几百年，一些来自希腊大陆的部落征服了这块90英里长、仅

cities that at last the conditions of success were present in such perfect proportion that civilization reached a point which has sometimes been equaled but never has been surpassed.

In the first place,these colonies were inhabited by the most active and enterprising elements from among a dozen different nations.

In the second place,there was a great deal of general wealth derived from the carrying trade between the old and the new world,between Europe and Asia.

In the third place,the form of government under which the colonists lived gave the majority of the freemen a chance to develop their talents to the very best of their ability.

If I do not mention the climate,the reason is this;that in countries devoted exclusively to commerce,the climate does not matter much. Ships can be built and goods can be unloaded,rain or shine. Provided it does not get so cold that the harbors freeze or so wet that the towns are flooded,the inhabitants will take very little interest in the daily weather reports.

But aside from this,the weather of Ionia was distinctly favorable to the development of an intellectual class. Before the existence of books and libraries,learning was handed down from man to man by word of mouth and the town-pump was the earliest of all social centers and the oldest of universities.

In Miletus it was possible to sit around the town-pump for 350 out of every 365 days. And the early Ionian professors made such excellent use of their climatic advantages that they became the pioneers of all future scientific development.

The first of whom we have any report,the real founder of modern science,was a person of doubtful origin. Not in the sense that he had robbed a bank or murdered his family and had fled to Miletus from parts unknown. But no one knew much about his antecedents.

数英里宽的多山地带，他们在那里建立了许多殖民城市，其中最著名的有以弗所、福基思、厄立特里亚和米利都。在这些城市，成功的条件最终以非常完美的比例呈现出来，以至于它们的文明发展到了很高程度，其他文明有时最多与之并肩，却从未能超越它们。

首先，这些殖民地居住了来自十多个不同民族的最活跃、最具进取心的人。

其次，这里拥有新老世界和欧亚大陆之间互通贸易所得的大量财富。

第三，代表殖民主利益的政府给了广大自由民机会，以充分发挥他们的个人才华。

如果我没有提到气候，不过是因为对于只从事商业的国家而言，气候无关紧要。无论晴天雨天，都可以造船，都可以卸货，只要不是冷得港口结冰，或者城市被洪水淹没，人们就不会在意每天的天气预报。

除此之外，爱奥尼亚的天气对文化的发展极其有利。在书籍和图书馆出现之前，知识靠人口耳相传，城镇的水井附近就成为最早的社交中心和最老的大学所在地。

在米利都，人们一年中有350天坐在水井周围。早期的爱奥尼亚教授充分利用了他们的气候优势，他们成了科学发展的先驱。

我们有记载的第一个人（现代科学的真正创立者），是一个背景值得怀疑的人物。这并不是说他抢了银行或谋杀了家人，并从无人知晓的地方逃到米利都来的。没有人知道他的祖先，不知道他是比奥夏人还是腓尼基人，或者说（用我们博学的

Was he a Boeotian or a Phoenician,a Nordic (to speak in the jargon of our learned racial experts) or a Semite?

It shows what an international center this little old city at the mouth of the Meander was in those days. Its population (like that of New York today) consisted of so many different elements that people accepted their neighbors at their face value and did not look too closely into the family antecedents.

Since this is not a history of mathematics or a handbook of philosophy,the speculations of Thales do not properly belong in these pages,except in so far as they tend to show the tolerance towards new ideas which prevailed among the Ionians at a time when Rome was a small market-town on a muddy river somewhere in a distant and unknown region,when the Jews were still captives in the land of Assyria and when northern and western Europe were naught but a howling wilderness.

In order that we may understand how such a development was possible,we must know something about the changes which had taken place since the days when Greek chieftains sailed across the Aegean Sea,intent upon the plunder of the rich fortress of Troy. Those farfamed heroes were still the product of an exceedingly primitive form of civilization. They were over-grown children who regarded life as one long,glorified rough-house,full of excitement and wrestling matches and running races and all the many things which we ourselves would dearly love to do if we were not forced to stick to the routine jobs which provide us with bread and bananas.

The relationship between these boisterous paladins and their Gods was as direct and as simple as their attitude towards the serious problems of every-day existence. For the inhabitants of high Olympus,who ruled the world of the Hellenes in the tenth century before our era,were of this earth earthy,and not very far removed from ordinary mortals. Exactly where and when and how man and his Gods had parted company was a more or

人类学专家的行话来说）是北欧人还是闪米特人。

这表明这个坐落于米安德尔山口的小小古城在当时是一个著名的世界中心。它的市民（就像今天的纽约）来自各个地方，因此人们凭表面印象来判断他们的邻居，而不会特别注意其家庭背景。

既然本书不是数学史或哲学手册，因此就不必过多地阐述泰勒斯其人了。但需要说明的是，他倾向于对新思想采取宽容的态度。这种宽容的态度曾盛行于爱奥尼亚，当时罗马还是偏远无名地区一条泥泞小河旁的小商镇，犹太人还是亚述人的俘虏，北欧和西欧还是野兽横行之地。

为了了解发展状况，我们必须了解自从希腊首领们渡过爱琴海，掠夺富庶的特洛伊城以来所发生的变化。当时，那些闻名遐迩的英雄仍然是最初级文明的产物，他们就像早熟的孩子，认为生命就是一场漫长而光荣的搏斗，充满了刺激的角斗、赛跑及诸如此类的竞技，而我们自己若不是为生存所迫而埋头苦干的话，也会乐意去做这些的。

这些热血沸腾的武士对待他们的上帝坦率而质朴，就像对待日常生活中的严肃问题一样。住在高大的奥林匹斯山上的诸神在公元前10世纪曾统治着希腊人的世界，他们都是地球上真实的形象，和普通人区别并不大。人和他们的上帝是在何时、何地及如何分道扬镳的，一直是未解之谜。即使如此，高居云端的上帝对拜倒在地面的臣民所怀有的情谊从未间断，并一直保持着亲切而富有个性的色彩，这赋

less hazy point,never clearly established. Even then the friendship which those who lived beyond the clouds had always felt towards their subjects who crawled across the face of the earth had in no way been interrupted and it had remained flavored with those personal and intimate touches which gave the religion of the Greeks its own peculiar charm.

Of course,all good little Greek boys were duly taught that Zeus was a very powerful and mighty potentate with a long beard who upon occasion would juggle so violently with his flashes of lightning and his thunderbolts that it seemed that the world was coming to an end. But as soon as they were a little older and were able to read the ancient sagas for themselves,they began to appreciate the limitations of those terrible personages of whom they had heard so much in their nursery and who now appeared in the light of a merry family-party-everlastingly playing practical jokes upon each other and taking such bitter sides in the political disputes of their mortal friends that every quarrel in Greece was immediately followed by a corresponding row among the denizens of the aether.

Of course in spite of all these very human short-comings,Zeus remained a very great God,the mightiest of all rulers and a personage whom it was not safe to displease. But he was“reasonable”in that sense of the word which is so well understood among the lobbyists of Washington. He was reasonable. He could be approached if one knew the proper way. And best of all,he had a sense of humor and did not take either himself or his world too seriously.

This was perhaps,not the most sublime conception of a divine figure,but it offered certain very distinct advantages. Among the ancient Greeks there never was a hard and fast rule as to what people must hold true and what they must disregard as false. And because there was no“creed”in the modern sense of the word,with adamantine dogmas and a class of professional priests,ready to enforce them with the help of the secular gallows,the people in different parts of the country were able to reshape their religious ideas and ethical conceptions as best suited their own individual tastes.

予了希腊宗教独特的魅力。

当然，所有出身良好的孩子都知道，宙斯是强大而万能的统治者，留着长胡子，偶尔狂暴地使出法力让电闪雷劈时，世界末日似乎就到了。孩子们稍稍长大并能够被自阅读古老的传说时，就开始分析这些可怕神灵的缺陷。他们还在摇篮时就听过这些神灵的故事，而现在这些神灵却出现在愉快的家庭晚会的灯光下——相互间不断地恶作剧，参与尘世朋友的政治争论，因各自不同观点而激烈争吵。因此，希腊尘世的每次争论必然会立即引起天国诸神之间的纷争。

当然，尽管具有人类的这些弱点，宙斯仍然是非常伟大的上帝、最强大的统治者和神灵，冒犯他可不安全。但他还是“通情达理”的，在华盛顿专门对议员进行游说的说客对这个词的含义了解得很清楚。宙斯通情达理，如果方法得当还可以疏通他。最主要的是，他具有幽默感，不把他自己和他的天国太当回事。

也许这并不是对一位神灵的最好评价，但它有着明显的好处。在古希腊，从未有森严的条例要求人们应该把哪些奉为真理，把哪些视为谬误。由于没有现代意义中的“信条”，没有僵化的教条和职业教士阶层（他们靠绞刑架强制推行教条），全国各地的民众都可以根据自己的喜好来修改他们的宗教思想和天国概念。

住在奥林匹斯山咫尺之遥的塞萨利人对自己可敬的邻居（奥林匹斯山诸神）的崇拜，当然远不如住在拉科尼亚湾一个遥远的村子里的阿索庇人。雅典人认为他们有守护神雅典娜的护佑，就可以对这位女神的父亲（宙斯）放肆随便了；而居住在

The Thessalians, who lived within hailing distance of Mount Olympus, showed of course much less respect for their august neighbors than did the Asopians who dwelled in a distant village on the Laconian Gulf. The Athenians, feeling themselves under the direct protection of their own patron saint, Pallas Athene, felt that they could take great liberties with the lady's father, while the Arcadians, whose valleys were far removed from the main trade routes, clung tenaciously to a simpler faith and frowned upon all levity in the serious matter of religion, and as for the inhabitants of Phocis, who made a living from the pilgrims bound for the village of Delphi, they were firmly convinced that Apollo (who was worshiped at that profitable shrine) was the greatest of all divine spirits and deserved the special homage of those who came from afar and still had a couple of drachmas in their pocket.

The belief in only one God which soon afterwards was to set the Jews apart from all other nations, would never have been possible if the life of Judaea had not centered around a single city which was strong enough to destroy all rival places of pilgrimage and was able to maintain an exclusive religious monopoly for almost ten consecutive centuries.

In Greece such a condition did not prevail. Neither Athens nor Sparta ever succeeded in establishing itself as the recognized capital of a united Greek fatherland. Their efforts in this direction only led to long years of unprofitable civil war.

No wonder that a race composed of such sublime individualists offered great scope for the development of a very independent spirit of thought.

The Iliad and the Odyssey have sometimes been called the Bible of the Greeks. They were nothing of the sort. They were just books. They were never united into "The Book." They told the adventures of certain wonderful heroes who were fondly believed to be the direct ancestors of the generation then living. Incidentally they contained a certain amount of religious information because the Gods, without exception, had taken sides in the

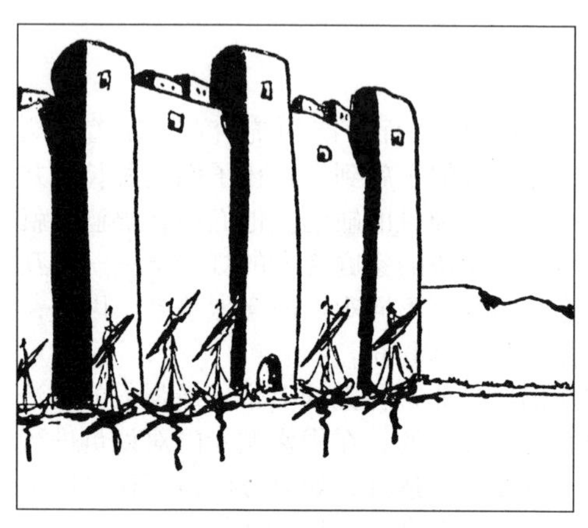

■ 商业城市

远离通衢大道的山谷中的阿卡德人却固执地坚持更淳朴的信仰，他们对所有轻浮地对待宗教这一严肃问题的人很不满。至于福西斯的居民，他们靠人们对德尔法村的朝圣维持生计，他们坚信阿波罗（这个在有利可图的圣地接受朝拜的天神）是所有天神中最伟大的，理应得到那些不远千里、口袋里还有几个钱的人的特殊崇拜。

如果犹太人不是聚集在一个城市，势力强大到足以击败所有与之竞争的朝圣地，并保持宗教垄断近千年，那么要让人们只信奉唯一的上帝（这一点使犹太人不久就和其他民族区别开来）是不可能的。

在希腊可没有这种条件。雅典和斯巴达都未能使自己成为希腊人公认的首都。他们的努力只导致了徒劳无益的长期内战。

个性如此强悍的民族能为独立思考精神的发展提供广阔的舞台，也就不足为怪了。

《伊利亚特》和《奥德赛》有时被称为“希腊人的圣经”。其实它们和《圣

quarrel and had neglected all other business for the joy of watching the rarest prizefight that had ever been staged within their domain.

The idea,however,that the works of Homer might either directly or indirectly have been inspired by Zeus or Minerva or Apollo never even dawned upon the Greek mind. These were a fine piece of literature and made excellent reading during the long winter evenings. Furthermore they caused children to feel proud of their own race.

And that was all.

In such an atmosphere of intellectual and spiritual freedom,in a city filled with the pungent smell of ships from all the seven seas,rich with fabrics of the Orient,merry with the laughter of a well fed and contented populace,Thales was born. In such a city he worked and taught and in such a city he died. If the conclusions which he reached differed greatly from the opinions held by most of his neighbors,remember that his ideas never penetrated beyond a very limited circle. The average Miletian may have heard the name of Thales,just as the average New Yorker has probably heard the name of Einstein. Ask him who Einstein is,and he will answer that he is a fellow with long hair who smokes a pipe and plays the fiddle and who wrote something about a man walking through a railroad train,about which there once was an article in a Sunday paper.

That this strange person who smokes a pipe and plays the fiddle has got hold of a little spark of truth which eventually may upset (or at least greatly modify) the scientific conclusions of the last sixty centuries,is a matter of profound indifference to the millions of easy-going citizens whose interest in mathematics does not reach beyond the conflict which arises when their favorite batsman tries to upset the law of gravity.

The text-books of ancient history usually get rid of the difficulty by printing"Thales of Miletus (640~546 B. C.),the founder of modern science."And we can almost see the

经》毫不相干，它们只是书而已，从未被列入“圣经”。书中讲述了某些传奇英雄的冒险，而这些英雄又总被认为是当时希腊人的祖先。它们包含了许多宗教知识，因为天神们都无一例外地在凡人的争吵中各自支持一方，尽情欣赏在自己版图上发生的罕见大厮杀而将其他事情抛诸脑后。

然而，希腊人的脑子里从未想过，荷马的著作是不是在宙斯、米纳瓦和阿波罗的直接或间接启示下才写成的。荷马史诗是光辉的文学篇章，是漫漫冬夜陪伴人们的优秀读物。此外，它们还使孩子们为自己的民族而感到骄傲。

这就是一切。

在这种知识和精神自由的氛围中，在这座弥漫着来自世界各地的船上发出的呛人气味、点缀着富丽堂皇的东方丝织品、洋溢着心满意足的人们的欢笑声的城市，泰勒斯降生了。他在这座城市工作、学习，并在这个城市离开人世。如果他的结论和大多数人的观点分歧很大，我们就不会忘记他的思想会有很大的局限性这一点。一般的米利都人都知道泰勒斯这个人，就像一般的纽约人都听过爱因斯坦的大名一样。如果问他爱因斯坦是谁，他会回答说爱因斯坦是个留着长头发、叼着烟斗、拉着小提琴的家伙，还写过关于一个人穿越火车的故事，这篇文章曾刊登在一家星期日的报纸上。

这个叼着烟斗、拉着小提琴的怪人抓住了真理那微弱的光芒，最终推翻了（至少大大改变了）过去6000年来的科学结论，但它并没有引起千百万慵懒的市民的注意。只有当他们喜欢的击球手试图推翻万有引力而受阻时，这些市民才会对数学感兴趣。

headlines in the"Miletus Gazette"saying,"Local graduate discovers secret of true science."

But just how and where and when Thales left the beaten track and struck out for himself,I could not possibly tell you. This much is certain,that he did not live in an intellectual vacuum,nor did he develop his wisdom out of his inner consciousness. In the seventh century before Christ,a great deal of the pioneer work in the realm of science had already been done and there was quite a large body of mathematical and physical and astronomical information at the disposal of those intelligent enough to make use of it.

Babylonian star-gazers had searched the heavens.

Egyptian architects had done considerable figuring before they dared to dump a couple of million tons of granite on top of a little burial chamber in the heart of a pyramid.

The mathematicians of the Nile Valley had seriously studied the behavior of the sun that they might predict the wet and dry seasons and give the peasants a calendar by which they could regulate their work on the farms.

All these problems,however,had been solved by people who still regarded the forces of nature as the direct and personal expression of the will of certain invisible Gods who administered the seasons and the course of the planets and the tides of the ocean as the members of the President's cabinet manage the department of agriculture or the post-office or the treasury.

Thales rejected this point of view. But like most well educated people of his day,he did not bother to discuss it in public. If the fruit vendors along the water front wanted to fall upon their faces whenever there was an eclipse of the sun and invoke the name of Zeus in fear of this unusual sight,that was their business and Thales would have been the last man to try to convince them that any schoolboy with an elementary knowledge of the behavior of heavenly bodies would have foretold that on the 25th of May of the year 585 B. C.,at

古代历史教科书通常会绕开这个难题，只印上“米利都的泰勒斯(公元前640~546年)，现代科学奠基人”。我们似乎也可以看到《米利都报》上的大字标题：“本地毕业生发现了真正科学的秘密。”

但泰勒斯究竟是何时、何地、怎样超越前人的老路并独自探索出新路的，我也不知道。但有一点是可以肯定的：他不是生活在没有知识的真空里，他的智慧也不是从内心想象出来的。公元前7世纪，科学领域的大量探索工作已经展开，有大量数学、物理学和天文学的资料供学者利用。

巴比伦的星象观察家已经在探索天空了。

埃及的建筑师在仔细计算之后，把一些重达百万吨的花岗石放在了金字塔内部小墓室的顶部。

尼罗河谷的数学家认真研究了太阳的运行，可以预测雨季和旱季，为农民提供了使农业耕作规律化的日历。

然而，解答了这些实际问题的人仍然认为，自然界的力量是某些看不见的神灵意志的直接表现。这些神灵掌管季节、星象运行和海潮，就像总统的内阁成员掌管农业部、邮政部或财政部一样。

泰勒斯反对这种观点。但他和同时代大多数受过良好教育的人一样，不愿在公开场合讨论它。如果海边的水果贩子遇到日食而趴倒在地，因害怕这种怪异的景象而祈求宙斯保佑，那是他自己的事。泰勒斯绝不会告诉他们说，任何稍有天体运行知识的学童都会预测到公元前585年5月25日会有日食，此时此刻月亮会位于地球和

such and such an hour,the moon would find herself between the earth and the sun and that therefore the town of Miletus would experience a few minutes of comparative darkness.

Even when it appeared (as it did appear) that the Persians and the Lydians had been engaged in battle on the afternoon of this famous eclipse and had been obliged to cease killing each other for lack of sufficient light,he refused to believe that the Lydian deities (following a famous precedent established a few years previously during a certain battle in the valley of Ajalon) had performed a miracle,and had suddenly turned off the light of Heaven that the victory might go to those whom they favored.

For Thales had reached the point (and that was his great merit) where he dared to regard all nature as the manifestation of one Eternal Will ,subject to one Eternal Law and entirely beyond the personal influence of those divine spirits which man was forever creating after his own image. And the eclipse,so he felt,would have taken place just the same if there had been no more important engagement that particular afternoon than a dog fight in the streets of Ephesus or a wedding feast in Halicarnassus.

Drawing the logical conclusions from his own scientific observations,he laid down one general and inevitable law for all creation and guessed (and to a certain extent guessed correctly) that the beginning of all things was to be found in the water which apparently surrounded the world on all sides and which had probably existed from the very beginning of time.

Unfortunately we do not possess anything that Thales himself wrote. It is possible that he may have put his ideas into concrete form (for the Greeks had already learned the alphabet from the Phoenicians) but not a page which can be directly attributed to him survives today. For our knowledge of himself and his ideas we depend upon the scanty bits of information found in the books of some of his contemporaries. From these,however,we

太阳之间，米利都城将会经历几分钟的相对黑暗。

■ 哲学家

这次著名日食发生（它的确发生过）的下午，波斯人和吕底亚人正在战场上厮杀；由于光线不足，他们停止了相互残杀。但泰勒斯不相信这是吕底亚诸神（效仿几年前在阿迦隆山谷战役中发生的著名先例）创造了奇迹，突然使天国的光芒熄灭，以便让他们支持的一方获胜。

泰勒斯达到了一种境界（这正是他的伟大业绩），那就是他敢于承认一切自然现象都是受永恒法则支配的，是永恒意志的具体体现，绝非人们想象出来的天神的支配所致。他认为，即使那个特殊的下午只有以弗所大街上的狗打架，或在哈利卡纳索斯举办一场婚宴，而没有更重大的事情发生，日食照样会出现。

通过自己的科学观察，泰勒斯得出了一个符合逻辑的结论。他推测（从某种程度上讲是正确的）万物皆起源于从四面八方包围这个世界并自创世之初就与世共存的水。

不幸的是，我们没有任何泰勒斯自己写的东西。他可能将他的思想写成作品

have learned that Thales in private life was a merchant with wide connections in all parts of the Mediterranean. That,by the way,was typical of most of the early philosophers. They were"lovers of wisdom."But they never closed their eyes to the fact that the secret of life is found among the living and that"wisdom for the sake of wisdom"is quite as dangerous as"art for art's sake"or a dinner for the sake of the food.

To them,man with all his human qualities,good and bad and indifferent,was the supreme measure of all things. Wherefore they spent their leisure time patiently studying this strange creature as he was and not as they thought that he ought to be.

This made it possible for them to remain on the most amicable terms with their fellow citizens and allowed them to wield a much greater power than if they had undertaken to show their neighbors a short cut to the Millennium.

They rarely laid down a hard and fast rule of conduct.

But by their own example they managed to show how a true understanding of the forces of nature must inevitably lead to that inner peace of the soul upon which all true happiness depends and having in this way gained the good-will of their community they were given full liberty to study and explore and investigate and were even permitted to venture within,those domains which were popularly believed to be the exclusive property of the Gods. And as one of the pioneers of this new gospel did Thales spend the long years of his useful career.

Although he had pulled the entire world of the Greeks apart,although he had examined each little piece separately,and had openly questioned all sorts of things which the majority of the people since the beginning of time had held to be established facts,he was allowed to die peacefully in his own bed,and if any one ever called him to account for his heresies,we fail to have record of the fact.

And once he had shown the way,there were many others eager to follow.

（因为希腊人已经从腓尼基人那里学会了字母），但他的文稿一点都没有保存下来。我们对他和他的思想的了解，全仰仗从他同时代人的书中找到的些许资料。然而，就靠这些资料，我们了解到泰勒斯是个商人，和地中海各地区的人有过广泛接触。顺便说一句，这是早期大多数哲学家的一大特征。他们是“智慧的恋人”。但他们从不忽视这一事实：生活的秘密就在生命中，并认为“为智慧而寻求智慧”的观点和“为艺术而艺术”“为食物而吃饭”一样极其危险。

在他们看来，世上各色人等好坏参差不齐，是衡量世间万物的最高标准。因此，他们在空闲时，会耐心地按人的本来面目去研究人这个奇怪的生物，而不是凭想象去研究。

这使他们能和周围的人相处融洽，而且远比让他们向人们指出通往太平盛世的捷径更有影响力。

他们极少提出限制人们行为的森严的清规戒律。

但他们以自己的榜样作用向人们表明，一旦真正理解了自然界的力量，就必然会获得灵魂深处（一切幸福都寄托于此）的安宁。以这种方式获得周围人的好感之后，他们便有了充分的自由去研究、探索和调查，甚至深入到一般被认为只有上帝才有权掌管的领域探险。作为这个新福音的先驱之一，泰勒斯把他有益的一生长期献给了这项事业。

尽管他分解了整个希腊世界，分别考查了每一个细小部分，并公开质疑自古以来大多数人认为天经地义的事情，但人们还是允许他在床上寿终正寝。即便有人曾

There was,for example,Anaxagoras of Clazomenae,who left Asia Minor for Athens at the age of thirty-six and spent the following years as a“sophist”or private tutor in different Greek cities. He specialized in astronomy and among other things he taught that the sun was not a heavenly chariot,driven by a God,as was generally believed,but a red-hot ball of fire,thousands and thousands of times larger than the whole of Greece.

When nothing happened to him,when no bolt from Heaven killed him for his audacity,he went a little further in his theories and stated boldly that the moon was covered with mountains and valleys and finally he even hinted at a certain“original matter”which was the beginning and the end of all things and which had existed from the very beginning of time.

But here,as many other scientists after him were to discover,he trod upon dangerous ground,for he discussed something with which people were familiar. The sun and the moon were distant orbs. The average Greek did not care what names the philosopher wished to call them. But when the professor began to argue that all things had gradually grown and developed out of a vague substance called“original matter”—then he went decidedly too far. Such an assertion was in flat contradiction with the story of Deucalion and Pyrrha,who after the great flood had re-populated the world by turning bits of stone into men and women. To deny the truth of a most solemn tale which all little Greek boys and girls had been taught in their early childhood was most dangerous to the safety of established society. It would make the children doubt the wisdom of their elders and that would never do. Hence Anaxagoras was made the subject of a formidable attack on the part of the Athenian Parents' League.

During the monarchy and the early days of the republic,the rulers of the city would have been more than able to protect a teacher of unpopular doctrines from the foolish hostility of the illiterate Attic peasants. But Athens by this time had become a full-fledged democracy and the freedom of the individual was no longer what it used to be.

让他对自己的异端邪说进行解释，我们也无据可查了。

一旦泰勒斯指明了方向，就有许多人热切地追随其后。

例如，克拉佐梅尼的阿那克萨哥拉在36岁时离开小亚细亚来到雅典，后来以“诡辩家”的身份度过余生，还在希腊几座城市当过私人教师。他专攻天文。他告诉学生，太阳不是人们通常认为的由天神驾驭的马车，而是一个又红又烫的火球，比整个希腊要大几千万倍。

结果什么事情都没有发生，天庭也没有因为他的放肆言论而用雷电劈死他。他在理论上又推进了一步，大胆提出，月亮表面被山脉和山谷覆盖着；最后他甚至暗示，自从开天辟地以来，就存在某种“源物”，它是万物的起源和归宿。

但是，正如他之后的其他科学家发现的那样，他进入了一个危险领域，因为他讨论的正是人们熟悉的事情。太阳和月亮太远了，平民百姓并不在乎哲学家如何称呼它们。但当这位教授开始提出世间万物都是从一个叫“源物”的原始物质中逐渐成长发展起来的时候，他就有点显得太过分了。这种论断和天神丢卡利翁和皮拉的故事完全背离——是天神在大洪水后用小石子变成了无数男女，让这个世界重新人丁兴旺起来。所有希腊孩子在童年时代就听过这个故事，因此否认这个无比庄重的故事的真实性，对现存社会的安全造成威胁。它还会让孩子们怀疑长辈的智慧，这绝对不行。于是，阿那克萨哥拉成了雅典父母同盟猛烈攻击的目标。

在君主制和共和制早期，城邦统治者或许有足够的力量保护一个宣扬不受欢迎的教义的老师，使其免受古雅典无知农民的愚蠢迫害。但此时的雅典民主制已发展

Furthermore,Pericles,just then in disgrace with the majority of the people,was himself a favorite pupil of the great astronomer,and the legal prosecution of Anaxagoras was welcomed as an excellent political move against the city's old dictator.

A priest by the name of Diopheites,who also was a ward-leader in one of the most densely populated suburbs,got a law passed which demanded"the immediate prosecution of all those who disbelieved in the established religion or held theories of their own about certain divine things."Under this law,Anaxagoras was actually thrown into prison. Finally,however,the better elements in the city prevailed. Anaxagoras was allowed to go free after the payment of a small fine and move to Lampsacus in Asia Minor where he died,full of years and honor,in the year 428 B. C.

His case shows how little is ever accomplished by the official suppression of scientific theories. For although Anaxagoras was forced to leave Athens,his ideas remained behind and two centuries later they came to the notice of one Aristotle,who in turn used them as a basis for many of his own scientific speculations. Reaching merrily across a thousand years of darkness,he handed them on to one Abul-Walid Muhammad ibn-Ahmad (commonly known as Averroës),the great Arab physician who in turn popularized them among the students of the Moorish universities of southern Spain. Then,together with his own observations,he wrote them down in a number of books. These were duly carried across the Pyrenees until they reached the universities of Paris and Boulogne. There they were translated into Latin and French and English and so thoroughly were they accepted by the people of western and northern Europe that today they have become an integral part of every

■ 希腊传说

到了极致，个性自由早已今非昔比。况且当时受大多数人鄙视的伯里克利[1]正是这位伟大天文学家的得意弟子，因此对阿那克萨哥拉的依法治罪受到了人们的欢迎，人们借此掀起了一场反对城邦旧独裁者的声势浩大的政治运动。

一个名叫奥菲特斯的教士（他在一个人口最稠密的郊区当行政长官）使一条法律获得了批准，该法律要求“对一切不相信现存宗教者或对一切神明坚持己见者立即治罪”。根据这条法律，阿那克萨哥拉真的被关入了大牢。但城市的开明势力最终占了上风，阿那克萨哥拉交了很小一笔罚款之后获释，并迁居到小亚细亚的朗萨库斯，在那里活了很长时间，名同皓月，直到公元前428年与世长辞。

他的例子表明，官方压制科学理论只会一无所获。因为阿那克萨哥拉虽然被迫离开了雅典，但他的思想留给了后世；而且在两个世纪之后，引起了一个叫亚里士多德的人的注意，并将它作为他的科学假设的基础。在经过千年的漫长黑暗之后，亚里士多德的思想又传给了伊本-艾默德（通常以阿威罗伊的名字而为人所知）。

[1] 古代雅典著名执政官和改革家，他执政期间被誉为希腊（雅典）的“黄金时代”。——译注

primer of science and are considered as harmless as the tables of multiplication.

But to return to Anaxagoras. For almost an entire generation after his trial,Greek scientists were allowed to teach doctrines which were at variance with popular belief. And then,during the last years of the fifth century,a second case took place.

The victim this time was a certain Protagoras,a wandering teacher who hailed from the village of Abdera,an Ionian colony in northern Greece. This spot already enjoyed a doubtful reputation as the birthplace of Democritus,the original"laughing philosopher,"who had laid down the law that"only that society is worth while which offers to the largest number of people the greatest amount of happiness obtainable with the smallest amount of pain,"and who therefore was regarded as a good deal of a radical and a fellow who should be under constant police supervision.

Protagoras,deeply impressed by this doctrine,went to Athens and there,after many years of study,proclaimed that man was the measure of all things,that life was too short to waste valuable time upon an inquiry into the doubtful existence of any Gods,and that all energies ought to be used for the purpose of making existence more beautiful and more thoroughly enjoyable.

This statement,of course,went to the very root of the matter and it was bound to shock the faithful more than anything that had ever been written or said. Furthermore it was made during a very serious crisis in the war between Athens and Sparta and the people,after a long series of defeats and pestilence,were in a state of utter despair. Most evidently it was not the right moment to incur the wrath of the Gods by an inquiry into the scope of their supernatural powers. Protagoras was accused of atheism,of"godlessness,"and was told to submit his doctrines to the courts.

Pericles,who could have protected him,was dead and Protagoras,although a scientist,felt little taste for martyrdom.

这是一位伟大的阿拉伯医学家，他在西班牙南部摩尔大学的学生中大力传播亚里士多德的思想。然后，他结合自己的观察，将它们写成了许多著作。这些书被及时运过比利牛斯山，一直送到巴黎大学和布伦大学。在那里，它们被译成拉丁文、法文和英文，西欧人和北欧人全盘接受了这些思想，以至于今天它们成了科学入门书的一个必要组成部分，被认为和乘法口诀表一样无害。

回到阿那克萨哥拉身上来。在他受审以后经过了几乎整整一代人的时间，希腊科学家获准教授与民众信仰有所分歧的学说。到公元前五世纪末，又发生了第二件事。

这次的受害者是普罗塔哥拉，他是个流浪教师，来自希腊北部殖民地爱奥尼亚的阿布德拉村。该地已因作为德谟克利特的出生地而声誉不佳。德谟克利特是最富创见的“微笑哲学家”，他提出了一条法则：“一个社会只有以最小的代价给绝大多数人提供最大的幸福，才是有价值的。”结果被视为激进分子，应该交给警察持续看管。

普罗塔哥拉深受这一思想的影响。他来到雅典，在那里经过几年研究，便宣称：人是衡量万物的准绳，生命太短暂了，不应耗费宝贵的时间去探讨神灵是否存在的问题，而应将全部精力用于创造更美好、更愉快的生活。

这一论述当然直奔问题的根本，肯定比以往任何文字或言论都更能动摇人们的信仰。何况这一理论是在雅典和斯巴达的战争处于关键时刻提出来的，人们长期遭受失败和疾病的折磨，已经陷入了极度的绝望。很显然，这时因质疑上帝的超凡能

He fled.

Unfortunately,on the way to Sicily,his ship was wrecked,and it seems that he was drowned,for we never hear of him again.

As for Diagoras,another victim of Athenian malevolence,he was really not a philosopher at all but a young writer who harbored a personal grudge against the Gods because they had once failed to give him their support in a law-suit. He brooded so long upon his supposed grievance that finally his mind became affected and he went about saying all sorts of blasphemous things about the Holy Mysteries which just then enjoyed great popularity among the people of northern Hellas. For this unseemly conduct he was condemned to death. But ere the sentence was executed,the poor devil was given the opportunity to escape. He went to Corinth,continued to revile his Olympian enemies,and peacefully died of his own bad temper.

And this brings us at last to the most notorious and the most famous case of Greek intolerance of which we possess any record,the judicial murder of Socrates.

When it is sometimes stated that the world has not changed at all and that the Athenians were no more broadminded than the people of later times,the name of Socrates is dragged into the debate as a terrible example of Greek bigotry. But today,after a very exhaustive study of the case,we know better and the long and undisturbed career of this brilliant but exasperating soap-box orator is a direct tribute to the spirit of intellectual liberty which prevailed throughout ancient Greece in the fifth century before our era.

For Socrates,at a time when the common people still firmly believed in a large number of divine beings,made himself the prophet of an only God. And although the Athenians may not always have known what he meant when he spoke of his"daemon" (that inner voice of divine inspiration which told him what to do and say),they were fully aware of

力而激怒上帝实在不是时候。普罗塔哥拉被指控为无神论者，被勒令屈服于法庭。

伯里克利本来可以保护他，但已不在人世。普罗塔哥拉尽管是科学家，却对殉道毫无兴趣。

他逃走了。

不幸的是，在前往西西里的路途中，他的船就失事了。他可能淹死了，因为再也没有他的消息。

至于迪亚哥拉斯（另一个遭到雅典人恶毒迫害的人），其实并不是哲学家，而是一个青年作家。由于神灵在一次官司中没有帮助他，他就把个人怨恨全都倾泻在他们身上。他长时间为自己假想的冤情沉思苦想，最终思想发生变化。他四处奔走，说着各种亵渎的语言，诽谤当时在希腊北部人中间深受敬仰的“神圣玄机”。由于这种不理智行为，他被判处死刑。但在临刑前，这个可怜虫得到机会逃跑了。他来到科林斯，继续诅咒他在奥林匹斯的敌人，终因脾气暴躁而一命呜呼。

我们最终看到了希腊人最臭名昭著、最著名的专制的例子。这就是对苏格拉底的死刑判决。对此我们有记载。

只要谈及世界依然没有改变，谈及雅典人的心胸和后人一样狭隘，人们必然会说出苏格拉底的名字，以此作为希腊人冥顽不化的可怕例证。但是今天经过对这个案例详尽的研究之后，我们了解得更多了。这位富有才华却又令人讨厌的街头演说家平凡的一生，对公元前5世纪盛行于古希腊的自由精神做出了直接贡献。

在普通百姓仍然坚信有许多天神的时代，苏格拉底把自己说成是某位神灵的

his very unorthodox attitude towards those ideals which most of his neighbors continued to hold in holy veneration and his utter lack of respect for the established order of things. In the end,however,politics killed the old man and theology (although dragged in for the benefit of the crowd) had really very little to do with the outcome of the trial.

Socrates was the son of a stone-cutter who had many children and little money. The boy therefore had never been able to pay for a regular college course,for most of the philosophers were practical fellows and often charged as much as two thousand dollars for a single course of instruction. Besides,the pursuit of pure knowledge and the study of useless scientific facts seemed to young Socrates a mere waste of time and energy. Provided a person cultivated his conscience,so he reasoned,he could well do without geometry and a knowledge of the true nature of comets and planets was not necessary for the salvation of the soul.

All the same,the homely little fellow with the broken nose and the shabby cloak,who spent his days arguing with the loafers on the corner of the street and his nights listening to the harangues of his wife (who was obliged to provide for a large family by taking in washing,as her husband regarded the gaining of a livelihood as an entirely negligible detail of existence),this honorable veteran of many wars and expeditions and ex-member of the Athenian senate was chosen among all the many teachers of his day to suffer for his opinions.

In order to understand how this happened,we must know something about the politics of Athens in the days when Socrates rendered his painful but highly useful service to the cause of human intelligence and progress.

All his life long (and he was past seventy when he was executed) Socrates tried to show his neighbors that they were wasting their opportunities;that they were living hollow and shallow lives;that they devoted entirely too much time to empty pleasures and

先知。尽管雅典人并不能完全理解他所谓的“精灵”（即告诉他该说什么和做什么的内心神灵的声音）意味着什么，但他们完全能注意到他对邻居们奉若神明的思想观念是持完全否定态度的，对既有习俗也极其不尊重。最后，当政者杀死了这位老人，而他的神学观点（尽管这种观点被牵强附会地用来说服民众）和审判结果实际上毫无关系。

■ 天文学家

苏格拉底是石匠的儿子。他父亲的子女很多，但收入微薄，因此苏格拉底没有钱进正规大学读书，因为当时的哲学家大都很现实，教单独一门课程经常要价不菲。此外，对年轻的苏格拉底来说，追求纯粹的知识、研究没用的科学现象只是浪费时间和精力。在他看来，一个人只要善于培植自己的良心，那么即便不懂几何学也会做得很好，了解彗星和行星的自然现象对于拯救灵魂来说也不是必要的。

然而，这个长着塌鼻梁、衣着邋遢的朴实的小个子，白天在街上和无业游民争论不休，晚上则在家听着妻子训斥（她为了养活一大家人而被迫给别人浆洗缝补，可是她丈夫却把谋生视为可以完全忽略的生存细节）；这个曾参加过多次战争和远征的受人尊敬的老兵；这个雅典元老院的前议

vain triumphs and almost invariably squandered the divine gifts with which a great and mysterious God had endowed them for the sake of a few hours of futile glory and self-satisfaction. And so thoroughly convinced was he of man's high destiny that he broke through the bounds of all old philosophies and went even farther than Protagoras. For whereas the latter had taught that"man is the measure of all things,"Socrates preached that"man's invisible conscience is (or ought to be) the ultimate measure of all things and that it is not the Gods but we ourselves who shape our destiny."

The speech which Socrates made before the judges who were to decide his fate (there were five hundred of them to be precise and they had been so carefully chosen by his political enemies that some of them could actually read and write) was one of the most delightful bits of commonsense ever addressed to any audience,sympathetic or otherwise.

"No person on earth,"so the philosopher argued,"has the right to tell another man what he should believe or to deprive him of the right to think as he pleases,"and further,"Provided that man remain on good terms with his own conscience,he can well do without the approbation of his friends,without money,without a family or even a home. But as no one can possibly reach the right conclusions without a thorough examination of all the pros and cons of every problem,people must be given a chance to discuss all questions with complete freedom and without interference on the part of the authorities."

Unfortunately for the accused,this was exactly the wrong statement at the wrong moment. Ever since the Peloponnesian war there had been a bitter struggle in Athens between the rich and the poor,between capital and labor. Socrates was a"moderate"—a liberal who saw good and evil in both systems of government and who tried to find a compromise which should satisfy all reasonable people. This,of course,had made him thoroughly unpopular with both sides but thus far they had been too evenly balanced to

员，却被从当时众多的教师中选出来，为了他的信仰而接受惩罚。

为了了解事情的经过，我们必须知道苏格拉底为了人类的进步事业而做出痛苦的牺牲（他后来被认为做出了极其有益的贡献）时，雅典的政治状况。

终其一生（苏格拉底被处死时已年逾七旬），苏格拉底都在试图告诉世人：他们正在浪费机会，他们的生活毫无意义，把过多的时间耗费在空洞的欢乐和虚无的胜利上，为了几小时的虚荣和自满而一味地挥霍伟大而神圣的上帝赐予的礼物。他完全相信人的崇高命运，这就彻底打破了一切旧哲学的藩篱，甚至比普罗塔哥拉走得还远。因为后者只是说："人是衡量万物的准绳。"苏格拉底却宣称："人的无形意识是（或应该是）万物的最终准绳；不是上帝，而是我们自己塑造了我们的命运。"

苏格拉底在那些法官面前的演讲（准确地说有500名法官，他们是苏格拉底的政敌精心挑选出来的，他们中有些人还会读书写字），对任何听众来说，都是最鼓舞人心的话语，而不论他们对此是持什么态度。

这位哲学家辩论说："世界上没有人有权力告诉别人应该信仰什么，或剥夺别人自由思考。"他还说："只要那个人有良知，那么即使没有朋友的赞同，没有金钱，没有妻小，甚至没有家庭，他也会成功。但若不彻底研究每个问题的来龙去脉，任何人都不可能得出正确的结论。因此人们必须有讨论所有问题的完全的自由，而且不受官方干涉。"

对苏格拉底这个被告来说，他不幸在错误的时间阐述了错误的论断。自从伯罗奔尼撒战争之后，在雅典富人与穷人、主人与仆人之间关系极度紧张。苏格拉底是

take action against him.

When at last in the year 403 B. C. the one-hundred-percent Democrats gained complete control of the state and expelled the aristocrats,Socrates was a doomed man.

His friends knew this. They suggested that he leave the city before it was too late and this would have been a very wise thing to do.

For Socrates had quite as many enemies as friends. During the greater part of a century he had been a sort of vocal"columnist,"a terribly clever busy-body who had made it his hobby to expose the shams and the intellectual swindles of those who regarded themselves as the pillars of Athenian society. As a result,every one had come to know him. His name had become a household word throughout eastern Greece. When he said something funny in the morning,by night the whole town had heard about it. Plays had been written about him and when he was finally arrested and taken to prison there was not a citizen in the whole of Attica who was not thoroughly familiar with all the details of his career.

Those who took the leading part in the actual trial (like that honorable grain merchant who could neither read nor write but who knew all about the will of the Gods and therefore was loudest in his accusations) were undoubtedly convinced that they were rendering a great service to the community by ridding the city of a highly dangerous member of the so-called"intelligentsia,"a man whose teaching could only lead to laziness and crime and discontent among the slaves.

It is rather amusing to remember that even under those circumstances,Socrates pleaded his case with such tremendous virtuosity that a majority of the jury was all for letting him go free and suggested that he might be pardoned if only he would give up this terrible habit of arguing,of debating,of wrangling and moralizing,in short,if only he would leave his neighbors and their pet prejudices in peace and not bother them with his eternal doubts.

个“温和分子”——一个既看到两种政权体系的利弊，又力图找到折中方案以满足所有理智人士的自由主义者。这当然让他在双方都不受欢迎，但他们那时候势均力敌而顾不上对付他。

终于到了公元前403年，彻头彻尾的民主派完全控制了国家，赶走了贵族，苏格拉底就难逃厄运了。

他的朋友知道了这事。他们建议他最好离开这座城市，不要太晚了，而且这样做是很明智的。

苏格拉底的敌人和朋友一样多。在大半个世纪里，他一直是个“口头评论家”，一个绝顶聪明的大忙人，以揭穿那些将自己标榜为雅典社会支柱的人的伪装和思想骗术为嗜好。结果，他的大名在整个希腊东部家喻户晓。他上午说的趣事，到晚上全城就都知道了。有人写了关于他的戏剧。当他最终被捕入狱时，整个雅典没有一人不对他一生的各个细节极其熟悉。

在实际审判中占主角的人（如那个既不会读又不会写，只因为知道上帝各项旨意，因此在起诉中最卖力的可敬的粮贩子），深信他们是在为社会做出伟大贡献，是在为城市除掉一个所谓“知识界”高度危险的人，一个其学说只能让奴隶学会懒惰、犯罪和不满的人。

非常有趣的是，即使在这种情况下，苏格拉底仍以精湛的口才为自己辩护，竟使得陪审团绝大多数人倾向于释放他，并且提出只要苏格拉底放弃辩论、争吵、说教的可怕习惯——简言之，只要他不再干涉别人，不再用他那无止境的疑问去打搅

But Socrates would not hear of it.

"By no means,"he exclaimed."As long as my conscience,as long as the still small voice within me,bids me go forth and show men the true road to reason,I shall continue to buttonhole whomsoever I happen to meet and I shall say what is on my mind,regardless of consequences."

After that,there was no other course but to condemn the prisoner to death.

Socrates was given a respite of thirty days. The holy ship which made an annual pilgrimage to Delos had not yet returned from its voyage and until then,the Athenian law did not allow any executions. The whole of this month the old man spent quietly in his cell,trying to improve his system of logic. Although he was repeatedly given the opportunity to escape,he refused to go. He had lived his life and had done his duty. He was tired and ready to depart. Until the hour of his execution he continued to talk with his friends,trying to educate them in what he held to be right and true,asking them to turn their minds upon the things of the spirit rather than those of the material world.

Then he drank the beaker of hemlock,laid himself upon his couch and settled all further argument by sleep everlasting.

For a short time,his disciples,rather terrified by this terrible outburst of popular wrath,thought it wise to remove themselves from the scene of their former activities.

But when nothing happened,they returned and resumed their former occupation as public teachers,and within a dozen years after the death of the old philosopher,his ideas were more popular than ever.

The city meanwhile had gone through a very difficult period. It was five years since the struggle for the leadership of the Greek peninsula had ended with the defeat of Athens and the ultimate victory of the Spartans. This had been a complete triumph of brawn over brain. Needless to say that it did not last very long. The Spartans,who never wrote a line

■ 普罗塔哥拉

他们，他就可以被赦免。

但苏格拉底不听这一套。

“没门儿！”他喊道，“只要我的良心和我体内微弱的心声，还在推动我前进，给人们指明通向理智的道路，我就要继续拉住我遇见的每一个人，说出我内心的想法，不论后果怎样。”

既然这样，就没有别的办法，只能判处这个囚犯死刑。

苏格拉底被缓刑30天。每年一度去朝拜戴洛斯的圣船还没有返航，雅典法律规定期间不准行刑。这位老人在单人牢房里安静地待了整整一个月，努力改进他的逻辑体系。虽然人们给了他多次逃跑的机会，但他都拒绝了。他已经尽了自己的职责，不枉此生。他累了，准备走了。直到行刑之际，他还在和朋友们谈话，用自己追求的真理教导他们，要求他们多考虑精神世界，而不是物质世界。

然后，他喝下毒药，躺在床上，让所有争论都随着他的长眠而宣告结束。

苏格拉底的门徒曾一度被公众可怕的愤怒吓坏了，觉得离开他们过去的活动场所不失为明智之举。

但什么都没发生，他们又回来了，重操旧业公开讲学。在这位老哲学家死后的

worth remembering or contributed a single idea to the sum total of human knowledge (with the exception of certain military tactics which survive in our modern game of football) thought that they had accomplished their task when the walls of their rival had been pulled down and the Athenian fleet had been reduced to a dozen ships. But the Athenian mind had lost none of its shrewd brilliancy. A decade after the end of the Peloponnesian war,the old harbor of the Piraeus was once more filled with ships from all parts of the world and Athenian admirals were again fighting at the head of the allied Greek navies.

Furthermore,the labor of Pericles,although not appreciated by his own contemporaries,had made the city the intellectual capital of the world—the Paris of the fourth century before the birth of Christ. Whosoever in Rome or Spain or Africa was rich enough to give his sons a fashionable education,felt flattered if the boys were allowed to visit a school situated within the shadow of the Acropolis.

For this ancient world,which we modern,people find so difficult to understand properly,took the problem of existence seriously.

Under the influence of the early Christian enemies of pagan civilization,the impression has gained ground that the average Roman or Greek was a highly immoral person who paid a shallow homage to certain nebulous Gods and for the rest spent his waking hours eating enormous dinners,drinking vast bumpers of Salernian wine and listening to the pretty prattle of Egyptian dancing girls,unless for a change he went to war and slaughtered innocent Germans and Franks and Dacians for the pure sport of shedding blood.

Of course,both in Greece and even more so in Rome,there were a great many merchants and war contractors who had accumulated their millions without much regard for those ethical principles which Socrates had so well defined before his judges. Because these people were very wealthy,they had to be put up with. This,however,did not mean that they

10多年里，他的思想比以前更受欢迎了。

与此同时，雅典经历了一段非常困难的时期。争夺希腊半岛领导权的战争已经五年了，战争以雅典人失败而斯巴达人最后获胜告终。这是一场体力战胜智力的胜利。不用说这是难以持久的。斯巴达人从未写过一句值得记住的话，也没有对人类的文化发展有过任何贡献（除了一些军事战术，它们保留在了我们当今的足球比赛中）。他们认为自己已经大功告成，因为对手的围墙被推倒了，雅典舰队也大大减少了。但雅典人丝毫没有丧失敏捷的才华。伯罗奔尼撒战争结束10年之后，古老的比雷埃夫斯港重新聚集了世界各地的船只，雅典海军将领在希腊联合舰队中再次冲锋在前。

何况伯里克利的努力虽然没有得到赏识，却使雅典成为世界文化的中心——正如公元前4世纪的巴黎一样。不管是罗马、西班牙或非洲的富人，只要想让他的孩子接受时髦的教育，那么即使孩子只被允许参观卫城附近的学校，家长也会飘飘然的。

我们现代人要正确理解古代社会非常困难，但那时候生存问题被看得很重要。

在异教文明早期基督教敌人的影响下，罗马人和希腊人被视为极其不道德的人。他们肤浅地崇拜一些古怪的神灵，剩下来的清醒时间就大吃大喝、暴餮天物，欣赏埃及舞女的妙歌曼舞；有时纯粹为了嗜血的乐趣，他们还出去打打仗，屠杀无辜的日耳曼人、法兰克人和达西雅人。

当然，希腊和罗马都有大量的商人和战争贩子（罗马甚至更多）。这些人积攒了百万财富，完全不顾苏格拉底在法官面前精辟阐述的伦理道德。因为这些人非常

enjoyed the respect of the community or were regarded as commendable representatives of the civilization of their day.

We dig up the villa of Epaphroditus,who amassed millions as one of the gang who helped Nero plunder Rome and her colonies. We look at the ruins of the forty room palace which the old profiteer built out of his ill-gotten gains. And we shake our heads and say,"What depravity !"

Then we sit down and read the works of Epictetus,who was one of the house slaves of the old scoundrel,and we find ourselves in the company of a spirit as lofty and as exalted as ever lived.

I know that the making of generalizations about our neighbors and about other nations is one of the most popular of indoor sports,but let us not forget that Epictetus,the philosopher,was quite as truly a representative of the time in which he lived as Epaphroditus,the imperial flunkey,and that the desire for holiness was as great twenty centuries ago as it is today.

Undoubtedly it was a very different sort of holiness from that which is practiced today. It was the product of an essentially European brain and had nothing to do with the Orient. But the"barbarians"who established it as their ideal of what they held to be most noble and desirable were our own ancestors,and they were slowly developing a philosophy of life which was highly successful if we agree that a clear conscience and a simple,straightforward life,together with good health and a moderate but sufficient income,are the best guarantee for general happiness and contentment. The future of the soul did not interest these people overmuch. They accepted the fact that they were a special sort of mammal which by reason of its intellectual application had risen high above the other creatures which crawled upon this earth. If they frequently referred to

富有，人们才被迫接受他们。但这并不等于他们拥有社会的尊重，或者被认为是当时值得赞扬的文化代表。

我们挖掘了埃帕菲罗迪特的别墅。作为帮助尼禄洗劫罗马及其殖民地的歹徒之一，这个人大发了横财。我们看着这个老投机商用不义之财建起来的有40间房屋的宫殿废墟，摇头叹道："多么腐败啊！"

然后，我们坐下来，读爱比克泰德[1]（他曾是埃帕菲罗迪特这个老恶棍的家奴）的著作，我们会发现自己在和人类最崇高的灵魂对话。

我知道，人们最喜欢在背后评论自己的邻居或邻国，但我们不要忘记，哲学家爱比克泰德是他所生活的那个时代的真正代表，正如埃帕菲罗迪特这个朝廷走狗也具有其代表性一样；而且2000年前人们追求尽善尽美的欲望和今天一样强烈。

毫无疑问，那是一种与今天迥然不同的尽善尽美，是一种基本上欧化的产物，和东方社会毫不相干。但那些建立了自己的理想并把它作为最崇高目标的"野蛮人"正是我们的祖先，他们慢慢发展出了一种生活哲学。如果我们赞同纯正的良心、简朴的生活，再加上健康的身体和适度而充足的收入是幸福和满足的最好保障的话，那么这种哲学就会被广为接受。这些人不会对灵魂的归宿很感兴趣，他们只是接受这样一个事实：自己是有文化的特殊动物，高居地球上的其他生物之上。他们常常谈到上帝，就像我们今天使用"原子""电子"或"乙醚"等词一样。万物

---

[1] 公元前1世纪希腊斯多葛派哲学家、教师。——译注

the Gods,they used the word as we use"atoms"or"electrons"or"aether."The beginning of things has got to have a name,but Zeus in the mouth of Epictetus was as problematical a value as x or y in the problems of Euclid and meant just as much or as little.

Life it was which interested those men and next to living,art.

Life,therefore,in all its endless varieties,they studied and following the method of reasoning which Socrates had originated and made popular,they achieved some very remarkable results.

That sometimes in their zeal for a perfect spiritual world they went to absurd extremes was regrettable,but no more than human. But Plato is the only one among all the teachers of antiquity who from sheer love for a perfect world ever came to preach a doctrine of intolerance.

This young Athenian,as is well known,was the beloved disciple of Socrates and became his literary executor.

In this capacity he immediately gathered all that Socrates had ever said or thought into a series of dialogues which might be truthfully called the Socratian Gospels.

When this had been done,he began to elaborate certain of the more obscure points in his master's doctrines and explained them in a series of brilliant essays. And finally he conducted a number of lecture courses which spread the Athenian ideas of justice and righteousness far beyond the confines of Attica.

In all these activities he showed such whole-hearted and unselfish devotion that we might almost compare him to St. Paul. But whereas St. Paul had led a most adventurous and dangerous existence,ever traveling from north to south and from west to east that he might bring the Good Tidings to all parts of the Mediterranean world,Plato never budged from his comfortable garden chair and allowed the world to come to him.

之源必须有一个名称，因此爱比克泰德口中的宙斯只是一切疑难问题的代号，就像欧几里得数学题中的*X*和*Y*，既可以含义很广，也可以很小。

■ 苏格拉底

那些人最感兴趣的是生活，仅次于生活的是艺术。

因此，他们研究包罗万象的生活，并遵循由苏格拉底创造并普及的推理方法，取得了优异的成绩。

他们有时因为追求完美的精神世界而走到荒唐的极端，这不免令人遗憾。但人无完人。不过，柏拉图是古代众多学者中唯一因对完美世界的挚爱而走向鼓吹不宽容教义人。

正如人们知道的那样，这个年轻的雅典人是苏格拉底的得意门生，也是他的思想的记录者。

他利用这一优势，随时将苏格拉底曾说过或想过的一切编成对话，这些完全可以被称为《苏格拉底福音书》。

完成这项工作之后，他开始详尽阐释老师的理论中比较深奥难解的观点，并写

Certain advantages of birth and the possession of independent wealth allowed him to do this.

In the first place he was an Athenian citizen and through his mother could trace his descent to no one less than Solon. Then as soon as he came of age he inherited a fortune more than sufficient for his simple needs.

And finally,his eloquence was such that people willingly traveled to the Aegean Sea if only they were allowed to follow a few of the lectures in the Platonic University.

For the rest,Plato was very much like the other young men of his time. He served in the army,but without any particular interest in military affairs. He went in for outdoor sports,became a good wrestler,a fairly good runner,but never achieved any particular fame in the stadium. Again,like most young men of his time,he spent a great deal of his time in foreign travel and crossed the Aegean Sea and paid a short visit to northern Egypt,as his famous grandfather Solon had done before him. After that,however,he returned home for good and during fifty consecutive years he quietly taught his doctrines in the shadowy corners of a pleasure garden which was situated on the banks of the river Cephissus in the suburbs of Athens and was called the Academy.

■ 苏格拉底之死

He had begun his career as a mathematician,but gradually he switched over to politics and in this field he laid the foundations for our modern school of government. He was at heart a confirmed optimist and believed in a steady process of human evolution. The life of man,so he taught,rises slowly from a lower plane to a higher one. From beautiful bodies,the world proceeds to beautiful institutions and from beautiful

了一系列才华横溢的文章来解释它们。最后他开了许多演讲课，将雅典人关于公正和正义的理想传播到了雅典以外的世界。

他在所有这些活动中表现出来的全力以赴和无私奉献精神，我们几乎可以将他和圣徒保罗相媲美。但圣徒保罗过着极其漂泊的日子，不停地从北到南、从西到东，把上帝的福音带到地中海各个地区；而柏拉图从未离开过他舒适花园的座椅，他让全世界都来向他请教。

良好的家世和足以使其独立的财产，让他能做到这点。

首先，他是雅典公民，从他母亲的血统可以直接追溯到梭伦[1]。其次，他一到法定年龄就继承了一笔足以过上优裕生活的财产。

最后，他口才非常出众，以至于那些获准在柏拉图大学哪怕只听他讲过几次课的人都情愿长途跋涉来到爱琴海。

至于其他方面，柏拉图和他那个时代的其他年轻人非常像。他当过兵，但对军事没有任何特殊的兴趣。他参加户外运动，是个摔跤赛跑好手，却从未在运动场上取得过好名次。和当时大多数年轻人一样，他也花了很多时间去国外旅行，曾横渡爱琴海，到埃及北部短暂观光，就像他著名的外祖父梭伦在他之前曾做过的那样。但他自从回国后再也没有外出过，在后来的50年内，他在一个景致宜人的花园的阴凉角落里

[1] 古雅典政治家和诗人，贵族出身。公元前594年担任执政官，进行政治经济改革。——译注

institutions to beautiful ideas.

This sounded well on parchment,but when Plato tried to lay down certain definite principles upon which his perfect state was to be founded,his zeal for righteousness and his desire for justice were so great that they made him deaf and blind to all other considerations. His Republic,which has ever since been regarded as the last word in human perfection by the manufacturers of paper Utopias,was a very strange commonwealth and reflected and continues to reflect with great nicety the prejudices of those retired colonels who have always enjoyed the comforts of a private income,who like to move in polite circles and who have a profound distrust of the lower classes,lest they forget"their place"and want to have a share of those special privileges which by right should go to the members of the"upper class."

Unfortunately the books of Plato enjoyed great respect among the medieval scholars of western Europe and in their hands the famous Republic became a most formidable weapon in their warfare upon tolerance.

For these learned doctors were apt to forget that Plato had reached his conclusions from very different premises than those which were popular in the twelfth and thirteenth centuries.

For instance,Plato had been anything but a pious man in the Christian sense of the word. The Gods of his ancestors he had always regarded with deep contempt as ill-mannered rustics from distant Macedonia. He had been deeply mortified by their scandalous behavior as related in the chronicles of the Trojan War. But as he grew older and sat and sat and sat in his little olive grove and became more and more exasperated by the foolish quarrels of the little city-states of his native land,and witnessed the utter failure of the old democratic ideal,he grew convinced that some sort of religion was necessary for the average citizen,or his imaginary Republic would at once degenerate into a state of

安静地传授他的教义，这个花园位于雅典郊区赛菲萨斯河畔，柏拉图学园由此得名。

柏拉图最初是一位数学家，但他逐渐转向政治学，并在这个领域为我们现代政治学说奠定了基础。他是个坚定的乐观主义者，相信人类进化是持续不断的。他教导说，人的生命是由较低级向较高级缓慢发展的，世界也从美好的实体发展为美好的制度，再从美好的制度上升为美好的思想。

这种思想写在羊皮纸上倒是不错，但当柏拉图试图制定某些具体原则，以此作为他的理想国的理论基础时，他追求公正、正义的热情和愿望就变得非常强烈，以至于他不能接受其他的想法。他所谓的共和国一直被纸上谈兵的乌托邦建设者们认为是适合人类生存最完美的世界。它是一个很奇特的共和国，已经并将继续反映那些退伍上校的微妙偏见，他们一直过着有充裕个人收入的舒适生活，喜欢参与政治，对下层社会非常不信任，免得忘了自己的“地位”，并想分享那些只有“上流社会”才有的特权。

不幸的是，柏拉图的书在西欧中世纪的学者中备受尊崇。在这些人手里，著名的共和国成了他们向宽容开战的非常可怕的武器。

这些知识渊博的学者健忘的是，柏拉图得出其结论的前提条件完全不同于12、13世纪。

例如，就基督教教义来说，柏拉图根本不是一个虔诚的人。对于他的祖先敬仰的神灵，他一直深恶痛绝，认为它们是来自偏远的马其顿的粗俗的乡巴佬。他曾为特洛伊战争纪年表中记载的有关神灵的丑恶行径深感羞辱。但当他走向成年，年复

rampant anarchy. He therefore insisted that the legislative body of his model community should establish a definite rule of conduct for all citizens and should force both freemen and slaves to obey these regulations on pain of death or exile or imprisonment. This sounded like an absolute negation of that broad spirit of tolerance and of that liberty of conscience for which Socrates had so valiantly fought only a short time before,and that is exactly what it was meant to be.

The reason for this change in attitude is not hard to find. Whereas Socrates had been a man among men,Plato was afraid of life and escaped from an unpleasant and ugly world into the realm of his own day dreams. He knew of course that there was not the slightest chance of his ideas ever being realized. The day of the little independent city-states,whether imaginary or real,was over. The era of centralization had begun and soon the entire Greek peninsula was to be incorporated into that vast Macedonian Empire which stretched from the shores of the Maritsa to the banks of the Indus River.

But ere the heavy hand of the conqueror descended upon the unruly democracies of the old peninsula,the country had produced the greatest of those many benefactors who have put the rest of the world under eternal obligation to the now defunct race of the Greeks.

I refer of course to Aristotle,the wonder-child from Stagira,the man who in his day and age knew everything that was to be known and added so much to the sum total of human knowledge that his books became an intellectual quarry from which fifty successive generations of Europeans and Asiatics were able to steal to their hearts' content without exhausting that rich vein of pure learning.

At the age of eighteen,Aristotle had left his native village in Macedonia to go to Athens and follow the lectures in Plato's university. After his graduation he lectured in a number of places until the year 336 B. C. when he returned to Athens and opened a school of his own in a garden near the temple of Apollo Lyceus,which became known as the Lyceum

一年地坐在他的小橄榄树园子里，被家乡各个小城邦之间的愚蠢争吵越来越激怒，并看到旧的民主理想彻底失败时，他逐渐相信，宗教对平民百姓是必不可少的，否则他的理想国就会立即陷于混乱状态。于是，他坚持认为，他的模范社会的立法机构应该制定出规范所有公民行为的明确准则，自由人和奴隶都必须遵守这些规范，否则就要被处死、流放或监禁。这像是对苏格拉底不久前还为之英勇奋斗的宽容精神和信仰自由的彻底否定，其实这正是柏拉图理论的本意。

这一态度变化的原因并不难找，因为苏格拉底扎根于大众，而柏拉图害怕生活，并且从令人厌烦的丑陋世界躲进了他自己臆想的王国。他当然知道，他的理想没有任何实现的可能。独立的小城邦时代——不论想象的还是实际的——已经过去了。中央集权的时代已经开始，不久，整个希腊半岛就将并入从马里查河岸一直延伸到印度河畔的广阔的马其顿帝国。

但在征服者的巨掌尚未征服这个古老半岛上难以驾驭的民主国家的时候，这个国家诞生了一位最伟大的思想家，他使整个世界永远怀念那个如今已消失的希腊民族。

我指的当然是亚里士多德，一个来自斯塔吉拉的神童，一个在当时就已经通晓许多不为人知的事情，并为人类知识宝库增添了丰富宝藏的人。他的书成为智慧的温泉，他以后的50代欧洲人和亚洲人都不必绞尽脑汁地学习，就可以从中获得让他们满意的精神食粮。

18岁时，亚里士多德离开马其顿的家乡，来到雅典，在柏拉图学园听课。毕业

and soon attracted pupils from all over the world.

Strangely enough,the Athenians were not at all in favor of increasing the number of academies within their walls. The town was at last beginning to lose its old commercial importance and all of her more energetic citizens were moving to Alexandria and to Marseilles and other cities of the south and the west. Those who remained behind were either too poor or too indolent to escape. They were the hidebound remnant of those old,turbulent masses of free citizens,who had been at once the glory and the ruin of the long-suffering Republic. They had regarded the"goings on"in Plato's orchard with small favor. When a dozen years after his death,his most notorious pupil came back and openly taught still more outrageous doctrines about the beginning of the world and the limited ability of the Gods,the old fogies shook their solemn heads and mumbled dark threats against the man who was making their city a by-word for free thinking and unbelief.

If they had had their own way,they would have forced him to leave their country. But they wisely kept these opinions to themselves. For this short-sighted,stoutish gentleman,famous for his good taste in books and in clothes,was no negligible quantity in the political life of that day,no obscure little professor who could be driven out of town by a couple of hired toughs. He was no one less than the son of a Macedonian court-physician and he had been brought up with the royal princes. And furthermore,as soon as he had finished his studies,he had been appointed tutor to the crown prince and for eight years he had been the daily companion of young Alexander. Hence he enjoyed the friendship and the protection of the most powerful ruler the world had ever seen and the regent who administered the Greek provinces during the monarch's absence on the Indian front watched carefully lest harm should befall one who had been the boon companion of his imperial master.

No sooner,however,had news of Alexander's death reached Athens than Aristotle's life

后，他在许多地方授课，直到公元前336年返回雅典，在阿波罗神庙附近一座花园开办了自己的学校，这就是亚里士多德讲学的学园，它很快就吸引了来自世界各地的学生。

奇怪的是，雅典人对于在自己的城堡兴建学园之事根本不感兴趣。当时的城邦开始丧失传统的商业重要地位，它所有精力旺盛的市民都搬到了亚历山大、马赛和其他城市。那些留下来的人，或者一贫如洗，或者懒惰成性。他们是老一辈狂暴自由民最墨守成规的残余分子，他们曾是苦难深重的共和国的荣耀，却也导致了它的毁灭。他们对柏拉图学园正在发生的事情没有好感。在柏拉图去世10多年后，他最著名的学生又回来了，公开讲授仍不被人们所接受的关于世界起源和神灵威力有限的教义。于是，老保守派严肃地摇着头，低声咒骂那个正在将他们的城邦变成思考自由和不拘信仰的场所的人。

如果按他们的意愿行事，他们就会把亚里士多德赶出国境。但他们明智地克制了自己。因为这位眼睛近视、身体矮胖的绅士以知识和衣着上的良好修养而闻名，在当时的政治生活中具有不可忽视的作用，而不是一两个雇用的打手就能把他赶出城邦的无名小教授。他不仅是马其顿宫廷医生的儿子，而且和王子们一起受过教育。更重要的是，他刚完成学业，就被任命为王太子的家庭教师。8年来，他和年轻的亚历山大日夜相伴。这样，他就赢得了有史以来最强大的统治者的友谊和保护。在亚历山大去印度前线期间，掌管希腊各省的摄政王对他照看周到，以免这位帝国主

was in peril. He remembered what had happened to Socrates and felt no desire to suffer a similar fate. Like Plato,he had carefully avoided mixing philosophy with practical politics. But his distaste for the democratic form of government and his lack of belief in the sovereign abilities of the common people were known to all. And when the Athenians,in a sudden outburst of fury,expelled the Macedonian garrison,Aristotle moved across the Euboean Sound and went to live in Calchis,where he died a few months before Athens was reconquered by the Macedonians and was duly punished for her disobedience.

At this far distance it is not easy to discover upon what positive grounds Aristotle was accused of impiety. But as usual in that nation of amateur orators,his case was inextricably mixed up with politics and his unpopularity was due to his disregard of the prejudices of a few local ward-bosses,rather than to the expression of any startlingly new heresies,which might have exposed Athens to the vengeance of Zeus.

Nor does it matter very much.

The days of the small independent republics were numbered.

Soon afterwards,the Romans fell heir to the European heritage of Alexander and Greece became one of their many provinces.

Then there was an end to all further bickering,for the Romans in most matters were even more tolerant than the Greeks of the Golden Age had been and they permitted their subjects to think as they pleased,provided they did not question certain principles of political expediency upon which the peace and prosperity of the Roman state had,since time immemorial,been safely built.

All the same there existed a subtle difference between the ideals which animated the contemporaries of Cicero and those which had been held sacred by the followers of such a man as Pericles. The old leaders of Greek thought had based their tolerance upon certain

宰的挚友受到伤害。

然而，亚历山大去世的消息刚传到希腊，亚里士多德的生命便陷入了危险中。他回想起苏格拉底的遭遇，不想遭受同样的下场。他像柏拉图那样，小心翼翼地避免把哲学和现实政治混为一谈。但他对民主政府的厌恶和对平民执政能力的不信任是众所周知的。当雅典人勃然大怒地赶走马其顿驻军时，亚里士多德便渡过尤比亚海峡，在卡尔基斯住了下来。在雅典再次被马其顿征服，并因其叛乱而受到惩罚之前几个月，他在卡尔斯基离开了人世。

已经过去这么久了，要找出亚里士多德被指控为不忠的确切背景可不容易。但通常情况下，在一个到处都是业余演说家的国度，他的活动必然会和政治盘根错节地纠缠在一起；而且他不受欢迎，是因为他对少数几个地方实力派的偏见的蔑视，而不是因为他散布了什么会使雅典遭到宙斯严厉惩罚的骇人听闻的新异端邪说。

但这已经无关紧要。

独立小城邦的日子已经屈指可数了。

不久，罗马人继承了亚历山大在欧洲的遗产，希腊成为他们众多行省中的一个。

然后，所有的争吵结束了，因为罗马人在许多事情上甚至比黄金时代的希腊人还要宽容。他们容许其臣民自由思考，但前提是臣民不能质疑政治上的某些随机应变原则，因为罗马政权自远古以来之所以能保持安定繁荣，全都有赖于这些原则。

西塞罗同时代的人所具有的思想，和伯里克利的追随者们所推崇的理想之间存

definite conclusions which they had reached after centuries of careful experiment and meditation. The Romans felt that they could do without the preliminary study. They were merely indifferent,and were proud of the fact. They were interested in practical things. They were men of action and had a deep-seated contempt for words.

If other people wished to spend their afternoons underneath an old olive tree,discussing the theoretical aspects of government or the influence of the moon upon the tides,they were more than welcome to do so.

If furthermore their knowledge could be turned to some practical use,then it was worthy of further attention. Otherwise,together with singing and dancing and cooking,sculpture and science,this business of philosophizing had better be left to the Greeks and to the other foreigners whom Jupiter in his mercy had created to provide the world with those things which were unworthy of a true Roman's attention.

Meanwhile they themselves would devote their attention to the administration of their ever increasing domains;they would drill the necessary companies of foreign infantry and cavalry to protect their outlying provinces;they would survey the roads that were to connect Spain with Bulgaria;and generally they would devote their energies to the keeping of the peace between half a thousand different tribes and nations.

Let us give honor where honor is due.

The Romans did their job so thoroughly that they erected a structure which under one form or another has survived until our own time,and that in itself is no mean accomplishment. As long as the necessary taxes were paid and a certain outward

柏拉图学园

在微妙的差别。希腊思想的老一代领袖把他们的宽容建立在某些明确的结论基础之上，这些结论是他们经过几个世纪的认真实践和冥思苦想才总结出来的。罗马人则认为，他们不必进行这方面的初步研究。他们对此毫不关心，而且对自己的行为引以为豪。他们对实用的东西感兴趣，注重行动，尤其蔑视空谈。

如果其他人愿意下午在老橄榄树下讨论统治理论或月亮对海潮的影响，罗马人是很欢迎的。

此外，如果外国人的知识有实践价值，那就会受到罗马人的进一步关注。至于哲学探讨，以及唱歌、跳舞、烹调、雕塑和科学等没有价值的事情，最好是留给希腊人或其他外国人，好心的朱庇特创造了他们，就是为了让他们去摆弄这些不值得正统罗马人关注的东西。

与此同时，罗马人要倾尽全力掌管日益扩大的领土；他们还要训练足够数量的外籍步兵和骑兵，以保卫他们的边沿各省，巡查连接西班牙和保加利亚的交通要道。他们通常要花很大精力，以维持几百个不同部落和民族之间的和平。

我们应该将荣誉送给值得送的人。

罗马人工作很精心，他们创建了一个政治体系，这个体系以这样或那样的形式一直延续至今，这本身就是个很伟大的成就。罗马的臣民只要缴纳必要的赋税，表

homage was paid to the few rules of conduct laid down by their Roman masters,the subject-tribes enjoyed a very large degree of liberty. They could believe or disbelieve whatever they pleased. They could worship one God or a dozen Gods or whole temples full of Gods. It made no difference. But whatever religion they chose to profess,these strangely assorted members of a world-encircling empire were forever reminded that the"pax Romana"depended for its success upon a liberal application of the principle of"live and let live."They must under no condition interfere either with their own neighbors or with the strangers within their gates. And if perchance they thought that their Gods had been insulted,they must not rush to the magistrate for relief."For,"as the Emperor Tiberius remarked upon one memorable occasion,"if the Gods think that they have just claims for grievance,they can surely take care of themselves."

And with such scant words of consolation,all similar cases were instantly dismissed and people were requested to keep their private opinions out of the courts.

If a number of Cappadocian traders decided to settle down among the Colossians,they had a right to bring their own Gods with them and erect a temple of their own in the town of Colossae. But if the Colossians should for similar reasons move into the land of the Cappadocians,they must be granted the same privileges and must be given an equal freedom of worship.

It has often been argued that the Romans could permit themselves the luxury of such a superior and tolerant attitude because they felt an equal contempt for both the Colossians and the Cappadocians and all the other savage tribes who dwelled outside of Latium. That may have been true. I don't know. But the fact remains that for half a thousand years,a form of almost complete religious tolerance was strictly maintained within the greater part of civilized and semi-civilized Europe,Asia and Africa and that the Romans developed a technique of statecraft which produced a maximum of practical results together with a

面上尊重罗马统治者定下的为数不多的行动准则，就可以享受广泛的自由。他们可以随心所欲地相信或不相信某事，可以信仰一个上帝或十几个上帝，甚至所有充斥各种神灵的庙宇，这都没有关系。但是，不管人们选择信仰什么，混居在这个世界性大帝国的形形色色的人们必须永远记住，“罗马和平”的实现有赖于公正地实施这样一条原则：“待人宽者，人亦待己宽。”在任何情况下，他们都不得干涉别人或自己大门内陌生人的事情。即使他们偶然认为自己信仰的神灵被亵渎了，也不必跑到官府那里去寻找解脱。“因为，”正如提庇留大帝在一次值得纪念的场合所说的：“如果这些神灵认为必须补偿他们遭受的损失，他们一定会照顾好自己的。”

正是有了这句不足道的安慰话，法庭可以拒绝处理所有这类案子，并要求人们不要为个人见解之类的问题打官司。

如果一群卡帕多西亚商人决定在哥罗西人的土地上定居，有权力信仰自己的上帝，并在哥罗西镇建造自己的庙宇。那么，如果哥罗西人为了类似的原因而搬到卡帕多西亚人的土地上居住时，他们也必须得到同样的权力和同等的信仰自由。

人们经常争辩说，罗马人之所以能够摆出这样一副至高无上的宽容姿态，是因为他们对哥罗西人、卡帕多西亚人及其他所有野蛮部落都同样轻视。这可能是正确的。我不能肯定。但事实是在500年中，近乎彻底的宗教宽容一直在文明和半文明的欧洲、亚洲和非洲绝大部分地区得到了严格维护；而且罗马人发展出了一种统治艺术：以最低限度的摩擦，换取巨大的实际成果。

minimum of friction.

To many people it seemed that the millennium had been achieved and that this condition of mutual forbearance would last forever.

But nothing lasts forever. Least of all,an empire built upon force.

Rome had conquered the world,but in the effort she had destroyed herself.

The bones of her young soldiers lay bleaching on a thousand battlefields.

For almost five centuries the brains of her most intelligent citizens had wasted themselves upon the gigantic task of administering a colonial empire that stretched from the Irish Sea to the Caspian.

At last the reaction set in.

Both the body and the mind of Rome had been exhausted by the impossible task of a single city ruling an entire world.

And then a terrible thing happened. A whole people grew tired of life and lost the zest for living.

They had come to own all the country-houses,all the town-houses,all the yachts and all the stage-coaches they could ever hope to use.

They found themselves possessed of all the slaves in the world.

They had eaten everything,they had seen everything,they had heard everything.

They had tried the taste of every drink,they had been everywhere,they had made love to all the women from Barcelona to Thebes. All the books that had ever been written were in their libraries. The best pictures that had ever been painted hung on their walls. The cleverest musicians of the entire world had entertained them at their meals. And,as children,they had been instructed by the best professors and pedagogues who had taught them everything there was to be taught. As a result,all food and drink had lost its taste,all books had grown dull,all women had become uninteresting,and existence itself

对许多人而言，太平盛世似乎来临了，相互宽容的状况似乎会持续到永远。

但没有什么东西能永远存在。至少建立在武力基础上的帝国是不能长久的。

罗马征服了世界，但同时毁灭了自己。

罗马帝国年轻战士的尸骨遍布上千个战场。

在近五个世纪中，社会精英们都把精力浪费在管理从爱尔兰海到黑海的殖民帝国这个庞大的工作中。

最后，副作用出现了。

以一个城市的体力和脑力统治全世界，这项事业拖垮了罗马。

随后，发生了一件可怕的事。人们逐渐厌恶了生活，失去了生活的热情。

他们已经占有了所有的乡村和城镇住房，拥有了他们曾希望使用的所有游艇和马车。

他们拥有了全世界的奴隶。

他们吃遍了每一样食物，看遍了所有美景，听到了所有妙音。

他们尝遍了每一种美酒，踏遍了所有的地方，玩遍了从巴塞罗那到底比斯的所有女人。世间所有用文字写成的书籍进入了他们的图书室，世界上画得最好的图画挂在他们墙上。全世界最卓越的音乐家在他们吃饭时为他们演奏。他们在童年时就接受最出色的教育。结果，所有的美味佳肴都失去了味道，所有的图书都变得枯燥乏味，所有的女人都失去了魅力，甚至生存本身也成为一种负担，许多人情愿寻找

had developed into a burden which a good many people were willing to drop at the first respectable opportunity.

There remained only one consolation,the contemplation of the Unknown and the Invisible.

The old Gods,however,had died years before. No intelligent Roman any longer took stock in the silly nursery rhymes about Jupiter and Minerva.

There were the philosophic systems of the Epicureans and the Stoics and the Cynics,all of whom preached charity and self-denial and the virtues of an unselfish and useful life.

But they were so empty. They sounded well enough in the books of Zeno and Epicurus and Epictetus and Plutarch,which were to be found in every corner store library.

But in the long run,this diet of pure reason was found to lack the necessary nourishing qualities. The Romans began to clamor for a certain amount of"emotion"with their spiritual meals.

Hence the purely philosophical"religions" (for such they really were,if we associate the idea of religion with a desire to lead useful and noble lives) could only appeal to a very small number of people,and almost all of those belonged to the upper classes who had enjoyed the advantages of private instruction at the hands of competent Greek teachers.

To the mass of the people,these finely-spun philosophies meant less than nothing at all. They too had reached a point of development at which a good deal of the ancient mythology seemed the childish invention of rude and credulous ancestors. But they could not possibly go as far as their so-called intellectual superiors and deny the existence of any and all personal Gods.

Wherefore they did what all half-educated people do under such circumstances. They paid a formal and outward tribute of respect to the official Gods of the Republic and then

一个体面的机会离开人世。

剩下一种兴趣，就是对未知世界的冥想。

然而，旧的上帝已在许多年前死了，聪明的罗马人不会再沉醉在幼儿园对丘比特和米纳瓦的愚蠢赞歌中。

伊壁鸠鲁学派[1]、斯多葛派[2]和昔尼克学派[3]的哲学体系已经出现，所有这些哲学体系都宣扬仁爱、克己、无私和有意义生活的美德。

但它们太空泛了。它们在齐诺、伊壁鸠鲁、爱比克泰德和普卢塔克的书中讲得倒是很动听，这些书在街头书店里比比皆是。

但从长远来看，这种纯理性的教义缺乏必要的营养成分。罗马人开始追求一种可以作为精神食粮的“情感”。

因此，这种纯哲学色彩的“宗教”（如果我们把宗教思想和追求有益的高尚生活的愿望联系起来，它们的确是哲学色彩的宗教）只能取悦一小部分人，这些人几乎全都属于上流社会，他们早已经享受到了能干的希腊教师个别授课的特殊待遇。

[1] 又称享乐主义学派，以其创始人伊壁鸠鲁而得名。其特点是终于师说，宣传快乐论学说。——译注

[2] 又称“画廊派”“斯多亚派”，因讲学场所称“斯多亚”而得名。该派主张宿命论，对基督教影响很大。——译注

[3] 又称“犬儒学派”。该派生活刻苦，时人讥之为“犬”，号召人们克己自制，把名利视为身外之物。——译注

betook themselves for real comfort and happiness to one of the many mystery religions which during the last two centuries had found a most cordial welcome in the ancient city on the banks of the Tiber.

The word"mystery"which I have used before was of Greek origin. It originally meant a gathering of"initiated people"—of men and women whose"mouth had been shut"against the betrayal of those most holy secrets which only the true members of the mystery were supposed to know and which bound them together like the hocus-pocus of a college fraternity or the cabalistic incantations of the Independent Order of Sea-Mice.

During the first century of our era,however,a mystery was nothing more nor less than a special form of worship,a denomination,a church. If a Greek or a Roman (if you will pardon a little juggling with time) had left the Presbyterian church for the Christian Science church,he would have told his neighbors that he had gone to"another mystery."For the word"church,"the"kirk,"the"house of the Lord,"is of comparatively recent origin and was not known in those days.

If you happen to be especially interested in the subject and wish to understand what was happening in Rome,buy a New York paper next Saturday. Almost any paper will do. Therein you will find four or five columns of announcements about new creeds,about new mysteries,imported from India and Persia and Sweden and China and a dozen other countries and all of them offering special promises of health and riches and salvation everlasting.

■ 亚里士多德

对普通百姓而言，这些冠冕堂皇的哲学思想却什么都不是。他们也发展到了这样一个阶段，认为大部分古代神话似乎都是粗俗而愚昧的祖先孩童般的发明。但他们还不可能赶上那些所谓的有智慧的人，还不能否认上帝的存在。

因此，他们做了所有知识浅薄的人在这种环境下会做的事情：表面上很正规地推崇共和国官方的上帝，实际上却为了寻求真正的安慰和幸福而信仰某些神秘宗教，这些宗教过去两个世纪在台伯河畔的古老城市中受到了最真诚的欢迎。

我上面用的“神秘”这个词源于希腊。它原来意味着一群“受到启示的人”——这些男女必须“守口如瓶”，不得把他们最神圣的秘密泄露出去。这些秘密只有他们才能知道，而且像大学兄弟会的咒语或海鼠独立教的秘密咒语一样，使人们结合在一起。

然而，在公元1世纪期间，神秘宗教只不过是一种特殊的崇拜形式、一种派别。如果一个希腊人或罗马人（请原谅时间上的小小混淆）已经离开长老会而加入基督科学教会，他就会告诉他的邻居，说他已经参加“另一个宗教”了。“教堂”“苏格兰长老会”和“贵族院”是比较新的词语，当时人们还不知道。

如果你碰巧对这个问题特别感兴趣，想知道当时罗马的情况，下周六就买一份纽约报纸，任何报纸都行。在这些报纸上，你会看到四五栏从印度、波斯、瑞典、中国及其他十多个国家引进的关于新教旨和新神秘宗教的广告，这些广告全都给人

Rome,which so closely resembled our own metropolis,was just as full of imported and domestic religions. The international nature of the city had made this unavoidable. From the vine-covered mountain slopes of northern Asia Minor had come the cult of Cybele,whom the Phrygians revered as the mother of the Gods and whose worship was connected with such unseemly outbreaks of emotional hilarity that the Roman police had repeatedly been forced to close the Cybelian temples and had at last passed very drastic laws against the further propaganda of a faith which encouraged public drunkenness and many other things that were even worse.

Egypt,the old land of paradox and secrecy,had contributed half a dozen strange divinities and the names of Osiris,Serapis and Isis had become as familiar to Roman ears as those of Apollo,Demeter and Hermes.

As for the Greeks,who centuries before had given unto the world a primary system of abstract truth and a practical code of conduct,based upon virtue,they now supplied the people of foreign lands who insisted upon images and incense with the far-famed"mysteries"of Attis and Dionysus and Orpheus and Adonis,none of them entirely above suspicion as far as public morals were concerned,but nevertheless enjoying immense popularity.

The Phoenician traders,who for a thousand years had frequented the shores of Italy,had made the Romans familiar with their great God Baal (the arch-enemy of Jehovah) and with Astarte his wife,that strange creature to whom Solomon in his old age and to the great horror of all his faithful subjects had built a"high place"in the very heart of Jerusalem;the terrible Goddess who had been recognized as the official protector of the city of Carthage during her long struggle for the supremacy of the Mediterranean and who finally after the destruction of all her temples in Asia and Africa was to return to Europe in the shape of a

们以健康、财富和灵魂永恒拯救的特殊许诺。

和我们的大都市相似，罗马充斥着外来的和本地的宗教。由于罗马的世界性地位，使这一点难以避免。从小亚细亚北部青藤覆盖的山坡上产生了对自然女神的崇拜，弗里吉亚人把自然女神尊崇为众神之母。伴随着崇拜自然女神而来的，是一些不合乎礼仪的感情狂欢。于是，罗马当局被迫一再关闭自然女神庙，最后还通过了一项果断的法律，禁止任何宗教活动，因为这种宗教只会鼓励公众喝得酩酊大醉，并做出其他更糟的事情。

埃及这块自相矛盾而又神秘的古老土地，产生了五六个怪诞不经的天神，奥赛利斯、塞拉皮斯和伊希斯的名字在罗马时代就像阿波罗、得墨忒耳和赫耳墨斯一样为人熟知。

至于希腊人，他们在几个世纪之前就为世人献上了抽象真理和行为法典的雏形体系。这时他们出于道德考虑，又向坚持偶像崇拜的外国居民提供了声名远播的艾蒂斯、狄俄尼索斯、俄耳甫斯和阿多尼斯等“神秘宗教”。从道德角度来说，这些神灵没有一个是尽善尽美的，但他们却颇受欢迎。

腓尼基商人在整整1000年的时间里经常去意大利海岸，使罗马人熟悉了他们伟大的上帝巴力（耶和华不共戴天之敌）和巴力的妻子阿斯塔特。为了这位神奇的女神，所罗门老年时在耶路撒冷中心建造了一个“高坛”，使他所有忠诚的臣民大为震惊。在争夺地中海最高权力的漫长斗争中，这个令人敬畏的女神一直被公认为是迦太基城的庇护者，她在亚洲和非洲的庙宇全被摧毁以后，又以最令人尊敬的基督

most respectable and demure Christian saint.

But the most important of all,because highly popular among the soldiers of the army,was a deity whose broken images can still be found underneath every rubbish pile that marks the Roman frontier from the mouth of the Rhine to the source of the Tigris.

This was the great God Mithras.

Mithras,as far as we know,was the old Asiatic God of Light and Air and Truth,and he had been worshiped in the plains of the Caspian lowlands when our first ancestors took possession of those wonderful grazing fields and made ready to settle those valleys and hills which afterwards became known as Europe. To them he had been the giver of all good things and they believed that the rulers of this earth exercised their power only by the grace of his mighty will. Hence,as a token of his divine favor,he sometimes bestowed upon those called to high offices a bit of that celestial fire by which he himself was forever surrounded,and although he is gone and his name has been forgotten,the kindly saints of the Middle Ages,with their halo of light,remind us of an ancient tradition which was started thousands of years before the Church was ever dreamed of.

But although he was held in great reverence for an incredibly long time,it has been very difficult to reconstruct his life with any degree of accuracy. There was a good reason for this. The early Christian missionaries abhorred the Mithras myth with a hatred infinitely more bitter than that reserved for the common,every day mysteries. In their heart of hearts they knew that the Indian God was their most serious rival. Hence they tried as hard as possible to remove everything that might possibly remind people of his existence. In this task they succeeded so well that all Mithras temples have disappeared and that not a scrap of written evidence remains about a religion which for more than half a thousand years was as popular in Rome as Methodism of Presbyterianism is in the United States of today.

教圣人的形象回到了欧洲。

但在所有神灵中还有一个最重要的神，他在军队中极受欢迎。在从莱茵河口到底格里斯河源头的罗马边界线的每一堆残砖破瓦下面，都会发现他的破碎金身。

这就是伟大的密斯拉神。

据我们所知，密斯拉是掌管光、空气和真理的古老的亚洲神，在里海低地平原受人崇拜。当时我们最早的祖先占有了那片牧草肥沃的土地，准备在山峰峡谷之间定居下来，这里后来成了人所共知的欧洲。密斯拉给了人类各种美好的东西，人们认为这块土地的统治者之所以能施展权力，完全是依靠他万能的旨意。密斯拉终日处在天火之中，作为天恩的象征，他有时会把一缕天火降在身居高职的人身上。虽然他早已离去，名字也被人们忘记了，但是中世纪那些仁慈的圣人头上的光环向我们提示了一个早在教堂问世1000年之前就已经形成的古老传统。

尽管密斯拉在相当长的时间里深受人们的崇敬，但要稍微准确地再现他的一生却非常困难。这是有其原因的。早期基督教传教士对密斯拉神话的仇恨要比对一般神话的仇恨更甚。他们明白，印度神是他们最凶恶的对手，因此他们竭尽所能地毁掉一切可能使人们想起他的存在的东西。他们的努力大见成效，所有的密斯拉神庙荡然无存，关于这一宗教的文字证据没有留下任何东西。这个宗教在500年中曾盛行于罗马，就像今天长老会和卫理公会在美国盛行一样。

不过，得益于一些亚洲资料，以及人们对一些废墟的仔细搜索（在炸药还没有发明之前，建筑物不可能被彻底摧毁），我们已经填补了这个空白，现在掌握了

However with the help of a few Asiatic sources and by a careful perusal of certain ruins which could not be entirely destroyed in the days before the invention of dynamite,we have been able to overcome this initial handicap and now possess a fairly accurate idea about this interesting God and the things for which he stood.

Ages and ages ago,so the story ran,Mithras was mysteriously born of a rock. As soon as he lay in his cradle,several nearby shepherds came to worship him and make him happy with their gifts.

As a boy,Mithras had met with all sorts of strange adventures. Many of these remind us closely of the deeds which had made Hercules such a popular hero with the children of the Greeks. But whereas Hercules was often very cruel,Mithras was forever doing good. Once he had engaged in a wrestling match with the sun and had beaten him. But he was so generous in his victory,that the sun and he had become like brothers,and were often mistaken for each other.

When the God of all evil had sent a drought which threatened to kill the race of man,Mithras had struck a rock with his arrow,and behold! plentiful water had gushed forth upon the parched fields. When Ahriman (for that was the name of the arch-enemy) had thereupon tried to achieve his wicked purpose by a terrible flood,Mithras had heard of it,had warned one man,had told him to build a big boat and load it with his relatives and his flocks and in this way had saved the human race from destruction. Until finally,having done all he could to save the world from the consequences of its own follies,he had been taken to Heaven to rule the just and righteous for all time.

Those who wished to join the Mithras cult were obliged to go through an elaborate form of initiation and were forced to eat a ceremonious meal of bread and wine in memory of the famous supper eaten by Mithras and his friend the Sun. Furthermore,they

■ 对立的宗教

关于这个有趣天神及其轶事的相当准确的情况。

密斯拉的故事要追溯到很久很久以前。密斯拉神秘地从一块岩石中出生了。他还睡在摇篮里，附近的几个牧羊人就来祭拜他，还送礼物逗他高兴。

密斯拉在孩提时代就经历了各种怪异的冒险，其中很多冒险使我们想起了一些事情，这些事情使赫拉克勒斯成了希腊孩子们最欢迎的英雄。但赫拉克勒斯总是那么残酷，而密斯拉总是与人为善。有一次他与太阳神角逐，把对方打翻在地。但是他胜而不骄，而是宽容大度地和太阳神成为手足兄弟，以至于人们经常将他们搞错。

当罪恶之神意欲毁灭整个人类而降下一场干旱的时候，密斯拉用他的箭射向一块岩石，顿时，泉涌般的水冲向了干裂的土地。当艾赫里曼（这是密斯拉不共戴天之敌、罪恶之神的名字）又想以一场可怕的洪水达到其卑鄙目的时，密斯拉得知了此事。他告诉了一个人，让他造一艘大船，把他的亲属和家禽都带上船，这样又把人类从毁灭中救了出来。最后，为了拯救世界，使其不致因自身的各种弊病而遭到恶报，他竭尽了力气，然后又升入天国，永远掌握着正义和公正。

were obliged to accept baptism in a font of water and do many other things which have no special interest to us,as that form of religion was completely exterminated more than fifteen hundred years ago.

Once inside the fold,the faithful were all treated upon a footing of absolute equality. Together they prayed before the same candle-lit altars. Together they chanted the same holy hymns and together they took part in the festivities which were held each year on the twenty-fifth of December to celebrate the birth of Mithras. Furthermore they abstained from all work on the first day of the week,which even today is called Sun-day in honor of the great God. And finally when they died,they were laid away in patient rows to await the day of resurrection when the good should enter into their just reward and the wicked should be cast into the fire everlasting.

The success of these different mysteries,the widespread influence of Mithraism among the Roman soldiers,points to a condition far removed from religious indifference. Indeed the early centuries of the empire were a period of restless search after something that should satisfy the emotional needs of the masses.

But early in the year 47 of our own era something happened. A small vessel left Phoenicia for the city of Perga,the starting point for the overland route to Europe. Among the passengers were two men not overburdened with luggage.

Their names were Paul and Barnabas.

They were Jews,but one of them carried a Roman passport and was well versed in the wisdom of the Gentile world.

It was the beginning of a memorable voyage.

Christianity had set out to conquer the world

那些想加入密斯拉崇拜行列的人，必须通过一种仪式，必须隆重吃一顿面包和酒作为礼餐，以纪念密斯拉和他的朋友太阳神一起享用的著名晚餐。还有，他们必须在圣水前接受洗礼，做很多在我们看来毫无特殊意义的事情，这种宗教形式早在1500年前就不见了。

一旦加入密斯拉崇拜的行列，所有虔诚信徒都会被同等相待。他们一起在同一个烛光明亮的祭台前祷告，一起唱同一首赞美诗，一同参加每年12月25日举行的庆祝密斯拉生日的节日。而且他们在每周的第一天不做任何工作，直到今天，我们仍然称这一天为“星期日”，以纪念这位伟大的天神。他们死后，尸体要摆放整齐，以等待末日审判。那时，好人会得到公正的报答，而恶人则被投入永恒的烈火中。

这形形色色的神话的成功，以及密斯拉在罗马士兵中的广泛影响，表明了人们对宗教的极大兴趣。实际上，罗马帝国在早期的几个世纪里，一直在不停地寻找某种能够满足民众精神需求的东西。

但是在公元47年，发生了一件事。一艘小船从腓尼基驶向佩加城，该城是通往欧洲的陆路起点。在乘客中有两个没有带行李的人。

他们的名字是保罗和巴拿巴。

他们是犹太人，但其中一人持有罗马护照，还通晓非犹太人的智慧。

这是一次值得纪念的旅程的开始。

基督教开始征服世界了。

CHAPTER Ⅲ THE BEGINNING OF RESTRAINT

The rapid conquest of the western world by the Church is sometimes used as proof definite that the Christian ideas must have been of divine origin. It is not my business to debate this point,but I would suggest that the villainous conditions under which the majority of the Romans were forced to live had as much to do with the success of the earliest missionaries as the sound common sense of their message.

Thus far I have shown you one side of the Roman picture—the world of the soldiers and statesmen and rich manufacturers and scientists,fortunate folks who lived in delightful and enlightened ease on the slopes of the Lateran Hill or among the valleys and hills of the Campania or somewhere along the bay of Naples.

But they were only part of the story.

Amidst the teeming slums of the suburbs there was little enough evidence of that plentiful prosperity which made the poets rave about the Millennium and inspired orators to compare Octavian to Jupiter.

There,in the endless and dreary rows of overcrowded and reeking tenement houses lived those vast multitudes to whom life was merely an uninterrupted sensation of hunger,sweat and pain. To those men and women,the wonderful tale of a simple carpenter in a little village beyond the sea,who had gained his daily bread by the labor of his own hands,who had loved the poor and downtrodden and who therefore had been killed by his cruel and rapacious enemies,meant something very real and tangible. Yes,they had all of them heard of Mithras and Isis and Astarte. But these Gods were dead,and they had

第3章　桎梏的开始

基督教迅速征服了西方世界，这件事有时被人们作为佐证，来强调基督教思想来源于天国。我并不想争论这个观点，只是想指出，大多数罗马人水深火热的生活和最早期传教士的成功颇有干系，就像困苦生活导致人们喜欢神话寓一样。

至此，我已向大家展示了罗马图画的一个方面——士兵、政客、企业家和科学富翁的世界，这是些幸运儿，他们住在拉特兰山山坡、坎帕尼亚山脉峡谷和那不勒斯海湾，过着幸福而文明的生活。

但他们只代表故事的一个方面。

在城郊多如牛毛的贫民窟里，却几乎难以看到那种使诗人欢呼太平盛世、激发演说家把奥克塔维安比喻成朱庇特的繁荣盛况。

就在那儿，就在那人头攒动、臭气冲天的一排排漫长无边、凄凉悲惨的租赁房屋中，住着的是一大群劳苦大众。对他们来说，生活不过是无休止的饥饿、流放和痛苦。在这些男女的眼里，只有一个朴实的木匠讲的精彩故事才是真实可信的。这个木匠住在大海对岸的一个小村庄，他用自己的双手劳动换来了每天的衣食，热爱贫苦之辈，因此被冷酷贪婪的敌人谋害了。的确，所有罗马人都知道密斯拉、伊希

died hundreds and thousands of years ago and what people knew about them they only knew by hearsay from other people who had also died hundreds and thousands of years ago.

Joshua of Nazareth,on the other hand,the Christ,the anointed,as the Greek missionaries called him,had been on this earth only a short time ago. Many a man then alive might have known him,might have listened to him,if by chance he had visited southern Syria during the reign of the Emperor Tiberius.

And there were others,the baker on the corner,the fruit peddler from the next street,who in a little dark garden on the Appian Way had spoken with a certain Peter,a fisherman from the village of Capernaum,who had actually been near the mountain of Golgotha on that terrible afternoon when the Prophet had been nailed to the cross by the soldiers of the Roman governor.

We should remember this when we try to understand the sudden popular appeal of this new faith.

It was that personal touch,that direct and personal feeling of intimacy and near-by-ness which gave Christianity such a tremendous advantage over all other creeds. That and the love which Jesus had so incessantly expressed for the submerged and disinherited among all nations and which radiated from everything he had said. Whether he had put it into the exact terms used by his followers was of very slight importance. The slaves had ears to hear and they understood. And trembling before the high promise of a glorious future,they for the first time in their lives beheld the rays of a new hope.

At last the words had been spoken that were to set them free.

No longer were they poor and despised,an evil thing in the sight of the great of this world.

On the contrary,they were the predilected children of a loving Father.

They were to inherit the earth and the fullness thereof.

斯和艾斯塔蒂，但这些神都死了，在千百年前就离开了人世，人们也只是根据千百年前就死了的人留下的传闻才知道了他们的事迹。

可是，拿撒勒的约书亚，基督，也就是被希腊传教士称为救世主的人不久前还活在世上。当时很多活着的人都知道他，在提庇留大帝统治时期，如果有人去过叙利亚南部，也许还听过他的演说。

还有其他人：街角的面包师和邻街的水果贩在亚壁古道旁边的黑暗小花园里曾与一个叫彼得的人说过话；伽百农村的一个渔夫曾去过各各他山附近，在先知被罗马士兵钉在十字架上的那个可怕的下午，曾目睹了此事。

如果我们要理解人们为什么突然热衷于新的信仰，就要记住这一点。

正是这种人的接触，正是这种亲密直接的私人感情，使基督教获得了高于其他教义的巨大优越性。耶稣的这种爱，表达了各国深受压迫、丧失权利的民众的呼声，并且传到了四面八方。他说的话是否使用与后人完全一样的词汇毫不重要，奴隶们能够理解。他们在崇高诺言面前战栗着，有生以来第一次看到了新希望的光芒。

他们终于盼到了使他们获得自由的话。在世界权势面前，他们不再是可怜、卑贱、可恶的生灵了。

相反，他们成了慈父的宠儿。

他们要继承这个世界以及属于它的富足的一切。

They were to partake of joys withheld from many of those proud masters who even then dwelled behind the high walls of their Samnian villas.

For that constituted the strength of the new faith. Christianity was the first concrete religious system which gave the average man a chance.

Of course I am not talking of Christianity as an experience of the soul—as a mode of living and thinking—and I have tried to explain how,in a world full of the dry-rot of slavery,the good tidings must spread with the speed and fury of an emotional prairie fire. But history,except upon rare occasions,does not concern itself with the spiritual adventures of private citizens,be they free or in bondage. When these humble creatures have been neatly organized into nations,guilds,churches,armies,brotherhoods and federations;when they have begun to obey a single directing head;when they have accumulated sufficient wealth to pay taxes and can be forced into armies for the purpose of national conquest,then at last they begin to attract the attention of our chroniclers and are given serious attention. Hence we know a great deal about the early Church,but exceedingly little about the people who were the true founders of that institution. That is rather a pity,for the early development of Christianity is one of the most interesting episodes in all history.

The Church which finally was built upon the ruins of the ancient empire was really a combination of two conflicting interests. On the one side it stood forth as the champion of those all-embracing ideals of love and charity which the Master himself had taught. But on the other side it found itself ineradicably bound up with that arid spirit of provincialism which since the beginning of time had set the compatriots of Jesus apart from the rest of the world.

In plain language,it combined Roman efficiency with Judaean intolerance and as a result it established a reign of terror over the minds of men which was as efficient as it was illogical.

To understand how this could have happened,we must go back once more to the days of

他们还要分享一直被住在萨姆奈别墅高墙之内骄横跋扈的人所独霸的欢乐。

新信仰的力量由此产生了。基督教是第一个给予普通人关怀的实实在在的宗教体系。

当然，我并不想把基督教说成是灵魂的感受——一种生活和思考的方式——我只是想说，在腐朽的奴隶制社会，这种好事情必然会以极快的速度点燃情感烈火，并得到传播。但是除了个别情况外，历史是不关注普通人的精神冒险的，不管他们是自由人还是奴隶。这些卑微的人被整齐地划分为民族、行会、教会、军队、兄弟会和同盟，当他们开始服从一个统一的指挥，积累了足够的财富来缴税，并被强招入伍为征服其他民族而战时，他们才会吸引编年史家的注意，受到重视。因此，尽管我们对早期基督教会了解很多，却对它的创始人知之甚少。这的确很遗憾，因为基督教的早期发展是最值得探讨的历史之一。

在古老帝国的废墟上最终建立起来的基督教堂，实际上是两个相冲突的利益结合的产物：一个代表友爱慈善理想的高峰，这是耶稣亲自教导的；另一个则代表狭隘的地方主义，由于它的根深蒂固的束缚，使得耶稣的同乡从一开始便与世界其他地方疏远了。

说得浅显些，这种地方主义将罗马人的效率和犹太人的专横联系在一起，结果建立了压抑人的思想的恐怖统治，虽然这种统治行之有效，却不合逻辑。

为了理解事情是如何发生的，我们必须再次回到保罗的年代和耶稣遇难后的

Paul and to the first fifty years after the death of Christ,and we must firmly grasp the fact that Christianity had begun as a reform movement within the bosom of the Jewish church and had been a purely nationalistic movement which in the beginning had threatened the rulers of the Jewish state and no one else.

The Pharisees who had happened to be in power when Jesus lived had understood this only too clearly. Quite naturally they had feared the ultimate consequences of an agitation which boldly threatened to question a spiritual monopoly which was based upon nothing more substantial than brute force. To save themselves from being wiped out they had been forced to act in a spirit of panic and had sent their enemy to the gallows before the Roman authorities had had time to intervene and deprive them of their victim.

What Jesus would have done had he lived it is impossible to say. He was killed long before he was able to organize his disciples into a special sect nor did he leave a single word of writing from which his followers could conclude what he wanted them to do.

In the end,however,this had proved to be a blessing in disguise.

The absence of a written set of rules,of a definite collection of ordinances and regulations,had left the disciples free to follow the spirit of their master's words rather than the letter of his law. Had they been bound by a book,they would very likely have devoted all their energies to a theological discussion upon the ever enticing subject of commas and semi-colons.

In that case,of course,no one outside of a few professional scholars could have possibly shown the slightest interest in the new faith and Christianity would have gone the way of so many other sects which begin with elaborate written programs and end when the police are called upon to throw the haggling theologians into the street,

At the distance of almost twenty centuries,when we realize what tremendous damage Christianity did to the Roman Empire,it is a matter of surprise that the authorities took practically no steps to quell a movement which was fully as dangerous to the safety of the state

头50年，而且我们要牢牢把握住这个事实：基督教是从犹太教内部的变革中产生的，是一场纯民族主义的运动，它从一开始就威胁到了犹太王国的统治者，而不是别人。

耶稣在世时，正在掌权的法利赛人清楚地知道这一点。他们自然十分害怕这种鼓动宣传的严重后果，因为它威胁说要对政府的精神垄断提出质疑，而这种垄断只是建立在野蛮的武力基础上的。为了不被赶走，他们惊慌失措地采取行动，在罗马当局还没来得及插手带走他们的对手之前，就把敌人送上了绞刑架。

谁也说不准，假如当时耶稣还活着，将会采取什么对策。他遇害时还没有把信徒组成一个教派，也没有写下任何东西告诉追随者应该怎样做。

结果证明，这倒成了福音。

由于没有文字形成的规定，没有明确的条例规则汇编，反而使信徒可以自由地遵循其导师的精神，而不是他的法规文字。如果他们被一本书束缚了，那他们很可能会把全部精力用在标点符号之类的迷人话题的讨论上。

当然，如果是这样，那么除了几个专业学者之外，就没有人会对新信仰感兴趣了，基督教就会重蹈其他众多教派的覆辙，以精心写成的文字纲领开始，最后以那些争吵不休的理论家被警察扔到大街上告终。

在过了近20个世纪之后，我们了解了基督教对罗马帝国的严重危害，但令人惊讶的是，既然它对国家安全的威胁就像匈奴人和哥特人的侵略一样，罗马当局竟

as an invasion by Huns or Goths. They knew of course that the fate of this eastern prophet had caused great excitement among their house slaves,that the women were forever telling each other about the imminent reappearance of the King of Heaven,and that quite a number of old men had solemnly predicted the impending destruction of this world by a ball of fire.

But it was not the first time that the poorer classes had gone into hysterics about some new religious hero. Most likely it would not be the last time,either. Meanwhile the police would see to it that these poor,frenzied fanatics did not disturb the peace of the realm.

And that was that.

The police did watch out,but found little occasion to act. The followers of the new mystery went about their business in a most exemplary fashion. They did not try to overthrow the government. At first,several slaves had expected that the common fatherhood of God and the common brotherhood of man would imply a cessation of the old relation between master and servant. The apostle Paul,however,had hastened to explain that the Kingdom of which he spoke was an invisible and intangible kingdom of the soul and that people on this earth had better take things as they found them,in expectation of the final reward which awaited them in Heaven.

Similarly,a good many wives,chafing at the bondage of matrimony as established by the harsh laws of Rome,had rushed to the conclusion that Christianity was synonymous with emancipation and full equality of rights between men and women. But again Paul had stepped forward and in a number of tactful letters had implored his beloved sisters to refrain from all those extremes which would make their church suspect in the eyes of the more conservative pagans and had persuaded them to continue in that state of semi-slavery which had been woman's share ever since Adam and Eve had been driven out of Paradise. All this showed a most commendable respect for the law and as far as the authorities were concerned,the Christian missionaries could therefore come and go at will and preach as

然没有采取任何实际行动。他们当然知道，正是这位东方先知导致了家奴的巨大骚动，女人们也喋喋不休地谈论上帝会很快重现，而且许多老人还一本正经地预言地球即将在一团火球中毁灭。

但这已经不是贫苦阶层第一次为了某个新的宗教人物而疯狂了，而且很可能也不是最后一次。只要警察密切关注，贫穷的狂热者就扰乱不了帝国的安宁。

情况就是这样。

警方的确戒备森严，但找不到诉诸武力的任何机会。新的宗教追随者以一种很值得效仿的方式在做自己的事情。他们并不想推翻政府。起初，有几个奴隶还期望上帝的父爱和人与人之间的兄弟之情会终止旧的主仆关系，但圣徒保罗赶忙来解释说，他所说的王国是看不见摸不着的灵魂王国，尘世的人最好对一切都逆来顺受，以期在天国得到好报。

同样，许多妻子也在对罗马法典规定的婚姻束缚进行抗争，她们得出结论说，基督教是解放、男女权力平等的同义词。但保罗又跳出来，以一连串娓娓动听的字眼恳求心爱的姐妹们不要走向极端，那样将会使保守的异教徒对教会产生疑心；而且他还劝她们继续维持半奴隶的状态，因为自从亚当和夏娃被逐出天堂以后，这一直是女人的本分。所有这些都表现了对法律的极大顺从，很值得效仿，因此对罗马当局来说，基督教传教士可以随意往来，因为他们的说教最符合当政者的口味和愿望。

best suited their own individual tastes and preferences.

But as has happened so often in history,the masses had shown themselves less tolerant than their rulers. Just because people are poor it does not necessarily follow that they are high-minded citizens who could be prosperous and happy if their conscience would only permit them to make those compromises which are held to be necessary for the accumulation of wealth.

And the Roman proletariat,since centuries debauched by free meals and free prize-fights,was no exception to this rule. At first it derived a great deal of rough pleasure from those sober-faced groups of men and women who with rapt attention listened to the weird stories about a God who had ignominiously died on a cross,like any other common criminal,and who made it their business to utter loud prayers for the hoodlums who pelted their gatherings with stones and dirt.

The Roman priests,however,were not able to take such a detached view of this new development.

The religion of the empire was a state religion. It consisted of certain solemn sacrifices made upon certain specified occasions and paid for in cash. This money went toward the support of the church officers. When thousands of people began to desert the old shrines and went to another church which did not charge them anything at all,the priests were faced by a very serious reduction in their salary. This of course did not please them at all,and soon they were loud in their abuse of the godless heretics who turned their backs upon the Gods of their fathers and burned incense to the memory of a foreign prophet.

But there was another class of people in the city who had even better reason to hate the Christians. Those were the fakirs,who as Indian Yogis and Pooughies and hierophants of the great and only mysteries of Isis and Ishtar and Baal and Cybele and Attis had for years made a fat and easy living at the expense of the credulous Roman middle classes. If the

但是，正像历史上经常发生的那样，群众表现出来的宽容精神却不如他们的统治者。因为他们贫困潦倒，即使良知准许他们为了必要的财富积累而做出妥协让步，他们也不会成为快慰和富足的品格高尚之人。

古罗马的最下层人，由于数世纪以来沉湎于免费的大吃大喝和职业拳击赛，都毫无例外地遵守着上述法则。起初，他们从那些一脸严肃的男男女女那儿获得了大量粗俗的快乐，这些男女全神贯注地听着耶稣像其他普通罪犯那样不光彩地死在十字架上的神奇故事，而且他们把为那些流氓无赖（他们朝耶稣投掷了无数石头和泥土）高声祈祷看成是自己的责任。

然而，罗马教士对这种新发展不能泰然处之。

罗马帝国奉行的宗教是国教，它包括在某些特定时节举行的隆重祭祀，人们要为此缴纳现钱。这些钱自然进了教堂主管的腰包。如果成千上万的人开始抛弃旧的圣地，而投奔另一个不收任何钱的教堂，教士的收入就会大大减少。这当然让他们不高兴，不久他们就竭力诽谤咒骂不信奉传统神灵的异教徒，说他们背叛了祖先的上帝，而且为了纪念异邦的先知而进香。

但城市中另一个阶层的人更有理由憎恨基督教。他们是些骗子，他们就像印度的瑜伽信奉者和伊希斯、阿施塔尔、巴力、自然女神和阿提斯神话中伟大而唯一的祭司长一样，年复一年地挥霍着偏听轻信的罗马中产阶级的钱，过着舒适奢侈的生活。假如基督教建立了一个竞争性组织，为他们自己的上天启示而收取一定的费

Christians had set up a rival establishment and had charged a handsome price for their own particular revelations,the guild of spook-doctors and palmists and necromancers would have had no reason for complaint. Business was business and the soothsaying fraternity did not mind if a bit of their trade went elsewhere. But these Christians—a plague upon their silly notions!—refused to take any reward. Yea,they even gave away what they had,fed the hungry and shared their own roof with the homeless. And all that for nothing! Surely that was going too far and they never could have done this unless they were possessed of certain hidden sources of revenue,the origin of which no one thus far had been able to discover.

Rome by this time was no longer a city of free-born burghers. It was the temporary dwelling place of hundreds of thousands of disinherited peasants from all parts of the empire. Such a mob,obeying the mysterious laws that rule the behavior of crowds,is always ready to hate those who behave differently from themselves and to suspect those who for no apparent reason prefer to live a life of decency and restraint. The hail-fellow-well-met who will take a drink and (occasionally) will pay for one is a fine neighbor and a good fellow. But the man who holds himself aloof and refuses to go to the wild-animal show in the Coliseum,who does not cheer when batches of prisoners of war are being dragged through the streets of the Capitoline Hill,is a spoil-sport and an enemy of the community at large.

When in the year 64 a great conflagration destroyed that part of Rome inhabited by the poorer classes,the scene was set for the first organized attacks upon the Christians.

At first it was rumored that the Emperor Nero,in a fit of drunken conceit,had ordered his capital to be set on fire that he might get rid of the slums and rebuild the city according to his own plans. The crowd,however,knew better. It was the fault of those Jews and Christians who were forever telling each other about the happy day when large balls of fire would descend from Heaven and the homes of the wicked would go up in flames.

Once this story had been successfully started,others followed in rapid succession. One

用，那么巫师、看手相者和巫术师行会是没有理由抱怨的。生意毕竟是生意，预言行业并不在意其他人也干这行。但这些基督徒却出了些该死的主意——他们竟拒绝收取任何报酬，甚至还把自己的东西送给别人，给饥饿者饭吃，把无家可归者请到家里住，而这一切竟不收任何钱。这太过分了，除非他们有某些私下的收入或尚未被发现的财源，否则他们不可能这样做。

这时的罗马已不再是自由民的城市了，它是来自帝国各地的成千上万失去了财产的农民的临时栖身之所。这些下层民众只知道服从统治大多数人行为的玄奥法则，却总是憎恨那些行为与众不同的人，并且对那些无缘无故想过体面而节制生活的人怀有戒心。时常喝上一杯酒、（偶尔）还替别人付钱的好心人的确是好邻居和好伙伴；但自命清高、拒绝去圆形大剧场看斗兽表演、不为在凯皮特林山的街道上游街的一批批战俘而欢呼的人，却成了扫兴的人和大众的公敌。

公元64年，一场大火烧毁了罗马贫民居住的地方，这一事件导致了对基督徒第一次有组织的进攻。

一开始有人谣传是喝得醉醺醺的尼禄皇帝异想天开，命令在首都放火，以便除掉贫民窟，按照他的计划重建罗马城。然而大家知道得很清楚。这是那些犹太人和基督徒干的，因为他们总是谈论那幸福的日子，那时天国大火球就会降临，这邪恶的世界将化为灰烬。

一旦这种说法有根有据，很快就会传开。一个老妇人听到了基督徒和死人说

old woman had heard the Christians talk with the dead. Another knew that they stole little children and cut their throats and smeared their blood upon the altar of their outlandish God. Of course,no one had ever been able to detect them at any of these scandalous practices,but that was only because they were so terribly clever and had bribed the police. But now at last they had been caught red-handed and they would be made to suffer for their vile deeds.

Of the number of faithful who were lynched upon this occasion,we know nothing. Paul and Peter,so it seems,were among the victims for thereafter their names are never heard again.

That this terrible outbreak of popular folly accomplished nothing,it is needless to state. The noble dignity with which the martyrs accepted their fate was the best possible propaganda for the new ideas and for every Christian who perished,there were a dozen pagans,ready and eager to take his place. As soon as Nero had committed the only decent act of his short and useless life (he killed himself in the year 68),the Christians returned to their old haunts and everything was as it had been before.

By this time the Roman authorities were making a great discovery. They began to suspect that a Christian was not exactly the same thing as a Jew.

We can hardly blame them for having committed this error. The historical researches of the last hundred years have made it increasingly clear that the Synagogue was the clearing-house through which the new faith was passed on to the rest of the world.

Remember that Jesus himself was a Jew and that he had always been most careful in observing the ancient laws of his fathers and that he had addressed himself almost exclusively to Jewish audiences. Once,and then only for a short time,had he left his native country,but the task which he had set himself he had accomplished with and by and for his fellow-Jews. Nor was there anything in what he had ever said which could have given the average Roman the impression that there was a deliberate difference between Christianity and Judaism.

What Jesus had actually tried to do was this. He had clearly seen the terrible abuses which had entered the church of his fathers. He had loudly and sometimes successfully protested

话；另一个人得知他们偷小孩，割断他们的喉咙，把血涂在稀奇古怪的上帝祭坛上。当然，没有任何人目睹这些丑恶的勾当，但这仅仅是因为基督徒太狡猾，已经用钱收买了警察。这次，他们终于被当场抓住了，他们必须为他们的罪恶行径接受惩罚。

有多少虔诚的教徒在这一事件中被私刑处死，我们毫无所知。或许保罗和彼得也是受害者，因为从这以后再也没有听到过他们的名字。

不用说，这场愚蠢的民众性的可怕大发泄自然一无所获。牺牲者接受厄运的高贵姿态是对新信仰的最好宣传。尼禄在短暂而无用的一生中做了唯一一件体面的事（这就是他在公元68年自杀）以后，基督徒马上重返旧土，一切依然如故。

这时的罗马当局有了大发现。他们开始怀疑，基督徒和犹太人是两码事。

我们很难责怪他们犯下的这种错误。近百年来的历史研究清晰地表明，犹太教堂其实是一个情报交换所，新信仰通过它传到了世界各地。

要记住，耶稣本人是犹太人，他一直小心谨慎地遵守着祖先的古老律法，几乎只对犹太听众演讲。他离开家乡只有一次，而且时间很短，但他为自己制定的使命却是与他的犹太同胞共同完成的，目的也是为了犹太同胞。他所说的话，没有任何蛛丝马迹会使普通罗马人感到基督教与犹太人有什么细微区别。

耶稣努力想做的实际上是下面这些：他已经清楚地看到各种可怕陋习进入了祖先的教堂，他曾经大声疾呼并有效地和这些陋习做了斗争。但他为之奋斗的只是内部的改革，他从未想过要成为一门新宗教的创始人。假如当时有人向他提到

against them. But he had fought his battles for reform from within. Never apparently had it dawned upon him that he might be the founder of a new religion. If some one had mentioned the possibility of such a thing to him,he would have rejected the idea as preposterous. But like many a reformer before his day and after,he had gradually been forced into a position where compromise was no longer possible. His untimely death alone had saved him from a fate like that of Luther and so many other advocates of reform,who were deeply perplexed when they suddenly found themselves at the head of a brand new party"outside"the organization to which they belonged,whereas they were merely trying to do some good from the"inside."

For many years after the death of Jesus,Christianity (to use the name long before it had been coined) was the religion of a small Jewish sect which had a few adherents in Jerusalem and in the villages of Judaea and Galilee and which had never been heard of outside of the province of Syria.

It was Gaius Julius Paulus,a full-fledged Roman citizen of Jewish descent,who had first recognized the possibilities of the new doctrine as a religion for all the world. The story of his suffering tells us how bitterly the Jewish Christians had been opposed to the idea of a universal religion instead of a purely national denomination,membership to which should only be open to people of their own race. They had hated the man who dared preach salvation to Jews and Gentiles alike so bitterly that on his last visit to Jerusalem Paul would undoubtedly have suffered the fate of Jesus if his Roman passport had not saved him from the fury of his enraged compatriots.

But it had been necessary for half a battalion of Roman soldiers to protect him and conduct him safely to the coastal town from where he could be shipped to Rome for that famous trial which never took place.

A few years after his death,that which he had so often feared during his lifetime and which he had repeatedly foretold actually occurred.

Jerusalem was destroyed by the Romans. On the place of the temple of Jehovah a

这样的事，他会认为这主意荒唐可笑。但就像在他前后的一些改革者一样，他逐渐陷入了不能再调和的境地。他的过早死亡反而使他免于遭受路德和其他许多改革者那样的命运，这些人本来也只想在“内部”做一点好事，可是当他们突然发现自己成为所属的组织“外部”的一个新团体的首领时，他们陷入了困境。

耶稣死后很多年，基督教（这个名字是很久以后才有的）是犹太教一个小教派，只在耶路撒冷、犹大村和加利利村有几个支持者，而且从未超出叙利亚省的范围。

正是犹太血统的罗马公民盖尤斯·朱利斯·保罗斯（即圣徒保罗）首先意识到这个新教义有可能成为全世界的宗教。他那饱受磨难的故事告诉我们，犹太基督徒是如何强烈反对将这个宗教世界化的。他们只希望它在本国享受统治地位，只对他们自己民族的人开放。他们深恨一视同仁地向犹太人和非犹太人宣扬灵魂拯救的人，因此保罗最后一次来到耶路撒冷时，如果不是他的罗马护照保护而使他免遭被怒火填膺的同乡撕成碎片的话，他肯定会和耶稣的下场一样。

不过还是有必要派出半个营的罗马士兵保护保罗，把他安全地带到港口城市，再从那里乘船回罗马参加那前所未有的著名审判。

他死了几年之后，他一生经常担心而又不断预言的事情真的发生了。

耶路撒冷被罗马人毁了，在耶和华神庙的所在地建起了祭祀朱庇特的新庙。城市的名字改为爱利亚首都，犹太也变成了叙利亚巴勒斯坦罗马行省的一部分。至于

new temple was erected in honor of Jupiter. The name of the city was changed to Aelia Capitolina and Judaea itself had become part of the Roman province of Syria Palaestina. As for the inhabitants,they were either killed or driven into exile and no one was allowed to live within several miles of the ruins on pain of death.

It was the final destruction of their holy city which had been so disastrous to the Jewish-Christians. During several centuries afterwards,in the little villages of the Judaean hinterland colonies might have been found of strange people who called themselves"poor men"and who waited with great patience and amidst everlasting prayers for the end of the world which was at hand. They were the remnants of the old Jewish-Christian community in Jerusalem. From time to time we hear them mentioned in books written during the fifth and sixth centuries. Far away from civilization,they developed certain strange doctrines of their own in which hatred for the apostle Paul took a prominent place. After the seventh century however we no longer find any trace of these so-called Nazarenes and Ebionites. The victorious Mohammedans had killed them all. And,anyway,if they had managed to exist a few hundred years longer,they would not have been able to avert the inevitable.

Rome,by bringing east and west and north and south into one large political union,had made the world ready for the idea of a universal religion. Christianity,because it was both simple and practical and full of a direct appeal,was predestined to succeed where Judaism and Mithraism and all of the other competing creeds were predestined to fail. But,unfortunately,the new faith never quite rid itself of certain rather unpleasant characteristics which only too clearly betrayed its origin.

The little ship which had brought Paul and Barnabas from Asia to Europe had carried a message of hope and mercy.

But a third passenger had smuggled himself on board.

He wore a mask of holiness and virtue.

But the face beneath bore the stamp of cruelty and hatred.

And his name was Religious Intolerance.

当地居民，或者被杀，或者被逐出家园，在废墟周围数英里内，不许有人居住。

这座曾给犹太基督徒带来过许多灾难的圣城终于被摧毁了。在以后的几个世纪，在犹太内地移民的一些小村子里会发现一些怪异的人，他们自称是“穷人”，正以极太的耐心和终日不断的祷告等待即将来临的世界末日。他们是耶路撒冷老犹太基督徒团体的残余。我们可以在15世纪和16世纪的书中不时地看到他们的身影。他们远离文明世界，形成了自己特有的怪诞的教义。在这种教义中，对使徒保罗的仇恨是其宗旨。但公元7世纪之后，我们再也没有发现这些所谓的拿撒勒人和爱比恩特人的踪迹。获胜的伊斯兰教徒把他们全杀了。不过，即使他们能再苟延残喘几百年，也无法使历史倒退。

罗马把东西南北聚集在一个大的政治联合体之下，使世界接受一个全球性宗教的条件渐渐成熟。基督教既简单又实用，教徒可以直接与上帝讲话，因此注定会成功；而犹太教、密特拉教以及所有其他参与竞争的宗教肯定会失败。但不幸的是，新信仰从未摈弃自身的一些不良特点，而这些特点显然是与其初衷相悖的。

一艘小船曾载着保罗和巴拿巴从亚洲来到欧洲，带来了希望和仁慈。

但另一个乘客也悄悄溜上了船。

它戴着神圣高贵的面纱。

面纱后面的嘴脸却是残忍和仇恨。

它的名字就是宗教专制。

CHAPTER Ⅳ THE TWILIGHT OF THE GODS

The early church was a very simple organization. As soon as it became apparent that the end of the world was not at hand,that the death of Jesus was not to be followed immediately by the last judgment and that the Christians might expect to dwell in this vale of tears for a good long time,the need was felt for a more or less definite form of government.

Originally the Christians (since all of them were Jews) had come together in the synagogue. When the rift had occurred between the Jews and the Gentiles,the latter had betaken themselves to a room in some one's house and if none could be found big enough to hold all the faithful (and the curious) they had met out in the open or in a deserted stone quarry.

At first these gatherings had taken place on the Sabbath,but when bad feeling between the Jewish Christians and the Gentile Christians increased,the latter began to drop the habit of keeping the Sabbathday and preferred to meet on Sunday,the day on which the resurrection had taken place.

These solemn celebrations,however,had borne witness to the popular as well as to the emotional character of the entire movement. There were no set speeches or sermons. There were no preachers. Both men and women,whenever they felt themselves inspired by the Holy Fire,had risen up in meeting to give evidence of the faith that was in them. Sometimes,if we are to trust the letters of Paul,these devout brethren"speaking with tongues,"had filled the heart of the great apostle with apprehension for the future. For most of them were simple folk without much education. No one doubted the sincerity of their impromptu exhortations but very often they got so excited that they raved like

第4章 诸神的黄昏

早期教会是很简单的组织。一旦人们明白世界末日并不是迫在眉睫，末日审判也不会在耶稣遇难以后立即到来，而且基督徒还要在灾难中煎熬很长时间时，人们就觉得需要某种形式的统治体系了。

最初基督徒（由于他们都是犹太人）都在犹太教堂集会。当犹太人和非犹太人产生冲突之后，非犹太人就到别人家的屋子里开会，如果找不到足够大的房子容纳所有虔诚（和好奇）的信徒，他们就在露天或废弃的石场开会。

起初这些会议都在星期六举行。但是当犹太基督徒与非犹太基督徒之间的感情恶化之后，非犹太基督徒便放弃了过安息日的习惯，而把耶稣复活的星期日作为聚会时间。

然而，这些庄严的仪式体现了公众特点和感情特点。没有固定的讲演或说教，也没有教士，所有男女只要感到内心被圣火激励，就可以在集会上站起来表白内心的信仰。如果我们相信保罗的描述，有时这些虔诚的弟兄“雄辩的口才”会使这位伟大的圣徒心里充满了对未来的希望。他们当中大多数人是普通百姓，没受过多少教育。没有人怀疑他们即席良言的真诚，但他们常常过于激动，以至于像疯子一样

maniacs and while a church may survive persecution,it is helpless against ridicule. Hence the efforts of Paul and Peter and their successors to bring some semblance of order into this chaos of spiritual divulgation and divine enthusiasm.

At first these efforts met with little success. A regular program seemed in direct contradiction to the democratic nature of the Christian faith. In the end,however,practical considerations supervened and the meetings became subject to a definite ritual.

They began with the reading of one of the Psalms (to placate the Jewish Christians who might be present). Then the congregation united in a song of praise of more recent composition for the benefit of the Roman and the Greek worshipers.

The only prescribed form of oration was the famous prayer in which Jesus had summed up his entire philosophy of life. The preaching,however,for several centuries remained entirely spontaneous and the sermons were delivered only by those who felt that they had something to say.

But when the number of those gatherings increased,when the police,forever on the guard against secret societies,began to make inquiries,it was necessary that certain men be elected to represent the Christians in their dealings with the rest of the world. Already Paul had spoken highly of the gift or leadership. He had compared the little communities which he visited in Asia and Greece to so many tiny vessels which were tossed upon a turbulent sea and were very much in need of a clever pilot if they were to survive the fury of the angry ocean.

And so the faithful came together once more and elected deacons and deaconesses,pious men and women who were the"servants"of the community,who took care of the sick and the poor (an object of great concern to the early Christians) and who looked after the property of the community and took care of all the small daily chores.

Still later when the church continued to grow in membership and the business of administration had become too intricate for mere amateurs,it was entrusted to a small group

大喊大叫。教会虽然顶得住迫害，却禁受不住冷嘲热讽。于是，保罗、彼得及他们的继承人不得不颇费力气地维持秩序，以抚平人们的精神世界和神圣热情所导致的混乱。

刚开始，这些努力收效甚微，因为规章制度和基督教信仰的民主精神似乎正好是对立的。不过人们最后还是考虑到实际情况，使集会成了固定仪式的东西。

人们以朗读一首赞美诗开始（为的是安抚可能在场的犹太基督徒）。然后，全体教徒合唱为罗马和希腊崇拜者而谱写的赞歌。

唯一预先拟好的演说，是耶稣倾注了一生哲学思想的著名祷文。然而，在几个世纪中，布道完全是自发的，只有那些感到心里有话要说的人才能登台说教。

但随着集会次数的增加，总是对秘密团体保持警惕的警察开始干涉了，因此有必要推选出某些人代表基督徒与外界打交道。保罗曾高度评价过领导的才能。他把他在亚洲和希腊走访过的小团体比作在波涛汹涌的大海中颠簸的小舟，如果要闯过怒涛汹涌的大海，就必须有聪明的领航员。

于是虔诚的信徒又聚集在一起，选出了男女执事。他们是些虔诚的男男女女，是团体的“仆人”，要照顾好病人和穷人（这是早期基督徒非常关心的事情），管理好集体财产，还要料理所有日常琐事。

再后来，教会成员越来越多，事务性管理对兼职的执事来说太复杂了，于是选了几位“老者”担当此任。他们的希腊称呼是“长老”，现在被称为“神父”。

of"elders."These were known by their Greek name of Presbyters and hence our word"priest."

After a number of years,when every village or city possessed a Christian church of its own,the need was felt for a common policy. Then an"overseer" (an Episkopos or Bishop) was elected to superintend an entire district and direct its dealings with the Roman government.

Soon there were bishops in all the principal towns of the empire,and those in Antioch and Constantinople and Jerusalem and Carthage and Rome and Alexandria and Athens were reputed to be very powerful gentlemen who were almost as important as the civil and military governors of their provinces.

In the beginning of course the bishop who presided over that part of the world where Jesus had lived and suffered and died enjoyed the greatest respect. But after Jerusalem had been destroyed and the generation which had expected the end of the world and the triumph of Zion had disappeared from the face of the earth,the poor old bishop in his ruined palace saw himself deprived of his former prestige.

And quite naturally his place as leader of the faithful was taken by the"overseer"who lived in the capital of the civilized world and who guarded the sites where Peter and Paul,the great apostles of the west,had suffered their martyrdom—the Bishop of Rome.

This bishop,like all others,was known as Father of Papa,the common expression of love and respect bestowed upon members of the clergy. In the course of centuries,the title of Papa however became almost exclusively associated in people's minds with the particular"Father"who was the head of the metropolitan diocese. When they spoke of the Papa or Pope they meant just one Father,the Bishop of Rome,and not by any chance the Bishop of Constantinople or the Bishop of Carthage. This was an entirely normal development. When we read in our newspaper about"the President"it is not necessary to add"of the United States."We know that the head of our government is meant and not the President of the Pennsylvania Railroad or the President of Harvard University or the President of the League of Nations.

过了些年，每个村庄和城市都有了自己的教堂，因此又有必要制定人们共同遵守的政策。于是选出了“总监”（即主教）来监督整个教区，并负责与罗马政府打交道。

不久，帝国的所有大都市都有了主教，安条克、君士坦丁堡、耶路撒冷、迦太基、罗马、亚历山大和雅典的主教都是很有权势的人物，他们和当地的军政长官几乎同样重要。

起初，掌管着耶稣当年曾经生活、受难并死去的地方的主教当然广受尊敬。但自从耶路撒冷被毁以及期待世界末日和天国成功的一代人从地球上消失之后，可怜的老主教在他荒废的宫殿里眼睁睁地看着自己被剥夺了原有的威望。

虔诚信徒首领的位置很自然地被“总监”代替了。“总监”住在文明世界的首都，守卫着西方伟大使徒保罗和彼得当年殉教的地方——他就是罗马大主教。

这个主教与其他主教一样，也被称为“神父”或“圣父”，这是对圣职人员表示热爱和尊敬的一般称呼。但在以后的几个世纪里，“圣父”这个头衔在人们心目中几乎只与主教管区的首领相联系。当人们提到“圣父”时，指的只是一个神父，即罗马的大主教，而绝不会是君士坦丁堡的主教或迦太基的主教。这是个非常自然的发展过程。当我们在报纸上看到“总统”一词时，没必要再加上“合众国”一词，因为我们知道这里指的是政府首脑，而不是宾夕法尼亚铁路局长或哈佛大学校

The first time the name occurred officially in a document was in the year 258. At that time Rome was still the capital of a highly successful empire and the power of the bishops was entirely overshadowed by that of the emperors. But during the next three hundred years,under the constant menace of both foreign and domestic invasions,the successors of Caesar began to look for a new home that would offer them greater safety. This they found in a city in a different part of their domains. It was called Byzantium,after a mythical hero by the name of Byzas who was said to have landed there shortly after the Trojan war. Situated on the straits which separated Europe from Asia and dominating the trade route between the Black Sea and the Mediterranean,it controlled several important monopolies and was of such great commercial importance that already Sparta and Athens had fought for the possession of this rich fortress.

Byzantium,however,had held its own until the days of Alexander and after having been for a short while part of Macedonia it had finally been incorporated into the Roman Empire.

And now,after ten centuries of increasing prosperity,its Golden Horn filled with the ships from a hundred nations,it was chosen to become the center of the empire.

The people of Rome,left to the mercy of Visigoths and Vandals and Heaven knows what other sort of barbarians,felt that the end of the world had come when the imperial palaces stood empty for years at a time;when one department of state after another was removed to the shores of the Bosporus and when the inhabitants of the capital were asked to obey laws made a thousand miles away.

But in the realm of history,it is an ill wind that does not blow some one good. With the emperors gone,the bishops remained behind as the most important dignitaries of the town,the only visible and tangible successors to the glory of the imperial throne.

And what excellent use they made of their new independence! They were shrewd politicians,for the prestige and the influence of their office had attracted the best brains of all Italy. They felt themselves to be the representatives of certain eternal ideas. Hence they

长、国联主席。

“教皇”这个名字第一次出现在正式文件中是公元258年。那时，罗马还是强盛帝国的首都，主教的势力完全处在皇帝的权势之下。但是在接下来的300年中，由于经常受到外侵内乱的威胁，凯撒的继承人开始寻找更加安全的新国土来建立自己的国家。他们在国土的另一个地方找到了一座城市，它叫拜占廷，是根据一个神话英雄拜扎斯的名字而得名的，据说特洛伊战争结束不久，拜扎斯曾在这里登陆。由于拜占廷位于几条将欧亚大陆分割开来的海峡之畔，控制着黑海和地中海之间的商业要道，因此它控制了几个重要的垄断项目，占据着非常重要的商业地位，以至于斯巴达人和雅典人为了争夺这个富足的要塞而打得不可开交。

然而，拜占廷在亚历山大时代以前一直是独立的。它沦为马其顿一部分不久，就被并入罗马帝国的版图。

现在经过1000年的财富积累，这个“金号角”海港中就挤满了来自上百个国家的船只，它被选为帝国的中心。

罗马人民只能听任哥特人、汪达尔人等野蛮人的宰割。当他们看到皇宫接连好几年空荡荡的，看到政府部门一个接一个搬到博斯普鲁斯海峡之滨，看到首都的居民竟要遵守在千里之外制定的法律时，他们感到世界末日已经来临了。

但是在历史的长河中，任何事情都是有得有失。皇帝走了，留下来的主教成了

were never in a hurry,but proceeded with the deliberate slowness of a glacier and dared to take chances where others,acting under the pressure of immediate necessity,made rapid decisions,blundered and failed.

But most important of all,they were men of a single purpose,who moved consistently and persistently towards one goal. In all they did and said and thought they were guided by the desire to increase the glory of God and the strength and power of the organization which represented the divine will on earth.

How well they wrought,the history of the next ten centuries was to show.

While everything else perished in the deluge of savage tribes which hurled itself across the European continent,while the walls of the empire,one after the other,came crumbling down,while a thousand institutions as old as the plains of Babylon were swept away like so much useless rubbish,the Church stood strong and erect,the rock of ages,but more particularly the rock of the Middle Ages.

The victory,however,which was finally won,was bought at a terrible cost.

For Christianity which had begun in a stable was allowed to end in a palace. It had been started as a protest against a form of government in which the priest as the self-appointed intermediary between the deity and mankind had insisted upon the unquestioning obedience of all ordinary human beings. This revolutionary body grew and in less than a hundred years it developed into a new super-theocracy,compared to which the old Jewish state had been a mild and liberal commonwealth of happy and carefree citizens.

And yet all this was perfectly logical and quite unavoidable,as I shall now try to show you.

Most of the people who visit Rome make a pilgrimage to the Coliseum and within those wind-swept walls they are shown the hallowed ground where thousands of Christian martyrs fell as victims of Roman intolerance.

But while it is true that upon several occasions there were persecutions of the adherents

最显赫的人物，他们是皇冠荣耀唯一看得见摸得着的继承人。

他们充分利用了这个新的毫无束缚的机会。教会的声望和影响吸引了意大利最有智慧的人，这使主教们变成了精明的政治家。他们觉得自己就是某些永恒信念的代表，因此他们没有必要那么急，而是采取潜移默化的方法，抓住机会即可；而不必像其他人那样，因为操之过急造成的压力而仓促作出决定，最后出错失败。

但最重要的是，主教们只有一个目标，只向一个目标坚韧不拔地前进。他们所做所说所想的一切，都是为了增加上帝的荣耀，为了使代表上帝意志的尘世教会更强大有力。

以后1000年的历史表明，他们的工作是卓有成效的。

当野蛮部落的洪水席卷欧洲大陆而毁坏了一切时，当帝国的围墙一面面倒坍时，当上千个像巴比伦平原那样古老的体制像垃圾一样冲散时，只有教会仍然坚强地屹立着，它是时代的坚石，更是中世纪的中流砥柱。

然而，虽然最终胜利，但代价却惨重。

基督教起源于马厩，却被允许在宫殿里寿终正寝。它本是以抗议政府发展起来的，但后来自命能沟通人神的神父坚持让每一个普通人无条件地服从教会。这个团体不断地成长，在不到100年的时间里竟发展成为新的拥有超级神权的政治集团。古老的犹太国家与之相比，反而成了幸福快乐的公民居住的自由的联邦。

然而这一切既合乎逻辑而又不可避免。下面我要进一步说明。

of the new faith,these had very little to do with religious intolerance.

They were purely political.

The Christian,as a member of a religious sect,enjoyed the greatest possible freedom.

But the Christian who openly proclaimed himself a conscientious objector,who bragged of his pacifism even when the country was threatened with foreign invasion and openly defied the laws of the land upon every suitable and unsuitable occasion,such a Christian was considered an enemy of the state and was treated as such.

That he acted according to his most sacred convictions did not make the slightest impression upon the mind of the average police judge. And when he tried to explain the exact nature of his scruples,that dignitary looked puzzled and was entirely unable to follow him.

A Roman police judge after all was only human. When he suddenly found himself called upon to try people who made an issue of what seemed to him a very trivial matter,he simply did not know what to do. Long experience had taught him to keep clear of all theological controversies. Besides he remembered many imperial edicts,admonishing public servants to use"tact"in their dealings with the new sect. Hence he used tact and argued. But as the whole dispute boiled down to a question of principles,very little was ever accomplished by an appeal to logic.

In the end,the magistrate was placed before the choice of surrendering the dignity of the law or insisting upon a complete and unqualified vindication of the supreme power of the state. But prison and torture meant nothing to people who firmly believed that life did not begin until after death and who shouted with joy at the idea of being allowed to leave this wicked world for the joys of Heaven.

The guerilla warfare therefore which finally broke out between the authorities and their Christian subjects was long and painful. We possess very few authentic figures upon the total

大多数游览罗马的人都要去瞻仰圆形大剧场，在被风吹拂的围墙里是一块凹陷的土地，数千名基督徒殉道者作为罗马专制的牺牲品，倒在了这里。

不过，尽管在那里的确发生过几次对新信仰拥护者的迫害，却都与宗教的不宽容无关。

这些迫害全都出于政治原因。

基督教作为一个宗教派别，享有最大的自由。

但是，基督徒公开宣称自己由于宗教信仰而拒服兵役，甚至当国家受到外国侵略时还大肆吹嘘和平主义，而且在各种场合公开诋毁土地法律，因此这种基督徒被视为国家的敌人，遭到了应有的处决。

基督徒是按照自己最神圣的信条行事的，可普通的警方法官却不管这个。当基督徒努力解释自己的道德本性时，长官大人却迷惑不解，完全不知道他们在说什么。

罗马的警方法官毕竟只是凡人。他突然发现自己应召来审判犯人，而犯人的官司在他看来却毫不重要时，他简直不知所措。经验告诉他，对神学中的所有争论应采取超然态度；而且他还记得，皇帝的许多敕令曾告诫公职人员，在和新教派打交道时要“策略”些，于是他用了各种手段进行理论。可是当全部争论集中到一个原则问题时，使用逻辑方法也就收效甚微了。

最后，行政长官面临两难的抉择：或者放弃法律的尊严，或者坚持对国家最高

number of victims. According to Origen,the famous church father of the third century,several of whose own relatives had been killed in Alexandria during one of the persecutions,"the number of true Christians who died for their convictions could easily be enumerated."

On the other hand,when we peruse the lives of the early saints we find ourselves faced by such incessant tales of bloodshed that we begin to wonder how a religion exposed to these constant and murderous persecutions could ever have survived at all.

No matter what figures I shall give,some one is sure to call me a prejudiced liar. I will therefore keep my opinion to myself and let my readers draw their own conclusions. By studying the lives of the Emperors Decius (249~251) and Valerian (253~260) they will be able to form a fairly accurate opinion as to the true character of Roman intolerance during the worst era of persecution.

Furthermore if they will remember that as wise and liberal minded a ruler as Marcus Aurelius confessed himself unable to handle the problem of his Christian subjects successfully,they will derive some idea about the difficulties which beset obscure little officials in remote corners of the empire,who tried to do their duty and must either be unfaithful to their oath of office or execute those of their relatives and neighbors who could not or would not obey those few and very simple ordinances upon which the imperial government insisted as a matter of self-preservation.

Meanwhile the Christians,not hindered by false sentimentality towards their pagan fellow-citizens,were steadily extending the sphere of their influence.

Late in the fourth century,the Emperor Gratian at the request of the Christian members of the Roman senate who complained that it hurt their feelings to gather in the shadow of a heathenish idol,ordered the removal of the statue of Victory which for more than four hundred years had stood in the hall built by Julius Caesar. Several senators protested. This

权力的完全而绝对服从。但监狱和折磨对那些教徒根本不算什么，他们坚信生命只有在死亡之后才会开始，还热烈欢呼能离开这个邪恶的世界去享受天国之乐。

因此，当局和基督教臣民之间爆发的游击战痛苦而漫长。我们没有全部死亡人数的官方数据。但依照公元3世纪著名神父奥利金（他的一些亲戚在亚历山大的一次迫害中被杀死）的说法，“为信念而死的真正基督徒的数目很容易统计出来”。

另一方面，我们只要仔细研究早期圣人的生平，就会发现许多鲜血淋淋的故事；因此我们不禁会感到奇怪，一个屡遭杀戮迫害的宗教究竟是如何保存下来的？

无论我提供什么样的数字，一定会有人指控我是心怀偏见的骗子。因此我保留自己的见解，让读者自己去得出结论。只要研究一下德西厄斯皇帝（249~251）和瓦莱里安皇帝（253~260年）的一生，那我们对迫害行为最猖獗时罗马专制的真正本性就会有比较清楚准确的结论了。

此外，如果读者还记得，就连马可·奥勒留皇帝这样开明睿智的君主都承认自己很难处理基督教臣民的问题，那么对帝国边远地区的无名小官来说，他们面临的困难就可想而知了。那些想尽忠职守的小官们不是必须背弃自己的就职誓词，就是必须处死自己的亲朋好友和邻居，因为这些人不能也不愿遵守帝国政府为了保存自己而制定的几项简单的法令。

与此同时，基督徒没有受同城异教臣民假惺惺的伤感的迷惑，而是稳步扩大自己的影响范围。

公元4世纪后期，格瑞提恩皇帝应罗马元老院基督徒的要求（这些人抱怨说，

did very little good and only caused a number of them to be sent into exile.

It was then that Quintus Aurelius Symmachus,a devoted patriot of great personal distinction,wrote his famous letter in which he tried to suggest a compromise.

"Why,"so he asked,"should we Pagans and our Christian neighbors not live in peace and harmony?We look up to the same stars,we are fellow-passengers on the same planet and dwell beneath the same sky. What matters it along which road each individual endeavors to find the ultimate truth?The riddle of existence is too great that there should be only one path leading to an answer."

He was not the only man who felt that way and saw the danger which threatened the old Roman tradition of a broadminded religious policy. Simultaneously with the removal of the statue of Victory in Rome a violent quarrel had broken out between two contending factions of the Christians who had found a refuge in Byzantium. This dispute gave rise to one of the most intelligent discussions of tolerance to which the world had ever listened. Themistius the philosopher,who was the author,had remained faithful to the Gods of his fathers. But when the Emperor Valens took sides in the fight between his orthodox and his non-orthodox Christian subjects,Themistius felt obliged to remind him of his true duty.

"There is,"so he said,"a domain over which no ruler can hope to exercise any authority. That is the domain of the virtues and especially that of the religious beliefs of individuals. Compulsion within that field causes hypocrisy and conversions that are based upon fraud. Hence it is much better for a ruler to tolerate all beliefs,since it is only by toleration that civic

■ 逃离罪恶的世界

在异教偶像的阴影下开会伤害了他们的感情），下令把那座矗立在凯撒建立的宫殿里长达400年之久的胜利女神像搬走。几个元老曾进行抗议，但无济于事，结果还导致他们中一些人被流放。

这时，一位享有非凡荣誉的忠诚爱国者昆图斯·奥勒留乌斯·塞玛楚斯挥笔写下一封著名的信，提出了一个折中的办法。

“为什么，”他问道，“我们异教徒不能和基督徒邻居和平相处呢？我们仰望的是同样的星辰，并肩走在同一块土地上，住在同一片天空之下。每个人自己选择寻求最终真理的道路又有什么关系？生存的奥秘太伟大了，通向答案的道路不可能只有一条。”

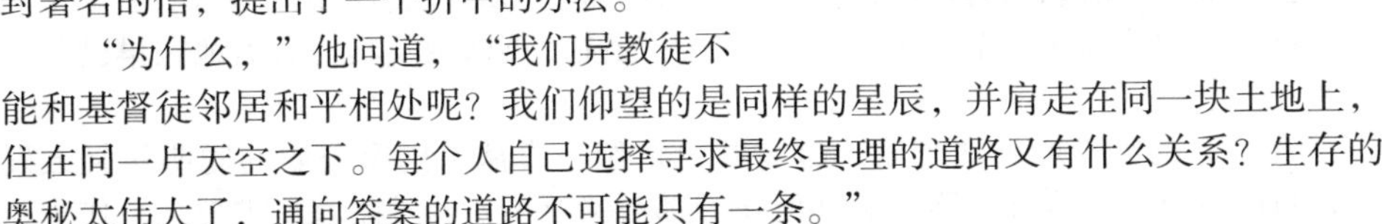

他并不是唯一这样分析问题并看出古罗马宗教开放的政策传统正在受到威胁的人。与此同时，随着罗马胜利女神像的搬迁，已经在拜占廷立足的两个敌对的基督教派之间爆发了激烈的争执。这次争执引起了世所未闻的关于宽容的最富有才智的讨论。哲学家西米斯提乌斯是讨论的发起人，他对祖先信奉的上帝忠贞不渝。但当瓦伦斯皇帝在正统与非正统的基督徒论战中偏袒一方时，他觉得必须让皇帝明白自己真正的职责。

他说：“有一个领域，任何统治者都休想在那里施展权威，这就是道德王国，

strife can be averted. Moreover,tolerance is a divine law. God himself has most clearly demonstrated his desire for a number of different religions. And God alone can judge the methods by which humanity aspires to come to an understanding of the Divine Mystery. God delights in the variety of homage which is rendered to him. He likes the Christians to use certain rites,the Greeks others,the Egyptians again others."

Fine words,indeed,but spoken in vain.

The ancient world together with its ideas and ideals was dead and all efforts to set back the clock of history were doomed beforehand. Life means progress,and progress means suffering. The old order of society was rapidly disintegrating. The army was a mutinous mob of foreign mercenaries. The frontier was in open revolt. England and the other outlying districts had long since been surrendered to the barbarians.

When the final catastrophe took place,those brilliant young men who in centuries past had entered the service of the state found themselves deprived of all but one chance for advancement. That was a career in the Church. As Christian archbishop of Spain,they could hope to exercise the power formerly held by the proconsul. As Christian authors,they could be certain of a fairly large public if they were willing to devote themselves exclusively to theological subjects. As Christian diplomats,they could be sure of rapid promotion if they were willing to represent the bishop of Rome at the imperial court of Constantinople or undertake the hazardous job of gaining the good will of some barbarous chieftain in the heart of Gaul or Scandinavia. And finally,as Christian financiers,they could hope to make fortunes administering those rapidly increasing estates which had made the occupants of the Lateran Palace the largest landowners of Italy and the richest men of their time.

We have seen something of the same nature during the last five years. Up to the year 1914 the young men of Europe who were ambitious and did not depend upon manual labor for their

尤其是个人宗教信仰方面。在那个领域实施强制，必然会导致建立在欺骗上的虚伪和皈依。因此，对统治者来说最好是容忍一切信仰，因为只有宽容才能防止公众冲突。况且，宽容是项神圣法则，上帝自己已经明确表明愿意容忍多种不同的宗教。也只有上帝能够判断人类用以理解神圣玄机的方法。上帝喜欢人们对他的形形色色的崇拜，喜欢基督徒采用的某种礼仪，也喜欢希腊人和埃及人采用的其他礼仪。"

这的确是金玉良言，但没有人听。

这个古老的世界连同它的思想和理想都已经死了，任何倒转历史时钟的企图都注定会失败。生活意味着进步，进步意味着磨难。旧的社会秩序正迅速崩溃。军队是一群叛乱的外国雇佣军。边境发生了公开叛乱。英格兰及其他边沿地区早已落入野蛮人之手。

当最后的灾难爆发的时候，过去几个世纪一直从事国家公职的聪明年轻人发现，自己只有一条晋升之路，而其他路子都被堵死了，这条路就是进教会。作为西班牙的基督教大主教，有望获得以前由地方长官控制的权力；作为基督教作者，只要全身心从事理论方面的研究，就能获得广泛的公众影响力；作为基督教外交官，只要愿意在君士坦丁堡皇宫里代表罗马教皇，或愿意冒险深入高卢或斯堪的那维亚内地，获得野蛮人酋长的友情，就可以平步青云。最后，要是当了基督教财务主管，还有望掌管那片曾使拉特兰宫的占有者成为意大利当时最大的地主和最富裕人家的快速致富的领地而大发横财。

我们在过去5年已经看到了本质相同的事情。直到1914年，那些野心勃勃、不想

support almost invariably entered the service of the state. They became officers of the different imperial and royal armies and navies. They filled the higher judicial positions,administered the finances or spent years in the colonies as governors or military commanders. They did not expect to grow very rich,but the social prestige of the offices which they held was very great and by the application of a certain amount of intelligence,industry and honesty,they could look forward to a pleasant life and an honorable old age.

Then came the war and swept aside these last remnants of the old feudal fabric of society. The lower classes took hold of the government. Some few among the former officials were too old to change the habits of a lifetime. They pawned their orders and died. The vast majority,however,surrendered to the inevitable. From childhood on they had been educated to regard business as a low profession,not worthy of their attention. Perhaps business was a low profession,but they had to choose between an office and the poor house. The number of people who will go hungry for the sake of their convictions is always relatively small. And so within a few years after the great upheaval,we find most of the former officers and state officials doing the sort of work which they would not have touched ten years ago and doing it not unwillingly. Besides,as most of them belonged to families which for generations had been trained in executive work and were thoroughly accustomed to handle men,they have found it comparatively easy to push ahead in their new careers and are today a great deal happier and decidedly more prosperous than they had ever expected to be.

What business is today,the Church was sixteen centuries ago.

It may not always have been easy for young men who traced their ancestry back to Hercules or to Romulus or to the heroes of the Trojan war to take orders from a simple cleric who was the son of a slave,but the simple cleric who was the son of a slave had something to give which the young men who traced their ancestry back to Hercules and

依靠手工劳动谋生的欧洲年轻人几乎都想挤入政府部门工作。他们在不同的帝国和皇家陆军、海军中当上了军官。他们把持着高级法官的位置，掌握着财政，或在殖民地当几年总督或军事司令官。他们并不指望变得很富有，但他们的官职带来了巨大的社会威望，只要足够聪明、勤奋和诚实，就可以过上美满的生活和令人尊敬的晚年。

然后爆发了战争，它把旧社会的封建结构的最后残余涤荡一空，下层阶层掌握了政权。有些前任官员太老了，难以改变一生形成的习惯，便典当了自己的勋章，离开了人世。然而，绝大多数人都接受了无法避免的事实。他们从小接受教育，把做生意当成低下职业，对此不屑一顾。也许做生意是门低贱职业，但他们必须选择是进办公室还是进贫民区。为信念而宁愿挨饿的人总是一小部分，因此大动乱后没过几年，我们便发现大多数前任军官和政府官员都心甘情愿地做起生意来，而十年前他们是绝不会涉足此事的。此外，由于他们大多数人出生于世代从政的家庭，都习惯于指挥别人，因此他们在新的行当中进展得比较容易，比自己所期望的更加幸福和富足。

工商业在今天的情形，正是教会在16世纪以前的写照。

要让一些年轻人（他们把自己的祖先追溯到赫拉克勒斯、罗慕路斯或特洛伊战争的英雄）接受一个奴隶出身的朴素牧师的教诲，可不那么容易；然而，这位奴隶出身的朴素牧师所奉献的东西，正是这些把祖先追溯到赫拉克勒斯、罗慕路斯或特洛伊战争英雄的年轻人所热切盼望的。因此，如果双方都是聪明人的话（他们很可能是这样），很快就能学到彼此的优点并和睦相处。因为这是历史的又一条奇怪法

Romulus and the heroes of the Trojan war wanted and wanted badly. And therefore if they were both bright fellows (as they well may have been) they soon learned to appreciate the other fellow's good qualities and got along beautifully. For it is one of the other strange laws of history that the more things appear to be changing,the more they remain the same.

Since the beginning of time it has seemed inevitable that there shall be one small group of clever men and women who do the ruling and a much larger group of not-quite-so-bright men and women who shall do the obeying. The stakes for which these two groups play are at different periods known by different names. Invariably they represent Strength and Leadership on the one hand and Weakness and Compliance on the other. They have been called Empire and Church and Knighthood and Monarchy and Democracy and Slavery and Serfdom and Proletariat. But the mysterious law which governs human development works the same in Moscow as it does in London or Madrid or Washington,for it is bound to neither time nor place. It has often manifested itself under strange forms and disguises. More than once it has worn a lowly garb and has loudly proclaimed its love for humanity,its devotion to God,its humble desire to bring about the greatest good for the greatest number. But underneath such pleasant exteriors it has always hidden and continues to hide the grim truth of that primeval law which insists that the first duty of man is to keep alive. People who resent the fact that they were born in a world of mammals are apt to get angry at such statements. They call us"materialistics"and"Cynics"and what not. Because they have always regarded history as a pleasant fairy tale,they are shocked to discover that it is a science which obeys the same iron rules which govern the rest of the universe. They might as well fight against the habits of parallel lines or the results of the tables of multiplication.

Personally I would advise them to accept the inevitable.

For then and only then can history some day be turned into something that shall have a practical value to the human race and cease to be the ally and confederate of those who profit by

则：事情表面变化越大，就越一成不变。

人类初始以来，就似乎有一条不可避免的规律，即小部分聪明的男女进行统治，而大部分不太聪明的男女则受制于人。这两类人在不同时代分别有不同的名字，其中一方总代表力量和领导，另一方则代表软弱和屈从，分别被称为帝国、教会、骑士、君主和民主、奴隶、农奴、无产者。但无论是在莫斯科，还是在伦敦、马德里和华盛顿，操纵人类发展事业的神秘法则都是一样的，因为它不受时间地点的限制。它常常以怪异的形式或伪装出现。它不止一次披上陈腐的外衣，高喊对人类的爱、对上帝的忠诚和给绝大多数人带来最大好处的谦卑愿望。但是在这宜人的外壳下面，却一直隐藏并继续隐藏着原始法则的严酷真理：它强调人的第一职责是生存。那些痛恨自己出生在哺乳动物世界这一事实的人很容易对这种论点产生反感。他们称我们是“唯物主义者”“愤世嫉俗者”，等等。因为他们一直把历史当作令人愉悦的神话故事，因此当他们发现历史也是一门科学（它受制于操纵宇宙其他事物的铁律）时，便大为震惊。他们也许还会反对平行线法则和乘法口诀表呢。

我个人奉劝他们还是接受不可改变的事实。

这样，也只有这样，历史总有一天才会变得对人类有实用价值，而不再是那些从种族偏见、部落专横和广大居民的无知中坐收渔利的人结成的联盟。

谁要是怀疑这种观点，就请在我前几页所写的这几个世纪的历史中寻找证据吧。

racial prejudice,tribal intolerance and the ignorance of the vast majority of their fellow citizens.

And if any one doubts the truth of this statement,let him look for the proof in the chronicles of those centuries of which I was writing a few pages back.

Let him study the lives of the great leaders of the Church during the first four centuries.

Almost without exception he will find that they came from the ranks of the old Pagan society,that they had been trained in the schools of the Greek philosophers and had only drifted into the Church afterwards,when they had been obliged to choose a career. Several of them of course were attracted by the new ideas and accepted the words of Christ with heart and soul. But the great majority changed its allegiance from a worldly master to a Heavenly ruler because the chances for advancement with the latter were infinitely greater.

The Church from her side,always very wise and very understanding,did not look too closely into the motives which had impelled many of her new disciples to take this sudden step. And most carefully she endeavored to be all things to all men. Those who felt inclined towards a practical and worldly existence were given a chance to make good in the field of politics and economics. While those of a different temperament,who took their faith more emotionally,were offered every possible opportunity to escape from the crowded cities that they might cogitate in silence upon the evils of existence and so might acquire that degree of personal holiness which they deemed necessary for the eternal happiness of their souls.

In the beginning it had been quite easy to lead such a life of devotion and contemplation.

The Church during the first centuries of her existence had been merely a loose spiritual bond between humble folks who dwelled far away from the mansions of the mighty. But when the Church succeeded the empire as ruler of the world,and became a strong political organization with vast real-estate holdings in Italy and France and Africa,there were less opportunities for a life of solitude. Many pious men and women began to harken back

请他研究一下最初4000年教会伟大领袖的生平。

他肯定会发现，教会领袖都出生于古老的异端社会的某些阶层，在希腊哲学家那里受过教育，只是到后来不得不选择一个职业时才转到教会。当然，他们中有几个人是受新思想的吸引而真心诚意地接受基督教诲的，但大多数人从效忠凡世主人转变为效忠天国统治者，则是因为后者晋升的机会更多。

就教会而言，它也总是通情达理，并不细究许多新信徒是出于什么动机而突然改奉基督教的，而是极其认真地为所有人做好事。那些向往实际利益和凡尘生活的人，会得到机会在政治经济领域大显身手。对那些情趣不同、对信仰情深义重的人，会寻找机会离开拥挤不堪的城市，以便在安静中深思生存的罪恶，以达到他们认为使灵魂获得永恒幸福必不可少的个人圣境。

起初，过上这种信仰上帝、沉思冥想的生活非常容易。

教会在最初的几个世纪只是对住在远离权力中心的下层百姓有松弛的精神约束。但是当教会继帝国之后成为世界的统治者，并成为一个在意大利、法国和非洲拥有大片肥沃土地的强大政治组织之后，过隐居生活的可能性便减少了。许多善男信女开始向往“旧日好时光”，那时所有真正的基督徒都可以把时间花在做善事和祷告上。为了重获幸福，他们人为地创造一些条件，再现那种自然形成的生活。

这场争取修道院式生活的运动起源于东方，它对社会在接下来1000年的政治经济的发展产生了巨大影响，并为教会镇压不信教者或异教徒的战争提供了一支忠诚

to the"good old days"when all true Christians had spent their waking hours in works of charity and in prayer. That they might again be happy,they now artificially recreated what once had been a natural development of the times.

This movement for a monastic form of life which was to exercise such an enormous influence upon the political and economic development of the next thousand years and which was to give the Church a devoted group of very useful shock-troops in her warfare upon heathen and heretics was of Oriental origin.

This need not surprise us.

In the countries bordering upon the eastern shores of the Mediterranean,civilization was very,very old and the human race was tired to the point of exhaustion. In Egypt alone,ten different and separate cycles of culture had succeeded each other since the first settlers had occupied the valley of the Nile. The same was true of the fertile plain between the Tigris and the Euphrates. The vanity of life,the utter futility of all human effort,lay visible in the ruins of thousands of bygone temples and palaces. The younger races of Europe might accept Christianity as an eager promise of life,a constant appeal to their newly regained energy and enthusiasm. But Egyptians and Syrians took their religious experiences in a different mood.

To them it meant the welcome prospect of relief from the curse of being alive. And in anticipation of the joyful hour of death,they escaped from the charnel-house of their own memories and they fled into the desert that they might be alone with their grief and their God and nevermore look upon the reality of existence.

For some curious reason the business of reform always seems to have had a particular appeal to soldiers. They,more than all other people,have come into direct contact with the cruelty and the horrors of civilization. Furthermore they have learned that nothing can be accomplished without discipline. The greatest of all modern warriors to fight the battles of the Church was a former captain in the army of the Emperor Charles V. And the man

的突击队。

对此我们不必惊讶。

濒临地中海东岸的国家，拥有古老的文明，而且人们已经筋疲力尽。仅仅在埃及，自从第一批居民在尼罗河谷住下来开始，就有十种不同文化此起彼伏，以不同的方式循环往复。在底格里斯河和幼发拉底河之间的肥沃平原也是这样。生活空虚无聊，人类所有的努力都徒劳无益，路旁边成千上万座庙宇和宫殿的废墟就是写照。欧洲年轻一代接受基督教，是因为它体现了对生活的强烈期望，激发了他们的精力和热情。但埃及人和叙利亚人对自己的宗教生活却有不同的看法。

对他们来说，宗教意味着从“活着”的痛苦中获得盼望许久的解脱。他们沉浸在对死亡的快乐时光的期待中，从他们记忆中的停尸场逃离出去，躲进沙漠，只与悲伤和上帝做伴，而不再理会现实生活。

出于某些难以理解的原因，改革似乎总能对士兵产生特殊的号召力。他们比其他人都更加直接地接触到文明的野蛮和恐怖。此外，他们还明白，没有纪律就一事无成。为教会而战的最伟大的现代勇士，是查理五世皇帝军队中的一个上尉。他第一个把精神落伍者组成了一个简单的组织，曾在君士坦丁大帝的军队中当过列兵。他名叫帕乔米乌斯，是个埃及人。他服完兵役后，加入到一小群隐居者当中，这些人的头目是一个叫安东尼的人，他与帕乔米乌斯来自同一个国家。这些隐居者离开城市，与沙漠上的豺狗和平相处。不过，由于隐居生活往往会产生各种奇怪的思想

who first gathered the spiritual stragglers into a single organization had been a private in the army of the Emperor Constantine. His name was Pachomius and he was an Egyptian. When he got through with his military service,he joined a small group of hermits who under the leadership of a certain Anthony,who hailed from his own country,had left the cities and were living peacefully among the jackals of the desert. But as the solitary life seemed to lead to all sorts of strange afflictions of the mind and caused certain very regrettable excesses of devotion which made people spend their days on the top of an old pillar or at the bottom of a deserted grave (thereby giving cause for great mirth to the pagans and serious reason for grief to the true believers) Pachomius decided to put the whole movement upon a more practical basis and in this way he became the founder of the first religious order. From that day on (the middle of the fourth century) hermits living together in small groups obeyed one single commander who was known as the"superior general"and who in turn appointed the abbots who were responsible for the different monasteries which they held as so many fortresses of the Lord.

Before Pachomius died in 346 his monastic idea had been carried from Egypt to Rome by the Alexandrian bishop Athanasius and thousands of people had availed themselves of this opportunity to flee the world,its wickedness and its too insistent creditors.

The climate of Europe,however,and the nature of the people made it necessary that the original plans of the founder be slightly changed. Hunger and cold were not quite so easy to bear under a wintry sky as in the valley of the Nile. Besides,the more practical western mind was disgusted rather than edified by that display of dirt and squalor which seemed to be an integral part of the Oriental ideal of holiness.

"What,"so the Italians and the Frenchmen asked themselves,"is to become of those good works upon which the early Church has laid so much stress?Are the widows and the orphans and the sick really very much benefited by the self-mortification of small groups of emaciated

矛盾，引起某些可悲的过度虔诚的行为，如爬到古老的石柱顶上或荒芜的坟墓里度日（这给了异教徒极大的笑料，使真正的信仰者伤心欲绝），于是帕乔米乌斯决定把整个运动建立在更加实际的基础上。这样，他就成了第一个宗教秩序的奠基者。从那时起（公元4世纪中叶），住在一起的小群隐居者都服从一个首领，称他为“总管”，他可以任命修道院院长管理不同的修道院，把林立的修道院当成了主的堡垒。

帕乔米乌斯死于公元346年。在他去世之前，他的隐修思想被亚历山大的阿塔纳修斯主教从埃及带到了罗马。数以千计的人借此机会，逃离了现实世界的邪恶和欲壑难填的债主的勒索。

然而，欧洲的气候和人们的本性使得创始人的最初计划必须稍做修改。在冰天雪地里，饥饿和寒冷不像在尼罗河谷那样容易忍受。此外，西方人很实际，作为神圣的东方理想的一个有机组成部分，所表现出来的既肮脏又邋遢的一面，不但不会让他们受到启发，反而让他们觉得恶心。

意大利人和法国人会这样扪心自问：“早期教会呕心沥血做的那些善事有什么用呢？几小群瘦弱的狂热分子住在千里之外深山老林的潮湿帐篷里禁欲苦修，难道寡妇、孤儿和病人就能真的从中受益吗？”

西方人坚持要把修道院体系改变得更合理些，这一改革要归功于一位住在亚平宁山脉的纳西亚镇人。他叫本尼迪克特，通称为圣人本尼迪克特。他的父母送他到罗马去上学，但这座城市使他的基督教灵魂充满了恐怖。他逃到了阿布鲁齐山的苏

zealots who live in the damp caverns of a mountain a million miles away from everywhere?"

The western mind therefore insisted upon a modification of the monastic institution along more reasonable lines,and credit for this innovation goes to a native of the town of Nursia in the Apennine mountains. His name was Benedict and he is invariably spoken of as Saint Benedict. His parents had sent him to Rome to be educated,but the city had filled his Christian soul with horror and he had fled to the village of Subiaco in the Abruzzi mountains to the deserted ruins of an old country palace that once upon a time had belonged to the Emperor Nero.

There he had lived for three years in complete solitude. Then the fame of his great virtue began to spread throughout the countryside and the number of those who wished to be near him was soon so great that he had enough recruits for a dozen full-fledged monasteries.

He therefore retired from his dungeon and became the lawgiver of European monasticism. First of all he drew up a constitution. In every detail it showed the influence of Benedict's Roman origin. The monks who swore to obey his rules could not look forward to a life of idleness. Those hours which they did not devote to prayer and meditation were to be filled with work in the fields. If they were too old for farm work,they were expected to teach the young how to become good Christians and useful citizens and so well did they acquit,themselves of this task that the Benedictine monasteries for almost a thousand years had a monopoly of education and were allowed to train most of the young men of exceptional ability during the greater part of the Middle Ages.

In return for their labors,the monks were decently clothed,received a sufficient amount of eatable food and were given a bed upon which they could sleep the two or three hours of each day that were not devoted to work or to prayer.

But most important,from an historical point of view,was the fact that the monks

■ 七山的罪孽之城

比亚克村，躲进了尼禄皇帝时代一座古老的乡村行宫的废墟中。

他在那里过了3年与世隔绝的生活，美德的盛名开始传遍整个乡村，希望与他接近的人很快激增，足以组建六七座完整的修道院。

于是，他告别了地牢，成为欧洲僧侣制度的立法人。他首先制定了法律，字里行间无不流露出他的罗马血统的痕迹。发誓遵守他的规定的僧侣可别指望过游手好闲的日子，在不做祷告和静思的时候，他们就得在田野里耕作。如果年纪太大而不能干农活了，就要教育年轻僧侣如何当一个好基督徒和有用的公民。他们恪尽职守，使本尼迪克特修道院在近1000年中独揽教育，在中世纪大部分时间里获准教育才能超群的年轻人。

作为劳动的报酬，僧侣们得到了体面的衣服、丰富可口的食物和床铺，每天不

ceased to be laymen who had merely run away from this world and their obligations to prepare their souls for the hereafter. They became the servants of God. They were obliged to qualify for their new dignity by a long and most painful period of probation and furthermore they were expected to take a direct and active part in spreading the power and the glory of the kingdom of God.

The first elementary missionary work among the heathen of Europe had already been done. But lest the good accomplished by the apostles come to naught,the labors of the individual preachers must be followed up by the organized effort of permanent settlers and administrators. The monks now carried their spade and their ax and their prayer-book into the wilderness of Germany and Scandinavia and Russia and far-away Iceland. They plowed and they harvested and they preached and they taught school and brought unto those distant lands the first rudimentary elements of a civilization which most people only knew by hearsay.

In this way did the Papacy,the executive head of the entire Church,make use of all the manifold forces of the human spirit.

The practical man of affairs was given quite as much of an opportunity to distinguish himself as the dreamer who found happiness in the silence of the woods. There was no lost motion. Nothing was allowed to go to waste. And the result was such an increase of power that soon neither emperor nor king could afford to rule his realm without paying humble attention to the wishes of those of his subjects who confessed themselves the followers of the Christ.

The way in which the final victory was gained is not without interest. For it shows that the triumph of Christianity was due to practical causes and was not (as is sometimes believed) the result of a sudden and overwhelming outburst of religious ardor.

The last great persecution of the Christians took place under the Emperor Diocletian.

Curiously enough,Diocletian was by no means one of the worst among those many

干活或不祷告的时候还能在床上睡两三个小时。

但从历史的角度来看，最重要的是，僧侣们不再是逃离现实世界和义务而为来世灵魂做准备的凡夫俗子，而是上帝的仆人。为了配得上新的尊称，他们必须在漫长痛苦的试用期内修炼自己，继而在传播上帝王国的力量和荣耀中承担起直接而积极的角色。

在欧洲异教徒中的初步传教工作已经完成了。但是为了不使教徒的成果化为乌有，个别传教士的劳动必须得到常住居民和官员们有组织的支持。于是僧侣们扛着铁锹和斧头，带着祷告书，来到德国、斯堪的那维亚、俄国和遥远冰岛的荒野之地。他们耕耘收获，布道办学，第一次为遥远的土地带来了文明的基本要素，而以前大多数人对它只是道听途说而已。

所有教会的最高管理者——罗马教皇，正是用这种方法激发了各种各样的人类精神力量。

务实的人可以得到机会，使自己有别于他人而名扬天下，正如做梦者能找到丛林静谧深处的幸福一样。没有白做的运动，也没有浪费的事情，它的结果就是权力的增长。不久，如果皇帝和国王不屈尊关注那些自认为基督追随者的臣民的要求，就难坐稳宝座。

取得最后胜利的方法也颇为有趣，因为它表明基督教的胜利是有现实原因的，绝不是（像有时候人们认为的）一时间迸发出来的势不可挡的宗教狂热的结果。

对基督徒的最后一次残酷迫害，发生在戴奥克里先皇帝统治时期。

potentates who ruled Europe by the grace of their body-guards. But he suffered from a complaint which alas! is quite common among those who are called upon to govern the human race. He was densely ignorant upon the subject of elementary economics.

He found himself possessed of an empire that was rapidly going to pieces. Having spent all his life in the army,he believed the weak point lay in the organization of the Roman military system,which entrusted the defenses of the outlying districts to colonies of soldiers who had gradually lost the habit of fighting and had become peaceful rustics,selling cabbages and carrots to the very barbarians whom they were supposed to keep at a safe distance from the frontiers.

It was impossible for Diocletian to change this venerable system. He therefore tried to solve the difficulty by creating a new field army,composed of young and agile men who at a few weeks' notice could be marched to any particular part of the empire that was threatened with an invasion.

This was a brilliant idea,but like all brilliant ideas of a military nature,it cost an awful lot of money. This money had to be produced in the form of taxes by the people in the interior of the country. As was to be expected,they raised a great hue and cry and claimed that they could not pay another denarius without going stone broke. The emperor answered that they were mistaken and bestowed upon his tax-gatherers certain powers thus far only possessed by the hangman. But all to no avail. For the subjects,rather than work at a regular trade which assured them a deficit at the end of a year's hard work,deserted house and home and family and herds and flocked to the cities or became hobos. His Majesty,however,did not believe in half-way measures and he solved the difficulty by a decree which shows how completely the old Roman Republic had degenerated into an Oriental despotism. By a stroke of his pen he made all government offices and all forms of handicraft and

让人倍感奇怪的是，戴奥克里先绝不是借助禁卫军之力统治欧洲的众多君主中最坏的一个，可是他遭到了统治者曾遭到的各种非难。他连最基础的经济知识都一窍不通。

他发现自己的帝国正在迅速走向瓦解。他戎马一生，深知弱点就在罗马的军事体制内部，这一体制把边界地区的防卫任务交给了占领地的士兵，而这些士兵已逐渐丧失了斗志，变成了爱好和平的乡下人，将白菜和胡萝卜卖给那些本来应该远离边界的野蛮人。

戴奥克里先不可能改变这个古老的体制。因此，为了解决当前困境，他建立了一支新型野战军，由年轻机敏的战士组成，几周之内就能开赴帝国任何遭受入侵的角落。

这是个绝妙的主意，但正如所有带军事色彩的好主意一样，它需要大笔可怕的开销。这些钱必须以赋税的方式由国内的老百姓缴纳。不出所料，老百姓群情激愤，大声疾呼，声称再要交钱就家徒四壁了。皇帝答复说他们误解了，并把以前只有刽子手才有的权力交给了收税官。但是一切都无济于事，因为各行各业的臣民辛辛苦苦干了一年，到头来却债务缠身，因此都抛家舍业，蜂拥到城里，或者干脆成为流浪汉。然而，皇帝陛下不想半途而废，又颁布了一项解决困难的法令，这表明古罗马共和国已经彻底堕落为东方专制主义国家。他一纸令下，所有政府机关和手工业、商业都变成了世袭职业。也就是说，官员的儿子注定要做官，不管愿意不愿意；面包师的儿子一定会成为面包师，即使他们在音乐或典当方面极有天赋；水手

commerce hereditary professions. That is to say,the sons of officers were supposed to become officers,whether they liked it or not. The sons of bakers must themselves become bakers,although they might have greater aptitude for music or pawn-broking. The sons of sailors were foredoomed to a life on shipboard,even if they were sea-sick when they rowed across the Tiber. And finally,the day laborers,although technically they continued to be freemen,were constrained to live and die on the same piece of soil on which they had been born and were henceforth nothing but a very ordinary variety of slaves.

To expect that a ruler who had such supreme confidence in his own ability either could or would tolerate the continued existence of a relatively small number of people who only obeyed such parts of his regulations and edicts as pleased them would be absurd. But in judging Diocletian for his harshness in dealing with the Christians,we must remember that he was fighting with his back against the wall and that he had good cause to suspect the loyalty of several million of his subjects who profited by the measures he had taken for their protection but refused to carry their share of the common burden.

You will remember that the earliest Christians had not taken the trouble to write anything down. They expected the world to come to an end at almost any moment. Therefore why waste time and money upon literary efforts which in less than ten years would be consumed by the fire from Heaven?But when the New Zion failed to materialize and when the story of Christ (after a hundred years of patient waiting) was beginning to be repeated with such strange additions and variations that a true disciple hardly knew what to believe and what not,the need was felt for some authentic book upon the subject and a number of short biographies of Jesus and such of the original letters of the apostles as had been preserved were combined into one large volume which was called the New Testament.

This book contained among others a chapter called the Book of Revelations and therein

的儿子必须在船板上漂流一生，即使他们在台伯河划船会晕船。最后，那些出卖苦力的工人虽然名义上仍然是自由的，但必须在出生地生老病死，因此和普通的奴隶没什么区别。

■ 君士坦丁大帝

指望一个对自己的能力极度自信的统治者，能够或者愿意容忍一小部分根据个人好恶去遵守或反对某些规定和法令的人继续存在，那就有点儿荒唐可笑了。但是在评价戴奥克里先对基督徒的残暴时，我们必须记住，他已经陷入了困境，有充分的理由怀疑数以百万计的臣民对他的忠诚，这些人只知道在皇帝的庇护下捞取好处，却拒绝替国家分忧解难。

还记得吗？最早的基督徒从未写过任何东西。他们本以为世界随时会毁灭，何必将时间和金钱浪费在那10年之内就会被天国大火焚烧殆尽的文学成就上呢？但是新天国并没有出现，基督的故事（经过100年的耐心等待之后）开始被人添枝加叶、改头换面地口口相传，虔诚的信徒变得

were to be found certain references and certain prophecies about and anent a city built on"seven mountains."That Rome was built on seven hills had been a commonly known fact ever since the days of Romulus. It is true that the anonymous author of this curious chapter carefully called the city of his abomination Babylon. But it took no great degree of perspicacity on the part of the imperial magistrate to understand what was meant when he read these pleasant references to the"Mother of Harlots"and the"Abomination of the Earth,"the town that was drunk with the blood of the saints and the martyrs,foredoomed to become the habitation of all devils,the home of every foul spirit,the cage of every unclean and hateful bird,and more expressions of a similar and slightly uncomplimentary nature.

Such sentences might have been explained away as the ravings of a poor fanatic,blinded by pity and rage as he thought of his many friends who had been killed during the last fifty years. But they were part of the solemn services of the Church. Week after week they were repeated in those places where the Christians came together and it was no more than natural that outsiders should think that they represented the true sentiments of all Christians towards the mighty city on the Tiber. I do not mean to imply that the Christians may not have had excellent reason to feel the way they did,but we can hardly blame Diocletian because he failed to share their enthusiasm.

But that was not all.

The Romans were becoming increasingly familiar with an expression which the world thus far had never heard. That was the word"heretics."Originally the name"heretic"was given only to those people who had"chosen"to believe certain doctrines,or,as we would say,a"sect."But gradually the meaning had narrowed down to those who had chosen to believe certain doctrines which were not held"correct"or"sound"or"true"or"orthodox"by the duly established authorities of the Church and which therefore,to use the language of the Apostles,were"heretical,unsound,false and eternally wrong."

无所适从了。于是，人们觉得在这方面需要一本权威性的书，便把耶稣的几篇短传和圣徒的亲笔信综合成一大卷书，这就是《新约》。

这本书中有一章叫《启示录》，它里面有关于一座建立在“七山”之上的城市的预言。自从罗慕路斯时代以来，人们就知道罗马建立在七山之上。的确，这个奇特章节的匿名作者小心谨慎地把他深为憎恶的那个城市称为巴比伦，但帝国官员还是敏锐地发现了这一点；他在书中读到了这座城市是“鸨母”和“地球的污点”，说这座城市浸满了圣人和牺牲者的鲜血，注定要成为所有魔鬼和邪恶灵魂的栖身之所，是一切肮脏可憎的鸟类的巢穴，还有许多诸如此类的贬抑词句。

这些言论可以被说成出自一个可怜的宗教狂热者的胡言乱语，他因为想起了过去50年来被杀害的许多朋友而被怒火蒙蔽了双眼。但这些句子是教堂庄严仪式的一部分，要周而复始地在基督徒聚会的地方传诵，因此旁观者自然会认为，这些话表达了基督徒对台伯河畔这座强大城市的真实感情。我并不是说基督徒没有充分的理由产生那样的感情，但我们也不能因为戴奥克里先没有产生这种热情而责备他。

但这并不是全部。

罗马人对一个闻所未闻的词语日益熟悉起来，这个词就是“异教徒”。起初，“异教徒”的名字只是用于那些“被选定”相信某些教义的人，或称一个“教派”。但渐渐地这一意思缩小到那些不信仰由正统教会权威制定的“正确”“合理”“真实”“正统”教义的人；或者用圣徒的话说，是“异端、谬误、虚假和永

The few Romans who still clung to the ancient faith were technically free from the charge of heresy because they had remained outside of the fold of the Church and therefore could not,strictly speaking,be held to account for their private opinions. All the same,it did not flatter the imperial pride to read in certain parts of the New Testament that"heresy was as terrible an evil as adultery,uncleanness,lasciviousness,idolatry,witchcraft,wrath,strife,murder,sedition and drunkenness"and a few other things which common decency prevents me from repeating on this page.

All this led to friction and misunderstanding and friction and misunderstanding led to persecution and once more Roman jails were filled with Christian prisoners and Roman executioners added to the number of Christian martyrs and a great deal of blood was shed and nothing was accomplished and finally Diocletian,in utter despair,went back to his home town of Salonae on the Dalmatian coast,retired from the business of ruling and devoted himself exclusively to the even more exciting pastime of raising great big cabbages in his back yard.

His successor did not continue the policy of repression. On the contrary,since he could not hope to eradicate the Christian evil by force,he decided to make the best of a bad bargain and gain the good will of his enemies by offering them some special favors.

This happened in the year 313 and the honor of having been the first to"recognize"the Christian church officially belongs to a man by the name of Constantine.

Some day we shall possess an International Board of Revisioning Historians before whom all emperors,kings,pontiffs,presidents and mayors who now enjoy the title of the"great"shall have to submit their claims for this specific qualification. One of the candidates who will have to be watched very carefully when he appears before this tribunal is the aforementioned Emperor Constantine.

This wild Serbian who had wielded a spear on every battle field of Europe,from

恒错误”的人。

几个仍抱着旧信仰不放的罗马人可以免遭异端邪说的指责，因为他们仍然待在基督教之外，而且严格来讲也不允许解释他们自己的观点。同样，《新约》中有些话也有伤皇帝的尊严，如“异端邪说是一种可怕的邪恶，犹如通奸、猥亵、淫荡、偶像崇拜、巫术、怒火、争斗、谋杀、叛乱和酗酒”，以及其他一些事情，出于礼貌，在此就不再重复了。

所有这些导致了摩擦和误解，摩擦和误解又导致了迫害。罗马监狱里又一次挤满了基督教囚徒，刽子手杀死了许多基督徒，虽然血流成河，却一无所获。最后，戴奥克里先陷入了绝望，放弃了皇帝宝座，回到了达尔马提亚马海岸的家乡萨洛尼亚，一心一意地做更有趣的事情——在后院里种大白菜消磨时光。

他的继承者没有继续镇压政策。相反，由于无望通过武力铲除基督教，他决定好好做一笔不光彩的交易，通过给敌人一些特殊好处来赢得好感。

这事发生在公元313年，君士坦丁大帝第一次以官方名义“承认”了基督教会。

如果我们有朝一日有一个“国际历史修正委员会”，所有皇帝、国王、教皇、总统、市长等享有“大”称号的人，都要以这个委员会的特定准绳来衡量，那么他们当中站在这个法庭前需要仔细审查的一位，就是上面提到的君士坦丁大帝。

这个狂野的塞尔维亚人在欧洲各个战场上挥舞着长矛，从英格兰的约克郡打到博斯普鲁斯海峡的拜占廷。他还杀死了自己的妻子、姐夫和外甥（一个7岁的男孩），

York in England to Byzantium on the shores of the Bosphorus,was among other things the murderer of his wife,the murderer of his brother-in-law,the murderer of his nephew (a boy of seven) and the executioner of several other relatives of minor degree and importance. Nevertheless and notwithstanding,because in a moment of panic just before he marched against his most dangerous rival,Maxentius,he had made a bold bid for Christian support,he gained great fame as the"second Moses"and was ultimately elevated to sainthood both by the Armenian and by the Russian churches. That he lived and died a barbarian who had outwardly accepted Christianity,yet until the end of his days tried to read the riddle of the future from the steaming entrails of sacrificial sheep,all this was most considerately overlooked in view of the famous Edict of Tolerance by which the Emperor guaranteed unto his beloved Christian subjects the right to"freely profess their private opinions and to assemble in their meeting place without fear of molestation."

For the leaders of the Church in the first half of the fourth century,as I have repeatedly stated before,were practical politicians and when they had finally forced the Emperor to sign this ever memorable decree,they elevated Christianity from the rank of a minor sect to the dignity of the official church of the state. But they knew how and in what manner this had been accomplished and the successors of Constantine knew it,and although they tried to cover it up by a display of oratorical fireworks the arrangement never quite lost its original character.

※ ※ ※ ※ ※ ※

"Deliver me,oh mighty ruler,"exclaimed Nestor the Patriarch unto Theodosius the Emperor,"deliver me of all the enemies of my church and in return I will give thee Heaven. Stand by me in putting down those who disagree with our doctrines and we in turn will stand by thee in putting down thine enemies."

There have been other bargains during the history of the last twenty centuries.

But few have been so brazen as the compromise by which Christianity came to power.

杀了其他一些地位低卑的亲戚。然而尽管如此，由于他在向自己最危险的对手马克辛提乌斯进攻时，为了获得基督徒的支持，他一时间惊慌失措地大加许愿，结果赢得了“第二个摩西”的声誉，亚美尼亚和俄国教会都推崇他为圣人。他无论生或死都是个野蛮人，虽然他表面上接受了基督教，但他至死都在试图通过蒸祭祀羊的内脏来预测未来吉凶。然而，人们忘记了这些，只是注意到了那部著名的《宽容法》。这位皇帝想通过它来保护可爱的基督教臣民“自由表达个人思想和集会不受干扰”的权利。

我在前面已经讲过，公元4世纪上半叶的教会领袖都是些现实的政治家，当他们终于使皇帝签署了这项永远值得纪念的法令时，基督教就从小教派的行列中上升到了尊贵的国教。但他们知道这一成果是怎样取得的，君士坦丁的继承者也知道，尽管他们想用伶牙俐齿来掩盖它，但终究纸包不住火。

※ ※ ※ ※ ※ ※

“交给我吧，强大的统治者，”内斯特主教对西奥多修斯皇帝说，“把教会的全部敌人都交给我吧，我将给你天堂。和我站在一起，把不赞成我们教义的人打倒；我们也将站在你这边，打倒你的敌人。”

在过去20个世纪的历史中，双方还有过其他交易。

但是这种无耻的妥协在历史上很少见，他正是这种妥协使基督教登上了权力顶峰。

CHAPTER V IMPRISONMENT

Just before the curtain rings down for the last time upon the ancient world,a figure crosses the stage which had deserved a better fate than an untimely death and the unflattering appellation of"the Apostate."

The Emperor Julian,to whom I refer,was a nephew of Constantine the Great and was born in the new capital of the empire in the year 331. In 337 his famous uncle died. At once his three sons fell upon their common heritage and upon each other with the fury of famished wolves.

To rid themselves of all those who might possibly lay claim to part of the spoils,they ordered that those of their relatives who lived in or near the city be murdered. Julian's father was one of the victims. His mother had died a few years after his birth. In this way,at the age of six,the boy was left an orphan. An older half-brother,an invalid,shared his loneliness and his lessons. These consisted mostly of lectures upon the advantages of the Christian faith,given by a kindly but uninspired old bishop by the name of Eusebius.

But when the children grew older,it was thought wiser to send them a little further away where they would be less conspicuous and might possibly escape the usual fate of junior Byzantine princes. They were removed to a little village in the heart of Asia Minor. It was a dull life,but it gave Julian a chance to learn many useful things. For his neighbors,the Cappadocian mountaineers,were a simple people and still believed in the gods of their ancestors.

第5章 囚 禁

当帷幕最后一次落在古代社会的时候，有一个人物出现在历史舞台上。他本该有更好的命运，但却过早地死去了，并且背着一个没人喜欢的“叛教者”的称号。

我指的是朱利安皇帝，君士坦丁大帝的侄子，他于公元331年出生在帝国的新首都。公元337年，他那声名显赫的叔叔死了，三个儿子立刻扑向他们共有的遗产，像饿狼般打成一团。

为了除掉那些可能要求分享遗产的人，他们命令杀死住在城里和附近的皇亲。朱利安的父亲就是受害者之一。他母亲生下他几年之后就死了。这样，他在六岁时就成了孤儿。一个体弱多病的表兄与他在一起读书，学的东西大部分都是宣扬基督信仰的好处，由和蔼但却平庸的尤斯比乌斯主教授课。

这两个孩子长大以后，大家觉得最好把他们送远些，免得引起别人注意，重蹈拜占廷小王子们的厄运。他们被送到小亚细亚中部的一个小村庄，生活虽然单调乏味，却使朱利安有机会学到不少有用的东西。因为他的邻居卡帕多西亚山民是朴实人，仍然信仰他们祖先的神灵。

在那里，朱利安根本没有机会担任什么要职。当他要求专心做研究时，得到了批准。

There was not the slightest chance that the boy would ever hold a responsible position and when he asked permission to devote himself to a life of study,he was told to go ahead.

First of all he went to Nicomedia,one of the few places where the old Greek philosophy continued to be taught. There he crammed his head so full of literature and science that there was no space left for the things he had learned from Eusebius.

Next he obtained leave to go to Athens,that he might study on the very spot hallowed by the recollections of Socrates and Plato and Aristotle.

Meanwhile,his half-brother too had been assassinated and Constantius,his cousin and the one and only remaining son of Constantine,remembering that he and his cousin,the boy philosopher,were by this time the only two surviving male members of the imperial family,sent for Julian,received him kindly,married him,still in the kindest of spirits,to his own sister,Helena,and ordered him to proceed to Gaul and defend that province against the barbarians.

It seems that Julian had learned something more practical from his Greek teachers than an ability to argue. When in the year 357 the Alamanni threatened France,he destroyed their army near Strassburg,and for good measure added all the country between the Meuse and the Rhine to his own province and went to live in Paris,filled his library with a fresh supply of books by his favorite authors and was as happy as his serious nature allowed him to be.

When news of these victories reached the ears of the Emperor,little Greek fire was wasted in celebration of the event. On the contrary,elaborate plans were laid to get rid of a competitor who might be just a trifle too successful.

But Julian was very popular with his soldiers. When they heard that their commander-in-chief had been ordered to return home (a polite invitation to come and have one's head

他首先来到尼科米迪亚，那是少数几个还在教授古希腊哲学的地方之一。他的脑子里装满了文学和科学，完全放弃了从尤斯比乌斯那儿学到的知识。

然后他获准去雅典，打算在苏格拉底、柏拉图和亚里士多德待过的圣地学习。

与此同时，他的表兄也被暗杀了。他的堂兄——君士坦丁唯一在世的儿子君士坦丁乌斯，想起只有他和他的堂弟——朱利安这位小哲学家是皇族中至今仅存的两个男性，便派人把他接回来，亲切地接待了他，还以极度的善意把自己的妹妹海伦娜嫁给他，并命令他去高卢抵御野蛮人。

看来朱利安从希腊老师那儿学到了比辩论更实用的东西。公元357年，阿拉曼尼人威胁法国，朱利安在斯特拉斯堡附近击垮了他们的军队，还巧用计谋把默兹河和莱茵河之间的土地纳入了自己的省份。他住进了巴黎，在图书室重新装满了自己喜爱的作家的书。尽管他生性严肃，这回却很高兴。

当这些胜利的消息传到皇帝耳朵中时，希腊却没有点燃庆祝的火焰。相反，他们制定了除掉对手的周密计划，因为朱利安有点儿太成功了。

但朱利安在士兵中享有崇高威望。他们一听到总司令要被召回（客气地请他回去，但回去就要斩首），便闯入他的宫殿，当即宣布他为皇帝；同时四处宣扬道，如果朱利安拒不接受就杀死他。

朱利安是个明智的人，他接受了这种拥戴。

即使是那时候，罗马的道路仍然秩序井然。朱利安以迅雷不及掩耳之势，把部队从法国中部开到了博斯普鲁斯海岸。但是在他到达首都之前，他获悉堂兄君士坦

cut off),they invaded his palace and then and there proclaimed him emperor. At the same time they let it be known that they would kill him if he should refuse to accept.

Julian,like a sensible fellow,accepted.

Even at that late date,the Roman roads must have been in a remarkably good state of preservation. Julian was able to break all records by the speed with which he marched his troops from the heart of France to the shores of the Bosphorus. But ere he reached the capital,he heard that his cousin Constantius had died.

And in this way,a pagan once more became ruler of the western world.

Of course the thing which Julian had undertaken to do was impossible. It is a strange thing indeed that so intelligent a man should have been under the impression that the dead past could ever be brought back to life by the use of force;that the age of Pericles could be revived by reconstructing an exact replica of the Acropolis and populating the deserted groves of the Academy with professors dressed up in togas of a bygone age and talking to each other in a tongue that had disappeared from the face of the earth more than five centuries before.

And yet that is exactly what Julian tried to do.

All his efforts during the two short years of his reign were directed towards the reestablishment of that ancient science which was now held in profound contempt by the majority of his people;towards the rekindling of a spirit of research in a world ruled by illiterate monks who felt certain that everything worth knowing was contained in a single book and that independent study and investigation could only lead to unbelief and hell fire;towards the requickening of the joy-of-living among those who had the vitality and the enthusiasm of ghosts.

Many a man of greater tenacity than Julian would have been driven to madness and

丁乌斯驾崩了。

就这样，一个异教徒又当上了西方世界的统治者。

■ 荒废的寺庙

朱利安要做的事情当然是不可能实现的。但奇怪的是，像他这样聪明的人竟然认为，已经逝去的东西可以借助某种力量复活；只要重建卫城的废墟、在荒芜的学园树林里重新住上教授、教授们穿着过时的宽外袍并相互用五个世纪以前就已经在世界上消失的语言交谈，伯里克利时代就可以复苏。

然而这正是朱利安想做到的。

在他执政的短暂两年时间里，想努力恢复当时大多数人都不屑一顾的古老科学；想重新点燃对僧侣统治的世界的研究热情，这些僧侣目不识丁，认为一切值得知道的东西都包括在一本书里，独立研究和调查只会导致信仰丧失和使地狱燃起烈火；还想重新点燃具有高度活力和热情的人的生活乐趣。

朱利安四面楚歌，许多比他更坚忍的人也会被这些反对之声逼入疯狂绝望的境地。至于朱利安，他在这种情况下快要崩溃了，但他至少暂时奉行了伟大祖先的

despair by the spirit of opposition which met him on all sides. As for Julian,he simply went to pieces under it. Temporarily at least he clung to the enlightened principles of his great ancestors. The Christian rabble of Antioch might pelt him with stones and mud,yet he refused to punish the city. Dull-witted monks might try to provoke him into another era of persecution,yet the Emperor persistently continued to instruct his officials"not to make any martyrs."

In the year 363 a merciful Persian arrow made an end to this strange career.

It was the best thing that could have happened to this,the last and greatest of the Pagan rulers.

Had he lived any longer,his sense of tolerance and his hatred of stupidity would have turned him into the most intolerant man of his age. Now,from his cot in the hospital,he could reflect that during his rule,not a single person had suffered death for his private opinions. For this mercy,his Christian subjects rewarded him with their undying hatred. They boasted that an arrow from one of his own soldiers (a Christian legionary) had killed the Emperor and with rare delicacy they composed eulogies in praise of the murderer. They told how,just before he collapsed,Julian had confessed the errors of his ways and had acknowledged the power of Christ. And they emptied the arsenal of foul epithets with which the vocabulary of the fourth century was so richly stocked to disgrace the fame of an honest man who had lived a life of ascetic simplicity and had devoted all his energies to the happiness of the people who had been entrusted to his care.

When he had been carried to his grave the Christian bishops could at last consider themselves the veritable rulers of the Empire and immediately began the task of destroying whatever opposition to their domination might remain in isolated corners of Europe,Asia and Africa.

开明原则。安条克的基督教众向他投掷石块和泥土，但他并没有惩罚这座城市。头脑迟钝的僧侣想激怒他再次掀起新的迫害悲剧，而朱利安皇帝却一再告诫官员们：“不要再有人流血牺牲了。”

公元363年，一支仁慈的波斯箭结束了朱利安奇怪的一生。

对于这位最后也是最伟大的异教徒统治者来说，这可能是最好的结局了。

如果他活得再长一些，他的宽容和对蠢行的憎恶会将他变为当时最专横的人。如今他躺在医院的病床上，能宽慰地回忆起在他统治期间，没有一个人因为个人见解而被处死。可是对他的这种仁慈，他的基督臣民却报之以永恒的仇恨。他们夸张地说是皇帝自己的士兵（一个基督徒士兵）射死了他，还精心谱写了赞歌来颂扬凶手。他们造谣说，朱利安死前已经承认了自己的错误，并承认了基督的权力。为了诋毁这位一生过着俭朴严谨的生活、全心全意为自己臣民谋取幸福的正人君子的名声，他们挖空心思地把公元4世纪盛行的污言秽语全都泼向了他。

朱利安被抬进坟墓之后，基督教的主教们终于可以自诩为帝国真正的统治者了。他们立即开始摧毁残存在欧洲、亚洲和非洲每个偏僻角落的反对势力。

在瓦伦提尼安和瓦伦斯兄弟联合执政的公元364年至公元378年，通过了一项法令，禁止所有罗马人向旧天神祭献牲畜。于是异教教士被剥夺了收入，必须另谋生路。

但这些规定和狄奥多斯皇帝颁布的法律相比还算是轻的。他规定，所有臣民不但要接受基督教义，而且只能接受“天主教”形式的基督教；他自己则成了天主教

Under Valentinian and Valens,two brothers who ruled from 364 to 378,an edict was passed forbidding all Romans to sacrifice animals to the old Gods. The pagan priests were thereby deprived of their revenue and forced to look for other employment.

But the regulations were mild compared to the law by which Theodosius ordered all his subjects not only to accept the Christian doctrines,but to accept them only in the form laid down by the"universal"or"Catholic"church of which he had made himself the protector and which was to have a monopoly in all matters spiritual.

All those who after the promulgation of this ordinance stuck to their"erroneous opinions"—who persisted in their"insane heresies"—who remained faithful to their"scandalous doctrines"—were to suffer the consequences of their willful disobedience and were to be exiled or put to death.

From then on the old world marched rapidly to its final doom. In Italy and Gaul and Spain and England hardly a pagan temple remained. They were either wrecked by the contractors who needed stones for new bridges and streets and city-walls and water-works,or they were remodeled to serve as meeting places for the Christians. The thousands of golden and silver images which had been accumulated since the beginning of the Republic were publicly confiscated and privately stolen and such statues as remained were made into mortar.

The Serapeum of Alexandria,a temple which Greeks and Romans and Egyptians alike had held in the greatest veneration for more than six centuries,was razed to the ground. There remained the university,famous all over the world ever since it had been founded by Alexander the Great. It had continued to teach and explain the old philosophies and as a result attracted a large number of students from all parts of the Mediterranean. When it was not closed at the behest of the Bishop of Alexandria,the monks of his diocese took the

的保护者，天主教垄断了人们所有的精神思想。

这项法律颁布之后，所有仍然坚持“错误观点”的人，仍然坚持“疯狂的异端邪说”的人，仍然信仰“可耻教义”的人，都要自食拒不服从法律的后果，或者被流放，或者被处死。

从那以后，旧世界快步走向了最后的灭亡。在意大利、高卢、西班牙和英格兰，异教徒的庙宇一座都不见了，不是被需要石头的建筑商拆去建造桥梁、街道、城墙和水利工程，就是被重新改造为基督徒的集会场所。成千上万座从共和国建立时开始积累下来的金制和银制神像，不是被公然没收，就是被偷盗，即使侥幸残存下来的也被打得粉碎。

六个多世纪以来一直深受希腊人、罗马人和埃及人尊崇的亚历山大的塞拉

新世界的帝国

matter into their own hands. They broke into the lecture rooms,lynched Hypatia,the last of the great Platonic teachers,and threw her mutilated body into the streets where it was left to the mercy of the dogs.

In Rome things went no better.

The temple of Jupiter. was closed,the Sibylline books,the very basis of the old Roman faith,were burned. The capitol was left a ruin.

In Gaul,under the leadership of the famous bishop of Tours,the old Gods were declared to be the predecessors of the Christian devils and their temples were therefore ordered to be wiped off the face of the earth.

If,as sometimes happened in remote country districts,the peasants rushed forth to the defense of their beloved shrines,the soldiers were called out and by means of the ax and the gallows made an end to such"insurrections of Satan."

In Greece,the work of destruction proceeded more slowly. But finally in the year 394,the Olympic games were abolished. As soon as this center of Greek national life (after an uninterrupted existence of eleven hundred and seventy years) had come to an end,the rest was comparatively easy. One after the other,the philosophers were expelled from the country. Finally,by order of the Emperor Justinian,the University of Athens was closed. The funds established for its maintenance were confiscated. The last seven professors,deprived of their livelihood,fled to Persia where King Chosroes received them hospitably and allowed them to spend the rest of their days peacefully playing the new and mysterious Indian game called"chess."

In the first half of the fifth century,archbishop Chrysostomus could truthfully state that the works of the old authors and philosophers had disappeared from the face of the earth. Cicero and Socrates and Virgil and Homer (not to mention the mathematicians and the

佩雍神庙被夷为平地。有一所从亚历山大大帝时代以来就闻名于世的大学仍然保留着，继续教授和解释古代哲学，结果吸引了大批来自地中海各地的学生。亚历山大的主教下谕不许关闭这所大学，但教区的僧侣自行其是。他们闯入教堂，私刑处死了最后一位伟大的柏拉图学派的教师西帕蒂娅，把她大卸八块扔到了街上喂狗。

罗马的情况也好不到哪里去。

朱庇特的庙宇被关闭了，古罗马信仰的经典《预言集》被付之一炬。首都成了一片废墟。

由著名主教图尔斯统治的高卢，旧天神被宣布为基督教义中魔鬼的前身，于是所有旧神的庙宇都从地球上消失了。

如果边远乡村的农民偶尔起来保卫自己敬爱的神庙，这时军队就会开来，用残暴武力平息“撒旦的叛乱”。

在希腊，破坏进行得慢一些。但是到公元394年，奥林匹克运动会终于被禁止。希腊国家这一生活中心（从未间断地进行了1170年）一终止，其他事情就更容易被扼杀了。哲学家一个接一个地被驱逐出境，最后查士丁尼皇帝一纸令下，雅典大学也被关了，维持其运转的基金被没收。最后七位教授失去了谋生之路，逃到了波斯。波斯国王乔思罗斯倒是热情地接待了他们，让他们过着宁静的晚年生活，玩一种叫“棋”的新颖神奇的印度游戏。

公元5世纪上半叶，克里索斯托大主教可以毫不夸张地宣称，古代作者和哲学家的著作已经从地球上消失了。西塞罗、苏格拉底、维吉尔和荷马（更不必说被所

astronomers and the physicians who were an object of special abomination to all good Christians) lay forgotten in a thousand attics and cellars. Six hundred years were to go by before they were called back to life,and in the meantime the world would be obliged to subsist on such literary fare as it pleased the theologians to place before it.

A strange diet,and not exactly (in the jargon of the medical faculty) a balanced one.

For the Church,although triumphant over its pagan enemies,was beset by many and serious tribulations. The poor peasant in Gaul and Lusitania,clamoring to burn incense in honor of his ancient Gods,could be silenced easily enough. He was a heathen and the law was on the side of the Christian. But the Ostrogoth or the Alaman or the Longobard who declared that Arius,the priest of Alexandria,was right in his opinion upon the true nature of Christ and that Athanasius,the bishop of that same city and Arius' bitter enemy,was wrong (of vice versa)—the Longobard or Frank who stoutly maintained that Christ was not"of the same nature"but of a"like nature only"with God (or vice versa)—the Vandal or the Saxon who insisted that Nestor spoke the truth when he called the Virgin Mary the"mother of Christ"and not the"mother of God"(or vice versa)—the Burgundian or Frisian who denied that Jesus was possessed of two natures,one human and one divine (or vice versa)—all these simpleminded but strong—armed barbarians who had accepted Christianity and were,outside of their unfortunate errors of opinion,staunch friends and supporters of the Church—these indeed could not be punished with a general anathema and a threat of perpetual hell fire. They must be persuaded gently that they were wrong and must be brought within the fold with charitable expressions of love and devotion. But before all else they must be given a definite creed that they might know for once and for all what they must hold to be true and what they must reject as false.

It was that desire for unity of some sort in all matters pertaining to the faith which

有基督徒恨之入骨的数学家、天文学家和物理学家）都被扔在阁楼和地窖里，被世人遗忘了。直到600年之后，这些人才重见光明；在此期间，人们只能听凭神学家的任意摆布。

这就像一种奇怪的节食，但（按医学行话讲）并不平衡。

至于基督教会，虽然战胜了异教敌人，却陷入了多重困境。大声疾呼要为自己的古老神灵烧香祭奠的高卢和卢西塔尼亚贫苦农民还是很容易被制服的。他们是异教徒，法律则支持基督徒。但要命的是，东哥特人、阿拉曼人和朗巴族人为亚历山大教士阿里乌斯关于基督真实面目的观点是否正确，而住在同一城市的阿里乌斯的死对头阿忒那修斯是否错误（或正好相反）而争得面红耳赤；朗巴族人和法兰克人就基督与上帝“并非同类，只是相像而已”这个问题争执不休；汪达尔人和萨克森人为尼斯特尔所说的圣母玛丽亚是“基督之母”而非“上帝之母”是否正确而打得不可开交；布尔戈尼人和弗利西人为耶稣是否具有半人半神的二重性而互不相让——所有这些四肢发达头脑简单、已经接受了基督教义的野蛮人虽然在观念上不幸误入歧途，但他们还是教会的坚定朋友和支持者，不能以一般的诅咒和永恒的地狱炼火去惩罚他们。他们必须用婉言说服，指出其错误，将他们带回具有仁爱和献身精神的信徒队伍中来。但是他们必须首先有明确教会宗旨，知道什么是对的，什么是错误而必须抛弃的。

由于人们要求把各种各样的信仰统一起来，因而导致了那次著名的集会，即我们所知道的“基督教世界范围联合会”或“全世界基督教大会”。自从公元4世纪

finally caused those famous gatherings which have become known as Oecumenical or Universal Councils,and which since the middle of the fourth century have been called together at irregular intervals to decide what doctrine is right and what doctrine contains the germ of heresy and should therefore be adjudged erroneous,unsound,fallacious and heretical.

The first of those Oecumenical councils was held in the town of Nicaea,not far from the ruins of Troy,in the year 325. The second one,fifty-six years later,was held in Constantinople. The third one in the year 431 in Ephesus. Thereafter they followed each other in rapid succession in Chalcedon,twice again in Constantinople,once more in Nicaea and finally once again in Constantinople in the year 869.

After that,however,they were held in Rome or in some particular town of western Europe designated by the Pope. For it was generally accepted from the fourth century on that although the emperor had the technical right to call together such meetings (a privilege which incidentally obliged him to pay the traveling expenses of his faithful bishops) that very serious attention should be paid to the suggestions made by the powerful Bishop of Rome. And although we do not know with any degree of certainty who occupied the chair in Nicaea,all later councils were dominated by the Popes and the decisions of these holy gatherings were not regarded as binding unless they had obtained the official approval of the supreme pontiff himself or one of his delegates.

Hence we can now say farewell to Constantinople and travel to the more congenial regions of the west.

The field of Tolerance and Intolerance has been fought over so repeatedly by those who hold tolerance the greatest of all human virtues and those who denounce it as an evidence of moral weakness,that I shall pay very little attention to the purely theoretical aspects of the case. Nevertheless it must be confessed that the champions of the Church follow a

■ 竞相匹敌的监狱

中叶以来，这种大会就不定期地召开，以决定哪些教义对，哪些教义带有异端邪说的萌芽，要被指为错误、谬论和异端。

第一届大会于公元325年在离特洛伊不远的尼西亚召开。56年后，第二届大会在君士坦丁堡举行。第三届大会于431年在以弗所召开。后来，大会连续在查尔斯顿开了几次，又在君士坦丁堡开了两次，在尼西亚开了一次，最后一届大会于公元869年又在君士坦丁堡召开。

但是从那以后，大会便在罗马或教皇指定的某个西欧城市召集。因为至公元四世纪以来，人们已经普遍承认了一个事实，即皇帝虽然有召集这种大会的权力（这一特权也迫使他为忠诚的主教出路费），可是权力强大的罗马主教提出的建议却必须予以高度重视。尽管我们不知道是谁主持了第一届尼西亚会议，但后来的会议都是由教皇主持的，这些神圣会议达成的决议不经教皇或他的代表批准就没有效力。

现在，我们可以告别君士坦丁堡，到西部气候更宜人的地方去看看。

宽容与专制之争一直没有停止过，一方认为宽容是人类的最高美德，另一方却诋毁它是道德观念衰弱的表现。我并不想从纯理论的角度去谈这个问题。不过

plausible line of reasoning when they try to explain away the terrible punishments which were inflicted upon all heretics.

"A church,"so they argue,"is like any other organization. It is almost like a village or a tribe or a fortress. There must be a commander-in-chief and there must be a definite set of laws and bylaws,which all members are forced to obey. It follows that those who swear allegiance to the Church make a tacit vow both to respect the commander-in-chief and to obey the law. And if they find it impossible to do this,they must suffer the consequences of their own decisions and get out."

All of which,so far,is perfectly true and reasonable.

If today a minister feels that he can no longer believe in the articles of faith of the Baptist Church,he can turn Methodist,and if for some reason he ceases to believe in the creed as laid down by the Methodist Church,he can become a Unitarian or a Catholic or a Jew,or for that matter,a Hindoo or a Turk. The world is wide. The door is open. There is no one outside his own hungry family to say him nay.

But this is an age of steamships and railroad trains and unlimited economic opportunities.

The world of the fifth century was not quite so simple. It was far from easy to discover a region where the influence of the Bishop of Rome did not make itself felt. One could of course go to Persia or to India,as a good many heretics did,but the voyage was long and the chances of survival were small. And this meant perpetual banishment for one's self and one's children.

And finally,why should a man surrender his good right to believe what he pleased if he felt sincerely that his conception of the

■ 异见者

必须承认，当教会的支持者在辩解对所有异教徒的残酷镇压时，倒是说得头头是道。

他们说："教会和任何其他组织一样，犹如一个村庄、一个部落或一片森林，必须有一名总指挥、一套明确的法律和规则，所有成员都必须遵守。凡是宣誓效忠教会的人，就等于发誓要尊敬总指挥，并遵守法律。如果他们做不到，那就要自食其果，从教会滚出去。"

迄今为止，这些都是非常正确合理的。

今天，一位牧师如果不再信仰浸礼会教派的教义，可以改信卫理公会，如果他因为某种原因而不再信仰卫理公会的教义，还可以改信唯一神教、天主教或犹太教，也可以改信印度教或伊斯兰教。世界广阔，大门敞开着，除了他饥肠辘辘的家人，别人不会反对他。

但这是轮船、火车和充满无限商机的时代。

idea of Christ was the right one and that it was only a question of time for him to convince the Church that its doctrines needed a slight modification?

For that was the crux of the whole matter.

The early Christians,both the faithful and the heretics,dealt with ideas which had a relative and not a positive value.

A group of mathematicians,sending each other to the gallows because they cannot agree upon the absolute value of x would be no more absurd than a council of learned theologians trying to define the undefinable and endeavoring to reduce the substance of God to a formula.

But so thoroughly had the spirit of self-righteousness and intolerance got hold of the world that until very recently all those who advocated tolerance upon the basis that"we cannot ever possibly know who is right and who is wrong"did so at the risk of their lives and usually couched their warnings in such careful Latin sentences that not more than one or two of their most intelligent readers ever knew what they meant.

而公元5世纪的世界却没有这么简单，当时罗马主教的影响无处不在。人们当然可以去波斯或印度，就像许多异教徒那样。但路途遥远，生还的机会渺茫，而且还意味着永远与家人分别。

最终如果一个人真的认为自己对基督的理解是正确的，对他而言说服教会稍微修改一下教义只是时间问题，那为什么还要放弃自由信仰的权利呢？

这正是整个问题的关键所在。

早期基督徒，不管是虔诚的还是异端的，都认为思想的价值只是相对的，而不是绝对的。

博学的神学家极力想说明无法解释的事情，想把上帝的本质归纳成公式，这就像一群数学家因为对*X*的绝对值难以达成一致而把对方送上绞刑架一样荒唐可笑。

但是，自以为是和专制的风气弥漫了整个世界。直到最近，如果有人说“我们永远不可能分辨孰对孰错”，并以此为依据来倡导宽容的话，还会有生命危险；因此他们通常会把忠告小心翼翼地隐含在拉丁文书本中，而能够理解他们意思的聪明读者却不会有几个人。

CHAPTER Ⅵ THE PURE OF LIFE

Here is a little problem in mathematics which is not out of place in a book of history.

Take a piece of string and make it into a circle,like this:

In this circle all diameters will of course be equal.

AB = CD = EF-GH and so on,ad infinitum.

But turn the circle into an ellipse by slightly pulling two sides. Then the perfect balance is at once disturbed. The diameters are thrown out of gear. A few like AB and EF have been greatly shortened. Others,and especially CD,have been lengthened.

Now transfer the problem from mathematics to history. Let us for the sake of argument suppose that

AB represents politics

CD " trade

EF " art

GH " militarism

In the figure I the perfectly balanced state,all lines are equally long and quite as much attention is paid to politics as to trade and art and militarism.

But in figure II (which is no longer a perfect circle) trade has got an undue advantage at the expense of politics and art has almost entirely disappeared,while militarism shows a gain.

Or make GH (militarism) the longest diameter,and the others will tend to disappear altogether.

You will find this a handy key to a great many historical problems.

第6章 生活的纯洁

这里讲一个在历史书中并非离题的数学小问题。

把一根绳子绕成圈，如图所示：

在这个圆圈中，各条直径当然是相等的。

AB=*CD*=*EF*=*GH*，等等，以此类推。

但是，轻轻地拉绳子两边，圆圈就变成了椭圆形，完美的平衡就会被破坏，各条直径变得参差不齐。*AB*和*EF*被大大缩短，其他线，尤其是*CD*却变长了。

现在把数学问题引申到历史问题中来。为了便于讨论，我们先假定：

*AB*代表政治；*CD*代表商业；*EF*代表艺术；*GH*代表军事

在图I中，是完美的平衡，所有线都一样长，对政治的关注与对商业、艺术和军事的关注是相同的。

但是在图II（它不再是完美的圆圈了）中，商业受到了特别优待，其代价是政治和艺术几乎完全销声匿迹，而军事却稍有发展。

或者使*GH*（军事）成为最长的线，而其他方面则趋于消亡。

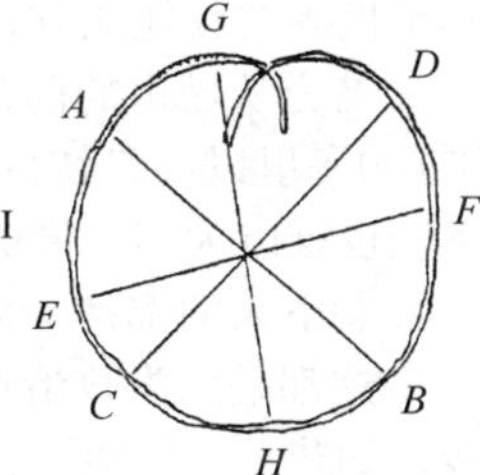

图I

Try it on the Greeks.

For a short time the Greeks had been able to maintain a perfect circle of all-around accomplishments. But the foolish quarrels between the different political parties soon grew to such proportions that all the surplus energy of the nation was being absorbed by the incessant civil wars. The soldiers were no longer used for the purpose of defending the country against foreign aggression. They were turned loose upon their own neighbors,who had voted for a different candidate,or who believed in a slightly modified form of taxation.

Trade,that most important diameter of all such circles,at first became difficult,then became entirely impossible and fled to other parts of the world,where business enjoyed a greater degree of stability.

The moment poverty entered through the front gate of the city,the arts escaped by way of the back door,never to be seen again. Capital sailed away on the fastest ship it could find within a hundred miles,and since intellectualism is a very expensive luxury,it was henceforth impossible to maintain good schools. The best teachers hastened to Rome and to Alexandria.

What remained was a group of second-rate citizens who subsisted upon tradition and routine.

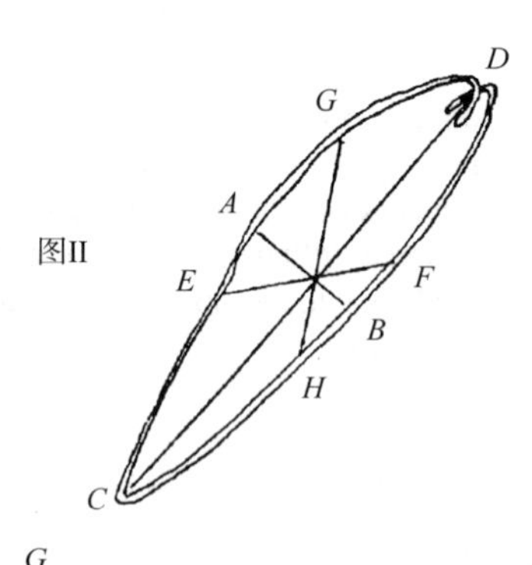

图II

And all this happened because the line of politics had grown out of all proportion,because the perfect circle had been destroyed,and the other lines,art,science,philosophy,etc. ,etc. ,had been reduced to nothing.

If you apply the circular problem to Rome,you will find that there the particular line called"political power"grew and grew and grew until there was nothing left of any of the others. The circle which had spelled the glory of the

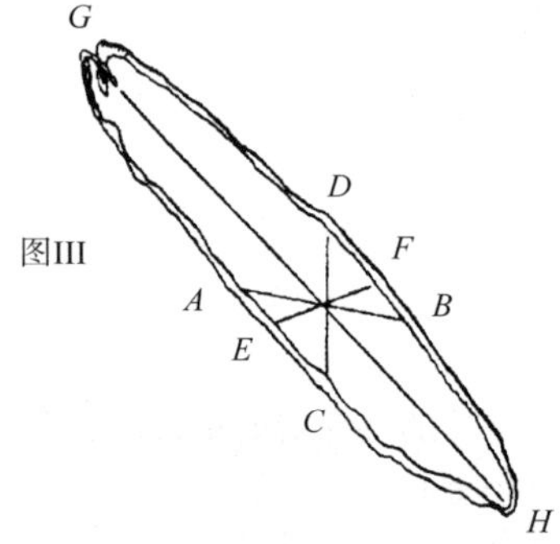

图III

你将会发现这就是解答许多历史问题的灵巧钥匙。

我们就用它来试一下希腊吧。

在短时间内，希腊还能够保持各行各业的完美圆圈。但是，不同政党之间的愚蠢争吵很快发展到不可收拾的地步，以至于无休无止的内战耗尽了整个国家原本阔绰的精力。士兵们不再被用来保卫国家抵御外来侵略。他们奉命向同胞开火，因为这些人投了另一位候选人的票，或者提出了希望有更好的赋税法等观点。

商业作为这类圆圈中最重要的直径，第一次感到了无法伸展，到完全走投无路时，便逃到了世界的其他地方，因为生意在那里更加稳定。

贫穷从城市的前门进来，艺术便从后门溜走了，从此不再露面。资本也乘坐周围100海里以内最快的船逃走了。由于知识等智力活动成了昂贵的奢侈品，因此好学校也难以为继。最优秀的教师匆匆逃奔到了罗马和亚历山大。

剩下来的都是一群二流公民，他们靠传统和常规生活着。

这都是因为政治这条线的增长超出了比例，完美的平衡的圆圈遭到破坏，其他线，如艺术、科学、哲学等，几乎不见踪影了。

Republic disappeared. All that remained was a straight,narrow line,the shortest distance between success and failure.

And if,to give you still another example,you reduce the history of the medieval Church to this sort of mathematics,this is what you will find.

The earliest Christians had tried very hard to maintain a circle of conduct that should be perfect. Perhaps they had rather neglected the diameter of science,but since they were not interested in the life of the world,they could not very well be expected to pay much attention to medicine or physics or astronomy,useful subjects,no doubt,but of small appeal to men and women who were making ready for the last judgment and who regarded this world merely as the anteroom to Heaven.

But for the rest,these sincere followers of Christ endeavored (however imperfectly) to lead the good life and to be as industrious as they were charitable and as kindly as they were honest.

As soon,however,as their little communities had been united into a single powerful organization,the perfect balance of the old spiritual circle was rudely upset by the obligations and duties of the new international responsibilities. It was easy enough for small groups of halfstarved carpenters and quarry workers to follow those principles of poverty and unselfishness upon which their faith was founded. But the heir to the imperial throne of Rome,the Pontifex Maximus of the western world,the richest landowner of the entire continent,could not live as simply as if he were a sub-deacon in a provincial town somewhere in Pomerania or Spain.

Or,to use the circular language of this chapter,the diameter representing "worldliness" and the diameter representing"foreign policy"were lengthened to such an extent that the diameters representing"humility"and"poverty"and"self-negation"and the other elementary Christian virtues were being reduced to the point of extinction.

如果把这个圆圈的问题应用于罗马，你就会发现，那条叫“政治权力”的特殊线条在不停地增长，直到其他所有线条都被挤掉了。于是，筑成共和国荣耀的圆圈消失了，剩下的只是一条细细的直线，也就是从成功到失败的最短距离。

再举一例。如果你把中世纪教会的历史简化成这种数学问题，就会发现下面的情况。

最早的基督徒曾经极力使自己的行为保持为完美的圆圈。也许他们忽略了科学的直径，不过既然他们对这个世界的生活不感兴趣，也就不要指望他们会过多地关注医学、物理或天文。有用的科学对于这些只想为末日审判做好准备、并认为尘世只是通往天堂前厅的男男女女来说，当然没有什么吸引力。

但对于基督的其他虔诚的追随者而言，他们却在想方设法（尽管很不完备）要过好日子。他们勤奋而仁慈，和善而诚实。

然而，当众多的小社团联合成一个单一的强大组织时，旧的精神圆圈的完美平衡就被新的世界性责任和义务无情地破坏了。半饥半饱的木匠和采石工人的信仰是建立在贫穷和无私的原则基础上的，要他们遵守这样的信条还很容易。可是罗马皇位继承人、西方世界的大祭司和整个欧洲大陆最富有的财主却不能像波美拉尼亚或西班牙某些外省城镇的小执事那样过简朴的生活。

或者用这一章的圆圈术语来讲，代表“世俗”和“对外政策”的直径伸展得太长，而代表“谦卑”“贫穷”“无私”和其他基督教基本美德的直径却日益缩短，甚至微乎其微了。

It is a pleasant habit of our time to speak patronizingly of the benighted people of the Middle Ages,who,as we all know,lived in utter darkness. It is true they burned wax tapers in their churches and went to bed by the uncertain light of a sconce,they possessed few books,they were ignorant of many things which are now being taught in our grammar schools and in our better grade lunatic asylums. But knowledge and intelligence are two very different things and of the latter,these excellent burghers,who constructed the political and social structure in which we ourselves continue to live,had their full share.

If a good deal of the time they seemed to stand apparently helpless before the many and terrible abuses in their Church,let us judge them mercifully. They had at least the courage of their convictions and they fought whatever they considered wrong with such sublime disregard for personal happiness and comfort that they frequently ended their lives on the scaffold.

More than that we can ask of no one.

It is true that during the first thousand years of our era,comparatively few people fell as victims to their ideas. Not,however,because the Church felt less strongly about heresy than she did at a later date,but because she was too much occupied with more important questions to have any time to waste upon comparatively harmless dissenters.

In the first place,there remained many parts of Europe where Odin and the other heathen gods still ruled supreme.

And in the second place,something very unpleasant had happened,which had wellnigh threatened the whole of Europe with destruction.

This"something unpleasant"was the sudden appearance of a brand-new prophet by the name of Mahomet,and the conquest of western Asia and northern Africa by the followers of a new God who was called Allah.

The literature which we absorb in our childhood full of"infidel dogs"and Turkish atrocities is apt to leave us under the impression that Jesus and Mahomet represented

我们这一代人有一个好习惯，那就是在谈到中世纪的愚昧时总带着一种包容态度，知道他们生活在无尽的黑暗之中。的确，他们在教堂里点蜡烛，在摇曳不定的烛光下起居，没有什么书，甚至不知道如今小学和稍好些的精神病院里教授的东西。不过，知识和智力是全然不同的东西，这些优秀的自由民很聪明，正是他们建立了我们现在仍在采用的政治和社会结构。

如果他们在很长的时间里面对其他人对教会的恶毒诋毁束手无策的话，我们评价他们时还是留点情吧。他们至少对自己的信念还是充满勇气的，他们会与他们认为错误的东西作战，完全不考虑个人幸福和舒适，以至于在断头台上结束自己的一生。

除此之外，我们不能提更多的要求了。

确实，在公元后1000年中，很少有人为自己的思想而牺牲。不过这并不是因为教会对异端的反感不如以前强烈，而是因为它有更重要的事情，无暇顾及那些相对无害的持不同观点的人。

首先，在欧洲许多地方，奥丁神和其他异教神仍然是最高统治者。

其次，发生了一件很不妙的事，它使整个欧洲几乎面临毁灭。

这件“不妙的事”就是突然出现了一个名叫穆罕默德的新先知，一群追随真主“安拉”的人征服了西亚和北非。

我们在孩提时代读到的充满了“异教徒”和土耳其人残酷恶行的文学故事，容易使我们认为耶稣和穆罕默德各自代表的思想是水火不容的。

ideals which were as mutually antagonistic as fire and water.

But as a matter of fact,the two men belonged to the same race,they spoke dialects which belonged to the same linguistic group,they both claimed Abraham as their great-great-grandfather and they both looked back upon a common ancestral home,which a thousand years before had stood on the shores of the Persian Gulf.

And yet,the followers of those two great teachers who were such close relatives have always regarded each other with bitter scorn and have fought a war which has lasted more than twelve centuries and which has not yet come to an end.

At this late day and age it is useless to speculate upon what might have happened,but there was a time when Mecca,the arch-enemy of Rome,might have easily been gained for the Christian faith.

The Arabs,like all desert people,spent a great deal of their time tending their flocks and therefore were much given to meditation. People in cities can drug their souls with the pleasures of a perennial county-fair. But shepherds and fisher folk and farmers lead solitary lives and want something a little more substantial than noise and excitement.

In his quest for salvation,the Arab had tried several religions,but had shown a distinct preference for Judaism. This is easily explained,as Arabia was full of Jews. In the tenth century B. C. ,a great many of King Solomon's subjects,exasperated by the high taxes and the despotism of their ruler,had fled into Arabia and again,five hundred years later in 586 B. C. ,when Nebuchadnezzar conquered Judah,there had been a second wholesale exodus of Jews towards the desert lands of the south.

Judaism,therefore,was well known and furthermore the quest of the Jews after the one and only true God was entirely in line with the aspirations and ideals of the Arabian tribes.

Any one in the least familiar with the work of Mahomet will know how much the Medinite had borrowed from the wisdom contained in some of the books of the Old Testament.

其实，这两个人属于同一个种族，说同一个语系的方言，都把亚伯拉罕奉为始祖，都可以追溯到同一个1000年前就矗立于波斯湾畔的祖籍。

然而，这两位伟大导师的追随者虽是近亲，却一直相互仇视，彼此之间的战争已经持续了12个世纪还多，至今尚未结束。

现在再做“假如”的猜想毫无意义，但的确曾有那么一段时间，罗马的死敌麦加差点儿接受了基督教。

阿拉伯人像所有沙漠民族一样，把大量时间用在放牧上，因此有充裕的时间沉思默祷。城里人可以从终年不断的乡镇集市中获得乐趣，而牧民、渔民和农夫过着孤独的生活，他们需要某种比热闹和刺激更实际的东西。

阿拉伯人在寻求救赎的过程中，尝试过好几种宗教，不过他们明显偏爱犹太教。这很容易解释，因为阿拉伯到处都是犹太人。公元前10世纪，所罗门国王的大批臣民因为对沉重的赋税和统治者的专制感到不满，逃到了阿拉伯。到了500年后的公元前586年，当尼布甲尼撒征服犹大国时，大批犹太人再次涌向南部沙漠地带。

犹太教由此为人们所熟知。而且犹太人只追求唯一真神，这与阿拉伯部落的志向和理想完全一致。

任何稍微读过穆罕默德著作的人都知道，麦地尼特从《旧约》的一些章节中借用了大量智慧。

以实玛利（他与母亲夏甲一起埋葬在阿拉伯中部的至圣所）的后裔并不敌视

Nor were the descendants of Ishmael (who together with his mother Hagar lay buried in the Holy of Holies in the heart of Arabia) hostile to the ideas expressed by the young reformer from Nazareth. On the contrary,they followed Jesus eagerly when he spoke of that one God who was a loving father to all men. They were not inclined to accept those miracles of which the followers of the Nazarene carpenter made so much. And as for the resurrection,they flatly refused to believe in it. But generally speaking,they felt very kindly disposed towards the new faith and were willing to give it a chance.

But Mahomet suffered considerable annoyance at the hands of certain Christian zealots who with their usual lack of discretion had denounced him as a liar and a false prophet before he had fairly opened his mouth. That and the impression which was rapidly gaining ground that the Christians were idol worshipers who believed in three Gods instead of one,made the people of the desert finally turn their backs upon Christianity and declare themselves in favor of the Medinese camel driver who spoke to them of one and only one God and did not confuse them with references to three deities that were"one"and yet were not one,but were one or three as it might please the convenience of the moment and the interests of the officiating priest.

Thus the western world found itself possessed of two religions,each of which proclaimed its own God to be the One True God and each of which insisted that all other Gods were impostors.

Such conflicts of opinion are apt to lead to warfare.

Mahomet died in 632.

Within less than a dozen years,Palestine,Syria,Persia and Egypt had been conquered and Damascus had become the capital of a great Arab empire.

Before the end of 656 the entire coast of northern Africa had accepted Allah as its divine ruler and in less than a century after the flight of Mahomet from Mecca to Medina,the Mediterranean had been turned into a Moslem lake,all communications between Europe

■ 第四次十字军东征

拿撒勒的年轻改革者的思想。相反，当耶稣说只有一个上帝，是所有人的慈父时，他们也热切地接受了他的说法。他们不愿意接受拿撒勒木匠（耶稣）的追随者大肆宣扬的那些奇迹。至于耶稣复活，他们根本就不相信。不过他们总体还是倾向于这一新信仰，愿意给它一席之地。

但是，穆罕默德在一伙基督教狂热分子手里吃了大苦头。这些缺乏判断力的人，没等他开口，就斥责他是骗子和伪先知。这件事再加上迅速广为流传的认为基督徒是崇拜三个而不是一个上帝的偶像崇拜者的说法，终于使沙漠居民放弃了基督教，并宣布自己更喜欢麦地那那个赶骆驼的人，他对他们只讲一个上帝，而不是搬出三个神来糊弄他们，一会儿合为一个上帝，一会儿又分为三个，全凭当时形势和官方教士的利益而定。

这样，西方世界便有了两种宗教，它们都宣称自己信奉的是唯一真神，而把其他神说成是骗子。

这些观点上的冲突很容易导致战争。

公元632年，穆罕默德去世。

and Asia had been cut off and the European continent was placed in a state of siege which lasted until the end of the seventeenth century.

Under those circumstances it had been impossible for the Church to carry her doctrines eastward. All she could hope to do was to hold on to what she already possessed. Germany and the Balkans and Russia and Denmark and Sweden and Norway and Bohemia and Hungary had been chosen as a profitable field for intensive spiritual cultivation and on the whole,the work was done with great success. Occasionally a hardy Christian of the variety of Charlemagne,well-intentioned but not yet entirely civilized,might revert to strong-arm methods and might butcher those of his subjects who preferred their own Gods to those of the foreigner. By and large,however,the Christian missionaries were well received,for they were honest men who told a simple and straightforward story which all the people could understand and because they introduced certain elements of order and neatness and mercy into a world full of bloodshed and strife and highway robbery.

But while this was happening along the frontier,things had not gone so well in the heart of the pontifical empire. Incessantly (to revert to the mathematics explained in the first pages of this chapter) the line of worldliness had been lengthened until at last the spiritual element in the Church had been made entirely subservient to considerations of a purely political and economic nature and although Rome was to grow in power and exercise a tremendous influence upon the development of the next twelve centuries,certain elements of disintegration had already made their appearance and were being recognized as such by the more intelligent among the laity and the clergy.

We modern people of the Protestant north think of a"church"as a building which stands empty six days out of every seven and a place where people go on a Sunday to hear a sermon and sing a few hymns. We know that some of our churches have bishops and occasionally

在不到12年的时间里，巴勒斯坦、叙利亚、波斯和埃及相继被征服，大马士革成为大阿拉伯帝国的首都。

到公元656年底之前，整个北非沿海都把安拉奉为神圣主宰。穆罕默德从麦加逃到麦地那之后不到一个世纪，地中海变成了伊斯兰教的一个内湖，欧洲和亚洲的一切交往都被切断了。直到17世纪末期，欧洲大陆一直处于被包围的状态。

在这种环境下，教会不可能把教义传到东方。它希望保住自己已经取得的成果。它选中了德国、巴尔干半岛诸国、俄罗斯、丹麦、瑞典、挪威、波希米亚和匈牙利，作为进行深入精神开发的肥沃土地，这项工作大获成功。偶尔也有像查理曼那样强悍的基督徒，虽然为了教会的利益，却用暴力手段屠杀了更喜欢异教神而不是外来上帝的臣民。不过，基督传教士大都是受欢迎的，因为他们是诚实的人，宣讲的东西简单明确，所有人都能理解，而且为充满流血、斗殴和拦路抢劫的世界带来了某些秩序、整洁和仁慈的因素。

虽然前方进展顺利，但是教会帝国内部却诸事不顺。（用本章开头的数学来讲）世俗的线条不断变长，直到最后教会的精神因素完全从属于纯政治和经济因素的考虑；尽管罗马的权力日益增加，对以后12个世纪的发展有巨大影响，但是土崩瓦解的某些因素已经显现，老百姓和教士当中的智者也看出了这一点。

现在，北方的新教徒把教堂看成一座房子，每七天中有六天空荡无人。到了星期日，人们去那里听布道和唱赞美诗。我们知道一些教堂有主教，这些主教偶尔在城里开会，那时我们周围就会有一群衣领翻到后面的和蔼的老绅士。我们可以从报纸上得

these bishops hold a convention in our town and then we find ourselves surrounded by a number of kindly old gentlemen with their collars turned backwards and we read in the papers that they have declared themselves in favor of dancing or against divorce,and then they go home again and nothing has happened to disturb the peace and happiness of our community.

We rarely associate this church (even if it happens to be our own) with the sum total of all our experiences,both in life and in death.

But in the Middle Ages this was altogether different. Then,the Church was something visible and tangible,a highly active organization which breathed and existed,which shaped man's destiny in many more ways than the State would ever dream of doing. Very likely those first Popes who accepted pieces of land from grateful princes and renounced the ancient ideal of poverty did not foresee the consequences to which such a policy was bound to lead. In the beginning it had seemed harmless enough and quite appropriate that faithful followers of Christ should bestow upon the successor of the apostle Peter a share of their own worldly goods. Besides,there was the overhead of a complicated administration which reached all the way from John o' Groat's to Trebizond and from Carthage to Upsala. Think of all the thousands of secretaries and clerks and scribes,not to mention the hundreds of heads of the different departments,that had to be housed and clothed and fed. Think of the amount spent upon a courier service across an entire continent;the traveling expenses of diplomatic agents now going to London,then returning from Novgorod;the sums necessary to keep the papal courtiers in the style that was expected of people who foregathered with worldly princes on a footing of complete equality.

All the same,looking back upon what the Church came to stand for and contemplating what it might have been under slightly more favorable circumstances,this development seems a great pity. For Rome rapidly grew into a gigantic super-state with a slight religious tinge and the pope became an international autocrat who held all the nations of western Europe in a

知他们已宣布提倡跳舞或反对离婚；然后他们又回到家里，我们的生活依然平静而幸福，没有任何干扰。

我们现在极少把这种教堂（即使它是我们自己的教堂）与我们的生死及所有活动相联系。

但是在中世纪情况完全不同。那时候，教会看得见摸得着，是一个高度活跃的组织，它会呼吸，也存在着，用国家做梦也不会想到的各种办法决定人的命运。第一批从慷慨的诸侯那里接受馈赠土地并放弃了古老的贫穷理想的教皇，很可能没有预见到这个政策会导致的后果。起初，基督的忠诚追随者向圣徒彼得的后继者赠送一些世俗礼物似乎很有益而且合情合理。然而，从约翰·奥格罗斯到特莱比赞德、从迦太基到乌普拉沙，到处都有复杂的监督管理体制。想想还有成千上万的秘书、牧师和抄写员，更不用说各个部门数以百计的大小头目，他们都要住房、穿衣、吃饭。还有横穿整个大陆的信使的费用，今天去伦敦、接着从诺夫哥罗德返回的外交使臣的旅行费用，以及为了保持教皇信使与世俗诸侯在一起时穿着体面、平起平坐所必需的总开支。

即使是这样，回顾一下教会本来代表什么，想想如果环境再好一些会出现什么情况，这种发展似乎是极大的遗憾。因为罗马很快变成了一个超级国家，而宗教色彩却只剩下一点点了，教皇则成了一位世界专制君主，控制着西欧各国的命运。与他相比，古代皇帝的统治反而显得温和大度。

bondage compared to which the rule of the old emperors had been mild and generous.

And then,when complete success seemed within certain reach,something happened which proved fatal to the ambition for world dominion.

The true spirit of the Master once more began to stir among the masses and that is one of the most uncomfortable things that can happen to any religious organization.

Heretics were nothing new.

There had been dissenters as soon as there had been a single rule of faith from which people could possibly dissent and disputes,which had divided Europe and Africa and western Asia into hostile camps for centuries at a time,were almost as old as the Church herself.

But these sanguinary quarrels between Donatists and Sabellianists and Monophysites and Manichaeans and Nestorians hardly come within the scope of this book. As a rule,one party was quite as narrow-minded as the other and there was little to choose between the intolerance of a follower of Arius and the intolerance of a follower of Athanasius.

Besides,these quarrels were invariably based upon certain obscure points of theology which are gradually beginning to be forgotten. Heaven forbid that I should drag them out of their parchment graves. I am not wasting my time upon the fabrication of this volume to cause a fresh outbreak of theological fury. Rather,I am writing these pages to tell our children of certain ideals of intellectual liberty for which some of their ancestors fought at the risk of their lives and to warn them against that attitude of doctrinary arrogance and cocksureness which has caused such a terrible lot of suffering during the last two thousand years.

But when I reach the thirteenth century,it is a very different story.

Then a heretic ceases to be a mere dissenter,a disputatious fellow with a pet hobby of his own based upon the wrong translation of an obscure sentence in the Apocalypse or the mis-spelling of a holy word in the gospel of St. John.

Instead he becomes the champion of those ideas for which during the reign of Tiberius a certain carpenter from the village of Nazareth went to his death,and behold! he stands revealed as the only true Christian !

就在教会似乎成功在望时，却出现了一些问题，它对教会统治世界的野心是致命的一击。

主的真正精神又一次在民众中崛起，这对于任何宗教组织都是很不舒服的事。

异教徒已经不是什么新事物了。

一旦出现人们可能反对的单一信仰统治，就会有持异见者。他们的争执与教会一样古老，它使欧洲、非洲和西亚在数世纪内成了相互敌视的阵营。

但是多纳特斯教派、撒比利乌教派、莫诺菲赛特教派、摩尼教派和尼斯特里教派之间的血腥争斗本书是不会讨论的。一般来讲，阿修斯的追随者的不宽容与阿塔那修斯信徒的不宽容都是一样的。

此外，这些争执总是围绕着一些模糊的神学问题，这些问题现在已经被逐渐遗忘了。我可不想把它们再从羊皮纸的坟墓中挖出来，也不想耗时费力地写出一本书来挑起神学的战火。我写这些只是想告诉子孙后代自由的信念，他们的祖先曾不惜牺牲为之奋斗。我还想告诫他们，不要养成教条主义的独断专行的态度。因为这种态度已经导致过去2000年来许多沉痛的灾难。

可是到了13世纪，情况大不一样了。

那时候的异教徒不再只是持不同见解的人，不再只是为《启示录》中哪句高深的话的误译或《圣约翰福音书》中哪个神圣字母的拼写错误而固执己见。

相反，他成了某些思想的斗士，在提庇留当政时期，一个来自拿撒勒村庄的木匠曾为之而死，而且，他站在那里，似乎他才是唯一真正的基督徒！

CHAPTER Ⅶ THE INQUISITION

IN the year 1198 a certain Lotario,Count of Segni,succeeded to the high honors which his uncle Paolo had held only a few years before and as Innocent III took possession of the papal chair.

He was one of the most remarkable men who ever resided in the Lateran Palace. Thirty-seven years old at the time of his ascension. An honor-student in the universities of Paris and Boulogne. Rich,clever,full of energy and high ambition,he used his office so well that he could rightly claim to exercise the"government not of the Church alone but of the entire world."

He set Italy free from German interference by driving the imperial governor of Rome from that city;by reconquering those parts of the peninsula which were held by imperial troops;and finally by excommunicating the candidate to the imperial throne until that poor prince found himself beset by so many difficulties that he withdrew entirely from his domains on the other side of the Alps.

He organized the famous fourth Crusade which never even came within sight of the Holy Land but sailed for Constantinople,murdered a goodly number of the inhabitants of that town,stole whatever could be carried away and generally behaved in such a way that thereafter no crusader could show himself in a Greek port without running the chance of being hanged as an outlaw. It is true that Innocent expressed his disapproval of these proceedings which shrieked to high Heaven and filled the respectable minority of Christendom with disgust and despair. But Innocent was a practical man of affairs.

第7章　宗教法庭

1198年，塞格尼公爵罗太里奥继承了他叔叔保罗在几年前才得到的崇高荣誉，以英诺森三世之名登上了教皇的宝座。

他是所有曾经入主过拉特兰宫的人当中最显赫的。他就任教皇时37岁，是巴黎大学和布伦大学的优秀学生，富有而聪明，精力充沛而抱负远大，善于使用权力，因此可以自称“不仅掌握着教会，还左右着整个世界”。

他把驻罗马的总督赶出了罗马城，再次征服了意大利半岛上由帝国军队控制的那部分地区，最后把皇位继承人逐出教会，使那个可怜的王子身陷困境，只好完全放弃了他在阿尔卑斯山那一侧的领地。通过这些，他使意大利摆脱了德国的掌控。

他组织了著名的第四次十字军东征，但这次东征从未到过“圣地”，而是奔向君士坦丁堡，屠杀了城里的大批居民，抢走了所有能带走的东西。由于他们的行径令人发指，以至于后来到希腊港口的十字军士兵无不担心被当作亡命徒绞死。英诺森三世的确表示过，不赞同这些残暴行径，它们使得少数德高望重的基督徒感到厌恶和绝望。但英诺森是个务实的人。他很快就接受了不可更改的事实，让一个威尼斯人去顶替君士坦丁堡主教的空缺。通过这个聪明策略，他使东正教再次处于罗马统治之下，同时赢得了威尼斯共和国的好感。从此，威尼斯把拜占廷领地看成是自己

He soon accepted the inevitable and appointed a Venetian to the vacant post of Patriarch of Constantinople. By this clever stroke he brought the eastern Church once more under Roman jurisdiction and at the same time gained the good will of the Venetian Republic which henceforth regarded the Byzantine domains as part of her eastern colonies and treated them accordingly.

In spiritual matters too,His Holiness showed himself a most accomplished and tactful person.

The Church,after almost a thousand years of hesitation,had at last begun to insist that marriage was not merely a civil contract between a man and a woman but a most holy sacrament which needed the public blessing of a priest to be truly valid. When Philip August of France and Alphonso IX of Leon undertook to regulate their domestic affairs according to their own particular preferences,they were speedily reminded of their duties and being men of great prudence they hastened to comply with the papal wishes.

Even in the high north,gained only recently for Christianity,people were shown in unmistakable manner who was their master. King Haakon IV (known familiarly among his fellow pirates as Old Haakon) who had just conquered a neat little empire including besides his own Norway,part of Scotland and all of Iceland,Greenland,the Orkneys and the Hebrides,was obliged to submit the somewhat tangled problem of his birth to a Roman tribunal before he could get himself crowned in his old cathedral of Trondhjem.

And so it went.

The king of Bulgaria,who invariably murdered his Greek prisoners of war,and was not above torturing an occasional Byzantine emperor,who therefore was not the sort of person one might expect to take a deep interest in religious matters,traveled all the way to Rome and humbly asked that he be recognized as vassal of His Holiness. While in England,certain barons who had undertaken to discipline their sovereign master were rudely informed that their charter was null and void because"it had been obtained by

的东方殖民地，随意发号施令。

在精神方面，教皇也表现出了极深的造诣和圆滑的策略。

在经过近1000年的犹豫之后，教会终于开始认为婚姻不只是男女之间的民事契约，而是一件神圣的事，必须在神父当众祝福后才真正生效。当法国的菲利普·奥古斯丁和莱昂的阿方索九世按照自己的好恶治理国家时，他们很快就得到教皇的警告，要记住自己的职责。他们都小心处世，立即遵从了教皇的旨意。

甚至在北方高地，尽管基督教刚刚传入，人们也准确无误地意识到谁是他们真正的主人。国王哈康四世（海盗同伙们习惯称他为“老哈康”）刚刚征服了一个小帝国，他的统治范围除了他所在的挪威之外，还有苏格兰的一部分、冰岛、格陵兰岛、奥克尼群岛和赫布里底群岛。但是他在旧天主教堂加冕之前，必须向罗马法庭交代清楚自己复杂的身世。

事态就这样发展下去。

保加利亚国王一味屠杀希腊战俘，有时还会折磨拜占廷的皇帝，因此他对宗教思想根本不感兴趣，但他还是赶赴罗马，谦卑地恳求当教皇的仆人。在英格兰，几个贵族想用一些规则来约束他们的国王，教会却粗暴地声明他们的宪章无效，因为“它是依靠武力获取的”；接着，他们又因为起草了那份著名的《大宪章》而被逐出了教会。

所有这些都表明，英诺森三世对那些敢于质疑教会法律的朴实的纺织工和目不

force"and next found themselves excommunicated for having given unto this world the famous document known as Magna Charta.

From all this it will appear that Innocent III was not the sort of person who would deal lightly with the pretensions of a few simple linen-weavers and illiterate shepherds who undertook to question the laws of his Church.

And yet,some there were found who had the courage to do this very thing as we shall now see.

The subject of all heresies is extremely difficult.

Heretics,almost invariably,are poor people who have small gift for publicity. The occasional clumsy little pamphlets they write to explain their ideas and to defend themselves against their enemies fall an easy prey to the ever watchful detectives of whatever inquisition happens to be in force at that particular moment and are promptly destroyed. Hence we depend for our knowledge of most heresies upon such information as we are able to glean from the records of their trials and upon such articles as have been written by the enemies of the false doctrines for the express purpose of exposing the new"conspiracy of Satan"to the truly faithful that all the world may be duly scandalized and warned against doing likewise.

As a result we usually get a composite picture of a longhaired individual in a dirty shirt,who lives in an empty cellar somewhere in the lowest part of the slums,who refuses to touch decent Christian food but subsists entirely upon vegetables,who drinks naught but water,who keeps away from the company of women and mumbles strange prophecies about the second coming of the Messiah,who reproves the clergy for their worldliness and wickedness and generally disgusts his more respectable neighbors by his ill-guided attacks upon the established order of things.

识丁的牧羊人提出的要求是不会轻易放过的。

不过，还是有一些人敢这样去做，正如我们将要看到的那样。

所有异端邪说都是令人极其费解的。

异教徒几乎都是贫苦大众，没有搞宣传的天赋。他们偶尔会写几本拙朴的小册子阐述自己的见解，以保护自己打击敌人，但它们马上就会被当时掌权的宗教法庭派出的机敏密探发现，并被立即销毁。因此我们只能凭借异端邪说的审判记录中的线索，以及他们的敌人为了杀一儆百，向虔诚信徒揭露的令全世界震惊的《新的撒旦阴谋》的文章来了解大多数异端邪说。

结果，对这些人我们通常会得到较复杂的印象：他们披头散发，衣衫褴褛，住在最下层贫民窟的空地窖里，拒绝接触崇高的基督食物，坚持只吃蔬菜，只喝白水，对女人避而远之，叨唠着救世主第二次下凡的奇怪预言，责骂教士的庸俗和邪恶，由于恶意攻击万物的既有规律而让他们体面的邻居感到厌恶。

当然，许多异教徒的确令人讨厌，而那似乎正是自命不凡的人应有的下场。

没错，很多异教徒是以非神圣的热情去追求神圣生活的。他们脏得像个魔鬼，臭气冲天，那些关于真正基督生活的怪诞思想通常会把他们家乡的平静生活搅乱。

不过，我们还是要赞扬他们的勇气和诚实。

他们可能所获无几，却失去了一切。

结果呢，他们失去了一切。

当然，这个世界上的一切都趋于有序化。最后，甚至那些根本不相信组织的

Undoubtedly a great many heretics have succeeded in making a nuisance of themselves,for that seems to be the fate of people who take themselves too seriously.

Undoubtedly a great many of them,driven by their almost unholy zeal for a holy life,were dirty,looked like the devil and did not smell pleasantly and generally upset the quiet routine of their home town by their strange ideas anent a truly Christian existence.

But let us give them credit for their courage and their honesty.

They had mighty little to gain and everything to lose.

As a rule,they lost it.

Of course,everything in this world tends to become organized. Eventually even those who believe in no organization at all must form a Society for the Promotion of Disorganization,if they wish to accomplish anything. And the medieval heretics,who loved the mysterious and wallowed in emotions,were no exception to this rule. Their instinct of self-preservation made them flock together and their feeling of insecurity forced them to surround their sacred doctrines by a double barrier of mystic rites and esoteric ceremonials.

But of course the masses of the people,who remained faithful to the Church,were unable to make any distinction between these different groups and sects. And they bunched them all together and called them dirty Manichaeans or some other unflattering name and felt that that solved the problem.

In this way did the Manichaeans become the Bolshevists of the Middle Ages. Of course I do not use the latter name as indicating membership in a certain well-defined political party which a few years ago established itself as the dominant factor in the old Russian Empire. I refer to a vague and ill-defined term of abuse which people nowadays bestow upon all their personal enemies from the landlord who comes to collect the rent down to the elevator boy who neglects to stop at the right floor.

人如果想有所成就，也必须成立一个“无组织促进会”。喜爱神话、沉湎于感情的中世纪异教徒也不例外。自我保护的天性使他们聚集在一起，不安全感迫使他们在自己神圣教义的外面裹上了两层玄奥神秘的礼拜和礼仪来打掩护。

■ 普罗旺斯

但是，大多数忠诚于基督教会的人却不能区别这些不同的组织和教派。他们把所有异教徒混为一谈，称他们是肮脏的摩尼教徒或其他不恭的东西，以为这样就能解决问题。

这样，摩尼教徒成了中世纪的布尔什维克。我当然不是指一个有明确纲领的政党，就像数年前在俄罗斯帝国确立了统治地位的那个政党。我是指一种含混不清的谩骂，如今人们也用它来诅咒所有的敌人，包括从收房租的房东到没有把电梯停在适当位置的电梯工。

对于中世纪的上等基督徒来说，摩尼教徒是最令人讨厌的家伙。可是由于没有真凭实据对他进行审判，所以就指控他为异端。这个方法和一般的法庭审判相比，既不怎么引人注意，也比较快，不过它常常稍欠准确，导致了大量的冤案。

A Manichaean,to a medieval super-Christian,was a most objectionable person. But as he could not very well try him upon any positive charges,he condemned him upon hearsay,a method which has certain unmistakable advantages over the less spectacular and infinitely slower procedure followed by the regular courts of law but which sometimes suffers from a lack of accuracy and is responsible for a great many judicial murders.

What made this all the more reprehensible in the case of the poor Manichaeans was the fact that the founder of the original sect,a Persian by the name of Mani,had been the very incarnation of benevolence and charity. He was an historical figure and was born during the first quarter of the third century in the town of Ecbatana where his father,Patak,was a man of considerable wealth and influence.

He was educated in Ctesiphon,on the river Tigris,and spent the years of his youth in a community as international,as polyglot,as pious,as godless,as material and as idealistically-spiritual as the New York of our own day. Every heresy,every religion,every schism,every sect of east and west and south and north had its followers among the crowds that visited the great commercial centers of Mesopotamia. Mani listened to all the different preachers and prophets and then distilled a philosophy of his own which was a mixturn-compositum of Buddhism,Christianity,Mithraism and Judaism,with a slight sprinkling of half a dozen old Babylonian superstitions.

Making due allowance for certain extremes to which his followers sometimes carried his doctrines,it can be stated that Mani merely revived the old Persijan myth of the Good God and the Evil God who are eternally fighting for the soul of man and that he associated the ancient God of Evil with the Jehovah of the Old Testament (who thus became his Devil) and the God of All Good Things with that Heavenly Father whom we find revealed within the pages of the Four Gospels. Furthermore (and that is where Buddhistic influence made itself

在可怜的摩尼教徒的案子中更应指责的是，这个教的创始人是个名叫摩尼的波斯人，他是宽厚和仁慈的化身。他是个历史人物，于公元3世纪之前25年出生在一个叫艾卡巴塔那的镇子里，他父亲帕塔克是那里很有钱财和影响的大人物。

他在底格里斯河畔的采斯雯受过教育，他青年时代所处的社会就像如今的纽约，具有国际性、语言混杂、人性虚伪、不信上帝和追求实利，并充满空想。在从四面八方赶来两河流域大商业中心的人群中，各种异端、宗教和教派都有自己的追随者。摩尼倾听着各种传教士和预言家的言论，把佛教、基督教、密特拉教和犹太教融合在一起，再掺上一些古巴比伦的迷信，形成了自己的一套哲学。

如果不考虑摩尼教徒有时会把摩尼教义推向极端，那么可以说摩尼只是复苏了古代波斯神话中的好上帝和坏上帝。坏上帝总是与人的灵魂作对，摩尼把古代的万恶之神与《旧约》中的耶和华相联系（于是耶和华变成了摩尼教的魔鬼），把洪福之神和四福音书中的“天父”相联系。而且（这里可以看到佛教的影响）摩尼认为，人的身躯是天性邪恶卑鄙之物，所有人都应该不断磨砺躯体，严格遵守节食和行为规范，以摈除自己的世俗野心，不至于沦入万恶之神的魔掌，不被炼狱烧为灰烬。结果，他恢复了一大批禁饮禁食的规矩，只让追随者喝凉水、吃干菜和死鱼。这后一项教义可能会让我们感到吃惊，不过教徒们一直认为，海里的冷血生物对人的不朽灵魂的损伤要比陆地上的热血亲族小一些，这些宁愿死也不愿吃一块牛排的人，吃起鱼来却津津有味，毫无愧疚感。

摩尼轻视女性，这表明他是个地地道道的东方人。他禁止信徒结婚，主张人类

felt) Mani believed that the body of man was by nature a vile and despicable thing;that all people should try to rid themselves of their worldly ambitions by the constant mortification of the flesh and should obey the strictest rules of diet and behavior lest they fall into the clutches of the Evil God (the Devil) and burn in Hell. As a result he revived a large number of taboos about things that must not be eaten or drunk and prescribed for his followers a menu composed exclusively of cold water,dried vegetables and dead fish. This latter ordinance may surprise us,but the inhabitants of the sea,being coldblooded animals,have always been regarded as less harmful to man's immortal soul than their warm-blooded brethren of the dry land,and the self-same people who would rather suffer death than eat a veal chop cheerfully consume quantities of fish and never feel a qualm of conscience.

Mani showed himself a true Oriental in his contempt for women. He forbade his disciples to marry and advocated the slow extinction of the human race.

As for baptism and the other ceremonies instituted originally by the Jewish sect of which John the Baptist had been the exponent,Mani regarded them all with horror and instead of being submerged in water,his candidates for holy orders were initiated by the laying on of hands.

At the age of twenty-five,this strange man undertook to explain his ideas unto all mankind. First he visited India and China where he was fairly successful. Then he turned homeward to bring the blessings of his creed to his own neighbors.

But the Persian priests who began to find themselves deprived of much secret revenue by the success of these unworldly doctrines turned against him and asked that he be killed. In the beginning,Mani enjoyed the protection of the king,but when this sovereign died and was succeeded by some one else who had no interest whatsoever in religious questions,Mani was surrendered to the priestly class. They took him to the walls of the

走向消亡。

至于对最初由犹太教创立、由施洗约翰发起的洗礼及其他仪式，摩尼则深恶痛绝；因而想入教的人不必将身体浸入水中，而是行按手礼。

25岁时，这个怪人开始向全人类解释他的思想。他首先来到印度和中国，在那里非常成功。然后他返回家乡，想把他的教义的祝福带给自己的同胞。

但是波斯教士们开始发现，摩尼教那些超凡脱俗的教义的成功使他们丧失了许多秘密收入，于是转而反对摩尼，要求处死他。起初，摩尼受到了国王的保护，但是老国王死后，新国王对宗教事务毫无兴趣，于是摩尼被交给了教士阶层去处置。他们把摩尼带到城墙下，把他钉在十字架上，还剥了他的皮挂在城门上示众，以警告那些对这个艾卡巴塔那预言家的异端邪说感兴趣的人。

由于和当局的激烈冲突，摩尼教自身也分崩离析了。但是这位预言家的思想火花像众多的精神流星，在欧洲和亚洲的广大土地上传播开来，在以后很多世纪里在朴实贫苦的百姓中继续产生着巨大反响，他们不自觉地捡起了摩尼的思想，仔细审视，发现它们很合自己的口味。

摩尼教具体是在何时以及怎样进入欧洲的，我也不清楚。

很可能它是经过小亚细亚、黑海和多瑙河来到欧洲，然后翻过阿尔卑斯山，很快在德国和法国受到了热烈欢迎。在那里，新教义的追随者给自己起了个东方名字“凯瑟利”，也就是“过纯洁生活的人”。这一让教会苦恼的教义迅速蔓延，以至在整个西欧，“凯赞”或“凯特”成了“异端邪说”的同义词。

town and crucified him and flayed his corpse and publicly exposed his skin before the city gate as an example to all those who might feel inclined to take an interest in the heresies of the Ecbatanian prophet.

By this violent conflict with the authorities,the Manichaean church itself was broken up. But little bits of the prophet's ideas,like so many spiritual meteors,were showered far and wide upon the landscape of Europe and Asia and for centuries afterwards continued to cause havoc among the simple and the poor who inadvertently had picked them up,had examined them and had found them singularly to their taste.

Exactly how and when Manichaeism entered Europe,I do not know.

Most likely it came by way of Asia Minor,the Black Sea and the Danube. Then it crossed the Alps and soon enjoyed immense popularity in Germany and France. There the followers of the new creed called themselves by the Oriental name of the Cathari,or"the people who lead a pure life,"and so widespread was the affliction that all over western Europe the word"Ketzer"or"Ketter"came to mean the same as"heretic."

But please don't think of the Cathari as members of a definite religious denomination. No effort was made to establish a new sect. The Manichaean ideas exercised great influence upon a large number of people who would have stoutly denied that they were anything but most devout sons of the Church. And that made this particular form of heresy so dangerous and so difficult of detection.

It is comparatively easy for the average doctor to diagnose a disease caused by microbes of such gigantic structure that their presence can be detected by the microscope of a provincial board-of-health.

But Heaven protect us against the little creatures who can maintain their incognito in the midst of an ultra-violet illumination,for they shall inherit the earth.

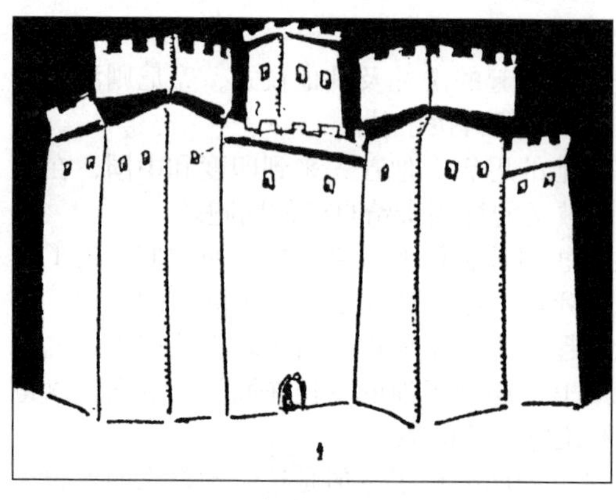

■ 彼得·沃尔多

不过，请不要认为“凯瑟利”是一个固定教派，根本没人试图建立一个新教派。摩尼教的思想对许多人产生了巨大影响，而这些人却仍然坚持自己是基督教会的虔诚信徒。这使这种特殊形式的异端邪说非常危险，而且难以察觉。

对于普通医生来说，要是某些病菌的体积大得在地方卫生部门的显微镜下就能看到，那么由这种病菌引起的疾病是比较容易诊断的。

但是上帝会保佑我们不受在紫外线下仍然能隐匿的小生物的侵害，因为上帝还要让世界延续下去。

从基督教的观点来看，摩尼教是最危险的社会瘟疫，它使教会上层人物充满了恐惧，这种恐惧是在各种常见的精神疾病面前体会不到的。

这也许不能公开说，但早期基督信仰的最坚定支持者的确表现出了这种病的征兆。就拿圣奥古斯丁来说吧，这个十字军里杰出、勇敢的人，这个曾奋勇争先摧毁异教的最后一座堡垒的人，据说内心却向着摩尼教。

Manichaeism,from the point of view of the Church,was therefore the most dangerous expression of all social epidemics and it filled the higher authorities of that organization with a terror not felt before the more common varieties of spiritual afflictions.

It was rarely mentioned above a whisper,but some of the staunchest supporters of the early Christian faith had shown unmistakable symptoms of the disease. Yea,great Saint Augustine,that most brilliant and indefatigable warrior of the Cross,who had done more than any one else to destroy the last stronghold of heathenism,was said to have been at heart considerable of a Manichaean.

Priscillian,the Spanish bishop who was burned at the stake in the year 385 and who gained the distinction of being the first victim of the law against heretics,was accused of Manichaean tendencies.

Even the heads of the Church seemed gradually to have fallen under the spell of the abominable Persian doctrines.

They were beginning to discourage laymen from reading the Old Testament and finally,during the twelfth century,promulgated that famous order by which all clergymen were henceforth condemned to a state of celibacy. Not to forget the deep impression which these Persian ideals of abstinence were soon to make upon one of the greatest leaders of spiritual reform,causing that most lovable of men,good Francis of Assisi,to establish a new monastic order of such strict Manichaean purity that it rightly earned him the title of the Buddha of the West.

But when these high and noble ideals of voluntary poverty and humility of soul began to filter down to the common people,at the very moment when the world was filled with the din of yet another war between emperor and pope,when foreign mercenaries,bearing the banners of the cross and the eagle,were fighting each other for the most valuable bits

普里西林是西班牙主教，他于公元385年被烧死在火刑柱上，因为他被指控倾向于摩尼教，由此成为《反对异教法》的第一个牺牲品。

就连基督教会的领袖似乎也渐渐被可怕的波斯教义吸引了。

他们开始劝阻不懂神学的门外汉不要读《旧约》；最后，在12世纪还宣布了著名的法令：所有神职人员都必须保持独身。不要忘记，这种波斯苦行思想很快就在精神变革的伟大领袖身上留下了深刻的烙印，使最受人爱戴的阿西斯的弗朗西斯制定了严格的摩尼教“纯洁”思想的新僧侣制度，这为他赢得了“西方的释迦牟尼”的头衔。

但是，当自愿贫穷和灵魂谦卑的高尚理想开始向普通大众渗透的时候，当皇帝与教皇的又一场战争一触即发的时候，当外国雇佣军各自扛着十字架和雄鹰旗帜你死我活地争夺地中海沿岸珍贵的弹丸之地的时候，当大批十字军携带从朋友和敌人那儿掠夺得来的不义之财蜂拥回国的时候，当修道院长住在奢华的宫殿并豢养了一群阿谀之徒的时候，当教士们匆忙念完清晨的弥撒赶去饱享狩猎早餐的时候，一件不妙的事情就要发生，而且真的发生了。

毫不奇怪，对基督教现状的公开不满首先出现在法国的一个地方，那里的古罗马文化传统虽然维持得最长，但是文明从来没有教化好野蛮人。

你可以在地图上找到这个地方。它叫普罗旺斯，由位于地中海、罗纳河和阿尔卑斯山之间的一个三角形组成。以前腓尼基人的殖民地马赛，过去曾是、现在依然是这个地区最重要的港口，这儿有不少富裕的城镇和乡村、肥沃的土地、充足的雨

of territory along the Mediterranean shores,when hordes of Crusaders were rushing home with the ill-gotten plunder they had taken from friend and enemy alike,when abbots lived in luxurious palaces and maintained a staff of courtiers,when priests galloped through the morning's mass that they might hurry to the hunting breakfast,then indeed something very unpleasant was bound to happen,and it did.

Little wonder that the first symptoms of open discontent with the state of the Church made themselves felt in that part of France where the old Roman tradition of culture had survived longest and where civilization had never been quite absorbed by barbarism.

You will find it on the map. It is called the Provence and consists of a small triangle situated between the Mediterranean,the Rhone and the Alps. Marseilles,a former colony of the Phoenicians,was and still is its most important harbor and it possessed no mean number of rich towns and villages. It had always been a very fertile land and it enjoyed an abundance of sunshine and rain.

While the rest of medieval Europe still listened to the barbaric deeds of hairy Teuton heroes,the troubadours,the poets of the Provence,had already invented that new form of literature which in time was to give birth to our modern novel. Furthermore,the close commercial relations of these Provencals with their neighbors,the Mohammedans of Spain and Sicily,were making the people familiar with the latest publications in the field of science at a time when the number of such books in the northern part of Europe could be counted on the fingers of two hands.

In this country,the back-to-early-Christianity movement had begun to make itself manifest as early as the first decade of the eleventh century.

But there had not been anything which,however remotely,could be construed into open rebellion. Here and there in certain small villages certain people were beginning to hint

水和阳光。

当中世纪欧洲的其他地区还在倾听长头发的条顿英雄的野蛮故事时，普罗旺斯的行吟诗人就已经发明了新的文学形式，它为我们现代小说奠定了基础。而且普罗旺斯人与邻邦西班牙和西西里的伊斯兰教徒有着密切的商业往来，这使人们能够及时了解科学领域的最新知识，而在欧洲北部这种书屈指可数。

在这个国家，再现早期基督教的运动在11世纪之前10年就开始变得明朗了。

但是无论如何，当时都不会有任何事情会导致人们公开反叛。在一些小村子里，一些人开始暗示说，教士应该像教民那样朴素无华；他们拒绝随领主奔赴疆场（啊，这让人想起了古代的牺牲者）；他们要学一点拉丁文，以便能自己阅读研究福音书；他们公然宣称不赞成死刑；他们否认“炼狱”的存在，在耶稣死后6个世纪时，“炼狱”就被官方宣布为基督天国的一部分；而且（这是最重要的细节）他们拒绝向教会缴纳什一税。

只要有可能，反对教士权威的叛逆首领就会被查出来，如果他们不听劝告，有时会被小心谨慎地处死。

但是邪恶继续蔓延，最后不得不召集普罗旺斯所有主教开会，讨论应该采取什么措施来阻止这场非常危险的煽动性骚动。他们激烈地讨论着，一直持续到1056年。

事情已经很清楚，普通形式的惩罚和逐出教会不会有任何效果。只要有机会在监狱紧锁的门后面表现他们基督徒的仁慈和宽厚信念，要过“纯洁生活”的淳朴乡下人就会高兴不已；如果有幸被判处死刑，他们会像羊羔一样顺从地走向火刑柱。

that their priests might live as simply and as unostentatiously as their parishioners;who refused (oh,memory of the ancient martyrs!) to fight when their lords went forth to war;who tried to learn a little Latin that they might read and study the Gospels for themselves;who let it be known that they did not approve of capital punishment;who denied the existence of that Purgatory which six centuries after the death of Christ had been officially proclaimed as part of the Christian Heaven;and who (a most important detail) refused to surrender a tenth of their income to the Church.

Whenever possible the ring leaders of such rebellions against clerical authority were sought out and sometimes,if they were deaf to persuasion,they were discreetly put out of the way.

But the evil continued to spread and finally it was deemed necessary to call together a meeting of all the bishops of the Provence to discuss what measures should be taken to put a stop to this very dangerous and highly seditious agitation. They duly convened and continued their debates until the year 1056.

By that time it had been plainly shown that the ordinary forms of punishment and excommunication did not produce any noticeable results. The simple country folk who desired to lead a"pure life"were delighted whenever they were given a chance to demonstrate their principles of Christian charity and forgiveness behind the locked doors of a jail and if perchance they were condemned to death,they marched to the stake with the meekness of a lamb. Furthermore,as always happens in such cases,the place left vacant by a single martyr was immediately occupied by a dozen fresh candidates for holiness.

Almost an entire century was spent in the quarrels between the papal delegates who insisted upon more severe persecutions and the local nobility and clergy who (knowing the true nature of their subjects) refused to comply with the orders from Rome and protested

况且，正如在这种情况下经常出现的那样，一个牺牲者留下的位置总会立即被十几个怀抱圣念的新人填补上。

■ 最后的沃尔多教徒

教会代表和地方贵族、牧师之间为此争吵了近百年。教会的代表坚持要采用更严厉的迫害，而地方贵族和牧师（由于了解老百姓的本意）则拒绝执行罗马的命令，并抗议说暴力只会鼓励异教徒更加坚定地反对理性的声音，因此是白费时间和精力。

到12世纪末期，这场运动得到了来自北方的新动力。

在与普罗旺斯隔罗纳河相望的里昂小镇，住着一位名叫彼得·沃尔多的商人。他严肃而善良，为人宽厚，一心想以救世主为榜样，简直都痴迷了。耶稣曾教导说，让骆驼钻进针眼也比让富有的年轻人进天堂容易。整整30代基督徒都极力想弄明白耶稣说这话时的确切含意。彼得·沃尔多却没有这样，他读了这句话便深信不疑。他把自己拥有的一切都分给了穷人，然后退出商界，不再积累新的财富。

that violence only encouraged the heretics to harden their souls against the voice of reason and therefore was a waste both of time and energy.

And then,late in the twelfth century,the movement received a fresh impetus from the north.

In the town of Lyons,connected with the Provence by way of the Rhone,there lived a merchant by the name of Peter Waldo. A very serious man,a good man,a most generous man,almost fanatically obsessed by his eagerness to follow the example of his Saviour. Jesus had taught that it was easier for a camel to pass through the eye of a needle than for a rich young man to enter the kingdom of Heaven. Thirty generations of Christians had tried to explain just what Jesus had actually meant when he uttered these words. Not so Peter Waldo. He read and he believed. He divided whatever he had among the poor,retired from business and refused to accumulate fresh wealth.

John had written,"Search ye the scriptures."

Twenty popes had commented upon this sentence and had carefully stipulated under what conditions it might perhaps be desirable for the laity to study the holy books directly and without the assistance of a priest.

Peter Waldo did not see it that way.

John had said,"Search ye the scriptures."

Very well. Then Peter Waldo would search.

And when he discovered that the things he found did not tally with the conclusions of Saint Jerome,he translated the New Testament into his own language and spread copies of his manuscript throughout the good land of Provence.

At first his activities did not attract much attention. His enthusiasm for poverty did not seem dangerous. Most likely he could be persuaded to found some new and very ascetic monastic order for the benefit of those who wished to lead a life of real hardships and who complained that the existing monasteries were a bit too luxurious and too comfortable.

施洗约翰写道：“你们应自寻圣经。”

20位教皇评论了这句话，并小心谨慎地规定，在什么情况下，俗人才能不经教士指点自行研究圣书。

彼得·沃尔多却不这么看。

施洗约翰已经说过：“你们应自寻圣经。”

那好吧，彼得·沃尔多就要自己去寻找。

当他发现自己找到的东西和圣吉罗姆的结论不一致的时候，他就把《新约》译成自己的语言，把手稿散发到普罗旺斯这块福地。

起初，他的活动并未引起很多人注意。他渴望贫穷的热情似乎没有危险。他很有可能被说服，为真正愿意过艰苦生活的人以及指责现存修道院有点儿太奢侈太舒服的人建立一种新型的修道院式禁欲条令。

罗马一直很善于为那些信仰过于狂热，却常常闹出乱子的人找到适当的发泄场所。

但是一切都要按照常规和先例行事。就此而言，来普罗旺斯的“纯洁人”和里昂的“穷人”当然做不到了。他们不仅没有告诉教皇他们的所作所为，甚至大胆地宣称，即使没有职业教士的指点，一个人也能成为完美的好基督徒，而且罗马主教在自己的司法权力之外没有权力告诉人们应该做什么和信仰什么，正如鞑靼的大公爵或巴格达的哈里发也没有这种权力一样。

Rome had always been very clever at finding fitting outlets for those people whose excess of faith might make them troublesome.

But all things must be done according to rule and precedent. And in that respect the"pure men"of the Provence and the"poor men"of Lyons were terrible failures. Not only did they neglect to inform their bishops of what they were doing,they even went further and boldly proclaimed the startling doctrine that one could be a perfectly good Christian without the assistance of a professional member of the priesthood and that the Bishop of Rome had no more right to tell people outside of his jurisdiction what to do and what to believe than the Grand Duke of Tartary or the Caliph of Bagdad.

The Church was placed before a terrible dilemma and truth compels me to state that she waited a long time before she finally decided to exterminate this heresy by force.

But an organization based upon the principle that there is only one right way of thinking and living and that all other ways are infamous and damnable is bound to take drastic measures whenever its authority is being openly questioned.

If it failed to do so it could not possibly hope to survive and this consideration at last compelled Rome to take definite action and devise a series of punishments that should put terror into the hearts of all future dissenters.

The Albigenses (the heretics were called after the city of Albi which was a hotbed of the new doctrine) and the Waldenses (who bore the name of their founder,Peter Waldo) living in countries without great political value and therefore not well able to defend themselves,were selected as the first of her victims.

The murder of a papal delegate who for several years had ruled the Provence as if it were so much conquered territory,gave Innocent III an excuse to interfere.

He preached a formal crusade against both the Albigenses and the Waldenses.

Those who for forty consecutive days would join the expedition against the heretics would

教会当时处于进退维谷的尴尬境地。说实话，它等了很长时间，最后才决定以武力来对付这个异端邪说。

但是，如果一个组织从根本上认为，只有一种正确的思想和生活方式，其他的都是可耻而值得诅咒的，那么当它的权威受到公开质疑时，它必然会采取极端措施。

如果教会做不到这一点，它就无法生存。这种想法终于迫使罗马采取果断行动，制定出一系列惩罚条例，以使将来所有的持异见者都感到恐惧。

阿尔比教徒（以阿尔比城命名的异教徒，该城是这个新教义的发源地）和沃尔多教徒（因其创始人彼得·沃尔多而得名）在这个国家的政治地位不高，因而不能很好地保护自己。他们被选中成为第一批牺牲品。

一个教皇代表统治了普罗旺斯好几年，他把这里当作被征服的土地而肆意妄为，他的被杀给教皇英诺森三世提供了干涉的借口。

他召集了一支正规十字军攻打阿尔比教徒和沃尔多教徒。

在40天内志愿加入讨伐异教徒远征军的人，还债时可以免交利息，可以赦免过去和将来的一切罪孽，也可以在一段时间内不受一般法庭的审判。这些条件很不错，极大地吸引了北欧人。

如果攻打普罗旺斯的富裕城市能够得到回报，而且在更短的时间内就能获得同等的荣耀，那北欧人为什么要不远千里去征战东方的巴勒斯坦呢？

be excused from paying interest on their debts;they would be absolved from all past and future sins and for the time being they would be exempted from the jurisdiction of the ordinary courts of law. This was a fair offer and it greatly appealed to the people of northern Europe.

Why should they bother about going all the way to Palestine when a campaign against the rich cities of the Provence offered the same spiritual and economic rewards as a trip to the Orient and when a man could gain an equal amount of glory in exchange for a much shorter term of service?

For the time being the Holy Land was forgotten and the worst elements among the nobility and gentry of northern France and southern England,of Austria,Saxony and Poland came rushing southward to escape the local sheriff and incidentally replenish its depleted coffers at the expense of the prosperous Provencals.

The number of men,women and children hanged,burned,drowned,decapitated and quartered by these gallant crusaders is variously given. I have not any idea how many thousands perished. Here and there,whenever a formal execution took place,we are provided with a few concrete figures,and these vary between two thousand and twenty thousand,according to the size of each town.

After the city of Béziers had been captured,the soldiers were in a quandary how to know who were heretics and who were not. They placed their problem before the papal delegate,who followed the army as a sort of spiritual adviser.

“My children,”the good man answered,“go ahead and kill them all. The Lord will know his own people.”

But it was an Englishman by the name of Simon de Montfort,a veteran of the real crusades,who distinguished himself most of all by the novelty and the ingenuity of his cruelties. In return for his valuable services,he afterwards received large tracts of land in the country which he had just pillaged and his subordinates were rewarded in proportion.

那时，“圣地”已被人们遗忘，法国北部、英国南部、奥地利、萨克森和波兰贵族绅士中的败类纷纷逃往南方，不但可以躲避地方长官，还可以重新装满他们的空钱箱，而把一切灾难加在富裕的普罗旺斯人身上。

被这些“勇敢的”十字军绞死、烧死、淹死、斩首或大卸八块的男女老幼难以计数，我也不清楚有几万人死了。各地在执行正式的大屠杀时很少提供具体数字，根据城镇规模大小，通常都在两千和两万之间。

贝兹埃城被占领后，十字军士兵分辨不出谁是异教徒，谁不是异教徒。他们把这个问题交给了随军的教皇代表精神顾问那里。

这个好心的家伙说：“孩子们，去吧，把他们都杀了。主知道谁是他的子民。”

有一个叫西蒙·德·蒙特福特的英国人，是个真正的十字军老兵。他以残暴成性和不断地以新花样杀戮掠夺而著称。作为对他“功绩”的报答，他得到了大片刚被他抢掠过的土地，他的部下也按“功”行赏。

剩下几个从大屠杀中幸存下来的沃尔多教徒，逃进了人迹罕至的庇埃德特山谷，并在那里建立了自己的教会，直至宗教改革时期。

阿尔比教徒没那么幸运。经过一个世纪的折磨和绞刑之后，他们的名字从宗教法庭的报告中消失了。不过三个世纪之后，他们的教义稍做修改之后又重新出现了，其倡导者是个名叫马丁·路德的萨克森教士。这个教派即将掀起一场改革，这

As for the few Waldenses who survived the massacre,they fled to the more inaccessible valleys of Piedmont and there maintained a church of their own until the days of the Reformation.

The Albigenses were less fortunate. After a century of flogging and hanging,their name disappears from the court reports of the Inquisition. But three centuries later,in a slightly modified form,their doctrines were to crop up again and propagated by a Saxon priest called Martin Luther,they were to cause that reform which was to break the monopoly which the papal super-state had enjoyed for almost fifteen hundred years.

All that,of course,was hidden to the shrewd eyes of Innocent□. As far as he was concerned,the difficulty was at an end and the principle of absolute obedience had been triumphantly re-asserted. The famous command in Luke xiv:23 where Christ tells how a certain man who wished to give a party,finding that there still was room in his banqueting hall and that several of the guests had remained away,had said unto his servant,"Go out into the highways and compel them to come in,"had once more been fulfilled.

"They,"the heretics,had been compelled to come in.

The problem how to make them stay in still faced the Church and this was not solved until many years later.

Then,after many unsuccessful experiments with local tribunals,special courts of inquiry,such as had been used for the first time during the Albigensian uprising,were instituted in the different capitals of Europe. They were given jurisdiction over all cases of heresy and they came to be known simply as the Inquisition.

Even today when the Inquisition has long since ceased to function,the mere name fills our hearts with a vague feeling of unrest. We have visions of dark dungeons in Havanna,of torture chambers in Lisbon,of rusty cauldrons and branding irons in the museum of Cracow,of yellow hoods and black masks,of a king with a heavy lower jaw leering at an endless row of old men and women,slowly shuffling to the gibbet.

场改革将打破教皇的超级帝国把持了近1500年的垄断。

当然，这一切都瞒过了英诺森三世机敏的眼睛，他还以为困难局面已经结束，绝对服从的信条已经成功地重新确立了。《路迦福音》第14章23节有一条著名的命令，耶稣在那里讲道，说是一个人想举办一场晚会，却发现宴席上还有空位子，几个客人还没有来，便对他的仆人说："到大路上去，把他们拉进来。"现在这条命令又一次执行了。

"他们"，也就是异教徒，被强行拉进来了。

教会面临着怎样留住他们的问题，直到许多年后这个问题才得以解决。

然后，由于地方法庭在很多案子中未能完成使命，因此诸如在第一次阿尔比教徒叛乱时所用的特别宗教法庭便在欧洲其他首都纷纷建立起来。它们专门审判所有异端邪说的案子，后来人们干脆称之为"宗教法庭"。

甚至在今天宗教法庭早已停止运转的时候，仅仅这个名字仍然会让我们极度不安。我们仿佛看见了哈瓦那的黑牢、里斯本的刑具室、克拉科夫博物馆的锈铁锅和烙铁、黄色的兜帽和黑色的面纱，以及一个下颚肥大的国王冷笑地看着一排排望不到边的老人慢慢地走向绞刑架。

19世纪后半叶的几部通俗小说的确使人们对宗教法庭令人发指的野蛮行径留有印象。我们可以去除其中百分之二十五的浪漫想象，再去除另外百分之二十五的异教徒的偏见，我们就会发现，剩下来的恐怖也足以证明某些人的说法——所有秘密

Several popular novels written during the latter half of the nineteenth century have undoubtedly had something to do with this impression of sinister brutality. Let us therefore deduct twenty-five per cent for the phantasy of our romantic scribes and another twenty-five for Protestant prejudice and we shall find that enough horror remains to justify those who claim that all secret tribunals are an insufferable evil and should never again be tolerated in a community of civilized people.

Henry Charles Lea has treated the subject of the Inquisition in eight ponderous volumes. I shall have to reduce these to two or three pages,and it will be quite impossible to give a concise account of one of the most complicated problems of medieval history within so short a space. For there never was an Inquisition as there is a Supreme Court or an International Court of Arbitration.

There were all sorts of Inquisitions in all sorts of countries and created for all sorts of purposes.

The best known of these was the Royal Inquisition of Spain and the Holy Inquisition of Rome. The former was a local affair which watched over the heretics in the Iberian peninsula and in the American colonies.

The latter had its ramifications all over Europe and burned Joan of Arc in the northern part of the continent as it burned Giordano Bruno in the southern.

It is true that the Inquisition,strictly speaking,never killed any one.

After sentence had been pronounced by the clerical judges,the convicted heretic was surrendered to the secular authorities. These could then do with him what they thought fit. But if they failed to pronounce the death penalty,they exposed themselves to a great deal of inconvenience and might even find themselves excommunicated or deprived of their support at the papal court. If,as sometimes happened,the prisoner escaped this fate and was

■ 牺牲

审判都是难以容忍的魔鬼，在文明世界是绝不可容忍的。

亨利·查理·李在煞费苦心写成的八卷书中讲述了宗教法庭的内容。我必须把这些内容压缩到两三页，要在这样短的篇幅内对中世纪最复杂的问题做精辟阐述是不可能的，因为宗教法庭并非只有一家，这和最高法院或国际仲裁法庭可不一样。

在不同的国家有形形色色的宗教法庭，它们又都是为了不同目的而设的。

在这些宗教法庭中，最著名的是西班牙的皇家宗教法庭和罗马的神圣宗教法庭。前者是一个地方性机构，监视伊比利亚半岛和美洲殖民地的异教徒。

后者的触角伸到了欧洲各地，在大陆北部烧死了圣女贞德，在南部烧死了乔达诺·布鲁诺。

严格地讲，宗教法庭真的没有杀过一个人。

not given over to the magistrates his sufferings only increased. For he then ran the risk of solitary confinement for the rest of his natural life in one of the inquisitorial prisons.

As death at the stake was preferable to the slow terror of going insane in a dark hole in a rocky castle,many prisoners confessed all sorts of crimes of which they were totally innocent that they might be found guilty of heresy and thus be put out of their misery.

It is not easy to write upon this subject without appearing to be hopelessly biased.

It seems incredible that for more than five centuries hundreds of thousands of harmless people in all parts of the world were overnight lifted from their beds at the mere whispered hearsay of some loquacious neighbors;that they were held for months or for years in filthy cells awaiting an opportunity to appear before a judge whose name and qualifications were unknown to them;that they were never informed of the nature of the accusation that was brought against them;that they were not allowed to know the names of those who had acted as witnesses against them;that they were not permitted to communicate with their relatives or consult a lawyer;that if they continued to protest their innocence,they could be tortured until all the limbs of their body were broken;that other heretics could testify against them but were not listened to if they offered to tell something favorable of the accused;and finally that they could be sent to their death without the haziest notion as to the cause of their terrible fate.

It seems even more incredible that men and women who had been buried for fifty or sixty years could be dug out of their graves,could be found guilty"in absentia"and that the heirs of people who were condemned in this fashion could be deprived of their worldly possessions half a century after the death of the offending parties.

But such was the case and as the inquisitors depended for their maintenance upon a liberal share of all the goods that were confiscated,absurdities of this sort were by

教士法官宣判之后，获罪的异教徒便被送交给世俗当局手里。当局可以采取他们认为合适的方式处置他。但是如果当局没有判处他死刑，便会给自己招致许多麻烦，甚至被逐出教会或失去教廷的支持。如果罪犯逃脱了这一劫难，没有被送到地方当局，就像有时曾发生过的那样，那么他遭受的磨难只会增加，因为他极可能会被囚禁在宗教法庭的某个牢房里，孤独地度过余生。

由于死在火刑柱上比在岩石城堡的黑牢里缓慢发疯的折磨要好受一些，因此许多囚犯招供了自己根本无辜的罪名，这样他们就可以被判处异端邪说罪而早日获得解脱。

谈论这个话题而不带偏见是很不容易的。

似乎不可思议的是，在五个多世纪的时间里，世界各地成千上万无辜平民仅仅由于某些多嘴的邻居道听途说而在半夜被从床上拖起来，在污秽的地牢里被关上几个月或几年，等待既不知姓名又不知身份的法官的审判。从来都没有人告诉他们因为什么被指控，他们也不许知道证人的名字，不许和亲戚联系，更不许请律师。如果他们坚持自己无罪，就会饱受折磨，直至四肢都被打断。别的异教徒可以作证控告他们，但要替被告说好话却是没有人听的。最后他们到死都不知道自己为何会遭此厄运。

更难以置信的是，已经入土五六十年的男女也会被从坟墓中挖出来，并以“缺席”的形式被判罪，这种被定罪的人的后代还要在罪犯死去半个世纪之后被剥夺财产。

no means an uncommon occurrence and frequently the grandchildren were driven to beggary on account of something which their grandfather was supposed to have done two generations before.

Those of us who followed the newspapers twenty years ago when Czarist Russia was in the heyday of its power,remember the agent provocateur. As a rule the agent provocateur was a former burglar or a retired gambler with a winning personality and a"grievance."He let it be secretly known that his sorrow had made him join the revolution and in this way he often gained the confidence of those who were genuinely opposed to the imperial government. But as soon as he had learned the secrets of his new friends,he betrayed them to the police,pocketed the reward and went to the next city,there to repeat his vile practices.

During the thirteenth,fourteenth and fifteenth centuries,southern and western Europe was overrun by this nefarious tribe of private spies.

They made a living denouncing those who were supposed to have criticized the Church or who had expressed doubts upon certain points of doctrine.

If there were no heretics in the neighborhood,it was the business of such an agent provocateur to manufacture them.

As he could rest assured that torture would make his victims confess,no matter how innocent they might be,he ran no risks and could continue his trade ad infinitum.

In many countries a veritable reign of terror was introduced by this system of allowing anonymous people to denounce those whom they suspected of spiritual deficiencies. At last,no one dared trust his nearest and dearest friends. Members of the same family were forced to be on their guard against each other.

The mendicant friars who handled a great deal of the inquisitorial work made excellent use of the panic which their methods created and for almost two centuries they lived on the fat of the land.

但这就是实际情况，因为宗教裁判官正是靠贪赃所有没收来的物品中饱私囊的，所以这种荒唐事就时有发生，比如某人时隔两代的祖父据说干过某件事而导致孙子沦为乞丐等。

读过20年前沙皇俄国处于全盛时期发行的报纸的人都记得密探。这种密探以前往往是窃贼或已洗手不干的赌徒，他们有着让人喜欢的个性和“悲伤”的情怀。他会故作神秘地让人知道他是由于痛心才参加革命的，这样他就经常能博得诚心反对帝国政府的人的信任。但他一旦探得新朋友的秘密时，就会向警察告密，把报酬装进腰包，再到下一个城市，在那里重演卑鄙的勾当。

在13、14和15世纪，南欧和西欧到处都是这种居心歹毒的私人密探。

他们靠告发那些据说批评教会或对教义中的某几点表示怀疑的人来谋生。

如果周围没有异教徒，这些密探就会人为地制造几个。

因为他确信，无论被告多么清白无辜，严刑拷打也会使他承认罪名。他没有任何风险，可以无休止地从事这一行业。

在许多国家，允许人们匿名告发他们认为思想不端的人，这种制度制造了真正的恐怖。最后，没有人敢相信即使是最亲密无间的朋友，一家人也要相互提防着。

掌管宗教法庭大量工作的行乞修道士充分利用了他们制造出来的恐惧，在近两个世纪里他们靠民脂民膏生活。

我们可以肯定地说，宗教改革的主要内在原因之一，就是广大民众对这些盛气凌人的乞丐深恶痛绝。这些人披着虔诚的外衣，强行闯入令人尊敬的市民家里，睡

Yes,it is safe to say that one of the main underlying causes of the Reformation was the disgust which a large number of people felt for those arrogant beggars who under a cloak of piety forced themselves into the homes of respectable citizens,who slept in the most comfortable beds,who partook of the best dishes,who insisted that they be treated as honored guests and who were able to maintain themselves in comfort by the mere threat that they would denounce their benefactors to the Inquisition if ever they were deprived of any of those luxuries which they had come to regard as their just due.

The Church of course could answer to all this that the Inquisition merely acted as a spiritual health officer whose sworn duty it was to prevent contagious errors from spreading among the masses. It could point to the leniency shown to all heathen who acted in ignorance and therefore could not be held responsible for their opinions. It could even claim that few people ever suffered the penalty of death unless they were apostates and were caught in a new offense after having forsworn their former errors.

But what of it?

The same trick by which an innocent man was changed into a desperate criminal could afterwards be used to place him in an apparent position of recantation.

The agent provocateur and the forger have ever been close friends.

And what are a few faked documents between spies?

在最舒适的床上，吃最好的饭菜，还喋喋不休地说他们应该被奉为上宾。他们只需要吓唬人们，如果他们没有得到理所应当的奢侈豪华，就要向宗教法庭告发施主，这样他们就可以维持舒适的生活。

针对这一切，教会当然可以答复说，宗教法庭只是承担思想健康检查官的作用，它立誓要尽的职责就是防止传染性错误思想在群众中传播。它可以向所有因无知而误入歧途的异教徒示以仁慈；它甚至还宣称，除了叛教者和屡教不改重新犯罪的人，几乎没有人被处死。

但是这又怎么样呢?

一条诡计就可以把无辜的人变为绝望的罪犯，同样可以用来使他进行表面的悔过自新。

密探和伪造者从来都是亲密的朋友。

而在这些奸细中间，几封伪造的文件又算得了什么?

CHAPTER Ⅷ THE CURIOUS ONES

Modern intolerance,like ancient Gaul,is divided into three parts;the intolerance of laziness,the intolerance of ignorance and the intolerance of self-interest.

The first of these is perhaps the most general. It is to be met with in every country and among all classes of society. It is most common in small villages and old-established towns,and it is not restricted to human beings.

Our old family horse,having spent the first twenty-five years of his placid life in a warm stable in Coley Town,resents the equally warm barn of Westport for no other reason than that he has always lived in Coley Town,is familiar with every stick and stone in Coley Town and knows that no new and unfamiliar sights will frighten him on his daily ambles through that pleasant part of the Connecticut landscape.

Our scientific world has thus far spent so much time learning the defunct dialects of Polynesian islands that the language of dogs and cats and horses and donkeys has been sadly neglected. But could we know what Dude says to his former neighbors of Coley Town,we would hear an outburst of the most ferocious equine intolerance. For Dude is no longer young and therefore is"set"in his ways. His horsey habits were all formed years and years ago and therefore all the Coley Town manners,customs and habits seem right to him and all the Westport customs and manners and habits will be declared wrong until the end of his days.

It is this particular variety of intolerance which makes parents shake their heads over the foolish behavior of their children,which has caused the absurd myth of"the good old

第8章　求知的人

与古高卢人一样，现代的不宽容可以分为三种情况：出于懒惰的不宽容、出于无知的不宽容和出于自私自利的不宽容。

其中第一种情况也许最普遍。在不同国家和不同阶层的社会里都能看到，在小村子和古老集市里更是常见，而且这种不宽容决不仅限于人类之间。

我们家的老马，在贩鱼镇温暖的马厩里平静地度过了25年的光景，对位于韦斯特伯特同样舒适的牲口棚却恨之入骨，理由很简单，就是因为它始终住在贩鱼镇，对这里的一砖一瓦都烂熟于胸，每天行进在康涅狄格州风景如画的土地上时不必担心受到陌生景物的惊扰。

迄今为止，我们的科学界耗费时日地研究着波利尼西亚群岛早已不复存在的方言，却令人遗憾地忽视了猫、狗、马和驴子的言语。不过，假如我们能听懂一匹名叫“杜德”的马与先前贩鱼镇邻居所说的话，我们就会听到一场马科动物不宽容语言的空前激烈的大爆发。“杜德”不再是小马驹，已经定型了，它的习性是日久天长形成的，这使得它觉得贩鱼镇的礼节、习惯和风俗样样称心如意；而这些礼节、习惯和风俗在韦斯特伯特则完全不是那么回事，至死它都会这样认为。

正是这种特定的不宽容，使父母对子女的愚蠢行为摇头叹息，使人们不可思

days";which makes savages and civilized creatures wear uncomfortable clothes;which fills the world with a great deal of superfluous nonsense and generally turns all people with a new idea into the supposed enemies of mankind.

Otherwise,however,this sort of intolerance is comparatively harmless.

We are all of us bound to suffer from it sooner or later. In ages past it has caused millions of people to leave home,and in this way it has been responsible for the permanent settlement of vast tracts of uninhabited land which otherwise would still be a wilderness.

The second variety is much more serious.

An ignorant man is,by the very fact of his ignorance,a very dangerous person.

But when he tries to invent an excuse for his own lack of mental faculties,he becomes a holy terror. For then he erects within his soul a granite bulwark of self-righteousness and from the high pinnacle of this formidable fortress,he defies all his enemies (to wit,those who do not share his own prejudices) to show cause why they should be allowed to live.

People suffering from this particular affliction are both uncharitable and mean. Because they live constantly in a state of fear,they easily turn to cruelty and love to torture those against whom they have a grievance. It was among people of this ilk that the strange notion of a predilected group of a"chosen people"first took its origin. Furthermore,the victims of this delusion are forever trying to bolster up their own courage by an imaginary relationship which exists between themselves and the invisible Gods. This,of course,in order to give a flavor of spiritual approbation to their intolerance.

For instance,such citizens never say,"We are hanging Danny Deever because we consider him a menace to our own happiness,because we hate him with a thousand hates and because we just love to hang him."Oh,no! They get together in solemn conclave and deliberate for hours and for days and for weeks upon the fate of said Danny Deever.

议地对那些“往日好时光”梦寐以求，使野蛮人和文明人都穿上了令人难受的衣服，连篇累牍的废话充斥着这个世界，常常会把那些持有新主张的人假想为人类的死敌。

不过，即便如此，这种不宽容相对来讲并无大碍。

我们大家或早或晚都会因为这种不宽容而受罪。在过去的岁月中，它使得成百上千的人背井离乡，现在它又是使那些渺无人烟的地方出现永久定居点的主要原因，否则那些地方至今仍然是一片荒芜。

第二种不宽容更为严峻。

无知之人仅凭他对事物的一无所知，便可以沦为极其危险的人物。

但是，如果他还搜肠刮肚地为自己的智力不足而百般辩驳，那就更令人恐怖了。因为他会在自己的灵魂里砌筑花岗岩堡垒，自以为是地从令人生畏的要塞高地向所有敌人（也就是那些不苟同于他的偏见的人）公然挑战，质问他们有什么理由活在这个世界。

遭受这种疾患的人既尖刻又卑劣。他们由于常年生活在恐惧之中，易于变得暴虐残忍，以折磨他们所憎恨的人为乐。正是在这帮人当中，首先出现了“上帝选民”的奇特念头。更何况这些人沉溺于幻觉，想象自己与无形的上帝有某种关联，以此为自己鼓劲，这样做的目的无非是为自己的不宽容寻求精神上的认同。

譬如，这些子民绝不会说：“我们要绞死丹尼·笛福，是因为我们认为他威胁了我们自身的幸福；或因为我们对他恨之入骨，抑或我们只是喜欢绞死他而已。”

When finally sentence is read,poor Danny,who has perhaps committed some petty sort of larceny,stands solemnly convicted as a most terrible person who has dared to offend the Divine Will (as privately communicated to the elect who alone can interpret such messages) and whose execution therefore becomes a sacred duty,bringing great credit upon the judges who have the courage to convict such an ally of Satan.

That good-natured and otherwise kind-hearted people are quite as apt to fall under the spell of this most fatal delusion as their more brutal and blood-thirsty neighbors is a commonplace both of history and psychology.

The crowds that gaped delightedly at the sad plight of a thousand poor martyrs were most assuredly not composed of criminals. They were decent,pious folk and they felt sure that they were doing something very creditable and pleasing in the sight of their own particular Divinity.

Had one spoken to them of tolerance,they would have rejected the idea as an ignoble confession of Moral weakness. Perhaps they were intolerant,but in that case they were proud of the fact and with good right. For there,out in the cold dampness of early morning,stood Danny Deever,clad in a saffron colored shirt and in a pair of pantaloons adorned with little devils,and he was going,going slowly but surely,to be hanged in the Market Place. While they themselves,as soon as the show was over,would return to a comfortable home and a plentiful meal of bacon and beans.

Was not that in itself proof enough that they were acting and thinking correctly?

Otherwise would they be among the

旧世界重新崛起

噢，不，绝不会这样！他们聚集在气氛庄严的秘密会所，一连几个小时、几天或几个星期详细研究上面提到的丹尼·笛福的命运。最后判决一俟宣读，这个可怜的丹尼也许只搞了些小偷小摸的行径，却俨然成了犯有重罪的最可怕的人物，他胆敢违背上帝的旨意（这些旨意只私下传授给上帝的选民，也只有他们才能解释这些信息），因而对他执行死刑成为一种神圣的职责，法官们于是也理直气壮地惩治撒旦的同伙。

生性善良、好心肠的人与野蛮粗鲁、嗜血成性的人一样，都会轻而易举地陷入这个最致命的幻觉之中，这在历史学和心理学领域早已司空见惯。

一群又一群的人兴致勃勃地观看着数以千计的牺牲者不幸罹难，当然不能认定这帮人就是罪犯；他们是体面、虔诚的普通百姓，而且他们确信自己是在上帝面前做一件值得欢欣鼓舞的事情。

如果有人向他们提到宽容，他们就会反对，好像这样就是自卑地默认他们在品格方面的缺陷。他们也许不够宽容，但在这种情况下，他们反而为此洋洋自得，还觉得理应如此。于是，在潮湿阴冷的晨曦里站立着丹尼·笛福，他穿着橘红色的衬衣和缀满小魔鬼的马裤，走向执行绞刑的市场，虽然步履缓慢，但却没有犹疑。示众一结束，人们就回到自己舒适的家中，好好享用一顿熏肉和豆角。

spectators?Would not the rôles be reversed?

A feeble argument,I confess,but a very common one and hard to answer when people feel sincerely convinced that their own ideas are the ideas of God and are unable to understand how they could possibly be mistaken.

There remains as a third category the intolerance caused by self-interest. This,of course,is really a variety of jealousy and as common as the measles.

When Jesus came to Jerusalem,there to teach that the favor of Almighty God could not be bought by the killing of a dozen oxen or goats,all those who made a living from the ceremonial sacrifices in the temple decried him as a dangerous revolutionist and caused him to be executed before he could do any lasting damage to their main source of income.

When Saint Paul,a few years later,came to Ephesus and there preached a new creed which threatened to interfere with the prosperity of the jewelers who derived great profit from the sale of little images of the local Goddess Diana,the Guild of the Goldsmiths almost lynched the unwelcome intruder.

And ever since there has been open warfare between those who depend for their livelihood upon some established form of worship and those whose ideas threaten to take the crowd away from one temple in favor of another.

When we attempt to discuss the intolerance of the Middle Ages,we must constantly remember that we have to deal with a very complicated problem. Only upon very rare occasions do we find ourselves confronted with only one manifestation of these three separate forms of intolerance. Most frequently we can discover traces of all three varieties in the cases of persecution which are brought to our attention.

That an organization,enjoying great wealth,administering thousands of square miles of land and owning hundreds of thousands of serfs,should have turned the full vigor of

这本身难道不足以证明他们的行动和思想是正确的吗？

不然他们怎么会站在观众席上？死者为何不能和他们调换一下位置呢？

我得说，这种经不起推敲的观点十分普遍，也难以应答，当人们坦诚地相信自己的想法就是上帝的意志时，让他们明白自己或许犯了什么错是根本办不到的。

余下的就是由自私自利引起的第三种不宽容，它实际上是嫉妒的一个变种，如麻疹一样普遍。

耶稣当年来到耶路撒冷教导人们说：屠杀十几头牛羊换不来万能的上帝的青睐。那些靠典礼祭祀活动谋生的人于是群起而攻之，诬陷他是危险的革命者，在他还没能从根本上损害他们巨额利益的时候，就把他处死了。

几年后，圣保罗来到以弗所，在那里宣扬一种新教义，它危及了珠宝商获利丰厚的买卖，这些人从制作和贩卖当地女神狄安娜的小塑像中大发横财，为此金匠行会差点用私刑处死这个不受欢迎的入侵者。

从那以后，一场公开争战在两拨人之间展开了：一拨人是那些依靠业已建立起来的某种宗教仪式谋生的人；另一拨人却主张把群众从一个庙宇引导到另一个庙宇去。

在我们试图讨论中世纪的不宽容时，必须不断提醒自己，我们不得不应对一个异常复杂的难题。这三种各不相同的不宽容，只有在极个别的情况下，我们才会遇到其单一的表现形态。在引起我们关注的迫害案例中，常常会找到三种情况并存的现象。

its anger against a group of peasants who had undertaken to reestablish a simple and unpretentious Kingdom-of-Heaven-on-Earth was entirely natural.

And in that case,the extermination of heretics became a matter of economic necessity and belonged to class C,the intolerance of self-interest.

But when we begin to consider another group of men who were to feel the heavy hand of official disapprobation,the scientists,the problem becomes infinitely more complicated.

And in order to understand the perverse attitude of the Church authorities towards those who tried to reveal the secrets of nature,we must go back a good many centuries and study what had actually happened in Europe during the first six centuries of our era.

The invasion of the Barbarians had swept across the continent with the ruthless thoroughness of a flood. Here and there a few pieces of the old Roman fabric of state had remained standing erect amidst the wastes of the turbulent waters. But the society that had once dwelled within these walls had perished. Their books had been carried away by the waves. Their art lay forgotten in the deep mud of a new ignorance. Their collections,their museums,their laboratories,their slowly accumulated mass of scientific facts,all these had been used to stoke the camp-fires of uncouth savages from the heart of Asia.

We possess several catalogues of libraries of the tenth century. Of Greek books (outside of the city of Constantinople,then almost as far removed from central Europe as the Melbourne of today) the people of the west possessed hardly any. It seems incredible,but they had completely disappeared. A few translations (badly done) of a few chapters from the works of Aristotle and Plato were all the scholar of that time could find when he wanted to familiarize himself with the thoughts of the ancients. If he desired to learn their language,there was no one to teach it to him,unless a theological dispute in Byzantium had driven a handful of Greek monks from their customary habitats and had forced them to

如果一个组织财力雄厚，掌管着千里土地，拥有不计其数的农奴，当一帮农民想要重新建立朴实的“人间天堂”时，它把所有的怒气都发泄在他们身上是再自然不过的。

于是，终止异端邪说就成为维护经济利益的必要之举，这属于不宽容的第三种——即自私自利的不宽容。

不过，当我们考虑到另一帮感受到来自官方禁令压力的科学家时，这个问题就变得更复杂了。

为了理解教会当局对揭示大自然奥秘的人所采取的刚愎自用的态度，我们得倒退若干个世纪，看看欧洲在公元1~6世纪究竟发生了什么。

野蛮人的入侵就像一场无情的滔天巨浪，席卷了整个欧洲大陆。在波涛汹涌的废弃物当中，依然残存着一些古罗马国家。但城墙里面的社会却湮灭了，典籍也被涤荡一空，当时人们所取得的艺术成果被无知的新泥沼所吞没。所有的收藏品、博物馆、图书馆和经年累月积累起来的科学资料，全被来自中亚的野蛮人付之一炬。

我们获得了公元10世纪图书馆的一些书目。至于古希腊的图书（君士坦丁堡除外，那时的君士坦丁堡被看成是远离欧洲中心的地方，就像如今的墨尔本那样遥远），在西方人手里几乎所剩无几。这说来似乎难以置信，但它们的确遗失殆尽了。一些篇章从亚里士多德和柏拉图的著作中被（非常拙劣地）翻译过来，成为那个时期想了解古人思想的学者们唯一的去处。即使学者们有意学习古希腊语，除了几个希腊僧侣外也没人给他们授课。这些僧侣是在拜占廷的神学争执中被驱逐出以

find a temporary asylum in France or Italy.

Latin books there were in great quantity,but most of those dated from the fourth and fifth centuries. The few manuscripts of the classics that survived had been copied so often and so indifferently that their contents were no longer understandable to any one who had not made a life study of paleography.

As for books of science,with the possible exception of some of the simplest problems of Euclid,they were no longer to be found in any of the available libraries and what was much more regrettable,they were no longer wanted.

For the people who now ruled the world regarded science with a hostile eye and discouraged all independent labor in the field of mathematics,biology and zoology,not to mention medicine and astronomy,which had descended to such a low state of neglect that they were no longer of the slightest practical value.

It is exceedingly difficult for a modern mind to understand such a state of affairs.

We men and women of the twentieth century,whether rightly or wrongly,profoundly believe in the idea of progress. Whether we ever shall be able to make this world perfect,we do not know. In the meantime we feel it to be our most sacred duty to try.

Yea,sometimes this faith in the unavoidable destiny of progress seems to have become the national religion of our entire country.

But the people of the Middle Ages did not and could not share such a view.

The Greek dream of a world filled with beautiful and interesting things had lasted such a lamentably short time! It

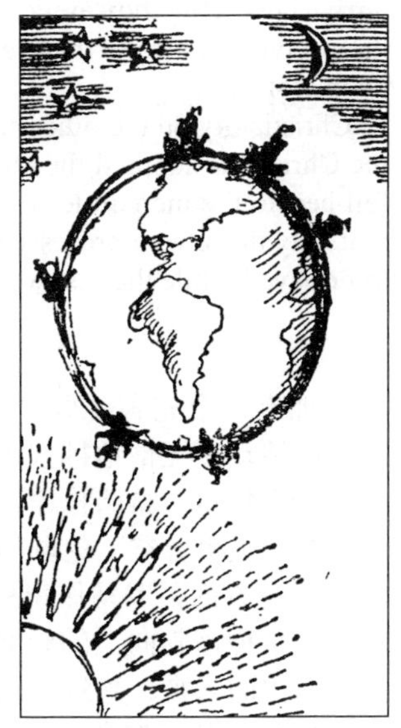

■ 这个圆圆的世界

往的栖身之所，而逃到法国或意大利来暂时寻求避难所的。

拉丁文的图书数量颇丰，但大部分介于公元4~5世纪之间。屈指可数的经典手稿，经屡次三番漫不经心地转抄，除非耗费毕生精力研究古文字体，否则没人能看得懂。

至于科学书籍，除去欧几里得有关最简单问题的书稿可能幸免于难之外，其余的书稿在任何图书馆里都踪影皆无。更可悲的是，人们对这些书的需求也颇为冷落。

当时大权在握的人用敌意的目光来审视科学，让那些在数学、生物学和动物学领域进行独立钻研的人感到气馁，更不必说医学和天文学了，它们地位低下，极受冷落，以至于丝毫没有实用价值。

想要现代人理解这种情形太难了。

20世纪的人，无论进步的主张正确与否，都深信不疑，尽管我们尚不知晓它能否使世界更趋于完美。同时，我们觉得“努力尝试”应成为我们最神圣的职责。

是的，我们坚信进步是不可规避的自然规律使然，有时它似乎已成为整个国家的国教。

但中世纪的人不会有，也不可能有类似的想法。

had been so rudely disturbed by the political cataclysm that had overtaken the unfortunate country that most Greek writers of the later centuries had been confirmed pessimists who,contemplating the ruins of their once happy fatherland,had become abject believers in the doctrine of the ultimate futility of all worldly endeavor.

The Roman authors,on the other hand,who could draw their conclusions from almost a thousand years of consecutive history,had discovered a certain upward trend in the development of the human race and their philosophers,notably the Epicureans,had cheerfully undertaken the task of educating the younger generation for a happier and better future.

Then came Christianity.

The center of interest was moved from this world to the other. Almost immediately people fell back into a deep and dark abyss of hopeless resignation.

Man was evil. He was evil by instinct and by preference. He was conceived in sin,born in sin,he lived in sin and he died repenting of his sins.

But there was a difference between the old despair and the new.

The Greeks were convinced (and perhaps rightly so) that they were more intelligent and better educated than their neighbors and they felt rather sorry for those unfortunate barbarians. But they never quite reached the point at which they began to consider themselves as a race that had been set apart from all others because it was the chosen people of Zeus.

Christianity on the other hand was never able to escape from its own antecedents. When the Christians adopted the Old Testament as one of the Holy Books of their own faith,they fell heir to the incredible Jewish doctrine that their race was“different”from all others and that only those who professed a belief in certain officially established doctrines could hope to be saved while the rest were doomed to perdition.

拥有一个充满美好、新奇事物的世界竟是令人如此伤悼的昙花一现的希腊梦想！政治动荡无情地摧残了这个梦想，它将这个不幸的国家搅得天翻地覆，以至于其后几百年里，希腊作家都成了悲观主义者，他们凝视着一度是乐土的废墟，绝望地成为“世事皆空”论调的信奉者。

另一方面，罗马作家从近千年延绵不断的历史中得出结论，从人类发展进程中找到了某种蓬勃向上的趋势。于是，罗马哲学家，如著名的伊壁鸠鲁派，为了更加美好幸福的未来，兴致勃勃地承担起教育年轻一代的职责。

随后，基督教来了。

人们的关注点从这个世界移到了另一个世界。几乎在瞬息之间，人类重新跌到毫无指望、逆来顺受的黑暗渊薮。

人是罪恶的。人的天性和癖好都是罪恶的。他沉溺于罪恶之中，在恶中生，在恶中长，最终在恶的救赎中结束生命。

但在新旧绝望之间存在一种差别。

希腊人坚信自己更富有智慧（可能的确如此），比邻国人受的教育更好，他们对那些不幸的野蛮人满怀悲悯。但是他们从不认为自己的民族由于是宙斯的选民而与其他民族有什么区别。

相反，基督教从未能摆脱自己的老祖宗。当基督徒采用《旧约》为自己信仰的圣书后，便继承了令人难以置信的犹太教的衣钵，认为自己的民族应有别于其他民族，只有信奉这种依法确立的教义的人才有希望获得拯救，而其他人则注定要

This idea was,of course,of enormous direct benefit to those who were lacking sufficiently in humility of spirit to believe themselves predilected favorites among millions and millions of their fellow creatures. During many highly critical years it had turned the Christians into a closely-knit,self-contained little community which floated unconcernedly upon a vast ocean of paganism.

What happened elsewhere on those waters that stretched far and wide towards the north and the south and the east and the west was a subject of the most profound indifference to Tertullian or St. Augustine,or any of those other early writers who were busily engaged in putting the ideas of their Church into the concrete form of written books. Eventually they hoped to reach a safe shore and there to build their city of God. Meanwhile,what those in other climes hoped to accomplish and to achieve was none of their concern.

Hence they created for themselves entirely new conceptions about the origin of man and about the limits of time and space. What the Egyptians and Babylonians and the Greeks and the Romans had discovered about these mysteries did not interest them in the least. They were sincerely convinced that all the old values had been destroyed with the birth of Christ.

There was for example the problem of our earth.

The ancient scientists held it to be one among a couple of billion of other stars.

The Christians flatly rejected this idea. To them,the little round disk on which they lived was the heart and center of the universe.

It had been created for the special purpose of providing one particular group of people with a temporary home. The way in which this had been brought about was very simple and was fully described in the first chapter of Genesis.

When it became necessary to decide just how long this group of predilected people had

沉沦。

对于那些严重缺乏谦卑精神的人来讲，相信自己是成千上万同类中得天独厚之辈，显然会给他们带来无数的直接利益。在许多关键时期，它促使基督徒成为联系紧密、自我隔离的小团体，在异教横流的大千世界超然世外。

对特图利安、圣奥古斯丁以及其他早期致力于把他们的教义写成著述的作家来说，汪洋肆意的世界的四面八方发生了什么，他们丝毫不感兴趣。他们希望最终抵达一处安全的海岸，在那儿建立上帝之城。至于其他人拼命要达到或完成的事情，则与他们毫不相干。

因此，他们为自己创造了有关人类起源和时空界限的全新概念。他们对埃及人、巴比伦人、希腊人和罗马人在此领域获得的神秘发现不闻不问。他们实实在在地认为，过去一切有价值的东西都随着基督的诞生而不复存在了。

譬如关于地球的问题。

古代科学家认为地球是几十亿个星球中的一个。

基督徒从根本上反对这个观点。在他们看来，他们借以生存的这个小圆盘是宇宙的核心。

创造地球的目的，就是为某一特定人群提供暂时的栖身之所。它的起源很简单，在《创世纪》第1章描写得一清二楚。

到了需要确定上帝偏爱的种族在地球上生活多久的时候，问题就变得更复杂了。从掩埋了的城市、绝迹的怪物到已经变成化石的植物，各方面的证据都显示了

been on this earth,the problem became a little more complicated. On all sides there were evidences of great antiquity,of buried cities,of extinct monsters and of fossilized plants. But these could be reasoned away or overlooked or denied or shouted out of existence. And after this had been done,it was a very simple matter to establish a fixed date for the beginning of time.

In a universe like that,a universe which was static,which had begun at a certain hour of a certain day in a certain year,and would end at another certain hour of a certain day in a certain year,which existed for the exclusive benefit of one and only one denomination,in such a universe there was no room for the prying curiosity of mathematicians and biologists and chemists and all sorts of other people who only cared for general principles and juggled with the idea of eternity and unlimitedness both in the field of time and in the realm of space.

True enough,many of those scientific people protested that at heart they were devout sons of the Church. But the true Christians knew better. No man,who was sincere in his protestations of love and devotion for the faith,had any business to know so much or to possess so many books.

One book was enough.

That book was the Bible,and every letter in it,every comma,every semicolon and exclamation point had been written down by people who were divinely inspired.

A Greek of the days of Pericles would have been slightly amused if he had been told of a supposedly holy volume which contained scraps of ill-digested national history,doubtful love poems,the inarticulate visions of half-demented prophets and whole chapters devoted

■ 无可辩驳的论证

大量生命古迹的存在。但这些可以被驳倒、视而不见、百般抵赖或完全抹杀。一切准备就绪后，再来确立一个具体的创世纪时间就容易多了。

在这样的宇宙当中，一切处于静止状态，它从某年某月某时开始，又将在某年某月某时终止。它的存在，仅是某个特定的独一无二教派的专利。在这个宇宙中，根本不会给那些探求的数学家、生物学家、化学家及诸如此类的人以任何余地。因为这帮人只对一般规律感兴趣，满脑子都是有关时空无涯的想法。

许多从事科学研究的人抗议说，在内心深处他们都是上帝虔诚的儿子，而事实上他们也的确如此。不过真正的基督徒却更加远见卓识。如果一个人如其所言地忠诚于自己挚爱的信仰的话，就不会想知道那么多事，也不会弄那么多书。

有一本书就足够了。

这本书就是《圣经》，其中的每个字、每个逗号、每个冒号及每个感叹号都是

to the foulest denunciation of those who for some reason or another were supposed to have incurred the displeasure of one of Asia's many tribal deities.

But the barbarian of the third century had a most humble respect for the"written word"which to him was one of the great mysteries of civilization,and when this particular book,by successive councils of his Church,was recommended to him as being without error,flaw or slip,he willingly enough accepted this extraordinary document as the sum total of everything that man had ever known,or ever could hope to know,and joined in the denunciation and persecution of those who defied Heaven by extending their researches beyond the limits indicated by Moses and Isaiah.

The number of people willing to die for their principles has always been necessarily limited.

At the same time the thirst for knowledge on the part of certain people is so irrepressible that some outlet must be found for their pent up energy. As a result of this conflict between curiosity and repression there grew up that stunted and sterile intellectual sapling which came to be known as Scholasticism.

It dated back to the middle of the eighth century. It was then that Bertha,wife to Pépin the Short,king of the Franks,gave birth to a son who has better claims to be considered the patron saint of the French nation than that good King Louis who cost his countrymen a ransom of eight hundred thousand Turkish gold pieces and who rewarded his subjects' loyalty by giving them an inquisition of their own.

When the child was baptized it was given the name of Carolus,as you may see this very day at the bottom of many an ancient charter. The signature is a little clumsy. But Charles was never much of a hand at spelling. As a boy he learned to read Frankish and Latin,but when he took up writing,his fingers were so rheumatic from a life spent fighting the

由那些得到神灵感应的人写成的。

伯里克利时代的希腊人，即便知道世上存在这么一本所谓的圣书也不会感兴趣。这本书中充斥着晦涩难懂的支鳞片爪的民族史、语焉不详的爱情诗篇、癫狂先知讳莫如深的描述以及出于某种原因而被惹恼了的人对诸多亚洲部落中某个神灵连篇累牍的恶意谩骂。

但是，公元3世纪的野蛮人却对“写下来的句子”顶礼膜拜。在他们看来，这是文明的奥秘之所在，于是当这本完美无瑕、非同凡响的书被教会委员会推荐给他们时，他们心甘情愿地全盘接受了，并把它视为人类业已掌握或期望能够知道的一切事物的总和。他们合起伙来，痛斥和迫害对天国持否定态度的人（这些人竟敢把探索的触角伸展到摩西和以赛亚规定的界线之外）。

甘愿为原则而死的人毕竟有限。

与此同时，有些人对知识的渴望是无法压抑的，一定要为积蓄已久的能量找到发泄的出口。在求知与压制的矛盾冲突中，结果产生了一株弱小枯萎的智力幼苗，这就是后来的“经院学派”。

这要追溯到公元8世纪中叶。法兰克国王、矮子丕平的妻子伯莎生了个儿子，他比善良的国王路易更有理由被认为是法兰西民族的圣主恩人，因为为了路易的获释，老百姓不得不交付了80万土耳其金币的赎金。作为对百姓忠诚的奖赏，路易恩准他们建立自己的法庭。

这孩子受洗礼时的教名叫卡罗鲁斯，在许多古宪章的结尾处都能看到他的签

Russians and the Moors that he had to give up the attempt and hired the best scribes of his day to act as his secretaries and do his writing for him.

For this old frontiersman,who prided himself upon the fact that only twice within fifty years had he worn"city clothes"(the toga of a Roman nobleman),had a most genuine appreciation of the value of learning,and turned his court into a private university for the benefit of his own children and for the sons and daughters of his officials.

There,surrounded by the most famous men of his time,the new imperator of the west loved to spend his hours of leisure. And so great was his respect for academic democracy that he dropped all etiquette and as simple Brother David took an active share in the conversation and allowed himself to be contradicted by the humblest of his professors.

But when we come to examine the problems that interested this goodly company and the questions they discussed,we are reminded of the list of subjects chosen by the debating teams of a rural high school in Tennessee.

They were very naive,to say the least. And what was true in the year 800 held equally good for 1400. This was not the fault of the medieval scholar,whose brain was undoubtedly quite as good as that of his successors of the twentieth century. But he found himself in the position of a modern chemist or doctor who is given complete liberty of investigation,provided he does not say or do anything at variance with the chemical and medical information contained in the volumes of the first edition of the Encyclopedia Britannica of the year 1768 when chemistry was practically an unknown subject and surgery was closely akin to butchery.

As a result (I am mixing my metaphors anyway) the medieval scientist with his tremendous brain capacity and his very limited field of experimentation reminds one somewhat of a Rolls-Royce motor placed upon the chassis of a flivver. Whenever he

名。不过查理对拼写始终不在行，笔迹有些拙劣。他在孩提时代学过法文和拉丁文，但只要提笔写字，他那早年由于在疆场同俄国人和摩尔人搏斗而患风湿病的手指就不听使唤，最终他不得不打消尝试的念头，雇用当时最好的抄手当秘书替他签字。

这个在50年里只穿过两次“都市服装”（罗马贵族穿的宽大外袍）并以此为荣的沙场老兵，最会评判学习的价值。为了教育自己的王族子孙和达观显贵的子嗣，他把宫廷变成了一所私立大学。

在这里，这个西方的新皇帝在当时周围众多名人的簇拥下，津津有味地打发自己的休闲时光。他极其崇拜学院式的民主，甚至屈尊降贵，并像朴实的大卫兄弟那样积极参与各种对话，允许地位最卑微的学者与之意见相左。

但是，当我们审视这些引发他们兴致、促使他们讨论的问题时，就会联想到田纳西州乡间中学辩论小组所选择的题目。

至少他们是很天真的。如果说公元800年的情况的确如此的话，那么公元1400年的情况也不例外。这并不能责备中世纪的学者，他们的头脑无疑和20世纪的后人一样敏锐。他们的处境和当代化学家、医生没什么两样，都享有调查研究的充分自由，但前提是他们不得有和1768年（那时化学还是不太为人知的科目，外科手术也常常与屠宰相提并论）颁布的第一部《不列颠百科全书》相悖的言论和做法。

结果（我有些混淆了自己的比喻），有着无限智力的中世纪科学家们仅在狭小的领域内做试验，就像在一辆廉价汽车的底盘上安装了一台劳斯莱斯汽车的先进

stepped on the gas,he met with a thousand accidents. But when he played safe and drove his strange contraption according to the rules and regulations of the road he became slightly ridiculous and wasted a terrible lot of energy without getting anywhere in particular.

Of course the best among these men were desperate at the rate of speed which they were forced to observe.

They tried in every possible way to escape from the everlasting observation of the clerical policemen. They wrote ponderous volumes,trying to prove the exact opposite of what they held to be true,in order that they might give a hint of the things that were uppermost in their minds.

They surrounded themselves with all sorts of hocus pocus;they wore strange garments;they had stuffed crocodiles hanging from their ceilings;they displayed shelves full of bottled monsters and threw evil smelling herbs in the furnace that they might frighten their neighbors away from their front door and at the same time establish a reputation of being the sort of harmless lunatics who could be allowed to say whatever they liked without being held too closely responsible for their ideas. And gradually they developed such a thorough system of scientific camouflage that even today it is difficult for us to decide what they actually meant.

That the Protestants a few centuries later showed themselves quite as intolerant towards science and literature as the Church of the Middle Ages had done is quite true,but it is beside the point.

The great reformers could fulminate and anathematize to their hearts' content,but they were rarely able to turn their threats into positive acts of repression.

The Roman Church on the other hand not only possessed the power to crush its enemies

马达，只要一踏油门便故障百出。等他能够安全操控、按章驾驶这辆不可思议的新玩意时，就变得令人感到荒唐可笑了，因为即便费了九牛二虎之力，也无法到达目的地。

当然，这些不得不遵循的进程，让这些人中的佼佼者彻底绝望了。

他们想方设法摆脱教会警察无休止的监视。他们编写了卷帙浩繁的作品，努力证明他们认为正确的事物对立面的错误，以便暗示萦绕在自己心头的那些想法。

他们做出各种掩人耳目的假象：穿上奇装异服，屋顶上挂满了鳄鱼，架子上摆满了装有怪物的瓶子，在炉子里烧些气味难闻的草药，以便把邻居从门前吓跑，他们这样做的同时也为自己赢得了一种名声，人们称他们是无害于人的神经病，可以随心所欲地胡说八道，而不必对自己的主张承担过多的相关责任。他们逐渐形成了一套完整的科学障眼法，直至今日我们也难以判断他们的真正意图是什么。

几个世纪之后，新教徒对科学和文学的不宽容，与中世纪教会所采取的行径如出一辙，这是毋庸置疑的，这里就不多说了。

那些伟大的宗教改革家可以毫无遮拦地严词谴责和大声责骂，却从未把恫吓转化成具体的镇压行动。

罗马教会却不然，它不仅拥有置异己于死地的权力，而且一俟时机成熟便会耀武扬威。

对我们其中的某些人而言，这种差别无足轻重，他们更愿意抽象地研讨宽容与否的理论价值。

but it made use of it,whenever the occasion presented itself.

The difference may seem trivial to those of us who like to indulge in abstract cogitations upon the theoretical values of tolerance and intolerance.

■ 新的一贯正确

But it was a very real issue to those poor devils,who were placed before the choice of a public recantation or an equally public flogging.

And if they sometimes lacked the courage to say what they held to be true,and preferred to waste their time on cross-word puzzles made up exclusively from the names of the animals mentioned in the Book of Revelations,let us not be too hard on them.

I am quite certain that I never would have written the present volume,six hundred years ago.

然而，对那些不得不作出选择的可怜虫来说，这种差别却产生了一个非常现实的问题，要么当众放弃信仰，要么当众承受鞭笞。

有些人会因缺乏勇气而在某些时刻不敢表达自己的真实想法，情愿把时间浪费在《启示录》动物名称的纵横填字游戏中，对于他们倒也不必太过苛求。

我敢肯定，假如倒退600年，我也不会写这本书。

CHAPTER IX THE WAR UPON THE PRINTED WORD

I find it increasingly difficult to write history. I am rather like a man who has been trained to be a fiddler and then at the age of thirty-five is suddenly given a piano and ordered to make his living as a virtuoso of the Klavier,because that too"is music."I learned my trade in one sort of a world and I must practice it in an entirely different one. I was taught to look upon all events of the past in the light of a definitely established order of things;a universe more or less competently managed by emperors and kings and arch-dukes and presidents,aided and abetted by congressmen and senators and secretaries of the treasury. Furthermore,in the days of my youth,the good Lord was still tacitly recognized as the ex-officio head of everything,and a personage who had to be treated with great respect and decorum.

Then came the war.

The old order of things was completely upset,emperors and kings were abolished,responsible ministers were superseded by irresponsible secret committees,and in many parts of the world,Heaven was formally closed by an order in council and a defunct economic hack-writer was officially proclaimed successor and heir to all the prophets of ancient times.

Of course all this will not last. But it will take civilization several centuries to catch up and by then I shall be dead.

Meanwhile I have to make the best of things,but it will not be easy.

Take the question of Russia. When I spent some time in that Holy Land,some twenty

第9章 向书开战

我发现写历史越来越困难了。我就像是某个人，他自幼学拉小提琴，可到了35岁时突然有人给了他一架钢琴，并要求他从此以键盘手身份谋生，理由是“那也是音乐”。我已经学会了某个领域的技巧，干的却是另一种完全不同的工作。我被教导要用既有的明确秩序去观察过去发生的事情，即这是一个由众议员、参议院和财政秘书辅佐的,由皇帝、国王、大公和总统（无论胜任与否）掌管的世界。更进一步讲，在我年轻的时候，大家仍然默认上帝是万物之尊，是必须推崇和供奉的人物形象。

后来，战争爆发了。

旧秩序被彻底推翻，皇帝和国王被废黜，责任大臣被不负责任的秘密委员会取代，天国的大门在世界许多地方被责令关闭，一个早就死去的经济学雇佣文人被官方认定为古往今来所有先知的继承人。

这一切当然不会持续太久，但文明却要花几个世纪才能重新赶上来，而那时我已不在人世了。

我必须充分利用现有的一切，但这并不容易。

就拿俄国的情形来说吧。大约20年前，我在这个“圣地”住了一段时间，那时我们得到的外国报纸中，总有四分之一的版面被涂抹得一片漆黑，技术上称之为

years ago,fully one quarter of the pages of the foreign papers that reached us were covered with a smeary black substance,known technically as"caviar."This stuff was rubbed upon those items which a careful government wished to hide from its loving subjects.

The world at large regarded this sort of supervision as an insufferable survival of the Dark Ages and we of the great republic of the west saved copies of the American comic papers,duly"caviared,"to show the folks at home what backward barbarians those far famed Russians actually were.

Then came the great Russian revolution.

For the last seventy-five years the Russian revolutionist had howled that he was a poor,persecuted creature who enjoyed no"liberty"at all and as evidence thereof he had pointed to the strict supervision of all journals devoted to the cause of socialism. But in the year 1918,the under-dog turned upper-dog. And what happened?Did the victorious friends of freedom abolish censorship of the press?By no means. They padlocked all papers and magazines which did not comment favorably upon the acts of the new masters,they sent many unfortunate editors to Siberia or Archangel (not much to choose) and in general showed themselves a hundred times more intolerant than the much maligned ministers and police sergeants of the Little White Father.

It happens that I was brought up in a fairly liberal community,which heartily believed in the motto of Milton that the"liberty to know,to utter and to argue freely according to our own conscience,is the highest form of liberty."

"Came the war,"as the movies have it,and I was to see the day when the Sermon on the Mount was declared to be a dangerous pro-German document which must not be allowed to circulate freely among a hundred million sovereign citizens and the publication of which would expose the editors and the printers to fines and imprisonment.

"鱼子酱"。这是因为小心翼翼的政府不愿让心爱的臣民知道那些被抹去的内容。

世人把这种监管看作是"黑暗时代"难以容忍的残余，而我们作为西方伟大共和国中的一分子，保留了几份滑稽的、涂有"鱼子酱"的美国报纸给本国老百姓看，是想让他们知道，那些名声在外的俄国人实际上是多么落后的野蛮人。

随后，伟大的俄国革命开始了。

在过去的75年里，俄国革命者怒吼着宣称自己是被剥削、被压迫的民众，根本享受不到任何"自由"。作为例证，他们指出那些投身于社会主义事业的刊物受到了严格监管。但等到了1918年，被压迫者变成了主导者。情形又怎样呢？获胜的自由盟友们取消了出版审查制度吗？这当然是不可能的。他们奉命关掉了所有不对新统治者的法令歌功颂德的报纸和杂志，把众多不幸的编撰人员发配到西伯利亚或名为"长天使"的地方（并不经常选用此地），与那些可恨的大臣和沙皇的警察们相比，他们总体上表现出超过百倍的不宽容。

我恰逢在较为自由的社会环境中生长，那里的人们打心底里相信弥尔顿的格言："自由之于求知、言论及凭借良知的辩论，乃是自由之最高表现形式。"

就像电影里描述的那样："开战了。"我看到了有朝一日即将到来的情景：《登山宝训》被宣布为前日耳曼人的危险文件，不许在广大民众中自行流传，那些编纂和印刷这些出版物的人将面临罚款或坐牢的威胁。

有鉴于此，放弃对历史的深入研究，改写短篇小说或从事房地产行业似乎更明智些。

In view of all this it would really seem much wiser to drop the further study of history and to take up short story writing or real estate.

But this would be a confession of defeat. And so I shall stick to my job,trying to remember that in a well regulated state,every decent citizen is supposed to have the right to say and think and utter whatever he feels to be true,provided he does not interfere with the happiness and comfort of his neighbors,does not act against the good manners of polite society or break one of the rules of the local police.

This places me,of course,on record as an enemy of all official censorship. As far as I can see,the police ought to watch out for certain magazines and papers which are being printed for the purpose of turning pornography into private gain. But for the rest,I would let every one print whatever he liked.

I say this not as an idealist or a reformer,but as a practical person who hates wasted efforts,and is familiar with the history of the last five hundred years. That period shows clearly that violent methods of suppression of the printed or spoken word have never yet done the slightest good.

Nonsense,like dynamite,is only dangerous when it is contained in a small and hermetically closed space and subjected to a violent impact from without. A poor devil,full of half-baked economic notions,when left to himself will attract no more than a dozen curious listeners and as a rule will be laughed at for his pains.

The same creature handcuffed to a crude and illiterate sheriff,dragged to jail and condemned to thirty-five years of solitary confinement,will become an object of great pity and in the end will be regarded and honored as a martyr.

But it will be well to remember one thing.

There have been quite as many martyrs for bad causes

■ 镇压

但这样做就等于认输。因而我要坚持工作，尽量提醒自己，在秩序良好的国度，每个正派的公民都应有表达、思考和阐述自己认为是正确事物的权利，只要没有干涉他人的幸福和安宁，没有采取有悖于社会文明礼仪的行为，也没有违背当地的法规就行。

这自然使我被记录在案，成为所有官方出版审查制度的敌人。依我看来，警方倒是应该监管那些仅为一己之私而印刷的黄色刊物。除此之外，我认为谁愿意印什么就由他去印吧。

我不是以理想主义者或改革家的身份这样说的，而是讨厌白费工夫，因为我非常熟悉过去500年的历史，并且讲求实际，所以才发表上述看法的。这段历史清楚地表明，采取暴力手段压制出版物或言论自由从来不会有什么好结果。

胡言乱语如同炸药，只有在狭小密封的容器里，加之外力敲打才会产生危险。如果听凭一个满肚子都是些半生不熟经济学概念的可怜虫去讲演，他至多只能招来几个好奇的听众，而他的苦心孤诣只会成为大家的笑柄。

同一个人，如果将其绑缚至粗鲁且目不识丁的地方官那里，就会被送进监狱，判处35年的单独监禁，他就会变成大家深刻同情的对象，最后还会被认为是牺牲者。

as martyrs for good causes. They are tricky people and one never can tell what they will do next.

Hence I would say,let them talk and let them write. If they have anything to say that is good,we ought to know it,and if not,they will soon be forgotten. The Greeks seem to have felt that way,and the Romans did until the days of the Empire. But as soon as the commander-in-chief of the Roman armies had become an imperial and semi-divine personage,a second-cousin to Jupiter and a thousand miles removed from all ordinary mortals,this was changed.

The crime of"laesa majestas,"the heinous offense of"offering insult to his Majesty,"was invented. It was a purely political misdemeanor and from the time of Augustus until the days of Justinian,many people were sent to prison because they had been a little too outspoken in their opinions about their rulers. But if one let the person of the emperor alone,there was practically no other subject of conversation which the Roman must avoid.

This happy condition came to an end. when the world was brought under the domination of the Church. The line between good and bad,between orthodox and heretical,was definitely drawn before Jesus had been dead more than a few years. During the second half of the first century,the apostle Paul spent quite a long time in the neighborhood of Ephesus in Asia Minor,a place famous for its amulets and charms. He went about preaching and casting out devils,and with such great success that he convinced many people of the error of their heathenish ways. As a token of repentance they came together one fine day with all their books of magic and burned more than ten thousand dollars worth of secret formulae,as you may read in the nineteenth chapter of the Acts of the Apostles.

This,however,was an entirely voluntary act on the part of a group of repentant sinners and it is not stated that Paul made an attempt to forbid the other Ephesians from reading or owning similar books.

Such a step was not taken until a century later.

Then,by order of a number of bishops convened in this same city of Ephesus,a book

但记住一件事情总是有好处的。

那就是为坏事“捐躯的人”与为好事献身的烈士一样多。他们是些狡诈的家伙，人们不知道他们下一步要干什么。

因此我主张，由他们去说去写吧。如果他们说的是些至理名言，我们就应该了解，否则很快会被忘掉。希腊人似乎意识到了这一点，罗马人在帝国时代之前也是如此行事的。但是一旦罗马军队的最高统帅成为帝王、半神半人的人物、朱庇特的远亲，并远远地与普通民众隔离开来时，事情就发生了改变。

“罔上之罪”，即谩骂君主的滔天大罪被确定下来了。这本该是政治上的一种不检点的行为，然而在奥古斯都到查士丁尼当政期间，许多人因此被投入监狱，因为他们对统治者的态度有些过于直率了。但如果人们把帝王束之高阁而不加理会，罗马实际上也就没什么可禁忌的话题了。

当世界进入教会统治时期之后，愉快的氛围戛然而止。

耶稣死后没几年，善恶之间、正统与异教之间就已经泾渭分明了。在公元1世纪后半叶，圣徒保罗在小亚细亚以弗所附近待了很长一段时间，那个地方以出护身符和符咒而闻名于世。保罗在此四处传教，驱逐恶魔，获得了极大的成功，使许多人承认自己异教行为的错误。作为忏悔的象征，在一个晴空万里的日子，人们带着魔法书聚集在一起，把价值1万多美元的秘密符咒付之一炬。在《使徒行传》第19章，你可以读到这些记载。

不过这完全是出于忏悔者的自愿，《使徒行传》上并没有记载保罗曾禁止其他以弗所的人阅读或拥有这些书籍。

containing the life of St. Paul was condemned and the faithful were admonished not to read it.

During the next two hundred years,there was very little censorship. There also were very few books.

But after the Council of Nicaea (325) when the Christian Church had become the official church of the Empire,the supervision of the written word became part of the routine duty of the clergy. Some books were absolutely forbidden. Others were described as"dangerous"and the people were warned that they must read them at their own risk. Until authors found it more convenient to assure themselves of the approval of the authorities before they published their works and made it a rule to send their manuscripts to the local bishops for their approbation.

Even then,a writer could not always be sure that his works would be allowed to exist. A book which one Pope had pronounced harmless might be denounced as blasphemous and indecent by his successor.

On the whole,however,this method protected the scribes quite effectively against the risk of being burned together with their parchment offspring and the system worked well enough as long as books were copied by hand and it took five whole years to get out an edition of three volumes.

All this of course was changed by the famous invention of Johann Gutenberg,alias John Gooseflesh.

After the middle of the fifteenth century,an enterprising publisher was able to produce as many as four or five hundred copies in less than two weeks' time and in the short period between 1453 and 1500 the people of western and southern Europe were presented with not less than forty thousand different editions of books that had thus far been obtainable only in some of the better stocked libraries.

The Church regarded this unexpected increase in the number of available books with

直至100年以后，才出现了这一幕。

到那时，仍然始于以弗所城，一些主教发出指令，凡载有圣徒保罗的书都是禁书，警告忠诚的信徒们不要阅读它们。

在此后200年中，问世的书籍寥寥无几。

但是尼西亚会议（公元325年）之后，基督教成为罗马帝国的国教，对文字的审查随之成为教士日常工作的一部分。有些书是绝对禁止的，还有些书则被称为“危险品”，阅读这类书籍的人被警告要自行承担风险。所以当作者们意识到，在作品出版之前应该先获得当局的批准时，这就形成了一种制度，手稿要送往当地的主教那里去审批。

即便如此，作者也不清楚是否自己的作品可以存留于世。一个教皇宣称此书无害，他的继任者却会斥其亵渎神灵和不够正派。

不过，这倒有效地保护了撰写人避免与自己写在羊皮纸上的作品一起被烧死的危险。只要图书还是依靠手抄，这项制度就不会寿终正寝，因为出版一套三卷本图书需要整整五年的时间。

然而，这一切都被约翰尼·古滕堡的著名发明改变了。人们戏称他为鸡皮疙瘩约翰。

15世纪中叶以后，有胆识的出版商在不足两星期内便能生产出400或500本图书。在1453~1500年这么短的时间内，西欧和南欧的读者竟获得了4万余册不同版本的图书，这相当于当时保存良好的图书馆历代藏书的总和。

教会对这些雨后春笋般出现的图书忧心忡忡。逮捕一个自抄《马太福音》的异

very serious misgivings. It was difficult enough to catch a single heretic with a single home made copy of the Gospels. What then of twenty million heretics with twenty million copies of cleverly edited volumes?They became a direct menace to all idea of authority and it was deemed necessary to appoint a special tribunal to inspect all forthcoming publications at their source and say which could be published and which must never see the light of day.

Out of the different lists of books which from time to time were published by this committee as containing"forbidden knowledge"grew that famous Index which came to enjoy almost as nefarious a reputation as the Inquisition.

But it would be unfair to create the impression that such a supervision of the printing-press was something peculiar to the Catholic Church. Many states,frightened by the sudden avalanche of printed material that threatened to upset the peace of the realm,had already forced their local publishers to submit their wares to the public censor and had forbidden them to print anything that did not bear the official mark of approbation.

But nowhere,except in Rome,has the practice been continued until today. And even there it has been greatly modified since the middle of the sixteenth century. It had to be. The presses worked so fast and furiously that even that most industrious Commission of Cardinals,the so-called Congregation of the Index,which was supposed to inspect all printed works,was soon years behind in its task. Not to mention the flood of rag-pulp and printers-ink which was poured upon the landscape in the form of newspapers and magazines and tracts and which no group of men,however diligent,could hope to read,let alone inspect and classify,in less than a couple of thousand years.

But rarely has it been shown in a more convincing fashion how terribly this sort of intolerance avenges itself upon the rulers who force it upon their unfortunate subjects.

Already Tacitus,during the first century of the Roman Empire,had declared himself against the persecution of authors as"a foolish thing which tended to advertise books

■ 书贩

教徒就很不易了，何况面对拥有2000万册巧妙编辑的图书的2000万异教徒呢？这对当权者的思想构成了极大威胁，看来只有指派一个特别法庭，从源头上审查这些即将发行的出版物，决定哪些可以出版，哪些永远不得面世。

从委员会对不同种类图书定期公布的带有“禁忌知识”的目录清单中，产生了臭名昭著的《禁书目录》。它与宗教法庭同样声名狼藉。

认为唯有天主教监管出版界，这是不公正的。许多国家，由于害怕危及国家安宁的出版物像雪片一样突然蜂拥而至，早已强迫地方出版商把书样递交公共检查机关，凡是没有加盖官方批准印章的书籍都不得出版。

不过除罗马外，没有一个国家把这种制度延续至今。即便如此，罗马也于16世纪中叶对其进行了大量修改。这些修改是迫不得已的。出版界的迅猛发展，使最为兢兢业业的红衣主教委员会（为审查各类印刷品而成立的所谓“《禁书目录》委员会”）应接不暇。除图书外，还没有将铺天盖地的报纸、杂志和小册子考虑进来，用在这些方面的纸浆油墨泛滥成灾。不用说审查分类了，就是再勤勉的人，阅读这些东西也需要花费几千年的时间。

which otherwise would never attract any public attention."

The Index proved the truth of this statement. No sooner had the Reformation been successful than the list of forbidden books was promoted to a sort of handy guide for those who Wished to keep themselves thoroughly informed upon the subject of current literature. More than that. During the seventeenth century,enterprising publishers in Germany and in the Low Countries maintained special agents in Rome whose business it was to get hold of advance copies of the Index Expurgatorius. As soon as they had obtained these,they entrusted them to special couriers who raced across the Alps and down the valley of the Rhine that the valuable information might be delivered to their patrons with the least possible loss of time. Then the German and the Dutch printing shops would set to work and would get out hastily printed special editions which were sold at an exorbitant profit and were smuggled into the forbidden territory by an army of professional book-leggers.

But the number of copies that could be carried across the frontier remained necessarily very small and in such countries as Italy and Spain and Portugal,where the Index was actually enforced until a short time ago,the results of this policy of repression became very noticeable.

If such nations gradually dropped behind in the race for progress,the reason was not difficult to find. Not only were the students in their universities deprived of all foreign text-books,but they were forced to use a domestic product of very inferior quality.

And worst of all,the Index discouraged people from occupying themselves seriously with literature or science. For no man in his senses would undertake to write a book when he ran the risk of seeing his work"corrected"to pieces by an incompetent censor or emendated beyond recognition by the inconsequential secretary of an Inquisitorial Board of Investigators.

Instead,he went fishing or wasted his time playing dominoes in a wine-shop.

Or he sat down and in sheer despair of himself and his people,he wrote the story of Don Quixote.

但是这种自作自受的不宽容，还不足以显示统治者强加在不幸臣民头上的不宽容的可怕。

罗马帝国的塔西陀在公元1世纪时就曾宣称反对迫害作者，认为“这是相当愚蠢的行径，原本无人问津的图书反而会因此大获瞩目”。

《禁书目录》验证了这个论断的正确。宗教改革刚刚获得成功，大批禁书的地位便骤然提升，成为那些想彻底通晓当代文学的读者非常便利的指南。还不止如此。16世纪德国和低地国家雄心勃勃的出版商在罗马长期设有耳目，专门搜集被禁止或被删节的最新书目，一旦到手，便立即由专门信使越过阿尔卑斯山和莱茵河谷，跋山涉水，以最快速度送到雇主手里。德国和荷兰的印刷厂随即马上开始工作，夜以继日抢印出特刊，然后再由一批训练有素的职业书贩偷偷将这些以暴利出售为目的的图书偷运到禁运国家。

不过偷运过境的书毕竟有限，而且在一些国家，如意大利、西班牙和葡萄牙，《禁书目录》直到前不久还在执行，这项压制政策的后果非常引人关注。

如果这些国家在追求进步的竞赛中落伍了，原因并不难找，因为这些国家在校大学生不但没有使用外国教科书的机会，就连强制采用的国内货也是些残次品。

最糟糕的是，《禁书目录》挫伤了人们投身科学研究和文学创作的激情，因为一个头脑正常的人不愿看到自己辛苦写出来的书被不称职的审查官“修正”得七零八落，或被不识轻重的宗教法庭调查委员会的秘书校订得面目全非。

他宁愿去钓鱼，或把时间消磨在酒馆多米诺骨牌游戏上。

他或许会坐下来，在失望之余，开始撰写堂吉诃德的故事。

CHAPTER X CONCERNING THE WRITING OF HISTORY IN GENERAL AND THIS BOOK IN PARTICULAR

In the correspondence of Erasmus,which I recommend most eagerly to those who are tired of modern fiction,there occurs a stereotype sort of warning in many of the letters sent unto the learned Desiderius by his more timid friends.

"I hear that you are thinking of a pamphlet upon the Lutheran controversy,"writes Magister X."Please be very careful how you handle it,because you might easily offend the Pope,who wishes you well."

Or again:"some one who has just returned from Cambridge tells me that you are about to publish a book of short essays. For Heaven's sake,do not incur the displeasure of the Emperor,who might be in a position to do you great harm."

Now it is the Bishop of Louvain,then the King of England or the faculty of the Sorbonne or that terrible professor of theology in Cambridge who must be treated with special consideration,lest the author be deprived of his income or lose the necessary official protection or fall into the clutches of the Inquisition or be broken on the wheel.

Nowadays the wheel (except for purposes of locomotion) is relegated to the museum of antiquities. The Inquisition has closed its doors these hundred years,protection is of little practical use in a career devoted to literature and the word"income"is hardly ever mentioned where historians come together.

第10章　历史写作的普遍性和本书的特殊性

我向那些已经厌倦现代小说的人们热诚地推荐伊拉斯谟的信札，在许多比他更为温顺的朋友寄给博学的德西德利乌斯的来信当中，都会提到一些典型的警告性言辞。

某行政长官写道："听说您正在考虑写一本有关路德之争的小册子。请您倍加小心，因为您可能非常容易冒犯教皇，而教皇希望您能万事平安。"

或者又有人说："某个刚从剑桥回来的人告诉我，说您正在计划出版一本短文集。看在上帝的份上，不要惹皇帝不高兴，他的态度会给您招致诸多伤害。"

一会儿是卢万的主教，一会儿是英格兰国王，一会儿是索邦大学的教师，一会儿又是剑桥大学可怕的神学教授，四面八方都得考虑周全，不然作者就会失去收入，丧失官方保护，或落入宗教法庭的桎梏，或被辗于车轮之下。

如今，作为刑具的轮子（除作为运载工具外）已陈列在博物馆的古董当中，宗教法庭也已关闭几百年了，对投身于文学的人而言，官方保护没多大实际用途，历史学家聚在一起时，更是对"收入"二字三缄其口。

不过，一旦私下里提到我要写一部《宽容史》时，一切就又一如既往地出现了，另一种形式的警告信件和劝谏便蜂拥至我那隐居的小屋。

But all the same,as soon as it was whispered that I intended to write a"History of Tolerance,"a different sort of letters of admonition and advice began to find their way to my cloistered cell.

"Harvard has refused to admit a negro to her dormitories,"writes the secretary of the S. P. C. C. P."Be sure that you mention this most regrettable fact in your forthcoming book."

Or again:"The local K. K. K. in Framingham,Mass. ,has started to boycott a grocer who is a professed Roman Catholic. You will want to say something about this in your story of tolerance."

And so on.

No doubt all these occurrences are very stupid,very silly and altogether reprehensible. But they hardly seem to come within the jurisdiction of a volume on tolerance. They are merely manifestations of bad manners and a lack of decent public spirit. They are very different from that official form of intolerance which used to be incorporated into the laws of the Church and the State and which made persecution a holy duty on the part of all good citizens.

History,as Bagehot has said,ought to be like an etching by Rembrandt. It must cast a vivid light upon certain selected causes,on those which are best and most important,and leave all the rest in the shadow and unseen.

Even in the midst of the most idiotic outbreaks of the modern spirit of intolerance which are so faithfully chronicled in our news sheets,it is possible to discern signs of a more hopeful future.

For nowadays many things which previous generations would have accepted as self-evident and which would have been passed by with the remark that"it has always been that way,"are cause for serious debate. Quite often our neighbors rush to the defense of ideas which would have been regarded as preposterously visionary and unpractical by our fathers and our grandfathers and not infrequently they are successful in their warfare upon some particularly obnoxious demonstration of the mob spirit.

This book must be kept very short.

"哈佛大学已拒绝让一个黑人进入她的宿舍了，"人口外溢预防控制与应对计划的一个书记官写道，"请务必在您即将出版的书中提一下这件最令人遗憾的事情。"

或者是："马萨诸塞州弗拉明汉地区的三K党已开始联合抵制一个杂货商人，因为他公开宣称自己是罗马天主教徒，您在撰写宽容故事的时候会就此说几句吧。"

诸如此类。

毋庸置疑，这太愚蠢了，愚昧到理应遭受谴责。不过它们似乎不应包含在论述宽容著作的范畴之内。它们只是一些没礼貌的行为，缺乏正派的公共意识，这与官方形式的不宽容大相径庭，官方的不宽容曾融入教会和国家的法律体系，把对良民百姓的迫害变成一项神圣的职责。

按照白哲特的说法，历史应该像伦勃朗的蚀刻画，必须对特定的事件投射生动的光辉，因为它们是最美好或最重要的，其余的一切就留在黑暗当中吧，让它们隐而不见。

在现代不宽容风气愚蠢爆发的过程中（报纸忠实地记载下了这一切），我们仍可以看到一些迹象，从而对未来充满信心。

许多老辈人认为理所当然、原本如此的事情本该被接受下来的，可是如今导致了激烈的争论。我们的邻居经常会急于维护自己的主张，而这些主张在我们的父辈和先祖那里却被认为是些荒诞无稽的幻想，毫无实际用处。在与下层民众的风俗陋习的战斗中，他们倒是经常获得成功。

这本书必须简明扼要。

手法老练的当铺老板的势利习气、至高无上的日耳曼民族颇具争议的荣光、边

I can't bother about the private snobbishness of successful pawnbrokers,the somewhat frayed glory of Nordic supremacy,the dark ignorance of backwoods evangelists,the bigotry of peasant priests or Balkan rabbis. These good people and their bad ideas have always been with us.

But as long as they do not enjoy the official support of the State,they are comparatively harmless and in most civilized countries,such a possibility is entirely precluded.

Private intolerance is a nuisance which can cause more discomfort in any given community than the combined efforts of measles,smallpox and a gossiping woman. But private intolerance does not possess executioners of its own. If,as sometimes happens in this and other countries,it assumes the rôle of the hangman,it places itself outside the law and becomes a proper subject for police supervision.

Private intolerance does not dispose of jails and cannot prescribe to an entire nation what it shall think and say and eat and drink. If it tries to do this,it creates such a terrific resentment among all decent folk,that the new ordinance becomes a dead letter and cannot be carried out even in the District of Columbia.

In short,private intolerance can go only as far as the indifference of the majority of the citizens of a free country will allow it to go,and no further. Whereas official intolerance is practically almighty.

It recognizes no authority beyond its own power.

It provides no mode of redress for the innocent victims of its meddlesome fury. It will listen to no argument. And ever again it backs up its decisions by an appeal to the Divine Being and then undertakes to explain the will of Heaven as if the key to the mysteries of existence were an exclusive possession of those who had been successful at the most recent elections.

If in this book the word intolerance is invariably used in the sense of official intolerance,and if I pay little attention to the private variety,have patience with me.

I can only do one thing at a time.

远地区福音传教士的孤陋寡闻、乡村牧师和巴尔干拉比（犹太传教士）的顽固僵化，这一切我都不会费力去讨论。这些好人和他们糟糕的想法总是出现在我们身边。

但是只要他们没有得到官方支持，他们相对来说倒也无害，而在最开明的国度，这种危害的可能性已被彻底消除了。

个人的不宽容是个讨厌的家伙，它令社团内部愈发不快，比麻疹、天花和饶舌妇加在一起惹的麻烦还要大。不过对于个人的不宽容不能采取刑法手段。如果允许不宽容的个人充当刽子手角色，就像有时在某些国家出现的情形，那他就超出了法律限度，真正成为警方关注的对象。

个人的不宽容不能设置监狱，也不能为整个国家规定人们必须想什么、说什么、吃什么和喝什么。如果真要这么做，就必然会招致所有正派乡亲的强烈怨愤，新法令就会形同虚设，即便在哥伦比亚地区也无法执行。

简而言之，个人的不宽容只能在自由国家大多数公民不介意的范围内走动，不可越此雷池。然而官方的不宽容却不然，它可是无所不及的。

它除自己的权利之外，不承认任何权威。

对无辜的受害者，它从未提供任何补救措施。它不听任何辩解，还求助于“神灵”来支持自己的决定，承担起解释上天意志的职责，好像打开生存之谜的钥匙为那些刚刚在大选中获胜的人所独有。

假如本书中“不宽容”一词总是意味着“官方不宽容”的话，假如我很少谈及个人不宽容的话，请您充分谅解。

我一次只能做一件事情。

CHAPTER XI RENAISSANCE

There is a learned cartoonist in our land who takes pleasure in asking himself,what do billiard-balls and crossword puzzles and bull-fiddles and boiled shirts and doormats think of this world?

But what I would like to know is the exact psychological reaction of the men who are ordered to handle the big modern siege guns. During the war a great many people performed a great many strange tasks,but was there ever a more absurd job than firing dicke Berthas?

All other soldiers knew more or less what they were doing.

A flying man could judge by the rapidly spreading red glow whether he had hit the gas factory or not.

The submarine commander could return after a couple of hours to judge by the abundance of flotsam in how far he had been successful.

The poor devil in his dug-out had the satisfaction of realizing that by his mere continued presence in a particular trench he was at least holding his own.

Even the artillerist,working his field-piece upon an invisible object,could take down the telephone and could ask his colleague,hidden in a dead tree seven miles away,whether the doomed church tower was showing signs of deterioration or whether he should try again at a different angle.

But the brotherhood of the big guns lived in a strange and unreal world of their own.

第11章 文艺复兴

在我们国家有一个博学的漫画家，他喜欢问自己，台球、纵横填字游戏、大提琴、浆洗的衬衫和门前的擦鞋垫对这个世界会是些什么看法呢?

不过，我想知道的是那些奉命掌控大规模现代攻城炮的人的心理。许多人在战争中执行着林林总总不可思议的任务，但还有比发射“大伯莎”榴弹炮更可笑的吗?

所有士兵都或多或少知道自己在干些什么。

飞行员可从腾空而起的红光中判断自己是否击中了燃气厂。

几小时后返航的潜艇指挥员可以通过漂浮物的多少来判断成果的大小。

壕沟里的可怜虫凭借自己还占据某个特定的战壕，从而意识到至少自己仍坚守阵地而沾沾自喜。

即便是野外炮兵，在向看不见的目标射击后，也可以拿起耳机向藏在7英里以外一颗枯树上的同伴询问，所要摧毁的教堂塔尖是否出现倒塌的迹象，是否需要调整角度再打一次。

但是，发射榴弹炮的弟兄们生活在怪异虚无的世界之中。即便获得了资深弹道专家的支持，他们仍不能预先知道他们痛痛快快射向天空的那些炮弹的命运究竟如

Even with the assistance of a couple of full-fledged professors of ballistics,they were unable to foretell what fate awaited those projectiles which they shot so blithely into space. Their shells might actually hit the object for which they were destined. They might land in the midst of a powder factory or in the heart of a fortress. But then again they might strike a church or an orphan asylum or they might bury themselves peacefully in a river of in a gravel pit without doing any harm whatsoever.

Authors,it seems to me,have much in common with the siege-gunners. They too handle a sort of heavy artillery. Their literary missiles may start a revolution or a conflagration in the most unlikely spots. But more often they are just poor duds and lie harmless in a nearby field until they are used for scrap iron or converted into an umbrella-stand or a flower pot.

Surely there never was a period in history when so much rag-pulp was consumed within so short a space as the era commonly known as the Renaissance.

Every Tomasso,Ricardo and Enrico of the Italian peninsula,every Doctor Thomasius,Professor Ricardus and Dominus Heinrich of the great Teuton plain rushed into print with at least a dozen duodecimos. Not to mention the Tomassinos who wrote pretty little sonnets in imitation of the Greeks,the Ricardinos who reeled off odes after the best pattern of their Roman grandfathers,and the countless lovers of coins,statuary,images,pictures,manuscripts and ancient armor who for almost three centuries kept themselves busy classifying,ordering,tabulating,listing,filing and codifying what they had just dug out of the ancestral ruins and who then published their collections in countless folios illuminated with the most beautiful of copper engravings and the most ponderous of wood-cuts.

This great intellectual curiosity was very lucrative for the Frobens and the Alduses and the Etiennes and the other new firms of printers who were making a fortune out of the invention which had ruined Gutenberg,but otherwise the literary output of the Renaissance did not

何。炮弹也许真的击中了所设定的目标，或许落在了兵工厂或在要塞中心。然而它们或许击中的是教堂或孤儿院，或许是安静地扎入河底的沙砾坑中，没有造成任何伤害。

依我所见，作家们在许多地方与攻城炮兵有许多相似之处。他们也在操纵一门重型火炮，他们的文学炮弹也许会点燃一场革命，也许在最出人意料的地点引起火灾。不过它们通常仅仅是些可怜的哑弹，无声无息地搁置在附近的田野里，最后被当成废铁，或用来制作成雨伞架和花盆。

历史上从没有哪个阶段像众所周知的“文艺复兴”时期那样，在如此短的时间内消耗了如此多的纸浆。

意大利半岛上的每一个托马索、里卡多和恩里科，日耳曼大平原上的每一个托马斯博士、里卡德和多米尼・海因里希教授，都匆匆忙忙地赶印出至少一打12开的作品，更甭说模仿希腊人谱写动人十四行诗的托马西诺之流，以及参照罗马先祖的佳文范本而提炼颂歌的里卡蒂诺之流，还有其他不计其数的热衷于古币、雕塑、肖像、书画、手稿和古代盔甲的人，他们投入了几乎整整三个世纪的时间，忙于把刚刚从前人废墟里挖掘出来的东西分类、整理、制表、登记、存档和编纂，然后再用大量的对开纸配以美丽的铜版画和精致的木版刻画，把它们印刷出来。

强烈的求知欲望使弗罗本、阿尔杜斯、埃帝安纳及其他新印刷公司发了财。他们从印刷术的发明中大捞油水，但这使得古滕堡公司破了产，但无论怎样，文艺复兴的文学作品在当时世界的状况下，即作家们所处的15、16世纪并没有产生巨大的

very greatly affect the state of that world in which the authors of the fifteenth and sixteenth centuries happened to find themselves. The distinction of having contributed something new was restricted to only a very few heroes of the quill and they were like our friends of the big guns. They rarely discovered during their own lifetime in how far they had been successful and how much damage their writings had actually done. But first and last they managed to demolish a great many of the obstacles which stood in the way of progress. And they deserve our everlasting gratitude for the thoroughness with which they cleaned up a lot of rubbish which otherwise would continue to clutter our intellectual front yard.

Strictly speaking,however,the Renaissance was not primarily a forward-looking movement. It turned its back in disgust upon the recent past,called the works of its immediate predecessors"barbaric" (or"Gothic"in the language of the country where the Goths had enjoyed the same reputation as the Huns),and concentrated its main interest upon those arts which seem to be pervaded with that curious substance known as the"classical spirit."

If nevertheless the Renaissance struck a mighty blow for the liberty of conscience and for tolerance and for a better world in general,it was done in spite of the men who were considered the leaders of the new movement.

Long before the days of which we are now speaking,there had been people who had questioned the rights of a Roman bishop to dictate to Bohemian peasants and to English yeomen in what language they should say their prayers,in what spirit they should study the words of Jesus,how much they should pay for an indulgence,what books they should read and how they should bring up their children. And all of them had been crushed by the strength of that superstate,the power of which they had undertaken to defy. Even when they had acted as champions and representatives of a national cause,they had failed.

影响。贡献出新思想的人仅限于为数不多的几个笔头英雄，他们像放榴弹炮的朋友们一样，几乎没能亲眼看见自己所取得成就的大小，或者其作品造成了怎样的负面作用。但总体来说，他们设法铲除了进步道路上的诸多藩篱，干净彻底地清除了堆积如山的垃圾，否则这些垃圾还会堆放在我们智慧的大杂院里，为此，他们值得我们永久的感激。

不过从严格意义上讲，文艺复兴最主要的并不是一场“复古”运动。对刚刚消失的过去，人们鄙视地转过脸去，称上一代人的作品为“野蛮”之作（或“哥特式”的，在一些国家的语言当中，哥特人和匈奴人等量齐观），人们的兴趣主要集中在艺术品上，因为艺术品中似乎蕴藏着一种叫作“古典精神”的神奇内涵。

假如说文艺复兴确实极大地推动了自由良知、宽容和更普遍的美好世界的话，它所实现的一切也并不是遵照所谓新运动领导者们的旨意为出发点的。

在此之前的很长时间里，就有人对罗马主教的权力提出质疑，他们何以能够强行规定波希米亚的农民和英格兰自由民用哪种语言祈祷，应以怎样的精神状态学习耶稣的教诲，为赎买自己的罪行而应支付多少钱，应该读些什么书，以及怎样教育子女。这帮公然质疑权力的人，全都被这个已经超越国家权力的力量所摧毁。即便他们当中的某些人曾担任民族运动的头领或代表，也难以逃脱失败的下场。

伟大的约翰·胡斯的骨灰余火未尽，就被扔进莱茵河受尽侮辱，这是对全世界发出的警告：教皇体制仍至高无上。

威克利夫的尸体被官方行刑者焚烧了，以此来告诉莱斯特郡卑微的农民，主教

The smoldering ashes of great John Huss,thrown ignominiously into the river Rhine,were a warning to all the world that the Papal Monarchy still ruled supreme.

The corpse of Wycliffe,burned by the public executioner,told the humble peasants of Leicestershire that councils and Popes could reach beyond the grave.

Frontal attacks,evidently,were impossible.

The mighty fortress of tradition,builded slowly and carefully during fifteen centuries of unlimited power,could not be taken by assault. The scandals which had taken place within these hallowed enclosures;the wars between three rival Popes,each claiming to be the legitimate and exclusive heir to the chair of Holy Peter;the utter corruption of the courts of Rome and Avignon,where laws were made for the purpose of being broken by those who were willing to pay for such favors;the utter demoralization of monastic life;the venality of those who used the recently increased horrors of purgatory as an excuse to blackmail poor parents into paying large sums of money for the benefit of their dead children;all these things,although widely known,never really threatened the safety of the Church.

But the chance shots fired at random by certain men and women who were not at all interested in ecclesiastical matters,who had no particular grievance against either pope or bishop,these caused the damage which finally made the old edifice collapse.

What the"thin,pale man"from Prague had failed to accomplish with his high ideals of Christian virtue was brought about by a motley crowd of private citizens who had no other ambition than to live and die (preferably at a ripe old age) as loyal patrons of all the good things of this world and faithful sons of the Mother Church.

They came from all the seven corners of Europe. They represented every sort of profession and they would have been very angry,had an historian told them what they were doing.

For instance,take the case of Marco Polo.

委员会和教皇仍掌控着墓地之外的一切。

正面攻破显然绝无可能。

“传统”的巨型堡垒是用特权，并经过15个世纪的精心打造而筑成的，外力休想攻占它。在栅栏深处出现的丑闻；三个对立教皇彼此宣称自己是圣彼得法定、唯一的继承人而大动干戈；罗马和阿维尼翁教廷腐败透顶，只要肯花钱就能买来为违法者定罪而制定的法律；修道士的堕落生活；中饱私囊之徒利用日益加剧的炼狱恐慌，要挟可怜的父母为死去的孩子缴纳大笔钱财。所有这些虽然人所共知，却不能真正危及教会的安全。

然而，一些对宗教事务毫无兴趣的男女，对教皇和主教也无切齿之恨的人们，他们胡乱开火，却使这座古老的大厦受到撞击，最终轰然倒塌。

来自布拉格的“瘦小苍白的人”（胡斯）未能实现的向往基督美德的崇高理想，却被一群杂七杂八的平民实现了。他们没有过高的奢望，只想在有生之年（最好是寿终正寝）为世上所有的善事提供忠实的赞助，做基督虔诚的儿子。

这帮人来自欧洲的各个角落，各行各业，假如有个历史学家指出他们所作所为的真实本意，他们还会为此烦恼不已。

以马可·波罗为例。

我们知道他是个伟大的旅行家，一个见多识广的人；而他那些对西部小城司空见惯的邻居们戏称他是“百万美元的马可”。每当他向人们讲述他所看到的宝塔那

We know him as a mighty traveler,a man who had seen such wondrous sights that his neighbors,accustomed to the smaller scale of their western cities,called him"Million Dollar Marc"and laughed uproariously when he told them of golden thrones as high as a tower and of granite walls that would stretch all the way from the Baltic to the Black Sea.

All the same,the shriveled little fellow played a most important rôle in the history of progress. He was not much of a writer. He shared the prejudice of his class and his age against the literary profession. A gentleman (even a Venetian gentleman who was supposed to be familiar with double-entry bookkeeping) handled a sword and not a goose-quill. Hence the unwillingness of Messire Marco to turn author. But the fortunes of war carried him into a Genoese prison. And there,to while away the tedious hours of his confinement,he told a poor scribbler,who happened to share his cell,the strange story of his life. In this roundabout way the people of Europe learned many things about this world which they had never known before. For although Polo was a simple-minded fellow who firmly believed that one of the mountains he had seen in Asia Minor had been moved a couple of miles by a pious saint who wanted to show the heathen"what true faith could do,"and who swallowed all the stories about people without heads and chickens with three legs which were so popular in his day,his report did more to upset the geographical theories of the Church than anything that had appeared during the previous twelve hundred years.

Polo,of course,lived and died a faithful son of the Church. He would have been terribly upset if any one had compared him with his near-contemporary,the famous Roger Bacon,who was an out and out scientist and paid for his intellectual curiosity with ten years of enforced literary idleness and fourteen years of prison.

And yet of the two he was by far the more dangerous.

For whereas only one person in a hundred thousand could follow Bacon when he went chasing rainbows,and spun those fine evolutionary theories which threatened to upset all

么高的黄金御座、犹如从巴尔干延伸到黑海那么远距离的大理石石墙时，总会引起人们的哄堂大笑。

正是这个瘦小的家伙，却在历史的进步中发挥了非常重要的作用。他不太像是个作家。他对从事文学也怀有他那个时代和阶层共有的偏见。一个绅士（即使是对图书生意了然于胸的威尼斯绅士）应该手握利剑而非要弄笔杆子，因此马可先生不愿意成为作家。但是，战争女神却把他带进了热那亚监狱。在那里，为了打发枯燥乏味的牢狱时光，他向一个恰巧同牢的可怜的三流作家讲述了自己传奇的一生，依靠这种转弯抹角的方法，欧洲人了解到许多过去闻所未闻的有关这个世界的事情。马可·波罗是个头脑简单的家伙，他曾固执地相信他在小亚细亚目睹过一座山被一个虔诚的圣人挪动了好几英里，借以向异教徒展示"真正的信仰所能达到的力量"；他也曾囫囵吞枣地记录了许多当时广为流传的故事，例如没有脑袋的人和三只腿的鸡。即便如此，他的游记对动摇教会的地理学理论却发挥了更为重要的作用，比此前12个世纪任何一件事情的影响都要大。

马可·波罗从生到死当然一直是教会的虔诚信徒，谁要是把他比作几乎是同时代的著名的罗吉尔·培根，他还会怒不可遏。培根是个地地道道的科学家，他为了追求知识，忍了整整十年的痛没有写作，还被关在监狱里整整14年。

不过这两个人中还是波罗更为危险。

在十万人中最多只有一个人会跟随培根追逐天上的彩虹，琢磨他那娓娓动听的

the ideas held sacred in his own time,every citizen who had been taught his ABCs Could learn from Polo that the world was full of a number of things the existence of which the authors of the Old Testament had never even suspected.

I do not mean to imply that the publication of a single book caused that rebellion against scriptural authority which was to occur before the world could gain a modicum of freedom. Popular enlightenment is ever the result of centuries of painstaking preparation. But the plain and straightforward accounts of the explorers and the navigators and the travelers,understandable to all the people,did a great deal to bring about that spirit of scepticism which characterizes the latter half of the Renaissance and which allowed people to say and write things which only a few years before would have brought them into contact with the agents of the Inquisition.

Take that strange story to which the friends of Boccaccio listened on the first day of their agreeable exile from Florence. All religious systems,so it told,were probably equally true and equally false. But if this were true,and they were all equally true and false,then how could people be condemned to the gallows for ideas which could neither be proven nor contradicted?

Read the even stranger adventures of a famous scholar like Lorenzo Valla. He died as a highly respectable member of the government of the Roman Church. Yet in the pursuit of his Latin studies he had incontrovertibly proven that the famous donation of"Rome and Italy and all the provinces of the West,"which Constantine the Great was supposed to have made to Pope Sylvester (and upon which the Popes had ever since based their claims to be regarded as super-lords of all Europe),was nothing but a clumsy fraud,perpetrated hundreds of years after the death of the Emperor by an obscure official of the papal chancery.

Or to return to more practical questions,what were faithful Christians,carefully reared in the ideas of Saint Augustine,who had taught that a belief in the presence of people on

进化理论以颠覆当时的神圣思想，而只学过ABC的平民百姓却可以从马可·波罗那儿得知世界上还存在着《旧约》的作者从未想到过的东西。

我并不是说在世界尚未获得一丝一毫的自由之前，仅靠出版一本书就能引起对《圣经》的权威性的反叛。对普通大众的启蒙开化是数世纪艰苦准备的结果。不过，探险家、航海家和旅行家的朴实讲述却很容易让人们理解，这促进了怀疑论精神的兴起。怀疑论是文艺复兴后期社会的特点，它允许人们去说去写那些在几年前还会被宗教法庭制裁的言论。

以薄伽丘的奇特故事为例，他的朋友们从佛罗伦萨出发，进行宜人的长足旅行，头一天便听到了这些故事。故事中说，所有宗教体制都可能有对有错。可是如果这个说法成立，所有宗教体制都对错相等，那么许多观点就无法证实或否定，既然如此，持各种观点的人为什么还要被判处绞刑呢？

读一读像洛伦佐·瓦拉这样著名的学者更奇特的探险经历吧。他死时是罗马教会政权中深受崇拜的高级官员。可是他在钻研拉丁文时却作出了无可辩驳的证明说，传说中关于君士坦丁大帝曾把“罗马、意大利和西方所有省份”赠给西尔维斯特教皇的说法（从那以后的历代教皇都以此为依据，在整个欧洲作威作福）只不过是个拙劣的骗局，是皇帝死去几百年后教廷里一个无名小官编造出来的。

或者，让我们回到更实际的话题上来，看看一直受圣奥古斯丁思想熏陶的那些虔诚的基督徒。圣奥古斯丁曾教导他们说，地球另一侧的人所持的信仰是亵渎和异

the other side of the earth was both blasphemous and heretical,since such poor creatures would not be able to see the second coming of Christ and therefore had no reason to exist,what indeed were the good people of the year 1499 to think of this doctrine when Vasco da Gama returned from his first voyage to the Indies and described the populous kingdoms which he had found on the other side of this planet?

What were these same simple folk,who had always been told that our world was a flat dial and that Jerusalem was the center of the universe,what were they to believe when the little"Vittoria"returned from her voyage around the globe and when the geography of the Old Testament was shown to contain some rather serious errors?

I repeat what I have said before. The Renaissance was not an era of conscious scientific endeavor. In spiritual matters it often showed a most regrettable lack of real interest. Everything during these three hundred years was dominated by a desire for beauty and entertainment. Even the Popes,who fulminated loudest against the iniquitous doctrines of some of their subjects,were only too happy to invite those self-same rebels for dinner if they happened to be good conversationalists and knew something about printing or architecture. And eager zealots for virtue,like Savonarola,ran quite as great a risk of losing their lives as the bright young agnostics who in poetry and prose attacked the fundaments of the Christian faith with a great deal more violence than good taste.

But throughout all these manifestations of a new interest in the business of living,there undoubtedly ran a severe undercurrent of discontent with the existing order of society and the restrictions put upon the development of human reason by the claims of an all-powerful Church.

Between the days of Boccaccio and those of Erasmus,there is an interval of almost two centuries. During these two centuries,the copyist and the printer never enjoyed an idle moment. And outside of the books published by the Church herself,it would be difficult to

端的，那些可怜的生灵不可能见到基督第二次降临，因而根本不应该活在世上。不过，当1499年达·伽马首航印度归来，描绘了他在地球另一端发现的人口稠密的王国时，这些善男信女又该如何看待圣奥古斯丁的教义呢?

同样是这群头脑简单的人，他们一直被告知说，世界是扁圆的，耶路撒冷是宇宙的中心。然而“维托利亚”号环球航行后平安返回，这表明《旧约》中的地理知识有不少严重错误，那么这些人应该相信什么呢?

我重复一下刚才所说的。文艺复兴不是自觉钻研科学的时代，在精神领域中也很遗憾缺乏真正的志趣。这300年里，在一切事物中占主导的是美和享乐。教皇虽然暴跳如雷地反对一些臣民的异端教旨，可是只要这些反叛者健谈，懂一点印刷和建筑学，他倒也十分乐于邀请他们共进晚餐。美德的热情鼓吹者（如萨瓦纳罗拉）和不可知论者冒有同样大的危险，年轻的不可知论者很聪明，用诗歌和散文抨击了基督信仰的基本观点，而且言辞激烈，绝不是和风细雨。

人们表露的是对生活的新向往，但是这里面却无疑蕴藏着一种潜在的不满——反对现存的社会秩序和拥有无上权力的教会对人类理性发展的束缚。

薄伽丘和伊拉斯谟之间隔了近两个世纪的时间。在这200年里，抄写匠和印刷商从未清闲过。除教会自己出版的图书外，所有重要的著作几乎无一不间接地暗示，由于野蛮入侵者造成的混乱局面取代了希腊和罗马的古代文明，西方社会落入了无知的僧侣掌管之下，世界便陷入了极为悲惨的灾难中。

find an important piece of work which did not contain some indirect reference to the sad plight into which the world had fallen when the ancient civilizations of Greece and Rome had beer superseded by the anarchy of the barbarian invaders and western society was placed under the tutelage of ignorant monks.

The contemporaries of Machiavelli and Lorenzo de' Medici were not particularly interested in ethics. They were practical men who made the best of a practical world. Outwardly they remained at peace with the Church because it was a powerful and far-reaching organization which was capable of doing them great harm and they never consciously took part in any of the several attempts at reform or questioned the institutions under which they lived.

But their insatiable curiosity concerning old facts,their continual search after new emotions,the very instability of their restless minds,caused a world which had been brought up in the conviction"We know"to ask the question"Do we really know?"

And that is a greater claim to the gratitude of all future generations than the collected sonnets of Petrarch or the assembled works of Raffael.

马基雅维里和洛伦佐·美第奇的同代人对伦理学并不很感兴趣。他们讲究实际，最会利用现实世界。他们表示要与教会和平共处，因为它的组织强大，魔爪甚长，会带来很大害处，所以他们从来不会有意识地参加改革的尝试，或对质疑管辖他们的制度。

但是对过去的事情，他们的求索之心总得不到满足，他们不断追求新的刺激，思想活跃极不安分。人们在这个世界上从小就坚信“我们知道”，但是从这时起，人们提出了这样的问题：“我们真的知道吗？”

这要比彼特拉克的十四行诗集和拉斐尔的画集更值得后世纪念。

CHAPTER XII THE REFORMATION

Modern psychology has taught us several useful things about ourselves. One of them is the fact that we rarely do anything actuated by one single motive. Whether we give a million dollars for a new university or refuse a nickel to a hungry tramp;whether we proclaim that the true life of intellectual freedom can only be lived abroad or vow that we will never again leave the shores of America;whether we insist upon calling black white or white black,there are always a number of divergent reasons which have caused us to make our decision,and way down deep in our hearts we know this to be true. But as we would cut a sorry figure with the world in general if we should ever dare to be quite honest with ourselves or our neighbors,we instinctively choose the most respectable and deserving among our many motives,brush it up a bit for public consumption and then expose it for all the world to behold as"the reason why we did so and so."

But whereas it has been repeatedly demonstrated that it is quite possible to fool most of the people most of the time,no one has as yet discovered a method by which the average individual can fool himself for more than a few minutes.

We are all of us familiar with this most embarrassing truth and therefore ever since the beginning of civilization people have tacitly agreed with each other that this should never under any circumstances be referred to in public.

What we think in private,that is our own business. As long as we maintain an outward air of respectability,we are perfectly satisfied with ourselves and merrily act upon the

第12章 宗教改革

现代心理学教会了我们一些有益于自身的东西，其中之一就是我们不会出于某一单个动机而去做一件事情。不论是向一所新建大学捐100万美元，还是拒绝给饥饿的流浪汉一个铜板；不论是叫嚷着国外才有真正理智自主的生活，还是发誓说永不再离开美国海岸；不论我们坚持把黑称作白，还是把白称作黑，总之是有一连串相互交错的理由促使我们作出决定的，这些理由深植心底，对此我们心知肚明。但是，假如我们勇于诚实地面对自己和周围人，我们就可能大体勾勒出一个在世上颇为可怜的形象。由此在众多动机当中，我们本能地选择出最体面、最值得钦佩的理由，刻意修饰一番以迎合公众心理，然后公之于众，坚称“这就是我们所作所为的理由”。

但是事实告诉我们，愚弄大多数人是可能的，但至今也没人能发明一种方法，让一个正常人欺骗自己，哪怕只有几分钟。

我们对这条最令人尴尬的真相谙熟于心，因此自从文明开始以来，人们便心照不宣地彼此达成默契，无论在怎样的情形下，决不能在公共场合戳穿它。

我们私下里怎样想，那是我们自己的事情。只要在外表上始终保持一副冠冕堂皇的外表，我们就会自我感觉良好，心甘情愿地按准则办事：“你相信我的鬼话，

principle"You believe my fibs and I will believe yours."

Nature,which has no manners,is the one great exception to this generous rule of conduct. As a result,nature is rarely allowed to enter the sacred portals of civilized society. And as history thus far has been a pastime of the few,the poor muse known as Clio has led a very dull life,especially when we compare it to the career of many of her less respectable sisters who have been allowed to dance and sing and have been invited to every party ever since the beginning of time. This of course has been a source of great annoyance to poor Clio and repeatedly in her own subtle way she has managed to get her revenge.

A perfectly human trait,this,but a very dangerous one and oftentimes very expensive in the matter of human lives and property.

For whenever the old lady undertakes to show us that systematic lying,continued during the course of centuries,will eventually play hob with the peace and happiness of the entire world,our planet is at once enveloped in the smoke of a thousand batteries,Regiments of cavalry begin to dash hither and yon and interminable rows of foot soldiers commence to crawl slowly across the landscape. And ere all these people have been safely returned to their respective homes or cemeteries,whole countries have been laid bare and innumerable exchequers have been drained down to the last kopek.

Very slowly,as I have said before,it is beginning to dawn upon the members of our guild that history is a science as well as an art and is therefore subject to certain of the immutable laws of nature which thus far have only been respected in chemical laboratories and astronomical observatories. And as a result we are now doing some very useful scientific house-cleaning which will be of inestimable benefit to all coming generations.

Which brings me at last to the subject mentioned at the head of this chapter,to wit:the Reformation.

我也相信你的。"

而大自然由于没有礼仪形态，它是这种仁慈法则中绝无仅有的一个例外，因而它很少被允许进入文明社会的神圣殿堂。由于历史历来就是少数人的消遣之物，这让可怜的克利俄女神生活得很是单调，尤其当我们拿她的职业与其不起眼的姐妹们比较时更是如此。她们可以唱歌跳舞，参加有史以来的每场聚会，这自然都让可怜的克利俄郁积于心，于是她间或采用一些隐蔽的方法来实施报复。

报复，心态是人类的禀赋天性，极具危险性，能造成人身和财产的巨大损失。

每当这个老妇人向我们展示数百年传承下来的那个自成体系的谎言时，邪恶精灵终将扰乱全世界的幸福和安宁，我们的星球也会随之笼罩在四起的狼烟之中。骑兵团开始横冲直撞，漫无边际的步兵部队缓慢地行进在阵地上。而当这些人最后回归到自己的家园或墓地时，有多少国家都变得满目疮痍，不计其数的金山银海花到最后也只剩下一个戈比。

所以，我的同行们开始意识到，历史既是艺术，也是科学，因而它听命于固有的自然法则，而这种法则迄今为止却只在化学实验室和天文台上受到尊重。于是，我们开始进行值得称道的科学园地大扫除，这将给未来的子孙带来无可估量的好处。

说到这里，才终于把我引到本章的主题，即宗教改革。

前不久，仍然只有两种观点来支持这场社会和精神领域的大变革，要么全盘肯定，要么全盘否定。

Until not so very long ago there were only two opinions regarding this great social and spiritual upheaval. It was either wholly good or wholly bad.

According to the adherents of the former opinion it had been the result of a sudden outbreak of religious zeal on the part of a number of noble theologians who,profoundly shocked by the wickedness and the venality of the papal super-state,had established a separate church of their own where the true faith was to be henceforward taught to those who were seriously trying to be true Christians.

Those who had remained faithful to Rome were less enthusiastic.

The Reformation,according to the scholars from beyond the Alps,was the result of a damnable and most reprehensible conspiracy on the part of a number of despicable princes who wanted to get unmarried and who besides hoped to acquire the possessions which had formerly belonged to their Holy Mother the Church.

As usual,both sides were right and both sides were wrong.

The Reformation was the work of all sorts of people with all sorts of motives. And it is only within very recent times that we have begun to realize how religious discontent played only a minor rôle in this great upheaval and that it was really an unavoidable social and economic revolution with a slightly theological background.

Of course it is much easier to teach our children that good Prince Philip was a very enlightened ruler who took a profound personal interest in the reformed doctrines,than to explain to them the complicated machinations of an unscrupulous politician who willingly accepted the help of the infidel Turks in his warfare upon other Christians. In consequence whereof we Protestants have for hundreds of years made a magnanimous hero out of an ambitious young

■ 抗议

前一种观点的支持者认为，这是一场宗教狂热的大爆发，一些品行高尚的神学人员，在震怒于教会上层的龌龊与腐败前提下，建立起专门属于自己的独立教堂，在那里向真正希望成为基督徒的人传授真正的信仰。

依然效忠于罗马的人并不如此热血沸腾。

依据那些来自阿尔卑斯山区域之外学者的观点，宗教改革是一场应该受到诅咒和谴责的阴谋，它的始作俑者是些令人鄙视的王子皇孙，他们要么想保持独身，要么觑视那些原本属于教会圣母的财产。

对此，通常的观点是，双方都是对的，双方又都是错的。

这场宗教改革是在不同动机驱使下，由各色人等共同完成的作品。直到最近人们才开始明白，宗教不满在这场大动乱中无足轻重，它实际上是一场不可避免的社会经济变革，神学的因素微乎其微。

如果我们教导子孙说，菲利浦王子是个开明的统治者，对改革教规深感兴趣，这比告诉孩子们说他是一个诡计多端、肆无忌惮的政客容易多了。在与其他基督徒的纷争当中，他竟然接受了土耳其异教徒的援助。于是几百年来，新教徒们便把一

landgrave who hoped to see the house of Hesse play the rôle thus far played by the rival house of Hapsburg.

On the other hand it is so much simpler to turn Pope Clement into a loving shepherd who wasted the last remnants of his declining strength trying to prevent his flocks from following false leaders,than to depict him as a typical prince of the house of Medici who regarded the Reformation as an unseemly brawl of drunken German monks and used the power of the Church to further the interests of his own Italian fatherland,that we need feel no surprise if such a fabulous figure smiles at us from the pages of most Catholic text-books.

But while that sort of history may be necessary in Europe,we fortunate settlers in a new world are under no obligation to persist in the errors of our continental ancestors and are at liberty to draw a few conclusions of our own.

Just because Philip of Hesse,the great friend and supporter of Luther,was a man dominated by an enormous political ambition,it does not necessarily follow that he was insincere in his religious convictions.

By no means.

When he put his name to the famous“Protest”of the year 1529,he knew as well as his fellow signers that the were about to“expose themselves to the violence of a terrible storm,”and might end their lives on the scaffold.

If he had not been a man of extraordinary courage,he would never have undertaken to play the rôle he actually played.

But the point I am trying to make is this:that it is exceedingly difficult,yes,almost impossible,to judge an historical character (or for that matter,any of our immediate neighbors) without a profound knowledge of all the many motives which have inspired him to do what he has done or forced him to omit doing what he has omitted to do.

个野心勃勃的伯爵粉饰成为宽宏大量的英雄；而他真正想要的，却是黑森家族取代自古以来便掌权的宿敌哈布斯堡家族。

另一方面，如果把主教克莱芒打扮成可爱的牧羊人，他风烛残年之际还要把自己所剩无几的气力都用在保护羊群不跟错头羊而误入歧途，这要比把他描写成典型的美第奇家族的王子更易于理解，该家族把宗教改革视为一群烂醉如泥的德国僧侣不光彩的闹剧，并运用教会力量扩大祖国意大利的利益。如果我们在天主教课本里看到这个微笑着的神奇人物，不必大惊小怪。

在欧洲如此记载历史可能是必要的，不过我们这些在新大陆定居的幸运者，没必要坚守欧洲大陆先祖的错误，应该理智地得出我们的结论。

不要因为黑森的菲利浦王子——路德的挚友和同盟，是个拥有巨大政治野心的人，就得出他对自己的宗教信仰不虔诚的论断。

事实绝非如此。

当他在1529年著名的《抗议》书上签字时，他和其他署名的人都明白，他们会“将自己暴露在暴风骤雨之中”，并有可能为此命丧断头台。

如果他不是个具有非凡勇气的人，就不可能发挥他实际上已经发挥了的作用。

不过我要指出的是，判断一个历史人物相当困难，几乎是难以企及的（或与此类似的情况，比如判断我们的一个近邻），除非我们对所有动机有深入了解：是什么激励他采取行动，又是什么迫使他止步不前的。

法国有句谚语：“了解一切即宽恕一切。”这似乎是个过于简化的解决办法。

The French have a proverb that"to know everything is to forgive everything."That seems too easy a solution. I would like to offer an amendment and change it as follows:"To know everything is to understand everything."We can leave the business of pardoning to the good Lord who ages ago reserved that right to himself.

Meanwhile we ourselves can humbly try to"understand"and that is more than enough for our limited human ability.

And now let me return to the Reformation,which started me upon this slight detour.

As far as I"understand"that movement,it was primarily a manifestation of a new spirit which had been born as a result of the economic and political development of the last three centuries and which came to be known as"nationalism"and which therefore was the sworn enemy of that foreign super-state into which all European countries had been forced during the course of the last five centuries.

Without the common denominator of some such grievance,it would never have been possible to unite Germans and Finns and Danes and Swedes and Frenchmen and Englishmen and Norsemen into a single cohesive party,strong enough to batter down the walls of the prison in which they had been held for such a long time.

If all these heterogeneous and mutually envious elements had not been temporarily bound together by one great ideal,far surpassing their own private grudges and aspirations,the Reformation could never have succeeded.

It would have degenerated into a series of small local uprisings,easily suppressed by a regiment of mercenaries and half a dozen energetic inquisitors.

The leaders would have suffered the fate of Huss. Their followers would have been killed as the little groups of Waldenses and Albigenses had been slaughtered before them. And the Papal Monarchy would have scored another easy triumph,followed by an era of

我想修改一下，变成“了解一切即理解一切”。还是把宽恕的权力留给那个善良的主吧，他在几个世纪之前就将这个权力留给了自己。

与此同时，对具备有限能力的人类来讲，彼此间能试着谦卑地去“理解”，就已经足够了。

现在还是回到宗教改革上来，开头的话题扯远了。

据我对这场运动的“理解”，它主要是过去300年间政治经济发展所引发的新思想的一种体现，被誉为“民族主义”，因而它与那个外来的国上之国（天主教廷）是不共戴天的敌人。在过去可恶的500年间，欧洲各国都被这个压迫势力所驱使。

要是没有同仇敌忾，就无法将德国人、芬兰人、丹麦人、瑞典人、法国人、英国人和挪威人紧密地联系在一起，就不可能形成足够的力量，来摧毁长期禁锢人类的铁壁铜墙。

如果没有一个伟大的理想，将这些各自为政、相互敌视的成员们暂时组织在一切，并凌驾于他们各自的吝啬和热望之上，宗教改革就不可能取得成功。

那样，宗教改革就会蜕变为一系列小规模的地方起义，只要一支雇佣军团和几个精力旺盛的宗教法官就可以轻而易举地把它们镇压下去。

宗教改革领袖便会重蹈胡斯的覆辙，他们的追随者们会像沃尔多派那样遭到清理，也会像阿尔比派那样遭到屠戮。教会王朝又会记录下一次易如反掌的胜利，随即就会出现一段恐怖统治时期，陪伴着那些犯有“违背教义”罪行的人。

Schrecklichkeit among those guilty of a"breach of discipline."

Even so,the great movement for reform only succeeded by the smallest of all possible margins. And as soon as the victory had been won and the menace which had threatened the existence of all the rebels had been removed,the Protestant camp was dissolved into an infinitesimal number of small hostile groups who tried on a greatly diminished scale to repeat all the errors of which their enemies had been guilty in the heyday of their power.

A French abbé (whose name I have unfortunately forgotten,but a very wise fellow) once said that we must learn to love humanity in spite of itself.

To look back from the safe distance of almost four centuries upon this era of great hope and even greater disappointment,to think of the sublime courage of so many men and women who wasted their lives on the scaffold and on the field of battle for an ideal that was never to be realized,to contemplate the sacrifice made by millions of obscure citizens for the things they held to be holy and then to remember the utter failure of the Protestant rebellion as a movement towards a more liberal and more intelligent world,is to put one's charity to a most severe test.

For Protestantism,if the truth must be told,took away from this world many things that were good and noble and beautiful and it added a great many others that were narrow and hateful and graceless. And instead of making the history of the human race simpler and more harmonious,it made it more complicated and less orderly. All that,however,was not so much the fault of the Reformation as of certain inherent weaknesses in the mental habits of most people.

They refuse to be hurried.

They cannot possibly keep up with the pace set by their leaders.

They are not lacking in good will. Eventually they will all cross the bridge that leads

即便如此，这场规模宏大的改革运动还是成功得极为侥幸。一旦胜利到手，一旦危及反抗者生命的威胁解除之后，清教徒的阵营便瓦解成无数个敌对的小山头，在各自大大缩小了的范围内，重复自己的敌人在鼎盛时期所犯下的所有罪行。

一位法国主教（很遗憾我把他的名字忘记了，但他是个颇具智慧的人）曾经说过，我们必须学会爱我们的同类，尽管人类有诸多缺点。

隔着近400年的距离，回首这个充满无数希望和失望的年代，去想象那无数男女的勇者之光，他们为了不可实现的理想，在绞刑架上捐躯，在战场上厮杀；默想那为了坚持神圣的事业而牺牲的百万民众；追忆那些为了一个更加自由、理性的世界而彻底失败了的清教徒反抗运动，这些所想所见，都会令人们的博爱之心经受到异乎寻常的考验。

如果一定要披露真相，那就是清教徒主义剥夺了这个世界上许多慷慨、高尚和美丽的东西，加进了太多狭隘、可恶和粗陋的成分。它不是使人类社会更加简约和谐，而是使它愈加繁杂无序。不过，与其说这是宗教改革的过错，倒不如说是由大多数人本身具有的弱点造成的。

他们拒绝仓促行事。

他们跟不上领导者设定的步伐。

他们并不缺乏善良，他们终将跨越通往新世界的桥梁。但是他们要选择自认为最佳的时机，而且尽其所能地携带祖先遗留下来的各种传说。

宗教改革原想在基督徒和上帝之间建立一种全新的关系，摈除过去的一切偏见

into the newly discovered territory. But they will do so in their own good time and bringing with them as much of the ancestral furniture as they can possibly carry.

As a result the Great Reform,which was to establish an entirely new relationship between the individual Christian and his God,which was to do away with all the prejudices and all the corruptions of a bygone era,became so thoroughly cluttered up with the medieval baggage of its trusted followers that it could move neither forward nor backward and soon looked for all the world like a replica of that papal establishment which it held in such great abhorrence.

For that is the great tragedy of the Protestant rebellion. It could not rise above the mean average of intelligence of the majority of its adherents.

And as a result the people of western and northern Europe did not progress as much as might have been expected.

Instead of a man who was supposed to be infallible,the Reformation gave the world a book which was held to be infallible.

Instead of one potentate who ruled supreme,there arose a thousand and one little potentates,each one of whom in his own way tried to rule supreme.

Instead of dividing all Christendom into two well defined halves,the ins and the outs,the faithful and the heretics,it created endless little groups of dissenters who had nothing in common but a most intense hatred for all those who failed to share their own opinions. Instead of establishing a reign of tolerance,it followed the example of the early Church and as soon as it had attained power and was firmly entrenched behind numberless catechisms,creeds and confessions,it declared bitter warfare upon those who dared to disagree with the officially established doctrines of the community in which they happened to live.

All this was,no doubt,most regrettable.

和腐败，可是其追随者的头脑完全被中世纪的包袱弄得乱七八糟，进退维谷，于是很快便发展成一个对它曾经深恶痛绝的教会组织相差无几的翻版。

万能的监狱

这便是清教徒起义的悲剧之所在。它没能从大多数支持者的平庸心智中摆脱出来。

结果，西欧和北欧并没有如料想的那样取得长足进展。

宗教改革未能产生出所谓完美无瑕的人，却给世界提供了一本被认为是毫无瑕疵的书；宗教改革没能产生一个无可企及的霸主，而是涌现出无数个各自为政的小头领，他们在自己管辖的范围内指点江山；宗教改革没能精心地把基督世界一分为二，一半界内一半界外，一半正统一半异端，而是创造出无数个持不同政见的小团体，彼此毫无共同之处，对所有与自己意见相左的人愤恨不已；宗教改革没能建立起一个更加宽容的统治政策，而是效法早期教会的范例，一旦权力到手，便紧紧地蜷缩在不计其数的宗教对答手册、教义和教规之后，并对那些胆敢反对所辖教区法定教义的人发动残酷

But it was unavoidable in view of the mental development of the sixteenth and seventeenth centuries.

To describe the courage of leaders like Luther and Calvin,there exists only one word,and rather a terrible word,"colossal."

A simple Dominican monk,a professor in a little tidewater college somewhere in the backwoods of the German hinterland,who boldly burns a Papal Bull and hammers his own rebellious opinions to the door of a church;a sickly French scholar who turns a small Swiss town into a fortress which successfully defies the whole power of the papacy;such men present us with examples of fortitude so unique that the modern world can offer no adequate comparison.

That these bold rebels soon found friends and supporters,friends with a purpose of their own and supporters who hoped to fish successfully in troubled waters,all this is neither here nor there.

When these men began to gamble with their lives for the sake of their conscience,they could not foresee that this would happen and that most of the nations of the north would eventually enlist under their banners.

But once they had been thrown into this maelstrom of their own making,they were obliged to go whither the current carried them.

Soon the mere question of keeping themselves above water took all of their strength. In far away Rome the Pope had at last learned that this contemptible disturbance was something more serious than a personal quarrel between a few Dominican and Augustinian friars,and an intrigue on the part of a former French chaplain. To the great joy of his many creditors,he temporarily ceased building his pet cathedral and called together a council of war. The papal bulls and excommunications flew fast and furiously. Imperial armies began

的战争。

所有这一切，毫无疑问，实在是太令人遗憾了。

但是考虑到16和17世纪社会发展的水平，这一切又是无法避免的。

要想形容像路德和加尔文这样的领导者的勇气，只有一个词，而且还是一个相当可怕的词：望而生畏。

一个是普通的多明我会的僧侣、一个位于德国边远落后地区一所滨海大学的教授，他大胆焚烧了一份教皇的训谕，用自己的叛逆思想敲击教会的大门；另一个是体弱多病的法国人，他把瑞士的一座小镇变成了堡垒，颇有成效地公然与教皇势力对抗。这样的人提供的有关"刚毅"的事例是如此卓尔不群，以至于当今世界找不到可与之匹敌的例证。

这些勇敢的造反者很快找到了盟友和支持者，但盟友们心怀叵测，支持者们浑水摸鱼，不过这些无关紧要。

当造反者拼出性命来为自己的良知一搏时，并没有预见到会天遂人愿，也没有料到北方大部分民族最终会云集到自己的旗帜之下。

但是他们一旦卷入自己掀起的巨大漩涡之后，也就不得不随波逐流了。

不久，仅仅为了让自己保持在水面上这样的小问题，就耗费了他们的全部力气。罗马教皇在千里之外终于了解到，这场卑鄙的动乱要比多明我会和奥古斯丁教派僧侣之间的争吵严重得多，这是法国牧师的一场阴谋。为了赢得众多资助人的欢心，教皇暂停了自己钟爱的大教堂的建设，召集成立了战事委员会。教皇的训谕和

to move. And the leaders of the rebellion,with their backs against the wall,were forced to stand and fight.

It was not the first time in history that great men in the midst of a desperate conflict lost their sense of proportion. The same Luther who at one time proclaims that it is“against the Holy Spirit to burn heretics,”a few years later goes into such a tantrum of hate when he thinks of the wickedness of those Germans and Dutchmen who have a leaning towards the ideas of the Anabaptists,that he seems to have lost his reason.

The intrepid reformer who begins his career by insisting that we must not force our own system of logic upon God,ends his days by burning an opponent whose power of reasoning was undoubtedly superior to his own.

The heretic of today becomes the arch-enemy of all dissenters of tomorrow.

And with all their talk of a new era in which the dawn has at last followed upon the dark,both Calvin and Luther remained faithful sons of the Middle Ages as long as they lived.

Tolerance did not and could not possibly show itself to them in the light of a virtue. As long as they themselves were outcasts,they were willing to invoke the divine right of freedom of conscience that they might use it as an argument against their enemies. Once the battle was won,this trusted weapon was carefully deposited in a corner of the Protestant junk-room,already cluttered with so many other good intentions that had been discarded as unpractical. There it lay,forgotten and neglected,until a great many years later,when it was discovered behind a trunk full of old sermons. But the people who picked it up,scraped off the rust and once more carried it into battle were of a different nature from those who had fought the good fight in the early days of the sixteenth century.

And yet,the Protestant revolution contributed greatly to the cause of tolerance. Not

教会驱逐令往来穿梭，十万火急。帝国的军队开拔了。造反的领导者们已无路可退，只能背水一战。

历史上不止一次地出现过，了不起的伟人在孤注一掷的争斗中会丧失公允的判断力。同一个路德，他曾经大声疾呼“烧死异教徒有悖圣意”，可几年之后，一想起邪恶的德国人和荷兰人竟然倾向于再洗礼派的思想，便恨得咬牙切齿，几乎到了失去理智的程度。

这个无畏的改革者在创业之初还坚持说，我们不应把自己的逻辑体系强加给上帝，最终却以烧死敌人的方式走向末路，因为这个敌人的智力明显胜其一筹。

今日的异教徒，他日变成了所有持不同政见者的公敌。

他们仍在喋喋不休地讨论着新纪元，那时曙光会终于降落在大地之上，然而加尔文和路德二人毕生都是中世纪传统的忠诚子孙。

在他们眼里，宽容从来不会也不可能闪烁出美德的光辉。他们遭受排挤的时候，还愿意向自由的良知祈求神圣的权力，把它作为与敌论战的武器。可一旦战胜了，这个深受信赖的武器便被小心翼翼地贮存在清教徒废品间的墙角，和其他诸多好想法挤一起，以不切实际的理由将其废弃。它闲置在那儿，被人遗忘，被人忽略，直到许多年后，它才再次从盛满旧说教的木箱子后面被发现。人们捡起它，擦去尘污，又一次带着它走向战场，但这与16世纪初期人们为之奋战的性质截然不同，其本质已经改变。

不过，清教徒革命还是为宽容事业做出了巨大贡献。这倒不是通过革命直接获

through what it accomplished directly. In that field the gain was small indeed. But indirectly the results of the Reformation were all on the side of progress.

In the first place,it made people familiar with the Bible. The Church had never positively forbidden people to read the Bible,but neither had it encouraged the study of the sacred book by ordinary laymen. Now at last every honest baker and candlestick maker could own a copy of the holy work;could peruse it in the privacy of his workshop and could draw his own conclusions without running the risk of being burned at the stake.

Familiarity is apt to kill those sentiments of awe and fear which we feel before the mysteries of the unknown. During the first two hundred years which followed immediately upon the Reformation,pious Protestants believed everything they read in the Old Testament from Balaam's ass to Jonah's whale. And those who dared to question a single comma (the“inspired”vowel-points of learned Abraham Colovius!) knew better than to let their sceptical tittering be heard by the community at large. Not because they were afraid any longer of the Inquisition,but Protestant pastors could upon occasion make a man's life exceedingly unpleasant and the economic consequences of a public ministerial censure were often very serious,not to say disastrous.

■ 两个监狱貌离神合

Gradually however this eternally repeated study of a book which was really the national history of a small nation of shepherds and traders was to bear results which Luther and Calvin and the other reformers had never foreseen.

If they had,I am certain they would have shared the Church's dislike of Hebrew and

取的，革命战场上的所得寥寥无几。宗教改革的成果全都间接地促进了各个方面的进步。

首先，它使人们了解了《圣经》。教会从未主动禁止人们阅读《圣经》，但也从未鼓励普通人研究这本神圣的书籍。如今每个诚实的面包师和烛台匠终于可以拥有一本自己的圣书了，他可以在工棚里独自研究它，也可以得出自己的结论，不必担忧会冒着被烧死在火刑柱上的风险。

这种阅读有助于抵消人们神奇事物面前在因一无所知所产生的敬畏和恐慌。在紧随宗教改革之后的两百年里，虔诚的清教徒相信自己从《旧约》中读到的一切，包括从巴兰的驴子到约拿的鲸鱼。如果什么人敢质疑哪怕是一个逗号（它是博学的阿伯拉罕·科洛威斯“受到神启后”写出来的），最好也别让大家听到他们怀疑的窃笑声。这倒不是因为他们仍然害怕宗教法庭，而是因为新教牧师有时会令他们的生活相当难堪，他们一个公开责难所导致的经济后果，即使不是灭顶之灾，也是相当惨重的。

这本被广泛阅读的书籍，实际上是由牧民和商人组成的一个小国的民族史，但是经过反复研读，它却使人收获了丰硕的成果，这恐怕是路德、加尔文以及其他改革者始料未及的。

假如他们预见到了，我肯定他们一定和教会一样讨厌希伯来语和希腊语，会

Greek and would have kept the scriptures carefully out of the hands of the uninitiated. For in the end,an increasing number of serious students began to appreciate the Old Testament as a singularly interesting book,but containing such dreadful and bloodcurdling tales of cruelty,greed and murder that it could not possibly have been inspired and must,by the very nature of its contents,be the product of a people who had still lived in a state of semi-barbarism.

After that,of course,it was impossible for many people to regard the Bible as the only font of all true wisdom. And once this obstacle to free speculation had been removed,the current of scientific investigation,dammed up for almost a thousand years,began to flow in its natural channel and the interrupted labors of the old Greek and Roman philosophers were picked up where they had been left off twenty centuries before.

And in the second place,and this is even more important from the point of view of tolerance,the Reformation delivered northern and western Europe from the dictatorship of a power which under the guise of a religious organization had been in reality nothing but a spiritual and highly despotic continuation of the Roman Empire.

With these statements,our Catholic readers will hardly agree. But they too have reason to be grateful to a movement which was not only unavoidable,but which was to render a most salutary service to their own faith. For,thrown upon her own resources,the Church made an heroic effort to rid herself of those abuses which had made her once sacred name a byword for rapacity and tyranny.

And she succeeded most brilliantly.

After the middle of the sixteenth century,no more Borgias were tolerated in the Vatican. The Popes as ever before continued to be Italians. A deflection from this rule was practically impossible,as the Roman proletariat would have turned the city upside down

小心谨慎地不使《圣经》落入尚未接触此书的人手里。到头来，越来越多的治学严谨的学生只是把《圣经》当作一本饶有兴趣却又晦涩难懂的书来欣赏，只是里面充斥了太多令人胆战心惊、毛骨悚然的残忍、贪婪和谋杀，不太可能是在神启下写成的，而从所包含内容的实质看，肯定是仍处于半野蛮状态下的作品。

自此以后，大多数人显然不会再把《圣经》看作唯一智慧的源泉。自由思考的障碍一旦扫除，堵塞近千年的科学探索的潮流便沿着自然形成的渠道流淌开来，一度中断的古希腊和古罗马哲学家的成果又从20个世纪前失落的地方被重新捡了回来。

其次，从宽容的角度来看，还有一个更为重要的缘由，那就是宗教改革把西欧和北欧从权力专制的桎梏中解救出来，这种专制特权披着宗教组织的外衣，事实上却是罗马帝国专制思想统治的延续。

天主教的读者们很难苟同上述观点。但他们同样有理由感怀于这场运动，因为它不仅是无法避免的，而且还给他们的信仰带来了不少好处。在所能得到的援助的帮助下，教会采取了英雄般的壮举来清除累积在自己身上的诟病，这些诟病使它的圣名成为贪婪和暴政的代名词。

她取得了无比辉煌的成就。

16世纪中叶以后，梵蒂冈不再容忍控制教会的波尔吉亚家族了。诚然，教皇和从前一样，仍然都是意大利人，要改变这种规矩实际上是不可能的，因为如果被授权挑选教皇的大主教们挑了一个德国人、法国人或其他任何国家的外籍人，意大利

if the cardinals entrusted with the election of a new pontiff had chosen a German or a Frenchman or any other foreigner.

The new pontiffs,however,were selected with great care and only candidates of the highest character could hope to be considered. And these new masters,faithfully aided by their devoted Jesuit auxiliaries,began a thorough house-cleaning.

The sale of indulgences came to an end.

Monastic orders were enjoined to study (and henceforth to obey) the rules laid down by their founders.

Mendicant friars disappeared from the streets of civilized cities.

And the general spiritual indifference of the Renaissance was replaced by an eager zeal for holy and useful lives spent in good deeds and in humble service towards those unfortunate people who were not strong enough to carry the burden of existence by themselves.

Even so,the greater part of the territory which had been lost was never regained. Speaking with a certain geographical freedom,the northern half of Europe remained Protestant,while the southern half stayed Catholic.

But when we translate the result of the Reformation into the language of pictures,the actual changes which took place in Europe become more clearly revealed.

During the Middle Ages there had been one universal spiritual and intellectual prison-house.

The Protestant rebellion had ruined the old building and out of part of the available material it had constructed a jail of its own.

呼吸的空间

的无产者就会把这座城市闹得天翻地覆。

新教皇的选举万分慎重，只有最德高望重的人才有希望当选。而这些新主人会在忠诚的耶稣会会士辅佐下，开始彻底的大清洗。

免罪符的买卖寿终正寝了。

修道院的秩序重新界定在研究法条上（也就是服从），这些法条是由修道院创始人定下的规矩。

在文明化的城市里，行乞僧人的踪影不见了。

取代普通民众对文艺复兴冷漠态度的，是一种对神圣和有意义生活的狂热追求，人们广结善缘，对那些不幸的、无力承担生活重压的人给予谦卑的关怀。

即使如此，已失去的大片疆土还是不可能收回来了。按地理疆界划分，北欧信奉了新教，南欧保住了天主教。

不过，如果我们把宗教改革的成果转化成图画来表述，那么欧洲实际发生的变化就一目了然。

中世纪，有一座集精神、智力于一体的监狱。

清教徒造反摧毁了那座旧建筑，并用现成的材料为自己建起了羁押所。

After the year 1517 there are therefore two dungeons,one reserved exclusively for the Catholics,the other for the Protestants.

At least that had been the original plan.

But the Protestants,who did not have the advantage of centuries of training along the lines of persecution and repression,failed to make their lockup dissenter-proof.

Through windows and chimneys and cellar-doors a large number of the unruly inmates escaped.

Ere long the entire building was a wreck.

At night the miscreants came and took away whole cartloads of stones and beams and iron bars which they used the next morning to build a little fortress of their own. But although this had the outward appearance of that original jail,constructed a thousand years before by Gregory the Great and Innocent III,it lacked the necessary inner strength.

No sooner was it ready for occupancy,no sooner had a new set of rules and regulations been posted upon the gates,than a wholesale walk-out occurred among the disgruntled trustees. As their keepers,now called ministers,had been deprived of the old methods of discipline (excommunication,torture,execution,confiscation and exile) they were absolutely helpless before this determined mob and were forced to stand by and look on while the rebels put up such a stockade as pleased their own theological preferences and proclaimed such new doctrines as happened to suit their temporary convictions.

This process was repeated so often that finally there developed a sort of spiritual no-man's-land between the different lockups where curious souls could roam at random and where honest people could think whatever they pleased without hindrance or molestation.

And this is the great service which Protestantism rendered to the cause of tolerance.

It reëstablished the dignity of the individual man.

1517年以后，出现了两座地牢，一座专为天主教徒准备，另一座是为清教徒准备的。

至少原定的计划是如此。

可是，清教徒由于没有受过长达数世纪的关于如何进行迫害和镇压的训练，他们没能起建立一个没有反对派的禁地。

通过窗子、烟囱和地牢的大门，大批狂妄之徒逃跑了。

没过多久，整个地牢的大厦成了残垣断壁。

到了夜晚，不法之徒返回来，整车地搬走石头、大梁和铁棍，次日早晨用它们为自己建造了一座小堡垒。它表面看起来虽然与千年前格里高利教皇和英诺森三世建造的监狱没什么两样，但却缺乏必要的内在控制力。

堡垒一旦投入使用，新规章制度贴在大门口，心怀不满的信徒们便纷纷出走了。监狱的看守人，即现在的牧师，由于从未掌管过旧式的惩治办法（逐出教会、酷刑、处决、罚没财产和流放），对那些铁了心的叛乱者只好因无能为力而袖手旁观，眼见着他们建起了符合自己神学意愿的防卫场所，并宣布了一套暂时恰巧能迎合他们信仰的新教义。

这一过程如此往复，直至在不同禁地之间形成了一个精神上的“无人区”，求索的灵魂可在此期间随意徜徉，正直的人们可以在此任意遐想，没有障碍和干扰。

这就是新教给宽容事业的巨大贡献。

它重建了人类的尊严。

CHAPTER XIII ERASMUS

In the writing of every book there occurs a crisis. Sometimes it comes during the first fifty pages. Upon other occasions it does not make itself manifest until the manuscript is almost finished. Indeed,a book without a crisis is like a child that has never had the measles. There probably is something the matter with it.

The crisis in the present volume happened a few minutes ago,for I have now reached the point where the idea of a work upon the subject of tolerance in the year of grace 1925 seems quite preposterous;where all the labor spent thus far upon a preliminary study appears in the light of so much valuable time wasted;where I would like best of all to make a bonfire of Bury and Lecky and Voltaire and Montaigne and White and use the carbon copies of my own work to light the stove.

How to explain this?

There are many reasons. In the first place,there is the inevitable feeling of boredom which overtakes an author when he has been living with his topic on a very intimate footing for too long a time. In the second place,the suspicion that books of this sort will not be of the slightest practical value. And in the third place the fear that the present volume will be merely used as a quarry from which our less tolerant fellow-citizens will dig a few easy facts with which to bolster up their own bad causes.

But apart from these arguments (which hold good for most serious books) there is in the present case the almost insurmountable difficulty of"system."

第13章 伊拉斯谟

写任何一本书都会出现类似危机的争议点，有时它出现在前50页，有时却直到稿子快要结束时才显现出来。的确，如果一本书没有这个点，就如同一个孩子没出过天花。

就在几分钟前，本书的争议点出现了，因为我刚刚才意识到，在1925年围绕宽容的议题来著书立说似乎是过于荒谬了，迄今为止我用于基础研究的努力，那些宝贵的时光都白白浪费掉了。我想最好还是用布里、莱基、伏尔泰、蒙田和怀特的著作来点火，连我自己的著作一同丢进火炉里去。

该如何解释这种情形呢?

原因很多。首先，由于作者与自己所选命题过于紧密地联系，时间久了，难免会感到枯燥无味；其次，是对这类书籍毫无实用价值的担忧；再则，就是害怕那些不够宽容的人利用此书中包含的一些简单事实，作为防卫自己不光彩行径的盾牌。

可是在上述所有原因之外（多数严肃书籍所遇到的情形大体如此），这本书还存在着一个无法克服的难题，那就是“结构”问题。

一本成功的书，必须首尾相连。本书有了开头，但是怎样才能有个结尾呢?

我可以列举出无数个骇人听闻的罪行，它们表面上是以公平和正义的名义，实

A story in order to be a success must have a beginning and an end. This book has a beginning,but can it ever have an end?

What I mean is this.

I can show the terrible crimes apparently committed in the name of righteousness and justice,but really caused by intolerance.

I can depict the unhappy days upon which mankind fell when intolerance was elevated to the rank of one of the major virtues.

I can denounce and deride intolerance until my readers shout with one accord,"Down with this curse,and let us all be tolerant!"

But there is one thing I cannot do. I cannot tell how this highly desirable goal is to be reached. There are handbooks which undertake to give us instruction in everything from after-dinner speaking to ventriloquism. In an advertisement of a correspondence course last Sunday I read of no less than two hundred and forty-nine subjects which the institute guaranteed to teach to perfection in exchange for a very small gratuity. But no one thus far has offered to explain in forty (or in forty thousand) lessons"how to become tolerant."

And even history,which is supposed to hold the key to so many secrets,refuses to be of any use in this emergency.

Yes,it is possible to compose learned tomes devoted to slavery or free trade or capital punishment or the growth and development of Gothic architecture,for slavery and free trade and capital punishment and Gothic architecture are very definite and concrete things. For lack of all other material we could at least study the lives of the men and women who had been the champions of free trade and slavery and capital punishment and Gothic architecture or those who had opposed them. And from the manner in which those excellent people had approached their subjects,from their personal habits,their

际上却是不宽容的结果。

我可以描述人类所经历的痛苦的日子，那时的不宽容已经被高高悬挂在美德之列。

我可以痛斥和嘲弄不宽容，直至我的读者们异口同声地疾呼："停止咒骂吧，让我们都宽容些！"

但有一件事我办不到。我无法知道这个崇高的、理想化的目标怎样才能实现。世上有不计其数的说明指南，给我们提供有关世间万物的指导，从饭后谈资到口技的训练。在上星期天的一份函授课程广告上，我看到至少有249门课程，学院保证提供完美的教学服务，而且费用低廉。但是至今没有人提出40个（或4万个）课程来讲明白"如何做到宽容"。

即便是历史，据说它拥有许多开启秘密的钥匙，却在这个关键时刻拒绝提供任何帮助。

的确，人们可以围绕诸如奴隶、自由贸易、死刑或哥特式建筑的发展等议题形成具有学术价值的大部头著作，因为奴隶、自由贸易、死刑和哥特式建筑都是些非常明确和具体的事情。即便无佐证资料，至少我们还可以研究那些大力宣扬或大力反对自由贸易、奴隶制和哥特式建筑的男男女女的生平。从这些优秀人物讲述自己的问题的方式，从他们的个人习性、社会关系及他们的饮食爱好，甚至从他们的穿着打扮等方面，我们都能看出他们的想法，他们是积极赞同的呢，还是坚决反对的。

associations,their preferences in food and drink and tobacco,yea,from the very breeches they had worn,we could draw certain conclusions about the ideals which they had so energetically espoused or so bitterly denounced.

But there never were any professional protagonists of tolerance. Those who worked most zealously for the great cause did so incidentally. Their tolerance was a by-product. They were engaged in other pursuits. They were statesmen or writers or kings or physicians or modest artisans. In the midst of the king business or their medical practice or making steel engravings they found time to say a few good words for tolerance,but the struggle for tolerance was not the whole of their careers. They were interested in it as they may have been interested in playing chess or fiddling. And because they were part of a strangely assorted group (imagine Spinoza and Frederick the Great and Thomas Jefferson and Montaigne as boon companions!) it is almost impossible to discover that common trait of character which as a rule is to be found in all those who are engaged upon a common task,be it soldiering or plumbing or delivering the world from sin.

In such a case the writer is apt to have recourse to epigrams. Somewhere in this world there is an epigram for every dilemma. But upon this particular subject,the Bible and Shakespeare and Izaak Walton and even old Benham leave us in the lurch. Perhaps Jonathan Swift (I quote from memory) came nearest to the problem when he said that most men had just enough religion to hate their neighbors but not quite enough to love them. Unfortunately that bright remark does not quite cover our present difficulty. There have been people possessed of as much religion as any one individual could safely hold who have hated their neighbors as cordially as the best of them. There have been others who were totally devoid of the religious

■ 那些可怕的小书

可是，从来就没有出现过专职的“宽容”倡导者。积极投身于伟大事业的人们只是偶尔涉足于此。他们的宽容只是一个副产品。他们从事的是其他方面的追求。他们是些政客、作家、国王、物理学家或朴实的艺术家。在处理国王事务、行医或在刻钢板画之余，他们会抽空为宽容说上一些美誉之词，但毕竟不是他们为之奋斗的终身事业。他们对此，类似在下棋或小提琴乐器方面的兴趣。由于这是一帮很奇怪的人，（试想斯宾诺莎、腓特烈大帝、托马斯·杰斐逊、蒙田这帮人竟然是好伙伴！）要想在他们彼此性情中找到共同点，几乎是不可能的。一般来说，致力于共同事业的人会有共同特征，无论是在疆场上，还是在科研领域或拯救世界逃离罪恶的事业中。

在这种情形下，作家倾向于求助警句。任何一种困境都会在世上的某个角落找到一句相应的警句。但是针对这个特定的议题，《圣经》、莎士比亚、艾萨克·沃尔顿和老贝哈姆都不能帮助我们摆脱困境。也许乔纳森·斯威夫特（按照我的记忆）最接近于这个题目，比如他说，大多数人的宗教信仰足以让他们恨他

instinct who squandered their affection upon all the stray cats and dogs and human beings of Christendom.

No,I shall have to find an answer of my own. And upon due cogitation (but with a feeling of great uncertainty) I shall now state what I suspect to be the truth.

The men who have fought for tolerance,whatever their differences,had all of them one thing in common;their faith was tempered by doubt;they might honestly believe that they themselves were right,but they never reached the point where that suspicion hardened into an absolute conviction.

In this day and age of super-patriotism,with our enthusiastic clamoring for a hundred-percent this and a hundred-percent that,it may be well to point to the lesson taught by nature which seems to have a constitutional aversion to any such ideal of standardization.

Purely bred cats and dogs are proverbial idiots who are apt to die because no one is present to take them out of the rain. Hundred-percent pure iron has long since been discarded for the composite metal called steel. No jeweler ever undertook to do anything with hundred-percent pure gold or silver. Fiddles,to be any good,must be made of six or seven different varieties of wood. And as for a meal composed entirely of a hundred-percent mush,I thank you,no!

In short,all the most useful things in this world are compounds and I see no reason why faith should be an exception. Unless the base of our"certainty"contains a certain amount of the alloy of"doubt,"our faith will sound as tinkly as a bell made of pure silver or as harsh as a trombone made of brass.

It was a profound appreciation of this fact which set the heroes of tolerance apart from the rest of the world.

As far as personal integrity went,honesty of conviction,unselfish devotion to duty and

们的邻居，而不足以爱他们。遗憾的是，这条真知灼见没能完全涉及我们目前的困难。有些人，他所拥有的宗教信仰并不逊于任何人，对他们的邻居却极其痛恨；还有些人，全无宗教信仰的天性，却对野猫、野狗和基督世界的人类倾注了他们的真挚情怀。

不行，我必须自己找到答案。经过深思熟虑（但仍有不确切的感觉），现在我要陈述我所认定的事实真相。

大凡为宽容而战的人，不论彼此怎样不同，他们必定有一点相同，即他们的信仰要经受怀疑的考验；他们可能实实在在地认为自己是对的，但从没有达到把疑惑扭转到完全信任的程度。

这是个具有非凡爱国情怀的时代，人们满怀激情地叫嚷着要百分之百地为此，要百分之百地为彼，但是我们不妨看看大自然给予我们的教训，它对任何标准化的看法似乎有着与生俱来的反感。

纯粹依靠人工喂养的猫狗是人所共知的笨蛋，如果没人把它们从雨里抱走，它们就会死掉。百分之百的纯铁早已被弃之不用，代替它的是混合钢金属。没有一个珠宝商会用百分之百的纯金或纯银来打造首饰。一把尚好的小提琴，必须采用六七种不同材质的木料来制作。即便仅仅是一顿饭，如果百分之百都是玉米糊糊的话，不胜感谢，但实在难以下咽。

一言以蔽之，世上最有用的东西全部都是合成体，我看不出为什么信仰会例外。除非在我们“肯定”的基础里掺入了一定量的“怀疑”的合成物，否则我们的

all the other household virtues,most of these men could have passed muster before a board of Puritan Inquisitors. I would go further than that and state that at least half of them lived and died in such a way that they would now be among the saints,if their peculiar trend of conscience had not forced them to be the open and avowed enemies of that institution which has taken upon itself the exclusive right of elevating ordinary human beings to certain celestial dignities.

But fortunately they were possessed of the divine doubt.

They knew (as the Romans and the Greeks had known before them) that the problem which faced them was so vast that no one in his right senses would ever expect it to be solved. And while they might hope and pray that the road which they had taken would eventually lead them to a safe goal,they could never convince themselves that it was the only right one,that all other roads were wrong and that the enchanting by-paths which delighted the hearts of so many simple people were evil thoroughfares leading to damnation.

All this sounds contrary to the opinions expressed in most of our catechisms and our text-books on ethics. These preach the superior virtue of a world illuminated by the pure white flame of absolute faith. Perhaps so. But during those centuries when that flame was supposed to be burning at its brightest,the average rank and file of humanity cannot be said to have been either particularly happy or extraordinarily comfortable. I don't want to suggest any radical reforms,but just for a change we might try that other light,by the rays of which the brethren of the tolerant guild have been in the habit of examining the affairs of the world. If that does not prove successful,we can always go back to the system of our fathers. But if it should prove to throw an agreeable luster upon a society containing a little more kindness and forbearance,a community less beset by ugliness and greed and hatred,a good deal would have been gained and the expense,I am sure,would be quite small.

信仰之声听起来就像纯银制成的钟一样叮当作响，或像铜制的长号一样刺耳。

正是基于对上述事实的深刻理解，才使得宽容的英雄们从世上脱颖而出。

他们中的大多数人，只要人品正直、忠诚职守、无私奉献，以及具备所有其他世俗认定的美德，原本都可以通过清教徒法官的考验的。我想讲得更清楚些，如果他们特殊的感知倾向没有迫使他们成为某个组织公开宣称的敌人的话，他们当中至少有一半人（活着的或死了的）可以纳入圣人之列，而正是这个组织赋予了自己把普通人加封为圣人的特权。

幸运的是，他们拥有了神圣的“怀疑”精神。

他们知道（一如先前古希腊人、古罗马人），自己所面临的问题坚不可摧，凭借准确的感官判断，谁都不该奢望自己能够解决这个问题。他们只能希望并求助于自己所选的道路能最终把自己带到安全地带；他们从来不相信自己的选择是唯一正确的，而其余路径只是通向诅咒的罪恶之途——那是些令无数普通人为之心驰神往的岔路歧途。

所有这些听起来与《宗教问答手册》和我们伦理教科书上的观点大相径庭。它们宣扬由绝对信仰的纯洁烈焰映照出世间最为崇高的美德。但是即便在这一烈焰燃烧得最耀眼的年代里，普通民众或者说就人类整体而言，都算不上特别愉快。我并不想推荐什么激进式改革方案，只是尝试着调试一下火候，这个恰当的火候就是让宽容成为兄弟会检验世间万物的一个日常规范。如果证明不成功，我们至少能回归到长老会原有的体系当中。但是如果通过证明得知它能够放射出宜人的光彩，让这个世界多一

And after this bit of advice,offered for what it is worth,I must go back to my history.

When the last Roman was buried,the last citizen of the world (in the best and broadest sense of the word) perished. And it was a long time before society was once more placed upon such a footing of security that the old spirit of an all-encompassing humanity,which had been characteristic of the best minds of the ancient world,could safely return to this earth.

That,as we saw,happened during the Renaissance.

The revival of international commerce brought fresh capital to the poverty stricken countries of the west. New cities arose. A new class of men began to patronize the arts,to spend money upon books,to endow those universities which followed so closely in the wake of prosperity. And it was then that a few devoted adherents of the"humanities,"of those sciences which boldly had taken all mankind as their field of experiment,arose in rebellion against the narrow limitations of the old scholasticism and strayed away from the flock of the faithful who regarded their interest in the wisdom and the grammar of the ancients as a manifestation of a wicked and impure curiosity.

Among the men who were in the front ranks of this small group of pioneers,the stories of whose lives will make up the rest of this book,few deserve greater credit than that very timid soul who came to be known as Erasmus.

For timid he was,although he took part in all the great verbal encounters of his day and successfully managed to make himself the terror of his enemies,by the precision with which he handled that most deadly of all weapons,the long-range gun of humor.

Far and wide the missiles containing the mustard-gas of his wit were shot into the enemy's country. And those Erasmian bombs were of a very dangerous variety. At a first glance they looked harmless enough. There was no sputtering of a tell-tale fuse. They had the appearance of an amusing new variety of fire-cracker,but God help those who took

份仁慈和忍让，少一些丑恶、贪婪和怨恨，那我们每人的所得都会十分丰厚，而我们的付出，我敢肯定，一定是微不足道的，或者说，是我们乐于付出的。

这仅是我提出的建议，接下来我们毋回到历史话题上来。最后一个古罗马人被掩埋之时，也就是广义范畴上最后一个公民的消亡之日。人类从此要经历漫长的岁月才能重新将人类社会安置在稳固的基石上，这个基石就是远古时代的博爱精神，它体现了远古时代先进的思想特征，这个博爱精神平安返回旷日持久。

正如我们所见到的，它发生在文艺复兴时期。

国际商业的复苏为西方饱受贫困之苦的国家输入了新鲜血液。新兴城市不断崛起，新贵们开始赞助艺术，慨然购书，还向那些应运而生的大学伸出援助之手。正是在此期间，一些彻底的“博爱思想”的捍卫者，大胆地把整个人类作为科学检验的对象，高举起反对故步自封的古典经院哲学的义旗，与那些固执己见者分道扬镳，这些顽固分子把人们研究古人智慧的兴致看作是由邪恶、心地不纯的好奇心所驱使的。

在这一小部分先驱者的前列，有这么一个人，他的故事将贯穿本书的其他章节，没有人能比这个拥有温和灵魂的人更值得我们信赖，他就是伊拉斯谟。

他虽然温和，但他却投身于当时最激烈的口诛笔伐的战役之中，并且让他的敌人为之胆寒，他准确地操控最具杀伤力的武器——远程“讽喻”炮。

由他的才智填充的芥子气弹在敌国的腹地深处炸响。而且这些伊拉斯谟式的炮弹别具一格。它一眼看去似乎毫无害处。没有噼啪作响的导火索，倒更像是一种赏

them home and allowed the children to play with them. The poison was sure to get into their little minds and it was of such a persistent nature that four centuries have not sufficed to make the race immune against the effects of the drug.

It is strange that such a man should have been born in one of the dullest towns of the mudbanks which are situated along the eastern coast of the North Sea. In the fifteenth century those water soaked lands had not yet attained the glories of an independent and fabulously rich commonwealth. They formed a group of little insignificant principalities,somewhere on the outskirts of civilized society. They smelled forever of herring,their chief article of export. And if ever they attracted a visitor,it was some helpless mariner whose ship had been wrecked upon their dismal shores.

But the very horror of a childhood spent among such unpleasant surroundings may have spurred this curious infant into that fury of activity which eventually was to set him free and make him one of the best known men of his time.

From the beginning of life,everything was against him. He was an illegitimate child. The people of the Middle Ages,being on an intimate and friendly footing both with God and with nature,were a great deal more sensible about such children than we are. They were sorry. Such things ought not to occur and of course they greatly disapproved. For the rest,however,they were too simple-minded to punish a helpless creature in a cradle for a sin which most certainly was not of its own making. The irregularity of his birth certificate inconvenienced Erasmus only in so far as both his father and his mother seem to have been exceedingly muddle-headed citizens,totally incapable of handling the situation and leaving their children to the care of relatives who were either boobs or scoundrels.

These uncles and guardians had no idea of what to do with their two little wards and after the mother had died,the children never had a home of their own. First of all they were

心悦目的新式花炮，但是让上帝保佑那些把这些玩意拿回家让孩子玩的人们吧！毒气肯定会潜入幼小的心灵，具有很强的依附性，整整四个世纪的时间都不足以让人类对这种毒药产生免疫。

这样一个人，竟出生在北海东海岸一个索然无味的泥滩小镇上，着实令人费解。15世纪时，这些被水浸泡的土地还没被独立富足的共和国的光芒普照，它们只是一群无足轻重的小公国，仍处于文明社会的边缘。他们经年累月闻着鲱鱼味，因为这是他们的主要出口商品。假使他们真的吸引来一个访问者，那也只能是个走投无路的水手，他的船只在这个昏暗的海岸上触礁了。

在如此恶劣的童年环境中形成的恐惧，激发了这个孩子的好奇和抗争意识，并最终使他获得自由，成为那个时代最了不起的人物之一。

他自出生以来就命运多舛。他是个私生子。中世纪的人，由于与上帝和自然更为紧密的联系，对待他这种孩子的态度要比现今敏感得多。人们为此深感遗憾。这种事既然本不该发生，人们当然也就坚决反对。不过除此之外，人们无论头脑怎样简单，也不可能因此而惩罚一个尚在襁褓中的孩子，这显然不是孩子的过错。伊拉斯谟非常规的出生并未对他造成很大不便，这仅仅表明他的父母也许是异常糊涂之人，根本不具备控制局面的能力，只好把他们的孩子甩给亲戚们照看，而这些亲戚不是笨蛋就是流氓。

这帮叔叔和监护人不知道该怎样打发他和另外一个被监护人，于是他们的母亲一死，两个小家伙就无家可归了。他们首先被送到代芬特尔城一所有名的学校，那

sent to a famous school in Deventer,where several of the teachers belonged to the Society of the Brothers of the Common Life,but if we are to judge by the letters which Erasmus wrote later in life,these young men were only"common"in a very different sense of the word. Next the two boys were separated and the younger was taken to Gouda,where he was placed under the immediate supervision of the head-master of the Latin school,who was also one of the three guardians appointed to administer his slender inheritance. If that school in the days of Erasmus was as bad as when I visited it four centuries later,I can only feel sorry for the poor kid. And to make matters worse,the guardians by this time had wasted every penny of his money and in order to escape prosecution (for the old Dutch courts were strict upon such matters) they hurried the infant into a cloister,rushed him into holy orders and bade him be happy because"now his future was secure".

The mysterious mills of history eventually ground this terrible experience into something of great literary value. But I hate to think of the many terrible years this sensitive youngster was forced to spend in the exclusive company of the illiterate boors and thick-fingered rustics who during the end of the Middle Ages made up the population of fully half of all monasteries.

Fortunately the laxity of discipline at Steyn permitted Erasmus to spend most of his time among the Latin manuscripts which a former abbot had collected and which lay forgotten in the library. He absorbed those volumes until he finally became a walking encyclopedia of classical learning. In later years this stood him in good stead. Forever on the move,he rarely was within reach

■ 鹿特丹

儿的一些教师加入了“共同生活兄弟会”，不过如果查一下伊拉斯谟当时的信件便可以得知，这些年轻人“是非常规意义上的共同”生活。随后，两个孩子分开了，弟弟被带到了豪达镇，直接处于拉丁学校校长的监管之下，他同时还是这个孩子所拥有的微薄财产的三个被指定管理者之一。如果伊拉斯谟当时的学校像四个世纪以后我所看到的那么破败的话，我只能为这可怜的孩子感到难受。更为糟糕的是，三个监护人此时已把孩子的每一分钱都挥霍掉了，为了逃避罪责（当时的荷兰法庭对这类事情严惩不贷），他们急忙把这个孤儿送进一所修道院，把他塞入僧侣之列，还祝他幸福，因为“他的前途终归有着落了”。

历史神秘的魔轮终于把这些可怕的经历研磨出了具有伟大文学价值的东西。但想起这个敏感的年轻人在那些年里，在完全封闭的情况下，被迫与那些目不识丁和粗手大脚的人混迹在一起，我的心情就特别郁闷，中世纪末期，无论哪所修道院，其半数左右的僧侣都是由这类人等充斥着的。

幸运的是，施泰恩修道院纪律松弛，这使得伊拉斯谟能用大部分时间阅读拉丁手稿，这些手稿是前任修道院长收集但遗忘在图书馆里的。他沉浸在那些鸿篇巨制当中，直至成为活的古典百科知识全书。这对他的将来大有裨益。不停地辗转颠簸

of a reference library. But that was not necessary. He could quote from memory. Those who have ever seen the ten gigantic folios which contain his collected works,or who have managed to read through part of them (life is so short nowadays) will appreciate what a"knowledge of the classics"meant in the fifteenth century.

Of course,eventually Erasmus was able to leave his old monastery. People like him are never influenced by circumstances. They make their own circumstances and they make them out of the most unlikely material.

And the rest of his life Erasmus was a free man,searching restlessly after a spot where he might work without being disturbed by a host of admiring friends.

But not until the fateful hour when with an appeal to the"lieve God"of his childhood he allowed his soul to slip into the slumber of death,did he enjoy a moment of that"true leisure"which has always appeared as the highest good to those who have followed the footsteps of Socrates and Zeno and which so few of them have ever found.

These peregrinations have often been described and I need not repeat them here in detail. Wherever two or more men lived together in the name of true wisdom,there Erasmus was sooner or later bound to make his appearance.

He studied in Paris,where as a poor scholar he almost died of hunger and cold. He taught in Cambridge. He printed books in Basel. He tried (quite in vain) to carry a spark of enlightenment into that stronghold of orthodox bigotry,the far-famed University of Louvain. He spent much of his time in London and took the degree of Doctor of Divinity in the University of Turin. He was familiar with the Grand Canal of Venice and cursed as familiarly about the terrible roads of Zeeland as those of Lombardy. The sky,the parks,the walks and the libraries of Rome made such a profound impression upon him that even the waters of Lethe could not wash the Holy City out of his memory. He was offered a liberal

使他很少接触到图书馆。不过这倒也无妨，因为他可以从自己的记忆中检索。但凡看过汇集他著作的十大本卷宗的人，或是只读了其中一部分书稿的人（现在的生活太短促了），一定会对15世纪的所谓“古典知识”赞叹不已。

当然，伊拉斯谟最后还是离开了那所古老的修道院。像他这样的人是不会囿于环境的，他们会营造出属于自己的环境，而且所选用材质也是最不可思议的。

伊拉斯谟此后的生活完全自由了，他永不停歇地寻求一个理想所在，以便安心工作，免受慕名而来的友人们的打扰。

可是直至弥留之际，他自童年时代就向“敬爱的上帝”提出的允许自己的灵魂融入死亡睡梦之乡的请求，只让他饱尝了一会儿“真正的清闲”。这对于紧步苏格拉底和齐诺后尘的人们来说，是一种难能可贵的体验，几乎很少有人能达到这一境界。

他的这些经历总会被人谈到，在此我就不赘述了。只要有两三个真正富有远见卓识的人聚到一起，无论在哪里，伊拉斯谟或早或晚一定会出现。

他在巴黎学习过，作为一个穷学生，他几乎在饥寒交迫中死去。他在剑桥教过书，在巴塞尔印过书，他还想（几乎是徒劳地）把启蒙之光带进东正教的堡垒——远近闻名的卢万大学。他在伦敦待过很长时间，并获得了都灵大学的神学博士学位。他对威尼斯大运河了如指掌，骂起泽兰的糟糕道路来就像是骂伦巴第的烂路那样熟稔于心。罗马的天空、公园、人行道和图书馆给他留下了深刻的印象，以至于遗忘河也不能把这座圣城从他的记忆中冲掉。只要他搬到威尼斯，便可得到一笔

pension if he would only move to Venice and whenever a new university was opened,he was sure to be honored with a call to whatever chair he wished to take or to no chair at all,provided he would grace the Campus with his occasional presence.

But he steadily refused all such invitations because they seemed to contain a threat of permanence and dependency. Before all things he wanted to be free. He preferred a comfortable room to a bad one,he preferred amusing companions to dull ones,he knew the difference between the good rich wine of the land called Burgundy and the thin red ink of the Apennines,but he wanted to live life on his own terms and this he could not do if he had to call any man“master.”

The rôle which he had chosen for himself was really that of an intellectual search-light. No matter what object appeared above the horizon of contemporary events,Erasmus immediately let the brilliant rays of his intellect play upon it,did his best to make his neighbors see the thing as it really was,denuded of all frills and divested of that“folly,”that ignorance which he hated so thoroughly.

That he was able to do this during the most turbulent period of our history,that he managed to escape the fury of the Protestant fanatics while keeping himself aloof from the fagots of his friends of the Inquisition,this is the one point in his career upon which he has been most often condemned.

Posterity seems to have a veritable passion for martyrdom as long as it applies to the ancestors.

“Why didn't this Dutchman stand up boldly for Luther and take his chance together with the other reformers?”has been a question which seems to have puzzled at least twelve generations of otherwise intelligent citizens.

The answer is,“Why should he?”

充足的养老金，威尼斯开办任何一所新大学，肯定会请他去，就任他所选课程的教职，即使他不愿任教，只要偶尔赏脸光顾一下校园亦可。

但他坚决回绝了诸如此类的邀请，因为这里面似乎含有一种束缚和依赖的威胁成分。而在世界万物当中，他首选的是自由。与其住在破败不堪的房屋，倒不如住在舒适宜人的房间；与其面对呆头呆脑的伙计，倒不如与志趣相投的伙伴为伍；他知道勃艮第的醇美佳酿与亚平宁淡色红墨水之间的区别，但他想按照自己的意愿来生活，如果他不得不称别人为“主人”的话，这一切就无从谈起了。

他为自己选定的角色是地地道道的智慧探照灯，一旦有什么标的物从现实的地平线上显现出来，他就立即让自己的智慧之光照在上面，尽力让旁人看清那东西的真面目，剥落掉它所有的伪装，戳穿它的愚蠢和人所痛恨的无知。

在动荡不堪的历史年代，伊拉斯谟能这样做，既规避了新教徒狂热分子的愤怒，又让自己摆脱了宗教法庭朋友们的束缚，成为他一生中最常被人指责的一点。

只要提起祖先，后代子孙似乎对那些曾经经历的磨难感兴趣，并且乐此不疲。

“这个荷兰人为什么不挺身而出支持路德呢？为什么不把握时机与其他改革者站在一起呢？”这个问题似乎至少让那些有识之士困惑了十二代之久。

历史的回答是：“为什么他偏要那么做呢？”

采取暴力非他本性，他从来没把自己看成是任何运动的领袖。他缺乏自以为是的满足感，而在那些承担着告知世界千年梦想该如何实现的职责的人中，这种自我良好的感觉相当普遍。他也从不认为，为了重新布置房间，非得把旧房子拆掉不

It was not in his nature to do violent things and he never regarded himself as the leader of any movement. He utterly lacked that sense of self-righteous assurance which is so characteristic of those who undertake to tell the world how the millennium ought to be brought about. Besides he did not believe that it is necessary to demolish the old home every time we feel the necessity of rearranging our quarters. Quite true,the premises were sadly in need of repairs. The drainage was old-fashioned. The garden was all cluttered up with dirt and odds and ends left behind by people who had moved out long before. But all this could be changed if the landlord was made to live up to his promises and would only spend some money upon immediate improvements. Beyond that,Erasmus did not wish to go. And although he was what his enemies sneeringly called a"moderate,"he accomplished quite as much (or more) than those out and out"radicals"who gave the world two tyrannies where only one had been before.

Like all truly great men,he was no friend of systems. He believed that the salvation of this world lies in our individual endeavors. Make over the individual man and you have made over the entire world!

Hence he made his attack upon existing abuses by way of a direct appeal to the average citizen. And he did this in a very clever way.

In the first place he wrote an enormous amount of letters. He wrote them to kings and to emperors and to popes and to abbots and to knights and to knaves. He wrote them (and this in the days before the stamped and self-addressed envelope) to any one who took the trouble to approach him and whenever he took his pen in hand he was good for at least eight pages.

In the second place,he edited a large number of classical texts which had been so often and so badly copied that they no longer made any sense. For this purpose he had been obliged to learn Greek. His many attempts to get hold of a grammar of that forbidden

■ 施泰恩修道院

可。是啊，房子亟待修缮，排水系统老化了，花园里更是被那些早年搬走的人扔下的破烂堆放得乱七八糟。可是，假如房主人答应履行诺言，花点钱立刻就会有改观。除此之外，伊拉斯谟不愿意采取行动。尽管他被敌人讥讽为“中庸”派，但与那些过了头的“激进派”相比，他的成就毫不逊色，甚至更胜一筹，世界上原本只有一个暴君，激进派却又送来一个。

和所有公认的伟人一样，伊拉斯谟对制度体系毫无好感。他认为拯救这个世界需要仰仗大家的努力，解放了个体，也就解救了世界。

因此他直接面对民众，对现存的弊端陋习展开有效进攻。他的手段相当高明。

首先，他写了大量的信笺，把它们送给国王、皇帝、教皇和修道院院长们，还有那些骑士和无业游民；写给那些所有他接触或知道的人们（那时还没有使用邮票，没有标注送达地址这一项），而且一旦他操笔在手，就会洋洋洒洒地至少写上至少8页。

其次，他编纂了大量的古典文集，由于反复抄录，加之字迹潦草，这些文集实

tongue was one of the reasons why so many pious Catholics insisted that at heart he must be as bad as a real heretic. This of course sounds absurd but it was the truth. In the fifteenth century,respectable Christians would never have dreamed of trying to learn this forbidden language. It was a tongue of evil repute like modern Russian. A knowledge of Greek might lead a man into all sorts of difficulties. It might tempt him to compare the original gospels with those translations that had been given to him with the assurance that they were a true reproduction of the original. And that would only be the beginning. Soon he would make a descent into the Ghetto to get hold of a Hebrew grammar. From that point to open rebellion against the authority of the Church was only a step and for a long time the possession of a book with strange and outlandish pothooks was regarded as ipso facto evidence of secret revolutionary tendencies.

Quite often rooms were raided by ecclesiastical authorities in search of this contraband,and Byzantine refugees who were trying to eke out an existence by teaching their native tongue were not infrequently forced to leave the city in which they had found an asylum.

In spite of all these many obstacles,Erasmus had learned Greek and in the asides which he added to his editions of Cyprian and Chrysostom and the other Church fathers,he hid many sly observations upon current events which could never have been printed had they been the subject of a separate pamphlet.

But this impish spirit of annotation manifested itself in an entirely different sort of literature of which he was the inventor. I mean his famous collections of Greek and Latin proverbs which he had brought together in order that the children of his time might learn to write the classics with becoming elegance. These so-called“Adagia”are filled with clever comments which in the eyes of his conservative neighbors were by no means what

际上已无多少参考价值了。为此，他被迫学习希腊文。他在掌握这种禁用文字语法方面进行的诸多尝试，令那些虔诚的天主教徒们坚信，他完全就是一个不亚于真正异教徒的坏家伙。这听起来当然不可思议，而事实上的确如此。15世纪令人敬重的基督徒，无论如何也想不到要学习什么禁用语言。拥有希腊知识会让一个人遭遇各种各样的麻烦，它会让人产生将现有福音书与原始版本进行比较的念头，而这些福音书已经被明确告知是基于最初版本翻译过来的。这只是类似事情的冰山一角。不久他就进入贫民窟去学习希伯来语语法，差点就要公开挑战教会权威了。在很长的一段时间里，拥有这本怪异莫测、字体潦草的书，便成为从事秘密革命的物证。

教会当局会时常抄家，突袭搜查违禁品，而拜占廷的避难者们通过教授本国语言来竭力维持自身的存在，即便他们在这座城市里找到了一个避难所，也会频繁地被驱逐出城。

尽管面对诸多阻碍，伊拉斯谟还是学会了希腊语，在他编纂圣希普里安、克里索斯托及其他神父的著作时加了一些注释，巧妙地夹杂了许多有关时事的评论，如果这些内容单独印刷成册的话，也许永远都不会有面世的机会。

这种调皮捣蛋式的注解体现了一种完全不同的文学风格，而伊拉斯谟正是它的发明人。我指的是他那著名的希腊和拉丁语谚语集，他把它们装订成册，为的是让同时代的孩子们能够通过学习古典文学来了解什么是崇尚高雅。这些所谓的“格言”蕴藏着机智的评论，在那些保守的邻居看来，无论如何不会出自一个与教皇关系密切的人。

one had the right to expect of a man who enjoyed the friendship of the Pope.

And finally he was the author of one of those strange little books which are born of the spirit of the moment,which are really a joke conceived for the benefit of a few friends and then assume the dignity of a great literary classic before the poor author quite realizes what he has done. It was called"The Praise of Folly"and we happen to know how it came to be written.

It was in the year 1515 that the world had been startled by a pamphlet written so cleverly that no one could tell whether it was meant as an attack upon the friars or as a defense of the monastic life. No name appeared upon the title page,but those who knew what was what in the world of letters recognized the somewhat unsteady hand of one Ulrich von Hutten. And they guessed right;for that talented young man,poet laureate and town bum extraordinary,had taken no mean share in the production of this gross but useful piece of buffoonery and he was proud of it. When he heard that no one less than Thomas More,the famous champion of the New Learning in England,had spoken well of his work,he wrote to Erasmus and asked him for particulars.

Erasmus was no friend of von Hutten. His orderly mind (reflected in his orderly way of living) did not take kindly to those blowsy Teuton Ritters who spent their mornings and afternoons valiantly wielding pen and rapier for the cause of enlightenment and then retired to the nearest pot-house that they might forget the corruption of the times by drinking endless bumpers of sour beer.

But von Hutten,in his own way,was really a man of genius and Erasmus answered him civilly enough. Yea,as he wrote,he grew eloquent upon the virtues of his London friend and depicted so charming a scene of domestic contentment that the household of Sir Thomas might well serve as a model for all other families until the end of time. It was in this letter that he mentions how More,himself a humorist of no small parts,had given him

最后，他写了一本书，这是众多不可思议的书籍中的一本，他的小书稿是在时代的感召下写成的，原本是为博得几个好友的一笑而写的笑话，后来却演变成连作者都未曾料想到的伟大的文学经典，这本书叫《愚人颂》，而我们恰巧知道这本书是如何写成的。

1515年，一本小册子轰动了世界。这本书写得相当巧妙，简直弄不清它是在攻击僧侣，还是在捍卫修行生活。封面上没有署名，但一些对文学世界了如指掌的人都可以看出，这是出自一个名叫乌尔里希·冯·赫顿的怪才之手。他们猜得对，正是这个有才华的年轻人、桂冠诗人、城市里闲极无聊之徒在这本于己毫无关联的书中，添加了最为插科打诨的部分，他还为此颇感自豪。他听说连英国新学术领袖托马斯·莫尔都称赞了他的书，便写信给伊拉斯谟，想特别请教他的看法。

伊拉斯谟对冯·赫顿并不了解。他是个有头脑的人（体现在他那有条不紊的生活当中），对那些邋里邋遢的条顿骑士无法恭维，他们整天豪情万丈地把气力都用在为启蒙事业鼓噪呐喊、临危助阵上，然后退缩到附近的小酒馆里，沉浸在酸啤酒之中，借以忘却荒废的时光。

不过，冯·赫顿的确是个天才，伊拉斯谟给他的回信也算是礼貌有加。是的，他写着写着，就因为表达对英国朋友的美德的看法而变得滔滔不绝起来，并且勾勒出一幅合家团圆的动人画面，以至于托马斯先生的家居生活堪称其他家庭的永世楷模。正是在这封信里，他提到了莫尔——这个十足的幽默家赋予了他写《愚人颂》的最初灵

the original idea for his"Praise of Folly"and very likely it was the good-natured horse-play of the More establishment (a veritable Noah's ark of sons and daughters-in-law and daughters and sons-in-law and birds and dogs and a private zoo and private theatricals and bands of amateur fiddlers) which had inspired him to write that delightful piece of nonsense with which his name is forever associated.

In some vague way the book reminds me of the Punch and Judy shows which for so many centuries were the only amusement of little Dutch children. Those Punch and Judy shows,with all the gross vulgarity of their dialogue,invariably maintained a tone of lofty moral seriousness. The hollow voiced figure of Death dominated the scene. One by one the other actors were forced to appear before this ragged hero and give an account of themselves. And one by one,to the everlasting delight of the youthful audience,they were knocked on the head with an enormous cudgel and were thrown on an imaginary scrap-heap.

In the"Praise of Folly,"the whole social fabric of the age is carefully taken apart while Folly,as a sort of inspired Coroner,stands by and favors the public at large with her comments. No one is spared. The whole of Medieval Main Street is ransacked for suitable characters. And of course,the go-getters of that day,the peddling friars of salvation with all their sanctimonius sales-talk,their gross ignorance and the futile pomposity of their arguments,came in for a drubbing which was never forgotten and never forgiven.

But the Pope and his cardinals and his bishops,incongruous successors to the poverty stricken fishermen and carpenters from the land of Galilee,were also on the bill and held the stage for several chapters.

The"Folly"of Erasmus however was a much more substantial personage than the usual Jack-in-the-Box of humorous literature. Throughout this little book (as indeed throughout everything he wrote) Erasmus preached a gospel of his own which one might call the philosophy of tolerance.

感，它可以和莫尔创立的善意的闹剧相提并论（一个名副其实的挪亚方舟，有儿子、儿媳、女儿、女婿、鸟、狗、私人动物园、私人剧院、乐队以及业余小提琴手），在此启发下，他写出了令人兴奋无比的无厘头闹剧，并使自己的名字永远与其联系在一起。

这本书使我隐约想起了英国木偶剧《庞奇和朱迪》，在好几个世纪里，它一直是荷兰儿童唯一的娱乐节目。大凡在庞奇和朱迪的表演中，对话里夹杂着大量的粗言秽语，但无一例外地又使用了一种严肃高雅的格调，用空腔嗓音说话的“死神”形象占据了整个舞台。演员们被迫逐一来到这位衣衫褴褛的主角面前，自我介绍一番。令小观众开心不已的是，他们要轮流被大木棒敲击脑袋，然后被扔进想象中的垃圾堆里。

在《愚人颂》中，整个社会的神秘面纱被小心地揭开了，其中的人物——“愚人”，是受到神启的验尸官，以旁观者的角度发表观点来取悦现场观众。没有任何人能逃脱。中世纪市面上形形色色的人物都被搜罗进角色当中。当然，那个时代的佼佼者，那些沿街兜售虚假救世神符的僧侣们，连同他们的无知和夸夸其谈的自我炫耀，全被写进书中，遭到了不容遗忘、不予宽恕的鞭挞。

还有那些与来自加利利的贫苦渔民和木匠毫无共同之处的继承者们，那些教皇、红衣主教和主教，也出现在声讨的清单上，并占据了舞台的大量情节。

不过，伊拉斯谟的愚人要比幽默文学中常见的玩偶形象更为生动丰满。贯穿这本小册子的（正如他一贯所表述的），是伊拉斯谟对自己那套哲理的大力弘扬，我

It was this willingness to live and let live;this insistence upon the spirit of the divine law rather than upon the commas and the semicolons in the original version of that divine law;this truly human acceptance of religion as a system of ethics rather than as a form of government which made serious-minded Catholics and Protestants inveigh against Erasmus as a“godless knave”and an enemy fo all true religion who“slandered Christ”but hid his real opinions behind the funny phrases of a clever little book.

This abuse (and it lasted until the day of his death) did not have any effect. The little man with the long pointed nose,who lived until the age of seventy at a time when the addition or omission of a single word from an established text might cause a man to be hanged,had no liking at all for the popular-hero business and he said so openly. He expected nothing from an appeal to swords and arquebusses and knew only too well the risk the world was running when a minor theological dispute was allowed to degenerate into an international religious war.

And so,like a gigantic beaver,he worked day and night to finish that famous dam of reason and common sense which he vaguely hoped might stem the waxing tide of ignorance and intolerance.

Of course he failed. It was impossible to stop those floods of ill-will and hatred which were sweeping down from the mountains of Germany and the Alps,and a few years after his death his work had been completely washed away.

But so well had he wrought that many bits of wreckage,thrown upon the shores of posterity,proved exceedingly good material for those irrepressible optimists who believe that some day we shall have a set of dykes that will actually hold.

Erasmus departed this life in July of the year 1536.

His sense of humor never deserted him. He died in the house of his publisher.

们可称之为“宽容的哲学”。

正是这种“与人方便，与己方便”的思想；正是这种对神圣法则精髓的坚持，而非对神圣教义中的细枝末节的纠缠；正是这种把宗教作为一种伦理体系，而不是作为某种统治形式来加以接受的思想，才使得头脑固执的天主教徒和新教徒痛斥伊拉斯谟是“无神的恶棍”，是所有真正宗教的敌人，他在那本诡辩的小册子里用滑稽的言辞掩盖自己“亵渎基督”的真实本意。

攻击（一直到他死）没起任何作用。在那个对既定文字稍加增减都会掉脑袋的年代里，这个尖鼻子的矮个子一直活到了70岁。他对风靡一时的英雄行径不感兴趣，也曾公开自己的看法。他从不指望从刀枪剑戟中有所收获，他清醒地认识到，假如任由神学上的小争执恶化成一场国际范围的宗教战争的话，世界将面临何等风险。

于是，他像个巨大的海狸，夜以继日地堆砌并构筑起理智和常识的堤坝，依稀地企望它能阻挡不断上涨的无知和偏执的洪水。

当然，他最终失败了。要想挡住来自日耳曼诸峰和阿尔卑斯山巅冲来的恶意和仇恨的洪流，根本是不可能的。他死后没几年，他的著作也被冲刷得不见踪影了。

不过，由于他的杰出贡献，许许多多沉船的骸骨又冲到了后人的岸边，成为永远无法抑制的乐观主义者的好材料。他们相信，总有一天，人类终将构筑起坚不可摧的拦洪大坝。

伊拉斯谟逝于1536年7月。

他的幽默感从未远离他。他死在了出版商的家里。

CHAPTER XIV RABELAIS

Social upheavals make strange bed-fellows.

The name of Erasmus can be printed in a respectable book intended for the entire family. But to mention Rabelais in public is considered little short of a breach of good manners. Indeed,so dangerous is this fellow that laws have been passed in our country to keep his wicked works out of the hands of our innocent children and that in many states copies of his books can only be obtained from the more intrepid among our book-leggers.

This of course is merely one of the absurdities which have been forced upon us by the reign of terror of a flivver aristocracy.

In the first place,the works of Rabelais to the average citizen of the twentieth century are about as dull reading as"Tom Jones"or"The House of the Seven Gables."Few people ever get beyond the first interminable chapter.

And in the second place,there is nothing intentionally suggestive in what he says. Rabelais used the common vocabulary of his time. That does not happen to be the common vernacular of our own day. But in the era of the bucolic blues,when ninety percent of the human race lived close to the soil,a spade was actually a spade and ladydogs were not"lady-dogs."

No,the current objections to the works of this distinguished surgeon go much deeper than a mere disapproval of his rich but somewhat outspoken collection of idioms. They are caused by the horror which many excellent people experience when they come face to

第14章 拉 伯 雷

社会动荡产生了奇特的同盟者。

伊拉斯谟的名字可以冠冕堂皇地印在书上供全家阅读。但在大庭广众之下谈及拉伯雷却是有失大雅的。这家伙的确十分危险，最后国家通过法律规定，禁止天真的儿童接触他邪恶的作品，而在许多国家，他的作品只能从那些胆子更大的书贩子那里才能获得。

显然，这不过是无能的专制和恐怖统治强加在我们头上的众多荒唐事件中的一件。

首先，拉伯雷的书对20世纪的普通百姓而言，就像《汤姆·琼斯》和《七个尖角的阁楼》一样枯燥无味。很少有人能读完那冗长不堪的第1章。

其次，他的言辞并没有多少启发性。拉伯雷采用的是他那个时代的通俗语言，如今却是不常用了。当时，百分之九十的人口都要依靠土地为生，一切就该直截了当，不必拐弯抹角，铁锹就是铁锹，母狗不会混同于“贵夫人的狗”。

不过，目前针对这位出色外科大夫作品的反对意见，绝不仅限于指责他大量采用过于直率的言辞，而实际上要深刻得多。这是因为许多杰出人物对习惯于抨击生活的人感到无比厌恶，而他又直截了当地表示拒绝做生活的俘虏。

face with the point of view of a man who point blank refuses to be defeated by life.

The human race,as far as I can make out,is divided into two sorts of people;those who say“yes”unto life and those who say“no.”The former accept it and courageously they endeavor to make the best of whatever bargain fate has handed out to them.

The latter accept it too (how could they help themselves?) but they hold the gift in great contempt and fret about it like children who have been given a new little brother when they really wanted a puppy or a railroad train.

But whereas the cheerful brethren of“yes”are willing to accept their morose neighbors at their own valuation and tolerate them,and do not hinder them when they fill the landscape with their lamentations and the hideous monuments to their own despair,the fraternity of“no”rarely extends this same courtesy to the parties of the first part.

Indeed if they had their own way,the“nays”would immediately purge this planet of the“yeas.”

As this cannot very well be done,they satisfy the demands of their jealous souls by the incessant persecution of those who claim that the world belongs to the living and not to the dead.

Dr. Rabelais belonged to the former class. Few of his patients or his thoughts ever went out to the cemetery. This,no doubt,was very regrettable,but we cannot all be grave-diggers. There have to be a few Poloniuses and a world composed exclusively of Hamlets would be a terrible place of abode.

As for the story of Rabelais' life,there was nothing very mysterious about it. The few details which are omitted in the books written by his friends are found in the works of his

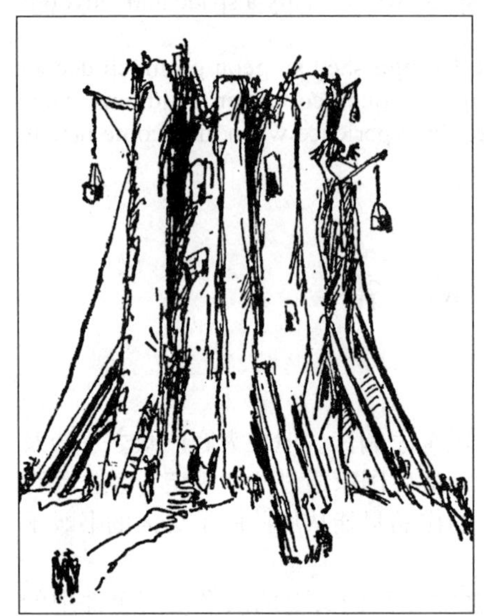

■ 旧大厦能维持我们的时代

依我看来，人可分为两种类型：一种人对生活说“行”，另一种说“不行”。前一种人勇于接受生活，无论讨价还价后命运赋予了什么，他们都努力获得最佳成果。

后一种人也接受生活（他们又能拿自己怎么办呢），但完全无视生活的给予，像孩子一样懊丧不已，他们原本想要的是木偶或小火车，结果却得了一个小弟弟。

“接受”派的快乐弟兄们乐意接受那些自持的郁郁寡欢的邻居，宽容他们，即使“不接受派”由着自己悲伤的性情而把大地涂抹得满目凄惶、阻碍重重，他们也不去加以阻拦。不过，“不接受派”却很少向“接受派”展示兄弟情怀。

事实上，一旦得到机会，“不接受”派便立即要把“接受”派从这个星球上清除掉。

这可不容易做到，于是“不接受”派为了满足自己嫉妒的心理，不断迫害那些认为“世界是属于生者而不属于死者”的人。

拉伯雷大夫属于第一种人，他的患者们，抑或他的思想，几乎都不会向往墓地。这无疑是件憾事，但似乎人们也不能都去做掘墓人。必须要有一些像波洛尼厄

enemies and as a result we can follow his career with a fair degree of accuracy.

Rabelais belonged to the generation which followed immediately upon Erasmus but he was born into a world still largely dominated by monks,nuns,deacons,and a thousand and one varieties of mendicant friars. He was born in Chinon. His father was either an apothecary or a dealer in spirits (which were different professions in the fifteenth century) and the old man was sufficiently well-to-do to send his son to a good school. There young Francois was thrown into the company of the scions of a famous local family called du Bellay-Langey. These boys,like their father,had a streak of genius. They wrote well. Upon occasion they could fight well. They were men of the world in the good sense of that oft misunderstood expression. They were faithful servitors of their master the king,held endless public offices,became bishops and cardinals and ambassadors,translated the classics,edited manuals of infantry drill and ballistics and brilliantly performed all the many useful services that were expected of the aristocracy in a day when a title condemned a man to a life of few pleasures and many duties and responsibilities.

The friendship which the du Bellays afterwards bestowed upon Rabelais shows that he must have been something more than an amusing table companion. During the many ups and downs of his life he could always count upon the assistance and the support of his former classmates. Whenever he was in trouble with his clerical superiors he found the door of their castle wide open and if perchance the soil of France became a little too hot for this blunt young moralist,there was always a du Bellay,conveniently going upon a foreign mission and greatly in need of a secretary who should be somewhat of a physician besides being a polished Latin scholar.

This was no small detail. More than once when it seemed that the career of our learned doctor was about to come to an abrupt and painful end,the influence of his old friends

斯这样饶舌的家伙，如果世上到处都是哈姆雷特，那地球就会成为一个令人可怕的居所。

至于拉伯雷的生平轶事，没什么特别神秘之处。在他朋友书中被忽略的情节，在他敌人的书里可以找到，因此总体说来，我们可以相当准确地了解他的一生。

拉伯雷所处的时代紧随伊拉斯谟之后，他所降临的世界仍被教士、修女、执事和各种类型的托钵僧们所把持。他出生在法国希侬，父亲不是个药剂师就是药酒商（这两种职业在15世纪并不相同），是个事业相当成功的人，能把儿子送到好学校里念书。年轻的弗朗西斯凭借着在那所学校就读，进入了杜贝拉——兰格家族后裔的圈子里。这是一个在当地颇有名望的家族，男孩子们像他们的父亲，具有一定的天赋，擅长写作，偶尔也能打漂亮仗。他们老于世故（这个词常被曲解，在这里是褒义），是国王忠诚的侍从，担当过无数公职，成为主教、红衣主教和大使，翻译古典作品，编辑炮兵步兵训练手册，出色地完成了那个时代拥有贵族头衔的人应履行的所有必要的职责。这个该诅咒的头衔让人必须担负起众多职责和义务，几乎没什么生活乐趣可言。

杜贝拉家族后来给予拉伯雷的友情表明，他绝不仅是一个陪他们消遣的食客。在跌宕起伏的人生境遇中，他总能得到老同学的提携和支持。只要他与教会当局发生摩擦，杜贝拉家族城堡的大门便向他敞开；一旦法国对这个年轻气盛的道德主义者偶尔变得不利时，总会有杜贝拉家族的某个成员恰好奉命前往国外，并急需一个秘书，这个人不仅要求是个造诣精深的拉丁学者，某种程度上还应是个大夫。

saved him from the fury of the Sorbonne or from the anger of those much disappointed Calvinists who had counted upon him as one of their own and who were greatly incensed when he pilloried the jaundiced zeal of their Genevan master as mercilessly as he had derided the three-bottled sanctity of his erstwhile colleagues in Fontenay and Maillezais.

Of these two enemies,the former was of course by far the more dangerous. Calvin could fulminate to his heart's content,but outside of the narrow boundaries of a small Swiss canton,his lightning was as harmless as a fire-cracker.

The Sorbonne,on the other hand,which together with the University of Oxford stood firmly for orthodoxy and the Old Learning,knew of no mercy when her authority was questioned and could always count upon the hearty cooperation of the king of France and his hangman.

And alas! Rabelais,as soon as he left school,was a marked man. Not because he liked to drink good wine and told funny stories about his fellow-monks. He had done much worse,he had succumbed to the lure of the wicked Greek tongue.

When rumor thereof had first reached the abbot of his cloister,it was decided to search his cell. It was found to be full of literary contraband,a copy of Homer,one of the New Testament,one of Herodotus.

This was a terrible discovery and it had taken a great deal of wire-pulling on the part of his influential friends to get him out of this scrape.

It was a curious period in the development of the Church.

Originally,as I told you before,the monasteries had been advance posts of civilization and both friars and nuns had rendered inestimable service in promoting the interest of the Church. More than one Pope,however,had foreseen the danger that might come from a too powerful development of the monastic institutions. But as so often happens,just because every one

这不是琐碎小事。这位博学大夫的生涯不止一次即将在不幸中戛然而止，是老朋友的干预才把他从索邦神学院的愤怒或彻底失望的加尔文主义者的怒火中解救出来。加尔文主义者本来把他视作是自己人，但他在大庭广众之下嘲讽加尔文派大师偏执的宗教热情，就像他在封特内和马耶塞讽刺他那“一瓶不满半瓶晃荡”的老同事一样，他的嘲讽让加尔文派很恼火。

在这两个敌人当中，索邦神学院当然更加危险。加尔文虽然可以尽兴地大声斥责，但在狭小的瑞士细长的边境线之外，他的雷霆之怒就会像爆竹一样毫无害处了。

与此相反，索邦神学院与牛津大学一道，固守正统和“旧学”，一旦他们的权威遭受质疑就毫无怜悯而言，而且他们还总能得到法兰西国王和国王刽子手们的鼎力支持。

嗨!拉伯雷一离开学校，就成了一个引人注目的人物。这不仅因为他爱喝好酒、爱拿同伴僧侣的趣事取乐。更糟糕的是，他已被邪恶的希腊文蛊惑了。

消息一传到他所在修道院院长的耳朵里，院长立即作出了搜查他住所的决定。他们发现了成堆的违禁书籍，一本《荷马史诗》，一本《新约》和一本希罗多德的书。

这真是一个可怕的发现，他那些有势力的朋友们费尽了幕后周折，才把他从困境中解救出来。

在教会发展史里，这是个奇妙的阶段。

起初，正如我前面所讲的，修道院是先进文明的落脚点，僧侣和修女们在促进

knew that something ought to be done about these cloisters,nothing was ever done.

Among the Protestants there seems to be a notion that the Catholic Church is a placid institution which is run silently and almost automatically by a small body of haughty autocrats and which never suffers from those inner upheavals which are an integral part of every other organization composed of ordinary mortals.

Nothing is further from the truth.

Perhaps,as is so often the case,this opinion has been caused by the misinterpretation of a single word.

A world addicted to democratic ideals is easily horrified at the idea of an"infallible" human being.

"It must be easy,"so the popular argument runs,"to administer this big institution when it is enough for one man to say that a thing is so to have all the others fall upon their knees and shout amen and obey him."

It is extremely difficult for one brought up in Protestant countries to get a correct and fair view of this rather intricate subject. But if I am not mistaken,the"infallible"utterances of the supreme pontiff are as rare as constitutional amendments in the United States.

Furthermore,such important decisions are never reached until the subject has been thoroughly discussed and the debates which precede the final verdict often rock the very body of the Church. Such pronunciamentos are therefore"infallible"in the sense that our own constitutional amendments are infallible,because they are"final"and because all further argument is supposed to come to an end as soon as they have been definitely incorporated into the highest law of the land.

If any one were to proclaim that it is an easy job to govern these United States because in case of an emergency all the people are found to stand firmly behind the Constitution,he

教会利益方面作出了无法估量的努力。但是，不止一个教皇已经预料到，发展得过于强大的修道院体制将是某种威胁。一如既往的是，大家都知道该对修道院采取某些措施，却迟迟不见采取行动。

在新教徒当中似乎有一种看法，即天主教会是个默默运行的平和的组织。是由一小撮高傲的贵族把持着的，内部从未遭受纷扰，而这些内讧在其他所有由普通平民组成的组织里却是与生俱来的。

这与事实相差甚远。

之所以会出现上述情形，可能是由于对一个词语的错误解读而造成的。

在一个热衷于民主理想的世界，人们容易被“绝对正确”的人所吓倒。

一个流行的观点认为：“一个大组织里只要一个人说了算，而其他所有人都跪下喊阿门，服从他，那么管理起来就容易多了。”

要想让一个在新教国家长大的人对这个复杂问题有一个正确公允的了解，可不是件容易的事。不过，如果我没有搞错的话，教皇发表“至圣”言辞的概率微乎其微，就像在美国宪法修订过程中众口一词一样难得。

更进一步地讲，如果未经彻底讨论，重大的决策是不会形成的，而最后法案形成之前的争论经常会动摇教会的根基。因此形成的公告也是“一贯正确的”，正如我们宪法的修订案也是不会有错的一样，因为它们是“最终”的，一旦这些争执意见被纳入国家的最高法典，所有进一步的争论都应结束。

如果有人因为一旦出现紧急情形，所有美国人都坚定地捍卫宪法，就断定管理

would be just as much in error as if he were to state that all Catholics who in supreme matters of faith recognize the absolute authority of their pope are docile sheep and have surrendered every right to an opinion of their own.

If this were true,the occupants of the Lateran and the Vatican palaces would have had an easy life. But even the most superficial study of the last fifteen hundred years will show the exact opposite. And those champions of the reformed faith who sometimes write as if the Roman authorities had been ignorant of the many evils which Luther and Calvin and Zwingli denounced with such great vehemence are either ignorant of the facts or are not quite fair in their zeal for the good cause.

Such men as Adrian VI and Clement VII knew perfectly well that something very serious was wrong with their Church. But it is one thing to express the opinion that there is something rotten in the state of Denmark. It is quite a different matter to correct the evil,as even poor Hamlet was to learn.

Nor was that unfortunate prince the last victim of the pleasant delusion that hundreds of years of misgovernment can be undone overnight by the unselfish efforts of an honest man.

Many intelligent Russians knew that the old official structure which dominated their empire was corrupt,inefficient and a menace to the safety of the nation.

They made Herculean efforts to bring about reforms and they failed.

How many of our citizens who have ever given the matter an hour's thought fail to see that a democratic instead of a representative form of government (as intended by the founders of the Republic) must eventually lead to systematized anarchy?

And yet,what can they do about it?

Such problems,by the time they have begun to attract public attention,have become so hopelessly complicated that they are rarely solved except by a social cataclysm. And

美国联邦诸州是件容易的事情的话，那他就和那些宣称天主教徒在关乎信仰的事情上完全听凭教皇权威的人犯了同样的错误，这些教徒都是驯服的羔羊，放弃了所有属于自己主张的权力。

如果事情果真如此，那些盘踞在罗马拉特兰宫和梵蒂冈宫殿里的人将生活得相当轻松。但即便对以往1500年的历史作最粗浅的研究，都会发现事实完全与此相反。那些宗教改革的急先锋们在文章中大谈路德、加尔文和茨温利大声疾呼的许多丑恶，好像罗马当权者对此全不知晓似的，其实这要么是出于他们的无知，要么是由于他们对美好事业的热情使他们失去了公正的判断力。

像艾德里安六世和克莱芒七世这些人，对教会自身出现的问题了如指掌。不过，指出丹麦王国里已滋生腐败是一回事，而纠正邪恶则是另一回事。即便可怜的哈姆雷特最后也了解到了这一点。

那个不幸的王子不会是美好幻觉的最后一个受害者。这种幻觉让人以为，仅靠一个诚实之人的无私努力，便能在一夜间纠正政府几百年积累的错误统治。

许多睿智的俄国人清楚，帝国陈腐的官僚统治腐败不堪，拖延无效，已危及了民族安全。

他们作出了赫拉克勒斯式无与伦比的努力，结果却失败了。

我们的同胞当中，有多少人即便花上一个小时进行思考，也仍然不明白代议制政府（正如共和国的缔造者希望的那样）取代民主制政府最终会导致大混乱呢？

而且，即便他们没有忽视这个事实，他们又能做些什么呢？

social cataclysms are terrible things from which most men shy away. Rather than run to such extremes,they try to patch up the old,decrepit machinery and meanwhile they pray that some miracle will occur which will make it work.

An insolent religious and social dictatorship,set up and maintained by a number of religious orders,was one of the most flagrant evils of the out-going Middle Ages.

For the so-many-eth time in history,the army was about to run away with the commander-in-chief. In plain words,the situation had grown entirely beyond the control of the popes. All they could do was to sit still,improve their own party organization,and meanwhile try to mitigate the fate of those who had incurred the displeasure of their common enemies,the friars.

Erasmus was one of the many scholars who had frequently enjoyed the protection of the Pope. Let Louvain storm and the Dominicans rave,Rome would stand firm and woe unto him who disregarded her command,"Leave the old man alone!"

And after these few introductory remarks,it will be no matter of surprise that Rabelais,a mutinous soul but a brilliant mind withal,could often count upon the support of the Holy See when the superiors of his own order wished to punish him and that he readily obtained permission to leave his cloister when constant interference with his studies began to make his life unbearable.

And so with a sigh of relief,he shook the dust of Maillezais off his feet and went to Montpellier and to Lyons to follow a course

■ 劝诱的全部办法

类似问题，如果到了引起公众注目的程度，就已经变得无可挽回地复杂起来，除非经历社会巨变，否则几乎无法解决。而社会动荡令多数人望而生畏。因此他们宁愿采取一些补救办法维持原本已经衰竭的机体，也不愿意采取如此极端的方式，同时祈盼着某种奇迹的发生，让一切都好起来。

由一系列宗教法规支撑组建起来的宗教专制独裁，是中世纪末期最臭名昭著的罪恶之一。

历史无数次地显示出“树倒猢狲散”（主帅一倒，全军溃逃）的局面。说得更直白些，就是最终局势已脱离了教皇的掌控。他们所能做的，就是静坐一旁，改善自己的组织，同时尽量阻止像他们共同的敌人托钵僧遇到的那样糟糕厄运的到来。

伊拉斯谟是多次得到教皇庇护的众多学者之一。无论是卢万大学的风暴还是多明我会修士的大放厥词，罗马始终坚定立场，并把那些无视其命令的人视为仇敌，命令他们：“让那个老人安生些吧！”

经过这些简单的介绍，我们了解了拉伯雷这个有着崇高智慧但又有着反叛精神的人，每次在他的上司想要惩罚他时，常常能仰仗梵蒂冈的支持也就不足为怪了。而且一旦他的学术研究持续遭到骚扰而使他的生活不堪重负时，他立即就能得到获准离开他所在的教堂。

in medicine.

Surely here was a man of extraordinary talents! Within less than two years the former Benedictine monk had become chief physician of the city hospital of Lyons. But as soon as he had achieved these new honors,his restless soul began to look for pastures new. He did not give up his powders and pills but in addition to his anatomical studies (a novelty almost as dangerous as the study of Greek) he took up literature.

Lyons,situated in the center of the valley of the Rhone,was an ideal city for a man who cared for belles lettres. Italy was nearby. A few days easy travel carried the traveler to the Provence and although the ancient paradise of the Troubadours had suffered dreadfully at the hands of the Inquisition,the grand old literary tradition had not yet been entirely lost. Furthermore,the printing-presses of Lyons were famous for the excellence of their product and her book stores were well stocked with all the latest publications.

When one of the master printers,Sebastian Gryphius by name,looked for some one to edit his collection of medieval classics,it was natural that he should bethink himself of the new doctor who was also known as a scholar. He hired Rabelais and set him to work. In rapid succession almanacs and chap-books followed upon the learned treatises of Galen and Hippocrates. And out of these inconspicuous beginnings grew that strange tome which was to make its author one of the most popular writers of his time.

The same talent for novelty which had turned Rabelais into a successful medical practitioner brought him his success as a novelist. He did what few people had dared to do before him. He began to write in the language of his own people. He broke with a thousand-year-old tradition which insisted that the books of a learned man must be in a tongue unknown to the vulgar multitude. He used French and,furthermore,he used the unadorned vernacular of the year 1532.

于是，带着一份释然，他拭去粘在鞋上的泥土，前往蒙彼利埃，然后去里昂，继续研究医学。

他的确是个有着超常天赋的人！在不到两年的时间里，这个本尼迪克特派的前任牧师一跃而成为里昂市政医院的主任医师。但是一旦获得了这些荣誉，他那不安分的灵魂又开始寻觅“新的牧场”。他并没有放弃自己的药粉和片剂，在解剖学（这是和希腊文同样危险的新学科）研究之外，他又选择了文学。

里昂位于罗纳河流域，是追求纯文学人士的理想所在。意大利距此不远。只需要几日的简短旅行，就能把一个游人由此带到普罗旺斯，这里曾是古代行吟诗人的乐园，在宗教裁判所的桎梏下这里横遭摧残，但伟大的文学传统并没有因之完全丧失。并且，里昂的印刷出版业以其制作精良而闻名，那里的书店还藏着所有最新的出版物。

一个名叫塞巴斯蒂安·格里弗斯的杰出出版商，在寻求一个中世纪文献的编校者，自然想到了这个以学者著称的新医生。他雇用了拉伯雷，让他着手工作。在盖伦和希波克拉底教派的学术论文之后，紧接着迅速出版了一系列年鉴和文集。这个不起眼的开端却促成了一部不可思议的巨著的产生，并使其作者成为那个时代最了不起的作家之一。

追求新奇事物的天资不但使拉伯雷成为著名的医生，还成为一名成功的小说家。他做了前人不敢问津的事：开始用自己民众的语言进行写作。他打破了千年来饱学之士的书必须采用粗俗的民众无从知晓的文字的旧传统。他用的是法语，是

I gladly leave it to the professors of literature to decide where and how and when Rabelais discovered his two pet heroes,Gargantua and Pantagruel. Maybe they were old heathenish Gods who,after the nature of their species,had managed to live through fifteen hundred years of Christian persecution and neglect.

Then again,he may have invented them in an outburst of gigantic hilarity.

However that be,Rabelais contributed enormously to the gayety of nations and greater praise no author can gain than that he has added something to the sum total of human laughter. But at the same time,his works were not funny books in the terrible modern sense of the word. They had their serious side and struck a bold blow for the cause of tolerance by their caricature of the people who were responsible for that clerical reign of terror which caused such untold misery during the first fifty years of the sixteenth century.

Rabelais,a skillfully trained theologian,was able to avoid all such direct statements as might have got him into trouble,and acting upon the principle that one cheerful humorist out of jail is better than a dozen gloomy reformers behind the bars,refrained from a too brazen exposition of his highly unorthodox opinions.

But his enemies knew perfectly well what he was trying to do. The Sorbonne condemned his books in unmistakable terms and the Parliament of Paris put him on their index and confiscated and burned all such copies of his works as could be found within their jurisdiction. But notwithstanding the activities of the hangman (who in those days was also the official book destroyer) the"Lives and Heroic Deeds and Sayings of Gargantua and his Sonne Pantagruel"remained a popular classic. For almost four centuries it has continued to edify those who can derive pleasure from a clever mixture of good-natured laughter and bantering wisdom and it will never cease to irritate those others who firmly believe that the Goddess of Truth,caught with a smile on her lips,cannot possibly be

1532年不加修饰的本地话。

至于拉伯雷何时、何地及如何发现他的两个心爱的主人公——卡冈都亚和庞大古埃，我很乐意留给文学教授们去研究，说不定这是两个异教的神灵，凭着天性，熬过了1500年来基督教的迫害和鄙视而幸免于难。

退一步讲，拉伯雷也可能是在一阵惊喜中创造了他们的。

无论如何，拉伯雷对民族欢乐有巨大贡献，他为人类的笑声增添了新鲜内容，人们对他的赞誉令任何作家都无法企及。与此同时，他的著作绝不是现代意义上令人无法承受的“趣味书”，它有其严肃的一面，通过对人物的讽刺描写，为宽容事业出了一记重拳。这些人物是宗教恐怖统治的罪魁祸首，他们炮制出了16世纪上半叶罄竹难书的苦难。

拉伯雷是一个训练有素的神学家，他规避了所有招惹麻烦的平铺直叙。他秉持的原则是：一个愉悦的幽默家，胜似监牢十多个阴郁的改革家。因此他会避免过分表露他那相当异端的观点。

而他的敌人对他的行径也是心知肚明。索邦神学院对其作品的谴责恰如其分，巴黎议会把他列入黑名单。他的书籍一经在管辖范围内发现，就全被没收和焚毁。不过，尽管刽子手活动频繁（当时刽子手也是法定的图书销毁人），《巨人传——英雄的业绩及生平，卡冈都亚的格言，以及来自德国松嫩的庞大古埃》仍然是畅销的经典作品。近四个世纪以来，它一直启迪着那些能够从善意的笑声和妙趣的智慧混合体中汲取乐趣的人。而对另一些人来说，它也一直在刺激着他们的神经。这些人顽固地认

a good woman.

As for the author himself,he was and is a"man of one book."His friends,the du Bellays,remained faithful to him until the end,but most of his life Rabelais practiced the virtue of discretion and kept himself at a polite distance from the residence of that Majesty by whose supposed"privilege"he published his nefarious works.

He ventured however upon a visit to Rome and met with no difficulties,but on the contrary was received with every manifestation of a cordial welcome. In the year 1550 he returned to France and went to live in Meudon. Three years later he died.

It is of course quite impossible to measure the exact and positive influence exercised by such a man. After all,he was a human being and not an electric current or a barrel of gasoline.

It has been said that he was merely destructive.

Perhaps so.

But he was destructive in an age when there was a great and crying need for a social wrecking crew,headed by just such people as Erasmus and Rabelais.

That many of the new buildings were going to be just as uncomfortable and ugly as the old ones which they were supposed to replace was something which no one was able to foresee.

And,anyway,that was the fault of the next generation.

They are the people we ought to blame.

They were given a chance such as few people ever enjoyed to make a fresh start.

May the Lord have mercy upon their souls for the way in which they neglected their opportunities.

为，只要“真理女神”的嘴边出现一丝笑意，她就不可能是个好女人。

至于作者本人，过去和现在都被看成是“一举成名”的作家。杜贝拉家族的朋友始终对他忠心耿耿。不过在人生的大多数时间里，拉伯雷一直很谨慎，他那离经叛道的著作虽然被认为是得到了大人物的“特殊照顾”才发表的，他对他们却保持着敬而远之的距离。

他还冒险去了一趟罗马，没有遇到任何阻碍，相反却处处受到热情的欢迎。1550年他回到法国，安居在默顿，于三年后辞世。

要准确衡量这样一个人所发挥的积极作用当然是不可能的，他毕竟是个人，不是电流，也不是一桶汽油。

有人说他仅仅是在摧毁。

也许正是如此。

但是时代迫切需要摧毁者来摧毁旧的，推进新的。而伊拉斯谟和拉伯雷是其中的领军人物。

他们打算要建许多新大厦来取代现存的东西，可是这些新房子仍像旧房子一样庸俗难看，这是人们始料未及的。

不管怎样，那是下一代人的过错。

我们该责备的是下一代人。

他们原本得到了改弦更张的机会，这几乎是千载难逢的良机。

他们错过了良机，愿上帝宽恕他们的灵魂吧！

CHAPTER XV NEW SIGNBOARDS FOR OLD

The greatest of modern poets saw the world as a large ocean upon which sailed many ships. Whenever these little vessels bumped against each other,they made a"wonderful music"which people call history.

I would like to borrow Heine's ocean,but for a purpose and a simile of my own. When we were children it was fun to drop pebbles into a pond. They made a nice splash and then the pretty little ripples caused a series of ever widening circles and that was very nice. If bricks were handy (which sometimes was the case) one could make an Armada of nutshells and matches and submit this flimsy fleet to a nice artificial storm,provided the heavy projectile did not create that fatal loss of equilibrium which sometimes overtakes small children who play too near the water's edge and sends them to bed without their supper.

In that special universe reserved for grown-ups,the same pastime is not entirely unknown,but the results are apt to be far more disastrous.

Everything is placid and the sun is shining and the water-wigglers are skating merrily,and then suddenly a bold,bad boy comes along with a piece of mill-stone(Heaven only knows where he found it!) and before any one can stop him he has heaved it right into the middle of the old duck pond and then there is a great ado about who did it and how he ought to be spanked and some say,"Oh,let him go,"and others,out of sheer envy of the kid who is attracting all the attention,pick up any old thing that happens to lie around

第15章 旧世界的新招牌

现代最伟大的诗人把世界视为千帆竞渡的一片汪洋，每当这些小船相互碰撞时便会发出“美妙的乐音”，而人们将其称为历史。

我愿意借鉴海涅关于大海的想象，不过是为了某个目的并让自己开心。在孩提时代，我们都喜欢往池塘里丢石子，觉得很好玩。石子能溅起美丽的浪花，小浪花逐渐成为扩大的圆圈，非常好看。如果手边有砖头（情形往往确实如此），人们就可以用果壳和火柴拼成无敌舰队，然后把这支脆弱的舰队投放到一个壮观的人工风暴之中。但要注意投掷这些重磅炮弹时千万不要失去平衡，否则离水太近的孩子会摔下去，结果被罚连晚饭都不让吃，只能去睡觉。

在专门为成人保留的世界里，同样的消遣并非没有，结局却更为惨痛。

一切都平静如常，阳光明媚，玩水者在欢快地玩耍。这时，突然有一个胆大的坏孩子抱着一块磨石来了（天晓得他是从哪儿找来的），别人还没来得及拦住他，他就已经用力把石头扔到了古老池塘的中间，接着一片大乱，大家问是谁干的，应该打他的屁股，而有些人则说：“放了他吧。”然而另外一些人出于对这个哗众取宠孩子的羡慕，也拾起周围现成的旧东西扔进水塘，此起彼伏，结果大家都成了落汤鸡。通常的结果是一片混战，几百万人因此打破了脑袋。

and they dump it into the water and everybody gets splashed and one thing leading to another,the usual result is a free-for-all fight and a few million broken heads.

Alexander was such a bold,had boy.

And Helen of Troy,in her own charming way,was such a bad,bold girl,and history is just full of them.

But by far the worst offenders are those wicked citizens who play this game with ideas and use the stagnant pool of man's spiritual indifference as their playground. And I for one don't wonder that they are hated by all right-thinking citizens and are punished with great severity if ever they are unfortunate enough to let themselves be caught.

Think of the damage they have done these last four hundred years.

There were the leaders of the rebirth of the ancient world. The stately moats of the Middle Ages reflected the image of a society that was harmonious in both color and texture. It was not perfect. But people liked it. They loved to see the blending of the brick-red walls of their little homes with the somber gray of those high cathedral towers that watched over their souls.

Came the terrible splash of the Renaissance and overnight everything was changed. But it was only a beginning. For just when the poor burghers had almost recovered from the shock,that dreadful German monk appeared with a whole cartload of specially prepared bricks and dumped them right into the heart of the pontifical lagoon. Really,that was too much. And no wonder that it took the world three centuries to recover from the shock.

The older historians who studied this period often fell into a slight error. They saw the commotion and decided that the ripples had been started by a common cause,which they alternately called

■ 环绕世界的大海

亚历山大就是这样一个胆大的坏孩子。

特洛伊的海伦非常漂亮，也是个任意胡为的坏女人。这种人在历史上随处可见。

但从古至今，最令人深恶痛绝的是那些卑鄙小人,他们以追求理想的名义玩着类似的游戏，把人们如一潭死水般麻木的精神作为用武之地。凡是思维正常的人都会对他们恨之入骨，他们一旦被捉住就会受到严惩。对此我一点都不奇怪。

想想过去近400年来他们造成的灾难吧。

他们是复辟旧世界的首领。中世纪庄严的护城河折射出了那个社会的面貌，它的色彩和条理都很和谐。尽管它不是完美无缺，但人们喜欢它，而且喜欢看自己小院的红砖墙与暗灰色的天主教堂交相辉映，居高临下的教堂塔楼庇护着他们的灵魂。

文艺复兴的滔天巨浪席卷而来，一夜间一切都面目全非。但这仅仅是开始。可怜的市民刚从惊愕中醒来，可怕的德国僧侣出现了。他们带着一大车特意准备的砖头，随即将砖头全都倒进了教皇的环礁湖心。说实话，这的确太过分了。难怪世界

the Renaissance and the Reformation.

Today we know better.

The Renaissance and the Reformation were movements which professed to be striving after a common purpose. But the means by which they hoped to accomplish their ultimate object were so utterly different that Humanist and Protestant not infrequently came to regard each other with bitter hostility.

They both believed in the supreme rights of man. During the Middle Ages the individual had been completely merged in the community. He did not exist as John Doe,a bright citizen who came and went at will,who sold and bought as he liked,who went to any one of a dozen churches (or to none at all,as suited his tastes and his prejudices). His life from the time of his birth to the hour of his death was lived according to a rigid handbook of economic and spiritual etiquette. This taught him that his body was a shoddy garment,casually borrowed from Mother Nature and of no value except as a temporary receptacle for his immortal soul.

It trained him to believe that this world was a half way house to future glory and should be regarded with that profound contempt which travelers destined for New York bestow upon Queenstown and Halifax.

And now unto the excellent John,living happily in the best of all possible worlds (since it was the only world he knew),came the two fairy god-mothers,Renaissance and Reformation,and said:"Arise,noble citizen,from now on thou art to be free."

But when John asked,"Free to do what?"the answers greatly differed.

"Free to go forth in quest of Beauty,"the Renaissance replied.

"Free to go in quest of Truth,"the Reformation admonished him.

"Free to search the records of the past when the world was truly the realm of men. Free

要用三个世纪的时间才从这场惊愕中恢复过来。

研究这段历史的老历史学家常常会犯小错误。他们看到了这些骚乱，断定这些波澜是起源于一个共同的原因，并将这一原因交替地称为文艺复兴或宗教改革。

如今我们对此有了更多的了解。

文艺复兴和宗教改革都宣称是在为同一个目标而奋斗。但它们寻求最终目标的手段大相径庭，以至于人文主义者和清教徒之间的恶意攻讦并不少见。

他们都相信人类具有至高无上的权力。在中世纪，个体已完全淹没于群体之中。那个精神抖擞、来去自由、按照自己喜好做买卖或自行挑选教堂（或者按照自己的喜好根本不去教堂）的人已经不复存在了。中世纪的人从生到死，都严格地遵循经济和精神礼节的小册子行事。这些规则教导他，身体是一件翻制的外衣，偶然从自然之母那儿借来，除了暂时安置灵魂之外，别无价值。

这些规则使他相信，这个世界只不过是通往天堂的驿站，对它可以不屑一顾，就像去纽约的旅客对皇后镇（新西兰）和哈利法克斯（加拿大）毫无兴致一样。

而那个自由的约翰在这个尽善尽美的世界（因为这是他所能了解的唯一的世界）幸福地生活着，这时来了两个神仙圣母——文艺复兴和宗教改革。她们说：“高贵的公民，起来吧，从现在开始你自由啦。”

约翰问道：“自由了能干什么？”结果她们的答案全然不同。

“自由了就可以追求美好的事物。”文艺复兴答道。

“自由了就可以探求真理。”宗教改革劝诫他。

to realize those ideals which once filled the hearts of poets and painters and sculptors and architects. Free to turn the universe into thine eternal laboratory,that thou mayest know all her secrets,"was the promise of the Renaissance.

"Free to study the word of God,that thou mayest find salvation for thy soul and forgiveness for thy sins,"was the warning of the Reformation.

And they turned on their heels and left poor John Doe in the possession of a new freedom which was infinitely more embarrassing than the thralldom of his former days.

Fortunately or unfortunately,the Renaissance soon made her peace with the established order of things. The successors of Phidias and Horace discovered that a belief in the established Deity and outward conformity to the rules of the Church were two very different things and that one could paint pagan pictures and compose heathenish sonnets with complete impunity if one took the precaution to call Hercules,John the Baptist,and Hera,the Virgin Mary.

They were like tourists who go to India and who obey certain laws which mean nothing to them at all in order that they may gain entrance to the temples and travel freely without disturbing the peace of the land.

But in the eyes of an honest follower of Luther,the most trifling of details at once assumed enormous importance. An erroneous comma in Deuteronomy might mean exile. As for a misplaced full stop in the Apocalypse,it called for instant death.

To people like these who took what they considered their religious convictions with bitter seriousness,the merry compromise of the Renaissance seemed a dastardly act of cowardice.

As a result,Renaissance and Reformation parted company,never to meet again.

Whereupon the Reformation,alone against all the world,buckled on the armor of

"自由了就可以探索过去，那时世界真正为人类所拥有。自由地实现理想，那曾是诗人、画家、雕塑家和建筑师一心追求的东西。自由地去把整个宇宙变成你永久的实验场，让你知道它所有的神奇奥秘。"文艺复兴许诺道。

"自由了就可以研究上帝的话语，你的灵魂会得到拯救，你的罪孽会得到饶恕。"宗教改革警告道。

她们转身离开了，留下可怜的他独享新自由。与以往被束缚的日子相比，眼前的新自由更令人迷惑彷徨。

无论幸运还是不幸，文艺复兴不久就与现存秩序和平共处了。菲狄亚斯和贺拉斯的后裔发现，信奉已经确立的上帝和表面顺从教规完全是两码事，只要小心地称颂赫拉克勒斯为施洗约翰，把天后赫拉称为圣母玛丽亚，就可以亵渎地画异教画，写异教诗歌，却不会受到惩罚。

这就像去印度的旅行者，只要遵守一些与己无关的法律，便能进入庙宇自由浏览，也不会搅乱了那片土地的安宁。

但在路德那些真正追随者的眼里，最微小的细节也要极其重视。《旧约・申命记》中错了一个逗号便可能意味着流放。要是在《启示录》里错了一个句号，就会立即被处死。

这种人对自己信仰的宗教至真至诚，在他们看来，文艺复兴皆大欢喜的折中方式是典型的懦夫行为。

结果，文艺复兴和宗教改革散伙了，彼此绝了交。

righteousness and made ready to defend her holiest possessions.

In the beginning,the army of revolt was composed almost exclusively of Germans. They fought and suffered with extreme bravery,but that mutual jealousy which is the bane and the curse of all northern nations soon lamed their efforts and forced them to accept a truce. The strategy which led to the ultimate victory was provided by a very different sort of genius. Luther stepped aside to make room for Calvin.

It was high time.

In that same French college where Erasmus had spent so many of his unhappy Parisian days,a black-bearded young Spaniard with a limp (the result of a Gallic gunshot) was dreaming of the day when he should march at the head of a new army of the Lord to rid the world of the last of the heretics.

It takes a fanatic to fight a fanatic.

And only a man of granite,like Calvin,would have been able to defeat the plans of Loyola.

Personally,I am glad that I was not obliged to live in Geneva in the sixteenth century. At the same time I am profoundly grateful that the Geneva of the sixteenth century existed.

Without it,the world of the twentieth century would have been a great deal more uncomfortable and I for one would probably be in jail.

The hero of this glorious fight,the famous Magister Joannes Calvinus (or Jean Calvini or John Calvin) was a few years younger than Luther. Date of birth:July 10,1509. Place of birth:the city of Noyon in northern France. Background:French middle class. Father:a small clerical

日内瓦

于是，宗教改革穿上“正义”的铠甲，单枪匹马地抵挡整个世界，时刻准备护卫自己最神圣的财富。

起初，叛军几乎都是日耳曼人。他们勇于战斗，不顾牺牲。但是，相互妒忌的毒牙及北方各国间的争吵很快削弱了他们的努力，最后被迫接受调停。最终导致胜利的计谋是由一个另类天才提出的。路德让位给了加尔文。

这真是恰逢其时。

在同一所法国学院，伊拉斯谟度过了许多不愉快的岁月，而另一个年轻的黑胡子西班牙人拖着一条跛腿（高卢人子弹让他受的伤），整日里梦想着有朝一日能亲率一支上帝的新军，把世界从最后的异端中解救出来。

需要一个狂热者去打败另一个狂热者。

只有像加尔文这样坚如磐石的人，才有可能击败罗耀拉的计划。

从个人角度而言，我很高兴自己没有生活在16世纪的日内瓦；不过同时我也为16世纪有日内瓦的存在而深感庆幸。

没有它，20世纪的世界可能会更加乌烟瘴气，而像我这样的人很可能会饱尝铁

official. Mother:the daughter of an innkeeper. Family:five sons and two daughters. Characteristic qualities of early education:thrift,simplicity,and a tendency to do all things in an orderly manner,not stingily,but with minute and efficient care.

John,the second son,was meant for the priesthood. The father had influential friends,and could eventually get him into a good parish. Before he was thirteen years old,he already held a small office in the cathedral of his home city. This gave him a small but steady income. It was used to send him to a good school in Paris. A remarkable boy. Every one who came in contact with him said,"Watch out for that youngster!"

The French educational system of the sixteenth century was well able to take care of such a child and make the best of his many gifts. At the age of nineteen,John was allowed to preach. His future as a duly established deacon seemed assured.

But there were five sons and two daughters. Advancement in the Church was slow. The law offered better opportunities. Besides,it was a time of great religious excitement and the future was uncertain. A distant relative,a certain Pierre Olivétan,had just translated the Bible into French. John,while in Paris,had spent much time with his cousin. It would never do to have two heretics in one family. John was packed off to Orleans and was apprenticed to an old lawyer that he might learn the business of pleading and arguing and drawing up briefs.

Here the same thing happened as in Paris. Before the end of the year,the pupil had turned teacher and was coaching his less industrious fellow-students in the principles of jurisprudence. And soon he knew all there was to know and was ready to start upon that course which,so his father fondly hoped,would some day make him the rival of those famous avocats who got a hundred gold pieces for a single opinion and who drove in a coach and four when they were called upon to see the king in distant Compiègne.

But nothing came of these dreams. John Calvin never practiced law.

窗生涯。

这场光荣之战的英雄是著名的约翰·加尔文，他比路德小几岁。1509年6月10日生于法国的北部城市努瓦永。他是法国中产阶级出身，父亲是个教会的小职员，母亲是饭店老板的女儿。家庭成员包括五个儿子、两个女儿。早期家庭教育的特征包括节俭、质朴、循规蹈矩、细致有效但不吝啬等。

约翰是家里的次子，原本打算当教士。他父亲结识了一些有势力的朋友，可以把他安排在好教区。他没满13岁就在本乡的教堂里做事，有一笔数额虽少却稳定的收入，这笔钱被用来送他到巴黎的好学校读书。这孩子很出众，凡是和他接触过的人都说："留心这个小伙子！"

16世纪的法国教育体制能够培养这样的孩子，并且尽量挖掘他的才能。19岁那年，他开始获准布道。看来他当一名执事的前景似乎已成定局。

但是家中有五儿两女，教堂的晋升又很缓慢，而司法界能提供更好的机会。况且宗教正逢骚乱之时，前途莫测。一个叫皮埃尔·奥利维坦的远亲刚刚把《圣经》译成法文。此时正在巴黎的约翰经常与他在一起。一个家庭有两个异教徒是绝对不行的，于是约翰便打起行囊前往奥尔良，做了一个老律师的学徒，学习申诉、辩护、起草文书等业务。

与在巴黎如出一辙的情形又出现了。到了年底，这个学生成了老师，指导那些不够刻苦的同学学习法学原理。他很快掌握了所需要的一切，可以做律师了。他父亲希望他有朝一日能成为那些著名律师的对手。这些律师发表一点儿意见就能得到

Instead,he returned to his first love,sold his digests and his pandects,devoted the proceeds to a collection of theological works and started in all seriousness upon that task which was to make him one of the most important historical figures of the last twenty centuries.

The years,however,which he had spent studying the principles of Roman law put their stamp upon all his further activities. It was impossible for him to approach a problem by way of his emotions. He felt things and he felt them deeply. Read his letters to those of his followers who had fallen into the hands of Catholics and who had been condemned to be roasted to death over slow burning coal fires. In their helpless agony they are as fine a bit of writing as anything of which we have a record. And they show such a delicate understanding of human psychology that the poor victims went to their death blessing the name of the man whose teaching had brought them into their predicament.

No,Calvin was not,as so many of his enemies have said,a man without a heart. But life to him was a sacred duty.

And he tried so desperately hard to be honest with himself and with his God that he must first reduce every question to certain fundamental principles of faith and doctrine before he dared to expose it to the touchstone of human sentiment.

When Pope Pius IV heard of his death,he remarked,"The power of that heretic lay in the fact that he was indifferent to money."If His Holiness meant to pay his enemy the compliment of absolute personal disinterestedness,he was right. Calvin lived and died a poor man and refused to accept his last quarterly salary because"illness had made it impossible for him to earn that money as he should have done."

But his strength lay elsewhere.

He was a man of one idea,his life centered around one all-overpowering impulse;the

上百个金币，而远在贡比埃涅的国王召见他们时，他们还要乘坐四轮马车前往。

可是这些梦想从未实现，约翰·加尔文从未干过法律工作。

相反，他又回到了自己最初的爱好，卖掉了法律汇编和法典，专心投入到神学著作当中，一丝不苟地开始完成自己的使命，这使他成为20个世纪以来最重要的历史人物之一。

不过，早年对罗马法典的研究在他以后的所有行为上都打下了烙印，他已不可能再凭感情来处理问题。他对事物充满感情，并感受至深。读一读他写给那些已落入天主教徒手里并被判处用炭火慢慢烤死的追随者的信吧。在表达无望的痛苦时，这些信是我们看到的有史以来最细腻的世间佳作。他在信中表达了对人类心理细致入微的理解，以至于那些可怜的受害者至死还在为这个人祝福，而正是由于这个人的教诲，才使他们陷入痛苦境地的。

不，加尔文并不像他众多敌人所说的那样是个铁石心肠的人。但生活对他而言是神圣的职责。

他竭尽全力对上帝和自己保持忠诚，对于所信仰的某些基本原理和教义，在把它们交付人类情感的试金石之前，自己首先必须消除所有的疑问。

教皇庇护四世得知他的死讯时说：“这个异教徒的力量在于他对金钱的漠视。”如果教皇是在称颂他毫无利己之心的死敌的话，那么他说对了。加尔文终生贫困潦倒，他曾拒绝接受最后一季的薪金，因为“疾病已使他不能再像从前那样挣钱了”。

desire to find the truth of God as revealed in the Scriptures. When he finally had reached a conclusion that seemed proof against every possible form of argument and objection,then at last he incorporated it into his own code of life. And thereafter he went his way with such utter disregard for the consequences of his decision that he became both invincible and irresistible.

This quality,however,was not to make itself manifest until many years later. During the first decade after his conversion he was obliged to direct all his energies toward the very commonplace problem of keeping alive.

A short triumph of the"new learning"in the University of Paris,an orgy of Greek declensions,Hebrew irregular verbs and other forbidden intellectual fruit had been followed by the usual reaction. When it appeared that even the rector of that famous seat of learning had been contaminated with the pernicious new German doctrines,steps were taken to purge the institution of all those who in terms of our modern medical science might be considered"idea carriers."Calvin,who,'twas said,had given the rector the material for several of his most objectionable speeches,was among those whose names appeared at the top of the list of suspects. His rooms were searched. His papers were confiscated and an order was issued for his arrest.

He heard of it and hid himself in the house of a friend.

But storms in an academic tea-pot never last very long. All the same,a career in the Church of Rome had become an impossibility. The moment had arrived for a definite choice.

In the year 1534 Calvin broke away from the old faith. Almost at the same moment,on the hills of Montmartre,high above the French capital,Loyola and

■ 罗耀拉

他的力量还表现在其他方面。

他是个信念始终如一的人，一生都以一个强大的推动力为中心：那就是探索《圣经》中体现出来的上帝的真理。当他最后得出自己认为不可辩驳的结论时，就把它纳入到了自己的生活准则中。从此他的言行就依此行事，完全无视自己的判断会引发怎样的后果，这使他成为不可战胜、不可阻挡之人。

然而这个品质直到许多年后才显现出来。在信念转变后的头十年，他不得不竭尽全力对付谋生这个最普通的问题。

“新学”在巴黎大学获得了短暂的胜利，希腊文词尾变化、希伯来文不规则动词和其他受禁的知识，这些成果全都引起了反响。就连端坐在博学宝辇上的教区长也受到了邪恶的日耳曼新教义的毒害。于是，人们采取措施，清洗那些现代医学会称之为“思想传播者”的人。据说加尔文曾把几篇最易引起异议的讲演稿交给了教区长，于是他的名字列在了嫌疑犯名单的前列。他的房间遭到搜查，文章被没收，逮捕他的命令也已签发。

他闻风藏到了朋友家里。

小学院的风波不会持续太久，但同时在罗马教会供职的可能性也没有了。做出

a handful of his fellow students were taking that solemn vow which shortly afterwards was to be incorporated into the constitution of the Society of Jesus.

Thereupon they both left Paris.

Ignatius set his face towards the east,but remembering the unfortunate outcome of his first assault upon the Holy Land,he retraced his steps,went to Rome and there began those activities which were to carry his fame (or otherwise) to every nook and corner of our planet.

John was of a different caliber. His Kingdom of God was bound to neither time nor place and he wandered forth that he might find a quiet spot and devote the rest of his days to reading,to contemplation and to the peaceful expounding of his ideas.

He happened to be on his way to Strassburg when the outbreak of a war between Charles V and Francis I forced him to make a detour through western Switzerland. In Geneva he was welcomed by Guillaume Farel,one of the stormy petrels of the French Reformation,fugitive extraordinary from all ecclesiastical and inquisitorial dungeons. Farel welcomed him with open arms,spoke to him of the wondrous things that might be accomplished in this little Swiss principality and bade him stay. Calvin asked time to consider. Then he stayed.

In this way did the chances of war decree that the New Zion should be built at the foot of the Alps.

It is a strange world.

Columbus sets forth to discover the Indies and stumbles upon a new continent.

Calvin,in search of a quiet spot where he may spend the rest of his days in study and holy meditation,wanders into a third-rate Swiss town and makes it the spiritual capital of those who soon afterwards turn the domains of their most Catholic Majesties into a

明确选择的时刻到了。

1534年，加尔文与旧信仰决裂了。几乎与此同时，在俯瞰法国首都的蒙马特尔山上，罗耀拉和几个追随他的学生也庄严宣誓，这些誓言后来被纳入耶稣会的法典之中。

接着，他们都离开了巴黎。

伊格那修（罗耀拉）向东而行，但想起自己第一次攻击圣地的不幸结局，他停下了脚步，来到了罗马。在那儿他着手工作，并使他的英名（或许并非如此）载誉史册，闻名四海。

约翰（加尔文）却是另外一种情形。他的天国不受时间地点的限制。他漫游四方，希望能找到一席安静之地，把余生都投入到阅读、思索以及和平地宣讲自己的主张上面。

他恰好行进在前往斯特拉斯堡的路上，由于查理五世和弗朗西斯一世之间正在交战，他被迫从瑞士西部绕行。在日内瓦，他受到了吉勒莫·法里尔的欢迎，法里尔是法国宗教改革中的海燕，是从长老会和宗教法庭的牢笼里逃出来的杰出代表。法里尔张开双臂迎接了他，告诉他在这个瑞士小公国里可以完成什么样的业绩，并请他留下来。加尔文先是要求能有一些时间考虑此事，随后留了下来。

就这样，为了躲避战争，新天国决定建在阿尔卑斯山脚下。

那是个奇特的世界。

哥伦布出发去寻找印度，却无意间发现了新大陆。

gigantic Protestant empire.

Why should any one ever read fiction when history serves all purposes?

I do not know whether the family Bible of Calvin has been preserved. But if it still exists,the volume will show considerable wear on that particular page which contains the sixth chapter of the book of Daniel. The French reformer was a modest man,but often he must have found consolation in the story of that other steadfast servant of the living God who also had been cast into a den of lions and whose innocence had saved him from a gruesome and untimely death.

Geneva was no Babylon. It was a respectable little city inhabited by respectable Swiss cloth makers. They took life seriously,but not quite so seriously as that new master who was now holding forth in the pulpit of their Saint Peter.

And furthermore,there was a Nebuchadnezzar in the form of a Duke of Savoy. It was during one of their interminable quarrels with the house of Savoy that the descendants of Caesar's Allobroges had decided to make common cause with the other Swiss cantons and join the Reformation. The alliance therefore between Geneva and Wittenberg was a marriage of convenience,an engagement based upon common interests rather than common affection.

But no sooner had the news spread abroad that"Geneva had gone Protestant,"than all the eager apostles of half a hundred new and crazy creeds flocked to the shores of Lake Leman. With tremendous energy they began to preach some of the queerest doctrines ever conceived by mortal man.

Calvin detested these amateur prophets with all his heart. He fully appreciated what a menace they would prove to the cause of which they were such ardent but ill-guided champions. And the first thing he did as soon as he had enjoyed a few months leisure was

加尔文在寻求一片静地以供研究和思索教义之用，他信马由缰地来到了瑞士一个三等小镇，并使它成为人们心目中的精神之都。人们很快就把天主教王国的大片领地变成了庞大的新教帝国。

既然读史能知晓一切，人们为何还要读小说？

不知道加尔文家里的《圣经》是否仍被保存着。如果有，人们会发现，书中载有丹尼尔书的第6章会磨损得特别厉害。这个法国改革家是个自律的人，但他也经常需要从其他坚定不移地侍奉永恒上帝的奴仆故事里寻求安慰——丹尼尔已被扔进狮穴，他的清白无辜挽救了他，使他免遭令人不寒而栗的死亡下场。

日内瓦不是巴比伦。这是个令人起敬的小城，住着体面的瑞士裁缝。他们严肃地对待生活，当然还比不上加尔文这位像圣彼得那样在讲坛上滔滔不绝地布道的新领袖。

另外，还有一个名叫尼布甲尼撒的萨伏伊公爵。正是在与萨伏伊家族无休止的争吵中，被凯撒征服的阿洛布洛克斯人的后裔才决定和瑞士其他地区联合起来，加入宗教改革运动。日内瓦和维滕堡的联合是一种互惠联姻，是在共同利益而非相互爱慕的基础上建立起来的联盟。

但是，日内瓦改奉新教的消息刚刚传开，就有总共不下50种热衷于各种新奇教义的教士们涌到了莱蒙湖边。他们干劲冲天，开始宣讲迄今为止人们所能想见的最为怪诞的教义。

加尔文打心底里厌恶这些业余预言家。他深知这些误入歧途的热情战士最终会

to write down as precisely and briefly as he could what he expected his new parishioners to hold true and what he expected them to hold false. And that no man might claim the ancient and timeworn excuse,"I did not know the law,"he,together with his friend Farel,personally examined all Genevans in batches of ten and allowed only those to the full rights of citizenship who swore the oath of allegiance to this strange religious constitution.

Next he composed a formidable catechism for the benefit of the younger generation.

Next he prevailed upon the Town Council to expel all those who still clung to their old erroneous opinions.

Then,having cleared the ground for further action,he set about to found him a state along the lines laid down by the political economists of the books of Exodus and Deuteronomy. For Calvin,like so many other of the great reformers,was really much more of an ancient Jew than a modern Christian. His lips did homage to the God of Jesus,but his heart went out to the Jehovah of Moses.

This,of course,is a phenomenon often observed during periods of great emotional stress. The opinions of the humble Nazarene carpenter upon the subject of hatred and strife are so definite and so clear cut that no compromise has ever been found possible between them and those violent methods by which nations and individuals have,during the last two thousand years,tried to accomplish their ends.

Hence,as soon as a war breaks out,by silent consent of all concerned,we temporarily close the pages of the Gospels and cheerfully wallow in the blood and thunder and the eye-for-an-eye philosophy of the Old Testament.

And as the Reformation was really a war and a very atrocious one,in which no quarter was asked and very little quarter was given,it need not surprise us that the state of Calvin was in reality an armed camp in which all semblance of personal liberty was gradually

给自己艰难推进的事业带来威胁。在经过几个月短暂的休憩后，他立即着手以最准确简洁的语言告诉新教民他所希望见到的是非曲直，谁都不能再用那个老掉牙的借口说："我不知道啊。"他和朋友法里尔一起，十个人为一组，亲自对全体日内瓦人进行检查，只有宣誓效忠这个神奇宗法的人才能享有全部公民权。

接着，为了有益于年轻人，他编写了一本足以令人敬畏的教义问答手册。

随即他又在市议会上获得成功，把所有依旧坚持错误观点的人驱逐出城。

在扫清前进道路的障碍之后，他按照政治经济学家在《出埃及记》和《申命记》中制定的规范，开始建立一个新的公国。像其他大多数改革者一样，与其说加尔文是个现代基督徒，还不如说他更像一个古犹太人。他口中叨念着基督耶稣的祷告词，心里却向往摩西的耶和华。

当然，在情绪动荡的年代，经常会看到这样的情形：那个卑微的拿撒勒木匠对仇恨和斗争有自己明确无误的看法，因此在他的观点和暴力行动之间根本不可能存在折中的办法。在过去的2000年，上至国家下到个人，都想通过暴力手段达到目的。

所以，战争一经爆发，相关人等都沉默了。人们暂时合上福音书，兴致勃勃地沉迷于《旧约》以牙还牙、以眼还眼哲学的血雨腥风之中。

由于宗教改革的确是一场相当残暴的战争，没人乞求宽恕，也没人给予宽恕，加尔文的王国实际上就是个全副武装的军营，任何个性自由的表现都逐渐被压制下去，对此我们毫不奇怪。

当然，这一切的取得并非没有巨大的阻力。1538年，组织中更为崇尚自由的分

suppressed.

Of course,all this was not accomplished without tremendous opposition,and in the year 1538 the attitude of the more liberal elements in the community became so threatening that Calvin was forced to leave the city. But in 1541 his adherents returned to power. Amidst the ringing of many bells and the loud hosannas of the deacons,Magister Joannes returned to his citadel on the river Rhone. Thereafter he was the uncrowned King of Geneva and the next twenty-three years he devoted to the establishment and the perfection of a theocratic form of government,the like of which the world had not seen since the days of Ezekiel and Ezra.

The word"discipline"according to the Oxford Concise Dictionary,means"to bring under control,to train to obedience and order,to drill."It expresses best the spirit which permeated the entire political-clerical structure of Calvin's dreams.

Luther,after the nature of most Germans,had been a good deal of a sentimentalist. The Word of God alone,so it seemed to him,would show a man the way to the life everlasting.

This was much too indefinite to suit the taste of the great French reformer. The Word of God might be a beacon light of hope,but the road was long and dark and many were the temptations that made people forget their true destination.

The minister,however,could not go astray. He was a man set apart. He knew all pitfalls. He was incorruptible. And if perchance he felt inclined to wander from the straight path,the weekly meetings of the clergy,at which these worthy gentlemen were invited to criticize each other freely,would speedily bring him back to a realization of his duties. Hence he was the ideal held before all those who truly aspired after salvation.

Those of us who have ever climbed mountains know that professional guides can upon occasion be veritable tyrants. They know the perils of a pile of rocks,the hidden dangers

子对加尔文形成了相当大的威胁，使他被迫离开了这座城市。但到了1541年，他的支持者们再度掌权。在一片钟鼓声和教士嘹亮的赞美声中，乔安尼斯行政长官又回到了罗纳河畔的城堡。从此，他成为日内瓦的无冕之王，在以后的23年里他致力于建立和完善神权政府机构，这是从以西结和以斯拉以来未曾出现过的。

按照《牛津简明大辞典》的解释，“纪律”一词意为：“接受控制，养成服从和秩序，并进行训练。”它准确地表达了贯穿于加尔文政教合一梦想的精神实质。

路德的本性和大多数日耳曼人一样，是个典型的感伤主义者。在他看来，上帝的话语本身就足以向人们指明通往永恒世界的道路。

这太不确切了，难以迎合法国改革家的口味。上帝的言辞可能是希望之灯，但是道路黑暗漫长，会有无数的诱惑使人忘记自己真正的目标。

然而这个新教牧师却不会迷失方向，他是个例外。他知道所有陷阱，也不会被收买。一旦他偶然想要偏离正道，每周的教士例会就很快能使他认清自己的责任。在这种会上，所有符合资格的先生都可以参加，自由地开展相互批评。于是他成为所有追求救赎的人心目中的理想人物。

爬过山的人都知道，职业导游有时会成为不折不扣的暴君。他们知道一堆岩石的险处，了解看似平常的雪地里暗藏的危险。因此在经过这些地段时，他们对其所监管的旅行团队拥有完全的指挥权，哪个愚蠢的旅客胆敢不听从命令，污言秽语就会劈头盖脸地倾泻下来。

加尔文理想王国的教士也有同样的责任感。他们对那些跌倒了请求帮助的人乐

of an innocent-looking snowfield. Wherefore they assume complete command of the party that has entrusted itself to their care and profanity raineth richly upon the head of the foolish tourist who dares to disobey their orders.

The ministers of Calvin's ideal state had a similar conception of their duties. They were ever delighted to extend a helping hand to those who stumbled and asked that they be supported. But when willful people purposely left the beaten track and wandered away from the flock,then that hand was withdrawn and became a fist which meted out punishment that was both quick and terrible.

In many other communities the dominies would have been delighted to exercise a similar power. But the civil authorities,jealous of their own prerogatives,rarely allowed the clergy to compete with the courts and the executioners. Calvin knew this and within his own bailiwick he established a form of church discipline which practically superseded the laws of the land.

Among the curious historical misconceptions which have gained such popularity since the days of the great war,none is more surprising than the belief that the French people (in contrast to their Teuton neighbors) are a liberty-loving race and detest all regimentation. The French have for centuries submitted to the rule of a bureaucracy quite as complicated and infinitely less efficient than the one which existed in Prussia in the pre-war days. The officials are a little less punctual about their office hours and the spotlessness of their collars and they are given to sucking a particularly vile sort of cigarette. Otherwise they are quite as meddlesome and as obnoxious as those in the eastern republic,and the public accepts their rudeness with a meekness that is astonishing in a race so addicted to rebellion.

Calvin was the ideal Frenchman in his love for centralization. In some details he almost approached the perfection for detail which was the secret of Napoleon's success. But

意施以援手。但对那些一意孤行、蓄意要离开沧桑正道的人，那伸出的援手就会抽回来变成拳头，给对方以迅疾而可怕的攻击。

在其他许多社团，牧师们也愿意行使类似的权力。但那些嫉妒他们特权的地方官员，几乎不允许牧师与法庭和刽子手分庭抗礼。加尔文对此谙熟于心，他在自己的管辖区域内建立了一套实际上已凌驾于现实法律之上的教规。

自大战以来，在对历史问题的诸多怪异的解读中，没有哪个说法比接下来的这个更令人吃惊：法国人（与条顿人相比）是热爱自由、憎恨所有监管的民族。几个世纪以来，法国一直处于官僚体制的统治之下，机构庞杂，与战前的普鲁士政府相比，效率更为低下。官员们迟到早退，衣冠不整，还抽着特别令人讨厌的卷烟。此外，他们还像东部共和国的政府官员们那样因爱管闲事而令人反感，公众对他们的粗鲁行径只能逆来顺

■ 新的暴政

unlike the great emperor,he was utterly devoid of all personal ambition. He was just a dreadfully serious man with a weak stomach and no sense of humor.

He ransacked the Old Testament to discover what would be agreeable to his particular Jehovah. And then the people of Geneva were asked to accept this interpretation of the Jewish chronicles as a direct revelation of the divine will.

Almost over night the merry city on the Rhone became a community of rueful sinners. A civic inquisition composed of six ministers and twelve elders watched night and day over the private opinions of all citizens. Whosoever was suspected of an inclination towards"forbidden heresies"was cited to appear before an ecclesiastic tribunal that he might be examined upon all points of doctrine and explain where,how and in what way he had obtained the books which had given him the pernicious ideas which had led him astray. If the culprit showed a repentant spirit,he might escape with a sentence of enforced attendance at Sunday School. But in case he showed himself obstinate,he must leave the city within twenty-four hours and never again show himself within the jurisdiction of the Genevan commonwealth.

But a proper lack of orthodox sentiment was not the only thing that could get a man into trouble with the so-called Consistorium. An afternoon spent at a bowling-alley in a nearby village,if properly reported (as such things invariably are),could be reason enough for a severe admonition. Jokes,both practical and otherwise,were considered the height of bad form. An attempt at wit during a wedding ceremony was sufficient cause for a jail sentence.

Gradually the New Zion was so encumbered with laws,edicts,regulations,rescripts and decrees that life became a highly complicated affair and lost a great deal of its old flavor.

Dancing was not allowed. Singing was not allowed. Card playing was not allowed. Gambling,of course,was not allowed. Birthday parties were not allowed. County fairs were not allowed. Silks and satins and all manifestations of external splendor were not

受，这对于一个醉心于反叛的民族来讲真是个奇迹。

就热衷于集权这一点来看，加尔文是个典型的法国人。他在某些细节方面近乎完美，而这些完美的细节正是拿破仑成功的秘籍。但与那个伟大皇帝不同，加尔文完全没有个人野心，他只是个极端认真的人，胃口不好，还缺乏幽默感。

他翻遍了《旧约》，寻找那些能够与他特指的耶和华保持一致的言辞，然后要求日内瓦人接受他对犹太历史的解读，将其视为上帝意志的直接反映。

一夜之间，罗纳河畔这座迷人的城市变成了悲哀的罪人的聚集地。一个由6位教士和12位长者组成的市政宗教法庭日夜监视着所有市民的私下言论。如果有谁被怀疑具有“异端”违禁倾向，便会被传讯到长老会法庭，逐一接受审查，并且需要解释清楚他是从哪里、如何以及用什么方式得到这些灌输错误思想并将其引入歧途的书籍的。如果被告有悔过自新的态度，可以通过强制参加主日学校的形式免予起诉。但是如果他表现得顽固不化，就必须在24小时内离开这座城市，永远不得在日内瓦联邦境内再度露面。

缺乏正统感并不是人们与所谓的“宗教法庭”之间发生矛盾的唯一原因。如果有人整个下午都在邻村玩滚木球，若是被人有意控告的话（常常会这样），就足以被严厉警告一番。不论是恶作剧还是真正的玩笑，都被看成是最恶毒的行为。婚礼上的各种取笑打闹更足以被判入狱。

渐渐地，梦想中的天国被法律、法令、规范、命令和政令所覆盖，生活因而变

allowed. What was allowed was going to church and going to school. For Calvin was a man of positive ideas.

The verboten sign could keep out sin,but it could not force a man to love virtue. That had to come through an inner persuasion. Hence the establishment of excellent schools and a first-rate university and the encouragement of all learning. And the establishment of a rather interesting form of communal life which absorbed a good deal of the surplus energy of the community and which made the average man forget the many hardships and restrictions to which he was submitted. If it had been entirely lacking in human qualities,the system of Calvin could never have survived and it certainly would not have played such a very decisive rôle in the history of the last three hundred years. All of which however belongs in a book devoted to the development of political ideas. This time we are interested in the question of what Geneva did for tolerance and we come to the conclusion that the Protestant Rome was not a whit better than its Catholic namesake.

The extenuating circumstances I have enumerated a few pages back. In a world which was forced to stand by and witness such bestial occurrences as the massacre of St. Bartholomew and the wholesale extermination of scores of Dutch cities,it was unreasonable to expect that one side (the weaker one at that) should practice a virtue which was equivalent to a self-imposed sentence of death.

This,however,does not absolve Calvin from the crime of having aided and abetted in the legal murder of Gruet and Servetus.

In the case of the former,Calvin might have put up the excuse that Jacques Gruet was seriously suspected of having incited his fellow citizens to riot and that he belonged to a political party which was trying to bring about the downfall of the Calvinists. But Servetus could hardly be called a menace to the safety of the community,as far as Geneva was concerned.

He was what the modern passport regulations call a“transient.”Another twenty-four

成了繁杂不堪的冗事，原有的乐趣几乎丧失殆尽。

不许跳舞，不许唱歌，不许玩扑克牌，赌博理所当然也被禁止。不许举办生日宴会，不许举办乡间集会，丝绸锦缎及所有外表华丽的东西皆属被禁之列。人们只许去教堂和学校，因为加尔文是个有着积极思想主张的人。

禁止标识能够驱逐罪孽，但不能强迫人们热爱美德，这必须经历一个内心自我劝慰的过程。因此，随之而来的是建立了优秀的中学、一流的大学，以及鼓励所有治学活动。此外，还建立了颇具趣味的集体生活，将人们过多的精力有效地吸引过来，使普通人忘记强压在自己身上的诸多磨难和限制。如果完全缺乏人性的话，加尔文的体制不可能存续下去，也不可能在近300年的历史中发挥这样决定性的作用。所有这些都要归功于一本论述政治思想发展的书。此时我们感兴趣的问题是，日内瓦为宽容事业贡献了什么。我们得出的结论是，日内瓦这个新教徒的罗马与天主教的罗马相比，丝毫没有优越之处。

我在前面已经历数了可以减轻罪孽的情形。在这样一个罪恶横行的世界——一个被迫目睹圣巴托洛缪大屠杀和许多荷兰城市被毁的世界，没有理由期待一方（弱的一方）践行宽容的美德，因为那等于自取灭亡。

但这并不能为加尔文的罪责进行开脱，他煽动法庭谋害了格鲁艾特和塞尔维特。

在前一个人的案子里，加尔文尚且可以借口说，雅克·格鲁艾特有煽动市民暴

hours and he would have been gone. But he missed his boat. And so he came to lose his life,and it is a pretty terrible story.

Miguel Serveto,better known as Michael Servetus,was a Spaniard. His father was a respectable notary-public (a semi-legal position in Europe and not just a young man with a stamping machine who charges you a quarter for witnessing your signature) and Miguel was also destined for the law. He was sent to the University of Toulouse,for in those happy days when all lecturing was done in Latin learning was international and the wisdom of the entire world was open to those who had mastered five declensions and a few dozen irregular verbs.

At the French university Servetus made the acquaintance of one Juan de Quintana who shortly afterwards became the confessor of the Emperor Charles V.

During the Middle Ages,an imperial coronation was a good deal like a modern international exhibition. When Charles was crowned in Bologna in the year 1530,Quintana took his friend Michael with him as his secretary and the bright young Spaniard saw all there was to be seen. Like so many men of his time,he was of an insatiable curiosity and he spent the next ten years dabbling in an infinite variety of subjects,medicine,astronomy,astrology,Hebrew,Greek,and,most fatal of all,theology. He was a very competent doctor and in the pursuit of his theological studies he hit upon the idea of the circulation of the blood. It is to be found in the fifteenth chapter of the first one of his books against the doctrine of the Trinity. It shows the one-sidedness of the theological mind of the sixteenth century that none of those who examined the works of Servetus ever discovered that this man had made one of the greatest discoveries of all ages.

If only Servetus had stuck to his medical practice! He might have died peacefully in his bed at a ripe old age.

But he simply could not keep away from the burning questions of his day,and having

动的重大嫌疑，他隶属于某个企图推翻加尔文主义的政党。但即便是从日内瓦所关注的情形来看，塞尔维特也难以被称作是对社会安全构成威胁的人。

按照现代护照的规定，他只是个“过境者”，24小时后离境，但他误了船，并为此丧了命。这真是个耸人听闻的故事。

麦克尔·塞尔维特（以麦克·塞尔维特这个名字更为人们所熟知）是个西班牙人，父亲是受人尊敬的公证人（这个职位在欧洲有关法律性质，而不是指拿着签章机看人家签了字就索取两毛五分钱的年轻人）。麦克尔注定也要从事法律工作，他被送进了图卢兹大学。在那些幸福的日子里，学习范围是国际性的，全都采用拉丁文授课，只要学会五个词尾变化和几个不规则动词，那么整个世界的智慧之门都会为其敞开。

塞尔维特在法国大学里认识了胡安·德·金塔纳。金塔纳不久成为查理五世的忏悔教父。

中世纪时期，帝王的加冕仪式很像现代国际展览会。当查理国王于1530年在波罗尼亚加冕时，金塔纳把他的朋友麦克尔带去做秘书。这个聪明的西班牙年轻人看到了所应了解的一切。与许多同时代的年轻人一样，他的好奇心永不满足，在未来的十年里，他接触了各种各样的学科，其中有医学、天文学、占星术、希伯来文和希腊文，以及最致命的神学。他是个很有潜力的医生，在神学研究的过程中，他萌发了血液循环的想法。这可以在他反对三位一体教义的第一本书的第15章中找到。

access to the printing shops of Lyons,he began to give vent to his opinions upon sundry subjects.

Nowadays a generous millionaire can persuade a college to change its name from Trinity College to that of a popular brand of tobacco and nothing happens. The press says,"Isn't it good of Mr. Dingus to be so generous with his money!"and the public at large shouts"Amen!"

In a world which seems to have lost all capacity for being shocked by such a thing as blasphemy,it is not easy to write of a time when the mere suspicion that one of its fellow citizens had spoken disrespectfully of the Trinity would throw an entire community into a state of panic. But unless we fully appreciate this fact,we shall never be able to understand the horror in which Servetus was held by all good Christians of the first half of the sixteenth century.

And yet he was by no means a radical.

He was what today we would call a liberal.

He rejected the old belief in the Trinity as held both by the Protestants and the Catholics,but he believed so sincerely (one feels inclined to say,so naively) in the correctness of his own views,that he committed the grave error of writing letters to Calvin suggesting that he be allowed to visit Geneva for a personal interview and a thorough discussion of the entire problem.

He was not invited.

And,anyway,it would have been impossible for him to accept. The Inquisitor General of Lyons had already taken a hand in the affair and Servetus was in jail. This inquisitor (curious readers will find a description of him in the works of Rabelais who refers to him as Doribus,a pun upon his name,which was Ory) had got wind of the Spaniard's blasphemies through a letter which a private citizen of Geneva,with the connivance of

所有检查过塞尔维特著作的人竟没有发现他拥有了有史以来最伟大的一个发现，这倒反衬出了16世纪的神学思想有多么偏执。

塞尔维特要是坚持医学研究该有多好啊！他本可以寿终正寝，安详地死在自己的床榻上。

但他就是不能避开那个时代争论最激烈的问题。由于与里昂印刷厂搭上了关系，这就使他有机会针对各种热点话题发表自己的观点。

如今一个慷慨的百万富翁能说服一所院校把“三位一体学院”的名称变成一种流行烟草的商标，而且还安然无事。宣传媒体会说：“丁古斯先生如此慷慨解囊，难道不好吗？”公众便齐声应和道：“阿门！”

由于当今世界似乎已经不再对亵渎神明之事感到震惊，因此要想描绘过去的情况绝非易事——那时，仅仅怀疑一个市民对三位一体说了些不敬之词，便足以使整个社会陷入恐慌。但是除非我们对这个事实有充分的体会，否则就无法理解16世纪上半叶塞尔维特在善良的基督徒心目中所造成的恐怖。

然而，他根本就不是个激进派。

他是我们现在所称的自由派。

他拒绝新教徒和天主教徒所秉承的三位一体的旧信仰。由于他坚信自己的正确看法，因此他犯了写信给加尔文这样极大的错误。他提议允许他访问日内瓦，并和加尔文进行私人会晤，就所有问题进行彻底讨论。

Calvin,had sent to his cousin in Lyons.

Soon the case against him was further strengthened by several samples of Servetus' handwriting,also surreptitiously supplied by Calvin. It really looked as if Calvin did not care who hanged the poor fellow as long as he got hung,but the inquisitors were negligent in their sacred duties and Servetus was able to escape.

First he seems to have tried to reach the Spanish frontier. But the long journey through southern France would have been very dangerous to a man who was so well known and so he decided to follow the rather round-about route via Geneva,Milan,Naples and the Mediterranean Sea.

Late one Saturday afternoon in August of the year 1553 he reached Geneva. He tried to find a boat to cross to the other side of the lake,but boats were not supposed to sail so shortly before the Sabbath day and he was told to wait until Monday.

The next day was Sunday. As it was a misdemeanor for both natives and strangers to stay away from divine service,Servetus went to church. He was recognized and arrested. By what right he was put into jail was never explained. Servetus was a Spanish subject and was not accused of any crime against the laws of Geneva. But he was a liberal in the matter of doctrine,a blasphemous and profane person who dared to have opinions of his own upon the subject of the Trinity. It was absurd that such a person should invoke the protection of the law. A common criminal might do so. A heretic,never! And without further ado he was locked up in a filthy and damp hole,his money and personal belongings were confiscated and two days later he was taken to court and was asked to answer a questionnaire containing thirty-eight different points.

The trial lasted two months and twelve days.

In the end he was found guilty of"heresies against the foundations of the Christian

他没被邀请。

其实他也不可能接受邀请，里昂的宗教大法官已插手此事，塞尔维特被关押入狱了。这个大法官是从一封信中捕捉到这个年轻人的亵渎行径的。这封信是在加尔文的怂恿下，由一个日内瓦人送到他在里昂的表亲手里的。

不久，塞尔维特的一些手稿进一步加剧了对他案情的不利，这也是加尔文偷偷提供的。看起来加尔文似乎真的不在乎由谁绞死这个可怜的家伙，只要他被绞死就行。但是宗教法官们玩忽职守，让塞尔维特逃脱了。

他先是试图穿越西班牙边境，但对他这样的公众人物而言，长途跋涉穿过法国南部将会是相当危险的，于是他决定绕道日内瓦、米兰，然后从那不勒斯到达地中海。

1553年8月的一个星期六的傍晚，他来到日内瓦。他本想搭船到湖对岸去，可是在安息日将近的时候是不开船的，他被告知要等到星期一。

第二天是星期日，无论当地人还是陌生人，逃避宗教礼拜仪式都是不端的行为。塞尔维特也去教堂了。他被人指认出来，遭到了逮捕。但判处他入狱的理由却从未解释清楚过。塞尔维特是西班牙公民，没有指控他违反日内瓦的任何法律。但他在教义上是个自由派，是个胆敢对三位一体发表自由言论的异端不敬分子。这种人想要援引法律的保护才是荒谬呢。普通犯人或许可以，异教徒却坚决不行！为了避免引发进一步混乱，他被锁进肮脏潮湿的地牢，钱财及随身物品全被没收。两天后，他被带上法庭，要求回答写有38个问题的问卷。

religion."The answers which he had given during the discussions of his opinions had exasperated his judges. The usual punishment for cases of his sort,especially if the accused were a foreigner,was perpetual banishment from the territory of the city of Geneva. In the case of Servetus an exception was made. He was condemned to be burned alive.

In the meantime the French tribunal had re-opened the case of the fugitive and the officials of the Inquisition had come to the same conclusion as their Protestant colleagues. They too had condemned Servetus to death and had dispatched their sheriff to Geneva with the request that the culprit be surrendered to him and be brought back to France.

This request was refused.

Calvin was able to do his own burning.

As for that terrible walk to the place of execution,with a delegation of arguing ministers surrounding the heretic upon his last journey,the agony which lasted for more than half an hour and did not really come to an end until the crowd,in their pity for the poor martyr,had thrown a fresh supply of fagots upon the flames,all this makes interesting reading for those who care for that sort of thing,but it had better be omitted. One execution more or less,what difference did it make during a period of unbridled religious fanaticism?

But the case of Servetus really stands by itself. Its consequences were terrible. For now it was shown,and shown with brutal clearness,that those Protestants who had clamored so loudly and persistently for"the right to their own opinions"were merely Catholics in disguise,that they were just as narrow-minded and cruel to those who did not share their own views as their enemies and that they were only waiting for the opportunity to establish a reign of terror of their own.

This accusation is a very serious one. It cannot be dismissed by a mere shrug of the shoulders and a"Well,what would you expect?"

审讯持续了两个月零十二天。

最终，他以“反对基督教基础教义的异端邪说”的罪名被判处有罪。在有关自己观点的辩论中，他的答案使法官暴跳如雷。

对这类案件的常规处罚，尤其是对外国人的处罚，是永远赶出日内瓦城的区域范围。但塞尔维特的案子却是例外。他被判处活活烧死。

与此同时，法国法庭也重新开庭审理这个逃亡者的案子，宗教法庭的官员们和新教徒的同僚们达成共识，他们同样判处塞尔维特死刑，并派出司法长官前往日内瓦，要求把罪犯提交给他带回法国。

要求被回绝了。

加尔文也能自行执行火刑。

去往刑场的道路的确艰难。在这个异教徒的最后行程中，一队牧师伴随左右，嘴里还喋喋不休地争辩着。罪犯痛苦挣扎持续了半个多小时仍没有完全终结，直到人们出于对这个可怜牺牲者的同情而向火焰里添加了柴枝为止。对于喜欢这类事情的人来说，这读起来倒是挺有意思的，不过还是不谈为好。死刑多一个少一个，在宗教肆无忌惮的年代又有什么不同呢?

塞尔维特案件的确有些特殊，它的后果相当可怕。它赤裸裸地表明，那些口口声声地叫嚷“拥有自己主张权力”的新教徒实际上不过是伪装的天主教徒，他们心胸狭隘，对待不同己见者就像对待敌人一样残酷无情；他们就是伺机想要建立起自己的恐怖统治。

We possess a great deal of information upon the trial and know in detail what the rest of the world thought of this execution. It makes ghastly reading. It is true that Calvin,in an outburst of generosity,suggested that Servetus be decapitated instead of burned. Servetus thanked him for his kindness,but offered still another solution. He wanted to be set free. Yea,he insisted (and the logic was all on his side) that the court had no jurisdiction over him,that he was merely an honest man in search for the truth and that therefore he had the right to be heard in open debate with his opponent,Dr. Calvin.

But of this Calvin would not hear.

He had sworn that this heretic,once he fell into his hands,should never be allowed to escape with his life,and he was going to be as good as his word. That he could not get a conviction without the co-operation of his arch-enemy,the Inquisition,made no difference to him. He would have made common cause with the pope if His Holiness had been in the possession of some documents that would further incriminate the unfortunate Spaniard.

But worse was to follow.

On the morning of his death,Servetus asked to see Calvin and the latter came to the dark and filthy dungeon that had served his enemy as a prison.

Upon this occasion at least he might have been generous;more,he might have been human.

He was neither.

He stood in the presence of a man who within another hour would be able to plead his case before the throne of God and he argued. He debated and sputtered,grew green and lost his temper. But not a word of pity,of charity,or kindliness. Not a word. Only bitterness and hatred,the feeling of"Serve you right,you obstinate scoundrel. Burn and be damned!"

这是个相当严厉的指控，不能只是耸耸肩，说“咳，你还能指望什么”就不了了之。

我们掌握了这次审判的大量资料，也详细知道外界是如何看待这次判决的。它读起来令人痛心。事实上，加尔文出于一时的仁慈，曾建议用砍头代替烧死塞尔维特。塞尔维特感谢了他的好意，却要求另一种解决方法。他要求获得自由。是的，他坚持认为（逻辑都在他这一方）法庭无权审判他，他只是探求真理的诚实之人，因此有权利在大庭广众之下与他的对手加尔文博士进行辩论。

但加尔文置若罔闻。

他曾发过誓，一旦这个异教徒落入自己手中，就决不让他活着逃脱，他要坚守誓言。如果没有他的头号敌人——宗教法庭的配合，他是无法给塞尔维特定罪的。但这无关紧要，如果教皇有可以进一步给那个不幸的西班牙人治罪的文件，他甚至可以与教皇携手合作。

还有更糟的事情。

在临死的那天早上，塞尔维特要求见加尔文，加尔文便来到了关押他的犯人的又黑又脏的地牢。

在这种情形下，他至少应该大度一点；更进一步地讲，他至少应该有点人性。

可是他两者全无。

站在这个一小时后就要在上帝面前申述案情的人面前，他争论着，辩解着，唾星四溅，脸色铁青，大发雷霆。没有一句同情、怜悯或善意之词，一个字都没有。只有恶毒和仇恨：“罪有应得，顽固的流氓。烧死你这个该死的家伙！”

※ ※ ※ ※ ※ ※

All this happened many,many years ago.

Servetus is dead.

All our statues and memorial tablets will not bring him back to life again.

Calvin is dead.

A thousand volumes of abuse will not disturb the ashes of his unknown grave.

They are all of them dead,those ardent reformers who during the trial had shuddered with fear lest the blasphemous scoundrel be allowed to escape,those staunch pillars of the Church who after the execution broke forth into paeans of praise and wrote each other,"All hail to Geneva! The deed is done."

They are all of them dead,and perhaps it were best they were forgotten too.

Only let us have a care.

Tolerance is like liberty.

No one ever gets it merely by asking for it. No one keeps it except by the exercise of eternal care and vigilance.

For the sake of some future Servetus among our own children,we shall do well to remember this.

※ ※ ※ ※ ※ ※

这是很多很多年以前的事。

塞尔维特死了。

所有的塑像和纪念碑都不能使其重生。

加尔文死了。

上千卷咒骂的书也不能搅动他那不为人知的墓穴里的骨灰。

狂热的宗教改革者在审判时浑身战栗，生怕亵渎的流氓逃掉；教会的中间分子在行刑后欢呼雀跃，相互写信道贺：“日内瓦万岁！采取行动啦！”

他们全都死了，人们最好还是把他们忘掉的好。

我们只需关注一件事。

宽容就如同自由。

一味乞求是无法得到它的。永远保持警惕才能拥有它。

为了子孙中的新的塞尔维特着想，我们要努力记住这一点。

CHAPTER XⅥ THE ANABAPTISTS

Every generation has a bogey-men all its own.

We have our"Reds."

Our fathers had their Socialists.

Our grandfathers had their Molly Maguires.

Our great-great-grandfathers had their Jacobins

And our ancestors of three hundred years ago were not a bit better off.

They had their Anabaptists.

The most popular"Outline of History"of the sixteenth century was a certain"World Book"or chronicle,which Sebastian Frank,soap-boiler,prohibitionist and author,living in the good city of Ulm,published in the year 1534.

Sebastian knew the Anabaptists. He had married into an Anabaptist family. He did not share their views,for he was a confirmed free-thinker. But this is what he wrote about them:"that they taught nothing but love and faith and the crucifixion of the flesh,that they manifested patience and humility under all suffering,assisted one another with true helpfulness,called each other brother and believed in having all things in common."

It is surely a curious thing that people of whom all those nice things could be truthfully said should for almost a hundred years have been hunted down like wild animals,and should have been exposed to all the most cruel punishments of the most bloodthirsty of centuries.

第16章　再洗礼教徒

每代人都有他们那个时代的异类。

我们这一代的异类是“赤党”。

父辈的异类是社会主义者。

祖父辈的异类是莫利·马格瑞斯。

曾曾祖父辈的异类是雅各宾派。

而且，我们300年前的祖先也不比他们的后代胜出多少。

他们的异类是再洗礼教徒。

16世纪最流行的《世界史纲》在某种意义上是一部“世界之书”或编年史，于1534年出版，作者塞巴斯蒂安·弗兰克，是一名制皂工、禁酒主义者和作家，生活在优美的城市乌尔姆。

塞巴斯蒂安熟知再洗礼教徒。他娶了一个出身再洗礼教家族的姑娘。作为坚定的自由思想者，他并不认同再洗礼教的观点。但是，塞巴斯蒂安这样描述再洗礼教徒：“除了爱和信仰，以及把人的肉体钉死在十字架上，他们没有传授任何东西；他们主张在任何困难面前都要有耐性和谦恭，真诚地帮助他人，彼此以兄弟相称，而且认为应该共同拥有一切。”

But there was a reason and in order to appreciate it you must remember certain facts about the Reformation.

The Reformation really settled nothing.

It gave the world two prisons instead of one,made a book infallible in the place of a man and established (or rather,tried to establish) a rule by black garbed ministers instead of white garbed priests.

Such meager results after half a century of struggle and sacrifice had filled the hearts of millions of people with desperate disappointment. They had expected a millennium of social and religious righteousness and they were not at all prepared for a new Gehenna of persecution and economic slavery.

They had been ready for a great adventure. Then something had happened. They had slipped between the wall and the ship. And they had been obliged to strike out for themselves and keep above water as best they could.

They were in a terrible position. They had left the old church. Their conscience did not allow them to join the new faith. Officially they had,therefore,ceased to exist. And yet they lived. They breathed. They were sure that they were God's beloved children. As such it was their duty to keep on living and breathing,that they might save a wicked world from its own folly.

Eventually they survived,but do not ask how!

Deprived of their old associations,they were forced to form groups of their own,to look for a new leadership.

But what man in his senses would take up with these poor fanatics?

As a result,shoemakers with second sight and hysterical midwives with visions and hallucinations assumed the rôle of prophets and prophetesses and they prayed and

毫不夸张地说，向往美好事物的人如野生动物一般被追杀了近百年，而且遭受了几个世纪以来最残酷的充满血腥味的各种惩罚。这确实是一件稀奇古怪的事。

但是，要想弄明白个中缘由，务必牢记关于宗教改革的一些事情。

事实上，宗教改革没有解决任何问题。

它给了世界不是一个而是两个牢狱，编一本绝对无误的书（《圣经》）来替代某个绝对无误的人（教皇），并且由黑衣牧师而不是白衣牧师来建立（不如说是试图建立）教规。

经历了半个世纪的奋斗和牺牲，如此微不足道的成就使得数百万人失望之极。他们期待一个具有社会正义感和宗教正义感的太平盛世，却根本没有料到会发生又一轮新的迫害和经济奴役。

他们已经准备进行一次伟大的冒险。就在那时，发生了一些事情。他们滑倒在码头和船的空隙里，却不得不持续挣扎，竭尽全力活下去。

他们的处境很糟糕。离开了旧教会，而良知不允许他们改变宗教信仰。为此，官方认为他们已经不存在，但他们还活着、呼吸着，并确信自己是上帝关爱的子民。正如继续活下去，不要停止呼吸，是他们的责任一样，他们同样有责任要将邪恶的世界从其自身的愚昧中拯救出来。

最终他们活下来了，但请不要问是怎样活下来的！

他们从旧的社团中脱离出来，被迫组建自己的组织，寻找新领袖。

但是，哪里会有清醒的人愿意和这些可怜的狂热者交往呢？

preached and raved until the rafters of their dingy meeting places shook with the hosannas of the faithful and the tip-staffs of the village were forced to take notice of the unseemly disturbance.

Then half a dozen men and women were sent to jail and their High and Mightinesses,the town councilors,began what was good-naturedly called"an investigation."

These people did not go to the Catholic Church. They did not worship in the Protestant kirk. Then would they please explain who they were and what they believed?

To give the poor councilors their due,they were in a difficult predicament. For their prisoners were the most uncomfortable of all heretics,people who took their religious convictions absolutely seriously. Many of the most respectable reformers were of this earth earthy and willingly made such small compromises as were absolutely necessary,if one hoped to lead an agreeable and respectable existence.

Your true Anabaptist was of a different caliber. He frowned upon all half-way measures. Jesus had told his followers to turn the other cheek when smitten by an enemy,and had taught that all those who take the sword shall perish by the sword. To the Anabaptists this meant a positive ordinance to use no violence. They did not care to dilly-dally with words and murmur that circumstances alter cases,that,of course,they were against war,but that this was a different kind of a war and that therefore they felt that for this once God would not mind if they threw a few bombs or fired an occasional torpedo.

A divine ordinance was a divine ordinance,and that was all there was to it.

And so they refused to enlist and refused to carry arms and in case they were arrested for their pacifism (for that is what their enemies called this sort of applied Christianity) they went willingly forth to meet their fate and recited Matthew xxvi:52 until death made an end to their suffering.

因此，有预见力的制鞋匠及充满幻觉和歇斯底里的助产士充当了先知或女先知的角色。他们祈祷、布道和咆哮，直到昏暗会场的椽木都随着忠诚的赞美声颤动起来，全村的法警都无法对这有失体面的骚扰视而不见。

接着，一些男人女人被送进监狱，有权有势的小镇议员开始了所谓的“调查”。

这些人不想去天主教堂，也不尊重新教的教会。因此，要麻烦他们解释清楚自己是什么人，信仰什么宗教。

说句公道话，可怜的议员们处在尴尬的困境中，因为这些囚犯是所有异教徒中最难对付的，他们对待自己的宗教信仰极其真诚。许多最值得尊敬的改革者都不能免俗，心甘情愿地做一些绝对有必要的小小妥协，从而过上既愉快又受尊重的生活。

然而，真正的再洗礼教徒具有出众的品质，他反对任何形式的妥协。耶稣告诉他的追随者，每当被敌人打时，要将另一侧脸也送过去让他打，并教导所有剑客，要做到剑毁人亡。对于再洗礼教徒来说，不能使用暴力是一条不容反抗的法令。他们不喜欢浪费时间去低声嘀咕“环境改变现实”的话题。当然，他们反对战争，但这是一场特殊的战争。而且他们感到，只有这一次，上帝不会介意他们是否投了几枚炸弹或偶尔引爆了一颗鱼雷。

神的命令就是神的命令，不过如此。

因此，他们拒绝入伍，拒绝携带武器。万一因为主张和平主义而被逮捕时（他们的敌人正是这样称呼这类实用基督教派别的），他们可以愉快地面对自己的命运，愉快地背诵《马太福音》第26章第52节，直到死亡终止了他们的苦难。

But anti-militarism was only a small detail in their program of queerness. Jesus had preached that the Kingdom of God and the Kingdom of Caesar were two entirely different entities and could not and should not be reconciled. Very well. These words were clear. Henceforth all good Anabaptists carefully abstained from taking part in their country's government,refused to hold public office and spent the time which other people wasted upon politics,reading and studying the holy scriptures.

Jesus had cautioned his disciples against unseemly quarrels and the Anabaptists would rather lose their rightful possessions than submit a difference of opinion to law court.

There were several other points which set these peculiar people apart from the rest of the world,but these few examples of their odd behavior will explain the suspicion and detestation in which they were held by their fat and happy neighbors who invariably mixed their piety with a dose of that comfortable doctrine which bids us live and let live.

Even so,the Anabaptists,like the Baptists and many other dissenters,might in the end have discovered a way to placate the authorities,if only they had been able to protect themselves from their own friends.

Undoubtedly there are many honest Bolshevists who dearly love their fellow proletarians and who spend their waking hours trying to make this world a better and happier place. But when the average person hears the word"Bolshevik,"he thinks of Moscow and of a reign of terror established by a handful of scholarly cut-throats,of jails full of innocent people and firing squads jeering at the victims they are about to shoot. This picture may be slightly unfair,but it is no more than

再洗礼教徒

但是，反战主义仅仅是他们怪诞计划中的一个小细节。耶稣教导说，上帝之国和凯撒之国是两个完全不同的实体，不能也不应该混为一谈。非常好，这样才算表达清楚了。因此，所有优秀的再洗礼教徒都谨慎地与自己家乡的乡村政府隔绝开来，拒绝担任公共职务，用他人浪费在政治上的时间来研读《圣经》。

耶稣曾告诫他的追随者们，不要有失体面地去争论。因而再洗礼教徒宁愿丢掉自己应得的利益，也不向法庭提出异议。

还有其他几点使得这些特殊的人与世隔绝。但是上面几个行为古怪的例子，足以解释他们为什么会引得那些心宽体胖的邻居怀疑和厌恶他们了。这些邻居总是把他们的信仰和“己待人宽人亦待己宽”这一令人愉快的教义混为一谈。

即便如此，再洗礼教徒也可以像洗礼教徒和许多其他异教徒一样，只要他们能够保护自己不受到朋友的伤害，最后也许能发现与官方和解的方法。

毋庸置疑，有许多真诚的布尔什维克主义者，他们由衷地爱着无产阶级朋友，试着用全部时间来使这个世界变得更美好更幸福。但是，一般人只要听到布尔什维克主义者，就会想到墨西哥，想到凶手建立的恐怖主义统治，想到住满无辜者的监

natural that it should be part of the popular myth after the unspeakable things which have happened in Russia during the last seven years.

The really good and peaceful Anabaptists of the sixteenth century suffered from a similar disadvantage. As a sect they were suspected of many strange crimes,and with good reason. In the first place,they were inveterate Bible readers. This,of course,is not a crime at all,but let me finish my sentence. The Anabaptists studied the scriptures without any discrimination and that is a very dangerous thing when one has a strong predilection for the Book of Revelation.

This strange work which even as late as the fifth century was rejected as a bit of"spurious writing"was just the sort of thing to appeal to people who lived during a period of intense emotional passions. The exile of Patmos spoke a language which these poor,hunted creatures understood. When his impotent rage drove him into hysterical prophecies anent the modern Babylon,all the Anabaptists shouted amen and prayed for the speedy coming of the New Heaven and the New Earth.

It was not the first time that weak minds gave way under the stress of a great excitement. And almost every persecution of the Anabaptists was followed by violent outbursts of religious insanity. Men and women would rush naked through the streets,announcing the end of the world,trying to indulge in weird sacrifices that the fury of God might be appeased. Old hags would enter the divine services of some other sect and break up the meeting,stridently shrieking nonsense about the coming of the Dragon.

Of course,this sort of affliction (in a mild degree) is always with us. Read the daily papers and you will see how in some remote hamlet of Ohio or Iowa or Florida a woman has butchered her husband with a meat cleaver because"she was told to do so"by the voice of an angel;or how an otherwise reasonable father has just killed his wife and eight

狱，想到嘲弄牺牲者临死时的刽子手。这个画面也许有一点不公平，但是，在过去7年，俄罗斯发生了一系列无法讲述的事情之后，这一画面理所当然地走进人们脑海，成为众人印象的一部分，这再自然不过了。

16世纪，这些原本善良平和的再洗礼教徒，在相似的不利条件下遭受着苦难。他们被怀疑成行为古怪的罪犯是有充分的理由的。首先，他们是《圣经》的忠实读者。当然，这根本就不是罪证，但是让我把话说完。再洗礼教徒研读《圣经》时不带任何偏见，但若是沉浸于《启示录》的话，则是十分危险的事。

甚至晚到15世纪时，《启示录》这部奇怪的著作仍被认为是“虚伪作品”而遭拒绝。正是这种东西，吸引了拥有强烈的感情冲动的人们。这些可怜的被追捕者能够听懂帕特摩斯岛上被流放者的语言。当疲惫的愤怒驱使他歇斯底里地预言现代巴比伦时，所有的再洗礼教徒大喊“阿门”，并为新天国和新世界的快点到来而祈祷。

在强大压力的刺激下，意志柔弱的人总会因无奈而做出让步的。而且，再洗礼教徒承受的迫害都伴随着宗教因疯狂而猛烈爆发的力量。男人女人在各条街道上裸奔，宣称世界末日的到来，竭力想用不可思议的自我牺牲来平息上帝的怒火。老巫婆进入到其他教派的礼拜仪式中，打断集会，尖叫着说什么撒旦就要来了，真是无稽之谈。

当然，这种冲突（属于温和程度）经常发生。在日报上，你会看到在俄亥俄州、爱荷华州或佛罗里达州某个偏远的小村庄，女人是怎样用切肉刀杀死自己丈夫

children in anticipation of the sounding of the Seven Trumpets. Such cases,however,are rare exceptions. They can be easily handled by the local police and they really do not have great influence upon the life or the safety of the Republic.

But what had happened in the year 1534 in the good town of Münster was something very different. There the New Zion,upon strictly Anabaptist principles,had actually been proclaimed.

And people all over northern Europe shuddered when they thought of that terrible winter and spring.

The villain in the case was a good-looking young tailor by the name of Jan Beukelszoon. History knows him as John of Leiden,for Jan was a native of that industrious little city and had spent his childhood along the banks of the sluggish old Rhine. Like all other apprentices of that day,he had traveled extensively and had wandered far and wide to learn the secrets of his trade.

He could read and write just enough to produce an occasional play,but he had no real education. Neither was he possessed of that humility of spirit which we so often find in people who are conscious of their social disadvantages and their lack of knowledge. But he was a very goodlooking young man,endowed with unlimited cheek and as vain as a peacock.

After a long absence in England and Germany,he went back to his native land and set up in the cloak and suit business. At the same time he went in for religion and that was the beginning of his extraordinary career. For he became a disciple of Thomas Münzer.

This man Münzer,a baker by profession,was a famous character. He was one of the three Anabaptist prophets who,in the year 1521,had suddenly made their appearance in Wittenberg that they might show Luther how to find the true road to salvation. Although

的，因为天使的声音“告诉她要这么做”；或者看到一个原本理性的父亲，又是怎样将妻子和八岁的孩子杀死的，因为他感觉听到了代表世界末日来临的“七支号角”的声音。然而，这是极少见的情况。当地警察会随意处置他们，当然，他们确实没对公众的生活和安全造成恶劣影响。

但是，1534年，在美丽的明斯特小镇发生了非常大的事情。按照再洗礼教的理论来说，实际上他们已经宣布了那里就是“新天国”。

而且，所有的北欧人一想到那个可怕的冬天和春天都会不寒而栗。

在这一事件中的反面人物是一个名为杰·比克赞的年轻英俊的裁缝。历史上称其为“莱顿的约翰”，因为他出生于那座以人们的勤劳著称的小城，并在缓缓流淌的莱茵河畔度过了他的孩提时代。他和那个时代所有的学徒工一样，云游四海，为了习得本行的秘籍而流浪远方。

虽然他没有受过正式教育，但他的读写水平足够用于即兴表演。通常人们意识到自己社会地位低下和知识欠缺时，会表现得很谦逊，可他不会。他是一个相当帅气的青年，无比鲁莽，如孔雀一般虚荣。

离开英国和德国很长一段时间以后，他回到故乡，做起了斗篷和外套生意。同时，他开始致力于宗教事业，那是他杰出事业的开端，因为他成了托马斯·闵采尔的信徒。

闵采尔是职业面包师，是个著名人物，也是三个再洗礼教的先知之一。1521年，这三个先知突然来到维滕堡，告诉路德怎样找到切实有效的拯救办法。即使他

they had acted with the best of intentions,their efforts had not been appreciated and they had been chased out of the Protestant stronghold with the request that never again they show their unwelcome selves within the jurisdiction of the Dukes of Saxony.

Came the year 1534 and the Anabaptists had suffered so many defeats that they decided to risk everything on one big,hold stroke.

That they selected the town of Münster in Westphalia as the spot for their final experiment surprised no one. Franz von Waldeck,the prince-bishop of that city,was a drunken bounder who for years had lived openly with a score of women and who ever since his sixteenth year had offended all decent people by the outrageous bad taste of his private conduct. When the town went Protestant,he compromised. But being known far and wide for a liar and a cheat,his treaty of peace did not give his Protestant subjects that feeling of personal security without which life is indeed a very uncomfortable experience. In consequence whereof the inhabitants of Münster remained in a state of high agitation until the next elections. These brought a surprise. The city government fell into the hands of the Anabaptists. The chairman became one Bernard Knipperdollinck,a cloth merchant by day and a prophet after dark.

The bishop took one look at his new councilors and fled.

It was then that John of Leiden appeared upon the scene. He had come to Münster as the apostle of a certain Jan Matthysz,a Haarlem baker who had started a new sect of his own and was regarded as a very holy man. And when he heard of the great blow that had been struck for the good cause,he remained to help celebrate the victory and purge the bishopric of all popish contamination. The Anabaptists were nothing if not thorough. They turned the churches into stone quarries. They confiscated the convents for the benefit of the homeless. All books except the Bible were publicly burned. And as a fitting climax,those

们是本着最好的意图来做这件事情的，但他们的付出没有得到认可，以致被逐出新教徒的大本营，永远不许在萨克森公爵的管辖区域内露面。

到了1534年，再洗礼教徒经历了无数挫折，因而他们决定要不顾一切代价，进行大力反击。

他们把威斯特伐利亚的明斯特镇选作最终的实验地，没有人对这一选择感到惊奇。那个城市兼任主教的公国君主弗朗兹·冯·瓦德克是一个醉鬼，长期毫无顾忌地与各种女人姘居，从16岁起，他那粗鲁且败坏的品性就让每一个体面的人深恶痛绝。当这座小镇转而信仰新教时，他妥协了。但是，他因说谎和欺骗而臭名远扬，他的求和意图让新教徒找不到安全感，没有安全感则不能体验到生活的安逸。结果，明斯特居民的这种极度骚动不安的状态一直持续到下一届选举。这倒带来了一件令人惊奇的事，那就是这个城市落入了再洗礼教的掌控之中。新当选的市政官是伯纳德·尼普多林克。他白天卖布，到了晚上就是一位先知。

主教瞧了瞧新长官，便落荒而逃。

接下来登场的是莱顿的约翰。从某种程度上来说，他是以约翰·马特兹的圣徒身份来到明斯特的。马特兹曾经开创了属于自己的教派，他是霍莱姆的一个面包师，被认为是一个非常虔诚的人。而且当他听说受到大力支持的正义事业抢占了绝对优势地位时，便留下来协助庆祝这场胜利，并坚持清除原天主教教主在教区的影响。他们把各个教堂都改造成采石场，没收了用来收容无家可归的人而建造的修道院。除了《圣经》以外，所有的书都被当众烧毁。并且，正义事业迎来了一个恰逢其时的高潮，那

who refused to be re-baptized after the Anabaptist fashion were driven into the camp of the Bishop,who decapitated them or drowned them on the general principle that they were heretics and small loss to the community.

That was the prologue.

The play itself was no less terrible.

From far and wide the high priests of half a hundred new creeds hastened to the New Jerusalem. There they were joined by all those who believed themselves possessed of a call for the great uplift,honest and sincere citizens,but as innocent as babes when it came to politics or statecraft.

The siege of Münster lasted five months and during that time,every scheme,system and program of social and spiritual regeneration was tried out;every new-fangled prophet had his day in court.

But,of course,a little town chuck full of fugitives,pestilence and hunger,was not a fit place for a sociological laboratory and the dissensions and quarrels between the different factions lamed all the efforts of the military leaders. During that crisis John the tailor stepped forward.

The short hour of his glory had come.

In that community of starving men and suffering children,all things were possible. John began his régime by introducing an exact replica of that old theocratic form of government of which he had read in his Old Testament. The burghers of Münster were divided into the twelve tribes of Israel and John himself was chosen to be their king. He had already married the daughter of one prophet,Knipperdollinck. Now he married the widow of another,the wife of his former master,John Matthysz. Next he remembered Solomon and added a couple of concubines. And then the ghastly farce began.

就是再洗礼教风潮席卷了天主教的阵营。从那之后，那些拒绝接受再次洗礼的人都被砍头或者淹死，因为，他们才是异教徒，他们死了对社会不会造成什么损失。

那只是序幕。

这场戏剧本身不能说不恐怖。

几十个信仰各种新教义的高级教士急急忙忙地从四面八方向新耶路撒冷赶去。在那里，所有自认为要求积极进取、诚实正直的市民都加入到他们中间来，但是说到政治或治国方略，这些市民就像小孩一样无知。

明斯特被围攻长达五个月。在那段时间里，每个关于社会和精神复活的计划、体系和议程都试验了一番，新涌现的先知们在议会上个个都显露了一把。

当然，一个充斥着逃亡、瘟疫和饥荒的小镇并不适合当作社会学实验室，而且派系之间的分歧与争议使得军事领导们的所有努力均付之东流。关键时刻，裁缝约翰站了出来。

他迎来了短暂的光辉时刻。

在那个社区，到处都是饥饿的人们和受苦难的孩子，任何事情都有发生的可能。约翰曾经在《旧约》中读到过关于旧神权政府的内容，他的统治以精确重现旧神权政府的方式开始了。明斯特镇的公民被分成12个犹太人部落，约翰本人则被选为他们的国王。他已经和尼普多林克先知的女儿结婚了。现在他又和另一位先知的遗孀结婚了——他前任主子约翰·马特兹的妻子。接着，他想起了所罗门，便又加了若干妃子。随后，糟糕透顶的闹剧便开始了。

All day long John sat on the throne of David in the market place and all day long the people stood by while the royal court chaplain read the latest batch of ordinances. These came fast and furiously,for the fate of the city was daily growing more desperate and the people were in dire need.

John,however,was an optimist and thoroughly believed in the omnipotence of paper decrees.

The people complained that they were hungry. John promised that he would tend to it. And forthwith a royal ukase,duly signed by His Majesty,ordained that all wealth in the city be divided equally among the rich and the poor,that the streets be broken up and used as vegetable gardens,that all meals be eaten in common.

So far so good. But there were those who said that some of the rich people had hidden part of their treasures. John bade his subjects not to worry. A second decree proclaimed that all those who broke a single law of the community would be immediately decapitated. And,mind you,such a warning was no idle threat. For this royal tailor was as handy with his sword as with his scissors and frequently undertook to be his own executioner.

Then came the period of hallucinations when the populace suffered from a diversity of religious manias;when the market place was crowded day and night with thousands of men and women,awaiting the trumpet blasts of the angel Gabriel.

Then came the period of terror,when the prophet kept up the courage of his flock by a constant orgy of blood and cut the throat of one of his own queens.

And then came the terrible day of retribution when two citizens in their despair opened the gates to the soldiers of the bishop and when the prophet,locked in an iron cage,was shown at all the Westphalian country fairs and was finally tortured to death.

A weird episode,but of terrible consequence to many a God-fearing and simple soul.

约翰整日坐在商业区的大卫王宝座上，人们则整日围在他的周围，听宫廷教士宣读最新条例。这一切来得很快很突然而迅猛，因为这座城市的命运正变得日益危急，而人们迫切需要改变这一状况。

然而，约翰是一个乐观主义者，而且完全相信白纸黑字的法令具有无限权威。

人们因饥饿而抗议，约翰承诺会解决这个问题。他毫不犹豫地以皇帝陛下的名义签署了一道圣旨，命令富人和穷人平分全城所有的财富，将各条街道推翻并改造成菜园，全城共吃一锅饭。

到此为止，一切顺利。但有人说，有些富人把一部分金银财宝藏起来了。约翰嘱咐他的臣民不要着急。于是颁布了第二条法令，无论是谁，只要违反了一条地方法规，立即杀头。但是，想想看，这样一条警告并不是无法实施的恐吓。因为这个皇家裁缝使起剑来跟使剪刀一样在行，而且经常自己充当刽子手。

接着，幻想阶段来临了，平民大众经受了各种宗教狂热的苦难，整个市场日夜挤满了成千上万的男女，等待着响起加百利天使的号角声。

后来，这个城市便进入了恐怖时期，这位先知用持续滥杀的手段来维持手下的勇气，甚至割断了一位王妃的喉咙。

可怕的报应很快就来了。两个市民在绝望中对天主教的士兵们敞开城门，被关进铁笼的先知在威斯特伐利亚的各个集市上亮相，并最终被拷打至死。

这是一段不可思议的记忆，但对于众多虔诚而又单纯的灵魂来说有着严重的后果。

From that moment on,all Anabaptists were outlawed. Such leaders as had escaped the carnage of Münster were hunted down like rabbits and were killed wherever found. From every pulpit,ministers and priests fulminated against the Anabaptists and with many curses and anathemas they denounced them as communists and traitors and rebels,who wanted to upset the existing order of things and deserved less mercy than wolves or mad dogs.

Rarely has a heresy hunt been so successful. As a sect,the Anabaptists ceased to exist. But a strange thing happened. Many of their ideas continued to live,were picked up by other denominations,were incorporated into all sorts of religious and philosophic systems,became respectable,and are today part and parcel of everybody's spiritual and intellectual inheritance.

It is a simple thing to state such a fact. To explain how it actually came about,that is quite a different story.

Almost without exception the Anabaptists belonged to that class of society which regards an inkstand as an unnecessary luxury.

Anabaptist history,therefore,was writ by those who regarded the sect as a particularly venomous kind of denominational radicalism. Only now,after a century of study,are we beginning to understand the great rôle the ideas of these humble peasants and artisans have played in the further development of a more rational and more tolerant form of Christianity.

But ideas are like lightning. One never knows where they will strike next. And what is the use of lightning rods in Münster,when the storm breaks loose over Sienna?

从那一刻开始，所有的再洗礼教徒都是歹徒。领袖们虽然已从明斯特大屠杀中逃走了，还是要像追捕兔子一样追捕他们，一旦抓住就地处决。各地的教长和牧师都一致怒斥再洗礼教徒，他们咒骂并指责再洗礼教徒为共产主义者、卖国贼和叛乱者，认为再洗礼教徒想要扰乱各项事物的现有秩序，比狼或疯狗更不值得怜悯。

几乎没有一个异端邪说被制服得如此彻底。再洗礼教不再作为一个教派而存在。但是奇怪的事情发生了。再洗礼教徒的许多思想继续存在，被其他教派继承，并被各种宗教和哲学体系所吸收，变得让人尊敬，也成为当今每个人精神和知识遗产的一部分。

要描述这样一个事实并不困难，但是要解释它实际上是怎么发生的却不容易。

几乎无一例外，再洗礼教徒都是把墨水瓶看成不必要的奢侈品的阶层。

因此，撰写再洗礼教历史的人，都将它看作十分恶毒的宗教激进主义。只是现在，经过了一个世纪的研究之后，我们才开始懂得，在进一步发展基督教精神理性与宽容的过程中，这些卑微的农民和工匠的思想扮演了伟大的角色。

但思想就像雷电，谁也不知道下一个出击的目标是哪里。而且，当风暴席卷整个锡耶纳时，明斯特的避雷针又有什么用呢?

CHAPTER XVII THE SOZZINI FAMILY

In Italy the Reformation had never been successful. It could not be. In the first place,the people of the south did not take their religion seriously enough to fight about it and in the second place,the close proximity of Rome,the center of a particularly well equipped office of the Inquisition,made indulgence in private opinions a dangerous and costly pastime.

But,of course,among all the thousands of humanists who populated the peninsula,there were bound to be a few black sheep who cared a great deal more for the good opinion of Aristotle than for that of Saint Chrysostom. Those good people,however,were given many opportunities to get rid of their surplus spiritual energy. There were clubs and coffee-houses and discreet salons where men and women could give vent to their intellectual enthusiasm without upsetting empires. All of which was very pleasant and restful. And besides,wasn't all life a compromise?Hadn't it always been a compromise?Would it not in all likelihood be a compromise until the end of time?

Why get excited about such a small detail as one's faith?

After these few introductory remarks,the reader will surely not expect to hear a loud fanfaronade or the firing of guns when our next two heroes make their appearance. For they are soft-spoken gentlemen,and go about their business in a dignified and pleasant way.

In the end,they are to do more to upset the dogmatic tyranny under which the world had suffered for such a long time than a whole army of noisy reformers. But that is one of those curious things which no one can foresee. They happen. We are grateful. But how it

第17章　索兹尼家族

在意大利，宗教改革从来未曾成功过，即使想成功也做不到。首先，南方人对宗教没有重视到要为它而战的程度；其次，罗马近在咫尺，这个宗教裁判所的中心，装备精良，这使得随心所欲地表达个人观点成为一种危险而代价昂贵的尝试。

但是，生活在半岛上的人道主义者成千上万，难免会有害群之马，他们更加关注亚里士多德提出的精辟见解，而不是圣克里索斯托的布道。然而，那些优秀人士有许多机会来消耗过剩的精力。在俱乐部、咖啡屋或是讲究礼节的沙龙，男人女人可以释放自己高智商的热情，而不让权贵们感到烦心，这一切让人感到轻松愉快。此外，生活不就是要折中么？它不就是一直都处于折中状态么？它会不会多半时候都处于折中状态，直到世界末日？

为什么要因为诸如某人的信仰那样的细枝末节而激动呢？

作完简短介绍之后，就是我们下面两位主角登场了。但是，读者压根就别指望能听到高声吹嘘或是枪炮开火的声音。因为他们是说话和气的绅士，处理起事情来高贵而优雅。

然而，在推翻令世人饱受苦难的独断专制政治的过程中，他们的功劳比整支闹哄哄的改革大军还要显著。这是众多无法预料的怪事中的一件。事情发生了，我们

comes about,that,alas,is something which we do not fully understand.

The name of these two quiet workmen in the vineyard of reason was Sozzini.

They were uncle and nephew.

For some unknown reason,the older man,Lelio Francesco,spelled his name with one"z"and the younger,Fausto Paolo,spelled his with two"zs."But as they are both of them much better known by the Latinized form of their name,Socinius,than by the Italian Sozzini,we can leave that detail to the grammarians and etymologists.

As far as their influence was concerned,the uncle was much less important than the nephew. We shall,therefore,deal with him first and speak of the nephew afterwards.

Lelio Sozini was a Siennese,the descendant of a race of bankers and judges and himself destined for a career at the bar,via the University of Bologna. But like so many of his contemporaries,he allowed himself to slip into theology,stopped reading law,played with Greek and Hebrew and Arabic and ended (as so often happens with people of his type) as a rationalistic mystic—a man who was at once very much of this world and yet never quite of it. This sounds complicated. But those who understand what I mean will understand without any further explanation,and the others would not understand,no matter what I said.

His father,however,seems to have had a suspicion that the son might amount to something in the world of letters. He gave his boy a check and bade him go forth and see whatever there was to be seen. And so Lelio left Sienna and during the next ten years,he traveled from Venice to Geneva and from Geneva to Zurich and from Zurich to Wittenberg and then to London and then to Prague and then to Vienna and then to Cracow,spending a few months or years in every town and hamlet where he hoped to find interesting company and might be able to learn something new and interesting. It was an age when people talked religion just as incessantly as today they talk business. Lelio must have collected a

满怀感激，至于它是怎样发生的，哎，那是我也不明白的。

这两个在理智的葡萄园中默默耕耘的人叫索兹尼。

他们是叔侄关系。

由于某些不为人知的原因，叔叔雷利奥·弗朗西斯科把自己的名字读作“Z”，年轻的侄子福斯图斯·保罗则用两个字母“ZS”作为自己的名字。但是，他俩更为人熟知的名字，是用拉丁语拼写的索西尼厄斯，而不是用意大利语拼写的索兹尼，我们把这个细节留给语法专家和语源学专家去琢磨。

就他们所产生的影响而言，叔叔显得不如侄子那么重要。因此，我们先来讨论叔叔，而后再说侄子。

雷利奥·索兹尼是锡耶纳人，出身银行家和法官世家，毕业于博洛尼亚大学，注定要走向律师生涯。但是他像许许多多同龄人一样，甘愿坠入神学的海洋，也不再读与法律相关的东西，还玩味起希腊语、希伯来语和阿拉伯语，最终（这样的事情经常发生在他这一类人身上）成为纯理性的神秘主义者——通晓世界之人，但却不是彻底地通晓。这听起来复杂了些。但是，我认为，能够理解这些话的人，则不必任何解释；而那些不能理解的人，无论说什么也是徒劳。

然而，他的父亲好像还觉得儿子没准能在世界文坛上混出点名堂。他给了儿子一张支票，让他去见见世面。于是，雷利奥离开了锡耶纳，在以后的10年里，他从威尼斯到日内瓦，又从日内瓦到苏黎世，再从苏黎世到维滕堡，还去过伦敦、布拉格、维也纳、克拉科夫，在各个城镇或小村庄过上几个月或是几年。他想要找到有

strange assortment of ideas and by keeping his ears open he was soon familiar with every heresy between the Mediterranean and the Baltic.

When,however,he carried himself and his intellectual luggage to Geneva,he was received politely but none too cordially. The pale eyes of Calvin looked upon this Italian visitor with grave suspicion. He was a distinguished young man of excellent family and not a poor,friendless wanderer like Servetus. It was said,however,that he had Servetian inclinations. And that was most disturbing. The case for or against the Trinity,so Calvin thought,had been definitely settled when the Spanish heretic was burned. On the contrary! The fate of Servetus had become a subject of conversation from Madrid to Stockholm,and serious-minded people all over the world were beginning to take the side of the anti-trinitarian. But that was not all. They were using Gutenberg's devilish invention to spread their views broadcast and being at a safe distance from Geneva they were often far from complimentary in their remarks.

Only a short while before a very learned tract had appeared which contained everything the fathers of the Church had ever said or written upon the subject of persecuting and punishing heretics. It had an instantaneous and enormous sale among those who"hated God,"as Calvin said,or who"hated Calvin,"as they themselves protested. Calvin had let it be known that he would like to have a personal interview with the author of this precious booklet. But the author,anticipating such a request,had wisely omitted his name from the titlepage.

It was said that he was called Sebastian Castellio,that he had been a teacher in one of the Geneva high schools and that his moderate views upon diverse theological enormities had gained him the hatred of Calvin and the approbation of Montaigne. No one,however,could prove this. It was mere hearsay. But where one had gone before,others might follow.

趣的同伴，并学到令自己感兴趣的新东西。那是一个无休止地讨论宗教的年代，就像如今的人们不停地谈论商务一样。雷利奥想必是汲取了不少新奇的观点，由于他细心关注，很快就熟悉了在地中海和波罗的海之间的每个异教。

但是，当他带着知识的行囊来到日内瓦时，他受到了礼貌却并不真诚的接待。加尔文那双失色的眼睛，极度怀疑地看着这位意大利的来访者。雷利奥是一位出身显赫的杰出青年，并不似塞尔维特信徒，如流浪汉那般贫穷冷漠。然而，据说他有塞尔维特信徒的倾向。那样最烦人不过了。根据加尔文的观点，当这位西班牙的异教徒被烧死时，支持或反对“三位一体”的冲突已被完全解决。但事实正相反！从马德里到斯德哥尔摩，塞尔维特的命运都已成为谈资，全世界思想认真的人们都开始站在了“反三位一体”的立场上。但那不是全部。他们用古腾堡可怕的发明（印刷术）来传播他们的观点，而且由于距日内瓦较远，他们总是言辞不恭。

不久前，一本博学的小册子问世了，其中涵盖了教会众神父曾经针对“迫害和惩罚异教徒”这一主题所说过或写过的每一件事情。在加尔文称之为“憎恨上帝”的人们和为自己抗议的“憎恨加尔文”的人们当中，该册子短期内大规模热销。加尔文很自然地想对这部珍贵小册子的作者进行个人访问。但是这位作者预先料到了这样的可能，明智地把自己的名字从扉页中删掉了。

据说作者名叫塞巴斯蒂安·卡斯特里奥，他曾是一位老师，在日内瓦的一所学校任教，而且他看待异教徒神学暴行的中庸观点，招来了加尔文的憎恨，却得到了蒙田的认可。然而，没有人能够证明这一点，这仅仅是道听途说。但是，只要有前

Calvin,therefore,was distantly polite to Sozzini,but suggested that the mild air of Basel would suit his Siennese friend much better than the damp climate of Savoy and heartily bade him Godspeed when he started on his way to the famous old Erasmian stronghold.

Fortunately for Calvin,the Sozzini family son afterwards fell under the suspicion of the Inquisition,Lelio was deprived of his funds and falling ill of a fever,be died in Zürich at the age of only thirty-seven.

Whatever joy his untimely demise may have caused in Geneva,it was short-lived.

For Lelio,besides a widow and several trunks of notes,left a nephew,who not only fell heir to his uncle's unpublished manuscripts but soon gained for himself the reputation of being even more of a Servetus enthusiast than his uncle had been.

During his younger years,Faustus Socinius had traveled almost as extensively as the older Lelio. His grandfather had left him a small estate and as he did not marry until he was nearly fifty,he was able to devote all his time to his favorite subject,theology.

For a short while he seems to have been in business in Lyons.

What sort of a salesman he made,I do not know,but his experience in buying and selling and dealing in concrete commodities rather than spiritual values seems to have strengthened him in his conviction that very little is ever gained by killing a competitor or losing one's temper if the other man has the better of a deal. And as long as he lived,he showed himself possessed of that sober common sense which is often found in a counting-house but is very rarely part of the curriculum of a religious seminary.

In the year 1563 Faustus returned to Italy. On his way home he visited Geneva. It does not appear that he ever paid his respects to the local patriarch. Besides,Calvin was a very sick man at that time. The visit from a member of the Sozzini family would only have disturbed him.

人走过，就不愁后继无人。

因此，加尔文对索兹尼的态度是礼貌但不热情。但他仍向这位来自锡耶纳的朋友建议道，巴塞尔温和的空气比萨瓦潮湿的气候要好得多，会更适合他。因而，当索兹尼向著名而又古老的伊拉斯谟派要塞出发时，加尔文却真诚地祝他一路平安。

对加尔文来说，幸运的是索兹尼叔侄后来引起了宗教裁判所的怀疑，雷利奥的财产被没收，还患上了发烧症，在苏黎世与世长辞，享年37岁。

无论他最终的逝去带给日内瓦人民怎样的欢欣，那也是短暂的。

雷利奥留下的，除了一位遗孀和几箱笔记以外，还有一个侄子，他的侄子不仅继承了叔叔还没来得及出版的手稿，而且很快就为自己赢得了声誉，甚至比他叔叔曾获得的热衷于塞尔维特的名声更响亮一些。

在年少的日子里，福斯图斯·索兹尼去过的地方几乎和老雷利奥一样多。他的爷爷留给他一个小庄园，而且由于他直到快50岁时才结婚，因此他能够把全部精力投放在自己热爱的神学事业上。

他好像还在里昂做过生意，不过时间不长。

我不知道他是怎样的商人，但是看得出来，他在买卖上的经验及经营具体商品而非精神财富的经验，使得他更加深信这一点，那就是消灭一个竞争对手或是在别人业务做得更好时大发脾气，并不能带来多少成就感。只要他活着，就会表现出那种只有在账房才能常常见到的清醒意识，这种表现在宗教神学院的圈子中却不常见。

1563年，福斯图斯回到了意大利。在回家途中，他去了趟日内瓦。他似乎并没

The next dozen years,young Socinius spent in the service of Isabella de' Medici. But in the year 1576 this lady,after a few days of matrimonial bliss,was murdered by her husband,Paolo Orsini. Thereupon Socinius resigned,left Italy for good and went to Basel to translate the Psalms into colloquial Italian and write a book on Jesus.

Faustus,so it appeared from his writings,was a careful man. In the first place,he was very deaf and such people are by nature cautious.

In the second place,he derived his income from certain estates situated on the other side of the Alps and the Tuscan authorities had given him a hint that it might be just as well for one suspected of"Lutheran leanings"not to be too bold while dealing with subjects which were held in disfavor by the Inquisition. Hence he used a number of pseudonyms and never printed a book unless it had been passed upon by a number of friends and had been declared to be fairly safe.

Thus it happened that his books were not placed on the Index. It also happened that a copy of his life of Jesus was carried all the way to Transylvania and there fell into the hands of another liberal-minded Italian,the private physician of a number of Milanese and Florentine ladies who had married into the Polish and Transylvanian nobility.

Transylvania in those days was the"far east"of Europe. A wilderness until the early part of the twelfth century,it had been used as a convenient home for the surplus population of Germany. The hard working Saxon peasants had turned this fertile land into a prosperous and well regulated little country with cities and schools and an occasional university. But it remained a country far removed from the main roads of travel and trade. Hence it had always been a favorite place of residence for those who for one reason or another preferred to keep a few miles of marsh and mountain between themselves and the henchmen of the Inquisition.

As for Poland,this unfortunate country has for so many centuries been associated with

有向当地主教表达问候。另外，加尔文那时得了重病，索兹尼家族成员的拜访只会让他徒增烦恼。

在接下来的十几年里，年轻的索兹尼都在为伊莎贝拉·德·美第奇效劳。但是在1576年，这位女士才过了几天幸福的婚姻生活，就被她的丈夫保罗·奥西尼杀害了。索兹尼立即辞职了，永远离开了意大利，去往巴塞尔，在那里将《诗篇》译成了通俗的意大利语，还写了一本关于耶稣的书。

从他的作品看来，福斯图斯是一个细心的人。首先，他是个聋子，而聋人的天性就是小心谨慎。

其次，他从位于阿尔卑斯山脉另一侧的某个庄园里获得收入，托斯坎纳当权者曾经给过他暗示，在谈论宗教裁判所不喜欢的话题时，不要太过鲁莽，不要像那些被怀疑有路德倾向的人那样。因此，他用了几个笔名，而且每本书在付印之前，都要经过若干位朋友的传阅，还得他们认为万无一失才行。

因此，他的书没被列为禁书。那本关于耶稣的书被不远千里地带到了特兰西瓦尼亚，落入了另一位意大利自由思想者手中，他是那些嫁给波兰和特兰西瓦尼亚贵族的米兰和佛罗伦萨女人的私人医生。

在那个时代，特兰西瓦尼亚是欧洲的“远东”。直到12世纪早期，它仍是一片荒凉之地，对德国过于茂盛的人口来说，那儿曾被看作是一个适宜落户的地方。在萨克森农民的辛勤耕作下，那块沃土变成了一个繁荣的、规划整齐的小国家，有城市、学校和一所临时大学。但是，这个国家仍缺乏运输和贸易交通要道。一个又一

the general idea of reaction and jingoism that it will come as an agreeable surprise to many of my readers when I tell them that during the first half of the sixteenth century,it was a veritable asylum for all those who in other parts of Europe suffered on account of their religious convictions.

This unexpected state of affairs had been brought about in a typically Polish fashion.

That the Republic for quite a long time had been the most scandalously mismanaged country of the entire continent was even then a generally known fact. The extent,however,to which the higher clergy had neglected their duties was not appreciated quite so clearly in those days when dissolute bishops and drunken village priests were the common affliction of all western nations.

But during the latter half of the fifteenth century it was noticed that the number of Polish students in the different German universities was beginning to increase at a rate of speed which caused great concern among the authorities of Wittenberg and Leipzig. They began to ask questions. And then it developed that the ancient Polish academy of Cracow,administered by the Polish church,had been allowed to fall into such a state of utter decay that the poor Polanders were forced to go abroad for their education or do without. A little later,when the Teuton universities fell under the spell of the new doctrines,the bright young men from Warsaw and Radom and Czenstochowa quite naturally followed suit.

And when they returned to their home towns,they did so as full-fledged Lutherans.

At that early stage of the Reformation it would have been quite easy for the king and the nobility and the clergy to stamp out this epidemic of erroneous opinions. But such a step would have obliged the rulers of the republic to unite upon a definite and common policy and that of course was directly in contradiction to the most hallowed traditions of this strange country where a single dissenting vote could upset a law which had the

个的理由，使某些人宁愿在自己和宗教裁判所的亲信之间保留一定的距离，因此对他们来说，那儿一直都是宜居之地。

至于波兰，世世代代以来，我们一想起这个不幸的国家，就会想起保守主义和沙文主义。令众多读者感到惊喜的是，我向他们所作的如下描述，在16世纪上半叶，对所有在欧洲其他地区遭受着各种宗教惩罚的人来说，它就是真正意义上的避难所。

典型的波兰风格造成了这一令人意外的局面。

在相当长的一段时期内，这个共和政府是整个大陆上因管理不善而声名远扬的国家。这几乎是众所周知的事实。然而，在那个时代，放荡的主教和醉醺醺的乡村牧师困扰着所有西方国家，因此波兰的上层教士玩忽职守的情况看上去似乎并不明显。

但是到15世纪下半叶，我们发现在德国大学里求学的波兰学生数量开始猛增，这让维滕堡和莱比锡的当权派产生了深深的忧虑。他们开始质问。后来事态发展到由波兰教会管理的古波兰克拉科夫学院堕落到了完全腐败的地步，以致可怜的波兰人只能出国求学，否则就没有学可上。一段时间以后，当条顿大学在新教义的符咒下衰落时，华沙、拉杜姆和捷斯托科瓦的聪明年轻人很自然地跟着出国求学。

当他们回到自己的家乡时，已经是羽翼颇丰的路德派了。

在宗教改革早期，对于波兰国王、贵族和教士来说，避免错误观念的传染是一件相当容易的事情。但是这一行动要求共和国的各位统治者团结在一个明确而普遍适用的方针政策下。这当然与这个奇怪的国家最虚伪的传统背道而驰，在这个国家，一张反对票就能推翻一条法律，哪怕这条法律已得到了会议其他所有成员的同意。

support of all the other members of the diet.

And when (as happened shortly afterwards) it appeared that the religion of the famous Wittenberg professor carried with it a by-product of an economic nature,consisting of the confiscation of all Church property,the Boleslauses and the Wladislauses and the other knights,counts,barons,princes and dukes who populated the fertile plains between the Baltic and the Black Sea began to show a decided leaning towards a faith which meant money in their pockets.

The unholy scramble for monastic real estate which followed upon the discovery caused one of those famous"interims"with which the Poles,since time immemorial,have tried to stave off the day of reckoning. During such periods all authority came to a standstill and the Protestants made such a good use of their opportunity that in less than a year they had established churches of their own in every part of the kingdom.

Eventually of course the incessant theological haggling of the new ministers drove the peasants back into the arms of the Church and Poland once more became one of the strongholds of a most uncompromising form of Catholicism. But during the latter half of the sixteenth century,the country enjoyed complete religious license. When the Catholics and Protestants of western Europe began their war of extermination upon the Anabaptists,it was a foregone conclusion that the survivors should flee eastward and should eventually settle down along the banks of the Vistula and it was then that Doctor Blandrata got hold of Socinius' book on Jesus and expressed a wish to make the author's acquaintance.

■ 索兹尼家族

著名的维滕堡教授（路德）的宗教出现时，相应产生了一个具有经济特性的副产品，其中一项内容就是，没收所有教会的财产。从波罗的海到黑海之间的肥沃平原上的博尔劳斯家族、乌拉蒂斯家族和其他骑士、伯爵、男爵、亲王和公爵，都对新教表现出坚定的倾向，因为他们这样做就可以保住自己的钱袋子。

在这种情况下，对修道院地产的邪恶掠夺便开始了，从而形成了著名的“过渡期”。自从有人类记载以来，波兰人就是靠这种“过渡期”拖延思索时间的。在这期间，所有权力都处于观望状态，新教徒便充分利用这个机会，不到一年就在全国各个角落建起了自己的教堂。

最终，新牧师无休止的神学争论使得农民又回到了天主教会的怀抱，波兰再一次成为天主教坚固的大本营。但是到16世纪下半叶，这个国家获得了允许全部宗教派别并存的特许。当西欧的天主教和新教都开始了消除再洗礼教的战争时，必然结局就是，幸存者东逃，最终在维斯瓦河沿岸定居下来。就在那时，布兰德拉塔医生得到了索兹尼那本关于耶稣的书，并想要结识该书的作者。

乔治是一位有才华的内科医生，意大利人。他从蒙彼利埃大学毕业，成为声名

Giorgio Blandrata was an Italian,a physician and a man of parts. He had graduated at the University of Montpellier and had been remarkably successful as a woman's specialist. First and last he was a good deal of a scoundrel,but a clever one. Like so many doctors of his time (think of Rabelais and Servetus) he was as much of a theologian as a neurologist and frequently played one rôle out against the other. For example,he cured the Queen Dowager of Poland,Bona Sforza (widow of King Sigismund),so successfully of the obsession that those who doubted the Trinity were wrong,that she repented of her errors and thereafter only executed those who held the doctrine of the Trinity to be true.

The good queen,alas,was gone (murdered by one of her lovers) but two of her daughters had married local noblemen and as their medical adviser,Blandrata exercised a great deal of influence upon the politics of his adopted land. He knew that the country was ripe for civil war and that it would happen very soon unless something be done to make an end to the everlasting religious quarrels. Wherefore he set to work to bring about a truce between the different opposing sects. But for this purpose he needed some one more skilled in the intricacies of a religious debate than he was himself. Then he had an inspiration. The author of the life of Jesus was his man.

He sent Socinius a letter and asked him to come east.

Unfortunately when Socinius reached Transylvania the private life of Blandrata had just led to so grave a public scandal that the Italian had been forced to resign and leave for parts unknown. Socinius,however,remained in this far away land,married a Polish girl and died in his adopted country in the year 1604.

These last two decades of his life proved to be the most interesting period of his career. For it was then that he gave a concrete expression to his ideas upon the subject of tolerance.

They are to be found in the so-called"Catechism of Rakow,"a document which Socinius

显赫的妇科专家。从始至终他都是桀骜不驯却又相当聪明的人。就像他那个时代的许多医生（如拉伯雷和塞尔维特）一样，他既是神经科专家又是神学家，所扮演的两个角色经常相互冲突。比如说，他非常成功地扭转了波兰王太后波娜·斯佛萨（西吉斯蒙德国王的遗孀）的臆断，之前她认为对“三位一体”持怀疑态度者是错误的，后来，她对自己的失误懊恼不已，仅仅处死了那些坚信“三位一体”教义的人。

这位优秀的王后已经逝去了（被她的一位情人谋杀了），但是她的两个女儿分别嫁给了当地的贵族。作为她们的医学顾问，布兰德拉塔给他寄居的那片土地上施加了深远的影响。他深知这个国家战争一触即发，除非采取一些措施来终结这场旷日持久的宗教争论。因此，他想方设法劝说各对抗教派休战。但是，为了达到这一目的，他需要一个比自己更有技巧去处理纷乱的宗教争论的人来帮忙。接着，他有了灵感。耶稣那本书的作者就是他要找的人。

他给索兹尼发了一封信，请他到东方来。

不幸的是，当索兹尼赶到特兰西瓦尼亚时，布兰德拉塔的私生活中一则相当不光彩的丑闻被曝光了，致使这个意大利人被迫辞职，去向不明。然而，索兹尼留在了这片遥远的土地上，与一位波兰姑娘结了婚，于1604年在这个国家死去。

他生命中的后20年被认为是他事业中最令人感兴趣的阶段。因为在那个时期，他具体阐述了自己的宽容思想。

在所谓的《拉科教义问答书》中可以找到这些阐述，这本书由索兹尼编著，他想把它当作一个宪章，写给那些希望这个世界越来越美好和希望今后不再有宗教纠

composed as a sort of common constitution for all those who meant well by this world and wished to make an end to future sectarian strife.

The latter half of the sixteenth century was an era of catechism,confessions of faith,credos and creeds. People were writing them in Germany and in Switzerland and in France and in Holland and in Denmark. But everywhere these carelessly printed little booklets gave expression to the ghastly belief that they (and they alone) contained the real Truth with a great big capital T and that it was the duty of all authorities who had solemnly pledged themselves to uphold this one particular form of Truth with a great big capital T to punish with the sword and the gallows and the stake those who willfully remained faithful to a different sort of truth (which was only written with a small t and therefore was of an inferior quality).

The Socinian confession of faith breathed an entirely different spirit. It began by the flat statement that it was not the intention of those who had signed this document to quarrel with anybody else.

"With good reason,"it continued,"many pious people complain that the various confessions and catechisms which have hitherto been published and which the different churches are now publishing are apples of discord among the Christians because they all try to impose certain principles upon people's conscience and to consider those who disagree with them as heretics."

Thereupon it denied in the most formal way that it was the intention of the Socinians to proscribe or oppress any one else on account of his religious convictions and turning to humanity in general,it made the following appeal:

"Let each one be free to judge of his own religion,for this is the rule set forth by the New Testament and by the example of the earliest church. Who are we,miserable people,that we would smother and extinguish in others the fire of divine spirit which God has kindled in them?Have any of us a monopoly of the knowledge of the Holy Scriptures?Why do we not

纷的人。

16世纪下半叶是教义问答广泛流传的时代，是进行信仰、信条和信念诠释的时代。在德国、瑞士、法国、荷兰和丹麦，人们都在写这类东西。但是，这些被散发到各个角落的草率印制的小册子，表达了一个糟糕透顶的观点——那就是，它们（而且只有它们）才代表真正的真理；而且当局郑重承诺要支持用超大大写字母T表示的真理，并且有责任用刀剑、恐吓和火刑柱来惩罚那些故意信仰其他真理（那些只是用小t书写，因而处于劣势地位的真理）的人。

索兹尼的信仰表明他具有另外一种完全不同的精神。他一开始便直奔主题：签署这份文件的人，没有想与他人发生争吵的意图。

它继续写道："许多虔诚的人不无道理地抱怨道，那些迄今为止已出版的和各教会正准备出版的各种教义和教义问答，正是在基督徒之间引发冲突的根源。因为他们都在尝试将某些原则强加于人们的良知之上，把与自己观念不一致的人视为异端。"

于是，它用最正式的方式申明，索兹尼派不会根据宗教观点来放纵或镇压其他任何人。针对广义的人性，它呼吁道：

"让每个人都有决定自己宗教信仰的自由，因为这是由《新约》在先前就设定的法则，而且最早的教会也是遵照这一法则行事的。我们这些不幸的人，有何资格去熄灭他人心中由上帝点燃的神圣灵魂之火呢？我们谁能垄断经文中的知识呢？为什么不牢记我们唯一的主是耶稣基督，彼此都是兄弟，谁也不能操纵他人的灵魂呢？纵使兄弟们当中有谁比其他人更有学问，但在自由和救世主面前，人人平等。"

remember that our only master is Jesus Christ and that we are all brothers and that to no one has been given power over the souls of others?It may be that one of our brothers is more learned than the others,yet in regard to liberty and the relationship with Christ we are all equal."

All this was very fine and very wonderful,but it was said three hundred years ahead of the times. Neither the Socinians nor any of the other Protestant sects could in the long run hope to hold their own in this turbulent part of the world. The counter-reformation had begun in all seriousness. Veritable hordes of Jesuit fathers were beginning to be turned loose upon the lost provinces. While they worked,the Protestants quarreled. Soon the people of the eastern frontier were back within the fold of Rome. Today the traveler who visits these distant parts of civilized Europe would hardly guess that,once upon a time,they were a stronghold of the most advanced and liberal thought of the age. Nor would he suspect that somewhere among those dreary Lithuanian hills there lies a village where the world was for the first time presented with a definite program for a practical system of tolerance.

Driven by idle curiosity,I took a morning off recently and went to the library and read through the index of all our most popular textbooks out of which the youth of our country learns the story of the past. Not a single one mentioned Socinianism or the Sozzinis. They all jumped from Social Democrats to Sophia of Hanover and from Sobieski to Saracens. The usual leaders of the great religious revolution were there,including Oecolampadius and the lesser lights.

One volume only contained a reference to the two great Siennese humanists but they appeared as a vague appendix to something Luther or Calvin had said or done.

It is dangerous to make predictions,but I have a suspicion that in the popular histories of three hundred years hence,all this will have been changed and that the Sozzinis shall enjoy the luxury of a little chapter of their own and that the traditional heroes of the Reformation shall be relegated to the bottom of the page.

They have the sort of names that look terribly imposing in footnotes.

这些说得太高尚、太精彩了，但是早了300年。无论是索兹尼派还是任何别的新教派，都不能在这个疯狂的世界长期坚持自己的立场。反对宗教改革的潮流在极其严峻的形势下萌芽了。许多耶稣会教士在茫然的边远地区变得放纵了。新教徒一边工作一边争吵。很快，东部边疆地区的人又重返罗马的老家。如今参观文明欧洲的边远地区的游客，几乎不能想象，这些地区从前是拥有那个时代最先进的自由思想的大本营，也很难想到在沉寂的立陶宛小山上，坐落着一个村庄，就在那里，世界上首次获得了践行宽容理念的明确方案。

最近，我被无聊的好奇心驱使，去了一趟图书馆，花了整个上午的时间，仔细阅读了所有流行的教科书，我国青年正是从这些教科书中了解历史的。没有一本书提到过索兹尼派或索兹尼叔侄，这些书只是从社会民主派跳到汉诺威的索菲娅，从索比斯基跳到撒拉森斯。而这场伟大的宗教改革的普通领导人都在这些书中出现，包括奥克兰帕迪乌斯和其他一些次要人物。

其中只有一卷书记载了这两位伟大的锡耶纳人文主义者，但也只是隐约地在附录中被提起，那些附录是关于路德或加尔文曾说过或做过的事情的。

我没有把握做出预言，但我怀疑，在300年后的通俗历史中，这一切都将发生改变，索兹尼叔侄会独自享有属于他们自己的小篇章，而宗教改革的传统主角则会被降至页脚。

索兹尼家族拥有那种即使在脚注中也看起来令人难忘的名字。

CHAPTER XVIII MONTAIGNE

In the Middle Ages it used to be said that city air made for freedom.

That was true.

A man behind a high stone wall could thumb his nose safely at baron and priest.

A little later,when conditions upon the European continent had improved so much that international commerce was once more becoming a possibility,another historical phenomenon began to make itself manifest.

Done into words of three syllables it read :"Business makes for tolerance."

You can verify this statement any day of the week and most of all on Sunday in any part of our country.

Winesberg,Ohio,can afford to support the Ku Klux Klan,but New York cannot. If the people of New York should ever start a movement for the exclusion of all Jews and all Catholics and all foreigners in general,there would be such a panic in Wall Street and such an upheaval in the labor movement that the town would be ruined beyond the hope of repair.

The same held true during the latter half of the Middle Ages. Moscow,the seat of a small grand ducal count,might rage against the pagans,but Novgorod,the international trading post,must be careful lest she offend the Swedes and Norwegians and the Germans and the Flemish merchants who visited her market place and drive them to Wisby.

A purely agricultural state could with impunity regale its peasantry with a series of festive autos dafé. But if the Venetians or the Genoese or the people of Bruges had started

第18章　蒙　　田

人们常常说，中世纪的城市氛围成就了自由。

确实如此。

置身于高墙之后的人可以毫无顾虑地嘲笑男爵和牧师。

此后不久，欧洲大陆的条件改善了许多，以致国际通商又一次成为可能，另一个历史性的现象开始显现出来。

用三个音节组成一句话来表示就是：“商业造就宽容。”

在我国任何地区的每一天，特别是星期天，这话都可以得到证明。

俄亥俄州的温斯堡可以支持三K党，但是纽约不行。如果纽约的人发起一场排斥全部犹太人、天主教徒和普通外国人的运动，就会带来华尔街经济大恐慌和工人罢工运动，将会导致这座城市彻底毁灭，丝毫没有复原的余地。

中世纪下半叶的情形也一样。莫斯科是一个大公爵的小小领地，在那里也许可以奋起反击异教徒。但是，国际贸易中心诺夫哥罗德事事小心谨慎，生怕冒犯了光顾她市场的瑞典、挪威、德国和佛兰德的商人，否则会把他们赶到维斯比去。

一个纯粹的农业国能够不费吹灰之力，就可以用过节般丰盛的自助餐来盛情款待全国农民兄弟。但是，只要威尼斯人、热那亚人或布鲁日人在自己内部开始一

a pogrom among the heathen within their walls,there would have been an immediate exodus of all those who represented foreign business houses and the subsequent withdrawal of capital would have driven the city into bankruptcy.

A few countries which were constitutionally unable to learn from experience (like Spain and the papal dominions and certain possessions of the Habsburgs),actuated by a sentiment which they proudly called"loyalty to their convictions,"ruthlessly expelled the enemies of the true faith. As a result they either ceased to exist altogether or dwindled down to the rank of seventh rate Ritter states.

Commercial nations and cities,however,are as a rule governed by men who have a profound respect for established facts,who know on which side their bread is buttered,and who therefore maintain such a state of spiritual neutrality that their Catholic and Protestant and Jewish and Chinese customers can do business as usual and yet remain faithful to their own particular religion.

For the sake of outward respectability Venice might pass a law against the Calvinists,but the Council of Ten was careful to explain to their gendarmes that this decree must not be taken too seriously and that unless the heretics actually tried to get hold of San Marco and convert it into a meeting-house of their own,they must be left alone and must be allowed to worship as they saw fit.

Their good friends in Amsterdam did likewise. Every Sunday their ministers fulminated against the sins of the"Scarlet Woman."But in the next block the terrible Papists were quietly saying mass in some inconspicuous looking house,and outside the Protestant chief-of-police

顶楼里的主

场针对异教徒的大屠杀，那么所有外国商业机构的代表，就会立马大批撤离，紧随其后资金也会被撤离，从而使这座城市走向崩溃。

天生就不会汲取经验（像西班牙、罗马教皇国和哈布斯堡王室的某些领地）的那些国家，被所谓的“忠诚于信念”的豪情所驱使，冷酷地驱逐了“真正信仰”的敌人。结果是他们虽继续生存，但体无完肤，或被降为第七等国家。

然而，商业国家和城市的管理者通常能够无条件尊重既定事实，还很清楚怎样决策才能获益。因此，他们维系着这样一个精神上中立的国家，以致天主教徒、新教徒、犹太人及中国顾客既可以和平常一样做生意，还能保持对自己个人信仰的忠诚。

为了维持外表的尊严，威尼斯打算通过一项法律来反对加尔文主义。但是十人委员会很细心地向他们的警察解释道，一定不能将这条法令看得过于认真，只要异教徒不以实际行动控制圣马可教堂，不至于想把它变为他们自己的礼拜堂，那就让他们去吧，不用管他们，而且他们可以崇拜任何看得顺眼的东西。

他们在阿姆斯特丹的好朋友就是这么做的。每到周日，新教的牧师就会以严词谴责罗马天主教的罪过。但是在紧邻的街区，可怕的天主教徒在不太显眼的屋子里

stood watch lest an over-zealous admirer of the Geneva catechism try to break up this forbidden meeting and frighten the profitable French and Italian visitors away.

This did not in the least mean that the mass of the people in Venice or Amsterdam ceased to be faithful sons of their respective churches. They were as good Catholics or Protestants as they had ever been. But they remembered that the good will of a dozen profitable heretics from Hamburg or Lübeck or Lisbon was worth more than the approbation of a dozen shabby clerics from Geneva or Rome and they acted accordingly.

It may seem a little far-fetched to connect the enlightened and liberal opinions (they are not always the same) of Montaigne with the fact that his father and grandfather had been in the herring business and that his mother was of Spanish-Jewish descent. But it seems to me that these commercial antecedents had a great deal to do with the man's general point of view and that the intense dislike of fanaticism and bigotry which characterized his entire career as a soldier and statesman had originated in a little fish-shop somewhere off the main quai of Bordeaux.

Montaigne himself would not have thanked me if I had been able to make this statement to his face. For when he was born,all vestiges of mere“trade”had been carefully wiped off the resplendent family escutcheon.

His father had acquired a bit of property called Montaigne and had spent money lavishly that his son might be brought up as a gentleman. Before he was fairly able to walk private tutors had stuffed his poor little head full of Latin and Greek. At the age of six he had been sent to high-school. At thirteen he had begun to study law. And before he was twenty he was a full-fledged member of the Bordeaux town council.

Then followed a career in the army and a period at court,until at the age of thirty-eight,after the death of his father,he retired from all active business and spent the last

平静地作弥撒，而新教徒的首席警察官就在外面站岗，以免那些对《日内瓦教义问答手册》过度热情的敬慕者闯入这个“犯禁”的集会，吓跑给这个城市带来好处的法国和意大利游客。

这并不意味着威尼斯或阿姆斯特丹的广大群众已不再是自己尊敬的教会的忠诚子民。他们仍像以前一样，是优秀的天主教徒或新教徒。但是他们明白，那十几个经商的异教徒的美好愿望（这些异教徒分别来自汉堡、吕贝克或里斯本）要比那十几个衣衫褴褛的传教士（他们来自日内瓦或罗马）更有价值，因此他们照前者的建议去做了。

要把蒙田开明而自由的观念（它们并不经常一致），与他父亲、祖父曾经是做鲱鱼生意的，而母亲是西班牙犹太人的后代等事实联系起来，仿佛有点牵强。但是依我看来，似乎长辈经商的经历与蒙田的世界观有着十分密切的联系；而且对宗教自有的狂热主义及偏执的强烈厌恶，也反映在他作为战士和政治家的整个生涯中，这种厌恶源自波尔多主码头旁一家小鱼铺。

如果我能当面跟蒙田说这些话，他本人是不会感激我的。因为他一出生，所有“从商”的残痕全部被仔仔细细地从辉煌的家族盾徽上清除掉了。

他的父亲得到了一块被称作“蒙田”的产业，便打算花巨资把自己的儿子培养成绅士。在蒙田刚会走路的时候，私人教师就把他那可怜的小脑袋塞满了拉丁语和希腊语。他6岁的时候就被送到中学，13岁时开始学习法律。20岁之前，他就已经是波尔多市议会的资深议员。

twenty-one years of his life,(with the exception of a few unwilling excursions into politics),among his horses and his dogs and his books and learned as much from the one as he did from the other.

Montaigne was very much a man of his time and suffered from several weaknesses. He was never quite free from certain affections and mannerisms which he,the fish-monger's grandson,believed to be a part of true gentility. Until the end of his days he protested that he was not really a writer at all,only a country gentleman who occasionally whiled away the tedious hours of winter by jotting down a few random ideas upon subjects of a slightly philosophic nature. All this was pure buncombe. If ever a man put his heart and his soul and his virtues and his vices and everything he had into his books,it was this cheerful neighbor of the immortal d'Artagnan.

And as this heart and this soul and these virtues and these vices were the heart and the soul and the virtues and the vices of an essentially generous,well-bred and agreeable person,the sum total of Montaigne's works has become something more than literature. It has developed into a definite philosophy of life,based upon common sense and an ordinary practical variety of decency.

Montaigne was born a Catholic. He died a Catholic,and in his younger years he was an active member of that League of Catholic Noblemen which was formed among the French nobility to drive Calvinism out of France.

But after that fateful day in August of the year 1572 when news reached him of the joy with which Pope Gregory XIII had celebrated the murder of thirty thousand French Protestants,he turned away from the Church for good. He never went so far as to join the other side. He continued to go through certain formalities that he might keep his neighbors' tongues from wagging,but those of his chapters written after the night of Saint

接着他在军队和法庭工作了一段时间，直到38岁，他父亲去世以后，他才从忙于各项事务的状态中退出，在马、狗和书中间度过了生命中余下的21年（除了几次勉强涉足于政治之外），并从中收获了不少东西。

蒙田是他那个时代的大人物，却因软弱而遭受苦难。作为这个鱼贩的孙子，他从来没有偏离过自己认为的真正属于绅士的东西，即爱心和礼节。直到死去的时候，他还一直说他根本就不是一个真正的作家，只是一个乡村绅士，通过草草记下一些稍稍触及哲学本质的杂想，消磨冗长乏味的冬日时光。所有这些纯粹是空话。如果一个人曾经把他的心、他的灵魂、他的美德、他的缺陷、他的所有一切都献给了自己的书，那么这个人就是不朽的达达尼昂那般令人愉悦的邻居。

而且，他的心、他的灵魂、他的美德、他的缺陷，都属于这个本质上慷慨、有教养又和蔼可亲的人。这正是蒙田著作的全部，已经成为比文学更重要的东西。它们以常识和普通情理为基础，已经发展成不容置疑的生活哲学。

蒙田从生下来到死都是天主教徒。他年轻的时候，活跃于天主教贵族社团，这个社团是在法国贵族驱逐加尔文派这一事件中形成的。

但是，在1572年8月那个要命的日子里，罗马教皇格列高利十三世举行了屠杀3万法国新教徒的庆典，欢腾的消息传到了蒙田那里，他为了自己的良心而永远脱离了教会。他从来都不会走向极端，而去加入其他派别。为了不让邻居饶舌，他继续遵守礼节，但在圣巴塞洛缪之夜以后，他的作品就和马可·奥勒留、爱比克泰特或其他希腊、罗马哲学家的作品差不多了。在《论良知的自由》这篇给人深刻印象的

Bartholomew might just as well have been the work of Marcus Aurelius or Epictetus or any of a dozen other Greek or Roman philosophers. And in one memorable essay,entitled"On the Freedom of Conscience,"he spoke as if he had been a contemporary of Pericles rather than a servant of Her Majesty Catherine de' Medici and he used the career of Julian the Apostate as an example of what a truly tolerant statesman might hope to accomplish.

It is a very short chapter. It is only five pages long and you will find it in part nineteen of the second book.

Montaigne had seen too much of the incorrigible obstinacy of both Protestants and Catholics to advocate a system of absolute freedom,which (under the existing circumstances) could only provoke a new outbreak of civil war. But when circumstances allowed it,when Protestants and Catholics no longer slept with a couple of daggers and pistols underneath their pillows,then an intelligent government should keep away as much as possible from interfering with other people's consciences and should permit all of its subjects to love God as best suited the happiness of their own particular souls.

Montaigne was neither the only,nor the first Frenchman who had hit upon this idea or had dared to express it in public. As early as the year 1560 ,Michel de l' Hôpital,a former chancellor of Catherine de' Medici and a graduate of half a dozen Italian universities (and incidentally suspected of being tarred with the Anabaptist brush) had suggested that heretics be attacked exclusively with verbal arguments. He had based his somewhat startling opinion upon the ground that conscience being what it was,it could not possibly be changed by force,and two years later he had been instrumental in bringing about that royal Edict of Toleration which had given the Huguenots the right to hold meetings of their

■ 蒙田

文章中，他说道，自己就好像是与伯里克利同时代的人，而不是法国凯瑟琳·德·美第奇陛下的奴仆。而且他还用变节者朱利安作为例子，认为真正宽容的政治家应向他学习。

这一章的篇幅很短，只有5页，在第2卷第19章。

蒙田见过太多的新教徒和天主教徒，他们以固执到无药可救的行动倡导绝对自由，这种自由体系（在现有的环境下）只会导致新的内战。但是，当环境允许的时候，当新教徒和天主教徒不再把匕首和手枪藏在枕头下睡觉时，一个充满智慧的政府就要尽可能地避免干预别人的思想，就要让所有的臣民依照最能使自己灵魂愉悦的方式去热爱上帝，这才最恰当不过了。

蒙田既不是唯一的，也不是第一个产生这种想法并敢于在公共场合表达这一观点的法国人。早在1560年，迈克尔·德·洛必达——凯瑟琳·德·美第奇女王的前任大臣和在多所意大利大学就读的毕业生（他因此被怀疑有再洗礼教派倾向）就

own,to call synods to discuss the affairs of their church and in general to behave as if they were a free and independent denomination and not merely a tolerated little sect.

Jean Bodin,a Parisian lawyer,a most respectable citizen (the man who had defended the rights of private property against the communistic tendencies expressed in Thomas More's“Utopia”),had spoken in a similar vein when he denied the right of sovereigns to use violence in driving their subjects to this or that church.

But the speeches of chancellors and the Latin treatises of political philosophers very rarely make best sellers. Whereas Montaigne was read and translated and discussed wherever civilized people came together in the name of intelligent company and good conversation and continued to be read and translated and discussed for more than three hundred years.

His very amateurishness,his insistence that he just wrote for the fun of it and had no axes to grind,made him popular with large numbers of people who otherwise would never dream of buying (or borrowing) a book that was officially classified under“philosophy.”

曾说，异教徒只适合用文字来攻击。他这个有点惊人的观点的理论依据是，他认为良知有自己本来的面目，不可能被武力改变。两年后，他促成了《宽容法令》的颁布，这个法令赋予了胡格诺教派举行自己的议会的权力，可以召开宗教会议讨论教会的重要事项，俨然就是一个自由独立的派别，而不仅仅是一个寄人篱下的小派别。

巴黎的律师让·布丹，是个值得尊敬的市民（此人为私人财产权利而辩护，反对托马斯·莫尔在《乌托邦》中所表现的共产主义倾向），在反对君权用于暴力驱赶臣民到其他教会时，他也用类似口吻说话。

但大臣们的演讲和政治家哲学家的拉丁语论文，鲜有能吸引人们眼球的。然而，无论在哪里，以智慧同仁聚会畅谈的名义走到一起来的文明人，都在阅读、翻译并讨论蒙田的著作，而且持续了300多年。

由于他正是为了兴趣才写书的，完全出自业余，并且持之以恒，这使他深受人们欢迎。不然，人们永远都不会想买（或借）一本被官方归类于“哲学”的书。

CHAPTER XIX ARMINIUS

The struggle for tolerance is part of the age-old conflict between"organized society"which places the continued safety of the"group"ahead of all other considerations and those private citizens of unusual intelligence or energy who hold that such improvement as the world has thus far experienced was invariably due to the efforts of the individual and not due to the efforts of the mass (which by its very nature is distrustful of all innovations) and that therefore the rights of the individual are far more important than those of the mass.

If we agree to accept these premises as true,it follows that the amount of tolerance in any given country must be in direct proportion to the degree of individual liberty enjoyed by the majority of its inhabitants.

Now in the olden days it sometimes happened that an exceptionally enlightened ruler spake unto his children and said,"I firmly believe in the principle of live and let live. I expect all my beloved subjects to practice tolerance towards their neighbors or bear the consequences."

In that case,of course,eager citizens hastened to lay in a supply of the official buttons bearing the proud inscription,"Tolerance first."

But these sudden conversions,due to a fear of His Majesty's hangman,were rarely of a lasting nature and only bore fruit if the sovereign accompanied his threat by an intelligent system of gradual education along the lines of practical every day politics.

Such a fortunate combination of circumstances occurred in the Dutch Republic during the latter half of the sixteenth century.

第19章　阿米尼乌斯

“有组织的社会”总是把“整体”安全置于其他顾虑之先，而才智过人或精力充沛的市民却坚持认为，这个世界到目前为止所历经的这些发展，要归功于个人的努力，而不是集体（集体的根本特性就是质疑所有革新），因此，个人的权力要比集体的权力重要得多。为宽容而战，正是发生在他们之间的持续已久的冲突的一部分。

如果我们把这些假设当作真理，那么它遵循这样一条规律，即国家的宽容程度在总体上会与多数居民个人享有的自由程度成正比。

在古老的年代里，不时地发生这样的事，一位格外开明的统治者对他的子民们说：“我坚信‘待人宽人亦待己宽’的原则。我希望，我所有深爱的臣民对待邻居要按照宽容原则行事，否则后果自负。”

如果是那样的话，很自然地，热心的臣民就会急忙贮备官方发行的底部刻有“宽容第一”的小圆徽章。

但是，这一转变是由于害怕陛下的刽子手而突然形成的，几乎不具可持续性。而且，国王只有在威吓的同时再建立起一整套逐级教育的明智体系，把它当作每天的政治活动，才能取得成效。

16世纪下半叶，如此幸运的环境出现在荷兰共和国。

In the first place the country consisted of several thousand semi-independent towns and villages and these for the greater part were inhabited by fishermen,sailors and traders,three classes of people who are accustomed to a certain amount of independence of action and who are forced by the nature of their trade to make quick decisions and to judge the casual occurrences of the day's work upon their own merits.

I would not for a moment claim that,man for man,they were a whit more intelligent or broadminded than their neighbors in other parts of the world. But hard work and tenacity of purpose had made them the grain and fish carriers of all northern and western Europe. They knew that the money of a Catholic was just as good as that of a Protestant and they preferred a Turk who paid cash to a Presbyterian who asked for six months' credit. An ideal country therefore to start a little experiment in tolerance and furthermore the right man was in the right place and what is infinitely more important the right man was in the right place at the right moment.

William the Silent was a shining example of the old maxim that"those who wish to rule the world must know the world."He began life as a very fashionable and rich young man,enjoying a most enviable social position as the confidential secretary of the greatest monarch of his time. He wasted scandalous sums of money upon dinners and dances,married several of the better known heiresses of his day and lived gayly without a care for the day of tomorrow. He was not a particularly studious person and racing charts interested him infinitely more than religious tracts.

The social unrest which followed in the wake of the Reformation did not at first impress him as anything more serious than still another quarrel between capital and labor,the sort of thing that could be settled by the use of a little tact and the display of a few brawny police constables.

But once he had grasped the true nature of the issue that had arisen between the

首先，这个国家有数千个半独立的城市和农村。这些地方的居民以渔民、水手和商人为主，从事这三种职业的人习惯于一定程度的独立行动，因为经商的职业特点迫使他们要迅速决策，要根据其自身情况判断日常工作中的偶然机遇。

虽说人与人之间存在差异，我也不能瞬间就断言，他们会比世界上其他地区的同类更聪明或心胸更开阔。但是，努力工作和不屈不挠的意志造就了整个北欧和西欧谷物和鱼类的搬运者。他们知道天主教徒的钱和新教徒的钱一样好用；相比之下，他们更喜欢支付现金的土耳其人，而不是要求赊账六个月的长老会教友。因此，这是一个可以进行宽容实验的小理想国，而且是合适的人处于合适的位置，而更重要的是合适的人在合适的时候处于合适的位置。

沉默者威廉是“欲统治世界之人，必先了解世界”这一古老谚语的光辉典范。作为当时最伟大君主的心腹秘书，他享有令人羡慕的社会地位，过着阔绰的时尚青年的生活。他在宴会和舞会上挥金如土，与数位当代著名女继承人结婚，生活放荡，不顾明日生计。他不算勤奋，对赛马排行榜的兴趣远远大过宗教手册。

宗教改革引起的社会动乱，并没有在一开始就引起他的注意，不过是发生在资本家与工人之间的又一轮争论。只要要要小手段，派几个威武的警察出面就可以解决了。

但是，当他领悟到摆在君主和臣民间的问题的真正本质时，这位和蔼可亲的大爵爷突然变成了十二分能干的领导者。他在布告中，三言两语就卖掉了豪宅、马匹、黄金餐具和乡村庄园（或在根本不知情的情况下直接充公了）。就所有的意图

sovereign and his subjects,this amiable grand seigneur was suddenly transformed into the exceedingly able leader of what,to all intents and purposes,was the prime lost cause of the age. The palaces and horses,the gold plate and the country estates were sold at short notice (or confiscated at no notice at all) and the sporting young man from Brussels became the most tenacious and successful enemy of the house of Habsburg.

This change of fortune,however,did not affect his private character. William had been a philosopher in the days of plenty. He remained a philosopher when he lived in a couple of furnished rooms and did not know how to pay for Saturday's clean wash. And just as in the olden days he had worked hard to frustrate the plans of a cardinal who had expressed the intention of building a sufficient number of gallows to accommodate all Protestants,he now made it a point to bridle the energy of those ardent Calvinists who wished to hang all Catholics.

His task was wellnigh hopeless.

Between twenty and thirty thousand people had already been killed,the prisons of the Inquisition were full of new candidates for martyrdom and in far off Spain new armies were being recruited to smash the rebellion before it should spread to other parts of the Empire.

To bell people who were fighting for their lives that they must love those who had just hanged their sons and brothers and uncles and grandfathers was out of the question. But by his personal example,by his conciliatory attitude towards those who opposed him,William was able to show his followers how a man of character can invariably rise superior to the old Mosaic law of an eye for an eye and a tooth for a tooth.

In this campaign for public decency he enjoyed the support of a very remarkable man. In the church of Gouda you may this very day read a curious monosyllabic epitaph which enumerates the virtues of one Dirck Coornhert,who lies buried there. This Coornhert was an interesting fellow. He was the son of well-to-do people and had spent many years of his youth

和目标来看，这项行动在那个时代一开始就注定要失败。这位布鲁塞尔花花公子，成了哈布斯堡王朝最顽强而又最有成就的敌人。

然而，财物的变化没有影响到他的个性。威廉在富足的时候是哲学家，当住在带家具的公寓里，还要为周六支付洗衣账单发愁的时候，他仍然是个哲学家。正是在那个久远的年代，他为挫败主教企图搭建数量多到足以容纳所有新教徒的绞刑架，这一计划他玩命工作。现在他的工作重点，就是打压那些想绞死全部天主教徒的冲动的加尔文派教徒。

他的目标几乎无望实现。

宗教裁判所的监狱关满了要殉难的新囚犯，遇害者有2万至3万。在遥远的西班牙，几支新部队正张罗着招兵买马，欲在谋反派势力快要扩张到帝国其他地区之前，就将它粉碎。

要提醒为自己的生活而奋斗的那些人，如果去爱亲手绞死了自己儿子、兄弟、叔叔和爷爷的人，是不可能的。但是，威廉以自身为例，以他对待叛党的宽容态度向追随者表明：有个性的人应该超越“以牙还牙”的古老摩西律法的境界。

在这场为实现公共道德而进行的战役中，他得到过一个相当卓越的人物的支持。你可以在豪达教会看到一段怪异的单音节字碑文，上面列举了迪尔克·库恩赫特的美德，他就在碑下长眠。库恩赫特是个有趣的家伙。他是小康人家的孩子，而且多年的青春都在国外的旅行中度过，获得了一些德国、西班牙和法国的第一手资料。他刚结束旅程返回故里，就爱上了一位身无分文的姑娘。他小心谨慎的父亲不

traveling in foreign lands and getting some first hand information about Germany,Spain and France. As soon as he had returned home from this trip he fell in love with a girl who did not have a cent. His careful Dutch father had forbidden the marriage. When his son married the girl just the same,he did what those ancestral patriarchs were supposed to do under the circumstances;he talked about filial ingratitude and disinherited the boy.

This was inconvenient,in so far as young Coornhert was now obliged to go to work for a living. But he was a young man of parts,learned a trade and set up as a copper-engraver.

Alas! once a Dutchman,always a dominie. When evening came,he hastily dropped the burin,picked up the goose-quill and wrote articles upon the events of the day. His style was not exactly what one would nowadays call"amusing."But his books contained a great deal of that amiable common sense which had distinguished the work of Erasmus and they made him many friends and brought him into contact with William the Silent who thought so highly of his abilities that he employed him as one of his confidential advisers.

Now William was engaged in a strange sort of debate. King Philip,aided and abetted by the Pope,was trying to rid the world of the enemy of the human race (to wit,his own enemy,William) by a standing offer of twenty-five thousand golden ducats and a patent of nobility and forgiveness of all sins to whomsoever would go to Holland and murder the arch-heretic. William,who had already lived through five attempts upon his life,felt it his duty to refute the arguments of good King Philip in a series of pamphlets and Coornhert assisted him.

That the house of Habsburg,for whom these arguments were intended,should thereby be converted to tolerance was of course an idle hope. But as all the world was watching the duel between William and Philip,those little pamphlets were translated and read everywhere and they caused a healthy discussion of many subjects that people had never before dared to mention above a whisper.

同意这门婚事。当儿子坚持和这位姑娘结婚时，在当时的环境下父亲按照族长的建议去做了——指责儿子不孝并要取消这孩子的继承权。

■ 争吵的教授们

年轻的库恩赫特迫于生计不得不出去工作，这多少有点困难。但他是个有才华的人，学了一门手艺，做起了铜器雕刻生意。

唉！只要是荷兰人，就永远会说教。每当夜幕降临，他就急急忙忙地放下刻刀，拾起鹅毛笔记录当天发生的事。他的风格不完全是现代人所称的“引人入胜”。但他的书包含了许多类似伊拉斯默作品所阐述的平易近人的常识，正是这一点让他结识了不少朋友，开始了与沉默者威廉的交往。威廉认为他的能力很强，因此雇佣他做自己的机要顾问。

现在，威廉卷入了一场奇怪的争论之中。菲利浦亲王在教皇的帮助和怂恿下，企图将人类的敌人斩草除根（也就是他自己的敌人威廉）。无论是谁，只要前往荷兰刺杀这个头号异教徒，都能得到一大笔赏金和贵族头衔，并宽恕其犯下的所有罪过。一生中经受过五次袭击的威廉觉得应该用一套小册子驳倒权威的菲利浦亲王，

Unfortunately the debates did not last very long. On the ninth of July of the year 1584 a young French Catholic gained that reward of twenty-five thousand ducats and six years later Coornhert died before he had been able to finish the translation of the works of Erasmus into the Dutch vernacular.

As for the next twenty years,they were so full of the noise of battle that even the fulminations of the different theologians went unheard. And when finally the enemy had been driven from the territory of the new republic,there was no William to take hold of internal affairs and three score sects and denominations,who had been forced into temporary but unnatural friendship by the presence of a large number of Spanish mercenaries,flew at each other's throats.

Of course,they had to have a pretext for their quarrel but who ever heard of a theologian without a grievance?

In the University of Leiden there were two professors who disagreed. That was nothing either new or unusual. But these two professors disagreed upon the question of the freedom of the will and that was a very serious matter. At once the delighted populace took a hand in the discussion and within less than a month the entire country was divided into two hostile camps.

On the one side,the friends of Arminius.

On the other,the followers of Gomarus.

The latter,although born of Dutch parents,had lived all his life in Germany and was a brilliant product of the Teuton system of pedagogy. He possessed immense learning combined with a total absence of ordinary horse-sense. His mind was versed in the mysteries of Hebrew prosody but his heart beat according to the rules of the Aramaic syntax.

His opponent,Arminius,was a very different sort of man. He was born in Oudewater,a

他得到了库恩赫特的支持。

小册子的矛头直指哈布斯堡王朝。但要是指望王室由此变得宽容，这个愿望就注定要落空了。然而，由于全世界都在观望威廉和菲利浦之间的这场决斗，在任何地方都可以读到那些翻译好的小册子。这些小册子还引起了涉及众多主题的热烈讨论，在此之前人们是从不敢公开提起这些主题的。

不幸的是，这场争论并没有持续多长时间。1584年7月9日，一个年轻的法国天主教徒挣到了菲利浦亲王的赏金。6年后，库恩赫特遇害了，还没来得及完成伊拉斯默作品的翻译。

此后20年，处处弥漫着战争的嘈杂，甚至各路神学家的争鸣都销声匿迹。最终，敌人被赶出了新共和国的领土，但却没有威廉那样的人来管理内部事务和三教九流，这些三教九流只是由于大批西班牙雇佣军的出现，才被迫暂时结成联盟的，现在他们又开始了互相攻击。

当然，他们必须为自己的争论找一个借口，但是又有哪个神学家没有一点抱怨呢？

在莱顿大学，有两位意见不统一的教授，这既不是什么新鲜事，也不是什么不同寻常的事。但是，这两位教授在“意志自由”这个问题上产生了分歧，那就是一件相当严重的事情。欢欣鼓舞的平民立即参与到这场讨论中来，而且不到一个月，整个国家就分成了两个敌对阵营。

一方是阿米尼乌斯的朋友。

little city not far away from that cloister Steyn where Erasmus had spent the unhappy years of his early manhood. As a child he had won the friendship of a neighbor,a famous mathematician and professor of astronomy in the University of Marburg. This man,Rudolf Snellius,had taken Arminius back with him to Germany that he might be properly educated. But when the boy went home for his first vacation he found that his native town had been sacked by the Spaniards and that all his relatives had been murdered.

That seemed to end his career but fortunately some rich people with kind hearts heard of the sad plight of the young orphan and they put up a purse and sent him to Leiden to study theology. He worked hard and after half a dozen years he had learned all there was to be learned and looked for fresh intellectual grazing grounds.

In those days,brilliant students could always find a patron willing to invest a few dollars in their future. Soon Arminius,provided with a letter of credit issued by certain guilds of Amsterdam,was merrily trotting southward in search of future educational opportunities.

As behooved a respectable candidate of theology,he went first of all to Geneva. Calvin was dead,but his man Friday,the learned Theodore Beza,had succeeded him as shepherd of the seraphic flock. The fine nose of this old heresy hunter at once detected a slight odor of Ramism in the doctrines of the young Dutchman and the visit of Arminius was cut short.

The word Ramism means nothing to modern readers. But three hundred years ago it was considered a most dangerous

■ 阿米尼乌斯

另一方是格玛鲁的追随者。

尽管格玛鲁是荷兰血统，但他在德国度过一生，而且是条顿教学体系下的得意门生。他有着渊博的学识，却又缺乏普通常识。他的大脑精通希伯来韵律学的奥秘，但他的心按照阿拉米语的语法规则跳动。

他的对手阿米尼乌斯却迥然不同。他出生于奥德沃特，是离泰恩修道院不远的一个小城市，伊拉斯默就在这个修道院度过了痛苦的少年时代。当阿米尼乌斯还只是个孩子时，就赢得了一位邻居、马尔堡大学著名数学家和天文学教授的友谊。此人叫鲁道夫·斯涅耳，他把阿米尼乌斯一同带回德国，在那里他可以受到正当的教育。但是，当这个孩子回到家乡过第一个假期时，就得知故乡已经沦陷于西班牙的魔爪，所有的亲人都遇害了。

这看起来好像会终结他的学业，但幸运的是，一些心地善良的有钱人听说了这个小孤儿的悲惨遭遇，便凑钱送他去莱顿大学学神学。他努力学习，六年后学到了全部可以学到的东西，就又寻找新的知识领地去了。

在那个时代，聪明的学生总是可以找到一个资助人愿意为他们的前途投资。很快，阿米尼乌斯带着由阿姆斯特丹几家行业协会开具的介绍信，愉快地跑去南方寻

religious novelty,as those who are familiar with the assembled works of Milton will know. It had been invented or originated (or what you please) by a Frenchman,a certain Pierre de la Ramie. As a student,de la Ramie had been so utterly exasperated by the antiquated methods of his professors that he had chosen as subject for his doctor's dissertation the somewhat startling text,"Everything ever taught by Aristotle is absolutely wrong."

Needless to say this subject did not gain him the good will of his teachers. When a few years afterwards he elaborated his idea in a number of learned volumes,his death was a foregone conclusion. He fell as one of the first victims of the massacre of Saint Bartholomew.

But his books,those pesky books which refuse to be assassinated together with their authors,had survived and Rame's curious system of logic had gained great popularity throughout northern and western Europe. Truly pious people however believed that Ramism was the password to Hades and Arminius was advised to go to Basel where"libertines" (a sixteenth century colloquialism meaning"liberals") had been considered good form ever since that unfortunate city had fallen under the spell of the quizzical Erasmus.

Arminius,thus forewarned,traveled northward and then decided upon something quite unusual. He boldly invaded the enemy's territory,studied for a few semesters in the University of Padua and paid a visit to Rome. This made him a dangerous person in the eyes of his fellow countrymen when he returned to his native country in the year 1587. But as he seemed to develop neither horns nor a tail,he was gradually taken back into their good favor and was allowed to accept a call as minister to Amsterdam.

There he made himself not only useful but he gained quite a reputation as a hero during one of the many outbreaks of the plague. Soon he was held in such genuine esteem that he was entrusted with the task of reorganizing the public school system of that big city and

找未来的教育机会了。

作为受人尊敬的神学继承人，他先来到日内瓦。加尔文已经死了，但是他忠心的仆人西奥多·伯撒接了他的班，成了纯洁羊群的牧羊人。这位捕捉异教徒的老猎手鼻子很灵敏，立即从这个荷兰青年的教义中嗅出了一点点拉米主义的气味，便缩短了阿米尼乌斯的拜访时间。

“拉米主义”这个词对于现代读者来说毫无意义。但300年前它被看作是一种危害相当大的宗教新观念，那些熟悉弥尔顿文集的人就能了解这一点。它由一位名叫皮埃尔·德·拉·拉米的法国人原创或发明（或者任凭你怎么想）。德·拉·拉米还是学生时，曾被教授陈旧的教学方式彻底激怒，于是他拟定了一个令人震惊的博士论文的题目——“亚里士多德教诲的每一件事情都是绝对错误的”。

不用说，这个题目不会让他在老师面前留下好印象。几年后，他在几本颇有见地的册子中详细阐述了自己的观点，因此他的死亡便成为意料之中的结局，圣巴托洛缪大屠杀第一轮的牺牲者中就有他。

但他那些可恶的书并没有随其作者一起消亡。拉米奇特的逻辑体系红透了整个北欧和西欧。然而，虔诚的人认为拉米主义简直就是通向地狱的密码。因而有人建议阿米尼乌斯去巴塞尔——这座不幸的城市自从受到遭人讥讽的伊拉斯谟的魔咒诱惑之后，一直把“自由思想家”（16世纪俗称“自由主义者”）当作好公民。

于是，得到警告的阿米尼乌斯向北而去，接着做出了一项不同寻常的决定。他大胆地踏入敌人的领地，在帕多瓦大学进修了几个学期，然后实地走访了罗马。这使

when in the year 1603 he was called to Leiden as a full-fledged prolessor of theology,he left the capital amidst the sincere regrets of the entire population.

If he had known beforehand what was awaiting him in Leiden,I am sure he would never have gone. He arrived just when the battle between the Infralapsarians and the Supralapsarians was at its height.

Arminius was both by nature and education an Infralapsarian. He tried to be fair to his colleague,the Supralapsarian Gomarus. But alas,the differences between the Supralapsarians and the Infralapsarians were such as allowed of no compromise. And Arminius was forced to declare himself an out and out Infralapsarian.

Of course,you will ask me what Supra-and Infralapsarians were. I don't know,and I seem unable to learn such things. But as far as I can make out,it was the age-old quarrel between those who believed (as did Arminius) that man is to a certain extent possessed of a free will and able to shape his own destinies and those who like Sophocles and Calvin and Gomarus taught that everything in our lives has been pre-ordained ages before we were born and that our fate therefore depends upon a throw of the divine dice at the hour of creation.

In the year 1600 by far the greater number of the people of northern Europe were Supralapsarians. They loved to listen to sermons which doomed the majority of their neighbors to eternal perdition and those few ministers who dared to preach a gospel of good will and charity were at once suspected of criminal weakness,fit rivals of those tender hearted doctors who fail to prescribe malodorous medicines and kill their patients by their kindness.

As soon as the gossiping old women of Leiden had discovered that Arminius was an Infralapsarian,his usefulness had come to an end. The poor man died under the torrent of abuse that was let loose upon him by his former friends and supporters. And then,as seemed unavoidable during the seventeenth century,Infralapsarianism and

得他在1587年回到祖国时，成为同胞眼中的危险人物。但他看上去既未生犄角也没长尾巴，渐渐地又重新获得了人们的欢心，还被允许担任阿姆斯特丹的新教牧师。

在那里，他不但发挥了自己应有的作用，在经历不断爆发的瘟疫之后，还赢得了英雄的美誉。很快，他受到了人们真诚的尊重，以致被委以一项重任——重组那座大城市的公立教育体系。1603年，作为羽翼丰满的神学教授，他被派去莱顿，在离开之际所有人都依依不舍。

如果他能预先知道莱顿等着他的将是什么，我确信他永远都不会去。他到达的时候，恰逢“堕落后预定论者”和“堕落前拯救论者”之间的战争正处于高潮阶段。

无论从本质还是从所受教育来讲，阿米尼乌斯都属于“堕落后预定论者”。他尝试要和他的同僚——“堕落前拯救论者”格玛鲁平起平坐。但是，唉，这两者之间的差异已经到了无法调和的地步。阿米尼乌斯被迫宣布自己是一个彻底的“堕落后预定论者”。

当然，你会问我，“堕落后预定论者”和“堕落前拯救论者”都是些什么。我不知道，而且我仿佛也无法理解这类东西。但是至少我可以作出如下总结：这是一场历经多年的争论，一方认为（正是阿米尼乌斯的观点）人在某种程度上拥有自由，并能决定自己的命运；另一方却认为，正如索福克勒斯、加尔文和格玛鲁所教导的，生命中每件事物在我们出生前数年就已经事先注定了，因此我们的命运取决于上帝在创造生命的刹那间随意投掷的骰子。

1600年，北欧人中“堕落前拯救论者”占多数。他们热衷听到的布道是，多数

Supralapsarianism made their entrance into the field of politics and the Supralapsarians won at the polls and the Infralapsarians were declared enemies of the public order and traitors to their country.

Before this absurd quarrel had come to an end,Oldenbarnevelt,the man who next to William the Silent had been responsible for the foundation of the Republic,lay dead with his head between his feet;Grotius,whose moderation had made him the first great advocate of an equitable system of international law,was eating the bread of charity at the court of the Queen of Sweden;and the work of William the Silent seemed entirely undone.

But Calvinism did not gain the triumph it had hoped.

The Dutch Republic was a republic only in name. It was really a sort of merchants' and bankers' club,ruled by a few hundred influential families. These gentlemen were not at all interested in equality and fraternity,but they did believe in law and order. They recognized and supported the established church. On Sundays with a great display of unction they proceeded to the large white-washed sepulchers which in former days had been Catholic Cathedrals and which now were Protestant lecture halls. But on Monday,when the clergy paid its respects to the Honorable Burgomaster and Town Councilor,with a long list of grievances against this and that and the other person,their lordships were"in conference"and unable to receive the reverend gentlemen. If the reverend gentlemen insisted,and induced (as frequently happened) a few thousand of their loyal parishioners to"demonstrate"in front of the town hall,then their lordships would graciously deign to accept a neatly written copy of the reverend gentlemen's complaints and suggestions. But as soon as the door had been closed upon the last of the darkly garbed petitioners,their lordships would use the document to light their pipes.

For they had adopted the useful and practical maxim of"once is enough and too

人注定要一刻不停地走向毁灭，如果有那么几个牧师胆敢宣称善意与仁慈的福音，立即会被怀疑为犯了软弱罪，恰如心慈手软的医生出于善良而不忍心开出恶臭的药方，结果却害死了病人一样。

当莱顿的长舌老妇一旦发现阿米尼乌斯是“堕落后预定论者”时，他便没有什么可利用之处了。这个可怜的人在从前的朋友和支持者的大肆辱骂声中死去。接着，“堕落后预定论者”和“堕落前拯救论者”都介入政坛，这在17世纪是必然的。“堕落前拯救论者”在选举中胜出，“堕落后预定论者”则被宣布为公共秩序的敌人和叛国者。

在这场荒唐的争吵结束之前，仅次于沉默者威廉的共和国奠基人奥登巴奈维特死了，死时头夹在双脚之间；因其适中的立场而成为国际法公平体系第一个伟大倡导者的格劳休斯，则在瑞典女王的王宫里过着寄人篱下的生活；沉默者威廉的计划看来完全破灭了。

但是，加尔文并没有如愿获胜。

荷兰共和国只是名义上的共和国。事实上，它是商人和银行家的俱乐部，由数百个有势力的家族统治。这些绅士对平等和友爱根本就不感兴趣，但他们相信法律和规则。他们认可并支持既有的教会。每逢星期天，他们总是充满热情并井然有序地进入宗教圣物储藏所，这些建筑用石灰粉刷过，过去曾是天主教堂，现在成了新教徒的布道厅。但是到了星期一，当牧师带着一份长长的名单去问候尊敬的镇长和小镇议员时（名单上列举了令牧师感到不满的人），官员们却又在“开会”，而不能接见这些牧

many"and they were so horrified by what had happened during the terrible years of the great Supralapsarian civil war that they uncompromisingly suppressed all further forms of religious frenzy.

Posterity has not always been kind to those aristocrats of the ledger. Undoubtedly they regarded the country as their private property and did not always differentiate with sufficient nicety between the interests of their fatherland and those of their own firm. They lacked that broad vision which goes with empire and almost invariably they were penny-wise and pound-foolish. But they did something which deserves our hearty commendation. They turned their country into an international clearing-house where all sorts of people with all sorts of ideas were given the widest degree of liberty to say,think,write and print whatever pleased them.

I do not want to paint too rosy a picture. Here and there,under a threat of ministerial disapprobation,the Town Councilors were sometimes obliged to suppress a secret society of Catholics or to confiscate the pamphlets printed by a particularly noisy heretic. But generally speaking,as long as one did not climb on a soap-box in the middle of the market place to denounce the doctrine of predestination or carry a big rosary into a public dining-hall or deny the existence of God in the South Side Methodist Church of Haarlem,one enjoyed a degree of personal immunity which for almost two centuries made the Dutch Republic a veritable haven of rest for all those who in other parts of the world were persecuted for the sake of their opinions.

Soon the rumor of this Paradise Regained spread abroad. And during the next two hundred years,the print shops and the coffee-houses of Holland were filled with a motley crew of enthusiasts,the advance guard of a strange new army of spiritual liberation.

师。如果牧师坚持说服数千个忠诚的教民在市政厅前“示威”（这种事情经常发生），官员们就会优雅地垂顾，接过牧师抄写整齐的诉苦书和建议书。但是，只要最后一位穿黑袍的请愿者转身离开，大门在他身后关上时，官员们就会用这些文稿来点烟斗。

他们已经采纳了“一次足矣，下不为例”这一行之有效的座右铭。况且，“堕落前拯救论者”在那几年掀起的可怕的大内战已经令他们惊恐万分，于是他们坚决镇压一切疯狂的宗教行为。

后人对这些贵族并无好感。毫无疑问，他们把国家看作私有财产，而且常常不能精确地区分祖国利益和自身固有利益之间的差别。他们缺乏治国的远见，差不多永远都是小事精明、大事糊涂的人。但是，他们也做过值得盛赞的事情。他们把自己的国家变成了国际中转站，在那里，思想迥异的人享有最大限度的自由，只要高兴，人们就可以说、写或出版任何东西。

我并不想描绘一幅太幸福的场景。迫于牧师指责的压力，各处的城市议会时常会镇压天主教的某个秘密社团，或没收某个嚣张异教徒印制的小册子。但是总的来说，只要不爬到集市中央的演讲台上公然指责宿命论的教义，不把天主教大串念珠带入公共餐厅，或不否认哈勒姆南方的卫理公会上帝的存在，便可保人身安全。近两个世纪，对于世界上其他地区因观点不同而遭到迫害的人们来说，荷兰共和国是名副其实的休养生息的天堂。

很快，这个“复乐园”的传闻被广泛传播。此后200年期间，荷兰的印刷厂和咖啡屋里挤满了各色宗教狂热分子，他们就是为精神解放而战的杰出新先锋。

CHAPTER X X BRUNO

It has been said (and with a good deal of reason) that the Great War was a war of non-commissioned officers.

While the generals and the colonels and the three-star strategists sat in solitary splendor in the halls of some deserted chateau and contemplated miles of maps until they could evolve a new bit of tactics that was to give them half a square mile of territory (and lose some thirty thousand men),the junior officers,the sergeants and the corporals,aided and abetted by a number of intelligent privates,did the so-called"dirty work"and eventually brought about the collapse of the German line of defense.

The great crusade for spiritual independence was fought along similar lines.

There were no frontal attacks which drew into action half a million soldiers.

There were no desperate charges to provide the enemy's gunners with an easy and agreeable target.

I might go even further and say that the vast majority of the people never knew that there was any fighting at all. Now and then,curiosity may have compelled them to ask who was being burned that morning or who was going to be hanged the next afternoon. Then perhaps they discovered that a few desperate individuals continued to fight for certain principles of freedom of which both Catholics and Protestants disapproved most heartily. But I doubt whether such information affected them beyond the point of mild regret and the comment that it must be very sad for their poor relatives to bear,that uncle had come to

第20章 布 鲁 诺

据说（有大量的根据）世界大战是那些没有军衔的军官们的战争。

将军、上校和三星级战略家们坐在某个荒废的别墅大厅幽暗的光线下，盯着几英尺大的地图冥思苦想，直到推演出一些新的战术，能帮他们争夺到半英里的领土（牺牲3000人才能换来），而那些下级军官、中士、下士却在一些机灵的列兵的帮助和教唆下，从事着所谓的“脏活”，最终导致了德国防线的崩溃。

为精神世界的独立而进行的伟大征战，情况与此类似。

没有投入几十万兵力的任何正面交战。

也没有孤注一掷的猛攻，为敌人的炮兵提供再明显不过的靶子。

我甚至可以更进一步地说，大多数人根本不知道外面早已战火纷飞。只是好奇心会不时地驱使人们关心早上刚刚有谁被烧死了，明天下午谁又将被绞死。接着，他们也许会发现，有几个喜欢铤而走险的亡命徒还在继续为几项自由法则而抗争，而这是天主教徒和新教徒都不愿支持的。不过，我想知道这消息是否真能让人们略感遗憾，并且说要是自己的叔父落得如此恐怖的下场，所有可怜的亲戚一定会痛不欲生。

事实不外乎于此。殉道者为高尚的事业甘愿奉献生命，当然不能用简简单单的

such a terrible end.

It could hardly have been otherwise. What martyrs actually accomplish for the cause for which they give their lives cannot possibly be reduced to mathematical formulae or be expressed in terms of amperes or horsepower.

Any industrious young man in search of a Ph. D. may read carefully through the assembled works of Giordano Bruno and by the patient collection of all sentences containing such sentiments as"the state has no right to tell people what to think"or"society may not punish with the sword those who dissent from the generally approved dogmas,"he may be able to write an acceptable dissertation upon"Giordano Bruno (1549~1600) and the principles of religious freedom. "

But those of us no longer in search of those fatal letters must approach the subject from a different angle.

There were,so we say in our final analysis,a number of devout men who were so profoundly shocked by the fanaticism of their day,by the yoke under which the people of all countries were forced to exist,that they rose in revolt. They were poor devils. They rarely owned more than the cloak upon their back and they were not always certain of a place to sleep. But they burned with a divine fire. Up and down the land they traveled,talking and writing,drawing the learned professors of learned academies into learned disputes,arguing humbly with the humble country folk in humble rustic inns,eternally preaching a gospel of good will,of understanding,of charity towards others. Up and down the land they traveled in their shabby clothes with their little bundles of books and pamphlets until they died of pneumonia in some miserable village in the hinterland of Pomerania or were lynched by drunken peasants in a Scotch hamlet or were broken on the wheel in a provincial borough of France.

布鲁诺去日内瓦

数学公式，也不能用安培和马力这样的术语来衡量他们的贡献。

任何正在攻读博士学位的勤奋学生可能会认真地拜读乔达诺·布鲁诺文集，通过耐心地搜集所有表达下面想法的句子，如“国家无权告诉人们应该想什么”和“社会不应该用剑来惩处那些对大众公认的信条持反对意见的人”，然后写出一篇可以被人接受的题为《乔达诺·布鲁诺（1549~1600年）和宗教自由原则》的论文。

但是，我们当中不再研究这些重要文学作品的人，必须从不同角度来看待这个问题。

正如我们在最后的分析中所表达的那样，一些虔诚的人由于对当时的宗教狂热主义和强加在各国百姓背上让他们不堪重负的道道枷锁深感震惊，于是起来造反。他们几乎一无所有，除了背上的披风以外，甚至连栖息之地都找不到。但是他们高举神圣的火把，来来回回地逡巡于大地之上，进行演讲，发表作品，把高等学府博学的教授也拉进了这场学术争执中。同时，他们还在普通的乡下酒馆里与出身卑微

And if I mention the name of Giordano Bruno,I do not mean to imply that he was the only one of his kind. But his life,his ideas,his restless zeal for what he held to be true and desirable,were so typical of that entire group of pioneers that he will serve very well as an example.

The parents of Bruno were poor people. Their son,an average Italian boy of no particular promise,followed the usual course and went into a monastery. Later he became a Dominican monk. He had no business in that order for the Dominicans were the most ardent supporters of all forms of persecution,the"police-dogs of the true faith,"as their contemporaries called them. And they were clever. It was not necessary for a heretic to have his ideas put into print to be nosed out by one of those eager detectives. A single glance,a gesture of the hand,a shrug of the shoulders were often sufficient to give a man away and bring him into contact with the Inquisition.

How Bruno,brought up in an atmosphere of unquestioning obedience,turned rebel and deserted the Holy Scriptures for the works of Zeno and Anaxagoras,I do not know. But before this strange novice had finished his course of prescribed studies,he was expelled from the Dominican order and henceforth he was a wanderer upon the face of the earth.

He crossed the Alps. How many other young men before him had braved the dangers of those ancient mountain passes that they might find freedom in the mighty fortress which the new faith had erected at the junction of the Rhone and the Arve!

And how many of them had turned away,broken hearted when they discovered that here as there it was the inner spirit which guided the hearts of men and that a change of creed did not necessarily mean a change of heart and mind.

Bruno's residence in Geneva lasted less than three months. The town was full of Italian refugees. These brought their fellow countryman a new suit of clothes and found him a job

的乡民们心平气和地交谈，并且一如既往地到处宣讲善意、理解和仁慈的道理。他们衣衫褴褛，提着成包的书和小册子，四处奔走，直到感染了肺炎，在波美拉尼亚某个穷乡僻壤的穷苦小村离开人世，或者在苏格兰小村庄被喝得醉醺醺的村民私刑处死，或者在法国的乡镇被车轮碾得粉碎。

如果我提及乔达诺·布鲁诺的名字，并非暗示他是唯一遭受这种苦难的人。不过，他的生活、他的思想、他为自己认为正确且高尚的事业所萌生的不息热情，的确堪称所有先驱的代表，所以他是个很好的例子。

布鲁诺的父母很穷，他们的儿子是个普通的意大利人，毫无前途可言，只是遵循着一般人的人生轨迹，进入了一家修道院。后来，他成了多明我会修士。他始终无法融入这个团体，因为多明我会教徒狂热地支持迫害行为，从而被那个时代的人称为“真正信仰的警犬”。而且他们都很机灵。其实，异端者无需将自己的观点公之于众，就可以让追踪的暗探看出蛛丝马迹。往往一个眼神、一个手势、一个耸肩，便足以将某人暴露无遗，并让他受到宗教法庭的特别“关照”。

布鲁诺成长于唯命是从的环境，我也弄不明白他究竟是如何变得叛逆，将《圣经》弃之不顾，却推崇齐诺和阿纳克萨哥拉的著作的。但是在这个性格怪异的新修士还没有完成规定的课程之前，就被多明我会除名了，从此成为流浪者，四处漂泊。

他翻过阿尔卑斯山。在他之前，有多少年轻人勇敢地穿过了那些古老的山口，希望从屹立在罗纳河和阿尔弗河交汇处、诞生了新信仰的大堡垒里找到自由啊！

as proofreader. In the evenings he read and wrote. He got hold of a copy of de la Ramée's works. There at last was a man after his own heart. De la Ramée believed too that the world could not progress until the tyranny of the medieval text-books was broken. Bruno did not go as far as his famous French teacher and did not believe that everything the Greeks had ever taught was wrong. But why should the people of the sixteenth century be bound by words and sentences that were written in the fourth century before the birth of Christ?Why indeed?

"Because it has always been that way,"the upholders of the orthodox faith answered him.

"What have we to do with our grandfathers and what have they to do with us?Let the dead bury the dead,"the young iconoclast answered.

And very soon afterwards the police paid him a visit and suggested that he had better pack his satchels and try his luck elsewhere.

Bruno's life thereafter was one endless peregrination in search of a place where he might live and work in some degree of liberty and security. He never found it. From Geneva he went to Lyons and then to Toulouse. By that time he had taken up the study of astronomy and had become an ardent supporter of the ideas of Copernicus,a dangerous step in an age when all the contemporary Bryans brayed,"The world turning around the sun! The world a commonplace little planet turning around the sun! Ho-ho and hee-hee! Who ever heard such nonsense?"

Toulouse became uncomfortable. He crossed France,walking to Paris. And next to England as private secretary to a French ambassador. But there another disappointment awaited him. The English theologians were no better than the continental ones. A little more practical,perhaps. In Oxford,for example,they did not punish a student when he

在他们之中，又有多少人发现，处处都有内在的精神力量支配着人们的心的时候，教条上的改变并不一定意味着心灵与精神的改变后，他们心灰意冷地转身离开了。

布鲁诺在日内瓦住了不足三个月。城里挤满了意大利难民，他们给这个同乡弄了套新衣服，还找了个校对员的工作。晚上的时候，他就埋头读书写作。他得到了一本德·拉·拉米的书，仿佛终于找到了志同道合的人。德·拉·拉米也相信，如果不打碎那些中世纪教科书中所宣扬的暴政，世界便不能取得进步。布鲁诺并没有像自己的著名法国老师那样思想极端，并不认为希腊人教授的一切一无是处。但是，生活在16世纪的人凭什么还要被那些在基督出生4个世纪之前就已诞生的字句束缚呢？这究竟为什么？

“因为一直都是这样啊！”正统信仰的支持者们回答道。

“我们与我们的父辈有什么关系，他们与我们又有什么关系呢？让死去的人死去吧！”这个年轻的反传统者回答道。

很快，警方便找上门，建议他最好收拾行装，到别的地方去混。

这之后，布鲁诺开始了一场没有休止的旅行，寻找具有一定程度的自由和安全的地方生活和工作，却未能如愿。他从日内瓦来到里昂，又漂泊到图卢兹。直到这时，他已经开始天文学的研究，成为哥白尼的热情支持者。这是危险的一步。在那个时代，人们都在狂吼：“世界绕着太阳转！世界是绕太阳转动的普通小行星！哈哈，谁听说过这一派胡言？”

committed an error against the teachings of Aristotle. They fined him ten shillings.

Bruno became sarcastic. He began to write brilliantly dangerous bits of prose,dialogues of a religious-philosophic-political nature in which the entire existing order of things was turned topsy turvy and submitted to a minute but none too flattering examination.

And he did some lecturing upon his favorite subject,astronomy.

But college authorities rarely smile upon professors who please the hearts of their students. Bruno once more found himself invited to leave. And so back again to France and then to Marburg,where not so long before Luther and Zwingli had debated upon the true nature of the transubstantiation in the castle of pious Elisabeth of Hungary.

Alas! his reputation as a"Libertine"had preceded him. He was not even allowed to lecture. Wittenberg proved more hospitable. That old stronghold of the Lutheran faith,however,was beginning to be overrun by the disciples of Dr. Calvin. After that there was no further room for a man of Bruno's liberal tendencies.

Southward he wended his way to try his luck in the land of John Huss. Further disappointment awaited him. Prague had become a Habsburg capital and where the Habsburg entered,freedom went out by the city gates. Back to the road and a long,long walk to Zürich.

There he received a letter from an Italian youth,Giovanni Mocenigo,who asked him to come to Venice. What made Bruno accept,I do not know. Perhaps the Italian peasant in him was impressed by the luster of an

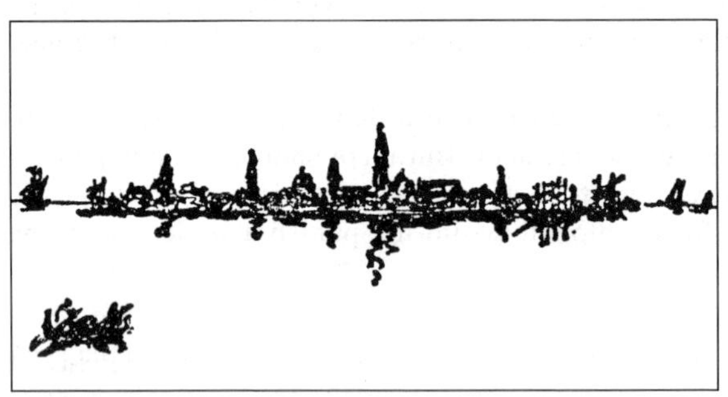

布鲁诺去威尼斯

在图卢兹也使他不自在。他横穿法国，步行到巴黎，接着又以法国大使私人秘书的身份来到英国。但等待他的又是无休无止的失望。英国神学家并不比欧洲大陆上那些人强到哪里去。也许，他们更注重实际一些。譬如在牛津大学，他们并不惩处敢于顶撞亚里士多德教诲的学生，只是罚他10个先令。

布鲁诺变得有些刻薄了。他开始撰写一些文采飞扬却又相当危险的小短文，还有那些以宗教、哲学、政治为内容的对话录；在这些对话录中，整个世界现存的秩序都被弄得乱七八糟，受到了细致而又毫无赞赏的检验。

他还专门为他喜爱的科目天文学作了一些演讲。

但是，受学生欢迎的教授无法得到学院当权者的肯定与欢迎。布鲁诺又一次被扫地出门。他回到法国，又到了马尔堡。不久之前，就在虔诚的匈牙利女王伊丽莎白的城堡里，路德和茨温利曾针对物质变化的实质进行了讨论。

哎！他的“自由思想家”的外号早就声名在外，甚至使他都不能给学生上课。事实证明，维滕堡更好客，可是这个路德信仰的古老根据地刚被加尔文博士的门徒占领和把持。从那之后，像布鲁诺这样有自由倾向的人再也找不到立锥之地了。

他向南走到约翰·胡斯的地盘去碰运气。然而，等待他的是新的失望。布拉格刚成为哈布斯堡王朝的首都，哈布斯堡王室一走进前门，自由便从后门出来。布鲁诺只好重新启程，长途步行到达苏黎世。

old patrician name and felt flattered by the invitation.

Giovanni Mocenigo,however,was not made of the stuff which had enabled his ancestors to defy both Sultan and Pope. He was a weakling and a coward and did not move a finger when officers of the Inquisition appeared at his house and took his guest to Rome.

As a rule,the government of Venice was terribly jealous of its rights. If Bruno had been a German merchant or a Dutch skipper,they would have protested violently and they might even have gone to war when a foreign power dared to arrest some one within their own jurisdiction. But why incur the hostility of the pope on account of a vagabond who had brought nothing to their city but his ideas?

It was true he called himself a scholar. The Republic was highly flattered,but she had scholars enough of her own.

And so farewell to Bruno and may San Marco have mercy upon his soul.

Seven long years Bruno was kept in the prison of the Inquisition.

On the seventeenth of February of the year 1600 he was burned at the stake and his ashes were blown to the winds.

He was executed on the Campo dei Fiori. Those who Know Italian may therein find inspiration for a pretty little allegory.

在那儿，他收到一封来自意大利年轻人乔瓦尼·莫塞尼哥的信，邀请他去威尼斯。究竟是什么原因让布鲁诺接受了他的邀请，我无从知晓。也许，这个意大利农民被这样一个古代贵族名字的光环深深折服，于是因为接到这个邀请而感到受宠若惊。

乔瓦尼·莫塞尼哥绝不是那种像他的祖先那样敢于挑战苏丹和教皇的人。当宗教法庭的官员要把他的客人布鲁诺从他家里带到罗马时，他连个屁都不敢放，十足的懦夫和胆小鬼。

威尼斯政府一贯珍惜它的权力。布鲁诺如果是个德国商人或荷兰船长，那么当外国军队胆敢在他们的地盘里随便抓人时，他们可能会强烈抗议，甚至诉诸战争。可是为了一个除了思想以外，不能给城市带来任何益处的流浪汉，犯得着去与教皇为敌吗？

没错，他自称学者，为此共和国也甚感荣幸，可惜她的学者已经泛滥了。

好吧，就和布鲁诺告别吧，愿圣马可宽恕他的灵魂。

布鲁诺在宗教法庭的监狱里被关了7年。

1600年2月17日，他被绑在火刑柱上烧死，骨灰随风飘散。

他是在坎普迪菲奥利被行刑的。懂意大利文的人，或许能找到一丝灵感，写一篇短小美妙的寓言。

CHAPTER XXI SPINOZA

There are certain things in history which I have never been able to understand and one of these is the amount of work done by some of the artists and literary men of bygone ages.

The modern members of our writing guild,with typewriters and dictaphones and secretaries and fountain pens,can turn out between three and four thousand words a day. How did Shakespeare,with half a dozen other jobs to distract his mind,with a scolding wife and a clumsy goose quill,manage to write thirty-seven plays?

Where did Lope de Vega,veteran of the Invincible Armada and a busy man all his life,find the necessary ink and paper for eighteen hundred comedies and five hundred essays?

What manner of man was this strange Hofkonzertmeister,Johann Sebastian Bach,who in a little house filled with the noise of twenty children found time to compose five oratorios,one hundred and ninety church cantatas,three wedding cantatas,and a dozen motets,six solemn masses,three fiddle concertos,a concerto for two violins which alone would have made his name immortal,seven concertos for piano and orchestra,three concertos for two pianos,two concertos for three pianos,thirty orchestral scores and enough pieces for the flute,the harpsichord,the organ,the bull fiddle and the French horn to keep the average student of music busy for the rest of his days.

Or again,by what process of industry and application could painters like Rembrandt and Rubens produce a picture or an etching at the rate of almost four a month during more than thirty years?How could an humble citizen like Antonio Stradivarius turn out five

第21章　斯宾诺莎

历史长河中的一些事情，我至今仍未弄懂。其中之一，便是以前的岁月中，艺术家和文学家的作品数量。

现代写作协会的成员在打字机、录音机、秘书和钢笔的帮助下，差不多每天能写三四千字。有许许多多的工作牵扯着他的精力，有个老婆在耳边唠叨烦扰，一支简陋的蘸水笔拖他的后腿，莎士比亚怎么还能完成37部剧本的创作呢？

洛浦·德·维加是西班牙“无敌舰队”的退役老兵，一生都忙忙碌碌，他又是从哪里弄来必需的墨水和纸张，写下1800部喜剧和500篇文章的呢？

那个奇怪的约翰·塞巴斯蒂安·巴赫又是什么样的人呢？他的小屋里有20个孩子打闹嬉笑，而他竟然能找到时间谱写5个清唱剧，190个教堂大合唱，3个婚礼大合唱，12支圣经歌，6支庄严弥撒曲，3部小提琴协奏曲，1部双小提琴协奏曲（仅此足以使他的名字永载史册），7部钢琴管弦乐队协奏曲，3部双钢琴协奏曲，2部三架钢琴的协奏曲，30部管弦乐谱，还谱写了大量的长笛、竖琴、风琴、提琴、法国号练习曲，足以让普通学生练一辈子的。

还有，伦勃朗和鲁本斯在30多年中，是怎样勤奋用功，以至于每个月都有4幅画或4幅蚀刻画诞生的呢？像安东尼奥·斯特拉迪瓦利这样毫不起眼的平民，怎样

hundred and forty fiddles,fifty violoncellos and twelve violas in a single lifetime?

I am not now discussing the brains capable of devising all these plots,hearing all these melodies,seeing all those diversified combinations of color and line,choosing all this wood. I am just wondering at the physical part of it. How did they do it?Didn't they ever go to bed?Didn't they sometimes take a few hours off for a game of billiards?Were they never tired?Had they ever heard of nerves?

Both the seventeenth and eighteenth centuries were full of that sort of people. They defied all the laws of hygiene,ate and drank everything that was had for them,were totally unconscious of their high destinies as members of the glorious human race,but they had an awfully good time and their artistic and intellectual output was something terrific.

And what was true of the arts and the sciences held equally true of such finicky subjects as theology.

Go to any of the libraries that date back two hundred years and you will find their cellars and attics filled with tracts and homilies and discussions and refutations and digests and commentaries in duodecimo and octodecimo and octavo,bound in leather and in parchment and in paper,all of them covered with dust and oblivion,but without exception containing an enormous if useless amount of learning.

The subjects of which they treated and many of the words they used have lost all meaning to our modern ears. But somehow or other these moldy compilations served a very useful purpose. If they accomplished nothing else,they at least cleared the air. For they either settled the questions they discussed to the general satisfaction of all concerned,or they convinced their readers that those particular problems could not possibly be decided with an appeal to logic and argument and might therefore just as well be dropped right then and there.

花一生的时间就做了540把小提琴、50把大提琴和12把中提琴的呢？

现在，我不是在讨论他们的头脑怎么能想出所有这些情节，听出所有这些旋律，看出各式各样的颜色和线条的组合，选择所有这些木材的。我只是对蕴含在这些作品中的体力感到惊奇。他们怎么做到这些的？他们从不睡觉吗？他们难道不打几小时的台球吗？他们从不疲倦吗？他们听说过“神经紧张”这个东西吗？

在17世纪和18世纪，这种人并不鲜见。他们把健康法则抛到九霄云外，大吃大喝，变得脑满肠肥，不管不顾作为人类的光荣一员，应当负有的崇高使命。但是，他们的人生如此恣意飞扬，他们的艺术和智力作品又是如此棒。

对于艺术和科学来说正确的，同样也会适用像神学之类如此吹毛求疵的领域。

如果你去任何一所200年前的图书馆，就会发现地下室和顶楼上都塞满了8开、12开和18开的，用皮革、羊皮纸和纸张装订着的各种宗教短论小册子，那是些布道书、讨论集、驳论、文摘和评论，上面堆满了灰尘，早已被人忘得一干二净。但是，这些书一律都写满了虽然广博实则无用的学问。

其中探讨的主题和使用的诸多词汇，对于现代人来说已经是历史云烟，毫无意义。可是，不知怎么回事，这些发了霉的汇编却发挥着如此大的作用。即使它们一无是处，但至少清洁了空气，因为它们或者解决了讨论的问题，从而使那些与此息息相关的人感到满意；或者使读者们相信，那些特殊的问题并不是求助于逻辑推理和辩论就能解决的，因此最好立即放下。

乍一听，这好像是假惺惺的恭维话。不过，我希望未来30世纪的批评家们在认

This may sound like a back-handed compliment. But I hope that critics of the thirtieth century shall be just as charitable when they wade through the remains of our own literary and scientific achievements.

※ ※ ※ ※ ※ ※

Baruch de Spinoza,the hero of this chapter,did not follow the fashion of his time in the matter of quantity. His assembled works consist of three or four small volumes and a few bundles of letters.

But the amount of study necessary for the correct mathematical solution of his abstract problems in ethics and philosophy would have staggered any normally healthy man. It killed the poor consumptive who had undertaken to reach God by way of the table of multiplication.

Spinoza was a Jew. His people,however,had never suffered the indignities of the Ghetto. Their ancestors had settled down in the Spanish peninsula when that part of the world was a Moorish province. After the reconquest and the introduction of that policy of"Spain for the Spaniard"which eventually forced that country into bankruptcy,the Spinozas had been forced to leave their old home. They had sailed for the Netherlands,had bought a small house in Amsterdan,had worked hard,had saved their money and soon were known as one of the most respectable families of the"Portuguese colony. "

If nevertheless their son Baruch was conscious of his Jewish origin,this was due more to the training he received in his Talmud school than to the gibes of his little neighbors. For the Dutch Republic was so chock full of class prejudice that there was little room left for mere race prejudice and therefore lived in perfect peace and harmony with all the alien races that had found a refuge along the banks of the North and Zuider Seas. And this was one of the most characteristic bits of Dutch life which contemporary travelers never failed to omit from their"Souvenirs de Voyage"and with good reason.

真审阅从我们这里流传下去的文学和科学成果时，也能这样仁慈。

※ ※ ※ ※ ※ ※

巴鲁克·德·斯宾诺莎是这一章的主角，他在数量上没有追赶时尚。他的全集只不过收录了三四个小册子和几捆书信。

但是，用正确的数学方法解决他的伦理学和哲学中的抽象问题，所必需的大量学习会使普通的健康人不堪重负。这样的重负也曾经杀死了试图通过乘法口诀表来接近上帝的可怜的肺病患者。

斯宾诺莎是犹太人。不过，那时的犹太人还没有遭受被单独隔离的侮辱。他们的祖先在西班牙半岛定居的时候，那里还是摩尔人居住的一个省。西班牙把它夺回之后，实施了“西班牙属于西班牙人”的政策，最后使整个国家陷入崩溃，斯宾诺莎一家也被迫背井离乡。他们从水路来到荷兰，在阿姆斯特丹买了幢小房子，辛勤地工作，聚敛财富，很快就成为“葡萄牙移民区”中最受尊敬的家庭之一。

如果他们的儿子巴鲁克突然对家族的犹太血统有所觉察，除去邻居小孩的时时讥讽之外，更要归结于在塔木德学校受到的教育。由于荷兰共和国被森严的阶级偏见所充斥，无暇顾及种族的偏见，所以那些在北海和须德海的海岸边找到避难所的外来民族能够平静且和谐地生活。这是荷兰生活的一大重要特点，现代的旅行者在撰写“游记”时绝不会遗漏这一点，这还是很合乎情理的。

甚至到了近代，在欧洲的其他大部分地方，犹太人和非犹太人的关系还是很

In most other parts of Europe,even at that late age,the relation between the Jew and the non-Jew was far from satisfactory. What made the quarrel between the two races so hopeless was the fact that both sides were equally right and equally wrong and that both sides could justly claim to be the victim of their opponent's intolerance and prejudice. In the light of the theory put forward in this book that intolerance is merely a form of self-protection of the mob,it becomes clear that as long as they were faithful to their own respective religions,the Christian and the Jew must have conceded each other as enemies. In the first place,they both of them maintained that their God was the only true God and that all the other Gods of all the other nations were false. In the second place,they were each other's most dangerous commercial rival. The Jews had come to western Europe as they had originally come to Palestine,as immigrants in search of a new home. The labor unions of that day,the Guilds,had made it impossible for them to take up a trade. They had therefore been obliged to content themselves with such economic makeshifts as pawnbroking and banking. In the Middle Ages these two professions,which closely resembled each other,were not thought fit occupations for decent citizens. Why the Church,until the days of Calvin,should have felt such a repugnance towards money (except in the form of taxes) and should have regarded the taking of interest as a crime,is hard to understand. Usury,of course,was something no government could tolerate and already the Babylonians,some forty centuries before,had passed drastic laws against the money changers who tried to make a profit out of other people's money. In several chapters of the Old Testament,written two thousand years later,we read how Moses too had expressly forbidden his followers to lend money at exorbitant rates of interest to any one except foreigners. Still later,the great Greek philosophers,including Aristotle and Plato,had given expression to their great disapproval of money that was born of other money. The Church fathers had been even more explicit upon this subject. All during the Middle Ages

糟糕，二者之间的争吵简直到了不可调和的程度，因为双方都各执一词，声称自己才是对方专横和偏见的受害者。按照本书提出的理论，不宽容是公众通常采取的自我保护的一种方法。很明显，只要基督徒和犹太人保持对各自宗教信仰的忠诚，就必定会视对方为敌人。首先，双方都坚持自己信奉的上帝才是唯一真正的上帝，其他民族信奉的上帝全是赝品。其次，双方都是具有极大威胁的商业对手。犹太人来到西欧，如同最初到巴勒斯坦一样，就像寻觅新家园的移民。当时的工会即“行会”不可能提供给他们谋生的空间，所以，作为权宜之计，他们甘愿开个相对经济合算的当铺和银行。这两种行当在中世纪别无二致，在人们眼里，正派的人是不屑于从事这种行业的。为什么直到加尔文时期，教会一直对金钱（税收除外）深恶痛绝，把拿利息看成是犯罪行为之一，这真令人匪夷所思！当然，没有一个政府会容许高利贷的存在。差不多早在40个世纪以前，巴比伦人就通过一项严苛的法律，对那些企图利用别人的钱来谋取私利的投机分子进行严惩。我们从2000年后写下的《旧约》中可以读到，摩西曾经明令禁止他的部下，把钱借给除了外国人之外的本地人，收取高利息，从而谋取暴利。这之后，包括亚里士多德和柏拉图在内的希腊大哲学家们都表示不赞同“借钱生钱”的行为，教会神父对这种事情的态度更加明确。在整个中世纪中，放债人一直受人唾弃。但丁甚至在地狱里为他这些银行家朋友们专门准备了一个小壁龛。

从理论上讲，当铺老板和他开银行的那些同僚们都是不受欢迎的公民，世界要

the money lenders were held in profound contempt. Dante even provided a special little alcove in his Hell for the exclusive benefit of his banker friends.

Theoretically perhaps it could he proved that the pawnbroker and his colleague,the man behind the"banco"were undesirable citizens and that the world would be better off without them. At the same time,as soon as the world had ceased to be entirely agricultural,it was found to be quite impossible to transact even the simplest business operations without the use of credit. The money lender therefore had become a necessary evil and the Jew,who (according to the views of the Christians) was doomed to eternal damnation any way,was urged to occupy himself with a trade which was necessary but which no respectable man would touch.

In this way these unfortunate exiles were forced into certain unpleasant trades which made them the natural enemy of both the rich and the poor,and then,as soon as they had established themselves,these same enemies turned against them,called them names,locked them up in the dirtiest part of the city and in moments of great emotional stress,hanged them as wicked unbelievers or burned them as renegade Christians.

It was all so terribly silly. And besides it was so stupid. These endless annoyances and persecutions did not make the Jews any fonder of their Christian neighbors. And as a direct result,a large volume of first-rate intelligence was withdrawn from public circulation,thousands of bright young fellows,who might have advanced the cause of commerce and science and the arts,wasted their brains and energy upon the useless study of certain old books filled with abstruse conundrums and hair-splitting syllogisms and millions of helpless boys and girls were doomed to lead stunted lives in stinking tenements,listening on the one hand to their elders who told them that they were God's chosen people who would surely inherit the earth and all the wealth thereof,and on the other hand being frightened to death by the curses of their neighbors who never ceased to inform them that they were pigs and only fit for the gallows or the wheel.

是没有他们将会更加美好，这也许可以被无数事实证明。同时，只要世界脱离了纯粹的农业社会，那么，不借助于信用贷款，就连最普通的生意都做不成。放债人虽然很邪恶，但也是不可或缺的，注定要遭天谴的犹太人（按照基督徒的看法）就会被迫从事一种必不可少，但体面人绝不会问津的行业。

这样，这些不幸的流浪者被迫从事那些令人不快的行当，这使得他们自然而然地和富人及穷人们对立起来。然后，他们一旦站稳脚跟，对方便会纷纷倒戈，点名谩骂他们，把他们锁在城市肮脏之地。在极度冲动的状况下，还会把他们当作不信教的恶棍绞死或作为基督教的叛徒烧死。

一切都是如此的愚蠢无知。无休无止的骚扰和迫害，并没能帮助犹太人获得他们四周那些信奉基督教的邻居们的喜爱。最直接的结果是，许多一流的智慧与才华从公共生活中消失了，成千上万天资聪慧的年轻人本来可以在商业、科学及艺术中有所作为，却把智慧和精力浪费在了研读那些深奥莫测的难题、有些吹毛求疵的关于演绎推理的旧书上。大批无助的男孩女孩注定要在发臭的小屋里受到畸形生活的煎熬，一边听老人说他们是上帝选定的、有权继承上帝土地和所有财富的幸运儿，一边却又听到邻居不停地骂他们是只配上绞架或刑车的猪猡，从而被吓得魂不附体。

要让那些注定在这种逆境中生活的人（不管是谁），保持用正常的态度看待生活，是不可能的。

在他们的基督徒同胞们一次又一次的逼迫下，犹太人只好采取疯狂的行动，

To ask that people (any people) doomed to live under such adverse circumstances shall retain a normal outlook upon life is to demand the impossible.

Again and again the Jews were goaded into some desperate act by their Christian compatriots and then,when white with rage,they turned upon their oppressors,they were called"traitors"and"ungrateful villains"and were subjected to further humiliations and restrictions. But these restrictions had only one result. They increased the number of Jews who had a grievance,turned the others into nervous wrecks and generally made the Ghetto a ghastly abode of frustrated ambitions and pent-up hatreds.

Spinoza,because he was born in Amsterdam,escaped the misery which was the birthright of most of his relatives. He went first of all to the school maintained by his synagogue (appropriately called"the Tree of Life") and as soon as he could conjugate his Hebrew verbs was sent to the learned Dr. Franciscus Appinius van den Ende,who was to drill him in Latin and in the sciences.

Dr. Franciscus,as his name indicates,was of Catholic origin. Rumor had it that he was a graduate of the University of Louvain and if one were to believe the best informed deacons of the town,he was really a Jesuit in disguise and a very dangerous person. This however was nonsense. Van den Ende in his youth had actually spent a few years at a Catholic seminary. But his heart was not in his work and he had left his native city of Antwerp,had gone to Amsterdam and there had opened a private school of his own.

He had such a tremendous flair for choosing the methods that would make his pupils like their classical lessons,that heedless of the man's popish past,the Calvinistic burghers of Amsterdam willingly entrusted their children to his care and were very proud of the fact that the pupils of his school invariably out-hexametered and out-declined the little boys of all other local academies.

Van den Ende taught little Baruch his Latin,but being an enthusiastic follower of all

当愤怒和怨气日积月累，逐渐达到白热化时，他们会起来反抗压迫者，从而被称为“叛徒”“不知报恩的小人”，还受到更变本加厉的欺侮和限制。这些限制只有一个结果，那就是心怀怨恨的犹太人越来越多，而其他人意志颓丧，使犹太区积聚了太多的严重受挫的激情及被压抑的仇恨。

斯宾诺莎在阿姆斯特丹出生，所以没有遭到大部分亲戚生来就遭到的苦难。他首先被送进犹太教会（更合适的称呼应该是“生命之树”）掌管的学校，学会希伯来文的动词变位以后，便被送到博学的弗朗西斯科·阿皮尼厄斯·范·登·恩德博士那儿攻读拉丁文和科学。

正如他的名字所显示的那样，弗朗西斯科博士出身于一个天主教徒家庭，有传言说他是卢万大学毕业生。按照城中消息灵通的教堂执事的说法，他是伪装的耶稣会成员，是个危险分子。这纯属无稽之谈！范·登·恩德年轻时确实在天主教神学院待过几年，但他并没有全心投入功课上。离开家乡安特卫普以后，他来到阿姆斯特丹，自己开办了一所私立学校。

他天赋过人，善于找到让学生们喜欢上古文课的办法。因此，阿姆斯特丹信奉加尔文教的市民们不顾他过去与天主教的恩怨，情愿把孩子托付给他。因为他教的孩子在掌握六韵步诗和变格上总比当地其他学校的学生更强，因此他感到无比的骄傲。

范·登·恩德教小巴鲁克拉丁文，但作为一个总是热情地追求科学领域的最新发现，并对乔达诺·布鲁诺崇拜得五体投地的人，他肯定会教给这孩子一些一般来

the latest discoveries in the field of science and a great admirer of Giordano Bruno,he undoubtedly taught the boy several things which as a rule were not mentioned in an orthodox Jewish household.

For young Spinoza,contrary to the customs of the times,did not board with the other boys,but lived at home. And he so impressed his family by his profound learning that all the relations proudly pointed to him as the little professor and liberally supplied him with pocket money. He did not waste it upon tobacco. He used it to buy books on philosophy.

One author especially fascinated him.

That was Descartes.

René Descartes was a French nobleman born in that region between Tours and Poitiers where a thousand years before the grandfather of Charlemagne had stopped the Mohammedan conquest of Europe. Before he was ten years old he had been sent to the Jesuits to be educated and he spent the next decade making a nuisance of himself. For this boy had a mind of his own and accepted nothing without"being shown. "The Jesuits are probably the only people in the world who know how to handle such difficult children and who can train them successfully without breaking their spirit. The proof of the educational pudding is in the eating. If our modern pedagogues would study the methods of Brother Loyola,we might have a few Descartes of our own.

When he was twenty years old,René entered military service and went to the Netherlands where Maurice of Nassau had so thoroughly perfected his military system that his armies were the post-graduate school for all ambitious young men who hoped to become generals. Descartes' visit to the headquarters of the Nassau prince was perhaps a little irregular. A faithful Catholic taking service with a Protestant chieftain! It sounds like high treason. But Descartes was interested in problems of mathematics and artillery

说不可能在正统的犹太家庭被提及的东西。

小斯宾诺莎一反当时的通习，没有和其他学生同住，而是住在家里。家人都被他渊博的学识震惊了，亲戚们自豪地称呼他为“小教授”，并毫不吝啬地给他塞零用钱。他倒是没把钱拿去买烟，而是买了哲学书。

有一个作者尤其吸引了他的注意力。

这就是笛卡尔。

勒内·笛卡尔是法国贵族，出生在图尔和普瓦提埃交界的地区。1000年前，查理大帝的祖父曾在这里阻止了穆罕默德对欧洲的侵略。他不满10岁就被送到耶稣会接受教育，一待就是10年。因为他很有主见，拒不接受那些没有经过证明的事物，这很让人生厌。也许耶稣会教士是这个世界上唯一能调教这种孩子的人。他们要在不挫伤其积极性的前提下，又能把孩子们训练得很成功。要检验布丁的滋味就要亲自尝一尝，办教育也是一样的道理。如果现代的老师们学会了耶稣会罗耀拉兄弟的方法，那么我们之中也一定会出现几个自己的笛卡尔了。

20岁时，笛卡尔开始服兵役，他到了荷兰，在那里，纳塞公国的莫里斯曾经彻底完善了他的军事体系，使他的军队成为有志当将军的年轻人的进修学校。笛卡尔去拜访纳塞亲王的司令部，也许有点不合规矩。一个虔诚的天主教徒怎能当新教徒首领的仆人！这听起来就像叛国罪。不过，好在笛卡尔并不怎么关心宗教和政治，只对数学和炮兵感兴趣。荷兰刚刚和西班牙达成休战协议，他便辞了职，来到慕尼黑，在巴伐利亚的天主教公爵麾下作战。

but not of religion or politics. Therefore as soon as Holland had concluded a truce with Spain,he resigned his commission,went to Munich and fought for a while under the banner of the Catholic Duke of Bavaria.

But that campaign did not last very long. The only fighting of any consequence then still going on was near La Rochelle,the city which the Huguenots were defending against Richelieu. And so Descartes went back to France that he might learn the noble art of siege-craft. But camp life was beginning to pall upon him. He decided to give up a military career and devote himself to philosophy and science.

He had a small income of his own. He had no desire to marry. His wishes were few. He anticipated a quiet and happy life and he had it.

Why he chose Holland as a place of residence,I do not know. But it was a country full of printers and publishers and bookshops and as long as one did not openly attack the established form of government or religion,the existing law on censorship remained a dead letter. Furthermore,as he never learned a single word of the language of his adopted country (a trick not difficult to a true Frenchman),Descartes was able to avoid undesirable company and futile conversations and could give all of his time (some twenty hours per day) to his own work.

This may seem a dull existence for a man who had been a soldier. But Descartes had a purpose in life and it seems that he was perfectly contented with his self-inflicted exile. He had during the course of years become convinced that the world was still plunged in a profound gloom of abysmal ignorance;that what was then being called science had not even the remotest resemblance to true science,and that no general progress would be possible until the whole ancient fabric of error and falsehood had first of all been razed to the ground. No small order,this. Descartes however was possessed of endless patience

然而，那场战争并没有持续多久，只在拉罗谢尔附近进行了唯一一场生死攸关的战役。在那里，胡格诺派正在抵御黎塞留。笛卡尔回到法国，以便学习一点高级的攻坚战术。可是他彻底厌倦了军营生活，决定告别戎马生涯，投身于哲学和科学研究。

他倒是有一笔小收入，却不想结婚，也别无所求，只盼望过一种安静快乐的生活，并且终于如愿以偿了。

他究竟出于什么原因选中荷兰作为居住地，我不太清楚。不过，这个国家处处可见印刷商、出版商和书店，只要不公开对现有的政府和宗教进行抨击，出版检查的法律就形同虚设。况且，他从未学会他所移居国家的文字（对真正的法国人来说，这种文字并不难），所以避开了那些饶舌的伙伴和没用的谈话，能够把全部时间（每天差不多20个小时）用在自己的工作上。

对于当过兵的人来说，这种生活实在是太枯燥了。但是，笛卡尔有自己的生活追求，似乎很满足这种类似自我折磨的流浪生活。随着光阴的流逝，他逐渐相信，深不可测的无知依然笼罩着整个世界，那个被人们称作“科学”的东西，其实连真正科学的皮毛都沾不上，不首先破除陈旧的错误和荒谬的东西，总体的进步就不可能实现。这可不是桩小工程。不过笛卡尔拥有极好的耐性。到了30岁，他开始给出了一套崭新的哲学体系。他被自己的成就深深激励，把几何学、天文学和物理学的内容加进了最初的大纲中。在工作中，他表现得不偏不倚，这使得天主教徒斥责他是加尔文派，而加尔文派骂他是无神论者。

and at the age of thirty he set to work to give us an entirely new system of philosophy. Warming up to his task he added geometry and astronomy and physics to his original program and he performed his task with such noble impartiality of mind that the Catholics denounced him as a Calvinist and the Calvinists cursed him for an atheist.

This clamor,if ever it reached him,did not disturb him in the least. He quietly continued his researches and died peacefully in the city of Stockholm,whither he had gone to talk philosophy with the Queen of Sweden.

Among the people of the seventeenth century,Cartesianism (the name under which his philosophies became known) made quite as much of a stir as Darwinism was to make among the contemporaries of Queen Victoria. To be a Cartesian in the year 1680 meant something terrible,something almost indecent. It proclaimed one an enemy of the established order of society,a Socinian,a low fellow who by his own confession had set himself apart from the companionship of his respectable neighbors. This did not prevent the majority of the intelligent classes from accepting Cartesianism as readily and as eagerly as our grandfathers accepted Darwinism. But among the orthodox Jews of Amsterdam,such subjects were never even mentioned. Cartesianism was not mentioned in either Talmud or Torah. Hence it did not exist. And when it became apparent that it existed just the same in the mind of one Baruch de Spinoza,it was a foregone conclusion that said Baruch de Spinoza would himself cease to exist as soon as the authorities of the synagogue had been able to investigate the case and take official action.

The Amsterdam synagogue had at that moment passed through a severe crisis. When little Baruch was fifteen years old,another Portuguese exile by the name of Uriel Acosta had arrived in Amsterdam,had forsworn Catholicism,which he had accepted under a threat of death,and had returned to the faith of his fathers. But this fellow Acosta had not been an ordinary Jew. He

■ 斯宾诺莎

这些喧嚷之声传到他的耳朵里，丝毫没有干扰他。他心平气和地继续自己的研究，最后安详地在斯德哥尔摩谢世。在那里，他曾经和瑞典女王高谈阔论过哲学等话题。

在17世纪，笛卡尔主义（因其哲学名扬天下）就像是维多利亚女王时代的达尔文主义，成为万众瞩目的焦点。在1680年，成为一名笛卡尔主义者是件可怕也很不光彩的事。它意味着某人站在社会制度的对立面，是索兹尼派教徒，是不能与体面人平起平坐的下等人。但是，这并没能阻止大部分知识分子像我们的前辈欣然热烈地接受达尔文主义一样，如饥似渴地接受笛卡尔主义。但是在阿姆斯特丹的正统犹太人中，没有人关注这样的问题。在塔木德和托拉赫，也没有人问津笛卡尔主义，因此它也就不存在。一经证明它存在于巴鲁克·德·斯宾诺莎的头脑里，结局自然不言而喻，即只要犹太教堂的权威人士能够出面调查此事，采取官方行动，斯宾诺莎也会同样不复存在。

was a gentleman accustomed to carry a feather in his hat and a sword at his side. To him the arrogance of the Dutch rabbis,trained in the German and Polish schools of learning,had come as a most unpleasant surprise,and he had been too proud and too indifferent to hide his opinions.

In a small community like that,such open defiance could not possibly be tolerated. A bitter struggle had followed. On the one side a solitary dreamer,half prophet,half hidalgo. On the other side the merciless guardians of the law.

It had ended in tragedy.

First of all Acosta had been denounced to the local police as the author of certain blasphemous pamphlets which denied the immortality of the soul. This had got him into trouble with the Calvinist ministers. But the matter had been straightened out and the charge had been dropped. Thereupon the synagogue had excommunicated the stiff-necked rebel and had deprived him of his livelihood.

For months thereafter the poor man had wandered through the streets of Amsterdam until destitution and loneliness had driven him back to his own flock. But he was not re-admitted until he had first of all publicly apologized for his evil conduct and had then suffered himself to be whipped and kicked by all the members of the congregation. These indignities had unbalanced his mind. He had bought a pistol and had blown his brains out.

This suicide had caused a tremendous lot of talk among the principal citizens of Amsterdam. The Jewish community felt that it could not risk the chance of another public scandal. When it became evident that the most promising pupil of the"Tree of Life"had been contaminated by the new heresies of Descartes,a direct attempt was made to hush things up. Baruch was approached and was offered a fixed annual sum if he would give his word that he would be good,would continue to show himself in the synagogue and would not publish or say anything against the law.

那时，阿姆斯特丹的犹太教会刚刚经历了一场严重的危机。小巴鲁克15岁的时候，一个名叫尤里尔·艾考斯塔的葡萄牙流亡者来到这里。他断然抛弃了曾在死亡威胁下被迫接受的天主教，转而皈依父辈们的宗教信仰。可是，这个艾考斯塔绝非犹太人中的等闲之辈，而是个习惯在帽子上插一根羽毛、腰上别一把剑的绅士。对他来说，那些在日耳曼和波兰学校受过训练的荷兰犹太教士所表现出的狂妄自大使他惊讶和恼怒。他为人也很骄傲中立，从不掩饰自己的观点。

在那样的小社会团体里，如此公开的蔑视是不可能被容忍的。于是，一场你死我活的斗争开始了，一方是清高的梦想家，既是先知又是贵族，另一方是铁面无情的法律卫士。

这场斗争终以悲剧结尾。

首先，艾考斯塔被人告发到当地警察局，说他写了几本否认灵魂不朽的亵渎神灵的小册子。这使他与加尔文派教士产生了矛盾。不过，事实很快澄清，随之控告也被撤销。于是，犹太教会把这个顽固的叛徒逐出教会，剥夺了他赖以生存的财产。

在接下来的几个月时间里，这个可怜虫流浪于阿姆斯特丹的街头，直到贫困和孤独又驱使他回到教会。但是，重新回去的首要条件是必须当众认罪，并且任所有教会成员鞭抽脚踢。这些侮辱造成了他的精神失常。他用买来的一支手枪，把自己的脑袋打开了花。

这一自杀事件引得阿姆斯特丹市民议论纷纷。犹太团体觉得实在不能冒险再惹

Now Spinoza was the last man to consider such a compromise. He curtly refused to do anything of the sort. In consequence whereof he was duly read out of his own church according to that famous ancient Formula of Damnation which leaves very little to the imagination and goes back all the way to the days of Jericho to find the appropriate number of curses and execrations.

As for the victim of these manifold maledictions,he remained quietly in his room and read about the occurrence in next day's paper. Even when an attempt was made upon his life by an over zealous follower of the law,he refused to leave town.

This came as a great blow to the prestige of the Rabbis who apparently had invoked the names of Joshua and Elisha in vain and who saw themselves publicly defied for the second time in less than half a dozen years. In their anxiety they went so far as to make an appeal to the town hall. They asked for an interview with the Burgomasters and explained that this Baruch de Spinoza whom they had just expelled from their own church was really a most dangerous person,an agnostic who refused to believe in God and who therefore ought not to be tolerated in a respectable Christian community like the city of Amsterdam.

Their lordships,after their pleasant habit,washed their hands of the whole affair and referred the matter to a subcommittee of clergymen. The sub-committee studied the question,discovered that Baruch de Spinoza had done nothing that could be construed as an offense against the ordinances of the town,and so reported to their lordships. At the same time they considered it to be good policy for members of the cloth to stand together and therefore they suggested that the Burgomasters ask this young man,who seemed to be so very independent,to leave Amsterdam for a couple of months and not to return until the thing had blown over.

From that moment on the life of Spinoza was as quiet and uneventful as the landscape

起另一场风波。当“生命之树”中最有前途的学生已经无疑被笛卡尔的异端邪说污染的时候，犹太教会就立即行动起来，试图加以遮掩。他们找巴鲁克密谈，只要他许诺乖乖的，在犹太教堂出现时不再妖言惑众，不再发表或散布任何反对法律的言论，就可以给他一笔固定的年金。

斯宾诺莎最无法容忍受人摆布，三言两语就回绝了这些提议。结果，根据著名的古老《惩处准则》，他被逐出教会。这个准则毫不给人思考的余地，通篇全是照搬耶利哥时代的字眼，大行诅咒谩骂之能事。

面对这些五花八门的诋毁，斯宾诺莎泰然处之，坐在屋里，从报纸上了解前一天发生的事。甚至当一个《准则》的狂热者想了结他的性命时，他也不肯离开。

这无疑沉重打击了犹太教士的威信，他们祈祷约书亚和以利沙这两位先知，却徒劳无功。在短短的几年里，他们仍然再次受到人们的公开挑战。他们心急火燎地向市政厅提出诉讼，要和市长见面，告诉他这个刚被赶出教会的巴鲁克·德·斯宾诺莎真的是个相当危险的人，是个不信仰上帝的“不可知论者”，在阿姆斯特丹这样受人尊敬的基督社团中，实在不应该容忍这种人的存在。

那些大老爷们仍然当老好人，对此置之不理，而是顺水推舟，交给基督教牧师的小组委员会全权处理。这个小组委员会经过研究，发现斯宾诺莎并没有做违反城市法律的事，便如实向市政府的官老爷作了禀报。同时，他们觉得一个教派的人能如此团结一致是件好事，便向市长建议，请这个似乎个性独立的年轻人离开阿姆斯特丹一些日子，等风声不那么紧了再回来。

upon which he looked from his bedroom windows. He left Amsterdam and hired a small house in the village of Rijnsberg near Leiden. He spent his days polishing lenses for optical instruments and at night he smoked his pipe and read or wrote as the spirit moved him. He never married. There was rumor of a love affair between him and a daughter of his former Latin teacher,van den Ende. But as the child was ten years old when Spinoza left Amsterdam,this does not seem very likely.

He had several very loyal friends and at least twice a year they offered to give him a pension that he might devote all his time to his studies. He answered that he appreciated their good intentions but that he preferred to remain independent and with the exception of an allowance of eighty dollars a year from a rich young Cartesian,he never touched a penny and spent his days in the respectable poverty of the true philosopher.

He had a chance to become a professor in Germany,but he declined. He received word that the illustrious King of Prussia would be happy to become his patron and protector,but he answered nay and remained faithful to the quiet routine of his pleasant exile.

After a number of years in Rijnsberg he moved to the Hague. He had never been very strong and the particles of glass from his half-finished lenses had affected his lungs.

He died quite suddenly and alone in the year 1677.

To the intense disgust of the local clergy,not less than six private carriages belonging to prominent members of the court followed the"atheist"to his grave. And when two hundred years later a statue was unveiled to his memory,the police reserves had to be called out to protect the participants in this solemn celebration against the fury of a rowdy crowd of ardent Calvinists.

So much for the man. What about his influence?Was he merely another of those industrious philosophers who fill endless books with endless theories and speak a language

从那以后，斯宾诺莎的生活一直风平浪静，就像他从卧室窗口看到的风景一样。他离开了阿姆斯特丹，在莱顿附近的莱茵斯堡小村里租了一间小房子，白天打磨光学仪器的镜头，晚上抽着烟斗，随性阅读或写作。他一直未婚。谣言说他和拉丁文老师范·登·恩德的女儿之间有私情，可是斯宾诺莎离开阿姆斯特丹时，那女孩才十岁，所以这简直是无稽之谈。

他有几个挚友，每年至少两次提出要给他一点接济，使他能把全部时间都投入到研究中。他回复他们，好意自己心领了，但他更愿意自力更生，除了接受一个有钱的笛卡尔主义信徒每年给他的80块钱外，不再多要一分钱，生活在真正哲学家应有的、让人肃然起敬的贫穷之中。

他曾经有机会去德国当教授，但他谢绝了。他得到消息，听说著名的普鲁士国王愿意当他的资助人和保护人，他也回绝了，继续坚持享受平静如常的流亡生活。

在莱茵斯堡住了几年后，他搬到海牙。他的身体一直不好，半成品镜头上的玻璃碎屑感染了他的肺。

1677年，他孑然一身，凄清孤苦地阖然而逝。

使当地教士极为愤慨的是，至少有6辆皇室成员专用的私人马车把这个“无神论者”送到墓地。200年后，当纪念他的雕像揭幕的时候，警察不得不大批出动去保护参加这个隆重仪式的人，使他们不致受到成群狂热的加尔文教徒的粗暴进攻。

这就是他。他究竟有什么影响呢？他难道是又一个只会把没完没了的理论写进成摞的书里、说一些话把奥马尔·卡亚姆气得暴跳如雷的勤奋哲学家吗？

which drove even Omar Khayyam to an expression of exasperated annoyance?

No,he was not.

Neither did he accomplish his results by the brilliancy of his wit or the plausible truth of his theories. Spinoza was great mainly by force of his courage. He belonged to a race that knew only one law,a set of hard and fast rules laid down for all times in the dim ages of a long forgotten past,a system of spiritual tyranny created for the benefit of a class of professional-priests who had taken it upon themselves to interpret this sacred code.

He lived in a world in which the idea of intellectual freedom was almost synonymous with political anarchy.

He knew that his system of logic must offend both Jews and Gentiles.

But he never wavered.

He approached all problems as universal problems. He regarded them without exception as the manifestation of an omnipresent will and believed them to be the expression of an ultimate reality which would hold good on Doomsday as it had held good at the hour of creation.

And in this way he greatly contributed to the cause of human tolerance.

Like Descartes before him,Spinoza discarded the narrow boundaries laid down by the older forms of religion and boldly built himself a new system of thought based upon the rocks of a million stars.

By so doing he made man what man had not been since the days of the ancient Greeks and Romans,a true citizen of the universe.

不，他不是。

他取得的成就绝不是靠出色的才智，或靠能言善辩阐述自己的理论换来的。他之所以伟大，全凭他的勇气。他属于这样一种人：他们只知道一种法则，那是在早已被忘却的遥远的黑暗年代里被定下的一套硬性规则，也是专为那些把解读宗教法典视为己任的职业教士们创立的精神专政体系。

在他生活的世界中，知识自由的思想与政治上的混乱几乎是同义词。

他知道他的逻辑体系既会得罪犹太人，也会得罪异教徒。

但是，他从来没有丝毫动摇。

他把所有问题都视为普遍问题，一无例外地把它们看作是无所不在的意志的体现，相信它们是纯粹的现实的表现，它在世界末日仍然像创世纪时一样有效。

这样，他为人类的宽容事业做出了巨大贡献。

如同先前的笛卡尔一样，斯宾诺莎摈弃了设置在旧的宗教形式之间的狭隘界线，在百万星辰的基石上勇敢地建立了自己崭新的思想体系。

这样一来，他使人类成了宇宙的真正公民，而这正是自从古希腊和古罗马时代以来人类就已失去了的。

CHAPTER XXII THE NEW ZION

There was little reason to fear that the works of Spinoza would ever be popular. They were as amusing as a textbook on trigonometry and few people ever get beyond the first two or three sentences of any given chapter.

It took a different sort of man to spread the new ideas among the mass of the people.

In France the enthusiasm for private speculation and investigation had come to an end as soon as the country had been turned into an absolute monarchy.

In Germany the poverty and the horror which had followed in the wake of the Thirty Years War had killed all personal initiative for at least two hundred years.

During the second half of the seventeenth century,therefore,England was the only one among the larger countries of Europe where further progress along the lines of independent thought was still possible and the prolonged quarrel between the Crown and Parliament was adding an element of instability which proved to be of great help to the cause of personal freedom.

First of all we must consider the English sovereigns. For years these unfortunate monarchs had been between the devil of Catholicism and the deep sea of Puritanism.

Their Catholic subjects (which included a great many faithful Episcopalians with a secret leaning towards Rome) were forever clamoring for a return to that happy era when the British kings had been vassals of the pope.

Their Puritan subjects on the other hand,with one eye firmly glued upon the example of

第22章　新的天国

没有理由害怕斯宾诺莎的著作会流传开来。这些书像三角学教科书那么有趣，然而不管哪个章节，很少有人能读三句以上。

需要另一种人在大众间传播新思想。

在法国，一旦国家转变成绝对君主专制，独立思考和调查的热情便结束了。

在德国，三十年战争带来的贫穷和恐怖扼杀了所有个人的创造力至少达200年。

因此，17世纪下半叶，英国是欧洲大国中唯一有可能在独立思考方面获得进步的国家，国王与国会的长期争吵增加了不安定的因素，这对个性自由的事业大有益处。

首先，我们必须分析英国君主。多年来，这些不幸的国王一直被夹在天主教的魔鬼和清教徒的汪洋大海之间。

他们的天主教臣民（包括许多暗地里倾向于罗马的忠诚圣公会教徒）一直叫嚷着要回到英国国王当教皇仆从的幸福时代。

然而，清教徒臣民却用另一只眼紧盯着日内瓦那个榜样，梦想有朝一日根本没有国王，英格兰将变成一个像蜷缩在瑞士山脉小角落的那个幸福联邦一样的国家。

Geneva,dreamed of the day when there should be no king at all and England should be a replica of the happy commonwealth tucked away in a little corner of the Swiss mountains.

But that was not all.

The men who ruled England were also kings of Scotland and their Scottish subjects,when it came to religion,knew exactly what they wanted. And so thoroughly were they convinced that they themselves were right that they were firmly opposed to the idea of liberty of conscience. They thought it wicked that other denominations should be suffered to exist and to worship freely within the confines of their own Protestant land. And they insisted not only that all Catholics and Anabaptists be exiled from the British Isles but furthermore that Socinians,Arminians,Cartesians,is short all those who did not share their own views upon the existence of a living God,be hanged.

This triangle of conflicts,however,produced an unexpected result. It forced the men who were obliged to keep peace between those mutually hostile parties to be much more tolerant than they would have been otherwise.

If both the Stuarts and Cromwell at different times of their careers insisted upon equal rights for all denominations,and history tells us they did,they were most certainly not animated by a love for Presbyterians or High Churchmen,or vice versa. They were merely making the best of a very difficult bargain. The terrible things which happened in the colonies along the Bay of Massachusetts,where one sect finally became all powerful,show us what would have been the fate of England if any one of the many contending factions had been able to establish an absolute dictatorship over the entire country.

Cromwell of course reached the point where he was able to do as he liked. But the Lord Protector was a very wise man. He knew that he ruled by the grace of his iron brigade and carefully avoided such extremes of conduct or of legislation as would have forced his

但那还不是全部。

统治英格兰的人也是苏格兰国王，苏格兰臣民在宗教方面很清楚自己需要什么。他们完全相信，自己坚决反对宗教信仰自由的观念是正确的。他们认为，在他们自己新教徒的土地上允许其他教派存在，而且还能信仰自由，这简直就是邪恶。他们坚持认为，不仅所有的天主教徒和再洗礼教徒应该被赶出不列颠群岛，而且索兹尼教徒、阿米尼乌斯教徒、笛卡尔主义者，总之所有不赞同他们观点（即存在一个活生生的上帝）的人，都应该被绞死。

但是，这个三角冲突产生了出乎意料的后果。它使得一些被迫在对立的教派之间保持中立的人变得比原来更宽容了，而他们原本没这么宽容的。

如果斯图亚特王朝和克伦威尔在其统治的不同时期都坚持各教派享有平等权利，而且历史告诉我们他们确实这样做了，那肯定不是他们对长老会教徒或高教会教徒有什么偏爱，或者是他们受到了那些教徒的爱戴。他们只是在一个非常困难的处境中争取最好的结果。在马萨诸塞湾殖民地发生的那件可怕的事情（即一个教派最后变得势力强大）告诉我们，如果英国众多相互争斗的小教派中的任何一派建立了全国范围的绝对专制，那么英格兰的命运将不堪设想。

克伦威尔当然达到了为所欲为的境地。但这个护国公是个很明智的人。他知道他的统治是靠铁军维持的，因此他会小心地避免一切有可能使反对派结盟反对他的过分行为或法令。然而他的宽容思想也仅止于此。

至于那些可恶的“无神论者”——也就是前面提到的索兹尼教徒、阿米尼乌斯

opponents to make common cause. Beyond that,however,his ideas concerning tolerance did not go.

As for the abominable"atheists"—the aforementioned Socinians and Arminians and Cratesians and other apostles of the divine right of the individual human being,their lives were just as difficult as before.

Of course,the English"Libertines"enjoyed one enormous advantage. They lived close to the sea. Only thirty-six hours of sickness separated them from the safe asylum of the Dutch cities. As the printing shops of these cities were turning out most of the contraband literature of southern and western Europe,a trip across the North Sea really meant a voyage to one's publisher and gave the enterprising traveler a chance to gather in his royalties and see what were the latest additions to the literature of intellectual protest.

Among those who at one time or another availed themselves of this convenient opportunity for quiet study and peaceful reflection,no one has gained a more deserving fame than John Locke.

He was born in the same year as Spinoza. And like Spinoza (indeed like most independent thinkers) he was the product of an essentially pious household. The parents of Baruch were orthodox Jews. The parents of John were orthodox Christians. Undoubtedly they both meant well by their children when they trained them in the strict doctrines of their own respective creeds. But such an education either breaks a boy's spirit or it turns him into a rebel. Baruch and John,not being the sort that ever surrenders,gritted their teeth,left home and struck out for themselves.

At the age of twenty Locke went to Oxford and there for the first time heard of Descartes. But among the dusty book-stalls of St. Catherine Street he found certain other volumes that were much to his taste. For example,there were the works of Thomas Hobbes.

教徒、笛卡尔主义者及其他人类神圣权力的信徒——其处境依然像从前一样艰难。

当然，英国的“自由思想者”有一个极大的优势。他们住在海边，只要36个小时就能渡船到达安全的避难所荷兰城市。由于这些荷兰城市的印刷厂正在出版大量南欧和西欧的禁书，因此穿越北海就意味着去出版商那儿，有胆量的人还可以得到一笔稿酬，还可以看一看反抗思想文学中有什么最新作品。

这些人当中，有人利用这个好机会进行宁静的研究和安宁的思索，其中最有名望的是约翰·洛克。

他和斯宾诺莎出生于同一年。他和斯宾诺莎（其实也像大多数独立的思想家）一样，出生于一个相当虔诚的家庭。斯宾诺沙的父母是正统的犹太人，约翰的母亲是正统的基督徒。他们用各自信仰的严格教义训练孩子，当然是出自好意。但这种教育不是摧毁孩子的心灵，就是将他们变成叛逆。斯宾诺沙和约翰都不是那种容易投降的人，他们紧咬牙离开了家，自谋生路去了。

20岁时，洛克来到牛津，他在那里第一次听说了笛卡尔。可是在圣凯瑟琳大街满是灰尘的书店里，他发现了另外一些更合自己口味的书，如托马斯·霍布斯的著作。

霍布斯是个有趣的人物，他以前曾在马格达朗学院求过学，是个不安分的人，到过意大利，和伽利略谈过话，与伟大的笛卡尔通过信，一生大部分时间住在欧洲大陆，为的是逃避清教徒的怒火。他偶尔写作，完成了一部巨著，包含了他对所有可以想到的问题的见解，该书有一个引人注目的书名：《利维坦：或曰教会国家和

An interesting figure,this former student of Magdalen College,a restless person who had visited Italy and had held converse with Galileo,who had exchanged letters with the great Descartes himself and who had spent the greater part of his life on the continent,an exile from the fury of the Puritans. Between times he had composed an enormous book which contained all his ideas upon every conceivable subject and which bore the inviting title of"Leviathan,or the Matter,Form and Power of a Commonwealth,Ecclesiastical and Civil."

This learned tome made its appearance when Locke was in his Sophomore year. It was so outspoken upon the nature of princes,their rights and most especially their duties,that even the most thorough going Cromwellian must approve of it,and that many of Cromwell's partisans felt inclined to pardon this doubting Thomas who was a full-fledged royalist yet exposed the royalist pretensions in a volume that weighed not less than five pounds. Of course Hobbes was the sort of person whom it has never been easy to classify. His contemporaries called him a Latitudinarian. That meant that he was more interested in the ethics of the Christian religion than in the discipline and the dogmas of the Christian church and believed in allowing people a fair degree of"latitude"in their attitude upon those questions which they regarded as non-essential.

Locke had the same temperament as Hobbes. He too remained within the Church until the end of his life but he was heartily in favor of a most generous interpretation both of life and of faith. What was the use,Locke and his friends argued,of ridding the country of one tyrant (who wore a golden crown) if it only led up to a fresh abuse of power by another tyrant (who wore a black slouch hat) ?Why renounce allegiance to one set of priests and then the next day accept the rule of another set of priests who were fully as overbearing and arrogant as their predecessors?Logic undoubtedly was on their side but such a point of view could not possibly be popular among those who would have lost their livelihood if the"latitude men"had been

新的天国

公民国家的性质、形式和权力》。

这本博学巨著问世的时候，洛克正读大学二年级。它毫不留情地揭示了诸侯的本质、权力，尤其是他们的责任，就连最彻底的克伦威尔派也不得不赞同，许多克伦威尔党人都倾向于宽赦这个持怀疑态度的托马斯，因为他尽管是个十足的保皇派，却在一本5磅多重的书中揭露了保皇派的虚伪。当然，霍布斯不是那种容易归类的人。他同时代的人称他是“宗教自由主义者”。也就是说，他更感兴趣的是基督教的伦理学，而不是基督教的教义和教条，而且认为应该让人们在那些不太重要的问题上有一定程度的“自由”。

洛克与霍布斯有相同的气质。他终生信教，却又从心底里赞同对生活和信仰做最宽容的解释。洛克和他的朋友们认为，国家摆脱一个（戴金冠的）暴君，如果只是导致另一个（戴黑色耷拉帽的）暴君来滥用权力，那又有什么用？为什么今天否认一帮教士的忠诚，而第二天又接受另一帮和其

successful and had changed a rigid social system into an ethical debating society?

And although Locke,who seems to have been a man of great personal charm,had influential friends who could protect him against the curiosity of the sheriffs,the day was soon to come when he would no longer be able to escape the suspicion of being an atheist.

That happened in the fall of the year 1683,and Locke thereupon went to Amsterdam. Spinoza had been dead for half a dozen years,but the intellectual atmosphere of the Dutch capital continued to be decidedly liberal and Locke was given a chance to study and write without the slightest interference on the part of the authorities. He was an industrious fellow and during the four years of his exile he composed that famous"Letter on Tolerance"which makes him one of the heroes of our little history. In this letter (which under the criticism of his opponents grew into three letters) he flatly denied that the state had the right to interfere with religion. The state,as Locke saw it (and in this he was borne out by a fellow exile,a Frenchman by the name of Pierre Bayle,who was living in Rotterdam at that time composing his incredibly learned one-man encyclopedia),the state was merely a sort of protective organization which a certain number of people had created and continued to maintain for their mutual benefit and safety. Why such an organization should presume to dictate what the individual citizens should believe and what not—that was something which Locke and his disciples failed to understand. The state did not undertake to tell them what to eat or drink. Why should it force them to visit one church and keep away from another?

The seventeenth century,as a result of the half-hearted victory of Protestantism,was an era of strange religious compromises.

The peace of Westphalia which was supposed to make an end to all religious warfare had laid down the principle that"all subjects shall follow the religion of their ruler."Hence in one six-by-

前任同样傲慢专横的教士的统治呢？从逻辑上讲这当然是对的，但对另外一些人而言，如果“自由主义者”一旦成功，把僵化的社会体系变成伦理辩论的社会，那么他们就会失去生计，因而这种观点在他们当中是不可能受欢迎的。

洛克虽然似乎很有个人魅力，有一些颇具影响的朋友能保护他不受地方长官的怀疑，但没过多久他还是不能再逃避“无神论者”的嫌疑了。

这是发生在1683年秋天的事，于是洛克来到阿姆斯特丹。斯宾诺莎去世已经六七年了，但荷兰首都的学术气氛还相当自由，洛克有机会学习和写作，而不受官方的任何干涉。他很勤奋，在外流亡的四年时间里写下了著名的《宽容信札》，这使他成为我们这本小历史书的主角之一。在这封信中（按照对反对派的批评需要而发展成了三封信），他断然否定国家有权干涉宗教。洛克认为（这一观点源于另一个流亡者，一个叫皮埃尔·贝尔的法国人，此人当时住在鹿特丹，正在独自编撰他那学识极其渊博的百科全书），国家只是一个保护性组织，由一批人创立和维持，以保护大家共同的利益和安全。为什么这样一个组织要发号施令让人信仰这个而不许信仰那个？这是洛克和他的信徒始终没有弄明白的。国家并没有规定他们应该吃什么喝什么，为什么它要强迫他们去这个教堂而不能去另一个教堂呢？

清教徒主义的不彻底的胜利，使17世纪成为一个奇怪的宗教妥协的时代。

被认为终止了所有宗教战争的《威斯特伐利亚和约》规定了一条原则：“所有臣民都必须服从统治者的宗教信仰。”这样一来，整个公国的臣民今天全是路德教徒（因为大公爵是路德教徒），而第二天又都成了天主教徒（因为当地男爵恰好是

nine principality all citizens were Lutherans (because the local grand duke was a Lutheran) and in the next they were all Catholics (because the local baron happened to be a Catholic).

"If,"so Locke reasoned,"the State has the right to dictate to the people concerning the future weal of their souls,then one-half of the people are foreordained to perdition,for since both religions cannot possibly be true (according to article I of their own catechisms) it follows that those who are born on one side of a boundary line are bound for Heaven and those who are born on the other side are bound for Hell and in this way the geographical accident of birth decides one's future salvation."

That Locke did not include Catholics in his scheme of tolerance is regrettable,but understandable. To the average Britisher of the seventeenth century Catholicism was not a form of religious conviction but a political party which had never ceased to plot against the safety of the English state,which had built Armadas and had bought barrels of gun-powder with which to destroy the parliament of a supposedly friendly nation.

Hence Locke refused to his Catholic opponents those rights which he was willing to grant to the heathen in his colonies and asked that they continue to be excluded from His Majesty's domains,but solely on the ground of their dangerous political activities and not because they professed a different faith.

One had to go back almost sixteen centuries to hear such sentiments. Then a Roman emperor had laid down the famous principle that religion was an affair between the individual man and his God and that God was quite capable of taking care of himself whenever he felt that his dignity had been injured.

The English people who had lived and prospered through four changes of government within less than sixty years were inclined to see the fundamental truth of such an ideal of tolerance based upon common sense.

天主教徒）。

洛克推论说："如果国家有权力决定人们灵魂的未来幸福，那么一半人都注定要进地狱，因为不可能两种宗教都正确（按照他们各自宗教手册第一条的说法），因此生在边界这边的肯定会进天堂，而生在另一边的则必然要下地狱。这样一来，出生时的地理位置便决定了一个人未来能否被拯救。"

洛克没有把天主教徒列入他的宽容计划中，这的确令人遗憾，不过可以理解。对17世纪的普通英国人而言，天主教不是一种宗教，而是一个政党，它从来没有停止过颠覆英国的安全，它建立了"无敌舰队"，还买来了大桶大桶的炸药，企图把这个友好国家的国会炸碎。

因此，洛克宁愿把权力交给殖民地的异教徒，也不想给天主教徒，而且要求将他们永远驱逐出英国的国土。但这也只是因为他们危险的政治活动，而不是因为他们有不同的信仰。

要听到这种看法，就必须回溯到几乎16个世纪以前。那时候，一个罗马皇帝曾经制定了一条著名的原则：宗教是人与上帝之间的事，如果上帝觉得自己的尊严受到了损害，自己会照顾好自己。

英国人在不到60年里经历了四个政府的更替，他们比较容易理解建立在常识基础上的宽容理想所包含的根本道理。

当奥兰治的威廉于1688年渡过北海时，洛克也紧跟着他坐第二条船来了，同船的还有英格兰新女王。从此，他过着平安无事的生活，直到72岁高龄去世，成为受

When William of Orange crossed the North Sea in the year 1688,Locke followed him on the next ship,which carried the new Queen of England. Henceforth he lived a quiet and uneventful existence and when he died at the ripe old age of seventy-two he was known as a respectable author and no longer feared as a heretic.

Civil war is a terrible thing but it has one great advantage. It clears the atmosphere.

The political dissensions of the seventeenth century had completely consumed the superfluous energy of the English nation and while the citizens of other countries continued to kill each other for the sake of the Trinity and prenatal damnation,religious persecution in Great Britain came to an end. Now and then a too presumptuous critic of the established church,like Daniel Defoe,might come into unpleasant contact with the law,but the author of"Robinson Crusoe"was pilloried because he was a humorist rather than an amateur theologian and because the Anglo-Saxon race,since time immemorial,has felt an inborn suspicion of irony. Had Defoe written a serious defense of tolerance,he would have escaped with a reprimand. When he turned his attack upon the tyranny of the church into a semi-humorous pamphlet entitled"The Shortest Way with Dissenters,"he showed that he was a vulgar person without a decent sense of the proprieties and one who deserved no better than the companionship of the pickpockets of Newgate Prison.

Even then Defoe was fortunate that he had never extended his travels beyond the confines of the British Isles. For intolerance having been driven from the mother country had found a most welcome refuge in certain of the colonies on the other side of the ocean. And this was due not so much to the character of the people who had moved into these recently discovered regions as to the fact that the new world offered infinitely greater economic advantages than the old one.

In England itself,a small island so densely populated that it offered standing room only

人尊敬的作者，而不再是让人害怕的异端了。

新世界的冬天

内战是件可怕的事，但它却有一大好处。它可以使空气清新。

17世纪的政治分歧完全耗尽了英国的多余精力。当其他国家的公民还在为“三位一体”和“生而入地狱”的问题相互残杀的时候，大不列颠的宗教迫害已近尾声。偶尔会有一个过于放肆的抨击教会的批评家像丹尼尔·笛福，也许会倒霉地触犯法律。但这位《鲁宾逊漂流记》的作者之所以被戴上枷锁，并非因为他是业余神学家，而是因为他是个幽默家，而且还因为盎格鲁-萨克森民族历来对讽刺就有天生的疑心。假如笛福写的是一本严肃维护宽容的书，他也可以逃脱责难。但是他把对教会暴政的攻击变成了一本名叫《持不同意见者的捷径》的半幽默的小册子，这表明他是个没有礼节观念的粗人，应该送到纽盖特监狱中去与小偷做伴。

尽管如此，笛福还是幸运的，因为他从没有被流放到不列颠群岛之外的地方去。专横从发源地英国被赶出去以后，在大洋彼岸的殖民地找到了备受欢迎的庇护

to the majority of her people,all business would soon have come to an end if the people had not been willing to practice the ancient and honorable rule of"give and take."But in America,a country of unknown extent and unbelievable riches,a continent inhabited by a mere handful of farmers and workmen,no such compromise was necessary.

And so it happened that a small communist settlement on the shores of Massachusetts Bay could develop into such a stronghold of self-righteous orthodoxy that the like of it had not been seen since the happy days when Calvin exercised the functions of Chief of Police and Lord High Executioner in western Switzerland.

The credit for the first permanent settlement in the chilly regions of the Charles River usually goes to a small group of people who are referred to as the Pilgrim Fathers. A Pilgrim,in the usual sense of the word,is one who"journeys to a sacred place as an act of religious devotion."The passengers of the Mayflower were not pilgrims in that sense of the word. They were English bricklayers and tailors and cord-wainers and blacksmiths and wheel-wrights who had left their country to escape certain of those hated"poperies"which continued to cling to the worship in most of the churches around them.

First they had crossed the North Sea and had gone to Holland where they arrived at a moment of great economic depression. Our school-books continue to ascribe their desire for further travel to their unwillingness to let their children learn the Dutch language and otherwise to see them absorbed by the country of their adoption. It seems very unlikely,however,that those simple folk were guilty of such shocking ingratitude and purposely followed a most reprehensible course of hyphenation. The truth is that most of the time they were forced to live in the slums,that they found it very difficult to make a living in an already over-populated country,and that they expected a better revenue from tobacco planting in America than from wool-carding in Leiden. Hence to Virginia they sailed,but having been thrown by adverse

场所。与其说这应该归因于刚刚搬到这些新发现的土地上的人们的性格，还不如说是因为新世界比旧世界更具有广阔的经济优势。

英格兰本身是个人口稠密的小岛，只为大部分人提供了小小的立足之地，如果人们不愿意再履行古老可敬的“平等交换”的规律，所有的生意都将终止。但是在美国，这是一个范围不知有多大、财富多得难以置信的国家，是一个只住了很少的农夫和工人的大陆，这种妥协就没有必要了。

因此，在马萨诸塞海岸的一个小团体发展成了一个防范坚固的自诩正确的正统堡垒。自从加尔文在瑞士西部充当了警察署长和最高审判长的幸福年代以来，这种情况还从未出现过。

在查理河的严寒地带首次永远定居的人通常是指一小群被称为“朝圣神父”的人。朝圣者一般是指“为了表示宗教虔诚而去圣地旅行的人”。按照这个意思讲，“五月花”号的旅客并不是朝圣者。他们是英国的砖瓦匠、裁缝、搓绳匠、铁匠和修车匠，他们为了逃离那些可恨的罗马天主教教义而离开了英国，这些教义仍在周围大多数教堂大行其道。

他们首先渡过北海来到荷兰，到达这里时正赶上经济大萧条。我们的教科书还说，他们决定继续旅行是因为不愿意让他们的孩子学荷兰语，否则他们就会被这个寄居国同化。然而，听起来似乎不可能的是，这些纯朴的人居然不图报恩，却跑去当受人指责的美国公民。事实上，他们大部分时间都不得不住在贫民窟里，在人口已经过于稠密的国家谋生的确很难，而在美国种烟草的收入要比在莱顿梳羊毛多

currents and bad seamanship upon the shores of Massachusetts,they decided to stay where they were rather than risk the horrors of another voyage in their leaky tub.

But although they had now escaped the dangers of drowning and seasickness,they were still in a highly perilous position. Most of them came from small cities in the heart of England and had little aptitude for a life of pioneering. Their communistic ideas were shattered by the cold,their civic enthusiasm was chilled by the endless gales and their wives and children were killed by an absence of decent food. And,finally,the few who survived the first three winters,good-natured people accustomed to the rough and ready tolerance of the home country,were entirely swamped by the arrival of thousands of new colonists who without exception belonged to a sterner and less compromising variety of Puritan faith and who made Massachusetts what it was to remain for several centuries,the Geneva on the Charles River.

Hanging on for dear life to their small stretch of land,forever on the verge of disaster,they felt more than ever inclined to find an excuse for everything they thought and did within the pages of the Old Testament. Cut off from polite human society and books,they began to develop a strange religious psyche of their own. In their own eyes they had fallen heir to the traditions of Moses and Gideon and soon became veritable Maccabees to their Indian neighbors of the west. They had nothing to reconcile them to their lives of hardship and drudgery except the conviction that they were suffering for the sake of the only true faith. Hence their conclusion (easily arrived at) that all other people must be wrong. Hence the brutal treatment of those who failed to share their own views,who suggested by implication that the Puritan way of doing and thinking was not the only right way. Hence the exclusion from their country of all harmless dissenters who were either unmercifully flogged and then driven into the wilderness or suffered the loss

许多，于是他们驶向弗吉尼亚，却遇上了逆风，再加上马萨诸塞岸边的水手技术又差，他们就决定留在那里，而不再乘着小漏船到海上冒险进行另一次恐怖航行了。

但是他们虽然逃脱了淹死和晕船的危险，却仍然处在高度的危险状态。他们大多数来自英国内地的小城镇，没有开创生活的能力。他们的共产思想被寒冷粉碎了，对城市的热情被不息的狂风吹得冰凉，妻子和孩子由于缺乏像样的食物而死去。最终，只有很少的人熬过了前三个冬天，秉性善良的他们习惯了家乡粗犷而质朴的宽容，完全被随后到来的好几千新殖民者吞没了。这些后来者全都是更严厉、更不妥协的清教徒，他们使马萨诸塞变成了查理河畔的日内瓦长达数世纪。

清教徒在弹丸之地挣扎谋生，总是面临着重重灾难，因此他们比以往任何时候都更想从《旧约》中找到他们所想所做的每件事情的依据。他们与礼仪社会和书籍一刀两断，开始形成他们自己一套奇怪的宗教精神。在他们看来，他们是摩西和基甸的后裔，很快会成为他们西部印第安邻居的马加比人（即救赎者）。他们没有办法慰藉自己艰苦乏味的生活，只能相信他们受难是为了唯一真正的信仰。他们还由此得出结论（很容易得出），其他人都是错误的。因此，若有人不赞同他们的观点，或含蓄地说清教徒的所作所为并不是唯一正确的，他就会遭到虐待。这些无辜的持异见者不是被无情地鞭打一顿后被赶到荒野里，就是被割去耳朵和舌头，还要被驱逐出境，除非他们万幸地在邻近的瑞典和荷兰殖民地找到避难所。

对于宗教自由和宽容事业来说，这块殖民地毫无贡献，它在这方面只不过是歪打正着罢了，这在人类进步的历史中倒是常见的。宗教专制的极端暴力导致了一

of their ears and tongues unless they were fortunate enough to find a refuge in one of the neighboring colonies which belonged to the Swedes and the Dutch.

No,for the cause of religious freedom or tolerance,this colony achieved nothing except in that roundabout and involuntary fashion which is so common in the history of human progress. The very violence of their religious despotism brought about a reaction in favor of a more liberal policy. After almost two centuries of ministerial tyranny,there arose a new generation which was the open and avowed enemy of all forms of priest-rule,which believed profoundly in the desirability of the separation of state and church and which looked askance upon the ancestral admixture of religion and politics.

By a stroke of good luck this development came about very slowly and the crisis did not occur until the period immediately before the outbreak of hostilities between Great Britain and her American colonies. As a result,the Constitution of the United States was written by men who were either freethinkers or secret enemies of the old-fashioned Calvinism and who incorporated into this document certain highly modern principles which have proved of the greatest value in maintaining the peaceful balance of our republic.

But ere this happened,the new world had experienced a most unexpected development in the field of tolerance and curiously enough it took place in a Catholic community,in that part of America now covered by the free state of Maryland.

The Calverts,who were responsible for this interesting experiment,were of Flemish origin,but the father had moved to England and had rendered very distinguished services to the house of Stuart. Originally they had been Protestants,but George Calvert,private secretary and general utility man to King James I,had become so utterly disgusted with the futile theological haggling of his contemporaries that he returned to the old faith. Good,bad or indifferent,it called black,black and white,white and did not leave the final

马里兰的基础

种主张更自由的政策的反作用。在将近两个世纪的教士专制之后，涌现了新的一代，他们是各种形式的教士统治的公开而可怕的敌人，坚决认为政教应该分离，蔑视祖辈将宗教和政治混为一体。

有点儿幸运的是，这个发展过程很缓慢，直到大不列颠和它的美洲殖民地的敌对刚要爆发之前，危机才出现。结果，起草美国宪法的人不是自由思想者就是旧式加尔文主义的秘密敌人，他们在这份文件里注入了某些很现代化的原则，实践证明这些原则在维持我们共和国的和平稳定上具有巨大价值。

可是在这以前，新世界在宽容领域里已经经历了一次未曾预料的发展，而且令人惊异的是它发生在天主教区里，在现在属于马里兰州的一个地方。

这一有趣的事件的主角是卡尔弗特父子。卡尔弗特原籍弗莱芒，但是父亲后来迁居到了英国，为斯图亚特王朝效劳，建立了卓越功勋。他们起初是新教徒，但是担任国王詹姆斯一世私人秘书和总管的乔治·卡尔弗特被同时代人毫无用处的神学争论搞得烦恼透顶，便又回到了古老的信仰上来。这种信仰无论好坏还是不好不坏，但它称黑为黑，称白为白，而不会把每项教义的最后裁定权交给一帮半文盲的教会执事。

settlement of every point of doctrine to the discretion of a board of semi-literate deacons.

This George Calvert,so it seems,was a man of parts. His backsliding (a very serious offense in those days!) did not lose him the favor of his royal master. On the contrary,he was made Baron Baltimore of Baltimore and was promised every sort of assistance when he planned to establish a little colony of his own for the benefit of persecuted Catholics. First,he tried his luck in Newfoundland. But his settlers were frozen out of house and home and his Lordship then asked for a few thousand square miles in Virginia. The Virginians,however,staunchly Episcopalian,would have naught of such dangerous neighbors and Baltimore then asked for a slice of that wilderness which lay between Virginia and the Dutch and Swedish possessions of the north. Ere he received his charter he died. His son Cecil,however,continued the good work,and in the winter of 1633~1634 two little ships,the Ark and the Dove,under command of Leonard Calvert,brother to George,crossed the ocean,and in March of 1634 they safely landed their passengers on the shores of the Chesapeake Bay. The new country was called Maryland. This was done in honor of Mary,daughter of that French king,Henry IV,whose plans for a European League of Nations had been cut short by the dagger of a crazy monk,and wife to that English monarch who soon afterwards was to lose his head at the hands of his Puritan subjects.

This extraordinary colony which did not exterminate its Indian neighbors and offered equal opportunities to both Catholics and Protestants passed through many difficult years. First of all it was overrun by Episcopalians who tried to escape the fierce intolerance of the Puritans in Massachusetts. Next it was invaded by Puritans who tried to escape the fierce intolerance of the Episcopalians in Virginia. And the two groups of fugitives,with the usual arrogance of that sort of people,tried hard to introduce their own"correct form of worship"into the commonwealth that had just offered them refuge. As"all disputes which might give rise to religious passions"were expressly forbidden on Maryland territory,the older colonists were entirely within their right when they bade both Episcopalians and Puritans to keep the

这个乔治·卡尔弗特似乎多才多艺，他的倒退（当时可是很严重的罪名！）并没有使他失去国王的恩宠。相反，他被封为巴尔的摩男爵，当他计划为受迫害的天主教徒建立一小块居住地时，国王还许诺给他提供各种帮助。他先在纽芬兰试运气，但是他派去的开拓者因为没有房子而差点儿冻死，于是他要求在弗吉尼亚给他几千平方英里土地。然而，弗吉尼亚人是顽固的圣公会教徒，他们也不要这些危险分子做邻居。巴尔的摩男爵接着要求得到位于弗吉尼亚和北边的荷兰、瑞典领地之间的一条荒野，但没等获准他就死了。他的儿子塞西尔继续这件好事，1633~1634年冬天，“方舟”号和“鸽子”号在乔治的兄弟列奥纳多的指挥下，穿越了大西洋，于1634年3月满载乘客安全抵达切萨皮克海湾。这个新地区叫马里兰，以法国国王亨利四世的女儿玛丽的名字命名。亨利四世本来计划建立一个欧洲各国的联盟，但是一个发疯的僧侣用匕首刺杀了亨利四世而使该计划破产了，玛丽成为英国国王的妻子，而这个国王不久又死于清教徒臣民之手。

这个与众不同的移民区并不根除印第安人，对天主教徒和新教徒也平等相待，度过了好几年困难时期。首先，该地区有很多圣公会教徒，他们是为了逃避马萨诸塞清教徒的残忍专制而来的。然后，清教徒也踏入这块移民区，他们则是为了逃避弗吉尼亚圣公会教徒的残忍专制而来的。这两伙亡命徒都是那种盛气凌人的家伙，都想把自己的“正确信仰”带进这个刚刚为他们提供避难所的地方。由于“所有可能引起宗教狂热的争执”在马里兰的土地上都被禁止，因此老移民完全有权力让圣公会教徒和清教徒都和平相处。但没过多久，家乡的保皇党和圆颅党的战争爆发，马里兰人害怕不管哪一方获胜，他们将会失去往日的自由。因此，1649年4月，在

peace. But soon afterwards war broke out in the home country between the Cavaliers and the Roundheads and the Marylanders feared that,no matter who should win,they would lose their old freedom. Hence,in April of the year 1649 and shortly after news of the execution of Charles I had reached them,and at the direct suggestion of Cecil Calvert,they passed their famous Act of Tolerance which,among other things,contained this excellent passage:

"That since the coercion of conscience in the matter of religion has often produced very harmful results in those communities in which it was exercised,for the more tranquil and pacific government in this province and for the better preservation of mutual love and unity among its inhabitants,it is hereby decided that nobody in this province who professes faith in Jesus Christ shall be disturbed,molested or persecuted in any way for reasons respecting his religion or the free exercise thereof."

That such an act could be passed in a country in which the Jesuits occupied a favorite position shows that the Baltimore family was possessed of remarkable political ability and of more than ordinary courage. How profoundly this generous spirit was appreciated by some of their guests was shown in the same year when a number of Puritan exiles overthrew the government of Maryland,abolished the Act of Tolerance and replaced it by an"Act Concerning Religion"of their own which granted full religious liberty to all those who declared themselves Christians"with the exception of Catholics and Episcopalians."

This period of reaction fortunately did not last long. In the year 1660 the Stuarts returned to power and once more the Baltimores reigned in Maryland.

The next attack upon their policy came from the other side. The Episcopalians gained a complete victory in the mother country and they insisted that henceforth their church should be the official church of all the colonies. The Calverts continued to fight but they found it impossible to attract new colonists. And so,after a struggle which lasted another generation,the experiment came to an end.

Protestantism triumphed

So did intolerance.

刚刚获悉查理一世被处以极刑之后，在塞西尔·卡尔弗特的直接倡议下，他们通过了著名的《宽容法》。其中有这样一段极其出色：

"鉴于在宗教问题上对思想的高压统治在所及的范围内常常产生非常有害的结果，为了本省政权的安定和平，为了保护本省居民相互之间的友爱和团结，特决定，不得以宗教或宗教信仰自由为理由，对本省任何信仰耶稣基督的人进行干扰、骚扰和迫害。"

在一个由耶稣会会士掌管重权的国家，能够通过这样一项法案，显示了巴尔的摩家族杰出的政治能力和非凡的勇气。然而，这种大度的精神是怎样受到某些客人赞扬的，在同一年就显示出来了：一伙清教徒流亡者推翻了马里兰的政权，废除了《宽容法》，代之以自己的《宗教法案》，它给予那些自称是基督徒的人以彻底的宗教自由，但"天主教徒和圣公会教徒除外"。

幸好这个反动时期持续得并不长。1660年，斯图亚特王朝重新当权，巴尔的摩派也重掌马里兰的统治。

对他们政策的又一次攻击来自另一面。圣公会教徒在宗主国获得了完全胜利，因此坚决要求把他们的教会变成所有殖民地的官方教会。卡尔弗特家族继续奋战，但他们看到要把新殖民地居民吸引到自己这边是不可能了。在经过整整一代人的斗争之后，这次试验宣告终止。

新教胜利了。

专制也占了上风。

CHAPTER X X Ⅲ THE SUN KING

The eighteenth century is usually referred to as an era of despotism. And in an age which believes in the dogma of democracy,despotism,however enlightened,is not apt to be regarded as a desirable form of government.

Historians who mean well by the human race are very apt to point the finger of scorn at that great monarch Louis XIV and ask us to draw our own conclusions. When this brilliant sovereign came to the throne,he inherited a country in which the forces of Catholicism and Protestantism were so evenly balanced that the two parties,after a century of mutual assassination (with the odds heavily in favor of the Catholics),had at last concluded a definite peace and had promised to accept each other as unwelcome but unavoidable neighbors and fellow citizens. The"perpetual and irrevocable"Edict of Nantes of the year 1598 which contained the terms of agreement,stated that the Catholic religion was the official religion of the state but that the Protestants should enjoy complete liberty of conscience and should not suffer any persecution on account of their belief. They were furthermore allowed to build churches of their own and to hold public office. And as a token of good faith,the Protestants were allowed to hold two hundred fortified cities and villages within the realm of France.

This,of course,was an impossible arrangement. The Huguenots were no angels. To leave two hundred of the most prosperous cities and villages of France in the hands of a political party which was the sworn enemy of the government was quite as absurd as if we should surrender Chicago and San Francisco and Philadelphia to the Democrats to make them accept a Republican administration,or vice versa.

第23章 太 阳 王

18世纪通常被称为专制的年代。在如今信仰民主的年代里，无论多么开明的专制，都不会是理想的政府。

即使那些总是说人类好话的历史学家，也都会对路易十四国王加以责难，然后让我们自己去得出结论。这个聪明的国王登上宝座的时候，在他继承的国家里天主教和新教徒势均力敌。这两派经过一个世纪的相互残杀（天主教徒大占便宜），最后终于达成了明确的和平，相互承诺，尽管对方不受欢迎，但既然是躲不开的邻居和公民，就要彻底接受对方。1598年发布的“永久而不可改变的”《南特敕令》包括了双方一致同意的各项协议，规定天主教为国教，新教徒可以充分享有信仰自由，不得因其信仰而遭受任何迫害。他们还获准建造自己的教堂并担任公职。为了表示对他们的信赖，新教徒还获准掌管法国境内200个要塞城市和村庄。

这当然是不可能实现的安排。胡格诺派教徒不是天使，把法国200多座繁荣的城市和乡村交给敌视政府的政党，简直和我们把芝加哥、旧金山和费城交给民主党人，以换取他们接受共和党人的统治一样荒谬，反之亦然。

黎塞留是统治过这个国家的智者，他看出了这一点。经过长期奋斗，他剥夺了

Richelieu,as intelligent a man as ever ruled a country,recognized this. After a long struggle he deprived the Protestants of their political power,but although a cardinal by profession,he scrupulously refrained from any interference with their religious freedom. The Huguenots could no longer conduct independent diplomatic negotiations with the enemies of their own country,but otherwise they enjoyed the same privileges as before and could sing paslms and listen to sermons or not as pleased them.

Mazarin,the next man to rule France in the real sense of the word,had followed a similar policy. But he died in the year 1661. Then young Louis XIV personally undertook to rule his domains,and there was an end to the era of good will.

It seems most unfortunate that when this brilliant if disreputable Majesty was forced for once in his life into the companionship of decent people he should have fallen into the clutches of a good woman who was also a religious fanatic. Francoise d'Aubigné,the widow of a literary hack by the name of Scarron,had begun her career at the French court as governess to the seven illegitimate children of Louis XIV and the Marquise de Montespan. When that lady's love philtres ceased to have the desired effect and the King began to show occasional signs of boredom,it was the governess who stepped into her shoes. Only she was different from all her predecessors. Before she agreed to move into His Majesty's apartments,the Archbishop of Paris had duly solemnized her marriage to the descendant of Saint Louis.

During the next twenty years the power behind the throne was therefore in the hands of a woman who was completely dominated by her confessor. The clergy of France had never forgiven either Richelieu or Mazarin for their conciliatory attitude towards the Protestants. Now at last they had a chance to undo the work of these shrewd statesmen and they went to it with a will. For not only were they the official advisers of the Queen,but they also became the bankers of the King.

新教徒的政治权利，却丝毫不干涉他们的宗教信仰自由，尽管他本人的职业是大主教。胡格诺派教徒不能再与国家的敌人进行单独的外交谈判了，但他们仍然享受和从前一样的权利，可以唱赞美诗，听布道，总之悉听尊便。

下一个真正的法国统治者是马萨林，他执行类似政策，但是他于1661年就死了。年轻的路易十四开始当政，人心向善的时代终止了。

非常不幸的是，这个聪明而又颇具争议的国王这一辈子只有一次不得不与正派人结交，没料想却落入了一个宗教狂热的女人手里。她叫弗朗科斯·多比娜，是御用文人斯科隆的遗孀。她一开始在宫中担任路易十四和蒙特斯丹侯爵夫人的七个私生子的家庭教师，等到那位侯爵夫人的春药已经丧失了魔力，国王开始表露出偶尔厌烦的时候，这位女教师便取而代之。她和国王以前所有情妇唯一不同的是，在同意搬入国王的居室之前，巴黎大主教为她和圣路易的婚礼举行了隆重的宗教仪式。

在以后的20年里，王位后面的权力全抓在这个女人手中，而她又完全受控于她的忏悔神父。法国的教士从来没有原谅过黎塞留和马萨林对基督徒的和善态度。现在他们终于有机会毁掉那些明智的政治家的成就了，便肆意胡为，因为他们不仅是王后的官方顾问，而且还是国王的银行家。

这是又一个奇怪的故事。

在过去的八个世纪里，修道院积攒了法国的大部分财富。因为国库开支与日俱增，而他们不必交税，因此他们拥有的大量过剩财产就尤其重要。国王陛下——他的荣耀比他的信誉大得多——抓住了这个大好机会，重新填满了自己的金库。他给

That again is a curious story.

During the last eight centuries the monasteries had accumulated the greater part of the wealth of France and as they paid no taxes in a country which suffered perpetually from a depleted treasury,their surplus wealth was of great importance. And His Majesty,whose glory was greater than his credit,made a grateful use of this opportunity to replenish his own coffers and in exchange for certain favors extended to his clerical supporters he was allowed to borrow as much money as he wanted.

In this way the different stipulations of the"irrevocable"Edict of Nantes were one by one revoked. At first the Protestant religion was not actually forbidden,but life for those who remained faithful to the Huguenot cause was made exasperatingly uncomfortable. Whole regiments of dragoons were turned loose upon those provinces where the false doctrines were supposed to be most strongly entrenched. The soldiers were billeted among the inhabitants with instructions to make themselves thoroughly detestable. They ate the food and drank the wine and stole the forks and spoons and broke the furniture and insulted the wives and daughters of perfectly harmless citizens and generally behaved as if they were in a conquered territory. When their poor hosts,in their despair,rushed to the courts for some form of redress and protection,they were laughed at for their trouble and were told that they had brought their misfortunes upon their own heads and knew perfectly well how they could get rid of their unwelcome guests and at the same time regain the good will of the government.

A few,a very few,followed this suggestion and allowed themselves to be baptized by the nearest village priest. But the vast majority of these simple people remained faithful to the ideals of their childhood. At last,however,when one after another their churches were closed and their clergy were sent to the galleys,they began to understand that they were

了支持他的教士一些特权，作为报答，他可以随意向教会借到他想要的钱。

就这样，“不可改变”的《南特敕令》被一项一项地取消了。起初新教徒的信仰还没有被禁止，但是坚持信仰胡格诺派事业的人总是不得安宁。据说一些省的错误教义极其顽固，于是整队的龙骑兵便开赴那里。士兵们得到命令，住在老百姓家中，发号施令，很让人讨厌。他们大吃大喝，偷走叉子和勺子，打坏家具，侮辱良家妇女，就像在被征服的土地上那样无恶不作。可怜的主人绝望之际跑去法庭要求保护，却因此受到嘲弄，还说他们是自作自受，自己应该知道怎样摆脱这些不受欢迎的客人，同时又能重新博得政府的好感。

只有很少很少的人听从了劝告，到最近的乡村牧师那里接受了天主教洗礼。但是绝大部分淳朴的人还是坚持自

■ 国王的废纸篓

doomed. Rather than surrender,they decided to go into exile. But when they reached the frontier,they were told that no one was allowed to leave the country,that those who were caught in the act were to be hanged,and that those who aided and abetted such fugitives were liable to be sent to the galleys for life.

There are apparently certain things which this world will never learn.

From the days of the Pharaohs to those of Lenin,all governments at one time or another have tried the policy of"closing the frontier"and none of them has ever been able to score a success.

People who want to get out so badly that they are willing to take all sorts of risks can invariably find a way. Hundreds of thousands of French Protestants took to the"underground route"and soon afterwards appeared in London or Amsterdam or Berlin or Basel. Of course,such fugitives were not able to carry much ready cash. But they were known everywhere as honest and hard working merchants and artisans. Their credit was good and their energy undiminished. After a few years they usually regained that prosperity which had been their share in the old country and the home government was deprived of a living economic asset of incalculable value.

Indeed,it is no exaggeration to say that the revocation of the Edict of Nantes was the prelude to the French Revolution.

France had been and still was a very rich country. But commerce and clericalism have never been able to coöperate.

From the moment that the French government surrendered to petticoats and cassocks,her fate was sealed. The same pen that decreed the expulsion of the Huguenots signed the death-warrant of Louis XVI.

幼就信仰的理想。最后，等他们的教堂一个接一个被关闭，教士被送去服苦役时，他们才开始明白他们这是命中注定的。他们没有投降，而是决定流亡，可是他们刚到边境，才得知谁也不许出走，被抓住的人就得被绞死，帮助逃跑的人也可能被送去终身做苦役。

显然，当时发生了一些世人永远不会知道的事。

从法老时代至今，所有政府也都不时“关闭边境”，但从来没有成功。

决意要走的人只要不惜冒各种危险，总是可以找到办法的。成千上万的法国新教徒通过“秘密途径”很快就来到伦敦、阿姆斯特丹、柏林或巴塞尔。当然，这些逃亡者没有什么钱，但他们是以忠诚肯干而闻名的商人和艺术家，他们的信誉很好，而且精力充沛，几年之后便重新发达起来，而这种繁盛本来是属于法国的，因此法国政府在经济上失去了无法计算的活资产。

事实上，说《南特敕令》的取缔是法国大革命的前奏，一点都不夸张。

法国曾经一直是个富庶的国家。但是商业和宗教从来没能合作过。

自从法国政权落入女人和教士手中那一刻起，命运就注定了。签署驱逐胡格诺教徒法令的那支笔，后来也签署了宣判路易十六的死刑令。

CHAPTER ⅩⅩⅣ FREDERICK THE GREAT

The house of Hohenzollern has never been famous for its love of popular forms of government. But ere the crazy strain of the Bavarian Wittelsbachs had tainted this soberminded family of bookkeepers and overseers,they rendered some very useful service to the cause of tolerance.

In part this was the result of a practical necessity. The Hohenzollerns had fallen heir to the poorest part of Europe,a half-populated wilderness of sand and forests. The Thirty Years War had left them bankrupt. They needed both men and money to start in business once more and they set out to get them,regardless of race,creed or previous condition of servitude.

The father of Frederick the Great,a vulgarian with the manners of a coal-heaver and the personal tastes of a bar-tender,could grow quite tender when he was called upon to meet a delegation of foreign fugitives."The more the merrier,"was his motto in all matters pertaining to the vital statistics of his kingdom and he collected the disinherited of all nations as carefully as he collected the six-foot-three grenadiers of his lifeguard.

His son was of a very different caliber,a highly civilized human being who,having been forbidden by his father to study Latin and French,had made a speciality of both languages and greatly preferred the prose of Montaigne to the poetry of Luther and the wisdom of Epictetus of that of the Minor Prophets. The Old Testament severity of his father (who ordered the boy's best friend to be decapitated in front of his window so as to teach him a

第24章 腓特烈大帝

霍亨佐伦王室从来没有因为喜欢平民执政的政府而出名。但是在巴伐利亚维特斯巴赫家族的疯狂气质侵蚀他们之前，这个由记账员和监工组成的家族还算头脑清醒，为宽容事业做了一些非常有益的贡献。

在某种程度上，这是实际需要的结果。霍亨佐伦王室继承了欧洲最穷的地方，有一半是漫无边际的沙地和森林。三十年战争使得那里的居民家破人亡。他们需要人力和资金重整家业。于是他们开始去寻找这一切，而不论其种族、信仰和以前的卑贱身份。

腓特烈大帝的父亲是个大老粗，言谈举止就活像采煤工，个人兴趣像酒吧女招待。不过，他会见外国逃亡者代表团的时候倒也礼数有加。在处理涉及王国重要统计数字的事情时，他的座右铭是“越多越好”。他小心谨慎地收集所有国家抛弃的东西，就像是在收集6.3英尺高的掷弹兵担任自己的警卫一样认真。

他的儿子与他完全不同，是个很有教养的人。父亲不允许他学习拉丁文和法文，可他偏偏精通了这两种语言。他喜欢蒙田的散文，讨厌路德的诗歌；喜欢爱比克泰德的智慧，讨厌天主教的无知。父亲按照《旧约》中的教义很严厉地对待孩子（为了让孩子学会服从，父亲命令把孩子最要好的朋友斩首在他窗前），却并没有

lesson in obedience) had not inclined his heart toward those Judaean ideals of rectitude of which the Lutheran and Calvinist ministers of his day were apt to speak with such great praise. He came to regard all religion as a survival of prehistoric fear and ignorance,a mood of subservience carefully encouraged by a small class of clever and unscrupulous fellows who knew how to make good use of their own preeminent position by living pleasantly at the expense of their neighbors. He was interested in Christianity and even more so in the person of Christ himself,but he approached the subject by way of Locke and Socinius and as a result he was,in religious matters at least,a very broad minded person,and could truly boast that in his country"every one could find salvation after his own fashion."

This clever saying he made the basis for all his further experiments along the line of Tolerance. For example,he decreed that all religions were good as long as those who professed them were upright people who led decent,law-abiding lives;that therefore all creeds must enjoy equal rights and the state must never interfere in religious questions,but must content herself with playing policeman and keeping the peace between the different denominations. And because he truly believed this,he asked nothing of his subjects except that they be obedient and faithful and leave the final judgment of their thoughts and deeds"to Him alone who knew the conscience of men"and of whom he (the King) did not venture to form so small an opinion as to believe him to be in need of that human assistance which imagines that it can further the divine purpose by the exercise of violence and cruelty.

In all these ideas,Frederick was a couple of centuries ahead of his day. His contemporaries shook their heads when the king gave his Catholic subjects a piece of land that they might build themselves a church right in the heart of his capital. They began to murmur ominous words of warning when he made himself the protector of the Jesuit

使儿子的心倾向于正直的犹太理想，那时路德派和加尔文派牧师都对犹太理想大加赞扬。腓特烈把所有的宗教都看作是史前的恐惧和无知状态的复苏，信教等于陷入一种奴性状态，被一小撮聪明却又无耻的家伙小心操纵着，他们知道怎样充分利用自己的优越地位，以损人利己来享乐。腓特烈不仅对基督教义感兴趣，而且对基督本人更感兴趣，但他是按照洛克和索兹尼的观点来看待这个问题的，所以至少在宗教问题上是个宽容大度的人，而且可以毫不夸张地说，在他的国家，“每个人都可以按照自己的方法寻求拯救”。

这个英明论断，为他沿着宽容的道路作将来所有的试验奠定了基础。例如，他颁布法令，只要承认自己是正直的人，过着正派和遵纪守法的生活，那么所有的宗教都是好的，因此所有的信念都必须享有同等权力，政府不得干涉宗教问题，只需要充当警察的角色，并维护不同教派之间的和平。因为他的确相信这一点，因此只要求臣民们顺从和忠诚，而把对思想和行为的最后审判留给上帝，“只有上帝才了解人的良知”。他（国王）从不对上帝作任何评论，以免使人们以为他需要人的帮助，也就是用暴力和凶残来推行神圣的目的。

腓特烈在所有的思想境界中，比他所处的年代早了两个世纪。当他在首都的中心给天主教徒们划出一块土地让他们自己修建教堂时，当时的人都不住地摇头。耶稣会的人从大多数天主教国家被赶了出来时，他又挺身保护他们，人们又开始咕哝着发出恶毒的警告。当他宣布道德和宗教完全是两码事，每个人只要交纳税款和服兵役，就可以随意信奉任何宗教时，人们已经明确认为他不是基督徒了。

order,which had just been driven out of most Catholic countries,and they definitely ceased to regard him as a Christian when he claimed that ethics and religion had nothing to do with each other and that each man could believe whatever he pleased as long as he paid his taxes and served his time in the army.

Because at that time they happened to live within the boundaries of Prussia,these critics held their peace,for His Majesty was a master of epigram and a witty remark on the margin of a royal rescript could do strange things to the career of those who in some way or another had failed to please him.

The fact however remains that it was the head of an unlimited monarchy,an autocrat of thirty years' standing,who gave Europe a first taste of almost complete religious liberty.

In this distant corner of Europe,Protestant and Catholic and Jew and Turk and Agnostic enjoyed for the first time in their lives equal rights and equal prerogatives. Those who preferred to wear red coats could not lord it over their neighbors who preferred to wear green coats,and vice versa.

And the people who went back for their spiritual consolation to Nicaea were forced to live in peace and amity with others who would as soon have supper with the Devil as with the Bishop of Rome.

That Frederick was entirely pleased with the outcome of his labors,that I rather doubt. When he felt his last hour approaching,he sent for his faithful dogs. They seemed better company in this supreme hour than the members of"the so-called human race." (His Majesty was a columnist of no mean ability.)

And so he died,another Marcus Aurelius who had strayed into the wrong century and who,like his great predecessor,left an heritage which was entirely too good for his successors.

由于当时他们恰好住在普鲁士境内，这些批评家都不敢乱来。因为陛下精通警句，谁要是在皇家法律上稍加评论，那么那些在某方面没能博得他欢心的人就会给自己造成不可预测的后果。

不过，事实上他是一个掌权30年的开明的专制君主，他第一次给欧洲带来了几乎彻底的宗教自由。

在欧洲这个偏僻的角落里，新教徒、天主教徒、犹太人、土耳其人和不可知论者第一次享有了平等的权利和平等的待遇。喜欢穿红衣服的人不能对穿绿衣服的人乱加评论，反之也如此。

那些回到尼西亚寻找精神安慰的天主教徒，被迫与那些宁愿和魔鬼也不愿和罗马主教共进晚餐的新教徒和平友好相处。

腓特烈是否真的很满意他的努力成果，我很怀疑。在他感到死期将至的时候，他让人把他忠实的狗叫来。在这最重要的时刻，狗看来是比“所谓的人类”更好的伴侣（陛下是一位能力很强的报刊专栏作者）。

他死了，这是另一个误入这个错误世纪的马可·奥勒留。像他的先辈一样，他给他的继承者们留下了一份丰厚的遗产。

CHAPTER XXV VOLTAIRE

In this day and age we hear a great deal of talk about the nefarious labors of the press agent and many good people denounce"publicity"as an invention of the modern devil of success,a new-fangled and disreputable method of attracting attention to a person or to a cause. But this complaint is as old as the hills. Events of the past,when examined without prejudice,completely contradict the popular notion that publicity is something of recent origin.

The prophets of the Old Testament,both major and minor,were past-masters in the art of attracting a crowd. Greek history and Roman history are one long succession of what we people of the journalistic profession call"publicity stunts."Some of that publicity was dignified. A great deal of it was of so patent and blatant a nature that today even Broadway would refuse to fall for it.

Reformers like Luther and Calvin fully understood the tremendous value of carefully pre-arranged publicity. And we cannot blame them. They were not the sort of men who could be happy growing humbly by the side of the road like the blushing daisies. They were very much in earnest. They wanted their ideas to live. How could they hope to succeed without attracting a crowd of followers?

A Thomas Kempis can become a great moral influence by spending eighty years in a quiet corner of a monastery,for scuh long voluntary exile,if duly advertised (as it was),becomes an excellent selling point and makes people curious to see the little book which was born of a lifetime of prayer and meditation. But a Francis of Assisi or a Loyola,who hope to see some

第25章　伏　尔　泰

在现今这个时代，对于“宣传家”令人生厌行为的声讨总是不绝于耳，众多正统人士都指责“宣传广告”是现代文明的罪恶发明之一，是一种将人们的注意力转移到某个人或某件事上去的，貌似新鲜实则拙劣无比的方法。当然，这样的抱怨已是陈言旧语。平心而论，如今人们普遍认为“宣传”是近些年的产物，其实这与过去的事实完全相反。

《旧约》中的先知们，无论大小，都曾是精通宣传造势之术的行家里手。用新闻专业的眼光来看，古希腊史和古罗马史便是“宣传绝招”造就的成功范例。当然，有些宣传还算光明正大，但大部分赤裸、粗劣的招数，甚至连现在的百老汇都不屑于使用。

路德和加尔文这样的改革者们当然明白精心策划的宣传的巨大作用。我们不能求全责备。他们当然不是那种像害羞的雏菊一样甘愿在路边谦卑且愉快生长的人。他们如此执着笃定，所以不吸引众人的跟随、追捧，又如何能让他们的思想永存呢?

一个叫托马斯·肯皮斯的人，因为独自一人在寺院的安静角落里待了整整80年，将在精神上对人们产生深远的影响。因为，如果这种长期的自我放逐被及时而

tangible results of their work while they are still on this planet,must willy-nilly resort to methods now usually associated with a circus or a new movie star.

Christianity lays great stress upon modesty and praises those who are humble of spirit. But the sermon which extols these virtues was delivered under circumstances which have made it a subject of conversation to this very day.

No wonder that those men and women who were denounced as the arch enemies of the Church took a leaf out of the Holy Book and resorted to certain rather obvious methods of publicity when they began their great fight upon the spiritual tyranny which held the western world in bondage.

I offer this slight explanation because Voltaire,the greatest of all virtuosos in the field of free advertisement,has very often been blamed for the way in which he sometimes played upon the tom-tom of public consciousness. Perhaps he did not always show the best of good taste. But those whose lives he saved may have felt differently about it.

And furthermore,just as the proof of the pudding is in the eating,the success or failure of a man like Voltaire should be measured by the services he actually rendered to his fellow-men and not by his predilection for certain sorts of dressing-gowns,jokes and wall-paper.

In an outburst of justifiable pride this strange creature once said,"What of it if I have no scepter?I have got a pen."And right he was. He had a pen. Any number of pens. He was the born enemy of the goose and used more quills than two dozen ordinary writers. He belonged to that class of literary giants who all alone and under the most adverse circumstances can turn out as much copy as an entire syndicate of modern sport writers. He scribbled on the tables of dirty country inns. He composed endless hexameters in the chilly guestrooms of lonely country houses. His scrawls littered the floors of dingy boarding-houses in Greenwich. He spattered ink upon the carpets of the royal Prussian

忠实地宣传出去，将成为一个巨大的“卖点”，驱使人们急切地去阅读那本记录了他花费一生的时间，冥思苦想得出的全部结晶的小册子。但是阿西斯的某一个叫弗朗西斯或罗耀拉的人，如果希望在有生之年看到自己有所作为，便会无可奈何地采取那些早就被某个马戏团或某个电影新星用滥了的招数。

基督教特别强调谦虚，尤其赞美那些为人低调的人。但是因为当时在宣扬时用了特定的方法，所以颂扬这些美德的布道至今仍是人们谈论的话题之一。

难怪那些被指责为教堂主要敌人的男男女女们，会从《圣经》上撕下来一页，并在抗争奴役整个西方世界的精神暴政时采用某种不加掩饰的宣传方法。

我提出这个不足挂齿的解释，是因为公共宣传领域里的大师伏尔泰，常常不择手段地利用公众意识上的空虚，因此经常受到批评。或许，他并不总是表现出最高雅的品味，但是那些被他拯救生命的人也许会持不同的意见。

并且，就像只有品尝之后才能点评布丁的味道一样，对于伏尔泰这样的人来说，成功或失败也只能通过他实际上为追随者做过哪些贡献来评判，而绝非依据他在衣着、玩笑和墙纸方面的嗜好。

出于强烈的自豪感，这个奇怪的人曾经说过：“没有王权又有什么关系呢？我有一支笔。”没错，他有笔，并且有许多支。他是鹅的天敌，他用过的鹅毛笔比20多个普通作家用过的还要多。他属于那种茕茕孑立的人，是在最艰险的逆境中也能保持高产的文学巨匠。他在肮脏的乡下客栈里伏案疾书，在乡村冰冷孤寂的客房里创作了无数的六步韵诗。他把稿纸铺满了他在格林尼治寄宿的屋子的破地板，把

residence and used reams of the private stationery which bore the monogram of the governor of the Bastille. Before he had ceased to play with a hoop and marbles,Ninon de Lenclos had presented him with a considerable sum of pocket-money that he might"buy some books,"and eighty years later,in the self-same town of Paris,we hear him ask for a pad of foolscap and unlimited coffee that he may finish yet one more volume before the inevitable hour of darkness and rest.

His tragedies,however,and his stories,his poetry and his treatises upon philosophy and physics,do not entitle him to an entire chapter of this book. He wrote no better verses than half a hundred other sonneteers of that era. As a historian he was both unreliable and dull,while his ventures in the realm of science were no better than the sort of stuff we find in the Sunday papers.

But as the brave and unyielding enemy of all that was stupid and narrow and bigoted and cruel,he wielded an influence which has endured until the beginning of the Great Civil War of the year 1914.

The age in which he lived was a period of extremes. On the one hand,the utter selfishness and corruption of a religious,social and economic system which had long since outlived its usefulness. On the other side,a large number of eager but overzealous young men and young women ready to bring about a millennium which was based upon nothing more substantial than their good intentions. A humorous fate dropped this pale and sickly son of an inconspicuous notary public into this maelstrom of sharks and pollywogs,and bade him sink or swim. He preferred to swim and struck out for shore. The methods he employed during his long struggle with adverse circumstances were often of a questionable nature. He begged and flattered and played the clown. But this was in the days before royalties and literary agents. And let the author who never wrote a potboiler

■ 伏尔泰去法国上学

墨水泼洒到普鲁士王室住宅的地毯上，还用了大量印有巴士底狱监狱长名字的私人信笺。在他歇下来玩滚铁环和弹子游戏之前，尼农·德·兰克罗曾送给他一笔数目可观的零用钱，让他“买一些书”。80年后，在同一个巴黎，我们听到他说要买一打大页书写纸和一些散装的咖啡，以便在无法遁逃的黑暗和长眠来临之前，再完成一部书稿。

然而，他写的悲剧、故事、诗歌以及关于哲学和物理的论文，都没有资格占据本书整整一章的篇幅。他的十四行诗并不比同时期的其他几十位诗人写得更好。作为历史学家，他不仅不可靠，而且还相当乏味。他在科学领域的探索也不比我们在星期日报纸上看到的废话强到哪里去。

但是作为一切愚蠢、狭隘、固执和残忍事物勇敢而坚强的敌人，他的影响一直持续到1914年第一次世界大战之前。

伏尔泰生活在一个激进的时代。即一方面，是一个充满极端自私而且宗教、社

throw the first stone !

Not that Voltaire would have been greatly worried by a few additional bricks. During a long and busy life devoted to warfare upon stupidity,he had experienced too many defeats to worry about such trifles as a public beating or a couple of well aimed banana peels. But he was a man of indomitable good cheer. If today he must spend his leisure hours in His Majesty's prison,tomorrow he may find himself honored with a high titulary position at the same court from which he has just been banished. And if all his life he is obliged to listen to angry village priests denouncing him as the enemy of the Christian religion,isn't there somewhere in a cupboard filled with old love letters that beautiful medal presented to him by the Pope to prove that he can gain the approbation of Holy Church as well as her disapproval?

It was all in the day's work.

Meanwhile he fully intended to enjoy himself hugely and crowd his days and weeks and months and years with a strange and colorful assortment of the most variegated experiences.

By birth Voltaire belonged to the better middle class.

His father was what for the lack of a better term we might call a sort of private trust company. He was the confidential handy-man of a number of rich nobles and looked after their legal and financial interests. Young Arouet (for that was the family name) was therefore accustomed to a society a little better than that of his own people,something which later in life gave him a great advantage over most of his literary rivals. His mother was a certain Mademoiselle d' Aumard. She had been a poor girl who did not bring her husband a cent of dowry. But she was possessed of that small“d”which all Frenchmen of the middle classes (and all Europeans in general and a few Americans in particular) regard with humble awe,and her husband thought himself pretty lucky to win such a prize. As for the son,he also basked in the reflected glory of his ennobled grandparents and as soon as he

会和经济制度腐败透顶的时代；另一方面，一大批激进但又过分热忱的青年男女，他们想建立一个太平盛世，却又不能脚踏实地，无非是痴人说梦罢了。令人啼笑皆非的命运将这个出生在毫不起眼的公证员家庭的、体弱多病的儿子扔进了极度混乱的大漩涡里，逼迫他要么沉下去，要么游上来。他当然选择向岸边奋力划水。长期以来，他这种同逆境作斗争的方法常常令人生疑。他乞求着，谄媚着，就像个小丑。但这都是发生在他没有获得版税和成为文学巨匠之前。就让这个从来不为混饭吃而粗制滥造的作者，率先向别人发难吧！

这倒不是说伏尔泰会担心砸向他的多余的砖块。在他投身于与愚蠢做斗争的漫长而繁忙的一生中，经历了无数次挫败，以至于不再顾及当众挨打或是挨了人家扔来的香蕉皮这类小事。他是一个大无畏的、充满无限斗志的勇士。如果他今天必须在陛下的监狱里打发日子，说不定明天就会在曾经失势的同一个宫廷里谋到一个名声显赫的职位。如果他的一生都必须被迫去听那些愤怒的乡村牧师骂他是基督教的敌人，那么，在塞满了旧情书的碗橱的某个角落里，说不定会扔着教皇颁发给他的一枚漂亮的勋章！这难道不能证明他既遭到了教会的非难，也受到了教会的抬举吗？

这并不足为奇。

与此同时，他决计纵情享受人生之乐，日复一日、年复一年地享受色彩斑斓、光怪陆离的生活。

伏尔泰出身于中等偏上阶层。

began to write,he exchanged the plebeian Francois Marie Arouet for the more aristocratic Francois Mane de Voltaire,but how and where he hit upon this surname is still a good deal of a mystery. He had a brother and a sister. The sister,who took care of him after his mother's death,he loved very sincerely. The brother,on the other hand,a faithful priest of the Jansenist denomination,full of zeal and rectitude,bored him to distraction and was one of the reasons why he spent as little time as possible underneath the paternal shingles.

Father Arouet was no fool and soon discovered that his little"Zozo"promised to be a handful. Wherefore he sent him to the Jesuits that he might become versed in Latin hexameters and Spartan discipline. The good fathers did their best by him. They gave their spindly-legged pupil a sound training in the rudiments of both the dead and living tongues. But they found it impossible to eradicate a certain bump of"queerness"which from the very beginning had set this child apart from the other scholars.

At the age of seventeen they willingly let him go,and to please his father,young Francois then took up the study of the law. Unfortunately one could not read all day long. There were the long hours of the lazy evenings. These hours Francois whiled away either writing funny little pieces for the local newspapers of reading his latest literary compositions to his cronies in the nearest coffee-house. Two centuries ago such a life was generally believed to lead straight to perdition. Father Arouet fully appreciated the danger his son was running. He went to one of his many influential friends and obtained for M. Francois a position as secretary to the French Legation at the Hague. The Dutch capital,then as now,was exasperatingly dull. Out of sheer boredom Voltaire began a love affair with the not particularly attractive daughter of a terrible old woman who was a society reporter. The lady,who hoped to marry her darling to a more promising party,rushed to the French minister and asked him to please remove this dangerous Romeo before the whole city

由于没有更合适的称谓，我们不妨称他父亲为开设私人信托公司的人。他是许多达官显贵的忠实心腹，为打点他们法律和财务上的利益而操劳。因此，年轻的阿鲁艾（这是他家的姓）对于比自己条件稍好些的阶层比较熟悉，这使他在后来的生活中超过了大多数文学对手。他的母亲是德·奥玛尔德小姐。她曾经是个穷姑娘，没给丈夫带来哪怕一分钱的嫁妆。但是她的姓前冠有一个小小的“德”字，所有中产阶级的法国人（和一般欧洲人，特别是为数不少的美国人）对此都肃然起敬，她丈夫觉得能获得这样的奖赏已经是三生有幸。至于他们的儿子伏尔泰，也浸润在贵族出身的外祖父给他带来的荣耀里。他刚开始写作，就把带有平民色彩的弗朗西斯·玛丽·阿鲁艾改为更有贵族气派的弗朗西斯·玛丽·德·伏尔泰，但是他如何、在什么地方改的这个姓，仍是不解之谜。他有一个哥哥和一个姐姐。伏尔泰非常喜欢姐姐，她在母亲去世后一直照料他。他哥哥是约翰逊教派的虔诚牧师，充满热诚，为人耿直，但伏尔泰讨厌他，这也是他尽量不在父亲的庇护下生活的一个原因。

父亲阿鲁艾并不傻，很快就发现他的小儿子实在是个大麻烦。为此，他把儿子送到耶稣会，期望他精通拉丁文六步韵诗，学会遵守斯巴达式的纪律。神父们十分称职，尽他们最大的努力引导他，给他们这个腿部细长的学生进行扎实且全面的训练，帮助他掌握已经消亡和仍然存在的语言的基本功。但是他们感到实在没法根除这孩子身上具备的那种使他与其他学生格格不入的“古怪”才能。

伏尔泰17岁的时候，教士们都很乐意让他离开。为了取悦父亲，年轻的伏尔泰开始学习法律。不幸的是，一个人不可能没日没夜地看书。晚上总有许多闲散的

knew about the scandal. His Excellency had troubles enough of his own and was not eager for more. He bundled his secretary into the next stagecoach for Paris and Francois,without a job,once more found himself at the mercy of his father.

In this emergency Maitre Arouet bethought himself of an expedient which was often used by such Frenchmen as had a friend at court. He asked and obtained a"lettre de cachet"and placed his son before the choice of enforced leisure in a jail or industrious application in a lawschool. The son said that he would prefer the latter and promised that he would be a model of industry and application. He was as good as his word and applied himself to the happy life of a free lance pamphleteer with such industry that the whole town talked about it. This was not according to the agreement with his papa and the latter was entirely within his rights when he decided to send his son away from the flesh-pots of the Seine and packed him off to a friend in the country,where the young man was to remain for a whole year.

There,with twenty-four hours leisure each day of the week (Sundays included) Voltaire began the study of letters in all seriousness and composed the first of his plays. After twelve months of fresh air and a very healthy monotony,he was allowed to return to the scented atmosphere of the capital and at once made up for lost time by a series of lampoons upon the Regent,a nasty old man who deserved all that was said about him but did not like this publicity the least little bit. Hence,a second period of exile in the country,followed by more scribbling and at last a short visit to the Bastille. But prison in those days,that is to say,prison for young gentlemen of Voltaire's social prominence,was not a bad place. One was not allowed to leave the premises but otherwise did pretty much as one pleased. And it was just what Voltaire needed. A lonely cell in the heart of Paris gave him a chance to do some serious work. When he was released,he had finished several

空余时间。伏尔泰不是为地方报纸撰写一些滑稽风趣的小文章，就是在附近的咖啡店为他的密友们朗读他的文学新作，以此来消磨时光。两个世纪以前，这种生活被大家认为会导致堕落、沉沦。父亲阿鲁艾充分意识到了儿子所冒的风险。他求助于一个颇有势力的朋友，为伏尔泰在海牙的法国使馆里谋得一份秘书工作。荷兰的首都，那时就和现在一样如出一辙，不是一般的索然无味。出于极度的无聊，伏尔泰开始和一个不算特别漂亮的女孩谈恋爱了。这女孩的母亲是一个社团记者、一个令人生畏的老女人。这位夫人希望把自己的女儿嫁给一个更有前途和出息的党徒，见状赶忙求助于法国大使，请求他在整个城市知道这件丑闻之前，就驱逐这个相当危险的罗密欧。大使阁下自己已经是泥菩萨过河，当然不想再惹上更多麻烦。于是，他把自己的秘书打发到下一辆前往巴黎的公共马车上。伏尔泰丢掉了工作，不得不再次落入父亲的掌控之中。

在此情急之时，阿鲁艾想到了一个常被那些有朋友在法庭工作的法国人使用的权宜之计。他申请并得到了一封“有封印的密信”，逼迫他儿子作出选择：要么到监狱去享受冷清和无聊，要么到法律学校发愤图强。儿子选择了后一种出路，并保证做一个勤奋和用功的典范。他倒是真的言而有信，投入到自由创作的幸福生活中，惹得整个镇子的人都对他的勤奋议论纷纷。这当然违背了与父亲达成的协议，惹得父亲大为光火，于是父亲在自己的权力范围之内，把儿子从塞纳河的欢场里揪出来，送到乡下的一位朋友家里待了一年。

在乡下，天天都有24小时的闲暇时间（包括星期日在内），伏尔泰开始非常认

plays and these were performed with such tremendous success that one of them broke all records of the eighteenth century and ran for forty-five nights in succession.

This brought him some money (which he needed badly) but it also established his reputation as a wit,a most unfortunate thing for a young man who still has to make his career. For hereafter he was held responsible for every joke that enjoyed a few hours' popularity on the boulevards and in the coffee-houses. And incidentally it was the reason why he went to England and took a post-graduate course in liberal statesmanship.

It happened in the year 1725. Voltaire had (or had not) been funny about the old but otherwise useless family of de Rohan. The Chevalier de Rohan felt that his honor had been assailed and that something must be done about it. Of course,it was impossible for a descendant of the ancient rulers of Brittany to fight a duel with the son of a notary public and the Chevalier delegated the work of revenge to his flunkeys.

One night Voltaire was dining with the Duc de Sully,one of his father's customers,when he was told that some one wished to speak to him outside. He went to the door,was fallen upon by the lackeys of my Lord de Rohan and was given a sound beating. The next day the story was all over the town. Voltaire,even on his best days,looked like the caricature of a very ugly little monkey. What with his eyes blackened and his head bandaged,he was a fit subject for half a dozen popular reviews. Only something very drastic could save his reputation from an untimely death at the hands of the comic papers. And as soon as raw beefsteak had done its work,M. de Voltaire sent his witnesses to M. le Chevalier de Rohan and began his preparation

■ 伏尔泰去英国上学

真地学习文学并且创作出了他的第一个剧本。12个月的清新空气和获益匪浅的健康而单调的生活之后，他被准许回到花天酒地的首都。他马上写了一系列针对摄政王的讽刺诗来弥补失去的光阴。其实，对于那个恶心的老家伙，无论怎么骂他都不过分，但是他一点也不喜欢这样的宣传。于是，伏尔泰这些胡言乱语给他招来了第二次流放，最后还不得不去巴士底狱待上一小段时间。但是当时的监狱，也就是说为像伏尔泰这样在社会上颇有名望的年轻绅士准备的监狱，并不太糟糕。囚犯不允许擅自离开房间，但是可以随心所欲地做自己喜欢的事。这正中伏尔泰的下怀。巴黎中心的宁静监牢为他提供了一些从事严肃工作的机会。他被释放的时候已经完成了好几个剧本，都取得了相当大的成功，其中一个打破了18世纪的所有纪录，接连上演了45个晚上。

这不仅使他赚到了一笔钱（他非常需要的），而且使他获得了才子的名号，这对于一个还在奔前程的年轻人来说是最不幸的，因为从此以后，他得为在林荫大道或是咖啡馆里开的每一个能在几小时内博得人们欢迎的玩笑负责。顺便提一句，这也是他前往英国进修自由党政治家研究生班的原因。

这事发生在1725年，伏尔泰对古老而又无用的罗汉家族开了（或者根本没开）几句玩笑，罗汉家族的骑士感到尊严受到了严重冒犯，决定必须给伏尔泰一个教

for mortal combat by an intensive course in fencing.

Alas! when the morning came for the great fight,Voltaire once more found himself behind the bars. De Rohan,a cad unto the last,had given the duel away to the police,and the battling scribe remained in custody until,provided with a ticket for England,he was sent traveling in a northwestern direction and was told not to return to France until requested to do so by His Majesty's gendarmes.

Four whole years Voltaire spent in and near London. The British kingdom was not exactly a Paradise,but compared to France,it was a little bit of Heaven.

A royal scaffold threw its shadow over the land. The thirtieth of January of the year 1649 was a date remembered by all those in high places. What had happened to sainted King Charles might (under slightly modified circumstances) happen to any one else who dared to set himself above the law. And as for the religion of the country,of course the official church of the state was supposed to enjoy certain lucrative and agreeable advantages,but those who preferred to worship elsewhere were left in peace and the direct influence of the clerical officials upon the affairs of state was,compared to France,almost negligible. Confessed Atheists and certain bothersome non-conformists might occasionally succeed in getting themselves into jail,but to a subject of King Louis XV the general condition of life in England must have seemed wellnigh perfect.

In 1729,Voltaire returned to France,but although he was permitted to live in Paris,he rarely availed himself of that privilege. He was like a scared animal,willing to accept bits of sugar from the hands of his friends,but forever on the alert and ready to escape at the slightest sign of danger. He worked very hard. He wrote prodigiously and with a sublime disregard for dates and facts,and choosing for himself subjects which ran all the way from Lima,Peru,to Moscow,Russia,he composed a series of such learned and popular

训。当然，让一个布列塔尼古代统治者的后代去和一个公证员的儿子进行决斗有点说不过去，于是这位骑士把复仇的任务交给了他的仆人们。

一天晚上，伏尔泰正与父亲的一个主顾苏里公爵一起吃饭，这时，有人告诉他外面有人要找他聊几句。他刚走到门口，就被罗汉爵士的仆人们狠狠地教训了一顿。第二天，这件事在镇子里不胫而走。就在他最风光的时候，伏尔泰看上去都像一只漫画上的丑陋的小猴子。尤其是他鼻青眼肿，头上缠满了绷带，便成为一些大众传媒津津乐道的谈资笑料。只有采取一种毅然决然的方法才能挽救他，使他不至于被漫画新闻弄得声名狼藉。在吃下去的生牛排的作用下，伏尔泰派了中间人去见罗汉骑士，然后开始刻苦地练习击剑，准备一场生死之战。

老天！当大战之日的早晨来临时，伏尔泰再次被送进了监狱。罗汉这个下流之辈，竟然把这场决斗转交给了警察。于是，决斗的勇士被监禁起来，直到拿到了一张去英国的船票，伏尔泰被流放到西北地区，并被严正告诫：没有得到陛下的宪兵的许可，他就不准返回法国。

伏尔泰在伦敦和伦敦的周边待了整整四年。不列颠王国并不是个完全意义上的天堂，但和法国比较起来，还算个小天堂。

王家断头台给这块土地投下了一片阴影。1649年1月30日是那些达官贵人永远难忘的日子。在死去的查理国王身上发生的事，同样会在任何胆敢凌驾于法律之上的人身上发生。至于国家的宗教，官方办的教堂必然要享受某种丰厚的礼遇和优待，但是拥有其他信仰的人也毫发无损。与法国相比，神职人员对国家事务的直接

histories,tragedies and comedies that at the age of forty he was by far the most successful man of letters of his time.

Followed another episode which was to bring him into contact with a different kind of civilization.

In distant Prussia,good King Frederick,yawning audibly among the yokels of his rustic court,sadly pined for the companionship of a few amusing people. He felt a tremendous admiration for Voltaire and for years he had tried to induce him to come to Berlin. But to a Frenchman of the year 1750 such a migration seemed like moving into the wilds of Virginia and it was not until Frederick had repeatedly raised the ante that Voltaire at last condescended to accept.

He traveled to Berlin and the fight was on. Two such hopeless egotists as the Prussian king and the French playwright could not possibly hope to live under one and the same roof without coming to hate each other. After two years of sublime disagreement,a violent quarrel about nothing in particular drove Voltaire back to what he felt inclined to call"civilization."

But he had learned another useful lesson. Perhaps he was right,and the French poetry of the Prussian king was atrocious. But His Majesty's attitude upon the subject of religious liberty left nothing to be desired and that was more than could be said of any other European monarch.

And when at the age of almost sixty Voltaire returned to his native land,he was in no mood to accept the brutal sentences by which the French courts tried to maintain order without some very scathing words of protest. All his life he had been greatly angered by man's unwillingness to use that divine spark of intelligence which the Lord on the sixth day of creation had bestowed upon the most sublime product of His handiwork. He

干预几乎不足挂齿。自认为是无神论者的人和某些老惹事的不信教的人，偶尔可能会被关到监狱里，不过对于路易十五的臣民们来说，英国的生活状况一般来说还是相当令人满意的。

1729年，伏尔泰回到法国，虽然获准可以在巴黎生活，但是他很少享受这种特权。他像一只惊慌失措的动物，乐意接受朋友们的施舍，哪怕只是一块白糖，却总是保持警觉，稍微觉察到一点风吹草动就会逃之夭夭。他努力地工作，保持高产，完全对时间和现实不管不顾，自己选定从秘鲁的利马到俄国的莫斯科的题材，写出了一系列内涵丰富、广受好评的历史剧、悲剧和喜剧。40岁时，他已经是名噪一时的文学家了。

接下来发生的另一个插曲，使伏尔泰接触到了另一种不同的文明。

在遥远的普鲁士，善良的腓特烈国王在乡村宫廷里被一帮乡巴佬簇拥着，肆无忌惮地打着呵欠，非常想找几个人陪他寻欢作乐。他对伏尔泰倾慕多时，多年来一直想邀请伏尔泰来柏林。但是对于1750年的法国人来说，这样的移居无异于迁到弗吉尼亚的蛮荒之地，直到腓特烈一再提高给他的待遇，伏尔泰这才屈尊赴约。

他来到柏林，矛盾也就随之开始了。普鲁士国王和这个法国剧作家都是不可救药的个人主义者，不可能在同一个屋檐下却相安无事。两年的拉锯战之后，一场毫无来由的争吵迫使伏尔泰回到了他奉为“文明”的法国。

不过伏尔泰收获颇丰。也许他是对的，普鲁士国王写的法国诗歌的确很蹩脚。但是国王陛下对宗教自由的态度是无可指责的，这就是他比欧洲任何君主更胜一筹

(Voltaire) hated and loathed stupidity in every shape,form and manner. The"infamous enemy"against whom he directed most of his anger and whom,Cato-like,he was forever threatening to demolish,this"infamous enemy"was nothing more or less than the lazy stupidity of the mass of the people who refused to think for themselves as long as they had enough to eat and to drink and a place to sleep.

From the days of his earliest childhood he had felt himself pursued by a gigantic machine which seemed to move through sheer force of lethargy and combined the cruelty of Huitzilopochtli with the relentless persistency of Juggernaut. To destroy or at least upset this contraption become the obsession of his old years,and the French government,to give this particular devil his due,ably assisted him in his efforts by providing the world with a choice collection of legal scandais.

The first one occurred in the year 1761.

In the town of Toulouse in the southern part of France there lived a certain Jean Calas,a shop-keeper and a Protestant. Toulouse had always been a pious city. No Protestant was there allowed to hold office or to be a doctor or a lawyer,a bookseller or a midwife. No Catholic was permitted to keep a Protestant servant. And on August 23rd and 24th of each year the entire community celebrated the glorious anniversary of the massacre of St. Bartholomew with a solemn feast of praise and thanksgiving.

Notwithstanding these many disadvantages,Calas had lived all his life in complete harmony with his neighbors. One of his sons had turned Catholic,but the father had continued to be on friendly terms with the boy and had let it be known that as far as he was concerned,his children were entirely free to choose whatever religion pleased them best.

But there was a skeleton in the Calas closet. That was Marc Antony,the oldest son. Marc was an unfortunate fellow. He wanted to be a lawyer but that career was closed

的地方。

直到将近60岁的时候，伏尔泰重回故土，他没有心情去接受严酷的判决，而法国的法庭正是靠这种不容任何反抗的判决来维持秩序的。上帝在创世纪的第六天赠予了他最伟大的作品（人类）以神圣的智慧之光，而人类偏偏弃之如敝屣，这使伏尔泰一生都耿耿于怀。他（伏尔泰）憎恶以各种形式、样子和态度表现出来的愚蠢。他把大部分愤恨都发泄在那些“邪恶的敌人”身上，像古罗马的政治家一样，总是威胁要消灭它。这个“邪恶的敌人”不是别的什么，就是“平常人的懒惰和愚蠢”。只要有吃有喝，有地方睡觉，这些人就从来不会思考，哪怕是为了他们自己。

从孩提时代开始，伏尔泰就感到自己被一架巨大的机器驱使着，这架机器看上去被一种毫无生气的力量操纵着，把阿兹特克人崇拜的神灵的残酷和“毁灭之王”毫无怜悯心的固执联系在了一起。摧毁或至少推翻这个稀奇古怪的东西，成了他老年时代孜孜以求的梦想。法国政府给了这个特殊的恶魔（伏尔泰）应有的一切，在这个世界上制造了种种法律上的丑闻，着实大大地帮了伏尔泰一把。

第一件事发生在1761年。

在法国南部的图卢兹城里，住着一个叫吉恩·卡拉斯的店主，他是个新教徒。图卢兹一直是个虔诚的城市，那儿的新教徒不许担任公职，也不许从事医生、律师、书商或是助产士的职业，天主教的家庭里不准雇用信奉新教的仆人。每年的8月23日和24日，全体居民举行庄严神圣的感恩宴来纪念大肆屠杀新教徒的圣巴托洛

to Protestants. He was a devout Calvinist and refused to change his creed. The mental conflict had caused an attack of melancholia and this in time seemed to prey upon the young man's mind. He began to entertain his father and mother with long recitations of Hamlet's well known soliloquy. He took long solitary walks. To his friends he often spoke of the superior advantages of suicide.

This went on for some time and then one night,while the family was entertaining a friend,the poor boy slipped into his father's storeroom,took a piece of packing rope and hanged himself from the doorpost.

There his father found him a few hours later,his coat and vest neatly folded upon the counter.

The family was in despair. In those days the body of a person who had committed suicide was dragged nude and face downward through the streets of the town and was hanged on a gibbet outside the gate to be eaten by the birds.

The Calas were respectable folks and hated to think of such a disgrace. They stood around and talked of what they ought to do and what they were going to do until one of the neighbors,hearing the commotion,sent for the police,and the scandal spreading rapidly,their street was immediately filled with an angry crowd which loudly clamored for the death of old Calas"because he had murdered his son to prevent him from becoming a Catholic."

In a little town all things are possible and in a provincial nest of eighteenth century France,with boredom like a black funeral pall hanging heavily upon the entire community,the most idiotic and fantastic yarns were given credence with a sigh of profound and eager relief.

The high magistrates,fully aware of their duty under such suspicious circumstances,at once arrested the entire family,their guests and their servants and every one who had

缪大惨案。

尽管环境恶劣艰险，卡拉斯一辈子倒是和左邻右舍相处融洽。他的一个儿子投奔了天主教，但是父亲仍然善待他的儿子，还让人们知道，就他自己来说，他家的孩子完全有自由皈依自己喜爱的宗教。

但是吉恩家还是发生了一件不可外扬的丑事，那就是他的大儿子麦克·安东尼。麦克是个不幸的人。他想成为一名律师，但是新教徒无法涉足这个职业。他是虔诚的加尔文主义者，还拒绝背叛自己的信条。思想上的强烈斗争使他患上了忧郁症，这位年轻人的心志也渐渐消殒。他开始大段大段地背诵哈姆雷特的著名独白来取悦父母，一个人长时间踯躅独行，并常常向朋友们宣扬自杀的好处。

这样持续了一段时间，直到一天晚上，家里人正在招待一个朋友，这个可怜的孩子悄然溜进父亲的储藏室，用一根打包的绳子在门梁上结束了自己的生命。

几小时以后，他父亲才发现了他，他的外套和衬衣都叠得整整齐齐放在柜子上。

全家人都陷入了绝望。那个年代，自杀的人要被扒得精光，脸朝下地被人拖着穿过城里的街道，然后绑在门外的绞刑架上喂鸟。

卡拉斯一家是体面人，当然不甘蒙羞。他们站成一圈，讨论应该做什么和准备做什么。这时，一个邻居听到了这场混乱，向警察通报了。丑闻迅速传开，这条街上马上挤满了愤怒的人群，他们大声呼喊要求处死老卡拉斯："因为他为了阻止儿子加入天主教，就干脆把他杀了。"

recently been seen in or near the Calas home. They dragged their prisoners to the town hall,put them in irons and threw them into the dungeons provided for the most desperate criminals. The next day they were examined. All of them told the same story. How Marc Antony had come into the house in his usual spirits,how he had left the room,how they thought that he had gone for one of his solitary walks,etc.,etc.

By this time,however,the clergy of the town of Toulouse had taken a hand in the matter and with their help the dreadful news of this bloodthirsty Huguenot,who had killed one of his own children because he was about to return to the true faith,had spread far and wide throughout the land of Languedoc.

Those familiar with modern methods of detecting crime might think that the authorities would have spent that day inspecting the scene of the murder. Marc Antony enjoyed quite a reputation as an athlete. He was twenty-eight and his father was sixty-three. The chances of the father having hanged his son from his own doorpost without a struggle were small indeed. But none of the town councilors bothered about such little details. They were too busy with the body of the victim. For Marc Antony,the suicide,had by now assumed the dignity of a martyr and for three weeks his corpse was kept at the town hall and thereupon it was most solemnly buried by the White penitents who for some mysterious reason had made the defunct Calvinist an ex-officio member of their own order and who conducted his embalmed remains to the Cathedral with the circumstance and the pomp usually reserved for an archbishop or an exceedingly rich patron of the local Basilica.

During these three weeks,from every pulpit in town,the good people of Toulouse had been urged to bring whatever testimony they could against the person of Jean Calas and his family and finally,after the case had been thoroughly thrashed out in the public press,and five months after the suicide,the trial began.

在小城镇里一切都有可能，而且在18世纪法国的乡下，无聊就像一个黑色的棺材，重重地压在人们的身上和心上，因而最光怪陆离的奇谈也不会受到怀疑，至少它们能使人们如释重负，缓解心中的压力。

高级地方官员完全明白在这种可疑的状况下自己的职责所在，于是立即逮捕了卡拉斯全家、他们的客人、佣人及最近去过或在卡拉斯家附近出现过的人。他们把犯人送到镇公所，给他们戴上镣铐，扔到专门为十恶不赦的囚犯而设的地牢里，第二天对他们进行盘问和调查。所有人的口供如出一辙，麦克·安东尼怎样不露声色地进了家门，怎样离开了房间，他们怎样一致认定他是去一个人散步，等等。

然而，这时图卢兹城的教士们却火上浇油，拜他们所赐，可怕的消息蔓延开来：这个嗜血成性的胡格诺派教徒就因为自己的儿子要皈依真正的信仰，就索性把他干掉了。

熟悉现代侦破方法的人们会认为，官方一定会在当天就勘察谋杀现场。麦克·安东尼身强力壮，像个运动员，这是众人皆知的事实。他28岁，父亲63岁，他父亲不经任何搏斗就轻而易举地把他挂到门柱上吊死，这种情况发生的可能性实在是微乎其微。但是没有一个镇议会议员为这微不足道的细节费尽思量，他们忙着处理受害者的尸体。因为麦克·安东尼的自杀被认为应当受到殉教者的待遇，他的尸体在礼堂里停放了三个星期，被身着白衣服的苦修会修士按最隆重的仪式埋葬了。他们出于某些不可思议的原因而把这个已死去的加尔文主义者当成了自己组织的成员，把涂抹了防腐剂的尸体隆重地送到大教堂，这种仪式通常只有大主教或当地天

One of the judges in a moment of great lucidity suggested that the shop of the old man be visited to see whether such a suicide as he described would have been possible,but he was overriden and with twelve votes against one,Calas was sentenced to be tortured and to be broken on the wheel.

He was taken to the torture room and was hanged by his wrists until his feet were a meter from the ground. Then his body was stretched until the limbs were"drawn from their sockets."(I am copying from the official report.) As he refused to confess to a crime which he had not committed,he was then taken down and was forced to swallow such vast quantities of water that his body had soon"swollen to twice its natural size. "As he persisted in his diabolical refusal to confess his guilt,he was placed on a tumbril and was dragged to the place of execution where his arms and legs were broken in two places by the executioner. During the next two hours,while he lay helpless on the block,magistrates and priests continued to bother him with their questions. With incredible courage the old man continued to proclaim his innocence. Until the chief justice,exasperated by such obstinate lying,gave him up as a hopeless case and ordered him to be strangled to death.

The fury of the populace had by this time spent itself and none of the other members of the family were killed. The widow,deprived of all her goods,was allowed to go into retirement and starve as best she could in the company of her faithful maid. As for the children,they were sent to different convents with the exception of the youngest who had been away at school at Nimes at the time of his brother's suicide and who had wisely fled to the territory of the sovereign city of Geneva.

The case had attracted a great deal of attention. Voltaire in his castle of Ferney (conveniently built near the frontier of Switzerland so that a few minutes' walk could carry him to foreign ground) heard of it but at first refused to be interested. He was forever at

主教大教堂最富有的资助人才有资格享受。

在这三个星期当中，城里每处布告都一再敦促图卢兹虔诚的人们提供揭发吉恩·卡拉斯和他们家的证据，在大众报刊彻底曝光了这个案件，即麦克自杀了五个月之后，审判终于开始了。

当时，一个审判官灵机一动，提出应该到这位老人的铺子里去看看，他所描述的那种自杀是否有发生的可能性，但他的提议被12票对1票否决了，卡拉斯被宣判施以车裂的酷刑。

卡拉斯被带到刑讯室吊起来，脚离地有一米高，然后四肢被拉到“脱臼为止”（我是抄自官方的报道）。由于他拒不承认自己根本没有犯过的罪行，就又被放了下来，灌了大量的水，一会儿，他的身体就肿胀得比“原来大了一倍”。他还是否认自己的罪行，就又被抬上死囚车送到刑场，在那儿刽子手要把他的胳膊和腿都撕成两半。在后来的两个小时里，他心灰意冷地躺在铁砧上，地方官和教士们还继续喋喋不休地质问这个，调查那个。老人以令人难以置信的勇气，继续为自己的无罪而辩护。首席执行官被这种固执的谎话弄得火冒三丈，便不再审理这个不可救药的案子，直接下令把他绞死。

直到这时，众人的愤怒才平息下来，他家里的人逃过一劫。卡拉斯的遗孀被剥夺了所有财产，被允许隐姓埋名，在忠心耿耿的佣人陪伴下，忍饥挨饿地度日。孩子们全都送到修道院，只有最小的孩子在哥哥自杀的时候正在尼姆读书，他很明智地跑到了主权城市日内瓦的境内。

loggerheads with the Calvinist ministers of Geneva who regarded his private little theater which stood within sight of their own city as a direct provocation and the work of Satan. Hence Voltaire,in one of his supercilious moods,wrote that he could not work up any enthusiasm for this so-called Protestant martyr,for if the Catholics were bad,how much worse those terribly bigoted Huguenots,who boycotted his plays! Besides,it seemed impossible to him (as to a great many other people) that twelve supposedly respectable judges would have condemned an innocent man to such a terrible death without very good reason.

But a few days later the sage of Ferney,who kept open house to all comers and no questions asked,had a visit from an honest merchant from Marseilles who had happened to be in Toulouse at the time of the trial and who was able to give him some first-hand information. Then at last he began to understand the horror of the crime that had been committed and from that moment on he could think of nothing else.

There are many sorts of courage,but a special order of merit is reserved for those rare souls who,practically alone,dare to face the entire established order of society and who loudly cry for justice when the high courts of the land have pronounced sentence and when the community at large has accepted their verdict as equitable and just.

Voltaire well knew the storm that would break if he should dare to accuse the court of Toulouse of a judicial murder,and he prepared his case as carefully as if he had been a professional attorney. He interviewed the Calas boy who had escaped to Geneva. He wrote to every one who could possibly know something of the inside of the case. He hired counsel to examine and if possible to correct his own conclusions,lest his anger and his indignation carry him away. And when he felt sure of his ground,he opened his campaign.

First of all he induced every man of some influence whom he knew within the realm of France (and he knew most of them) to write to the Chancellor of the Kingdom and ask for

这个案子引起了极大关注。伏尔泰居住在费内的城堡里（城堡建得离瑞士的边界很近，只有几分钟的路程就可以出国），听到了这个案件，一开始他拒绝深究其中缘由。他一直与瑞士信奉加尔文主义的牧师们不和，他们也把伏尔泰建在他们自己城里的那个小小的私人戏院视为一种明目张胆的挑衅，是恶魔故意搞的鬼。因此，伏尔泰怀着孤傲的心境，提笔写道：这个所谓的新教殉难者并不能激起他的任何兴趣，因为如果天主教不道德的话，那么一意孤行的胡格诺教徒拒绝看他的戏剧，就更不可饶恕！此外，在他看来（如同大多数人的看法一样），那12个似乎很受人尊敬的法官，要说他们无缘无故就把一个无辜的人判处死刑，似乎不太可能。

几天后，费内的这位来者不拒、极其好客的圣人遇到了从马赛来的一个诚实商人，这个商人在审判期间正好在图卢兹，他向伏尔泰提供了一些第一手的资料。终于，伏尔泰开始觉察到这一已经犯下的罪行的可怕后果，从此以后，这成了他心里的头等大事。

勇气有许多种，但那些敢于独自挑战整个社会的既定规则，并且在最高法庭已作了宣判，被整个社会认为是合法和公正的时候，仍敢大声疾呼正义的人，才是最值得敬佩的。

伏尔泰清楚地知道，如果他敢于控告图卢兹法庭犯有司法谋杀罪，大风暴就会降临。他像一个职业律师那样，精心准备自己的诉讼。他访问了卡拉斯家那个跑到日内瓦的孩子。他给每个可能知道内情的人写信。他还雇用了辩护人来检查和修改他的结论，以免自己由于满腔怒火和义愤而丧失了理智。等他觉得证据确凿时，就

a revision of the Calas case. Then he set about to find the widow and as soon as she had been located,he ordered her to be brought to Paris at his own expense and engaged one of the best known lawyers to look after her. The spirit of the woman had been completely broken. She vaguely prayed that she might get her daughters out of the convent before she died. Beyond that,her hopes did not extend.

Then he got into communication with the other son who was a Catholic,made it possible for him to escape from his school and to join him in Geneva. And finally he published all the facts in a short pamphlet entitled"Original Documents Concerning the Calas Family,"which consisted of letters written by the survivors of the tragedy and contained no reference whatsoever to Voltaire himself.

Afterwards,too,during the revision of the case,he remained carefully behind the scenes,but so well did he handle his publicity campaign that soon the cause of the Calas family was the cause of all families in all countries of Europe and that thousands of people everywhere (including the King of England and the Empress of Russia) contributed to the funds that were being raised to help the defense.

Eventually Voltaire gained his victory,but not until he had fought one of the most desperate battle of his entire career.

The throne of France just then was occupied by Louis XV of unsavory memory. Fortunately his mistress hated the Jesuits and all their works (including the Church) with a most cordial hatred and was therefore on the side of Voltaire. But the King loved his ease above all other things and was greatly annoyed at all the fuss made about an obscure and dead Protestant. And of course as long as His Majesty refused to sign a warrant for a new trial,the Chancellor would not

■ 卡拉斯

开始了这场战斗。

首先，伏尔泰推动每一个在法国有影响的人（他认识其中的大部分人）给国务大臣写信，要求重审卡拉斯案件。然后，他开始寻找卡拉斯的遗孀；找到她以后，又慷慨解囊把她带到巴黎，聘请了一个最有名的律师照看她。这个女人的精神已经完全崩溃了，她呆呆地祈祷着，在她死之前把女儿们从修道院里领出来。除此之外，她别无所求。

然后，伏尔泰又和卡拉斯那个信奉天主教的儿子取得了联系，帮助他逃出学校，到日内瓦找他。最后，他把所有的事实以题为《关于卡拉斯家庭的最原始材料》的小册子出版了，这个小册子收录了这场悲剧的幸存者们的书信，一点也没有涉及伏尔泰自己。

后来，在重审这个案件的过程中，伏尔泰还是审慎地躲在幕后。但是他成功地策划了这场宣传战，不久，卡拉斯家的诉讼就成为欧洲所有国家以及其家庭关心的事情，各地成千上万的人（包括英格兰国王和俄国沙皇）都为了帮助被告而积极捐款。

最后，伏尔泰取得了胜利，这是他一生中最艰苦的一仗。

take action,and as long as the Chancellor would not take action,the tribunal of Toulouse was perfectly safe and so strong did they feel themselves that they defied public opinion in a most high-handed fashion and refused to let Voltaire or his lawyers have access to the original documents upon which they had based their conviction.

During nine terrible months,Voltaire kept up his agitation until finally in March of the year 1765 the Chancellor ordered the Tribunal of Toulouse to surrender all the records in the Calas case and moved that there be a new trial. The widow of Jean Calas and her two daughters,who had at last been returned to their mother,were present in Versailles when this decision was made public. A year later the special court which had been ordered to investigate the appeal reported that Jean Calas had been done to death for a crime which he had not committed. By herculean efforts the King was induced to bestow a small gift of money upon the widow and her children. Furthermore the magistrates who had handled the Calas case were deprived of their office and it was politely suggested to the people of Toulouse that such a thing must not happen again.

But although the French government might take a luke-warm view of the incident,the people of France had been stirred to the very depths of their outraged souls. And suddenly Voltaire became aware that this was not the only miscarriage of justice on record,that there were many others who had suffered as innocently as Calas.

In the year 1760 a Protestant country squire of the neighborhood of Toulouse had offered the hospitality of his house to a visiting Calvinist minister. For this hideous crime he had been deprived of his estate and had been sent to the galleys for life. He must have been a terribly strong man for thirteen years later he was still alive. Then Voltaire was told of his plight. He set to work,got the unfortunate man away from the galleys,brought him to Switzerland where his wife and children were being supported by public charity and

当时，声名狼藉的路易十五正好是法国国王。幸亏他的情妇对耶稣会和他们所做的一切（包括教堂在内）深恶痛绝，因此站到了伏尔泰一边。但是国王把享乐看得高于一切，人们对一个已经死去的地位低下的新教徒还在喋喋不休，这使他很恼火。当然，国王只要不签署新的判决，大臣就不敢采取行动；只要大臣不轻举妄动，图卢兹法庭就安然无事。图卢兹自认为很强大，用高压手段阻止伏尔泰和他的律师接近判决的原始档案。

在这恐怖的九个月里，伏尔泰坚持不懈地开展鼓动工作。最后，在1765年3月，大法官要求图卢兹法庭交出所有关于卡拉斯案件的记录，并提议进行新的审判。当这项决定公之于众时，吉恩·卡拉斯的遗孀和终于回到她身边的两个女儿都来到了凡尔赛。一年以后，受命调查这个上诉案件的特别法庭向世人公布说，吉恩·卡拉斯完全是被冤死的。人们经过巨大的努力，总算说服国王赐给卡拉斯的遗孀和孩子们一小笔钱。此外，审判卡拉斯案件的地方官们都引咎辞职，这无异于向图卢兹人民发出警告：下不为例。

虽然法国政府对这件事采取了温和的态度，但是法国人民的内心激起了愤怒。伏尔泰突然意识到这并不是有记录可查的、仅此一件的冤假错案，一定还有许许多多像卡拉斯那样无辜的人蒙受了不白之冤。

1760年，图卢兹附近一个新教徒乡绅在家里盛情款待了一位前来拜访的加尔文派牧师。因为这桩骇人听闻的罪行，他付出了惨重代价，他被剥夺了财产，并被罚终身当划船苦工。他一定是个非常强壮的人，因为13年后他居然还活着。别人告诉

looked after the family until the crown was induced to surrender a part of the confiscated property and the family were given permission to return to their deserted homestead.

Next came the case of Chaumont,a poor devil who had been caught at an open-air meeting of Protestants and who for that crime had been dispatched to the galleys for an indeterminate period,but who now,at the intercession of Voltaire,was set free.

These cases,however,were merely a sort of grewsome hors d'oeuvre to what was to follow.

Once more the scene was laid in Languedoc,that long suffering part of France which after the extermination of the Albigensian and Waldensian heretics had been left a wilderness of ignorance and bigotry.

In a village near Toulouse there lived an old Protestant by the name of Sirven,a most respectable citizen who made a living as an expert in medieval law,a lucrative position at a time when the feudal judicial system had grown so complicated that ordinary rent-sheets looked like an income tax bland.

Sirven had three daughters. The youngest was a harmless idiot,much given to brooding. In March of the year 1764 she left her home. The parents searched far and wide but found no trace of the child until a few days later when the bishop of the district informed the father that the girl had visited him,had expressed a desire to become a nun and was now in a convent.

Centuries of persecution had successfully broken the spirit of the Protestants in that part of France. Sirven humbly answered that everything undoubtedly would be for the best in this worst of all possible worlds and meekly accepted the inevitable. But in the unaccustomed atmosphere of the cloister,the poor child had soon lost the last vestiges of reason and when she began to make a nuisance of herself,she was returned to her own people. She was then in a state of terrible mental depression and in such continual horror

了伏尔泰他的困境。伏尔泰又着手于这项工作，把这个不幸的人从船上弄走，送到瑞士；他妻子儿女也在那儿，靠政府施舍度日。伏尔泰一直照料他们全家，直到政府退还了他们一部分没收的财产，并允许他们回到荒废的家宅为止。

下一个是绍蒙的案件。这个可怜的人在参加新教徒的露天会上被抓了起来。由于这个罪名，他被遣送到船上当无期的划船苦工，但是后来经过伏尔泰的多方斡旋，他被释放了。

然而，这些案件对于下面发生的情况来说，不过是小事一桩。

事情发生的地点还是在法国阿尔比派和沃尔多派异教徒灭绝之后，长期遭受蹂躏的苦难之地朗格多克，那里到处都是无知和偏见的荒野。

在图卢兹附近的一个村庄里，住着一位名叫塞文的老新教徒，他很受人们的尊敬，在中世纪的法律研究方面颇有建树，并以此谋生。在封建司法制度下已经变得非常复杂，连普通的租契看起来都像所得税申报单一样的年代，这种工作能赚大钱。

塞文有三个女儿。最小的是个不谙世事的傻子，专门爱瞎琢磨。1764年3月，她离开了家。父母四处寻找，但是音信全无。几天之后，当地的主教告诉塞文说，他的女儿拜访了他，表示要当修女，现在待在一个女修道院里。

几个世纪的迫害已经使法国这个地方的新教徒的精神完全崩溃了。塞文毕恭毕敬地回答说，在这个最糟糕的世界里，每件事无疑都会有最好的结果，并恭顺地接受了不可避免的命运。但是，在修道院不平常的气氛里，这个可怜的孩子很快就丧

of voices and spooks that her parents feared for her life. A short time afterwards she once more disappeared. Two weeks later her body was fished out of an old well.

At that time Jean Calas was up for trial and the people were in a mood to believe anything that was said against a Protestant. The Sirvens,remembering what had just happened to innocent Jean Calas,decided not to court a similar fate. They fled and after a terrible trip through the Alps,during which one of their grandchildren froze to death,they at last reached Switzerland. They had not left a moment too soon. A few months later,both the father and the mother were found guilty (in their absence) of the crime of having murdered their child and were ordered to be hanged. The daughters were condemned to witness the execution of their parents and thereafter to be banished for life.

A friend of Rousseau brought the case to the notice of Voltaire and as soon as the Calas affair came to an end,he turned his attention to the Sirvens. The wife meanwhile had died. Remained the duty of vindicating the husband. It took exactly seven years to do this. Once again the tribunal of Toulouse refused to give any information or to surrender any documents. Once more Voltaire had to beat the tomtom of publicity and beg money from Frederick of Prussia and Catherine of Russia and Poniatowski of Poland before he could force the crown to take an interest. But finally,in the seventy-eighth years of his own life and in the eighth year of this interminable lawsuit,the Sirvens were exonerated and the survivors were allowed to go back to their homes.

So ended the second case.

The third one followed immediately.

In the month of August of the year 1765 in the town of Abbeville,not far from Amiens,two crucifixes that stood by the side of the road were found broken to pieces by an unknown hand. Three young boys were suspected of this sacrilege and orders were

失了最后一点理智，等她开始遭到所有人的鄙夷时，就被送回到了家人的身边。那时，她的精神非常沮丧，总是害怕人们的声音和魔鬼，她的父母焦急万分。没过多久，她再次失踪了。两个星期后，人们从一口旧井里把她的尸体打捞了出来。

当时，吉恩·卡拉斯的案件正在审理之中，对新教徒的诽谤之词大家都深信不疑。塞文一家还记得发生在无辜的吉恩·卡拉斯身上的悲剧，坚决不想再重蹈覆辙。他们落荒而逃，在穿过阿尔卑斯山的艰险旅行中，他的一个小孙子冻死了。最后，他们还是到达了瑞士。但一切太迟了。几个月之后，父母被扣上残害自己孩子的罪名（在他们逃亡期间），并下令将其绞死。女儿们被判处亲眼看见父母的死刑，然后被终身流放。

卢梭的一个朋友把这个案件告诉了伏尔泰，卡拉斯案件一结束，他就马上投入到塞文一家的案件上。这时塞文的妻子已经死了，剩下的任务只是为她的丈夫辩护。这足足花了整整七年的时间。图卢兹法庭再次拒绝提供任何信息和资料，伏尔泰只好又一次借助宣传的力量，请求普鲁士国王腓特烈二世、俄国女皇叶卡捷琳娜二世、波兰的波尼亚托夫斯基捐款，直到迫使国王过问这件事。但是，最后在伏尔泰78岁那年，也就是他不屈不挠上诉的第八个年头，塞文终于得以昭雪，幸存的家人也获准重返家园。

第二个案件就这样结束了。

第三个案子接踵而来。

1765年8月，在离亚眠城不远的阿布维尔镇子里，两个竖在路边的十字架不知

given for their arrest. One of them escaped and went to Prussia. The others were caught. Of these,the older one,a certain Chevalier de la Barre,was suspected of being an atheist. A copy of the Philosophical Dictionary,that famous work to which all the great leaders of liberal thought had contributed,was found among his books. This looked very suspicious and the judges decided to look into the young man's past. It was true they could not connect him with the Abbeville case but had he not upon a previous occasion refused to kneel down and uncover while a religious procession went by?

De la Barre said yes,but he had been in a hurry to catch a stagecoach and had meant no offense.

Thereupon he was tortured,and being young and bearing the pain less easily than old Calas,he readily confessed that he had mutilated one of the two crucifixes and was condemned to death for"impiously and deliberately walking before the Host without kneeling or uncovering,singing blasphemous songs,tendering marks of adoration to profane books,"and other crimes of a similar nature which were supposed to have indicated a lack of respect for the Church.

The sentence was so barbarous (his tongue was to be torn out with hot irons,his right hand was to be cut off,and he was to be slowly burned to death,and all that only a century and a half ago!) that the public was stirred into several expressions of disapproval. Even if he were guilty of all the things enumerated in the bill of particulars,one could not butcher a boy for a drunken prank! Petitions were sent to the King,ministers were besieged with requests for a respite. But the country was full of unrest and there must be an example,and de la Barre,having undergone the same tortures as Calas,was taken to the scaffold,was decapitated (as a sign of great and particular favor) and his corpse,together with his Philosophical Dictionary and some volumes by our old friend Bayle,were publicly burned by the hangman.

It was a day of rejoicing for those who dreaded the evergrowing influence of the

被谁折断了。三个年轻的男孩子被怀疑犯了如此大逆不道的渎圣罪，所以被下令逮捕起来。其中一个逃到了普鲁士，剩下的两个被抓住了。这两个人当中，年纪大一点的名叫谢瓦利埃·德·拉·巴尔，被怀疑是无神论者。在他的藏书里发现了一本《哲学辞典》，所有自由思想大师的结晶都汇集在这本著名的辞典里。这一点就很值得怀疑，法官们决定调查这个年轻人的成长史。没错，他们确实不能把他和阿布维尔案件联系在一起，但是当初一支宗教队伍路过时，他不是没有下跪和脱帽致敬吗？

巴尔承认了罪行，但是解释说当时他正忙着赶乘一辆公共马车，绝非有意冒犯。

于是，他遭到了严刑拷打，由于年轻，他不如老卡拉斯那样容易忍受折磨，很快就承认自己毁坏了其中的一个十字架。于是，由于他“不虔诚，并故意在圣体前走路而不下跪，不脱帽，并且唱有辱圣灵的歌，对渎神的书表现出喜爱的倾向”，还有如此种种据说不尊敬教会的罪行，被判处了死刑。

判决非常野蛮（要把他的舌头用烧得通红的铁块撕下来，剁掉右手，并要被慢慢烧死，这是一个半世纪之前才会使用的手段！），激起了民众的非议和抨击。即使犯了起诉书中的所有罪行，也不能用这种惨绝人寰的方法来残害一个醉酒后恶作剧的年轻人！人们向国王请愿，政府被请求缓刑的呼声包围了。但是国家局势动荡不安，必须杀一儆百。于是，巴尔经受了和卡拉斯相同的折磨后，被送上断头台斩首了（这表明已给了他巨大且特别的恩惠）。他的尸体连同他的《哲学辞典》及我们的老朋友拜勒的一些书都被刽子手们当众付之一炬。

Sozzinis and the Spinozas and the Descartes. It showed what invariably happened to those ill-guided young men who left the narrow path between the right and the wrong and followed the leadership of a group of radical philosophers.

Voltaire heard this and accepted the challenge. He was fast approaching his eightieth birthday,but he plunged into the case with all his old zeal and with a brain that burned with a clear white flame of outraged decency.

De la Barre had been executed for"blasphemy."First of all,Voltaire tried to discover whether there existed a law by which people guilty of that supposed crime could be condemned to death. He could not find one. Then he asked his lawyer friends. They could not find one. And it gradually dawned upon the community that the judges in their unholy eagerness had"invented"this bit of legal fiction to get rid of their prisoner.

There had been ugly rumors at the time of de la Barre's execution. The storm that now arose forced the judges to be very circumspect and the trial of the third of the youthful prisoners was never finished. As for de la Barre,he was never vindicated. The review of the case dragged on for years and when Voltaire died,no decision had as yet been reached. But the blows which he had struck,if not for tolerance at least against intolerance,were beginning to tell.

The official acts of terror instigated by gossiping old women and senile courts came to an end.

Tribunals that have religious axes to grind are only successful when they can do their work in the dark and are able to surround themselves with secrecy. The method of attack followed by Voltaire was one against which such courts had no means of defense.

Voltaire turned on all the lights,hired a voluminous orchestra,invited the public to attend,and then bade his enemies do their worst.

As a result,they did nothing at all.

对于那些害怕索兹尼、斯宾诺莎和笛卡尔不断增长的影响的人来说，这倒是欢欣鼓舞的一天。它警告那些误入歧途的年轻人，如果偏离了正确与错误之间这条狭窄的道路，进而追随一小撮激进的哲学家，这就是应有的下场。

伏尔泰听说这一切之后，接受了挑战。他马上就要过80岁生日了，但他还是凭借一如既往的热情和燃烧着填膺火焰的头脑，投身到这个案件中。

巴尔由于“亵渎神圣”而被处死。伏尔泰首先要找出是否有这样一条法律，人们犯了假设的罪就能够被处死。他没有找到，接着他又询问他的律师朋友们。他们同样也找不到。真相渐渐大白，那些充满邪恶的狂热的法官“创造”了这样一个合法的“事实”，以便除掉犯人。

在处决巴尔的时候，到处流传着不堪入耳的谣言。现在出现的这场风暴迫使法官们不得不审时度势，对第三个年轻犯人的审判迟而未决。至于巴尔，他一直未能洗冤。复审案件拖拖拉拉持续了很多年，到伏尔泰去世的时候，仍然没有任何定论。但是他发起的这些重拳——它们即使不是为了宽容，至少也是为了反对不宽容——已经开始奏效了。

受爱搬弄是非的老妇人和没落的法庭鼓吹而引发的官方的恐怖行为到此结束了。

怀有宗教私心的法庭只有在黑暗中偷偷摸摸地行事，保留各种秘密，才能获得成功。伏尔泰采取的这种进攻方法，法庭一点办法都没有。

伏尔泰张灯结彩，还雇用了大型乐队，邀请众人来参加，逼得敌人走投无路。

结果，敌人什么也做不了了。

CHAPTER X X VI THE ENCYCLOPEDIA

There are three different schools of statesmanship. The first one teaches a doctrine which reads somewhat as follows:"Our planet is inhabited by poor benighted creatures who are unable to think for themselves,who suffer mental agonies whenever they are obliged to make an independent decision and who therefore can be led astray by the first ward-heeler that comes along. Not only is it better for the world at large that these 'herd people' be ruled by some one who knows his own mind,but they themselves,too,are infinitely happier when they do not have to bother about parliaments and ballot-boxes and can devote all their time to their workshops,their children,their flivvers and their vegetable gardens."

The disciples of this school become emperors,sultans,sachems,sheiks and archbishops and they rarely regard labor unions as an essential part of civilization. They work hard and build roads,barracks,cathedrals and jails.

The adherents of the second school of political thought argue as follows:"The average man is God's noblest invention. He is a sovereign in his own right,unsurpassed in wisdom,prudence and the loftiness of his motives. He is perfectly capable of looking after his own interests,but those committees through which he tries to rule the universe are proverbially slow when it comes to handling delicate affairs of state. Therefore,the masses ought to leave all executive business to a few trusted friends who are not hampered by the immediate necessity of making a living and who can devote all their time to the happiness of the people."

第26章 百科全书

有三种不同的政治家学派。第一种教导的法则大致是这样的："我们这个星球上挤满了可怜而愚昧无知的人，他们不能自行思考，每当需要自己做出决策的时候就头脑发昏，会被第一个游说拉票的政客引入歧途。如果这些民众被某个了解自己思想的人统治，对整个世界来说就不仅是一件好事，而且他们自己也会感到更幸福，因为他们不必再过问议会和投票的事，可以全力关心他们的作坊、孩子、廉价小汽车和菜园子。"

这一学派的信徒成了皇帝、苏丹、巨头、酋长、大主教，他们很少把劳工组织看作文明的主要部分。他们努力工作，修筑公路、营房、大教堂和监狱。

第二种政治思想流派的倡导者持如下观点："普通人是上帝最高尚的发明。上帝本身就是统治者，拥有超凡绝伦的智慧、审慎和高尚的动机。他完全有能力照看好自己的利益，但是他想通过一个委员会来统治世界，可是这个委员会在处理一些棘手的国家问题时慢得出奇却是尽人皆知的。因此，人们应该把所有的管理事务交给几位可以信赖的朋友，他们不会被养家糊口的问题所羁绊，能用全部时间为人们谋求福祉。"

不用说，这种光辉理想的鼓吹者就是寡头政府、独裁者、第一执政官和护国公

Needless to say the apostles of this glorious ideal are the logical candidates for the job of oligarch,dictator,first consul and Lord prorector.

They work hard and build roads and barracks,but the cathedrals they turn into jails.

But there is a third group of people. They contemplate man with the sober eye of science and accept him as he is. They appreciate his good qualities,they understand his limitations. They are convinced from a long observation of past events that the average citizen,when not under the influence of passion or self-interest,tries really very hard to do what is right. But they make themselves no false illusions. They know that the natural process of growth is exceedingly slow,that it would be as futile to try and hasten the tides or the seasons as the growth of human intelligence. They are rarely invited to assume the government of a state,but whenever they have a chance to put their ideas into action,they build roads,improve the jails and spend the rest of the available funds upon schools and universities. For they are such incorrigible optimists that they believe that education of the right sort will gradually rid this world of most of its ancient evils and is therefore a thing that ought to be encouraged at all costs.

And as a final step towards the fulfillment of this ideal,they usually write an encyclopedia.

Like so many other things that give evidence of great wisdom and profound patience,the encyclopedia-habit took its origin in China. The Chinese Emperor K'ang-hi tried to make his subjects happy with an encyclopedia in five thousand and twenty volumes.

Pliny,who introduced encyclopedias in the west,was contented with thirty-seven books.

The first fifteen hundred years of the Christian era produced nothing of the slightest value along this line of enlightenment. A fellow-countryman of Saint Augustine,the African Felix Capella,wasted a great many years of his life composing something which

的候选人。

他们努力工作，修筑公路和营房，却把教堂变成了监狱。

但是第三种人是人民。他们用理性的科学眼光观察人，按照人的真面目去接受他。他们赞赏人的好品质，也了解人的局限性。通过对过去历史的长期观察，他们认为一般人只要不受狂热或自私的影响，的确能竭尽全力地做正确的事情。但是，他们对自己不抱任何虚假的幻想。他们知道生长的自然过程非常缓慢，要想加快人类智慧的增长就像试图加快潮流或季节一样徒劳无功。他们也很少应邀执掌政权，但是每当有机会把他们的思想付诸行动时，他们就开始修筑公路、改造监狱，并把剩余的钱用在学校和大学上。因为他们都是坚定不移的乐观主义者，相信正确的教育将会逐步消除这个世界上遗留下来的大部分古老弊病，所以这样的事业应得到不遗余力的支持。

作为实现这个理想的最后一步，他们通常是写一部百科全书。

像其他许多需要巨大智慧和相当忍耐力的事情一样，撰写百科全书的习惯起源于中国。中国的康熙皇帝想用一部5020卷的百科全书博得臣民的欢心。

第一个将百科全书引进西方的是普林尼，他给世人留下了一部37卷的百科全书《博物志》。

基督教时代的最初1500年，在启蒙方面没有贡献任何有价值的东西。圣奥古斯丁的一个同乡、非洲人菲利克斯·卡佩拉花费了许多年写了一些东西，并把它们奉为汇集了各种知识的宝库。为了使人们更容易记住他提供的许多有趣事情，他采用

he held to be a veritable treasure house of miscellaneous knowledge. In order that people might the more easily retain the many interesting facts which he presented to them,he used poetry. This terrible mass of misinformation was duly learned by heart by eighteen successive generations of medieval children and was held by them to be the last word in the fields of literature,music and science.

Two hundred years later a bishop of Sevilla by the name of Isidore wrote an entirely new encyclopedia and after that,the output increased at the regular rate of two for every hundred years. What has become of them all,I do not know. The book-worm (most useful of domestic animals) has possibly acted as our deliverer. If all these volumes had been allowed to survive,there would not be room for anything else on this earth.

When at last during the first half of the eighteenth century,Europe experienced a tremendous outbreak of intellectual curiosity,the purveyors of encyclopedias entered into a veritable Paradise. Such books,then as now,were usually compiled by very poor scholars who could live on eight dollars a week and whose personal services counted for less than the money spent upon paper and ink. England especially was a great country for this sort of literature and so it was quite natural that John Mills,a Britisher who lived in Paris,should think of translating the successful"Universal Dictionary"of Ephraim Chambers into the French language that he might peddle his product among the subjects of good King Louis and grow rich. For this purpose he associated himself with a German professor and then approached Lebreton,the king's printer,to do the actual publishing. To make a long story short,Lebreton,who saw a chance to make a small fortune,deliberately swindled his partner and as soon as he had frozen Mills and the Teuton doctor out of the enterprise,continued to publish the pirated edition on his own account. He called the forthcoming work the"Encyclopédie ou Dictionnaire Universel des Arts et des Sciences"and issued a series

了诗歌的手法。这一大堆可怕的错误信息却被中世纪以后连续18代子孙记住了，他们把它当成了文学、音乐和科学领域的权威。

200年以后，塞维利亚一个叫艾西多尔的主教撰写了一部崭新的百科全书，从那以后百科全书以每100年2部的平均速度增长。这些书的结局我一无所知。蛀虫（最有用的家养动物）可能担当了我们的搬运工。如果这些书全都保存下来，地球上就没有其他东西的立足之地了。

最后，在18世纪上半叶，欧洲经历了一场声势浩大的求知运动，百科全书的作家们进入了真正的天国。这些书和现在的一样，通常是由贫穷的学者们编写，他们靠每星期8美元生活，个人生活消费比纸和墨水的钱还要少。英国尤其是这种文学的伟大国家，所以生活在巴黎的英国人约翰·米尔斯自然想到要把伊弗雷姆·钱伯斯的成功作品《通用辞典》译成法文，以便向善良的路易国王的臣民兜售他的作品，好捞些油水。出于这个目的，他和一位德国教授合作，然后又接近国王的印刷商雷伯莱顿，让他承担实际的出版工作。长话短说，雷伯莱顿看到了这个发笔小财的商机，就故意欺骗他的合伙人，米尔斯和那个条顿医生刚赶走，他就单独继续出版盗版。他把即将出版的著作称为《艺术与科学万能百科全书辞典》，并印发了一系列颇能吸引顾客的精美书介，预订单很快就填满了。

然后，他雇用了法兰西大学一名哲学教授担任总编辑，买了大量的纸张静待佳音。

不幸的是，撰写一部百科全书并不像雷伯莱顿当初想象的那样简单。教授写

of beautiful prospectuses with such a tremendous selling appeal that the list of subscribers was soon filled.

Then he hired himself a professor of philosophy in the Collège de France to act as his editor-in-chief,bought a lot of paper and awaited results.

Unfortunately,the work of writing an encyclopedia did not prove as simple as Lebreton had thought. The professor produced notes but no articles,the subscribers loudly clamored for Volume I and everything was in great disorder.

In this emergency Lebreton remembered that a"Universal Dictionary of Medicine"which had appeared only a few months before had been very favorably received. He sent for the editor of this medical handbook and hired him on the spot. And so it happened that a mere encyclopedia became the"Encyclopédie. "For the new editor was no one less than Denis Diderot and the work which was to have been a hack job became one of the most important contributions of the eighteenth century towards the sum total of human enlightenment.

Diderot at that time was thirty-seven years old and his life had been neither easy nor happy. He had refused to do what all respectable young Frenchmen were supposed to do and go to a university. Instead,as soon as he could get away from his Jesuit teachers,he had proceeded to Paris to become a man of letters. After a short period of starvation (acting upon the principle that two can go hungry just as cheaply as one) he had married a lady who proved to be a terribly pious woman and an uncompromising shrew,a combination which is by no means as rare as some people seem to believe. But as he was obliged to support her,he had been forced to take all sorts of odd jobs and to compile all sorts of books from"Inquiries concerning Virtue and Merit"to a rather disreputable rehash of Boccaccio's"Decameron. "In his heart,however,this pupil of Bayle remained faithful to

出了一大堆笔记，但没有编成词条，预订者大吵大闹非要得到第一卷，一切变得一团糟。

■ 编写百科全书的人

在这紧急时刻，雷伯莱顿想起了几个月前出版的《医学通用辞典》颇受欢迎。他找到了这部医学手册的编辑，当即雇用了他。这样，一本某一专科的全书变成了《百科全书》。这个新编辑不是别人，正是丹尼斯·狄德罗。这项本来极其乏味的工作成了18世纪启发人类智慧的最重要的贡献之一。

狄德罗那时37岁，他的生活既不轻松也不幸福。他拒绝做所有体面的年轻法国人应做的事，也不想上大学。相反，他一离开耶稣会的老师，就到巴黎当了一个文人。经过短时间的忍饥挨饿的生活（按照两个人挨饿和一个人挨饿是一样的逻辑）之后，他和一个极其虔诚、不可理喻的悍妇结了婚，这种结合并不是像有的人认为

his liberal ideals. Soon the government (after the fashion of governments during times of stress) discovered that this inoffensive looking young author maintained grave doubts about the story of creation as rendered in the first chapter of Genesis and otherwise was considerable of a heretic. In consequence whereof Diderot was conducted to the prison of Vincennes and there held under lock and key for almost three months.

It was after his release from jail that he entered the service of Lebreton. Diderot was one of the most eloquent men of his time. He saw the chance of a lifetime in the enterprise of which he was to be the head. A mere rehash of Chambers' old material seemed entirely beneath his dignity. It was an era of tremendous mental activity. Very well! Let the Encyclopedia of Lebreton contain the latest word upon every conceivable subject and let the articles be written by the foremost authorities in every line of human endeavor.

Diderot was so full of enthusiasm that he actually persuaded Lebreton to give him full command and unlimited time. Then he made up a tentative list of his coöperators,took a large sheet of foolscap and began,"A:the first letter of the alphabet,etc.,etc."

Twenty years later he reached the Z and the job was done. Rarely,however,has a man worked under such tremendous disadvantages. Lebreton had increased his original capital when he hired Diderot,but he never paid his editor more than five hundred dollars per year. And as for the other people who were supposed to lend their assistance,well,we all know how those things are. They were either busy just then,or they would do it next month,or they had to go to the country to see their grandmother. With the result that Diderot was obliged to do most of the work himself while smarting under the abuse that was heaped upon him by the officials of both the Church and the State.

Today copies of his Encyclopedia are quite rare. Not because so many people want them but because so many people are glad to get rid of them. The book which a century

的那样罕见。但是他得养活她，不得不做各种各样稀奇古怪的工作，编辑各种各样的书，从《关于美德与优点的探讨》到声名颇为不佳的薄伽丘的《十日谈》的修订。然而，这个拜勒的学生在心底里还是忠于他的自由思想。不久政府（像所有处于艰难时期的政府一样）发现这个长相并不难看的年轻作者对《创世记》第一章描述的创世故事持有严重的怀疑；此外，他还是一个重要的异教徒。结果，狄德罗被关进了温塞纳监狱，被监禁了将近三个月。

直到从监狱释放以后，狄德罗才为雷伯莱顿效力。狄德罗是当时最能言善辩的人。他在这个事业中看到了出人头地的机会。仅仅改编钱伯斯的旧资料似乎有些降低身份。这是个思想极其活跃的时期。太好了！雷伯莱顿的百科全书要让每一个可以想到的主题都涵盖最新结论，并且词条要让各领域最有权威的专家撰写。

狄德罗热情高涨，他终于说服雷伯莱顿让他全权负责，而且不限制时间。然后，他列出了一份暂定的合作人名单，拿出一张大页纸，开始写道："A：字母表的第一个字母……"

20年后，他写到了Z，工作总算完成了。然而，很少有人能在这种极为不利的条件下工作。雷伯莱顿雇用狄德罗时已经增加了他的原始资本，但他每年给编辑的钱从不超过500美元。至于那些本以为可以提供帮助的人，唉，我们都知道情况会是怎样的：他们要么当时很忙，要么是下个月再说，要么是去乡下探望祖母。所以，尽管教会和政府官员的谩骂使狄德罗感到痛苦，他仍然得亲自完成大部分工作。

and a half ago was howled down as a manifestation of a pernicious radicalism reads today like a dull and harmless tract on the feeding of babies. But to the more conservative element among the clergy of the eighteenth century,it sounded like a clarion call of destruction,anarchy,atheism and chaos.

Of course,the usual attempts were made to denounce the editor-in-chief as an enemy of society and religion,a loose reprobate who believed neither in God,home or the sanctity of the family ties. But the Paris of the year 1770 was still an overgrown village where every one knew every one else. And Diderot,who not only claimed that the purpose of life was"to do good and to find the truth,"but who actually lived up to this motto,who kept open house for all those who were hungry,who labored twenty hours a day for the sake of humanity and asked nothing in return but a bed,a writing desk and a pad of paper,this simple-minded,hardworking fellow was so shining an example of those virtues in which the prelates and the monarchs of that day were so conspicuously lacking,that it was not easy to attack him from that particular angle. And so the authorities contented themselves with making his life just as unpleasant as they possibly could by a continual system of espionage,by everlastingly snooping around the office,by raiding Diderot's home,by confiscating his notes and occasionally by suppressing the work altogether.

These obstructive methods,however,could not dampen his enthusiasm. At last the work was finished and the"Encyclopédie"actually accomplished what Diderot had expected of it—it became the rallying point for all those who in one way or another felt the spirit of the new age and who knew that the world was desperately in need of a general overhauling.

It may seem that I have dragged the figure of the editor slightly out of the true perspective.

Who,after all,was this Denis Diderot,who wore a shabby coat,counted himself happy

现在，他的百科全书的版本已经非常罕见了。这倒不是因为许多人想得到，而是因为许多人都想除之而后快。一个半世纪之前，这本书就作为毒害至深的激进主义的代表而被强行压制了，可是今天读起来却像一本教人们喂养婴儿的书一样单调而无害。但是对18世纪教士中更保守的人来说，这部书就像吹响了毁灭、无政府、无神论和无秩序的嘹亮号角。

当然，人们通常会指责总编辑是社会和宗教的敌人，是既不相信上帝和家庭，又不相信神圣家庭关系的放荡恶棍。但是1770年的巴黎还只是一个过度发展的乡村，人们彼此之间都很了解。狄德罗不但主张生活的目的应该是“做好事和寻找真理”，而且真正实践了这一座右铭。他慷慨救济饥饿的人，为人类每天工作20个小时，除了一张床、一个写字台和一叠纸外，从没有要过任何回报。这个思想纯净、工作努力的人，正是这些美德的光辉榜样，而这正是当时的高级教士和君王明显欠缺的，因此要从这个特殊角度攻击他并非易事。于是，官方就想方设法找他的麻烦，不停地监视他，在他的办公室周围打探情况，抄狄德罗的家，没收他的笔记，有时干脆强行制止他工作。

然而，这些障碍都不能压抑他的热情。工作终于完成了，正如狄德罗期望的那样，《百科全书》竣工了。对于那些在某种程度上嗅到了新时代气息、知道世界亟须翻天覆地的大变化的人来说，《百科全书》成了他们重整旗鼓的转折点。

看起来我有点夸大了这位编辑的真实形象。

毕竟还是这个狄德罗，穿着一身破旧的衣服，当他那富有而聪明的朋友霍尔

when his rich and brilliant friend,the Baron D' Holbach,invited him to a square meal once a week,and who was more than satisfied when four thousand copies of his book were actually sold?He lived at the same time as Rousseau and D'Alembert and Turgot and Helvétius and Volney and Condorcet and a score of others,all of whom gained a much greater personal renown than he did. But without the Encyclopédic these good people would never have been able to exercise the influence they did. It was more than a book,it was a social and economic program. It told what the leading minds of the day were actually thinking. It contained a concrete statement of those ideas that soon were to dominate the entire world. It was a decisive moment in the history of the human race.

France had reached a point where those who had eyes to see and ears to hear knew that something drastic must be done to avoid an immediate catastrophe,while those who had eyes to see and ears to hear yet refused to use them,maintained with an equal display of stubborn energy that peace and order could only be maintained by a strict enforcement of a set of antiquated laws that belonged to the era of the Merovingians. For the moment,those two parties were so evenly balanced that everything remained as it had always been and this led to strange complications. The same France which on one side of the ocean played such a conspicuous rôle as the defender of liberty and freedom and addressed the most affectionate letters to Monsieur Georges Washington (who was a Free Mason) and arranged delightful weekend parties for Monsieur le Ministre,Benjamin Franklin,who was what his neighbors used to call a"sceptic"and what we call a plain atheist,this country on the other side of the broad Atlantic stood revealed as the most vindictive enemy of all forms of spiritual progress and only showed her sense of democracy in the complete impartiality with which she condemned both philosopher and peasant to a life of drudgery and privation.

Eventually all this was changed.

巴赫男爵每星期请他去大吃一顿的时候，他就会高兴得手舞足蹈。当4000册书销售一空时，他不是非常满意吗？他和卢梭、达兰贝尔、杜尔哥、爱尔维修、沃尔尼、孔多塞及其他许多人生活在同一个时代，所有这些人都比他享有高得多的个人声誉。但是如果没有《百科全书》，这些好人就不可能发挥他们已经发挥了的影响。这不仅仅是一本书，它是一部社会和经济纲领。它表明了当时先进思想的真实思想，具体陈述了不久之后就会统治整个世界的思想。它是人类历史上的决定性时刻。

有耳朵、有眼睛的人都知道，法国已经到了紧要关头，必须采取某种有力措施避免即将到来的灭顶之灾，然而这些有耳朵有眼睛的人拒绝这样做，而且非常固执地坚持说，和平和秩序只能靠严格执行墨洛温王朝那套已经废弃的法律来维护。当时，这两个党派势均力敌，一切都保持着原样，这却导致了奇怪的复杂情况。大洋彼岸的法国作为自由的卫士发挥了重要的作用，它给乔治·华盛顿先生（一名共济会成员）写了一封最亲切的信，并且为本杰明·富兰克林大使先生安排了一个愉快的周末晚会，邻居们习惯称富兰克林为“怀疑论者”，我们称他为朴素的无神论者。这个屹立在大西洋对岸的国家，作为所有进步思想最凶残的仇敌而屹立在那里，只有在决定哲学家和农民都要过同样辛苦贫困的生活时，她才表现出完全不带偏见的民主意识。

最后，所有这一切都改变了。

然而，没有人能预料到变化的方式。因为这场打算清除非宫廷人士精神和社会

But it was changed in a way which no one had been able to foresee. For the struggle that was to remove the spiritual and social handicaps of all those who were born outside the royal purple was not fought by the slaves themselves. It was the work of a small group of disinterested citizens whom the Protestants,in their heart of hearts,hated quite as bitterly as their Catholic oppressors and who could count upon no other reward than that which is said to await all honest men in Heaven.

The men who during the eighteenth century defended the cause of tolerance rarely belonged to any particular denomination. For the sake of personal convenience they sometimes went through certain outward motions of religious conformity which kept the gendarmes away from their writing desks. But as far as their inner life was concerned,they might just as well have lived in Athens in the fourth century B.C. or in China in the days of Confucius.

They were often most regrettably lacking in a certain reverence for various things which most of their contemporaries held in great respect and which they themselves regarded as harmless but childish survivals of a bygone day.

They took little stock in that ancient national history which the western world,for some curious reason,had picked out from among all Babylonian and Assyrian and Egyptian and Hittite and Chaldean records and had accepted as a guide-book of morals and customs. But true disciples of their great master,Socrates,they listened only to the inner voice of their own conscience and regardless of consequences,they lived fearlessly in a world that had long since been surrendered to the timid.

障碍的战斗不是奴隶自己打响的，这是一小群公正无私的人的事业，新教徒对这些人恨之入骨，就像天主教压迫者痛恨他们一样。而这一小群人并没有别的希望，据说只是期待所有诚实的人都能进天堂。

在18世纪，保卫宽容事业的人很少属于某个特殊的派别。为了个人方便起见，他们有时也参加一些表面上的宗教活动，好把宪兵从他们的写字台前赶走。但就他们的内心活动而言，他们更像是生活在公元前4世纪的雅典或是孔子时代的中国。

他们常常遗憾自己缺乏对各种事物的敬畏感，而他们同时代大部分人对此是很敬畏的，他们还认为这些只是过去遗留下来的虽然无害却很幼稚的东西。

他们很少注意西方世界出于某些好奇的原因而从巴比伦人、亚述人、埃及人、赫梯人和迦勒底人的历史中挑选出来作为道德和习俗教科书的古代民族史。但是大师苏格拉底的真正信徒们，只倾听自己内心的呼唤，根本不顾后果，他们无所畏惧地生活在一个早已变得胆小怯懦的世界里。

CHAPTER XXVII THE INTOLERANCE OF REVOLUTION

The ancient edifice of official glory and unofficial misery known as the Kingdom of France came crashing down on a memorable evening in the month of August of the year of grace 1789.

On that hot and sultry night,after a week of increasing emotional fury,the National Assembly worked itself into a veritable orgy of brotherly love. Until in a moment of intense excitement the privileged classes surrendered all those ancient rights and prerogatives which it had taken them three centuries to acquire and as plain citizens declared themselves in favor of those theoretical rights of man which henceforth would be the foundation-stone for all further attempts at popular self-government.

As far as France was concerned,this meant the end of the feudal system. An aristocracy which is actually composed of the"aristoi,"of the best of the most enterprising elements of society,which boldly assumes leadership and shapes the destinies of the common country,has a chance to survive. A nobility which voluntarily retires from active service and contents itself with ornamental clerical jobs in diverse departments of government is only fit to drink tea on Fifth Avenue or run restaurants on Second.

The old France therefore was dead.

Whether for better or for worse,I do not know.

But it was dead and with it there passed away that most outrageous form of an invisible

第27章　革命的不宽容

那座标志着达官贵人的荣誉和平民百姓的痛苦的大厦——法兰西王国——终于在1798年8月一个值得纪念的晚上倒塌了。

在那个天气闷热的晚上，经过民众一周以来持续上升的愤怒风潮的影响，国民议会沉浸在真正的兄弟般博爱的狂欢之中。直到这个群情激昂的时刻，特权阶层才交出了他们花了三个世纪才获得的所有古老权力和特权；广大民众宣布支持人权理论，这将为以后的民众自治奠定基石。

就法国而言，这意味着封建制度的终结。一个贵族阶层如果真的由社会上最具有进取心的人组成，能勇敢地承担起领导权，并决定这个国家的命运，那它就得到了继续生存的机会。至于那些甘愿退出公职，满足于在政府各个部门做一点冠冕堂皇的教士工作的贵族，只配去纽约第五大道喝茶或在第二大道开饭馆。

因此，旧的法兰西死了。

这到底是福是祸，我不知道。

但是它死了，随着它一起死去的还有看不见的最残暴的统治，自从黎塞留时代以来，教会一直把这种统治强加在圣·路易斯的天主教后代身上。

事实上，人类现在获得了一次绝无仅有的好机会。

government which the Church,ever since the days of Richelieu,had been able to impose upon the anointed descendants of Saint Louis.

Verily,now as never before,mankind was given a chance.

Of the enthusiasm which at that period filled the hearts and souls of all honest men and women,it is needless to speak.

The millennium was close at hand,yea,it had come.

And intolerance among the many other vices inherent in an autocratic form of government was for good and all to be eradicated from this fair earth.

Allons,enfants de la patrie,the days of tyranny are gone!

And more words to that effect.

Then the curtain went down,society was purged of its many iniquities,the cards were re-shuffled for a new deal and when it was all over,behold our old friend Intolerance,wearing a pair of proletarian pantaloons and his hair brushed à la Robespierre,a-sitting side by side with the public prosecutor and having the time of his wicked old life.

Ten years ago he had sent people to the scaffold for claiming that authority maintaining itself solely by the grace of Heaven might sometimes be in error.

Now he hustled them to their doom for insisting that the will of the people need not always and invariably be the will of God.

A ghastly joke!

But a joke paid for (after the nature of such popular fancies) with the blood of a million innocent bystanders.

What I am about to say is unfortunately not very original. One can find the same idea couched in different if more elegant words in the works of many of the ancients.

In matters pertaining to man's inner life there are,and apparently there always have

当时，所有诚实的男男女女都满怀激情，这是不言自明的。

太平盛世近在咫尺，甚至可以说已经到来了。

植根于独裁政府的专制及其种种邪恶，从此全都要被从这个公正的地球上永远清除掉。

前进吧，祖国的孩子们，暴政的时代一去不复返了！

对于它的后果还有许多说词。

然后，帷幕落下来了，社会上许多不公正被荡涤一空，一切都重新洗牌。当这一切都过去以后，我们的老朋友“不宽容”又出现了，它穿着无产者的裤子，梳着罗伯斯比尔式的发型，与检察官并肩坐在一起，安享它罪恶的晚年。

10年前，如果有人说当权者只是靠上帝的垂青度日，而且有时也会出错，那么“不宽容”就会把说这话的人送上断头台。

现在，谁要是坚持认为人民的意愿不一定总是上帝的意愿，那么“不宽容”也会把他们推向毁灭。

多么可怕的玩笑啊！

然而这个玩笑（大家还都喜欢它）的代价却是100万无辜旁观者的鲜血。

不幸的是，我要讲的不是什么新鲜事。你可以从许多古典作家的著作中找到以不同形式表达的更文雅的词句。

在人类的内心精神方面，一直明显地存在、现在及将来很可能永远存在着两种完全不同的类型。

been,and most likely there always will be two entirely different varieties of human beings.

A few,by dint of endless study and contemplation and the serious searching of their immortal souls will be able to arrive at certain temperate philosophical conclusions which will place them above and beyond the common worries of mankind.

But the vast majority of the people are not contented with a mild diet of spiritual"light wines."They want something with a kick to it,something that burns on the tongue,that hurts the gullet,that will make them sit up and take notice. What that"something"is does not matter very much,provided it comes up to the above-mentioned specifications and is served in a direct and simple fashion and in unlimited quantities.

This fact seems to have been little understood by historians and this has led to many and serious disappointments. No sooner has an outraged populace torn down the stronghold of the past (a fact duly and enthusiastically reported by the local Herodoti and Taciti),than it turns mason,carts the ruins of the former citadel to another part of the city and there remolds them into a new dungeon,every whit as vile and tyrannical as the old one and used for the same purpose of repression and terror.

The very moment a number of proud nations have at last succeeded in throwing off the yoke imposed upon them by an"infallible man"they accept the dictates of an"infallible book."

Yea,on the very day when Authority,disguised as a flunkey,is madly galloping to the frontier,Liberty enters the deserted palace,puts on the discarded royal raiment and forthwith commits herself to those selfsame blunders and cruelties which have just driven her predecessor into exile.

It is all very disheartening,but it is an honest part of our story and must be told.

■ 革命

少数人通过持续不断地学习和思考，以及对不朽灵魂的严肃追寻，将会悟出某些温和适度的哲学结论，它将帮助他们摆脱人类常见的苦恼。

但是大多数人并不满足精神上的“淡酒”。他们想找些富有刺激、燃烧舌头、伤到喉咙并使他们坐起来打起精神的东西。至于那“东西”是什么并不重要，只要它能达到上述要求，能采用直截了当的方法而且没有数量限制就行。

历史学家似乎不懂得这个事实，这导致了许多严重的令人大失所望的事情。愤怒的民众刚刚摧毁了过去的堡垒（当地的希罗多德和塔西佗之流及时而热情地报道了这件事），就摇身一变成了泥瓦匠，把旧城堡的废墟运往城市的另一端，将它们重新建成一个地牢，它的邪恶残暴和旧堡垒完全一样，也是用于镇压和恐怖的同样目的。

恰好在这个时候，一些自尊心很强的民族终于摆脱了由那些“一贯正确的人”强加在他们头上的枷锁，但又接受了一本“一贯正确的书”的统治。

是的，就在国王路易十六装扮成仆人，骑着马向边境狂奔的同一天，自由进入了这座被遗弃的宫殿，穿上了被遗弃的皇袍，又重蹈覆辙地犯错误，做残忍之事，而正是这些人迫使其前任刚刚被驱逐出境的。

No doubt the intentions of those who were directly responsible for the great French upheaval were of the best. The Declaration of the Rights of Man had laid down the principle that no citizen should ever be disturbed in the peaceful pursuit of his ways on account of his opinion,"not even his religious opinion,"provided that his ideas did not disturb the public order as laid down by the various decrees and laws.

This however did not mean equal rights for all religious denominations. The protestant faith henceforth was to be tolerated,Protestants were not to be annoyed because they worshiped in a different church from their Catholic neighbors,but Catholicism remained the official,the"dominant"Church of the state.

Mirabeau,with his unerring instinct for the essentials of political life,knew that this far famed concession was only a half-way measure. But Mirabeau,who was trying to turn a great social cataclysm into a one-man revolution,died under the effort and many noblemen and bishops,repenting of their generous gesture of the night of the fourth of August,were already beginning that policy of obstructionism which was to be of such fatal consequence to their master the king. And it was not until two years later in the year 1791 (and exactly two years too late for any practical purpose) that all religious sects including the Protestants and the Jews,were placed upon a basis of absolute equality and were declared to enjoy the same liberty before the law.

From that moment on,the rôles began to be reversed. The constitution which the representatives of the French people finally bestowed upon an expectant country insisted that all priests of whatsoever faith should swear an oath of allegiance to the new form of government and should regard themselves strictly as servants of the state,like the school-teachers and postal employees and light-house keepers and customs officials who were their fellow-citizens.

这一切都令人沮丧，但这是我们故事中真实的一部分，必须公之于众。

毫无疑问，那些对法国大革命负有直接责任的人出发点是非常好的。《人权宣言》规定的原则是，任何公民依照自己的观点，“包括宗教观点”，安静地寻求自己的生活方式时，只要他的观点不扰乱由各项法令和法律制定的社会秩序，就不应受到干预。

然而，这并不意味着所有的宗教派别都享有同等权力。新教从此以后得到了宽容，新教徒不会因为和天主教徒不在同一个教堂做礼拜而遭到任何打搅，但天主教仍然是官方“占统治地位”的国教。

米拉博尔在认识政治生活本质方面有准确无误的本能，他知道这个远近闻名的让步只是一种折中的办法。他试图把一场社会大变革变成一个人的革命，结果却劳累而死。许多贵族和主教很后悔他们在8月4日晚上作出的宽宏大量的表示，便开始采取设置障碍的政策，却给他们的国王主子造成了致命的后果。直到两年以后的1791年（整整两年对于任何实际目的来说都太迟了），所有宗教派别（包括新教徒和犹太人）才获得了完全平等的权利，被宣布在法律面前享有同等自由。

从那时开始，各种角色开始颠倒过来。法国人民的代表给这个充满希望的国家制订的宪法要求所有教士，无论怀有什么信仰，都必须宣誓忠诚于新政权领导，都应该把自己视为国家的公仆，就像他们的同胞，如学校的教师、邮局雇员、灯塔看守人和海关官员一样。

教皇庇护六世反对这样做。新宪法关于神职人员的规定直接践踏了自1516年以

Pope Pius VI objected. The clerical stipulations of the new constitution were in direct violation of every solemn agreement that had been concluded between France and the Holy See since the year 1516. But the Assembly was in no mood to bother about such little trifles as precedents and treaties. The clergy must either swear allegiance to this decree or resign their positions and starve to death. A few bishops and a few priests accepted what seemed inevitable. They crossed their fingers and went through the formality of an oath. But by far the greater number,being honest men,refused to perjure themselves and taking a leaf out of the book of those Huguenots whom they had persecuted during so many years,they began to say mass in deserted stables and to give communion in pigsties,to preach their sermons behind country hedges and to pay clandestine visits to the homes of their former parishioners in the middle of the night.

Generally speaking,they fared infinitely better than the Protestants had done under similar circumstances,for France was too hopelessly disorganized to take more than very perfunctory measures against the enemies of her constitution. And as none of them seemed to run the risk of the galleys,the excellent clerics were soon emboldened to ask that they,the non-jurors,the"refractory ones"as they were popularly called,be officially recognized as one of the"tolerated sects"and be accorded those privileges which during the previous three centuries they had so persistently refused to grant to their compatriots of the Calvinist faith.

The situation,for those of us who look back at it from the safe distance of the year 1925,was not without a certain grim humor. But no definite decision was taken,for the Assembly soon afterwards fell entirely under the denomination of the extreme radicals and the treachery of the court,combined with the stupidity of His Majesty's foreign allies,caused a panic which in less than a week spread from the coast of Belgium to

来法国和罗马教廷签订的各项正式协定。但是国民公会可没有心情考虑先例或条约这类小事。教士要么宣誓效忠宪法，要么辞职饿死。有几个主教和教士接受了这个看来不可避免的命运。他们双手合十，履行了正式的宣誓仪式。但是绝大多数教士是诚实人，他们拒绝发假誓。他们效仿被自己迫害了许多年的胡格诺派，开始在荒废的马厩里作弥撒，在猪圈里交流思想，在乡下的篱笆后面传经布道，并且在夜深人静的时候到他们以前教民的家里进行秘密拜访。

一般来说，他们在类似遭遇下比新教徒过的好很多，因为法国已是一片混乱，难以采取更多有效的方法对付反对宪法的人。由于他们似乎都不想冒着上断头台的危险，所以那些杰出的神职人员（人们一般称他们是不肯宣誓效忠的顽固分子）很快就壮着胆子要求官方承认自己是“被容忍的宗派”，并要求得到他们在过去三个世纪坚决拒绝交给同胞加尔文教徒的特权。

如果我们从1925年这样安全的距离来回顾当时的形势，就会发现一种冷幽默。但是官方并没有采取明确的措施，因为国民公会很快被极端的激进分子完全控制了。由于法庭的背信弃义，加上国王陛下那些外国盟友的愚蠢，结果导致了一场大恐慌，它在不到一个星期的时间里就从比利时海岸扩散到了地中海海滨，并导致了从1792年9月2日至7日的一系列大屠杀。

从那时起，这场革命注定要堕落为一种恐怖统治。

当饥饿的民众开始怀疑他们的领袖正在制造一场大阴谋，要把国家出卖给敌人时，哲学家们试图通过循序渐进的手段取得成功的努力化成了泡影。紧接着发生的

the shores of the Mediterranean and which was responsible for that series of wholesale assassinations which raged from the second to the seventh of September of the year 1792.

From that moment on the Revolution was bound to degenerate into a reign of terror.

The gradual and evolutionary efforts of the philosophers came to naught when a starving populace began to suspect that their own leaders were engaged in a gigantic plot to sell the country to the enemy. The explosion which then followed is common history. That the conduct of affairs in a crisis of such magnitude is likely to fall into the hands of unscrupulous and ruthless leaders is a fact with which every honest student of history is sufficiently familiar. But that the principal actor in the drama should have been a prig,a model-citizen,a hundred-percenting paragon of Virtue,that indeed was something which no one had been able to foresee.

When France began to understand the true nature of her new master,it was too late,as those who tried in vain to utter their belated words of warning from the top of a scaffold in the Place de la Concorde could have testified.

Thus far we have studied all revolutions from the point of view of politics and economics and social organization. But not until the historian shall turn psychologist or the psychologist shall turn historian shall we really be able to explain and understand those dark forces that shape the destinies of nations in their hour of agony and travail.

There are those who hold that the world is ruled by sweetness and light. There are those who maintain that the human race respects only one thing,brute force. Some hundred years from now,I may be able to make a choice. This much,however,seems certain to us,that the greatest of all experiments in our

革命的宽容

剧变在历史上也就不足为奇了。在这样危急的时刻，处理事务的权力很容易落在粗鲁而无情的领导人手里，这也是每一个熟谙历史的学生都很熟悉的情况。但是这出戏的主角竟然是个正人君子，是个公民楷模，是个百分之百的美德的化身，这的确是没有人会预料到的。

等法国开始明白新主人的真正本质时，已经太晚了，在协和广场的绞架上徒费口舌地发出过时警告的人可以证明这些。

到此为止，我们已从政治、经济和社会组织这几个角度研究了所有的革命，但是只有等历史学家变成了心理学家，或心理学家变成了历史学家，我们才能真正解释和理解那些在极度痛苦和危急的时刻决定国家命运的黑暗力量。

有些人认为是愉快和光明统治着世界。有些人认为人类只尊崇一件事——暴力。从现在起几百年后，我可能会作出一个选择。然而，有一点对我们来说似乎是肯定的，那就是在我们社会学的实验室里最伟大的实验，也即法国革命是对暴力的

sociological laboratory,the French revolution,was a noisy apotheosis of violence.

Those who had tried to prepare for a more humane world by way of reason were either dead or were put to death by the very people whom they had helped to glory. And with the Voltaires and Diderots and the Turgots and the Condorcets out of the way,the untutored apostles of the New Perfection were left the undisputed masters of their country's fate. What a ghastly mess they made of their high mission !

During the first period of their rule,victory lay with the out-an-dout enemies of religion,those who had some particular reason to detest the very symbols of Christianity;those who in some silent and hidden way had suffered so deeply in the old days of clerical supremacy that the mere sight of a cassock drove them into a frenzy of hate and that the smell of incense made them turn pale with long forgotten rage. Together with a few others who believed that they could disprove the existence of a personal God with the help of mathematics and chemistry,they set about to destroy the Church and all her works. A hopeless and at best an ungrateful task but it is one of the characteristics of revolutionary psychology that the normal becomes abnormal and the impossible is turned into an every day occurrence. Hence a paper decree of the Convention abolishing the old Christian calendar;abolishing All Saints' Days;abolishing Christmas and Easter;abolishing weeks and months and re-dividing the year into periods of ten days each with a new pagan Sabbath on every tenth. Hence another paper pronunciamento which abolished the worship of God and left the universe without a master.

But not for long.

However eloquently explained and defended within the bare rooms of the Jacobin club,the idea

■ 罗伯斯比尔

神圣崇拜。

那些想通过理性建立一个更人性化的世界的人，不是寿终正寝，就是被他们曾给予荣誉的人处死。随着伏尔泰、狄德罗、杜尔哥、孔多塞这些人的销声匿迹，新至善论的无知倡导者成了国家命运无可争议的主人。可是他们把这项崇高的使命弄得一团糟!

在他们统治的第一阶段，胜利掌握在宗教的敌人手里。这些人出于某些特殊的原因而痛恨基督教的象征。他们在教士专权的旧时代默默地忍受着巨大痛苦，一看到教士穿的黑长袍就恨之入骨，烧香的气味使他们的脸色发白，勾起他们早已忘却的怒火。还有些人认为，可以借助数学和化学来反对上帝的存在。他们和这些人一起开始着手摧毁教会和它所有的成就。这是件毫无希望的事，或最多是一场徒劳无功的任务，但它是革命心理的一个特点，即正常的变成了不正常的，不可能的事变成了每天都要发生的事。于是，一纸法律公文废除了基督教的旧历，废除了万圣节，废除了圣诞节和复活节，废除了星期和月份，重新将一年划分为十天一段，每十天就有一个异教徒的安息日。接着，又出现了一纸声明，禁止崇拜上帝，使世界失去了主人。

但这种局势持续的时间并不长。

of a limitless and empty void was too repellent to most citizens to be tolerated for more than a couple of weeks. The old Deity no longer satisfied the masses. Why not follow the example of Moses and Mahomet and invent a new one that should suit the demands of the times?

As a result,behold the Goddess of Reason!

Her exact status was to be defined later. In the meantime a comely actress,properly garbed in ancient Greek draperies,would fill the bill perfectly. The lady was found among the dancers of his late Majesty's corps de ballet and at the proper hour was most solemnly conducted to the high altar of Notre Dame,long since deserted by the loyal followers of an older faith.

As for the blessed Virgin who,during so many centuries,had stood a tender watch over all those who had bared the wounds of their soul before the patient eyes of perfect understanding,she too was gone,hastily hidden by loving hands before she be sent to the limekilns and be turned into mortar. Her place had been taken by a statue of Liberty,the proud product of an amateur sculptor and done rather carelessly in white plaster. But that was not all. Notre Dame had seen other innovations. In the middle of the choir,four columns and a roof indicated a"Temple of Philosophy"which upon state occasions was to serve as a throne for the new dancing divinity. When the poor girl was not holding court and receiving the worship of her trusted followers,the Temple of Philosophy harbored a"Torch of Truth"which to the end of all time was to carry high the burning flame of world enlightenment.

The"end of time"came before another six months.

On the morning of the seventh of May of the year 1794 the French people were officially informed that God had been reestablished and that the immortality of the soul

在雅各宾俱乐部空荡荡的房子里，不论人们怎样滔滔不绝地辩解，这种虚无缥缈的主张对大部分公民来说还是很不得人心，大部分人连两个星期都无法忍受。旧上帝满足不了大众的要求，为什么不效仿摩西和穆罕默德，制造出一个合乎时代要求的新上帝呢？

结果，理智女神出现了！

她的真实身份后来才弄明白。在当时，一个标致的女演员穿上合适的古希腊服装，就会完全符合人们的要求。这个女士是从前任国王陛下的芭蕾舞团舞蹈演员中找到的。在一个适当的机会，她被隆重地送到了早已被旧信仰追随者抛弃的巴黎圣母院高大的祭坛上。

至于那位被赐福的圣母，许多世纪以来一直站在祭坛上，用完全理解的宽容的目光温柔地守护着灵魂受到创伤的人们。现在她也消失了，在被送进石灰窑变成灰浆之前，被慈爱的人匆忙藏了起来。她的位置被自由女神的塑像取而代之。自由女神像是一个业余雕塑家的得意之作，用白色的石膏粗糙雕塑而成。但这并不是全部，巴黎圣母院还产生了其他发明。在唱诗班中间，四个柱子和一个屋顶象征着“哲学神殿”，它在国家的重大日子里就成了新“舞神”的宝座。当这个可怜的女孩子不主持仪式、不接受忠诚追随者的崇拜时，哲学神殿就高高燃起“真理的火炬”，意在高举世界文明的焰火，直到世界末日。

但“世界末日”不到六个月就来临了。

1794年5月7日早晨，法国人民被正式告知“上帝又重新确立了”，灵魂的不朽

was once more a recognized article of faith. On the eighth of June,the new Supreme Being (hastily constructed out of the second-hand material left behind by the late Jean Jacques Rousseau) was officially presented to his eager disciples.

Robespierre in a new blue waistcoat delivered the address of welcome. He had reached the highest point of his career. The obscure law clerk from a third rate country town had become the high priest of the Revolution. More than that,a poor demented nun by the name of Catherine Théot,revered by thousands as the true mother of God,had just proclaimed the forthcoming return of the Messiah and she had even revealed his name. It was Maximilian Robespierre;the same Maximilian who in a fantastic uniform of his own designing was proudly dispensing reams of oratory in which he assured God that from now on all would be well with His little world.

And to make doubly sure,two days later he passed a law by which those suspected of treason and heresy (for once more they were held to be the same,as in the good old days of the Inquisition) were deprived of all means of defense,a measure so ably conceived that during the next six weeks more than fourteen hundred people lost their heads beneath the slanting knife of the guillotine.

The rest of his story is only too well known.

As Robespierre was the perfect incarnation of all he himself held to be Good (with a capital G) he could,in his quality of a logical fanatic,not possibly recognize the right of other men,less perfect,to exist on the same planet with himself. As time went by,his hatred of Evil (with a capital E) took on such proportions that France was brought to the brink of depopulation.

Then at last,and driven by fear of their own lives,the enemies of Virtue struck back and in a short but desperate struggle destroyed this Terrible Apostle of Rectitude.

又一次成为公认的信仰。6月8日，新上帝（用已故的让·雅克·卢梭遗留下的旧材料匆忙塑造出来的）正式展现在热忱的信徒面前。

罗伯斯比尔身着一件新蓝马甲，发表了欢迎词。他已经达到了职业生涯的最高峰。这位来自三流乡村小镇的、默默无闻的法律执事，成了法国革命的高级教士。除此之外，一个名叫凯瑟琳·泰奥特的可怜的精神错乱的修女被千百万人拥戴为上帝的真正母亲，她刚刚宣布了救世主即将到来，甚至还透露了救世主的名字，这就是马克西米利安·罗伯斯比尔。这个马克西米利安穿着自己设计的奇装异服，正在高傲地发表演讲。他在演讲中向上帝保证，从今以后他所掌管的小世界一定会好起来。

为了双保险，两天后，他又通过了一项法律，规定凡是被怀疑犯有叛国罪和异教罪的人（二者又一次被视为等同，就像宗教法庭旧日好时光一样）要被剥夺一切为自己辩护的权利。这一措施非常奏效，在接下来的六个星期中，就有1400多人丧命。

剩下的事情，大家都很清楚。

由于罗伯斯比尔是所有他认为美好的东西（“G”要大写）的完美化身，因此在富有理性的狂热本性的支使下，他不可能承认其他不够完美的人有权和他在同一个星球上生活。随着时间的推移，他对罪恶（“E”要大写）的仇恨发展到了使法国濒临人口灭绝的边缘。

最后，由于担心生命安全，美德的敌人开始回击。在一场短暂的殊死搏斗中，

Soon afterwards the force of the Revolution had spent itself. The constitution which the French people then adopted recognized the existence of different denominations and gave them the same rights and privileges. Officially at least the Republic washed her hands of all religion. Those who wished to form a church,a congregation,an association,were free to do so but they were obliged to support their own ministers and priests and recognize the superior rights of the state and the complete freedom of choice of the individual.

Ever since,the Catholics and Protestants in France have lived peacefully side by side.

It is true that the Church never recognized her defeat,continues to deny the principle of a division of state and church (see the decree of Pope Pius IX of December 8th,1864) and has repeatedly tried to come back to power by supporting those political parties who hope to upset the republican form of government and bring back the monarchy or the empire. But these battles are usually fought in the private parlors of some minister's wife,or in the rabbit-shooting-lodge of a retired general with an ambitious mother-in-law.

They have thus far provided the funny papers with some excellent material but they are proving themselves increasingly futile.

这个正直得可怕的信徒被处死了。

之后不久，法国革命的力量耗尽了。法国人民当时采用的宪法承认了不同宗派的存在，并赋予它们平等的特权，至少从官方来说共和国不再干预宗教事务了。那些希望建立教堂、圣会和联盟的人可以自由地去做自己想做的事，但是他们必须支持自己的教士和牧师，并承认国家至高无上的权力和完全自由的个人选择。

从那时起，法国的天主教徒和新教徒开始和平共处。

教会的确从未承认过自己的失败，而且继续拒绝政教分离的原则（见1864年12月8日罗马教皇庇护九世的教令），不断支持那些妄图颠覆共和国体制、恢复君主制或帝国的政党，以图重掌大权。但这些战斗一般都是在一些大臣夫人的客厅里，或者是在退伍将军及其野心勃勃的岳母打兔子的山林小屋里进行的。

迄今为止，他们为趣味报纸提供了极好的素材，但这愈加证明了他们的枉费心机。

CHAPTER XXVIII LESSING

On the twentieth of September of the year 1792 a battle was fought between the armies of the French Revolution and the armies of the allied monarchs who had set forth to annihilate the terrible monster of insurrection.

It was a glorious victory,but not for the allies. Their infantry could not be employed on the slippery hillsides of the village of Valmy. The battle therefore consisted of a series of solemn broadsides. The rebels fired harder and faster than the royalists. Hence the latter were the first to leave the field. In the evening the allied troops retreated northward. Among those present at the engagement was a certain Johann Wolfgang von Goethe,aide to the hereditary Prince of Weimar.

Several years afterwards this young man published his memoirs of that day. While standing ankle-deep in the sticky mud of Lorraine,he had turned prophet. And he had predicted that after this cannonade,the world would never be the same. He had been right. On that ever memorable day,Sovereignty by the grace of God was blown into limbo. The Crusaders of the Rights of Man did not run like chickens,as they had been expected to do. They stuck to their guns. And they pushed those guns forward through valleys and across mountains until they had carried their ideal of"Liberty,Equality and Fraternity"to the further-most corners of Europe and had stabled their horses in every castle and church of the entire continent.

It is easy enough for us to write that sort of sentence. The revolutionary leaders have been dead for almost one hundred and fifty years and we can poke as much fun at them as we like. We can even be grateful for the many good things which they bestowed upon this world.

But the men and women who lived through those days,who one morning had gaily

第28章 莱　　辛

1792年9月20日，一场战斗在法国革命军和奉命剿灭这场可怕暴动的君主联盟军之间打响了。

这是一次辉煌的胜利，但胜者不是联军。联军步兵在瓦尔密村滑溜溜的山坡上没有用武之地。因此，战斗变成了一连串炮战。可是叛军的炮火比皇家军队更猛烈、更迅速，因此后者率先撤离了战场，晚上就向北方撤退了。参加这场战斗的士兵中，有一个名叫约翰·沃夫冈·冯·歌德的人，他是世袭魏玛公爵的助手。

几年后，这个年轻人出版了关于这一天的回忆录。当时，他站在洛林的齐踝深、又稠又黏的泥浆里，却变成了一个预言家。他预言说，经过这场炮战，世界将不再是原来的样子。他说得对。在永远值得记忆的那一天，神授君权被吹到了地狱的边缘。人权战士们并没有如人们预想的那样像逃之夭夭的小鸡。他们挺着枪，推着炮，穿过山谷，越过高山，一直把“自由、平等、博爱”的思想带到欧洲最边远的角落，把他们的马拴在整个大陆的每座城堡和教堂里。

对我们来说，写这样的词句倒是很容易。这场革命的领导者已经死去将近150年了，我们可以尽情地嘲弄他们。我们甚至还可以感谢他们赋予这个世界的许多好东西。

但经历了那些日子的男男女女们不可能对这场市民动乱保持公正的观点。他们曾在某天早晨在自由之树下面欢快地起舞，但在以后的三个月中又像城市下水道

danced around the Tree of Liberty and then during the next three months had been chased like rats through the sewers of their own city,could not possibly take such a detached view of those problems of civic upheaval. As soon as they had crept out of their cellars and garrets and had combed the cobwebs out of their perukes,they began to devise measures by which to prevent a reoccurrence of so terrible a calamity.

But in order to be successful reactionaries,they must first of all bury the past. Not a vague past in the broad historical sense of the word but their own individual"pasts"when they had surreptitiously read the works of Monsieur de Voltaire and had openly expressed their admiration for the Encyclopédie. Now the assembled works of Monsieur de Voltaire were stored away in the attic and those of Monsieur Diderot were sold to the junk-man. Pamphlets that had been reverently read as the true revelation of reason were relegated to the coal-bin and in every possible way an effort was made to cover up the tracks that betrayed a short sojourn in the realm of liberalism.

Alas,as so often happens in a case like that when all the literary material has been carefully destroyed,the repentant brotherhood overlooked one item which was even more important as a telltale of the popular mind. That was the stage. It was a bit childish on the part of the generation that had thrown whole cartloads of bouquets at"The Marriage of Figaro"to claim that they had never for a moment believed in the possibilities of equal rights for all men,and the people who had wept over"Nathan the Wise"could never successfully prove that they had always regarded religious tolerance as a misguided expression of governmental weakness.

The play and its success were there to convict them of the opposite.

The author of this famous key play to the popular sentiment of the latter half of the eighteenth century was a German,one Gotthold Ephraim Lessing. He was the son of a Lutheran clergyman and had studied theology in the University of Leipzig. But he had felt little inclination for a religious career and had played hooky so persistently that his

里的耗子一样被到处追赶。他们刚从地窖和阁楼里爬出来，梳理了假发上的蛛网之后，就开始想方设法，避免重演这种可怕的灾难。

但是为了当成功的反对者，他们首先必须掩盖过去。这不是广义历史学意义上的那个含糊的过去，而是他们自己的“过去”——他们偷偷摸摸地阅读伏尔泰先生的书，并公开表示对《百科全书》的钦佩。现在，伏尔泰先生的书被束之高阁，狄罗德先生的书被卖给了废品贩子，曾经被虔诚地拜读过的揭示真理的小册子也被扔进了煤箱。为了掩盖可能暴露他们曾在自由主义领域里逗留过的任何蛛丝马迹，他们用尽了一切可能的办法。

哎呀，就像在类似情形下经常发生的那样，当所有文学作品被细心地毁灭之后，这些忏悔的兄弟会却忽视了一件事情，这件事比泄露大家的心思更重要——这就是戏剧舞台。曾经为《费加罗的婚礼》献过整车鲜花的那一代人，现在却宣布他们从没有相信过人人平等的理想有可能实现，那也太幼稚了。曾为《聪明的南森》流过泪的人，现在再也无法证实，他们一直认为宗教宽容是政府软弱无能的误导的结果。

这出戏和它的成功，证明了正好相反的情况。

这出解释18世纪后期民众感情的著名戏剧的作者，是一个名叫戈思霍尔德·伊弗雷姆·莱辛的德国人。他是一名路德派牧师的儿子，在莱比锡大学攻读过神学。但是他不愿意以宗教为职业，经常逃学。他父亲听说此事之后，把他叫回家，让他选择是马上退学还是写一份到医学系学习的申请书。戈思霍尔德对当医生和当牧师一样不感兴趣，他保证做到父亲的每项要求，又回到了莱比锡，继续为他喜爱的演员朋友们作担保。当这些朋友从城里离开之后，莱辛为了避免因负债而被捕，不得

father heard of it,had told him to come home and had placed him before the choice of immediate resignation from the university or diligent application as a member of the medical department. Gotthold,who was no more of a doctor than a clergyman,promised everything that was asked of him,returned to Leipzig,went surety for some of his beloved actor friends and upon their subsequent disappearance from town was obliged to hasten to Wittenberg that he might escape arrest for debt.

His flight meant the beginning of a period of long walks and short meals. First of all he went to Berlin where he spent several years writing badly paid articles for a number of theatrical papers. Then he engaged himself as private secretary to a rich friend who was going to take a trip around the world. But no sooner had they started than the Seven Years' war must break out. The friend,obliged to join his regiment,had taken the first post-chaise for home and Lessing,once more without a job,found himself stranded in the city of Leipzig.

But he was of a sociable nature and soon found a new friend in the person of one Eduard Christian von Kleist,an officer by day and a poet by night,a sensitive soul who gave the hungry ex-theologian insight into the new spirit that was slowly coming over this world. But von Kleist was shot to death in the battle of Kunersdorf and Lessing was driven to such dire extremes of want that he became a columnist.

Then followed a period as private secretary to the commander of the fortress of Breslau where the boredom of garrison life was mitigated by a profound study of the works of Spinoza which then,a hundred years after the philosopher's death,were beginning to find their way to foreign countries.

All this,however,did not settle the problem of the daily Butterbrod. Lessing was now almost forty years old and wanted a home of his own. His friends suggested that he be appointed keeper of the Royal Library. But years before,something had happened that had made Lessing persona non grata at the Prussian court. During his first visit to Berlin he had made the acquaintance of Voltaire. The French philosopher was nothing if not

不逃到维滕堡。

他的逃跑意味着长时间的步行和饥饿的开始。他先来到柏林，在那里为几家戏剧类报纸写了几年的廉价书稿。后来，他又给一个准备环球旅行的富人朋友当私人秘书。他们刚一出发，七年战争就爆发了。这个朋友被迫从军，坐上第一辆邮政马车回了家乡。莱辛再次失业，在莱比锡城流浪。

但莱辛是个善于交际的人，不久又结交了一个新朋友，名叫爱德华·克里斯蒂娜·冯·克莱斯特。这是一个白天当官、晚上写诗、有一个敏感灵魂的人。他给了这个饥饿的前神学家洞察力，使他看到了正在慢慢遍布这个世界的新精神。但是克莱斯特在库内尔道夫战役中中弹身亡，莱辛被逼到了绝境，只得当了一名专栏作家。

接下来的一段时间，莱辛又当了布雷斯勒要塞指挥官的私人秘书。由于驻防生活很无聊，他认真钻研了斯宾诺莎的著作。这些作品在这位哲学家去世100年之后，才开始流传到国外。

然而，所有这一切还是解决不了日常温饱的问题。莱辛现在快40岁了，他想要一个自己的家。他的朋友建议他去当皇家图书馆的管理员。但是许多年前发生的事已经使莱辛成为不受普鲁士宫廷欢迎的人。他第一次访问柏林时就结识了伏尔泰。这个法国哲学家极为慷慨，没有任何“体系”观念，他允许这个年轻人借阅当时正准备出版的《路易十四的世纪》的手稿。不幸的是，当莱辛匆匆忙忙离开柏林时，（完全出于偶然）把手稿包在了自己的行李中。伏尔泰本来就对吝啬的普鲁士宫廷劣质的咖啡和硬板床极为恼火，便马上大喊大叫说自己被偷了。那个年轻德国人偷

generous and being a person without any idea of"system"he had allowed the young man to borrow the manuscript of the"Century of Louis XIV,"then ready for publication. Unfortunately,Lessing,when he hastily left Berlin,had (entirely by accident) packed the manuscript among his own belongings. Voltaire,exasperated by the bad coffee and the hard beds of the penurious Prussian court,immediately cried out that he had been robbed. The young German had stolen his most important manuscript,the police must watch the frontier,etc.,etc.,etc.,after the manner of an excited Frenchman in a foreign country. Within a few days the postman returned the lost document,but it was accompanied by a letter from Lessing in which the blunt young Teuton expressed his own ideas of people who would dare to suspect his honesty.

This storm in a chocolate-pot might ,have easily been forgotten,but the eighteenth century was a period when chocolate-pots played a great rôle in the lives of men and women and Frederick,even after a lapse of almost twenty years,still loved his pesky French friend and would not hear of having Lessing at his court.

And so farewell to Berlin and off to Hamburg,where there was rumor of a newly to be founded national theater. This enterprise came to nothing and Lessing in his despair accepted the office of librarian to the hereditary grand duke of Brunswick. The town of Wolfenbüttel which then became his home was not exactly a metropolis,but the grand-ducal library was one of the finest in all Germany. It contained more than ten thousand manuscripts and several of these were of prime importance in the history of the Reformation.

Boredom of course is the main incentive to scandal mongering and gossip. In Wolfenbüttel a former art critic,columnist and dramatic essayist was by this very fact a highly suspicious person and soon Lessing was once more in trouble. Not because of anything he had done but on account of something he was vaguely supposed to have done,to wit:the publication of a series of articles attacking the orthodox opinions of the old school of Lutheran theology.

走了他最重要的手稿，警方必须监视边界，等等。就像在异地他乡的激动的法国人所做的那样。没过几天，邮递员带回了丢失的稿件，但里面还有莱辛写的一封信，这个直率、年轻的条顿人在信中对那些敢怀疑他的诚实的人表达了自己的不满。

这场小小的风波本应该很容易被忘记，但18世纪是小事件在男男女女的生活中发挥巨大作用的时期。即使是在近20年之后，腓特烈大帝仍然喜欢他那位爱找麻烦的法国朋友（伏尔泰），所以也就不愿让莱辛到他的宫廷中来。

于是，莱辛告别柏林来到汉堡。在汉堡有个谣传，说要新建一座国家剧院。这项计划未能实现，莱辛在绝望中接受了在世袭的布伦斯威克公爵的图书馆当馆员的工作。那时他居住的沃尔芬布特尔城不是真正的大城市，但是大公爵的图书馆在全德国是首屈一指的。它保存了1万多部手稿，其中好几部是宗教改革史上最重要的文献。

无聊当然是导致丑闻交易和流言蜚语的主要原因。在沃尔芬布特尔城，以前曾经当过艺术批评家、专栏作家和戏剧随笔作家的人很令人怀疑，因此莱辛不久再次陷入困境。这倒不是因为他做了什么事，而是因为有人含糊地推测他发表了一系列攻击旧派路德神学正统观点的文章。

这些说教（因为它们就是说教）实际上是汉堡一位前任大臣撰写的，但是布伦斯威克大公爵对于在他的领地里开展一场宗教战的前景感到惶恐不安，便命令他的图书管理员谨慎行事，远离一切争议。莱辛按照主人的要求做了。然而，当时谁也没有说过不允用戏剧的形式讨论这个问题，于是莱辛开始工作，通过舞台的形式重新阐述他的看法。

These sermons (for sermons they were) had actually been written by a former Hamburg minister,but the grand duke of Brunswick,panic stricken at the prospect of a religious war within his domains,ordered his librarian to be discreet and keep away from all controversies. Lessing complied with the wishes of his employer. Nothing,however,had been said about treating the subject dramatically and so he set to work to re-valuate his opinions in terms of the stage.

The play which was born out of this small-town rumpus was called"Nathan the Wise. "The theme was very old and I have mentioned it before in this book. Lovers of literary antiquities can find it (if Mr. Sumner will allow them) in Boccaccio's"Decameron"where it is called the"Sad Story of the Three Rings"and where it is told as follows:

Once upon a time a Mohammedan prince tried to extract a large sum of money from one of his Jewish subjects. But as he had no valid reason to deprive the poor man of his property,he bethought himself of a ruse. He sent for the victim and having complimented him gracefully upon his learning and wisdom,he asked him which of the three most widely spread religions,the Turkish,the Jewish and the Christian,he held to be most true. The worthy patriarch did not answer the Padishah directly but said,"Let me,oh great Sultan,tell you a little story. Once upon a time there was a very rich man who had a beautiful ring and he made a will that whichever of his sons at the time of his death should be found with that ring upon his finger should fall heir to all his estates. His son made a like will. His grandson too,and for centuries the ring changed hands and all was well. But finally it happened that the owner of the ring had three sons whom he loved equally well. He simply could not decide which of the three should own that much valued treasure. So he went to a goldsmith and ordered him to make two other rings exactly like the one he had. On his death-bed he sent for his children and gave them each his blessing and what they supposed was the one and only ring. Of course,as soon as the father had been buried,the three boys all claimed to be his heir because they had The Ring. This led to many quarrels and finally

在这个小镇娱乐室里诞生的戏剧就是《聪明的南森》。这部戏剧主题非常古老，我在本书前面提到过它。喜欢古典文学的人能在薄伽丘的《十日谈》中找到它（如果萨姆勒先生允许的话）。在《十日谈》中它被称为《三个戒指的悲惨故事》，里面是这样说的：

很久很久以前，有一位伊斯兰教的王子想从他的一个犹太臣民那里敲诈一大笔钱。但是他没有正当理由剥夺这个可怜人的财产，就想出了一条诡计。他派人找来这个受害者，先是大大地赞赏了他的学识和智慧，然后问他，在伊斯兰教、犹太教和基督教这三种流传最广的宗教中，他认为哪一个最真实？这个令人尊敬的人没有正面回答王子，而是说："噢，伟大的苏丹，让我给你讲个小故事吧！从前，有一个很有钱的人，他有一枚漂亮的戒指。他立下遗嘱说，他死的时候，无论哪个儿子手指上带着这枚戒指，就将继承他的全部财产。他的儿子也立了同样的遗嘱，他的孙子也一样。几百年来，这枚戒指换了一个又一个主人，一直保存完好。但是最后碰巧有一个主人，他有三个儿子，他都同样爱他们，因此他很难决定哪一个应该拥有这无价珍宝。于是，他找到一个金匠，让他做了两枚和自己的一模一样的戒指。快要咽气的时候，他把三个孩子都叫来，为每个人祝福，他们也都认为自己是那枚戒指唯一的继承人。父亲刚一下葬，三个孩子当然都宣布自己是继承人，因为他们都有那枚戒指。这导致了许多争吵，最后他们把这件事交给法官裁决。由于这三枚戒指一模一样，即使是法官也无法断定哪枚是真的，于是这个案子就一直拖了下来，而且很可能要拖到世界末日。阿门。"

莱辛用这个古老的民间故事来证明他的观点：没有一种宗教可以垄断真理；人

they laid the matter before the Kadi. But as the rings were absolutely alike,even the judges could not decide which was the right one and so the case has been dragged on and on and very likely will drag on until the end of the world. Amen."

Lessing used this ancient folk-tale to prove his belief that no one religion possessed a monopoly of the truth,that it was the inner spirit of man that counted rather than his outward conformity to certain prescribed rituals and dogmas and that therefore it was the duty of people to bear with each other in love and friendship and that no one had the right to set himself upon a high pedestal of self-assured perfection and say,"I am better than all others because I alone possess the Truth."

But this idea,much applauded in the year 1778,was no longer popular with the little princelings who thirty years later returned to salvage such goods and chattels as had survived the deluge of the Revolution. For the purpose of regaining their lost prestige,they abjectly surrendered their lands to the rule of the police-sergeant and expected the clerical gentlemen who depended upon them for their livelihood to act as a spiritual militia and help the regular cops to restablish law and order.

But whereas the purely political reaction was completely successful,the attempt to reshape men's minds after the pattern of fifty years before ended in failure. And it could not be otherwise. It was true that the vast majority of the people in all countries were sick and tired of revolution and unrest,of parliaments and futile speeches and forms of taxation that had completely ruined commerce and industry. They wanted peace. Peace at any price. They wanted to do business and sit in their own front parlors and drink coffee and not be disturbed by the soldiers billeted upon them and forced to drink an odious extract of oak-leaves. Provided they could enjoy this blessed state of well-being,they were willing to put up with certain small inconveniences such as saluting whoever wore brass buttons,bowing low before every imperial letter-box and saying"Sir"to every assistant official chimney-sweep.

But this attitude of humble obedience was the result of sheer necessity,of the need for

的内心精神比他表面上遵奉某种规定的仪式和教条更重要，因此人们的任务就是友爱、和睦地相处，任何人都无权把自己视为完美无缺的偶像，也无权宣布："我比其他人都好，因为只有我掌握着真理。"

但是这个在1778年曾备受赞许的思想，在30年后的小诸侯国里却不再受欢迎。这些小诸侯在大革命的浪潮中都极力设法保住残存的财产和牲畜。为了重获他们已经失去的声望，他们卑怯地把自己的土地交给警察管理，并期望那些依赖他们谋生的牧师先生能担当精神卫兵，帮助正规军重建法律和秩序。

但其实是纯粹政治上的反动取得了完全胜利，那些试图按照50年前的模式重新塑造人们精神的努力以失败告终了，不会有其他的结局。诚然，所有国家的大多数群众对革命、骚乱、议会、毫无意义的演讲和完全遭到破坏的工商业的各种税收已经感到厌恶和疲倦了。他们想要和平，可以不惜一切代价。他们想做生意，坐在自己的客厅里喝咖啡，不再受到住在家里的士兵的骚扰，不再被迫喝从橡树叶上挤出的令人作呕的汁水。如果能享受到这种幸福愉快的生活，他们宁愿容忍一些小小的不方便，例如向每个穿制服的人行礼，在每个皇家信箱前面鞠躬，并用"先生"来称呼宫廷清扫烟囱的工人。

但这种谦卑顺从的态度完全是出于迫切的需要，出于在经过漫长而动荡不安的年代后要有一个短暂的喘息之机。那时，每天早晨都会出现新制服、新的政治纲领、新的法规政策和新的统治者，既有天上的又有地上的。然而，如果从这种一般的奴性姿态，从对上帝任命的主人的高声欢呼中就推断人们在心灵深处已经忘记了曾经撞击过他们头脑和心胸的格朗中士的新教义的擂鼓声，那可就错了。

a short breathing space after the long and tumultuous years when every new morning brought new uniforms,new political platforms,new police regulations and new rulers,both of Heaven and earth. It would be erroneous,however,to conclude from this general air of subservience,from this loud hurraying for the divinely appointed masters,that the people in their heart of hearts had forgotten the new doctrines which the drums of Sergeant Le Grand had so merrily beaten into their heads and hearts.

As their governments,with that moral cynicism inherent in all reactionary dictatorships,insisted chiefly upon an outward semblance of decency and order and cared not one whit for the inner spirit,the average subject enjoyed a fairly wide degree of independence. On Sunday he went to church with a large Bible under his arm. The rest of the week he thought as he pleased. Only he held his tongue and kept his private opinions to himself and aired his views when a careful inspection of the premises had first assured him that no secret agent was hidden underneath the sofa or was lurking behind the tile stove. Then however he discussed the events of the day with great gusto and sadly shook his head when his duly censored,fumigated and sterilized newspaper told him what new idiotic measures his masters had taken to assure the peace of the realm and bring about a return to the status quo of the year of grace 1600.

What his masters were doing was exactly what similar masters with an imperfect knowledge of the history of human nature under similar circumstances have been doing ever since the year one. They thought that they had destroyed free speech when they ordered the removal of the cracker-barrels from which the speeches that had so severely criticized their government had been made. And whenever they could,they sent the offending orators to jail with such stiff sentences (forty,fifty,a hundred years) that the poor devils gained great renown as martyrs,whereas in most instances they were scatter-brained idiots who had read a few books and pamphlets which they had failed to understand.

Warned by this example,the others kept away from the public parks and did their grumbling in obscure wine shops or in the public lodging houses of overcrowded cities

因为他们的政府具有一切反动独裁者所固有的玩世不恭，主要要求表面上的体面端庄和秩序，而不怎么关心人们的内心世界，所以平民百姓享有很大程度的自由。星期日，他会胳膊下夹一大本《圣经》去教堂，剩下那几天便可以随心所欲地思考。但他们必须保持缄默，保留个人见解，在发表言论之前要先仔细查看一下，保证沙发底下或炉子后边没有藏暗探。然而，尽管他们可以兴致勃勃地谈论当日发生的事情，但从经过正式审查、反复推敲、消过毒的报纸上他们又得知，主人又采取了新的愚蠢方法来保证王国的和平，以便重返1600年的体面年代时，他们又会伤心地摇头。

他们的主人所做的，正是自公元元年以来所有对人类本性的历史一无所知的主人们在类似的情况下一直在做的事情。他们认为，只要下令搬走人们站在上面发表攻击政府的激烈言词的装饼干的大桶，就能摧毁言论自由。因此只要有可能，他们就把出言不逊的演讲者送进监狱，从严宣判（40年、50年或100年的监禁），这些可怜的人因此得到了烈士的声誉。不过在大多数情况下，这些主人不过是浮躁的白痴，只读过几本书和一些小册子，甚至根本就没有看懂。

受到这种例子的警告，其他人都远离了公共场所，躲到偏僻的酒馆或拥挤的城市的公共旅店里去发牢骚，他们确信在这里有谨慎的听众，他们在这里的影响比在公共讲台上更具有无限震撼力。

上帝以其智慧赋予某人一点点权力，而这个人却时刻担心失去自己的官方声望，世界上再也没有什么比这更可怜的。一个国王可以失去他的王位，并且对这场打断他枯燥无味的日常生活的有趣小插曲报以一笑。不论他是戴着男仆褐色的圆顶

where they were certain of a discreet audience and where their influence was infinitely more harmful than it would have been on a public platform.

There are few things more pathetic in this world than the man upon whom the Gods in their wisdom have bestowed a little bit of authority and who is in eternal fear for his official prestige. A king may lose his throne and may laugh at a misadventure which means a rather amusing interruption of a life of dull routine. And anyway he is a king,whether he wears his valet's brown derby or his grandfather's crown. But the mayor of a third rate town,once he has been deprived of his gavel and his badge of office,is just plain Bill Smith,a ridiculous fellow who gave himself airs and who is now laughed at for his troubles. Therefore woe unto him who dares to approach such a potentate pro tem without visible manifestations of that reverence and worship due to so exalted a human being.

But those who did not stop at burgomasters,but who openly questioned the existing order of things in learned tomes and handbooks of geology and anthropology and economics,fared infinitely worse.

They were instantly and dishonorably deprived of their livelihood. Then they were exiled from the town in which they had taught their pernicious doctrines and with their wives and children were left to the charitable mercies of the neighbors.

This outbreak of the reactionary spirit caused great inconvenience to a large number of perfectly sincere people who were honestly trying to go to the root of our many social ills. Time,however,the great laundress,has long since removed whatever spots the local police magistrates were able to detect upon the professorial garments of these amiable scholars. Today,King Frederick William of Prussia is chiefly remembered because he interfered with the teachings of Emanuel Kant,that dangerous radical who taught that the maxims of our own actions must be worthy of being turned into universal laws and whose doctrines,according to the police reports,appealed only to"beardless youths and idle babblers. "The Duke of Cumberland has gained lasting notoriety because as King of Hanover he exiled a certain Jacob Grimm who had signed a protest against"His Majeaty's

礼帽，还是戴着他祖父的王冠，他终究是一个国王。但是，对于一个三流城市的市长来说，一旦被剥夺了小木槌和办公室的徽章，那他就只是一位普通人，一个可笑的自以为是的人，一个被人们嘲笑陷入困境的人。因此，谁要是胆敢接近这样一个大人物，却没有向他表示应有的尊敬和崇拜，谁就会大难临头。

但是那些跟市长过不去，公开在学术巨著、地质学、人类学和经济学作品中质疑现存秩序的人，他们的处境更糟。

他们立即被屈辱地剥夺了生计，然后被从他们曾散布过有毒教义的镇子里赶了出去，妻子儿女全靠邻居的施舍度日。

这种反动精神的大爆发，给一大批极其真诚、本想根除诸多社会弊病根源的人带来了极大的不便。然而，时间这位伟大的洗衣女，早已把粘在这些和善学者们制服上的、能被地方警察发现的污迹洗掉了。今天，普鲁士的腓特烈·威廉之所以能够被人记住，主要是因为他干涉了危险的激进分子伊曼纽尔·康德的学说。康德教诲说，我们的行动准则必须变成具有普遍性的准则。按照警方的记录，他的教义只能吸引“稚嫩的青年和游手好闲的告密者”。坎伯兰公爵之所以一直臭名远扬，就是因为他作为汉诺威国王，流放了一位名叫雅各布·格瑞姆的人——这个人在一份《陛下非法取消国家宪法》的抗议书上签过字。梅特涅的名声也不好，因为他竟然连音乐领域也不放过，曾经审查过舒伯特的音乐。

可怜的老奥地利!

现在，奥地利已经死亡，不复存在了，整个世界都对这个“快乐帝国”相当

unlawful abrogation of the country's constitution. "And Metternich has retained a certain notoriety because he extended his watchful suspicion to the field of music and once censored the music of Schubert.

Poor old Austria!

Now that it is dead and gone,all the world feels kindly disposed towards the"gay empire"and forgets that once upon a time it had an active intellectual life of its own and was something more than an amusing and well-mannered county-fair with excellent and cheap wine,atrocious cigars and the most enticing of waltzes,composed and conducted by no one less than Johann Strauss himself.

We may go even further and state that during the entire eighteenth century Austria played a very important rôle in the development of the idea of religious tolerance. Immediately after the Reformation the Protestants had found a fertile field for their operations in the rich province between the Danube and the Carpathian Mountains. But this had changed when Rudolf II became emperor.

This Rudolf was a German version of Spanish Philip,a ruler to whom treaties made with heretics were of no consequence whatsoever. But although educated by the Jesuits,he was incurably lazy and this saved his empire from too drastic a change of policy.

That came when Ferdinand II was chosen emperor. This monarch's chief qualification for office was the fact that he alone among all the Habsburgs was possessed of a few sons. Early during his reign he had visited the famous House of the Annunciation,bodily moved in the year 1291 by a number of angels from Nazareth to Dalmatia and hence to central Italy,and there in an outburst of religious fervor he had sworn a dire oath to make his country one-hundred-percent Catholic.

He had been as good as his word. In the year 1629 Catholicism once more was proclaimed the official and exclusive faith of Austria and Styria and Bohemia and Silesia.

Hungary having been meanwhile married into that strange family,which acquired vast

■ 莱辛

友好，忘记了它从前也有过积极的思想生活，这是比充满乐趣、装潢一新的乡村集市上物美价廉的酒、劣质的雪茄和由约翰·施特劳斯本人作曲和指挥的迷人的华尔兹更加珍贵的东西。

我们甚至可以说，整个18世纪，奥地利在传播宗教宽容思想上扮演了非常重要的角色。宗教改革运动之后，新教徒马上在多瑙河和喀尔巴阡山脉之间的富裕省份找到了一块肥沃的土地作为他们施展拳脚的地方。但是当鲁道夫二世当上皇帝之后，一切都变了。

这位鲁道夫是西班牙菲利普的德国化身，对他来说，和异教徒签订的条约没有任何约束。虽然他接受的是耶稣会的教育，但他懒得不可救药，这倒使他的帝国避免了政策上的剧烈变化。

这种剧变在费迪南德二世当选皇帝时发生了。他继承君位的主要资格，是在哈布斯堡王族中，只有他儿子较多。他在统治初期还参观了有名的天使报喜馆，这个建筑是1291年被一群从拿撒勒到达尔马提亚的天使们搬迁到意大利中心的。在这

quantities of European real estate with every new wife,an effort was made to drive the Protestants from their Magyar strongholds. But backed up by the Transylvanians,who were Unitarians,and by the Turks,who were heathen,the Hungarians were able to maintain their independence until the second half of the eighteenth century. And by that time a great change had taken place in Austria itself.

The Habsburgs were loyal sons of the Church,but at last even their sluggish brains grew tired of the constant interference with their affairs on the part of the Popes and they were willing for once to risk a policy contrary to the wishes of Rome.

In an earlier part of this book I have already told how many medieval Catholics believed that the organization of the Church was all wrong. In the days of the martyrs,these critics argued,the Church was a true democracy ruled by elders and bishops who were appointed by common consent of all the parishioners. They were willing to concede that the Bishop of Rome,because he claimed to be the direct successor of the Apostle Peter,had been entitled to a favorite position in the councils of the Church,but they insisted that this power had been purely honorary and that the popes therefore should never have considered themselves superior to the other bishops and should not have tried to extend their influence beyond the confines of their own territory.

The popes from their side had fought this idea with all the bulls,anathemas and excommunications at their disposal and several brave reformers had lost their lives as a result of their bold agitation for greater clerical decentralization.

The question had never been definitely settled,and then during the middle of the eighteenth century,the idea was revived by the vicargeneral of the rich and powerful archbishop of Trier. His name was Johann von Hontheim,but he is better known by his Latin pseudonym of Febronius. Hontheim had enjoyed the advantages of a very liberal education. After a few years spent at the University of Louvain he had temporarily forsaken his own people and had gone to the University of Leiden. He got there at a time when that

里，他爆发出一种宗教狂热，发毒誓要把他的国家变成百分之百的天主教国家。

他恪守了诺言。1629年，天主教再一次被宣布为奥地利、斯蒂里亚、波希米亚和西里西亚官方唯一的宗教。

与此同时，匈牙利与这个奇怪的家族建立了婚姻关系，每个新妻子都带来了大片欧洲地产，于是费迪南德就开始把新教徒从马扎尔人集中居住的地区赶出去。但是，在特兰西瓦尼亚一神论教徒和土耳其异教徒的支持下，匈牙利直到18世纪下半叶仍保持着独立。这时，奥地利内部发生了巨大变化。

哈布斯堡王室是教会的忠实子民，但最后就连思想最迟钝的人也对教皇的不断干涉产生了厌烦，他们很想冒险制定一项违背罗马意愿的政策。

在本书比较早的篇幅里我已经讲过，许多中世纪的天主教徒认为教会体制是完全错误的。这些批评者认为，在殉道者的时代，教会是真正的民主机构，它由年长者和主教掌管，而这些人正是由教区居民推选的。他们愿意承认罗马主教，因为他（主教）自称是圣徒彼得的直接继承人，有权在教会委员会中占显著的位置。但是他们坚持认为这种权力只是纯粹荣誉性的，因此教皇不应该认为自己比其他主教优越，不应把其影响扩展到自己的领地之外。

教皇从自身利益出发，与所有的投机分子、被教会诅咒或驱逐出教的人一起，全力反对这种思想。结果，好几个勇敢的改革者由于大胆地倡导教会分权而丧命。

这个问题一直没有完全解决，后来在18世纪中叶，这种思想被有钱有势的特利尔市代理主教给复苏了。他叫约翰·冯·霍特姆，但他的拉丁文笔名福布罗尼乌斯更为人所知。他受过自由思想的教育。在卢万大学学习几年之后，他暂时离开家人

old citadel of undiluted Calvinism was beginning to be suspected of liberal tendencies. This suspicion had ripened into open conviction when Professor Gerard Noodt,a member of the legal faculty,had been allowed to enter the field of theology and had been permitted to publish a speech in which he had extolled the ideal of religious tolerance.

His line of reasoning had been ingenious,to say the least.

"God is allpowerful,"so he had said."God is able to lay down certain laws of science which hold good for all people at all times and under all conditions. It follows that it would have been very easy for him,had he desired to do so,to guide the minds of men in such a fashion that they all of them should have had the same opinions upon the subject of religion. We know that He did not do anything of the sort. Therefore,we act against the express will of God if we try to coerce others by force to believe that which we ourselves hold to be true."

Whether Hontheim was directly influenced by Noodt or not,it is hard to say. But something of that same spirit of Erasmian rationalism can be found in those works of Hontheim in which he afterwards developed his own ideas upon the subject of episcopal authority and papal decentralization.

That his books were immediately condemned by Rome (in February of the year 1764) is of course no more than was to be expected. But it happened to suit the interests of Maria Theresa to support Hontheim and Febronianism or Episcopalianism,as the movement which he had started was called,continued to flourish in Austria and finally took practical shape in a Patent of Tolerance which Joseph II,the son of Maria Theresa,bestowed upon his subjects on the thirteenth of October of the year 1781.

Joseph,who was a weak imitation of his mother's great enemy,Frederick of Prussia,had a wonderful gift for doing the right thing at the wrong moment. During the last two hundred years the little children of Austria had been sent to bed with the threat that the Protestants would get them if they did not go to sleep at once. To insist that those same infants henceforth regard their Protestant neighbors (who,as they all knew,had horns and a long black tail),as their

到莱顿大学读书。他到达那里时，正值这个纯加尔文主义的老城堡开始被怀疑有自由主义倾向。等到一位法律部门的成员杰拉德教授获准进入神学界，并发表演讲赞扬宗教宽容的理想的时候，这种怀疑就演变成了公开的罪证。

至少可以说，他的推理方法具有创造性。

他说："上帝是万能的。他有能力制定对所有人在任何时间、任何情况下都适用的科学法规。所以，只要他想做，就可以很容易地引导人们的思想，使所有人在宗教问题上持相同的观点。我们知道，上帝并没有这么干。因此，如果我们用武力迫使别人相信我们认为是正确的东西，我们就违背了上帝的明确旨意。"

很难说霍特姆是否受到了伊拉斯谟的直接影响，但是从霍特姆的著作中可以发现与伊拉斯谟理性主义思想相似的东西。他后来在这些著作中就主教权限和罗马教皇公权的问题上发展了自己的思想。

不出所料，他的书当然马上（1764年2月）受到了罗马的非难。但这正好符合玛丽亚·特雷莎的利益，因此她支持了霍特姆发起的这场被称为费布罗尼主义或主教统治主义的运动。该运动继续在奥地利繁荣发展，最后形成了实用的《宽容特许权》，玛丽亚·特雷莎的儿子约瑟夫二世在1781年10月13日把它赐给了自己的臣民。

约瑟夫是他母亲的大敌普鲁士国王腓特烈的一个脆弱翻本，他有一项惊人的才能，那就是在错误时刻做出正确的事情。在过去200年中，奥地利的孩子入睡时经常被大人吓唬说，要是不赶紧睡觉，新教徒就会把他抓走。因此，要让孩子们把新教徒邻居（就像他们知道的那样，新教徒长着角和一条长长的黑尾巴）当作亲如手

dearly beloved brothers and sisters was to ask the impossible. All the same,poor,honest,hard working,blundering Joseph,forever surrounded by a horde of uncles and aunts and cousins who enjoyed fat incomes as bishops and cardinals and deaconesses,deserves great credit for this sudden outburst of courage. He was the first among the Catholic rulers who dared to advocate tolerance as a desirable and practical possibility of statecraft.

And what he did three months later was even more startling. On the second of February of the year of grace 1782 he issued his famous decree concerning the Jews and extended the liberty then only enjoyed by Protestants and Catholics to a category of people who thus far had considered themselves fortunate when they were allowed to breathe the same air as their Christian neighbors.

Right here we ought to stop and let the reader believe that the good work continued indefinitely and that Austria now became a Paradise for those who wished to follow the dictates of their own conscience.

I wish it were true. Joseph and a few of his ministers might rise to a sudden height of common sense,but the Austrian peasant,taught since time immemorial to regard the Jew as his natural enemy and the Protestant as a rebel and a renegade,could not possibly overcome that old and deep-rooted prejudice which told him to regard such people as his natural enemies.

A century and a half after the promulgation of these excellent Edicts of Tolerance,the position of those who did not belong to the Catholic Church was quite as unfavorable as it had been in the sixteenth century. Theoretically a Jew and a Protestant could hope to become prime ministers or to be appointed commander-in-chief of the army. And in practice it was impossible for them to be invited to dinner by the imperial boot-black.

So much for paper decrees.

足的兄弟姐妹是根本不可能的。同样，总是被叔伯、姑妈和表亲（他们与主教、红衣主教和女执事一样享受着荣华富贵）包围着的可怜、诚实、勤奋、易犯错误的约瑟夫，他那突如其来的勇气很值得赞扬。在天主教统治者中，他是第一个敢于宣称宽容是治理国家的理想而实用的财富的人。

他在三个月后做的事情更令人震惊。1782年2月2日，他颁布了有关犹太人的著名法令，把只有新教徒和天主教徒才享有的自由权利扩展到了那些直到这时才认为自己是幸运儿的犹太人，他们获准可以和基督徒邻居呼吸同样的空气。

我们应该在这儿停笔，让读者相信这个好事还在不确定地延续着。奥地利现在成了那些希望追随自己的良心行事的人的天堂。

我希望这是真的。约瑟夫和他的几位大臣可能在观念上达到了一个突然的高度，但是奥地利的农民自古以来就一直被教导说，犹太人是他们的天敌，新教徒是叛教者，所以他们不可能克服将这些人当作天敌的根深蒂固的偏见。

杰出的《宽容法令》已经颁布一个半世纪了，可是非天主教徒的地位仍然和16世纪一样糟糕。从理论上说，一个犹太人或一个新教徒可以指望当首相或被任命为军队总司令。但实际上，他们连和皇帝的擦鞋匠吃一顿饭的机会都没有。

关于这一纸法令，就讲这些吧。

CHAPTER X X IX TOM PAINE

Somewhere or other there is a poem to the effect that God moves in a mysterious way,his wonders to perform.

The truth of this statement is most apparent to those who have studied the history of the Atlantic seaboard.

During the first half of the seventeenth century the northern part of the American continent was settled by people who had gone so far in their devotion to the ideals of the Old Testament that an unsuspecting visitor might have taken them for followers of Moses,rather than disciples of the words of Christ. Cut off from the rest of Europe by a very wide and very stormy and very cold expanse of ocean,these pioneers had set up a spiritual reign of terror which had culminated in the witch-hunting orgies of the Mather family.

Now at first sight it seems not very likely that those two reverend gentlemen could in any way be held responsible for the very tolerant tendencies which we find expounded with such able vigor in the Constitution of the United States and in the many documents that were written immediately before the outbreak of hostilities between England and her former colonies. Yet such is undoubtedly the case,for the period of repression of the seventeenth century was so terrible that it was bound to create a furious reaction in favor of a more liberal point of view.

This does not mean that all the colonists suddenly sent for the collected works of Socinius and ceased to frighten little children with stories about Sodom and Gomorrah. But their

第29章　汤姆·潘恩

在某个地方流传着一首诗，它的大意是，上帝用一种神秘的方式创造了他的种种奇迹。

对于研究过大西洋沿海地区历史的人来说，这一说法的真实性是很明显的。

17世纪上半叶，美洲大陆北部住着一批对《旧约》理想极其崇拜的人，不知内情的参观者还可能把他们当作摩西的追随者，而不是基督言论的信徒。浩瀚汹涌、寒气袭人的大西洋把这些开拓者与欧洲国家决然隔开了，他们在美洲大陆建立了一种恐怖的精神统治，并在对马瑟家族的大规模追捕中达到了顶点。

现在乍一看，似乎不大可能把这种宽容的倾向和这两位令人起敬的绅士联系在一起，而在英国与她从前的殖民地之间的敌对情绪爆发前，这种宽容倾向在《美国宪法》和其他许多文件里又讲得明明白白。真实的情况是，由于17世纪有一段时期的镇压非常可怕，便注定会造成支持更加自由的思想的强烈反作用。

这并不是说，所有的殖民主义者都突然派人去收集索兹尼的作品，不再用所多玛和蛾摩拉这两个罪恶之地和罪恶之城的故事来吓唬小孩子。但是他们的领导几乎都是新思想的代表，他们都很有能力、很有策略，把自己的宽容思想写在羊皮纸纲领中，新的独立民族的大厦即将在这上面拔地而起。

leaders were almost without exception representatives of the new school of thought and with great ability and tact they infused their own conceptions of tolerance into the parchment platform upon which the edifice of their new and independent nation was to be erected.

They might not have been quite so successful if they had been obliged to deal with one united country. But colonization in the northern part of America had always been a complicated business. The Swedish Lutherans had explored part of the territory. The French had sent over some of their Huguenots. The Dutch Arminians had occupied a large share of the land. While almost every sort and variety of English sect had at one time or another tried to found a little Paradise of its own in the wilderness between the Hudson Bay and the Gulf of Mexico.

This had made for a variety of religious expression and so well had the different denominations been balanced that in several of the colonies a crude and rudimentary form of mutual forbearance had been forced upon a people who under ordinary circumstances would have been forever at each other's throats.

This development had been very unwelcome to the reverend gentlemen who prospered where others quarreled. For years after the advent of the new spirit of charity they had continued their struggle for the maintenance of the old ideal of rectitude. They had achieved very little but they had successfully estranged many of the younger men from a creed which seemed to have borrowed its conceptions of mercy and kindliness from some of its more ferocious Indian neighbors.

Fortunately for our country,the men who bore the brunt of battle in the long struggle for freedom belonged to this small but courageous group of dissenters.

Ideas travel lightly. Even a little two-masted schooner of eighty tons can carry enough new notions to upset an entire continent. The American colonists of the eighteenth century

如果他们必须对付一个统一的国家，他们很可能不会这么成功。但是在美洲北部进行殖民一直是件很复杂的事情。瑞士的路德派开辟了一部分土地，法国派来了一些胡格诺教徒，荷兰的阿米尼乌斯教徒占领了一大块土地，而英国几乎每个宗派都争先恐后地想在哈得孙湾和墨西哥湾之间的荒凉地带找到自己的小天堂。

■ 汤姆·潘恩

这促进了各种教派的发展，不同宗派之间便保持了很好的平衡。在一些殖民地，人们被迫接受了最原始而初级的互相容忍，而在一般情况下他们非拼个你死我活不可。

对于那些在别人争吵之际发财的体面绅士来说，这种局面当然不受欢迎。在新的仁爱精神出现许多年之后，他们仍然在为维持旧的正直理想而坚持战斗。虽然他们一无所获，却成功地使年轻人疏远了一种信条，这个信条似乎是从比它更野蛮的印第安邻居有关仁慈善良的概念中借来的。

were obliged to do without sculpture and grand pianos,but they did not lack for books. The more intelligent among the people in the thirteen colonies began to understand that there was something astir in the big world,of which they had never heard anything in their Sunday sermons. The booksellers then became their prophets. And although they did not officially break away from the established church and changed little in their outer mode of life,they showed when the opportunity offered itself that they were faithful disciples of that old prince of Transylvania,who had refused to persecute his Unitarian subjects on the ground that the good Lord had expressly reserved for himself the right to three things:"To be able to create something out of nothing;to know the future;and to dominate man's conscience."

And when it became necessary to draw up a concrete political and social program for the future conduct of their country,these brave patriots incorporated their ideas into the documents in which they placed their ideals before the high court of public opinion.

It would undoubtedly have horrified the good citizens of Virginia had they known that some of the oratory to which they listened with such profound respect was directly inspired by their arch-enemies,the Libertines. But Thomas Jefferson,their most successful politician,was himself a man of exceedingly liberal views and when he remarked that religion could only be regulated by reason and conviction and not by force or violence;or again,that all men had an equal right to the free exercise of their religion according to the dictates of their conscience,he merely repeated what had been thought and written before by Voltaire and Bayle and Spinoza and Erasmus.

And later when the following heresies were heard:"that no declaration of faith should be required as a condition of obtaining any public office in the United States,"or"that Congress should make no law which referred to the establishment of religion or which prohibited the free exercise thereof,"the American rebels acquiesced and accepted.

对我们国家来说，幸运的是，在这场争取自由的长期斗争中，首当其冲的是一批人数虽少却敢持不同政见的大无畏的人。

思想悄无声息地传播开来，甚至一艘80吨重的双桅小帆船就可以携带足够多的新思想，使整个大陆陷入混乱。18世纪的美洲殖民主义者没有什么雕塑和大钢琴，但他们并不缺乏书籍。13个殖民地中的开明人士开始明白，这个大千世界正在发生骚乱，而这在星期日的布道中是听不到的。那时的书商成了他们的先知。尽管他们没有公开脱离已有的教会，表面的生活也没有任何变化，但是时机一到，他们立即就表示自己是特兰西瓦尼亚老王储最忠实的信徒。这位老王储拒绝迫害坚持“一神论”的臣民，理由是因为仁慈的上帝已经明确地给自己保留了做三件事的权力：“创造新事物，预知未来，支配人的良知。”

当需要制订一个具体的政治和社会纲领，以便将来治理国家时，这些勇敢的爱国者就把自己的思想写进了文件里，接受公共舆论这个高级法庭的检验。

如果弗吉尼亚善良的公民知道他们曾恭敬地倾听的一些演讲是由他们不共戴天的敌人自由思想者在直接操纵的话，他们一定会吓得要死。然而，最成功的政治家托马斯·杰斐逊本人就是一个思想非常自由的人，当他表示宗教只能用理性和说服力，而不能用武力或暴力来管理时；或者，当他又说所有的人都有同等权利按照自己的意志自由选择宗教时，他仅仅是在重复以前伏尔泰、拜勒、斯宾诺莎和伊拉斯谟已经想过并写在其作品中的思想而已。

后来，当人们又听到如下异端邪说“在美国谋求任何公职都不需要把宣布信仰

In this way the United States came to be the first country where religion was definitely separated from politics;the first country where no candidate for office was forced to show his Sunday School certificate before he could accept the nomination;the first country in which people could,as far as the law was concerned,worship or fail to worship as they pleased.

But here as in Austria (or anywhere else for that matter) the average man lagged far behind his leaders and was unable to follow them as soon as they deviated the least little bit from the beaten track. Not only did many of the states continue to impose certain restrictions upon those of their subjects who did not belong to the dominant religion,but the citizens in their private capacity as New Yorkers or Bostonians or Philadelphians continued to be just as intolerant of those who did not share their own views as if they had never read a single line of their own Constitution. All of which was to show itself soon afterwards in the case of Thomas Paine.

Tom Paine rendered a very great service to the cause of the Americans.

He was the publicity man of the Revolution.

By birth he was an Englishman;by profession,a sailor;by instinct and training,a rebel.

He was forty years old before he visited the colonies. While on a visit to London he had met Benjamin Franklin and had received the excellent advice"to go west. "In the year 1774,provided with letters of introduction from Benjamin himself,he had sailed for Philadelphia and had helped Richard Bache,the son-in-law of Franklin,to found a magazine,the"Pennsylvania Gazette."

Being an inveterate amateur politician,Tom had soon found himself in the midst of those events that were trying men's souls. And being possessed of a singularly well-ordered mind,he had taken hold of the ill-assorted collection of American grievances and had incorporated them into a pamphlet,short but sweet,which by a thorough application

作为条件”或“国会不应该使用法律手段干涉宗教的建立或者禁止自由运用宗教”时，美国的起义者们默许并接受了这种方法。

就这样，美国成为第一个宗教和政治明确分离的国家，成为第一个公职候选人在接受任命时不必出示主日毕业证的国家，成为第一个在法律上人民可以随意信仰或不信仰宗教的国家。

但是这里就像在奥地利（或其他存在这种问题的地方）一样，平民百姓比领袖们落后得多，领袖们稍微有一点偏离既定路线，他们就追赶不上了。许多州不仅继续对那些不属于主导宗教组织的百姓施加某些限制，而且纽约、波士顿或费城的人在私人生活中对那些好像从未读过一句本国宪法的持不同信仰者极不宽容。所有这些不久就体现在汤姆·潘恩事件上。

汤姆·潘恩为美国的事业做出了巨大的贡献。

他是美国独立战争的宣传家。

从出身讲，他是英国人，职业是水手；从先天和后天所受的教育来看，他是个反叛者。

他访问各殖民地时已经40岁了。有一次参观伦敦时，他遇见了本杰明·富兰克林，接受了“西行”的杰出建议。1774年，他带着本杰明的亲笔介绍信，起航前往费城，帮助富兰克林的女婿理查德·贝奇创办了《费城公报》杂志。

作为一个老牌业余政治家，汤姆很快就发现自己处在了考验人的灵魂的重大事件之中。不过，他的头脑非常有条理。他收集了关于美国人各种不满情绪的材料，

of"common sense"should convince the people that the American cause was a just cause and deserved the hearty coöperation of all loyal patriots.

This little book at once found its way to England and to the continent where it informed many people for the first time in their lives that there was such a thing as"an American nation"and that it had an excellent right,yea,it was its sacred duty to make war upon the mother country.

As soon as the Revolution was over,Paine went back to Europe to show the English people the supposed absurdities of the government under which they lived. It was a time when terrible things were happening along the banks of the Seine and when respectable Britishers were beginning to look across the Channel with very serious misgivings.

A certain Edmund Burke had just published his panic-stricken"Reflections on the French Revolution."Paine answered with a furious counter-blast of his own called"The Rights of Man"and as a result the English government ordered him to be tried for high treason.

Meanwhile his French admirers had elected him to the Convention and Paine,who did not know a word of French but was an optimist,accepted the honor and went to Paris. There he lived until he fell under the suspicion of Robespierre. Knowing that at any moment he might be arrested and decapitated,he hastily finished a book that was to contain his philosophy of life. It was called"The Age of Reason."The first part was published just before he was taken to prison. The second part was written during the ten months he spent in jail.

Paine believed that true religion,what he called"the religion of humanity,"had two enemies,atheism on the one hand and fanaticism on the other. But when he gave expression to this thought he was attacked by every one and when he returned to America in 1802 he was treated with such profound and relentless hatred that his reputation as a"dirty little atheist"has survived him by more than a century.

写成了一个小册子，篇幅不长，但写得让人爱读。这本小册子完全通过“常识”，使人们相信美国的事业是正义的，应当得到所有忠诚爱国者的全心全意合作。

这本小册子马上传到了英国和欧洲大陆，许多人有生以来第一次知道有这么一个“美利坚民族”，这个民族完全有理由，而且具有神圣的职责——向它的宗主国开战。

独立战争刚一结束，潘恩就回到欧洲，给英国人民展示了他们政府那些充满假象的谬论。当时，塞纳河两岸正发生着可怕的事情，体面的英国人开始满怀忧虑地观望着海峡对岸的情况。

一个叫埃德蒙·伯克的人刚发表了满怀惊恐的《对法国大革命的反思》。潘恩马上义愤填膺地以《人的权利》进行回击。结果，英国政府下令以叛国罪对他进行审问。

与此同时，他的法国崇拜者们却选他进入国会。潘恩对法语一窍不通，但他是个乐观主义者，接受了这项荣誉，来到了巴黎。他在这儿一直住到被罗伯斯比尔怀疑为止。潘恩知道自己随时有可能被捕或丧命，就赶忙完成了一本汇集他的人生哲学的书。这本书叫《理性时代》，第一部分是在他入狱之前发表的，第二部分是他待在监狱的十个月期间完成的。

潘恩认为，真正的宗教（他称之为“人性的宗教”）有两个敌人，一个是无神论，另一个是宗教狂热主义。但是他在表达这个思想时，受到了大家的攻击。当他于1802年返回美国时，遭到了人们极大的仇视，以至于他那“肮脏的小无神论者”

It is true that nothing happened to him. He was not hanged or burned or broken on the wheel. He was merely shunned by all his neighbors,little boys were encouraged to stick their tongues out at him when he ventured to leave his home,and at the time of his death he was an embittered and forgotten man who found relief for his anger in writing foolish political tracts against the other heroes of the Revolution.

This seems a most unfortunate sequel to a splendid beginning.

But it is typical of something that has repeatedly happened during the history of the last two thousand years.

As soon as public intolerance has spent its fury,private intolerance begins.

And lynchings start when official executions have come to an end.

的名声直到他去世之后还持续了一个多世纪。

他没出什么事，这倒是真的。他既没有被绞死或烧死，也没有在轮子上被分尸。他只是被众人所抛弃；当他鼓足勇气要出门时，人们就怂恿小孩子朝他伸舌头。他去世的时候，已经变成了被人唾弃遗忘的人。他撰写了一些反对独立战争中其他英雄的愚蠢小册子来发泄自己的愤怒。

对于一个光辉的开端来说，这似乎是极其不幸的结局。

但这是在过去2000年的历史中反复发生的典型事件。

一旦公众的不宽容刚发泄完愤怒，个人的不宽容又开始了。

当官方的死刑宣告终止时，私刑又开始了。

CHAPTER X X X THE LAST HUNDRED YEARS

Twelve years ago it would have been quite easy to write this book. The word "Intolerance,"in the minds of most people,was then almost exclusively identified with the idea of"religious intolerance"and when a historian wrote that"so and so had been a champion of tolerance"it was generally accepted that so and so had spent his life fighting the abuses of the Church and the tyranny of a professional priesthood.

Then came the war.

And much was changed in this world.

Instead of one system of intolerance,we got a dozen.

Instead of one form of cruelty,practiced by man upon his fellowmen,we got a hundred.

And a society which was just beginning to rid itself of the horrors of religious bigotry was obliged to put up with the infinitely more painful manifestations of a paltry form of racial intolerance and social intolerance and a score of petty forms of intolerance,the existence of which had not even been suspected a decade ago.

※ ※ ※ ※ ※ ※

This seems very terrible to many good people who until recently lived in the happy delusion that progress was a sort of automatic timepiece which needed no other winding than their occasional approbation.

They sadly shake their heads,whisper"Vanity,vanity,all is vanity!"and mutter disagreeable things about the cussedness of the human race which goes everlastingly to

第30章 最后一百年

20年前写这本书一定很容易。那时，“不宽容”这个词在大多数人的头脑中几乎和“宗教不宽容”的意思完全一样；当历史学家写“某人是宽容的捍卫者”时，人们通常会认为他毕生都在反对教会滥用权力和职业教士的暴虐专横。

然后，战争爆发了。

世界发生了很大变化。

我们得到的不是一种不宽容的制度，而是十几种。

一个人施加给同伴的残酷，形式不止一种，而是100种。

一个社会刚开始摆脱宗教偏执的恐怖，又必须忍受无限多的更加痛苦的种族不宽容、社会不宽容及许多不足挂齿的不宽容。对于它们的存在，十年前人们连想都没想过。

※ ※ ※ ※ ※ ※

对许多好人来说，直到最近他们还生活在愉快的幻觉之中，认为发展是一种自动时钟，只要有他们的偶尔赞许就不用再上发条，这似乎太可怕了。

他们悲伤地摇着头，嘟囔着：“虚荣，虚荣，所有这一切都是虚荣！”他们还抱怨人类本性所表现出来的令人讨厌的固执，人类永远都在求知，却总是拒绝

school,yet always refuses to learn.

Until,in sheer despair,they join the rapidly increasing ranks of our spiritual defeatists,attach themselves to this or that or the other religious institution (that they may transfer their own burden to the back of some one else),and in the most doleful tones acknowledge themselves beaten and retire from all further participation in the affairs of their community.

I don't like such people.

They are not merely cowards.

They are traitors to the future of the human race.

※ ※ ※ ※ ※ ※

So far so good,but what is the solution,if a solution there be?

Let us be honest with ourselves.

There is not any.

At least not in the eyes of a world which asks for quick results and expects to settle all difficulties of this earth comfortably and speedily with the help of a mathematical or medical formula or by an act of Congress. But those of us who have accustomed ourselves to consider history in the light of eternity and who know that civilization does not begin and end with the twentieth century,feel a little more hopeful.

That vicious circle of despair of which we hear so much nowadays(“man has always been that way,”“man always will be that way,”“the world never changes,”“things are just about the same as they were four thousand years ago,”) does not exist.

It is an optical illusion.

学会。

直到完全绝望的时候，他们才加入迅速增长的精神失败主义者的行列，依附于这个那个或其他的宗教协会（他们可以把自己的包袱转移到别人身上），用最沉闷的语调宣布自己失败了，并且不再参与以后的一切社会事务。

我不喜欢这种人。

他们不仅仅是懦夫。

他们还是人类未来的背叛者。

※ ※ ※ ※ ※ ※

到现在为止，解决的办法是什么，如果有解决的办法的话？

我们对自己要诚实。

没有任何解决的办法。

至少在一个人们要求立竿见影，希望借助数学或医药公式，或者国会的一个法案迅速而轻松地解决地球上所有困难的世界是看不到解决办法的。但是我们那些习惯用发展的眼光看待历史的人，以及那些知道文明不会随着20世纪的到来而开始或结束的人，会觉得还有些希望。

现在，我们听到的许多悲哀绝望的论断（如“人类一向是那样”“人类将永远那样”“世界从未有过变化”“情况和4000年前的完全一样”），都是不符合事实的。

这是一个视觉错觉。

The line of progress is often interrupted but if we set aside all sentimental prejudices and render a sober judgment upon the record of the last twenty thousand years (the only period about which we possess more or less concrete information) we notice an indubitable if slow rise from a condition of almost unspeakable brutality and crudeness to a state which holds the promise of something infinitely nobler and better than what has ever gone before and even the ghastly blunder of the Great War can not shake the firm conviction that this is true.

※ ※ ※ ※ ※ ※

The human race is possessed of almost incredible vitality.

It has survived theology.

In due time it will survive industrialism.

It has lived through cholera and plague,high heels and blue laws.

It will also learn how to overcome the many spiritual ills which beset the present generation.

※ ※ ※ ※ ※ ※

History,chary of revealing her secrets,has thus far taught us one great lesson.

What the hand of man has done,the hand of man can also undo.

It is a question of courage,and next to courage,of education.

※ ※ ※ ※ ※ ※

That of course sounds like a platitude. For the last hundred years we have had"education"driven into our ears until we are sick and tired of the word and look longingly back to a time when people could neither read nor write but used their surplus

进步的道路常常中断。但是，我们如果把感情上的偏见置于一边，对过去两万年的历史作个冷静的评价（仅这段时期我们或多或少掌握了一点具体材料），就会注意到一种虽然缓慢但却毋庸置疑的发展，事情总是从几乎无法形容的野蛮和粗鲁状态走向相比过去无限高尚和完善的境界，甚至世界大战的可怕错误也无法动摇这个坚定的看法，这是千真万确的。

※ ※ ※ ※ ※ ※

人类拥有几乎难以置信的生命力。

它在宗教信仰中幸存下来了。

总有一天，它的寿命将超过工业主义。

它经历了霍乱和瘟疫、残酷迫害和清教徒法规。

它还将学会如何克服困扰目前这一代人的诸多精神罪恶。

※ ※ ※ ※ ※ ※

历史谨慎地揭示了自己的秘密，已经给我们上了一堂伟大的课。

人自己制造的东西，也可以亲手将它毁灭。

这首先是一个勇气的问题，接下来才是教育的勇气。

※ ※ ※ ※ ※ ※

当然，这听起来像是老生常谈。在这最后100年里，“教育”灌满了人们的耳朵，直到我们厌恶这个词，渴望回到过去那个人们既不会读也不会写，但是能用多余的智力偶尔进行独立思考的时代。

intellectual energy for occasional moments of independent thinking.

But when I here speak of"education"I do not mean the mere accumulation of facts which is regarded as the necessary mental ballast of our modern children. Rather,I have in mind that true understanding of the present which is born out of a charitable and generous knowledge of the past.

In this book I have tried to prove that intolerance is merely a manifestation of the protective instinct of the herd.

A group of wolves is intolerant of the wolf that is different (be it through weakness or strength) from the rest of the pack and invariably tries to get rid of this offending and unwelcome companion.

A tribe of cannibals is intolerant of the individual who by his idiosyncrasies threatens to provoke the wrath of the Gods and bring disaster upon the whole village and brutally relegates him or her to the wilderness.

The Greek commonwealth can ill afford to harbor within its sacred walls a citizen who dares to question the very fundaments upon which the success of the community has been built and in a poor outburst of intolerance condemns the offending philosopher to the merciful death of poison.

The Roman state cannot possibly hope to survive if a small group of well-meaning zealots is allowed to play fast and loose with certain laws which have been held indispensable ever since the days of Romulus,and much against her own will she is driven into deeds of intolerance which are entirely at variance with her age-old policy of liberal aloofness.

The Church,spiritual heir to the material dominions of the ancient Empire,depends

我这里所说的“教育”，不是指纯粹的事实积累（这被看作是我们现代儿童必需的精神库存）。我想说的是对现时的真正理解，它孕育于对过去的善意大度的了解之中。

在这本书中，我已经力图证明，不宽容仅仅是人类自我保护本能的一种表现。

一群狼不会容忍一只与众不同的狼（因为它的弱小或强壮），它们一定会努力除掉这个前来冒犯的、不受欢迎的伙伴。

在一个吃人的部落，谁的喜好要是会激怒上帝，给整个村庄带来灾难，部落就不会容忍他，会把他野蛮地流放到荒野。

希腊城邦也不敢向一个竟敢质疑社会赖以生存的基础的人提供避难所。在一次极为不幸的不宽容的爆发中，那位犯错的哲学家（苏格拉底）就被仁慈地判处饮毒而死。

如果允许一小群无恶意的狂热者践踏自从罗慕路斯时代以来就不可缺少的某些法律，那么罗马帝国就不可能生存下去，因此它只得违背自己的意愿，被迫采取一些不宽容的做法，而这与它古老的自由中立政策是背道而驰的。

教会作为这个古老帝国实际版图的精神继承人，它的生存全是靠最恭顺的臣民的绝对而毫无疑义的服从，因此它被迫走向镇压与凶残的极端，以至于许多人宁可忍受土耳其人的残酷，也不愿意要基督教的仁慈。

反对教会暴虐的伟大战士总是处于重重困境之中，但是他们要想维持自己的统治，就必须对所有的精神革新或科学试验表现出不宽容。于是借着“改革”的名

for her continued existence upon the absolute and unquestioning obedience of even the humblest of her subjects and is driven to such extremes of suppression and cruelty that many people prefer the ruthlessness of the Turk to the charity of the Christian.

The great insurgents against ecclesiastical tyranny,beset by a thousand difficulties,can only maintain their rule if they show themselves intolerant to all spiritual innovations and scientific experiments and in the name of"Reform"they commit (or rather try to commit) the self-same mistakes which have just deprived their enemies of most of their former power and influence.

And so it goes throughout the ages until life,which might be a glorious adventure,is turned into a horrible experience and all this happens because human existence so far has been entirely dominated by fear.

※ ※ ※ ※ ※ ※

For fear,I repeat it,is at the bottom of all intolerance.

No matter what form or shape a persecution may take,it is caused by fear and its very vehemence is indicative of the degree of anguish experienced by those who erect the gallows or throw fresh logs upon the funeral pyre.

※ ※ ※ ※ ※ ※

Once we recognize this fact,the solution of the difficulty immediately presents itself.

Man,when not under the influence of fear,is strongly inclined to be righteous and just.

Thus far he has had very few opportunities to practice these two virtues.

But I cannot for the life of me see that this matters overmuch. It is part of the necessary development of the human race. And that race is young,hopelessly,almost ridiculously young. To ask that a certain form of mammal,which began its independent career only a

义，他们又犯了（或者试图犯）自己的敌人刚刚犯过的错误，正是这些错误使他们的敌人丢掉了先前的大部分权力和影响。

多少个时代过去了，生命本来是一场光辉的历程，却变成了一场可怕的经历。这一切之所以发生，是因为迄今为止人类的生存完全被恐怖所支配。

※ ※ ※ ※ ※ ※

我重复一遍，恐惧正是所有不宽容的根源。

无论迫害的方法和形式是什么，它都是由恐惧造成的，那些支起绞刑架或把新鲜的原木扔向火刑柴堆的人所经历的痛苦程度，就集中表现了这种恐惧。

※ ※ ※ ※ ※ ※

一旦我们认清了这个事实，就马上有了解决难题的方法。

在没有恐惧影响的时候，人是很倾向于正直和正义的。

但是迄今为止，他还很少有机会实践这两项美德。

我在有生之年是看不到这件事情的实现了。这是人类发展的必然阶段。人类毕竟还年轻，而且毫无希望，甚至年轻得荒唐可笑。要求在几千年前才开始独立生活的哺乳动物具备这些只有随着年龄和经验的增长才能累积的美德，似乎既不合理，也不公正。

而且，它会使我们的观点出现偏差。

当我们应该有耐心的时候，它却使我们变得愤怒。

few thousand years ago should already have acquired those virtues which go only with age and experience,seems both unreasonable and unfair.

And furthermore,it warps our point of view.

It causes us to be irritated when we should be patient.

It makes us say harsh things where we should only feel pity.

※ ※ ※ ※ ※ ※

In the last chapters of a book like this,there is a serious temptation to assume the rôle of the prophet of woe and indulge in a little amateur preaching.

Heaven forbid !

Life is short and sermons are art to be long.

And what cannot be said in a hundred words had better never be said at all.

※ ※ ※ ※ ※ ※

Our historians are guilty of one great error. They speak of prehistoric times,they tell us about the Golden Age of Greece and Rome,they talk nonsense about a supposedly dark period,they compose rhapsodies upon the tenfold glories of our modern era.

If perchance these learned doctors perceive certain characteristics which do not seem to fit into the picture they have so prettily put together,they offer a few humble apologies and mumble something about certain undesirable qualities which are part of our unfortunate and barbaric heritage but which in due course of time will disappear,just as the stage-coach has given way before the railroad engine.

It is all very pretty but it is not true. It may flatter our pride to believe ourselves heir to the ages. It will be better for our spiritual health if we know ourselves for what we are—contemporaries of the folks that lived in caves,neolithic men with cigarettes and Ford

当我们只应该表示怜悯时，它却使我们说出刻薄的话来。

※ ※ ※ ※ ※ ※

在这样一本书的最后几章，会存在一种极大的诱惑力，那就是去承担悲哀的预言家的角色，沉迷于业余的说教之中。

这是老天爷都不允许的！

生命是短暂的，而布道却易于冗长。

用100个字表达不了的意思，还是不说为好。

※ ※ ※ ※ ※ ※

我们的历史学家犯了一个大错误。他们高谈阔论史前时代，告诉我们古希腊和古罗马的黄金时代，随意编造一段假设的黑暗时期，为比我们现代还要繁荣十倍的辉煌大唱赞歌。

如果这些学识渊博的博士偶然发现，人类的某些性格似乎不太适合他们巧妙拼凑而成的那幅图画，他们就会谦卑地道歉几声，低声嘟哝说，某些不受欢迎的品质不幸是过去野蛮时代遗留下来的，但时机一到，这种情况就会像公共马车让位于火车一样，全都消失殆尽了。

这一切很动听，但不是真实的。它可以满足我们的自尊心，使我们相信自己是时代的继承人。如果我们知道自己是什么人——是住在山洞里的人的当代化身，是叼着香烟、驾驶着福特汽车的新石器时代的人，是坐着电梯上公寓大厦的穴居

cars,cliff-dwellers who reach their homes in an elevator.

For then and only then shall we be able to make a first step toward that goal that still lies hidden beyond the vast mountain ranges of the future.

※ ※ ※ ※ ※ ※

To speak of Golden Ages and Modern Eras and Progress is sheer waste of time as long as this world is dominated by fear.

To ask for tolerance,as long as intolerance must of need be an integral part of our law of self-preservation,is little short of a crime.

The day will come when tolerance shall be the rule,when intolerance shall be a myth like the slaughter of innocent captives,the burning of widows,the blind worship of a printed page.

It may take ten thousand years,it may take a hundred thousand.

But it will come,and it will follow close upon the first true victory of which history shall have any record,the triumph of man over his own fear.

Westport,Connecticut
July,19,1925

人——那对我们的精神健康会更好些。

到那时，也只有到那时，我们才能朝着那个还隐藏在广阔的未来山岭另一侧的目标迈出第一步。

※ ※ ※ ※ ※ ※

只要这个世界还被恐惧所控制，谈论黄金时代、现代时期和人类进步，纯粹是在浪费时间。

只要不宽容是人类自我保护法则的必要部分，要求宽容简直是犯罪。

当屠杀无辜俘虏、烧死寡妇和盲目崇拜一纸文字等不宽容行为成为神话的时候，宽容一统天下的日子就将来临了。

这可能需要1万年，也可能需要10万年。

但是它终将会到来，而且将紧随着载入史册的、人类征服自身恐惧的第一次真正胜利而到来。

康涅狄格州　西港
1925年7月19日